BLANDINA SEGALE, THE NUN WHO RODE ON BILLY THE KID

SLEUTHING A FOISTED FRONTIER FABLE

BY
GALE COOPER

GELCOUR BOOKS

OTHER BILLY THE KID BOOKS BY GALE COOPER:

BILLY AND PAULITA: THE SAGA OF BILLY THE KID, PAULITA MAXWELL, AND THE SANTA FE RING

BILLY THE KID'S WRITINGS, WORDS, AND WIT

THE LOST PARDON OF BILLY THE KID: AN ANALYSIS FACTORING IN THE SANTA FE RING, GOVERNOR LEW WALLACE'S DILEMMA, AND A TERRITORY IN REBELLION

THE SANTA FE RING VERSUS BILLY THE KID: THE MAKING OF AN AMERICAN MONSTER

BILLY THE KID'S PRETENDERS: BRUSHY BILL & JOHN MILLER

CRACKING THE BILLY THE KID CASE HOAX: THE STRANGE PLOT TO EXHUME BILLY THE KID, CONVICT SHERIFF PAT GARRETT OF MURDER, AND BECOME PRESIDENT OF THE UNITED STATES

THE COLD CASE BILLY THE KID MEGAHOAX: A RASCALLY REPLAY OF THE BILLY THE KID CASE'S FORENSIC FLIMFLAM AND BRUSHY BILL'S BILLY THE KID BAMBOOZLE

COVER AND BOOK DESIGN BY GALE COOPER

COVER CREDIT PHOTO: For portrait image by unknown photographer of Sister Blandina Segale of the Sisters of Charity Order, Courtesy of the New Mexico History Museum's Palace of the Governors Photo Archives (NMHM/DCA), Negative Number 067735

COPYRIGHT © 2018 Gale Cooper
All Rights Reserved.

SECOND EDITION

*Reproductions, excerpts, or transmittals
of the author's original cover or text
are prohibited in any form whatsoever
without written permission of the author.
Infringers will be prosecuted
to the fullest extent of the law.*

ISBN: 978-1-949626-06-3 HARDCOVER
ISBN: 978-1-949626-07-0 PAPERBACK
Library of Congress Control Number: 2018909422

FIRST EDITION
COPYRIGHT © 2017 Gale Cooper

GELCOUR BOOKS
2270D Wyoming Boulevard NE
Suite 217
Albuquerque, NM 87112

WEBSITE
GaleCooperBillytheKidBooks.com

ORDERING THIS BOOK
Amazon.com, BarnesandNoble.com, bookstores

Printed in the United States of America
on acid free paper

For Billy Bonney,
a Lincoln County War freedom fighter,
whose enemies named him
"Billy the Kid"

CONTENTS

PREFACE xi
AUTHOR'S FOREWORD xiii
METHODOLOGY xv
ACKNOWLEDGEMENTS xv

1
HOAXBUSTING HIJACKERS OF BILLY THE KID'S HISTORY

INTRODUCTION 3
THE LURE OF BILLY THE KID'S FAME 4
OTHER HOAXBUSTING 5
BILLY THE KID HOAXERS' HANDICAPS 6
BLANDINA SEGALE'S HISTORICAL IMPASSE 8
QUESTIONING BLANDINA'S BOOK 9

2
THE NUN'S TALE OF "BILLY THE KID"

OVERVIEW 13
THE LIFE OF BLANDINA SEGALE 14
BLANDINA SEGALE'S TALE OF HERSELF
    AND "BILLY THE KID" 18
THE 1948 EDITION OF *AT THE END OF
    THE SANTA FE TRAIL* 19
BLANDINA'S 14 "BILLY THE KID" ENTRIES 22
BLANDINA'S CITING OF OTHER HISTORICAL
    FIGURES RELEVANT TO BILLY THE KID 30
ANALYSIS OF BLANDINA'S 14 "BILLY THE KID"
    ENTRIES 36
BLANDINA'S "BILLY THE KID" PROBLEM 47

3
MEDIA MAGNET OF A NUN PAL OF "BILLY THE KID"

FRIENDSHIP OF A POSSIBLE SAINT AND A
    CERTAIN SINNER GRABS MEDIA ATTENTION 51
EIGHT DECADES OF RISING MEDIA CRESCENDO 58
TV, FILM, AND BLANDINA 71

4
THE REAL BILLY THE KID

THE HISTORY OF BILLY BONNEY 75
BILLY BONNEY'S CONTEMPORARY FRIENDS 100
A TERRITORY IN REBELLION 108
BLANDINA'S GREAT INJUSTICE 110
BLANDINA'S MAKE-BELIEVE WORLD 111

5
SLEUTHING BLANDINA'S PUBLISHED "BILLY THE KID" CLAIMS

MEETING BLANDINA'S PETITIONER FOR SAINTHOOD 117
BACK TO THE FIRST EDITION OF 1932 120
CHECKING THE LATER EDITIONS OF
　AT THE END OF THE SANTA FE TRAIL 137
BACK TO THE FIRST PUBLICATION: "AT THE END
　OF THE SANTA FE TRAIL"
　MAGAZINE ARTICLES 138
BACK TO THE ORIGINAL JOURNAL 164
SUMMARY OF DATE AND TEXT ALTERATIONS
　IN PUBLISHED JOURNAL 166

6
SLEUTHING BLANDINA'S SECOND-HAND SOURCES FOR HER "BILLY THE KID" CLAIMS

RESEARCH AND THE NUN 173
WRITING IN JOURNAL STYLE RATHER THAN
　WRITING A JOURNAL 179
USING 20th CENTURY WRITINGS OF PAT GARRETT
　AND WALTER NOBLE BURNS FOR
　THE "19th CENTURY JOURNAL" 185
ALSO USING EARLY HISTORIAN RALPH EMERSON
　TWITCHELL 202
USING CONTEMPORARY NEWSPAPERS AS
　SOURCES FOR "BILLY THE KID'S GANG"
　AND OUTLAWRY 205
INDIRECT USE OF SECRET SERVICE REPORTS FOR
　THE KID'S GANG" AND OUTLAWRY 239

USING CONTEMPORARY PRESS AS SOURCES FOR
  "BILLY THE KID'S" THREAT TO LEW WALLACE 242
USING CONTEMPORARY PRESS AS SOURCES FOR
  LEW WALLACE INTERVIEWING BILLY THE KID 252
USING AN 1881 DIME NOVEL ON "BILLY THE KID" 263
USING HOLLYWOOD WESTERNS 266

7

SLEUTHING BLANDINA'S FIRST-HAND ACCOUNTS OF CONTACTS WITH "BILLY THE KID" AND RELATED OTHERS

A HOAXER'S RISK OF EXPOSURE WITH
  FIRST-HAND ACCOUNTS 271
MANY ENCOUNTERS WITH "BILLY THE KID'S
  GANG MEMBER SCHNEIDER" 272
FIRST ENCOUNTER WITH ON-THE-LOOSE
  "BILLY THE KID" 277
SECOND ENCOUNTER WITH ON-THE-LOOSE
  "BILLY THE KID" 281
SANTA FE JAIL MEETING WITH
  "BILLY THE KID" 284
FIRST-HAND ENCOUNTER WITH VICTORIO 302
FIRST-HAND ENCOUNTERS JUST IN
  VERITAS MAGAZINE 303

8

BLANDINA'S BACKERS' "TWO BILLY THE KIDS" THEORY

RATIONALIZING BLANDINA'S "BILLY THE KID"
  CLAIMS 309
THE "BILLY THE KID" MONIKER 310
PAT GARRETT'S DENIAL OF OTHER
  "BILLY THE KID'S" 319
DIME NOVEL FABRICATION OF BILLY LeROY
  AS "BILLY THE KID" 320
MODERN THROWBACK TO DAGGETT'S
  DIME NOVEL FAKERY OF
  "TWO BILLY THE KIDS" 343
BIOGRAPHY OF THE REAL ARTHUR POND,
  ALIAS BILLY LEROY 351
REAL BILLY LeROY's CONTEMPORARY PRESS 354

SEEKING OTHER OUTLAWS IN THE NEWS
  FOR BLANDINA 360

9
CRACKING THE NUN'S TALE HOAX

CRACKING THE NUN'S TALE HOAX 377
WEIGHING IN BLANDINA'S HOAXING INTENT 382
THE REAL BILLY THE KID IN HUMOROUS SIMPATICO 412
FRIENDLY SHOWDOWN ON SEPTEMBER 30, 2017 413
SUMMARY OF THE NUN'S TALE HOAX 423
CONCLUSION: "POPCORN HOAXING" AND
  THE "MARIA PROBLEM" 426
POSTSCRIPT: 2018 426

SOURCES AND INDEX

ANNOTATED BIBLIOGRAPHY
  Sources For Blandina Segale 429
  Sources For Other Billy the Kid Hoaxes 439
  General Historical References for William Bonney aka
    Billy the Kid 439
  Historical Organizations (Period) 440
  New Mexico Territory Rebellions Against the
    Santa Fe Ring 449
  Historical Figures (Period) 456
INDEX 515

PREFACE

Well, I'm back in the saddle to give my two bits for another book on Billy the Kid by this here author. This time she's saving that boy - really named Billy Bonney - from yarns as shy of the truth as a fish is of feathers. And me being a fictional New Mexican old-timer lets me speak my mind without looking over my shoulder - if you get my drift.

I tell you what: just when you thinks you'se seen everything, there up and comes something else. First, this here author took on a loco old-timer Texan from the last century who called hisself "Brushy Bill" - instead of his acktual name, "Oliver Roberts" - and made up that he was Billy the Kid, which needed making up that Sheriff Pat Garrett didn't kill Billy when he did on July 14, 1881. Then "Brushy" got him a writer for his fake book. And there are damn fools - excuse the French - who believe "Brushy's" tomfoolery to this day.

Then this here author wrangled for years to stop a modern campaign against the truth by a crooked New Mexico Governor in cahoots with crooked lawmen, crooked judges, and crooked lawyers, rustling Billy's history for a publicity stunt with crooked DNA papers from their crooked exhumations. They called it the "Billy the Kid Case." And they figered that "Brushy's" fool believers would back them if they said they'd prove he was Billy with their fake DNA. And they was right.

Now this here author has stumbled on a yarn topping all those past fellas. Some nun from Billy's day wrote her a book in the 1930's, when she was long in tooth, boasting how brave she was when she was a whipper-snapper in the Old West cause she stood up to killer-outlaw Billy the Kid - and got to be his pal. Cept she never met him. So some say she acktually mixed-up some fergetible Colorado bad-man, and figered he was Billy the Kid. Seems to me, if she survived the Old West, she had the smarts to put two and two together and figer that famous Billy would acktually get her story into a book better then some fergittable outlaw. And it did.

But that's just the front end of the strangest shenanigans in the history of Billy's coat-tail-riders since he got to shake hands with old St. Pete with Garrett's assistance. Seems folks see this nun - named Sister Blandina Segale - as an upcoming winner for sainthood. And I'd bet you ain't surprised if I said that the newspapers hitched her name - that nobody heard of - to Billy the Kid - that everybody heard of. So this may be a first for them at the Vatican to hear about Billy the Kid along with this nun, Blandina. And now some TV company is making programs on her frontier adventures. You tell me if you think they'll leave out Billy the Kid!

Now, I'd grant that maybe this nun, Sister Blandina, was more mixed-up then lying, and didn't know which end of a cow quits the ground first. But the worst part isn't dumbness, or even tall tales by her and by them backing her. The worst part is that they'se heading into territory that makes this here author cross as a snapping turtle: painting real Billy as some blood-thirsty road agent who scalped people; when he was acktually a freedom fighter in the Lincoln County War, who got his bad repartation from lying Santa Fe Ring politicians - who he was fighting and who won that War by playing dirty. So whether old Blandina wanted to do it or not, she ended up on the bad guys' side: namely helping them peddle their outlaw Billy the Kid hijinks right up to now.

So it all comes down to this here book having to set the record straight for Billy. And, as usual, this here author is making no friends jumping on people like a roadrunner on a rattler. And if old Blandina ends up a saint - with her tall tale written off - she may be the strangest enemy of all the other riled-up hoaxers this here author has roped: angry on high - real high. But if this here author was looking for friends, I have something to say to her: "You just gather enemies by siding with Billy. Billy hisself proved that. Ain't his grave crowded side-by-side with two of his pals that Garrett shot when he kept on missing Billy hisself?

So I say, 'Good luck, Missy. And you'se lucky that them backing Blandina is a hell of a lot nicer - excuse the French - then them other hoaxer varmints from Texas and New Mexico you already faced at high noon.

       Vern Blanton Johnson, Jr.
       Lincoln, Lincoln County, New Mexico

AUTHOR'S FOREWORD

The last thing I wanted to write was another exposé of a Billy the Kid hoax. They are unpleasant, being selfish profiteering based on the scornful assumption that people can be duped; and they damage to the real history. But the outrageous, almost 90 year old Nun's Tale Hoax was about to get a big boost by that nun's backing for sainthood; with a TV series joining in.

For almost 20 years, it has been my privilege to publish the revisionist history of Billy Bonney aka Billy the Kid, using over 40 thousand pages of archival documents and books, hundreds of expert consultants, and my background as a Harvard Medical School educated M.D. forensic psychiatrist.

My goal has been to document the magnificent freedom fight of the Lincoln County War, from which teenaged, brilliant, and charismatic Billy Bonney emerged as the people's hero. That required my exposing the corrupt political cabal of the Santa Fe Ring, and documenting New Mexico Territory's anti-Ring rebellions of the 1870's. That also necessitated exposing hoaxes hijacking Billy the Kid's famous history and hiding the truth.

This Nun's Tale Hoax, originating in the 19th century, is not only the first, the most peculiar, and the longest-running Billy the Kid hoax, but is also a veritable matryoshka nesting doll naively incorporating other Billy the Kid hoaxes to formulate its claims. It is now 141 years old - from its first 1876 fable - and is still doing tremendous damage to the true history.

Its apparent creator was a Sister of Charity of Cincinnati, Ohio, nun, Blandina Segale, a missionary to the 19th century Southwest. During her 21 years there, she allegedly kept a journal to share her adventures, trials and tribulations, humanitarian achievements, and unshakable faith with her sister and fellow Sister of Charity nun, Justina. That journal was published as a magazine serial from 1926 to 1931. In 1932, it was released as a book titled *At the End of the Santa Fe Trail*. And new editions followed into the 21st century.

Blandina's journal gained popular appeal by her first-hand accounts of befriending "Billy the Kid," as being a heinous outlaw and sadistic murderer. Undetected in her day of near total ignorance of Billy the Kid history, and perpetuated to the present, was that her relationship was fabricated. But it guaranteed Blandina continuous media attention. The stakes rose over the past few years as her publicity soared with her petition for her sainthood progressing to the Vatican.

Hoaxbusting the Nun's Tale Hoax was in order. But this exposé turned out to be a different experience for me than my past confrontations. I had exposed mid-20th century imposters, Oliver "Brushy Bill" Roberts and John Miller in my 2010 book, *Billy the Kid's Pretenders: Brushy Bill and John Miller*. Those mentally ill old-timers had claimed to be Billy the Kid, and had obtained profiteering hoaxing authors to promote them.

I had exposed a 21st century Billy the Kid Case DNA hoax in my 2014 book, *Cracking the Billy the Kid Case Hoax: The Strange Plot to Exhume Billy the Kid, Convict Sheriff Pat Garrett of Murder, and Become President of the United States*. That hoax used "Brushy's" fabricated claims of not being shot by Pat Garrett to conduct illegal exhumations for fraudulent DNA matchings to "prove" that "Brushy" was a surviving Billy Bonney. It was promulgated by scoundrels: a corrupt New Mexico governor, colluding lawmen, a rogue history professor, beholden judges, and complicit media. The hoaxers covered-up evidence of their crimes; gobbled taxpayer money to stonewall my whistleblower litigation; and were propelled by publicity, profiteering, and political ambitions as they garnered articles and TV programs.

The Nun's Tale Hoax was different. Those involved with promoting Blandina Segale for sainthood wanted to know the truth about her "Billy the Kid" claims, and freely shared information from the Sisters of Charity of Cincinnati, Ohio, archives.

That honorable openness and access to information from Blandina's backers allowed me to sleuth a conclusion that will hopefully be used to clarify the legacy of that unusual and devout woman.

Gale Cooper, M.D.
Sandia Park, New Mexico

METHODOLOGY

THE NUN'S WORDS: Blandina Segale's alleged Old West journal entries are repeated for each of their published editions for clarity and for comparisons of any text alterations. So when page numbers are given, they are accompanied by the copyright date; for example: (1948, Pages 79-80).

PRIMARY DOCUMENTS: Primary documents are presented with italics for handwriting, two column newsprint for articles, and in distinctive font for books. For Billy Bonney's personal letters, his idiosyncratic spellings are retained without a [sic] notation. The same is done for contemporary newspaper articles and Secret Service reports of Azariah Wild.

COMMENTARY: As guideposts, highlighted summaries for "Sleuthing Hoaxbusting Clues" and "Smoking Guns for a Hoax" are provided; boldfaced and bracketed "Author's Notes" add emphasis; and the "Bibliography" is annotated. For one chart, Billy the Kid is abbreviated as BTK.

FACILITATIONS: Bibliography entries are arranged chronologically. For navigation within the book, internal page references are provided. Page numbers are also given for certain reference book citations where the reader might want to check for themselves.

ACKNOWLEDGMENTS

Overriding is my debt to Billy Bonney, whose freedom fighting cause, courage, intelligence, and joie de vivre are my inspiration.

Thanks goes to honorable powerhouse, Allen Sánchez, Petitioner for the Cause of Sainthood of Blandina Segale; to his historical investigator, Peso Chavez; and to his personal assistant, Norma Evans, for shared information and determination to find the truth. Superlative research facilitation came from Sisters of Charity of Cincinnati's archivist, Veronica Buchanan.

Period newspaper research for Colorado was assisted by Kerry Baldwin of History Colorado Center, Collections and Library; and by private researcher, Laura Ruttum Senturia. Period newspaper research for New Mexico was assisted by Laura Calderone of the New Mexico State Library in Santa Fe.

Historical bedrock is from books by Frederick Nolan on Billy the Kid, the Lincoln County War, and John Henry Tunstall; by Leon Metz on Pat Garrett, and by Jerry Weddle on Billy Bonney's adolescence. National Archive specialists used for Billy the Kid and period research are Clarence Lyons, Wayne DeCesar, and Fred Romanski at the Civilian Records Branch; Dr. Milt Gustafson at the Civilian Records Branch Classification; Janice Wiggins at the Justice Department; Joseph Schwarz at the Department of Interior; and Michael Sampson at the Secret Service Library Counterfeit Division. Teri Caid, Manager of the St. James Hotel in Cimarron, New Mexico, confirmed that there is no evidence that Billy the Kid ever visited that hotel; and that false claim is being removed from their website.

Collections used for Billy the Kid sources were at the Las Cruces, New Mexico State University Library's Rio Grande Historical Collections' Herman B. Weisner Papers, ca. 1957-1992; the Albuquerque, University of New Mexico Center for Southwest Studies' Thomas Benton Catron Collection; the Midland, Texas Nita Stewart and J. Evert Haley Memorial Library and Historical Center; the Santa Fe, New Mexico, Fray Angélico Chávez Historical Library; and the Indianapolis, Indiana Historical Society's Lew and Susan Wallace Collection.

1

HOAXBUSTING HIJACKERS OF BILLY THE KID'S HISTORY

INTRODUCTION

SLEUTHING HOAXBUSTING CLUES: An historical hoax is a deliberate attempt to trick people with false information. It is detectable by contradiction of known facts, over-elaborated presentation, and the hoaxer's motives ranging from attention-seeking to riches.

The Nun's Tale Hoax, which claimed that the published journal of a 19th century Sisters of Charity of Cincinnati nun, Blandina Segale, presented her long relationship with Billy Bonney aka Billy the Kid - when no such relationship existed - is arguably the strangest of all historical fabrications about that famous Old West youth.

Webster's Dictionary states that a hoax is "an act intended to trick or dupe" or "something accepted or established by fraud or fabrication." So a hoax has to fool people intentionally. It follows that a hoaxer has a motive, and that is usually personal gain ranging from fame to riches.

When sleuthing an historical hoax, one must distinguish it from an honest mistake. Real hoaxes have tell-tale signs of being attention-grabbing, claiming first person participation, over-elaboration, and using sources to feign reality; as follows:

1) **Attention-grabbing:** The motive for hoaxing is usually self aggrandizement or profit. That necessitates claims that are extreme enough for other people to take notice.

2) **First person participation:** Hoaxers put themselves into the action to shine by reflected glory.

3) **Over-elaboration:** Because fiction is hard to create, most hoaxers err on the side of over-embellishing by fantasized details; and, thereby, resemble confabulators.

Real confabulators are not purposeful liars; they have a mental disorder. Confabulation, according to Harold Kaplan's and Benjamin Sadock's *Synopsis of Psychiatry*, is "unconscious filling of gaps in memory by imagined or untrue experiences." Hoaxers do the same thing to fill in facts for their fictions.

4) **Research:** Hoaxers of history try to align their tall tales to historical events. They often do research for their fables and sprinkle in historic names. But parroting tell-tale errors from their secret sources gives them away.

LURE OF BILLY THE KID'S FAME

In his own lifetime, William Henry "Billy" Bonney aka Billy the Kid became so famous that he could read and comment on his own press. He was arguably one of the first national media stars. To his readership, he was either a hero of the Lincoln County War's people's uprising against the corrupt land-grabbing Santa Fe Ring, or a villain in that Ring's propaganda myth of his being a gang-leading murdering desperado - thus offering something for everyone.

And the momentum of Billy's fame never ceased, being meteorically propelled by his dramatic death at only 21 on July 14, 1881 by an ambush bullet from Sheriff Pat Garrett in the Maxwell family mansion in Fort Sumner, New Mexico.

Billy's killer cashed in immediately on the fame. In 1882, Patrick Floyd "Pat" Garrett - with alcoholic, failed journalist Ashmun "Ash" Upson, his boarder in his Roswell, New Mexico, home as his ghostwriter - published *The Authentic Life of Billy the Kid The Noted Desperado of the Southwest, Whose Deeds of Daring and Blood Made His Name a Terror in New Mexico, Arizona, and Northern Mexico by Pat F. Garrett, Sheriff of Lincoln County, N.M., by Whom He was Finally Hunted Down and Captured by Killing Him, A Faithful and Interesting Narrative.* Limited by Garrett's and Upson's minimal knowledge of Billy Bonney's life history and Lincoln County War issues, it compensated by fictional dramatizing in the dime novel tradition. But it set the hysterically hyperbolic tone of the outlaw myth which plagued Billy's history ever since.

Billy himself objected to this unjust trend in a December 12, 1880 letter to Governor Lew Wallace, writing:

> *I noticed in the Las Vegas Gazette a piece which stated that, Billy "the" Kid, the name by which I am known in the Country was the captain of a Band of Outlaws who hold Forth at the Portales. There is no such Organization in Existence. So the Gentleman must have drawn very heavily on his Imagination.*

Things only got worse as Billy's posthumous fame burgeoned. In 1926, another journalist, Walter Noble Burns, published his *The Saga of Billy the Kid*. He used his imagination and Garrett as sources; though he also interviewed old-timers from Billy's life, being unaware that they kept self-protective secrets about the Santa Fe Ring and real reasons that Billy Bonney had to be killed. Burns's book was essentially a latter-day dime novel: a morality tale rabidly opposed to the demonic "outlaw Billy the Kid."

By the late 1930's, the first legitimate Billy the Kid historians were conducting scholarly research; and Billy's old-timer contemporaries were getting their memoirs published by advertising their erstwhile friendships with Billy.

That trend toward truth-seeking was counterbalanced by the opposite. Old-timer freeloaders and dementia-sufferers, seeking fame and fortune, began to hijack Billy's history by publishing, with hoaxing authors, faked first-person accounts of either having known Billy, or of being Billy the Kid by surviving Pat Garrett's shooting to live to old age. And those shenanigans have continued, with variations, to modern-day opportunistic backers of those old fraudsters.

OTHER HOAXBUSTING

I have made it my task to protect Billy Bonney's history by debunking Billy the Kid hoaxes. My book, *Billy the Kid's Pretenders: Brushy Bill and John Miller*, came out in 2010, exposing those two mentally disordered old men - both posing as "Billy the Kids" who survived Pat Garrett's shooting - who had acquired hoaxing authors. And in 2014, was published my *Cracking the Billy the Kid Case Hoax: The Strange Plot to Exhume Billy the Kid, Convict Pat Garrett of Murder, and Become President of the United States* - about a forensic DNA hoax, which was a throw-back scam, using faked DNA and illegal exhumations, with intent to claim that Oliver "Brushy Bill" Roberts was provable as having been Billy the Kid.

Then, in 2015, I first read on the internet about a 19th century nun named Blandina Segale, whose Old West journal was published in 1932 as a book titled *At the End of the Santa Fe Trial*. That book achieved multiple reprints largely because of her surprising tales of befriending an horrific, scalping murderer, highwayman outlaw she identified as "Billy the Kid." Her present surge of attraction arose from her sainthood petition, bestowing saint-and-sinner allure to her alleged frontier gambits with "Billy the Kid." She already had one TV program from the 1960's, and another was now in the making. I smelled another hoax.

BILLY THE KID HOAXERS' HANDICAPS

Billy the Kid history hoaxers have built-in handicaps for painting themselves into his history. They are making a first-person narrative, without first-person experience. That forces faking, which has smoking gun signs; as follows:

1) If you are a person, or know a person, you would have accurate knowledge of that person. Wrong information is a smoking gun for hoaxing.

2) If you are writing a diary or journal, its dates would be correct. Wrong dates are a smoking gun for hoaxing.

3) If you are constructing an historical hoax, you need sources. If your source has fake information, and you repeat it, it is a smoking gun for your hoaxing. Old-timer Billy the Kid hoaxers lived before scholarly history books on him. But there were dime novel-like renditions, which exposed hoaxers who copied their fabricated claims to smoking gun errors.

4) A claimant's obvious motive for fame or fortune, coupled with questionable credibility, is a smoking gun for hoaxing.

When exposing hoaxed history, one looks for these smoking gun mistakes. A sure-fire exposure of an historical hoax is demonstrating facts contradicting its fictions. Here is an example. When I exposed Billy the Kid imposter, Oliver "Brushy Bill" Roberts, for my books *Billy the Kid's Pretenders* and *Cracking the Billy the Kid Case Hoax*, I sleuthed the false information propounded by "Brushy." His hoax was that Pat Garrett never killed him - as "Billy the Kid" - at the famous time of a little before midnight on July 14, 1881, in Fort Sumner, New Mexico. That would have made "Brushy" an old-timer surviving Billy. So he demanded, in 1950, from New Mexico's Governor, Thomas Jewett Mabry, the pardon promised originally to Billy the Kid in 1879 by Governor Lew Wallace, but withheld.

"Brushy" appeared to be a true confabulator, loquaciously ad-libbing his life as Billy the Kid," as told to his hoaxing author, William Morrison, for a 1955 book, *Alias Billy the Kid*, published after "Brushy's" death. Both "Brushy" and Morrison suffered from lack of legitimate history books on Billy the Kid and the Lincoln County War; all published years later. So subject and author had to wing it, hoping equally ignorant readers would miss their tricks.

"Brushy" obviously had to give his version of the fateful night of July 14, 1881 in which he, as "Billy the Kid," faced lethally motivated Sheriff Pat Garrett, but was not killed. So, with his mentally deranged and garrulous manner of elaborating minute details, "Brushy" declared **it was a dark and moonless night**, causing Garrett to mistake "Brushy's" buddy - a factitious "Billy Barlow" - for him when shooting the fatal bullet. That made "Billy Barlow" the corpse buried in Billy Bonney's Fort Sumner grave.

There was a problem with this concoction besides the fact that there was a nighttime vigil for real Billy's corpse attended by the 200 Fort Sumner residents, who knew and recognized him; and besides the fact that the Coroner's Jury Report for Billy Bonney identified him. "Brushy's" big problem for his tale was that **on the night of July 14, 1881, the moon was just about full**. And it rose oddly at about 10 p.m., staying near the horizon in huge moon illusion, and leaving Fort Sumner almost as light as day. In fact, Garrett's Deputy, John William Poe, who did not know Billy, commented on the bright moonlight when he described seeing the boy approaching him at his stake-out position at the Maxwell family mansion's site of the imminent ambush killing. It was definitely not a dark and moonless night, as anyone present would have known.

So "the dark and moonless night" error was "Brushy's" smoking gun for fakery. Such errors, exposed by juxtaposition with reality, are the armamentarium of hoaxbusting.

BLANDINA SEGALE'S HISTORICAL IMPASSE

Blandina's book, *At the End of the Santa Fe Trail*, was published in the heyday of Billy the Kid identity hoaxes. Billy's burgeoning national popularity, with the guarantee of book publication to old-timer writers having first-hand contact with him, made him prey for profiteering hijacking.

But that same period had no authoritative history books on Billy Bonney and the Lincoln County War. In fact, the central role of the deadly Santa Fe Ring in that history remained unexplored until my own revisionist history books from 2008 to the present. In particular, perspective on Billy's Lincoln County Was freedom fighter role against the Santa Fe Ring was in my 2017, *The Lost Pardon of Billy the Kid: An Analysis Factoring in the Santa Fe Ring, Governor Lew Wallace's Dilemma, and a Territory in Rebellion*; and in my upcoming *The Santa Fe Ring: The Making of an American Monster*.

Blandina Segale was dead 16 years by the 1957 publication of early researcher-historian, William Keleher's, *Violence in Lincoln County 1869-1881*, with his discoveries of actual documents, like Billy Bonney's Coroner's Jury Report.

But it required the more sophisticated and massive research of British historian, Frederick Nolan, for Billy the Kid history to enter the authoritative and comprehensive scholarly realm. Nolan began with publication of his 1965 *The Life and Death of John Henry Tunstall*. In the 1990's, he released the foundation history books on the subject: his 1992 *The Lincoln County War: A Documentary History* and his 1998 *The West of Billy the Kid*, with its extensive photo-archive.

Billy's childhood and early adolescence were largely unknown until 1993 with Jerry Weddle's *Antrim is My Stepfather's Name: The Boyhood of Billy the Kid*.

A bibliography in the 1948 edition of Blandina's *At the End of the Santa Fe Trail*, in fact, listed the main Billy the Kid sources available at her time: the 1927 reprint of Pat Garrett's 1882 *The Authentic Life of Billy the Kid* and Walter Noble Burns's 1926 *The Saga of Billy the Kid*. In 1948, it was still too early to realize that Garrett's book used dramatic fabrications with added historical names, for lack of factual knowledge. And Burns's book, lacking bibliography or index, and copying misinformation from Garrett's original 1882 printing of *The Authentic Life of Billy the Kid*, remained largely fiction. So Garrett and Burns, if cribbed for Blandina's book, could reveal smoking guns for hoaxing.

QUESTIONING BLANDINA'S BOOK

At the start, I wondered if Blandina Segale's *At the End of the Santa Fe Trial* was actually her own hoax. It was possible that a later editor added Billy the Kid tales without her knowledge to expand readership. It was hard for me to conceive of a nun hoaxing Billy the Kid! And a saint hoaxing Billy the Kid took the concept to another realm.

The only certainty I had from the start was that her book's claims of criminal depravity of her "Billy the Kid" had severely damaged the true history. And the current media thrust, with a TV series, was flooding the public with her throw-back fakery to the original lurid and prejudicial Billy the Kid press and outlaw notoriety.

SMOKING GUNS FOR A HOAX: Blandina's published Old West journal's claims of "Billy the Kid's" outlaw depravity are incompatible with her knowing him first-hand. A publicity motive might have tempted her - or a later editor - to insert fables about him into the text of her entries.

2

THE NUN'S TALE OF "BILLY THE KID"

OVERVIEW

SLEUTHING HOAXBUSTING CLUES: Researching Blandina Segale's life, as well as studying her published "Billy the Kid" journal entries, was the start of an evaluation as to motives and claims related to hoaxing.

Blandina Segale was six months older than Sheriff Pat Garrett, Billy the Kid's killer. She outlived murdered Garrett by 33 years. In 1932, when her Old West journal was first published as the book titled *At the End of the Santa Fe Trail*, it capitalized on Billy and Pat's fame to spice up her tale of being a 19th century missionary nun in Colorado and New Mexico Territories by inserting herself into their history as a friend and moral goad of "Billy the Kid."

At the End of the Santa Fe Trail was republished in 1948, seven years after Blandina's death, and rode the public's enthusiasm for her "Billy the Kid" scenes by featuring them in introductions, and by adding an illustration of the famous Billy the Kid tintype. After that edition, the book has had more reprints, which all capitalized on her "Billy the Kid" connection and added an actual photo of his tintype.

Because of Billy the Kid claims, Blandina penetrated broader media. *Topix* comic books featured her adventure with him in 1949. In 1966, a CBS special on another of her outlaw encounters became the TV program, "The Fastest Nun in the West" - henceforth borrowed as a catchy phrase for her headlines about her alleged "Billy the Kid" contacts.

In 2013, her promoters for sainthood recycled her claims of knowing Billy the Kid, and garnered international press and a new TV series. By then, however, there was more than an inkling that she never knew him. So her promoters rationalized her misinformation by claiming that she meant *another* "Billy the Kid;" while the press largely ignored that convoluted and inconvenient alteration, and continued with the original story.

By 2017, an *Albuquerque Journal* article about her planned TV series proclaimed: "Sister Blandina TV pilot filming in New Mexico." Not content with "[t]he series follows the life of Sister Blandina, a 19th century nun who resided in New Mexico and has a deep history in the state," the reporter proclaimed:

> [Blandina] **visited and cared for Billy the Kid** and other prisoners confined **in the main prison in Santa Fe** ...
>
> Sister Blandina is a nun that **interacted with everyone from Billy the Kid** to Mark Twain.

Blandina, like Billy the Kid hoaxer, Oliver "Brushy Bill" Roberts, who emerged just eight years after her death, knew almost no real history of Billy Bonney while making her claims. But first, it was necessary to understand her better to put her use of Billy the Kid into perspective.

THE LIFE OF BLANDINA SEGALE

Sister Belinda Segale was born as Rosa Maria Segale on January 23, 1850, the youngest of five children, in the small village of Cicagna, in northern Italy near Genoa. She turned five during her family's immigration to join a small Genoese community in Cincinnati, Ohio. After grammar schooling, she attended Mount St. Vincent Academy, a Sisters of Charity of Cincinnati school. In 1866, after graduating at 16, she entered their order. She chose the name "Blandina," after Saint Blandina, a martyred Christian slave girl in ancient Rome who, 1,689 years earlier, had been tortured in an amphitheater by scourging, burning, and bull goring, until fatally stabbed. Rosa Maria's sister, Maria Maddelena, entered the Sisters of Charity at the same time, becoming Sister Justina.

Blandina first taught for the Sisters of Charity in Dayton and Steubenville, Ohio, parochial schools. In 1872, at 22, she was sent alone by her order to Trinidad, Colorado Territory, as a missionary and teacher. She would remain in the frontier's Southwest for 21 years.

On November 30, 1872, before departing Ohio, Blandina began a journal for her sister, Justina, to record her frontier experiences; and she maintained it throughout her stay.

She arrived in Trinidad on December 9, 1872, two years after the tiny town's founding; and stayed until 1877, after building a school there. To this Colorado period, she dated her alleged first meetings with "Billy the Kid" and his "gang."

In 1877, she was transferred by the Sisters of Charity to New Mexico Territory's Santa Fe, where she founded St. Vincent Hospital and Orphan Asylum and ministered to the poor, miners, railway construction workers, orphans, Hispanic people, and Native Americans until 1881. This was the time in which she claimed to visit "Billy the Kid" in the Santa Fe jail.

In 1881, she was transferred to New Mexico Territory's Albuquerque, where she founded and constructed St. Vincent Academy, a Sisters of Charity Mission and a Wayfarers' House, taught school, and defended rights of Native Americans and Mexicans.

In 1889, she was returned to Trinidad, Colorado, for a failed campaign to enable Sisters of Charity to wear their religious garments when teaching at the local public school. She stayed until 1892, when she was transferred to Pueblo, Colorado, where she remained till 1893.

She was brought back to Ohio in 1894, being in Fayetteville and Cincinnati. In 1897, she and her fellow nun and sister, Justina, founded the Santa Maria Institute - called America's first Catholic Settlement House - to minister to Italian immigrants for the Sisters of Charity in Cincinnati, Ohio. Its progressive social services addressed trafficking of girls and juvenile delinquency. It also worked in prisons; gave religious instruction; provided a soup kitchen; had a day nursery and drama club; gave English, Italian, and citizenship classes; provided lessons in arts and crafts and sewing; and briefly cared for orphans. Blandina also founded the Santa Maria Institute's magazine, utilizing the sophisticated Bruce Publishing Company in Milwaukee, Wisconsin, for its printing; first as *Veritas* magazine, then as *The Santa Maria* magazine.

From 1900 to 1901, Blandina was returned by her order to Albuquerque, and was involved in founding St. Joseph Hospital there.

From 1926 to 1931, and back in Cincinnati, utilizing Bruce Publishing Company printing options of her Santa Maria Institute, Blandina first published her memoir journal of the Southwest in serialized form in the Institute's magazine as "At the End of the Santa Fe Trail." During creation of the articles, she disposed of her original journal. It was in this period, on July 31, 1929, that her sister, Justina, died at 83 following an appendectomy. In 1932, the magazine articles were edited and republished as a book, retaining the title: *At the End of the Santa Fe Trial.*

In 1931, at 81, Blandina went to Rome as a petitioner for sainthood of Mother Elizabeth Seton. Her local *Cincinnati Post* reporter wrote in his column "Life as He Sees It" that: "Sister Blandina is saint enough herself." She also successfully petitioned for the sainthood of Kateri Tekakwitha.

At 83, in 1933, Blandina retired to the Sisters of Charity motherhouse. She died at 91 on February 23, 1941.

On June 29, 2014, 73 years, 4 months, and 6 days after Blandina's death, Allen Sánchez, CEO/President of Catholic Health Initiatives (CHI) St. Joseph's Children Community Health in Albuquerque, New Mexico, became the Petitioner for the Cause of Sister Blandina for Sainthood. St. Joseph's Hospital, the foundation institution for CHI, was itself begun by Blandina. The path for her sainthood started officially by posting of a decree on the doors of Santa Fe's Basilica Cathedral of St. Francis of Assisi. Allen Sánchez described the process in his "Preface" to the 2014 edition of her *At the End of the Santa Fe Trail.* The Archbishop of Santa Fe, Michael J. Sheehan, opened her Cause. At this time, by Allen Sánchez's efforts, Blandina Segale has attained the first step towards canonization by becoming a Servant of God.

And for an August 31, 2015 article by a Catholic News Agency reporter, Mary Rezac, titled "Nuns, guns and the Wild West - the extraordinary tale of Sr. Blandina," Allen Sánchez listed one of several, required, inexplicable miracles proving Blandina's beneficent post-death intercessions. There was a premature, moribund baby with a heart defect and collapsed lungs, whose parents prayed to Blandina; and four days later the baby was declared free of illness.

But Blandina's public claim to fame was summarized in her Wikipedia profile's abstract of her own journal's *At the End of the Santa Fe Trail*, stating:

> During her missionary work [in Trinidad, Colorado], she met, among others, Billy the Kid ... She came to learn from one of her students that a member of the gang led by the famed outlaw Billy the Kid had been seriously wounded, and had been left alone to die in a shack ... [S]he received a tip that Billy the Kid was coming to her town to scalp the four doctors who had refused to treat his friend's gunshot wound. Segale nursed the friend to health, and when Billy came to Trinidad, Colorado, to thank her, she asked him to abandon his violent plan. He agreed.
>
> [Later] Billy the Kid and his gang attempted to rob the covered wagon in which she was traveling on the frontier. When he looked inside, he saw Segale. At that, Billy the Kid simply tipped his hat and rode off in deference to ... the debt he owed her.
>
> [And] [s]he visited and took care of Billy the Kid and other prisoners confined in the main prison in [Santa Fe] New Mexico.

So Sister Blandina's life of religious devotion, service, and posthumous miracles had a quirk: it featured an Androcles-and-the-lion tale of a holy person taming a beast. That quirk was a big problem, since Blandina never met her beast: Billy the Kid. Her dates, locations, and information do not match Billy Bonney's. That leaves a hole in her seamlessly honorable and achieving life, and opens the question of her being a very unusual hoaxer. And the only way to decide for or against her is to scrutinize her own presentation and its later incarnations to determine her responsibility - or someone else's - for the Nun's Tale Hoax of "Billy the Kid."

BLANDINA SEGALE'S TALE OF HERSELF AND "BILLY THE KID"

BACKGROUND OF BLANDINA'S BOOK

Blandina Segale first published her Old West journal as a serial titled "At the End of the Santa Fe Trail" in *Veritas* - later *The Santa Maria* - the magazine of the Santa Maria Institute of Cincinnati, Ohio. She and her sister, Justina, had founded that Institute in 1897, and founded the magazine in 1926, when Blandina began her series. Her series ended in 1931.

In 1932, she republished her magazine articles as a book by the Columbian Press of Columbus, Ohio, which retained the title as *At the End of the Santa Fe Trail*. Its copyright page states that it was prepared with Blandina's "cooperation." It had woodcut illustrations of places and buildings done by Blandina's niece, Maria Cordano Becker.

In 1948, seven years after Blandina's death, a revised edition was published by Bruce Publishing Company of Milwaukee, Wisconsin. This edition enlisted a Sisters of Charity nun, named Therese Martin, to provide Blandina's biography, and to add introductory comments, footnotes, bibliography, and index. It also inserted an illustration of Billy Bonney's famous tintype, which was captioned "Billy the Kid."

A 1996 edition, with new preface and with photo of the Billy Bonney tintype replacing the illustration of that tintype, was published by the Sisters of Charity of Cincinnati, Ohio.

In 2014, the most recent edition was published by the Sisters of Charity of Cincinnati, Ohio. Its new "Preface" is by Blandina's Petitioner for the cause of her sainthood, Allen Sánchez.

From its magazine origin, *At the End of the Santa Fe Trail* rode on the publishing trend in the first half of the 20th century in which first-hand contact with Billy the Kid guaranteed printing of your writings. That opportunity was used by other "frontier figure" authors who legitimately knew Billy Bonney; like George Coe, Dr. Henry Hoyt, and John Meadows. Pat Garrett's 1882 book about Billy Bonney and killing him, got its reprinting in 1927. And Governor Lew Wallace, after betraying his 1879 pardon promise to Billy, spent his life getting long articles published on his fabricated "adventures" with the "outlaw Kid." Even addled old-timer pretender, Oliver "Brushy Bill" Roberts, got a hoaxing author and publisher for the 1955 book about his *being Billy the Kid.*

Billy Bonney was, and is, a source of insatiable fascination. Blandina certainly knew that impact when she told her tales of her frontier life, calling him "**the greatest murderer in the Southwest.**" And there is no doubt that she presented her "Billy the Kid" as the real Billy Bonney, stating: "**I learned his proper name - William H. Bonney.**" That made her stand out in her day. Then it gave her a place in the burgeoning media business in film and TV about the Old West and its famous Billy the Kid. And it has provided the publicity hook for Blandina's quest for sainthood in our day.

THE 1948 EDITION OF
AT THE END OF THE SANTA FE TRAIL

To evaluate Blandina Segale's journal writings, I wanted to start with the 1932 first edition of *At the End of the Santa Fe Trail*, that being when she was alive and taking responsibility for it by her "**cooperation.**" I reasoned that subsequent editions could have been edited to beef-up, or to add de novo, the Billy the Kid content after her death.

But I quickly learned that the 1932 book was a rare limited edition, and was unavailable. So my sleuthing had to start with its 1948 second edition, published seven years after her death.

That edition reprinted her "Original Author's Note" from the 1932 book. Blandina had written:

> Into the keeping of this Journal of my life in the Southwest, there never entered the thought of its publication. The reward for the work was to come if Sister Justina and myself would meet and read it together.

Importantly for this analysis as to hoaxing, Blandina had also implied participation of others in producing her book, since her responsibilities running the Santa Maria Institute and ministering to its the Cincinnati, Ohio, Italian immigrant clients left her "no time" to "re-write it" from the magazine articles, as she had written in her "Author's Note; " stating:

> [T]he crowded hours that allowed no time for the leisurely writing of my Journal still prevail for me; and I realized if the urgent requests for the book were to be met, **my wish to re-write it must be set aside.**

BLANDINA'S EDITOR

Indeed, for the 1948 edition, Blandina did have an editor. The Sisters of Charity of Cincinnati archives identify her as Sister Therese Martin of that order. Noteworthy is that Sister Therese was not present when the 1932 edition was written.

The 1948 edition was published by the Bruce Publishing Company of Milwaukee, Wisconsin, the press originally chosen by Blandina herself for printing of her Santa Maria Institute magazine. This edition uses Therese Martin's text, in addition to Blandina's own, to introduce her more fully to readers and to advertise her journal's appeal. Sister Therese wrote:

> This simple story of the missionary work of a Sister of Charity in the Southwest of territorial days rivals in many of its pages the most thrilling romances written of that period.

Sister Therese clearly believed that some of that thrill came from Blandina's contact with "Billy the Kid," since she effused:

> [Blandina] is seen [in her journal entries] fearlessly confronting the notorious outlaw, "Billy the Kid," demanding safety for the physicians of Trinidad, [Colorado,] whose lives he threatened, and not only winning his confidence but inspiring him

with respect for every member of the religious garb. Who shall say what effect her ministrations to a neglected member of his band of outlaws may have had on the soul of this misguided youth?

Sister Therese provided a "Life Sketch of Sister Blandina Segale 1850-1941," introductory texts for each section, "Footnotes," "Bibliography," and "Index."

Sister Therese's introduction to "Part I, Trinidad" puts "Billy the Kid" front-and-center; stating:

> Sister Blandina was the first person to stop lynching laws in Trinidad [Colorado]. **Nor did she quail when she asked Billy the Kid and his gang not to scalp Trinidad's four physicians, although Billy had come to Trinidad for the express purpose of killing these four men.** (1948, Pages 11-12)

Sister Therese's introduction to "Part II, Santa Fe," also features "Billy the Kid," stating:

> **[Blandina] visited Billy the Kid** and other prisoners **in the Santa Fe jail** ... In spite of the flagrant spread of evil in the Territory, she carried on courageously, even gaily. (1948, Page 82)

Presumably for Therese Martin, "Billy the Kid," as part of that "evil," had elicited Blandina's courage.

As to Territorial Governor Wallace, who betrayed his pardon promise to Billy Bonney, unaware Sister Therese wrote:

> [The last governor's] successor, Lew Wallace, is above reproach, a man of strong principles and a student of humanity. (1948, Page 83)

Added to this 1948 edition by Therese Martin is a bad illustration of the tintype of Billy Bonney on its page 210a, captioned "Billy the Kid." Some of her footnotes pertain to

Billy the Kid. And an added bibliography leaves no doubt that Blandina - or Therese Martin, or someone else - had researched William Bonney. Cited are the two main history books on him available at the time: Walter Noble Burns's 1926 *The Saga of Billy the Kid* and Patrick Floyd Garrett's 1927 reprint of his 1882 *The Authentic Life of Billy the Kid*. They would have been available in Blandina's lifetime. But, if they were her personal copies, they are no longer in the Sisters of Charity archive of her collected papers. And unfortunately for her and/or for Therese Martin, if they copied them, these books were largely fictionalized.

BLANDINA'S 14 "BILLY THE KID" ENTRIES

The 1948 edition of *At the End of the Santa Fe Trail* has journal entries addressed to Justina, and dated variably by: month, day, and year; month and year; or a religious day with its year. The text is peppered, from beginning to end of the book, with evenly spaced references to "Billy the Kid;" and, thus, maintains dramatic literary momentum with him as a punch-line - as if intentionally placed. Of the entries, 11 are second-hand reporting about "Billy the Kid" and his "gang." Three are elaborate first-hand accounts. Blandina's 14 entries - numbered for reference - are as follows:

1948 "BILLY THE KID" ENTRY 1

For her long "September, 1876" entry, from Trinidad, Colorado, Blandina makes her first "Billy the Kid" reference, and also uses the names "Bill's Gang" and "Billy the Kid's Gang;" as follows:

> My scattered notes on **"Billy the Kid's Gang"** are condensed, and someday you [Justina] will be thrilled by their perusal.
>
> *The Trinidad Enterprise* – the only paper published here – in its last issue gave an exciting description of

how **a member of "Bill's Gang"** painted red the town of Cimarron ...

Yesterday one of the Vigilant Committee came to where I was ... and said: ... "I want you to see one of **'Billy's gang,'** the one who caused such fright in Cimarron ...

Billy's accomplice headed toward us.

He was mounted on a spirited stallion ... and was dressed as the *Torreros* (Bull-Fighters) dress in old Mexico. Cowboy's sombrero, fantastically trimmed, red velvet knee breaches, green velvet short coat, long sharp spurs, gold and green saddle cover. A figure of six feet three ... The impression made on me was of intense loathing, and I will candidly acknowledge, of fear also. (1948, Pages 67-68)

1948 "BILLY THE KID" ENTRY 2

The "September, 1876" entry continued about the gigantic "gang member," now left in Trinidad by the gang with a bullet in his thigh after a gunfight with another gang member named "Happy Jack," whom he shot dead. Blandina calls him "Schneider" - with no first name - and she was nursing him. To her he confessed his robberies, murders, and a scalping; presumably all comparable crimes of his leader, "Billy the Kid."

Caring for "Schneider" led to Blandina's first reported meeting with "Billy the Kid." (1948, Pages 70-71) She wrote:

[At another visit, o]ur patient lost no time in telling me that **Billy and the "gang"** are to be here, Saturday at 2 P.M., and I'm going to tell you why they are coming ...

[He said,] "Well, the 'gang' is going to scalp the four of [the town's physicians] ... because none of them would extract the bullet from my thigh." ...

Saturday, 2 P.M. came, and I went to meet Billy and his gang ... The introduction was given. I can only remember, "**Billy, our Captain,** and Chism ..."

The leader, Billy, has steel-blue eyes, peach complexion, is young, one would take him to be seventeen – innocent-looking, save for the corners of his eyes, which tell a set purpose, good or bad ... My glance took this description in while "Billy" was saying: "We are all glad to see you, Sister, and I want to say, it would give me pleasure to do you a favor." ...

I took the hand saying: "I understand you have come to scalp our Trinidad physicians, which act I ask you to cancel." ...

"Not only [do I grant] that, Sister, but at any time my pals and I can serve you, you will find us ready."

I thanked him and left the room. (1948, Pages 74-75)

Therese Martin's fanciful footnote to this entry adds:

Billy was angry because Sister Blandina knew his purpose in coming to Trinidad. He felt that he and his gang had been betrayed by the sick member.

1948 "BILLY THE KID" ENTRY 3

From Trinidad, Blandina's entry dated "Feast of All Saints, 1876," described "Billy the Kid's" then dying "gang member, Schneider," in the context of Billy the Kid's "gang;" stating:

This is the ninth month of our work with this patient who now never mentions "the Gang," though Trinidad often hears of the atrocities committed by it – **only say "Billy the Kid" and every individual is at attention** ...

Billy and his gang are terrorizing the country between this place and La Glorieta, the historic battleground of Texans and Mexicans. (1948, Page 78)

1948 "BILLY THE KID" ENTRY 4

When Blandina got her Sisters of Charity transfer notice to leave Trinidad and go to Santa Fe, she followed her "December 16, 1876" entry from Trinidad, with an entry from Tiptonville, New Mexico, the following Tuesday, making it December 19th, and being about people's fears about her journey south because of "Billy the Kid." She wrote:

> "Billy's Gang" is quite active on the plains ...
> When we arrived at Aqua Dulce - Sweetwater - all at the place were **prepared to fight the Gang and leader**, if attacked ... Whatever may have been the thoughts of those prepared to defend their lives, we were not molested. (1948, Pages 79-80)

1948 "BILLY THE KID" ENTRY 5

From Santa Fe, in an entry dated "Fourth week in May, 1877," Blandina wrote about "Billy the Kid's gang," stating:

> Most Rev. Archbishop Lamy wishes me to go with the Staab family to the terminus of the railroad, which is five miles west of Trinidad, Colorado ... Everybody is concerned about our going. Mr. [Adolph] Staab spoke to Sister [Augustine] and myself about the **danger of travel (at the present time) on the Santa Fe Trail, owing to Billy the Kid's gang**. He told us that the gang is attacking every mail coach and private conveyance ...
> **If you ever get this journal, you will see how very little fear I have of Billy's gang. Even if "Billy" has mustered new pals, I'm marked for protection as well as anyone wearing my garb.** (1948, Pages 95-96)

1948 "BILLY THE KID" ENTRY 6

Visiting Trinidad, and planning her return trip to Santa Fe, for her "June 9, 1877" entry, Blandina wrote again about being told of the dangers of "Billy the Kid;" then encountering him. She wrote:

> "The Kid is attacking the coaches or anything of profit that comes this way," [the man] answered. **The "Kid" means Billy the Kid and gang ... [But I retorted:] "I have no more fear than if the gang did not exist."** (1948, Page 97)

Blandina then described her second encounter with "Billy the Kid" - by himself, and intercepting their coach on that trip. She wrote:

> I shifted my big bonnet, so that when he did look [inside the carriage], he could see the Sisters. Our eyes met; he raised his large-brimmed hat with a wave and a bow, looked his recognition, fairly flew a distance of about three rods, and then stopped to give us some of his wonderful antics and bronco maneuvers. **The rider was the famous "Billy, the Kid!"** (1948, Page 98)

1948 "BILLY THE KID" ENTRY 7

Back in Santa Fe, for "October 1, 1878," Blandina wrote more about "Billy the Kid" and his "gang," while dropping other historical names relevant to Billy Bonney: Lew Wallace, John Tunstall, and Lawrence Murphy. She wrote:

> Our new Governor is **General Lewis [sic - Lew] Wallace.** It is difficult to predict anything about him, except that he has a difficult task before him. Not the least of which will be to check the depredations being committed by **Billy and his gang.**

The work of the "Gang" is arousing the anger of good men. Mr. Tunstall, a rancher, was brutally murdered by "Cattle King" Major L.G. Murphy's men.

"Billy," cowboy for Tunstall, witnessed the deed and swore to shoot down like a dog every man he could find who had a part in the murder of his friend.

Here was a man with qualities to make him great, smothering his best instincts to become a murderer and an outlaw. (1948, Page 113)

1948 "BILLY THE KID" ENTRY 8

From Santa Fe, for "January, 1880," Blandina wrote about "Billy the Kid's" sought capture, playing up just two past brief encounters by calling him "my old acquaintance." She wrote:

My old acquaintance, "Billy the Kid," is using his gun freely. The people of the Territory are aroused and demand his capture, dead or alive. Rewards have been offered for his capture.

Our Governor, Lewis [sic - Lew] Wallace, has shown heroic bravery by going to Lincoln County to try to pacify the storm. He had a number of interviews with "Billy," but to no effect. New rewards have been offered both by the Governor and the people to capture Billy." (1948, Page 145)

1948 "BILLY THE KID" ENTRY 9

From Santa Fe, dated "July 23, 1880," Blandina wrote about "Billy the Kid," stating:

"Billy the Kid is playing high pranks. The Governor and the people in the Territory have offered big rewards for his capture, dead or alive. (1948, Page 167)

1948 "BILLY THE KID" ENTRY 10

From Santa Fe, dated "March, 1881," Blandina wrote about "Billy the Kid," stating:

> Unfortunate "Billy the Kid!" His marauding has drawn the attention of the whole Territory, and the "Kid" is as confident of safety as though he had a battalion at his command. It has been bruited about that he intends undoing Governor Wallace. Friends of law and order are on the *qui vive* that no harm come to the author of *Ben Hur*. (1948, Page 172)

1948 "BILLY THE KID" ENTRY 11

From Santa Fe, dated "April 24, 1881," Blandina wrote about "Billy the Kid" being in the Santa Fe jail, stating:

> The murderer [of a "tenderfoot" she had warned about showing off wealth by fancy dressing] was intoxicated and is now **in jail with "Billy the Kid," who attempted to carry out his threat against Governor Wallace, but the latter was well guarded by every honest man in the Territory – hence Billy's capture.** My first free hours will be to visit the prisoners. (1948, Page 173)

1948 "BILLY THE KID" ENTRY 12

From Santa Fe, dated "May 16, 1881," Blandina wrote about her third encounter with "Billy the Kid," by visiting him in the Santa Fe jail, and declaring him "the greatest murderer of the Southwest." She wrote:

I have just returned from the jail. The two prisoners were chained hands and feet, but **the "Kid" besides being cuffed hands and feet, was also fastened to the floor** ... When I got into the prison-cell and "Billy" saw me, he said – **as though we had met yesterday instead of four years ago** – "I wish I could place a chair for you, Sister ..."

After a few minutes talk, the "Kid" said to me:

"Do what you can for Kelly [the other prisoner who killed the fancy-dressed "tenderfoot"] ... this is his first offense, and he was not himself when he did it. I'll get out of this; you will see, Sister."

Think, dear Sister Justina, how many crimes might have been prevented, had someone had influence over "Billy" after his first murder ... Finding himself captain and dictator, with no religious principles to check him, **he became what he is – the greatest murderer of the Southwest.**

I marvel at the assurance of the chained youth. No one can surmise how he can escape punishment this time. Mr. Kelly, his companion prisoner, is much dejected – fully realizing the enormity of his crime. Were not the doings of these two captives publicly known, I would not mention them – for what a prisoner says to me remains my property. (1948, Page 173)

1948 "BILLY THE KID" ENTRY 13

From Albuquerque, on "September 8, 1881," Blandina wrote about the killing of "Billy the Kid;" along with some childhood history and his "proper name - William H. Bonney" - stating:

Poor, poor **"Billy the Kid,"** was shot by Sheriff **Patrick F. Garrett** of Lincoln County. That ends the career of one who **began his downward course at the age of twelve years by taking revenge for the insult that had been offered to his mother.**

Only now have I learned his proper name – **William H. Bonney.** (1948, Page 186)

A Therese Martin footnote to this entry states: "Billy the Kid was killed July 14, 1881 at Maxwell's ranch."

1948 "BILLY THE KID" ENTRY 14

Back in Trinidad, Colorado, for her entry dated "August, 1889," Blandina reminisced about "Billy the Kid," stating:

Trinidad has lost its frontier aspect. The jail is [now] built to hold its inmates. **Billy the Kid's gang is dissolved.** (1948, Page 278)

BLANDINA'S CITING OF OTHER HISTORICAL FIGURES RELEVANT TO BILLY THE KID

SLEUTHING HOAXBUSTING CLUES: Blandina's journal entries reference other historical figures relevant to Billy the Kid's history. They also need to be evaluated for willful misinformation to explore a hoaxing pattern.

As noted above, John Tunstall, Lawrence Murphy, and Lew Wallace, key figures in Billy Bonney's history, were cited by Blandina. Additional references she made in journal entries relevant to Billy Bonney were are follows:

LEW WALLACE

New Mexico Territorial Governor Lew Wallace is mentioned four times, though with omission of his pardon promise to Billy Bonney.

1948 LEW WALLACE ENTRY 1

From Santa Fe, Blandina's journal entry for "October 1, 1878" calls Lew Wallace "Lewis," which was not the name he used, and states:

> Our new Governor is General **Lewis [sic -Lew] Wallace.** It is difficult to predict anything about him, except that he has a difficult task before him. Not the least of which will be to check the depredations being committed by Billy and his gang. (1948, Page 113)

Therese Martin's footnote adds: "Appointed by president Hayes, he was inaugurated on October 1, 1878 at Santa Fe."

1948 LEW WALLACE ENTRY 2

From Santa Fe, Blandina's journal entry for "January, 1880" presents esoteric information about Lew Wallace's intervention in Lincoln County following the disorganization after the Lincoln County War, as well as his having contact with "Billy." Blandina wrote:

> Our Governor, **Lewis [sic - Lew] Wallace,** has shown heroic bravery by going to Lincoln County to try to pacify the storm. **He had a number of interviews with "Billy,"** but to no effect. New rewards have been offered both by the Governor and the people to capture Billy." (1948, Page 145)

1948 LEW WALLACE ENTRY 3

From Santa Fe, Blandina's journal entry for "March, 1881" shows that she was aware that Lew Wallace was writing his religious historical novel titled *Ben-Hur: A Tale of the Christ.* Blandina wrote:

> [Billy the Kid's] marauding has drawn the attention of the whole Territory ... It has been bruited about that he intends undoing Governor **Wallace.** Friends of law and order are on the *qui vive* that no harm come to the author of *Ben Hur.* (1948, Page 172)

LEW WALLACE ENTRY 4

From Albuquerque, Blandina's journal entry for "April 24, 1881," states:

> The murderer was intoxicated and is now in jail with "Billy the Kid," who **attempted to carry out his threat against Governor Wallace,** but the latter was well guarded by every honest man in the Territory – hence Billy's capture. (1948, Page 173)

THOMAS BENTON CATRON

Blandina cites her attorney, Thomas Benton Catron - without apparent awareness that this lawyer-politician headed the deadly land-grabbing Santa Fe Ring.

1948 THOMAS BENTON CATRON ENTRY 1:

From Santa Fe, Blandina's journal entry for "1886" calls Catron her lawyer, stating:

> I consulted with **Mr. T.B. Catron, who has been from the beginning our counselor-in-law,** besides being considered **the "Legal Light" of our Territory.** (1948, Page 259)

A Therese Martin footnote adds: "Thomas B. Catron, born October 6, 1840, Lafayette County, Missouri. Fought in the Civil War. Appointed United States Attorney by President Grant."

Blandina's "1886" entry about a meeting at Catron's office - which was in Santa Fe's central plaza, and adjacent to the Palace of the Governors which housed Lew Wallace - introduces Catron's law partners, who mocked another lawyer who was legally opposing Blandina. She wrote:

> [I]n walked every lawyer in the building ... Mr. [William] **Thornton**, one of Catron's firm, wanted to know if I had been intimidated by that threatening letter [blocking her school warrants, which were receipts for paying teachers at the Albuquerque public school she founded]. Mr. [Frank] **Clancy** [another partner] said: "What are you going to do about it?" All seemed to enjoy the "threat." ...
> Mr. Catron [said:] "[N]ow rest assured those school warrants will be legalized" [backed legally]. (1948, Page 260)

1948 THOMAS BENTON CATRON ENTRY 2

For Blandina, Catron was an heroic figure – besides being the above mentioned " 'Legal Light' of our Territory." On September 21, 1881, from Albuquerque, she wrote:

> The capital [of the Territory] will never be moved from Santa Fe while **Mr. Thomas B. Catron** lives. (1948, Page 188)

SANTA FE RING

Blandina was aware of the Santa Fe Ring, though not of its crimes. In fact, she moved in that circle of powerful men to accomplish funding and constructing her buildings.

1948 SANTA FE RING ENTRY 1

From Santa Fe, Blandina wrote for "July 16" [1879]:

> One belonging to the **"Santa Fe Ring"** political, of course – came to ask me to visit "Big Jim" who is in jail for the murder of a policeman. (1948, Page 133)

1948 SANTA FE RING ENTRY 2

Her entry for the "January, 1880" section from Santa Fe, elaborated on the Santa Fe Ring as follows:

> There are two political parties here, Republicans and Democrats. The first party goes by the name of the **"Santa Fe Ring."** This party has been doing things to suit themselves, so the Democrats say. (1948, Pages 149-150)

1948 MAXWELL'S RANCH

Her entry for "January 25, 1877" from Santa Fe, was about the Maxwell family, still living in Cimarron in 1865. Both Blandina and Therese Martin seemed unaware that the Maxwells moved to Fort Sumner in 1870. Blandina wrote:

> Maxwell's ranch in New Mexico was reached in the evening of September 11 [1865 by traveling Sisters of Charity entering the Territory] ...
> Early rising among a certain industrial class of natives [Mexicans] was proverbial, and Mrs. Maxwell belonged to that class ... She was inconsolable to find the Sisters had been in the coach during the night ... The Maxwell family is noted for hospitality. There the American, the native, the Indian are all made to feel at home.

LAND-GRABBERS

1948 LAND-GRABBER ENTRY 1

Blandina seemed unaware that her Ringite friends, like Catron, were the Hispanic land grant "land-grabbers," whom she deplored. Her idiosyncratic concept was that dishonest individuals cheated Hispanic property owners by making them sign an X on documents they could not read. She was apparently ignorant of the scale of millions of acres acquired by Catron and his cronies. She wrote on "September 21, 1881":

> I am going to make a further prediction. The "land-grabbers" will do tremendous havoc among our native population, both spiritually and financially ... (1948, Page 188)
>
> When the men from the States come out West to dispossess the poor natives of their lands, they used many subterfuges. One was to offer the owner of the land a handful of silver coins for the small service of making a mark on a paper. The mark was a cross, which was accepted as a signature, and by which the unsuspecting natives deeded away their lands. By this means, many a poor family was robbed of all its possessions. (1948, Page 194)

1948 LAND-GRABBER ENTRY 2

From Albuquerque, for "May, 1883," Blandina naively described Catron as generously offering her a huge tract of land for an Industrial School she hoped to build. She appeared unaware that the land Catron owned or controlled was from the Santa Fe Ring's "grabbing." Blandina wrote:

> Lawyer Catron told me he had a large grant of land. "Select a thousand acres and they are yours in fee simple, for your Industrial School," he said to me. (1948, Page 197)

1948 DR. ROBERT LONGWILL

Blandina was equally unaware that Dr. Robert Longwill was a Santa Fe Ring member, who was believed by citizens in Colfax County's Cimarron to be complicit in the 1875 murder of anti-Ring activist Reverend Franklin Tolby. Thomas Benton Catron allegedly shielded Longwill from prosecution; and Longwill resettled from Cimarron to Santa Fe. There, he became head of Blandina's hospital staff.

From Santa Fe, for "August 16 [1879]," Blandina wrote about using Longwill, as her head of the staff (1948, Page 140), to autopsy a man she had nursed there in her hospital. She wrote:

> As this case baffled the physicians, Dr. Longwill proposed a post-mortem. (1948, Page 138)

1948 VICTORIO

The Mimbres Apache Chief Victorio fought against unjust take-over of his tribal lands. From Albuquerque, for "February 2, 1886," Blandina wrote:

> Not only is Gerónimo riding at large, but Victorio and other captains also. (1948, Page 244)

ANALYSIS OF BLANDINA'S 14 "BILLY THE KID" ENTRIES

SLEUTHING HOAXBUSTING CLUES: Blandina's 1948 published "Billy the Kid" journal entries from At the End of the Santa Fe Trail paint a specific image of "Billy the Kid" as a depraved murderous desperado minimally tamed by exposure to her faith-based goodness. The entries' dating, locations, and events provide fodder for historical scrutiny as to their veracity.

1948 "BILLY THE KID" ENTRY 1

For her "September, 1876" entry, from Trinidad, Colorado, Blandina makes her first "Billy the Kid" reference, and also uses the names "Bill's Gang" and "Billy the Kid's Gang;" as follows:

> My scattered notes on **"Billy the Kid's Gang"** are condensed, and someday you [Justina] will be thrilled by their perusal.
>
> *The Trinidad Enterprise* – the only paper published here – in its last issue gave an exciting description of how **a member of "Bill's Gang"** painted red the town of Cimarron ...
>
> Yesterday one of the Vigilant Committee came to where I was ... and said: ... "I want you to see one of **'Billy's gang,'** the one who caused such fright in Cimarron ...
>
> **Billy's accomplice** headed toward us.
>
> He was mounted on a spirited stallion ... and was dressed as the *Torreros* (Bull-Fighters) dress in old Mexico. Cowboy's sombrero, fantastically trimmed, red velvet knee breaches, green velvet short coat, long sharp spurs, gold and green saddle cover. A figure of six feet three ... The impression made on me was of intense loathing, and I will candidly acknowledge, of fear also. (1948, Pages 67-68)

[AUTHOR'S NOTE: Billy Bonney was never in Colorado, and in 1876 was living in Bonita, Arizona. He departed there on August 17, 1877. In addition, he never had a gang; but one was invented for him in Santa Fe Ring newspaper propaganda beginning in 1880. And Anglo cowboys and outlaws did not wear Hispanic costumes like those described here. Also, the *Trinidad Enterprise* did not exist in 1876; the local paper was the *Enterprise and Chronicle*.]

1948 "BILLY THE KID" ENTRY 2

The "September, 1876" entry continued about the gigantic "gang member," now left in Trinidad by the gang with a bullet in his thigh after a gunfight with another gang member named "Happy Jack," whom he shot dead. Blandina calls him "Schneider" - with no first name - and she was nursing him. That led to her first reported meeting with "Billy the Kid." (1948, Pages 70-71) Blandina wrote:

[At another visit, o]ur patient [Schneider] lost no time in telling me that Billy and the "gang" are to be here, Saturday at 2 P.M., and I'm going to tell you why they are coming ...

"Well, the 'gang' is going to scalp the four of [the town's physicians] ... because none of them would extract the bullet from my thigh." ...

Saturday, 2 P.M. came, and I went to meet Billy and his gang ... The introduction was given. I can only remember, "**Billy, our Captain**, and Chism ..."

The leader, Billy, has steel-blue eyes, peach complexion, is young, one would take him to be seventeen – innocent-looking, save for the corners of his eyes, which tell a set purpose, good or bad ... My glance took this description in while "Billy" was saying: "We are all glad to see you, Sister, and I want to say, it would give me pleasure to do you a favor." ...

I took the hand saying: "I understand you have come to scalp our Trinidad physicians, which act I ask you to cancel." ...

"Not only [do I grant] that, Sister, but at any time my pals and I can serve you, you will find us ready."

I thanked him and left the room. (1948, Pages 74-75)

Therese Martin's footnote to this entry states: "Billy was angry because Sister Blandina knew his purpose in coming to Trinidad. He felt that he and his gang had been betrayed by the sick member."

[AUTHOR'S NOTE: Billy Bonney was never in Colorado, and in 1876 was in Bonita, Arizona. Furthermore, scalping was associated with Native Americans and bounty hunters who took their scalps to prove kills. Giving Billy a young appearance is no stretch, given the moniker "Kid." The footnote shows the elaboration of Blandina's "Billy the Kid" claims after her death.]

1948 "BILLY THE KID" ENTRY 3

From Trinidad, Blandina's entry dated "Feast of All Saints, 1876," described Billy the Kid's then dying "gang member," in context of "Billy the Kid's gang," stating:

> This is the ninth month of our work with this patient who now never mentions **"the Gang,"** though Trinidad often hears of the atrocities committed by it – **only say "Billy the Kid" and every individual is at attention** ...
>
> **Billy and his gang are terrorizing the country** between this place and La Glorieta, the historic battleground of Texans and Mexicans. (1948, Page 78)

[AUTHOR'S NOTE: Billy Bonney was never in Colorado, and in 1876 was in Bonita, Arizona. He was never in the area between Trinidad and Glorieta Pass, in New Mexico Territory (except during train transport in December of 1880 to the Santa Fe jail). He had no gang.]

1948 "BILLY THE KID" ENTRY 4

When Blandina traveled from Trinidad to Santa Fe, she made an entry for December 19, 1876 from Tiptonville, New Mexico, about fears of Billy the Kid. She wrote:

"Billy's Gang" is quite active on the plains ...

When we arrived at Aqua Dulce – Sweetwater – all at the place were **prepared to fight the Gang and leader**, if attacked ... Whatever may have been the thoughts of those prepared to defend their lives, we were not molested. (1948, Pages 79-80)

[AUTHOR'S NOTE: Billy Bonney was never in Colorado or northern New Mexico, and in 1876 was in Bonita, Arizona. He was never in the area described. And he had no gang.]

1948 "BILLY THE KID" ENTRY 5

From Santa Fe, in an entry dated "Fourth week in May, 1877," Blandina wrote about Billy the Kid's "gang," stating:

Most Rev. Archbishop Lamy wishes me to go with the Staab family to the terminus of the railroad, which is five miles west of Trinidad, Colorado ... Everybody is concerned about our going. Mr. [Adolph] Staab spoke to Sister and myself about the **danger of travel (at the present time) on the Santa Fe Trail**, owing to Billy the Kid's gang. He told us that the gang is attacking every mail coach and private conveyance ...

If you ever get this journal, you will see how very little fear I have of Billy's gang. Even if "Billy" has mustered new pals, I'm marked for protection as well as anyone wearing my garb. (1948, Pages 95-96)

[AUTHOR'S NOTE: In May of 1877, Billy Bonney was still in Bonita, Arizona; and did not leave there for New Mexico Territory until August 17, 1877. And he never rode the northern New Mexico Territory portion of the Santa Fe Trail. He had no gang.]

1948 "BILLY THE KID" ENTRY 6

Visiting Trinidad, and planning her return trip to Santa Fe, for her "June 9, 1877" entry, Blandina wrote again about being told of the dangers of "Billy the Kid;" and then encountering him. She wrote:

"The Kid is attacking the coaches or anything of profit that comes this way," [the man] answered. **The "Kid" means Billy the Kid and gang ... [But I retorted:] "I have no more fear than if the gang did not exist."** (1948, Page 97)

In the same entry, Blandina then described her second personal encounter with "Billy the Kid" - alone and intercepting their coach. She wrote:

I shifted my big bonnet, so that when he did look [inside the carriage], he could see the Sisters. Our eyes met; he raised his large-brimmed hat with a wave and a bow, looked his recognition, fairly flew a distance of about three rods, and then stopped to give us some of his wonderful antics and bronco maneuvers. **The rider was the famous "Billy, the Kid!"** (1948, Page 98)

[AUTHOR'S NOTE: In June of 1877, Billy Bonney was still in Bonita, Arizona; and did not leave for New Mexico Territory until August 17, 1877. And he never rode in the described area. And he had no gang. As fanciful as the bull-fighter costumed "gang member," is Blandina's "Billy the Kid" character implausibly and idiotically performing "wonderful antics and bronco maneuvers" just for her while taking the obvious outlaw risk: being shot by the men in the Staab group, who could be assumed to recognize him.]

1948 "BILLY THE KID" ENTRY 7

From Santa Fe, for "October 1, 1878," Blandina wrote more about "Billy the Kid" and his "gang," while dropping other historical names relevant to Billy Bonney: Lew Wallace, John Tunstall, and Lawrence Murphy. She wrote:

> Our new Governor is **General Lewis [sic -Lew] Wallace.** It is difficult to predict anything about him, except that he has a difficult task before him. Not the least of which will be to check the depredations being committed by **Billy and his gang.**
>
> **The work of the "Gang" is arousing the anger of good men. Mr. Tunstall,** a rancher, was brutally murdered by "Cattle King" **Major L.G. Murphy's** men.
>
> "Billy," cowboy for **Tunstall,** witnessed the deed and swore to shoot down like a dog every man he could find who had a part in the murder of his friend.
>
> Here was a man with qualities to make him great, smothering his best instincts to become a murderer and an outlaw. (1948, Page 113)

[AUTHOR'S NOTE: The historical names are not quite correct, and are dropped for feigned historical veracity. Wallace was called Lew, not Lewis. Lawrence Murphy was not a cattle king. Murphy did not murder Tunstall. Billy Bonney's Lincoln County War fighting was against the Santa Fe Ring, not just acting to avenge John Tunstall's murder. And in October of 1878, Billy was in Tascosa, Texas, selling stock rustled from Ringites. And Billy had no gang.]

1948 "BILLY THE KID" ENTRY 8

From Santa Fe, dating her entry as "January, 1880," Blandina wrote about "Billy the Kid" and his sought capture, calling him "my old acquaintance." She wrote:

43

My old acquaintance, "Billy the Kid," is using his gun freely. The people of the Territory are aroused and demand his capture, dead or alive. **Rewards have been offered** for his capture.

Our Governor, Lewis Wallace, has shown heroic bravery by going to Lincoln County to try to pacify the storm. **He had a number of interviews with "Billy," but to no effect. New rewards have been offered** both by the Governor and the people to capture Billy." (1948, Page 145)

[AUTHOR'S NOTE: In January of 1880, there were no rewards offered for Billy the Kid. And Wallace had met with Billy Bonney in Lincoln in March of 1879 to make the pardon bargain, which Billy honored and Wallace betrayed. The entry is concocted from later reference sources and is not date-related.]

1948 "BILLY THE KID" ENTRY 9

From Santa Fe, dated "July 23, 1880," Blandina wrote about "Billy the Kid," stating:

"Billy the Kid is playing high pranks. The Governor and the people in the Territory have **offered big rewards** for his capture, dead or alive. (1948, Page 167)

[AUTHOR'S NOTE: In July of 1880, there were no rewards offered for Billy Bonney.]

1948 "BILLY THE KID" ENTRY 10

From Santa Fe, dated "March, 1881," Blandina wrote about "Billy the Kid," stating:

Unfortunate "Billy the Kid!" His marauding has drawn the attention of the whole Territory, and the "Kid" is as confident of safety as though he had a battalion at his command. It has been bruited about that he intends undoing Governor Wallace. Friends of law and order are on the *qui vive* that no harm come to the author of *Ben Hur*. (1948, Page 172)

[AUTHOR'S NOTE: In March of 1881, Billy Bonney was either in the Santa Fe jail (until the 28th) or was in Mesilla for his hanging trial. And Lew Wallace fabricated the vendetta of Billy the Kid against himself in his own newspaper articles.]

1948 "BILLY THE KID" ENTRY 11

From Santa Fe, with entry of "April 24, 1881," Blandina wrote about "Billy the Kid" being in the Santa Fe jail, stating:

The murderer [of a "tenderfoot" she had warned about showing off wealth by fancy dressing] was intoxicated and is now **in jail with "Billy the Kid," who attempted to carry out his threat against Governor Wallace, but the latter was well guarded by every honest man in the Territory – hence Billy's capture.** My first free hours will be to visit the prisoners. (1948, Page 173)

[AUTHOR'S NOTE: Billy Bonney's capture by Pat Garrett on December 22, 1880 had nothing to do with Lew Wallace - aside from the betrayed pardon promise that would have removed Billy's Lincoln County War indictments and need for any capture. And on April 24, 1881, Billy was incarcerated in Lincoln's courthouse-jail, and four days from his great escape from it. He had been taken from the Santa Fe jail on March 28, 1881 for his hanging trials in Mesilla. He was not returned to the Santa Fe jail, but was transported to the Lincoln courthouse-jail to await hanging on May 13, 1881.]

1948 "BILLY THE KID" ENTRY 12

From Santa Fe, dated "May 16, 1881," Blandina wrote about her third personal encounter with "Billy the Kid," by visiting him in the Santa Fe jail, and declaring him "the greatest murderer of the Southwest." She wrote:

> I have just returned from the jail. The two prisoners were chained hands and feet, but **the "Kid" besides being cuffed hands and feet, was also fastened to the floor** ... When I got into the prison-cell and "Billy" saw me, he said – **as though we had met yesterday instead of four years ago** – "I wish I could place a chair for you, Sister ..."
>
> After a few minutes talk, the "Kid" said to me:
>
> "Do what you can for Kelly [the other prisoner who killed the fancy-dressed "tenderfoot"] ... this is his first offense, and he was not himself when he did it. I'll get out of this; you will see, Sister."
>
> Think, dear Sister Justina, how many crimes might have been prevented, had someone had influence over "Billy" after his first murder ... Finding himself captain and dictator, with no religious principles to check him, **he became what he is – the greatest murderer of the Southwest.**
>
> I marvel at the assurance of the chained youth. No one can surmise how he can escape punishment this time. Mr. Kelly, his companion prisoner, is much dejected – fully realizing the enormity of his crime. Were not the doings of these two captives publicly known, I would not mention them – for what a prisoner says to me remains my property. (1948, Page 173)

[AUTHOR'S NOTE: Billy Bonney was not in the Santa Fe jail in May of 1881. He was on the run after his Lincoln jailbreak on April 28, 1881.]

1948 "BILLY THE KID" ENTRY 13

From Albuquerque, on "September 8, 1881," Blandina wrote about the killing of "Billy the Kid;" along with some childhood history and his "proper name - William H. Bonney" - stating:

> Poor, poor **"Billy the Kid," was shot by Sheriff Patrick F. Garrett** of Lincoln County. That ends the career of one who **began his downward course at the age of twelve years by taking revenge** for the insult that had been offered to his mother.
>
> Only now have I learned his proper name - **William H. Bonney.** (1948, Page 186)

A Therese Martin footnote to this entry stated: "Billy the Kid was killed July 14, 1881 at Maxwell's ranch."

[AUTHOR'S NOTE: Billy Bonney did not commit murder at 12 years old. And Blandina confirms here that he was the "Billy" she had been writing about as "Billy the Kid."]

1948 "BILLY THE KID" ENTRY 14

Back in Trinidad, Colorado, for her entry dated "August 1889," Blandina reminisced about "Billy the Kid," stating:

> Trinidad has lost its frontier aspect. The jail is [now] built to hold its inmates. **Billy the Kid's gang is dissolved.** (1948, Page 278)

[AUTHOR'S NOTE: Billy Bonney was never in Trinidad, Colorado. He never had a gang.]

BLANDINA'S "BILLY THE KID" PROBLEM

The 1948 edition of *At the End of the Santa Fe Trail* leaves no doubt that its journal entries presented Blandina Segale as having associated with nationally famous Billy Bonney as Billy the Kid, who was additionally placed in the context of the Lincoln County War and historical figures associated with that period. Blandina herself called her "Billy the Kid" "William H. Bonney." And on page 210a, is a full-page illustration of the tintype of Billy Bonney, attributed to the collection of the Museum of New Mexico, where it was obtained.

The problem for these claims is that Blandina's description of "Billy the Kid's" activities, locations, gang, and dates have nothing to do with the historical Billy Bonney. It is clear that Blandina never personally knew Billy the Kid. And her second-hand entries have a quality of research from available sources. Furthermore, the even distribution of the "Billy the Kid" entries from beginning to end of the text implies literary placement rather than historical reporting in a real journal.

And that disconnect from reality applies to other historical figures. For example, Blandina's February 2, 1886 entry from Albuquerque referenced Victorio not only by second-hand information, but by her alleged encounter with his depredations at a mining camp the day before a visit of hers. But Victorio was killed in Old Mexico in October of 1880, six years earlier. Blandina had written:

> Not only is Gerónimo riding at large, but Victorio and other captains also.
> **Last week Sister Catherine and myself visited one of the grading camps and stood on a mound where, the day before, Victorio had scalped two of the working men.** Everyone in the camp was as quiet as though nothing had occurred. (1932, Page 244)

Worrisome questions arise. What was Blandina doing with her claims? Was she a boastful sibling, intending to impress her sister, Justina, some day with her jaunty daring and power to convert black-hearted desperados? Was she an addled lady, not able to distinguish one "outlaw" from another? Was she an unaware victim of unauthorized editing, with artful insertion by someone else - like a Therese Martin - of spicy tales to keep her narrative going?

And now that Blandina is in the running for sainthood, will her promoters capitalize on big name Billy the Kid, to garner media buzz to publicize her cause?

Will the currently planned TV series on Blandina likewise capitalize on sure-fire ratings boost of a Billy the Kid character?

And given the false claims in the journal, does this boil down to a true Billy the Kid hoax, joining others which attempted to hijack his fame?

It remains to be seen if these nun's tales will rank as the oddest example of a Billy the Kid identity theft as the Nun's Tale Hoax.

What I needed to do next was to go back to versions published during Blandina's lifetime. There were magazine articles and the first edition of *At the End of the Santa Fe Trail*. If they lacked the "Billy the Kid" entries, Blandina would be vindicated. One could conclude that a later editor, like Therese Martin, added the famous characters - including Billy the Kid - to broaden the frontier tales' public appeal.

SMOKING GUNS FOR A HOAX: Blandina's dated journal entries for "Billy the Kid" and Victorio in the 1948 edition of At the End of the Santa Fe Trail do not correspond to historical reality. But was Blandina their author? Would the entries in the 1932 edition, created in her lifetime, prove to be different from those in 1948? And would the original magazine articles further clarify responsibility for authorship? But as of the 1948 book, it was clear that a Billy the Kid hoax existed. Only its author was uncertain.

3

MEDIA MAGNET OF A NUN PAL OF "BILLY THE KID"

FRIENDSHIP OF A POSSIBLE SAINT AND A CERTAIN SINNER GRABS MEDIA ATTENTION

SLEUTHING HOAXBUSTING CLUES: Blandina's published Old West journal lured press and film by her connection to famous Billy the Kid. Naysayers were ignored to retain that attention-grabbing formula, guaranteeing public misinformation to the present.

FIRST ENCOUNTER WITH BLANDINA SEGALE

I was first introduced to Blandina Segale by a November 13, 2015 *DailyMail.com* Associated Press article titled " 'The Fastest Nun in the West': Nun who got Billy the Kid to back down and then became his friend moves up sainthood path." It claimed that Blandina had "helped a member of Billy the Kid's gang," that "Billy the Kid had been mad but she had induced him not to seek revenge on doctors," and that "she befriended the infamous Wild West outlaw and later visited him in jail." I was irritated by what looked like an obvious hoax. But I did nothing.

TAKING ACTION AGAINST A HOAX

What spurred me to action was a March 22, 2017, *Albuquerque Journal* article by an Adrian Gomez, Arts and Entertainment Editor, announcing: "Sister Blandina TV pilot filming in New Mexico." The *Albuquerque Journal* had already backed corrupt Governor Bill Richardson and his complicit lawmen for their Billy the Kid Case DNA hoax. It was not a credible seal of approval. Gomez now wrote:

[Blandina] visited and cared for Billy the Kid and other prisoners confined in the main prison in Santa Fe ... Allen Sanchez [her petitioner for sainthood] ... said, ... **Sister Blandina is a nun that interacted with everyone from Billy the Kid to Mark Twain.**

PRELIMINARY RESEARCH

Quick internet search showed me that on July 13, 2016, a DailyMail.com article had already declared: "Nun who Stopped Billy the Kid from scalping 4 doctors to become subject of new TV series." It had a large illustration of Billy Bonney's famous tintype. That ridiculous and scurrilous claim of Billy's intent to scalp doctors made me angry. And its crazy misinformation was poised to do public damage to the legitimate history of Billy Bonney. The subtitles stated:

- Saint Hood Productions based in Albuquerque, New Mexico, is scheduled Wednesday to announce new project around Sister Blandina Segale

- She was a 19th-Century nun whose clashes with Old West outlaws and work with immigrants has been the stuff of legend

- **She reported a tip that Billy the Kid was coming to her town to scalp four doctors who refused to threat his friend's gunshot wound**

- **Segale nursed the friend to health, and when Billy went to Trinidad to thank her, she convinced him to abandon his violent plan.**

- The Roman Catholic Church is examining Segale for Sainthood

This blarney was horrifying. Billy Bonney was never in Colorado. He was a freedom fighter in New Mexico Territory's Lincoln County War, and was outlawed by the victorious corrupt Santa Fe Ring, determined to kill him. The article had identified the players and the plan:

[Saint Hood Productions'] "At the End of the Santa Fe Trail" **aims to be a fictional account based on Segale's life and will use material from her 1932 book with the same name** ...

Allen Sanchez, president and CEO of CHI St. Joseph's Children – an Albuquerque community health organization born of Segale's work – said the nun is a perfect subject for a television series since many of the same issues she faced still resonate ...

Thomas Sanchez, executive producer and director of the Segale production, said 98 percent of the cast and crew will be from New Mexico. "I am honored to tell Sister Blandina's story," he said. "This task requires lots of attention to history."

So Allen Sánchez and Thomas Sanchez were people I had to meet. I was worried about the loop-hole of Saint Hood Productions' claim of "a fictional account based on Segale's ... 1932 book." It looked like a crafty way to use her Billy the Kid claims, and then say, "It's just fiction, folks." That was how to trick people, while taking no responsibility for the hoax.

This reporting also ignored an exposé four years earlier, on October 12, 2012, in *The American Catholic*, by a Donald R. McClarey, titled: "Sister Blandina and the Original Billy the Kid." McClarey debunked her Billy the Kid contact claims. He rationalized that she actually knew an outlaw named Arthur Pond aka William LeRoy; who, McClarey said, was also known as "Billy the Kid" - and was the "original" Billy the Kid! To excuse Blandina's misinformation, he concluded that she had had confused the two Billy's in her old age. So he wrote:

> One of the many outlaws who terrorized the area [in Colorado] was Arthur Pond aka William LeRoy, sometimes known as Billy the Kid, and who was celebrated as King of the American Highwaymen by the "penny dreadful" novelist Richard K. Fox who released a heavily fictionalized biography of him immediately after his death, conflating his exploits with those of the more famous Billy the Kid. (**Sister Blandina in later life confused LeRoy with William**

H. Bonney, the more famous Billy the Kid, who operated in New Mexico a few years later. Sister Blandina had known the outlaw only by his nickname and didn't realize there were two Billy the Kids, who died within months of each other in 1881.) ...

Sister Blandina encountered the original Billy the Kid for the last time in May of 1881 while he was being held in the Santa Fe jail ... LeRoy [and his fellow incarcerated brother] were both hung by a lynch mob that broke into the jail.

Another recent reporter who stayed clear of Billy the Kid intoxication, and picked Billy LeRoy, was a Hannah Nordhaus, writing for the November, 2016 edition of *Smithsonian Magazine* with the title: "Making the Case for the Next American Saint: Sister Blandina Segale showed true grit while caring for orphans and outlaws in New Mexico." After interviewing Peso Chavez, a Santa Fe private investigator assisting Allen Sánchez in researching Sister Blandina's history, Nordhaus reflected Chavez's doubt about Blandina's "Billy" being Billy Bonney, and adopted his and Sánchez's use of the "two Billy the Kid's" excuse. Nordhaus wrote:

> Chavez's research was complicated by the fact that **there were two Billy the Kid's roaming the high desert in 1877: William Bonney,** the famous Billy, who did most of his outlawing in southern New Mexico and eastern Arizona, and **William LeRoy –** the not-so-famous Billy – who terrorized northern New Mexico. Chavez created a chart tracking dates and Billy-sightings, and determined that it was likely the second Billy who spared my great-great-grandfather [a stage coach robbery] thanks to Blandina's intervention.

So investigator, Peso Chavez, was added to my list of people to contact to stop the Nun's Tale Hoax.

MORE BILLY THE KID HYPE FOR SAINTHOOD

I soon realized that Billy the Kid had been consistently used as the media hook for Blandina's story. Even her progress up the path of sainthood to Servant of God had hawked their alleged relationship.

It was an ongoing theme in Sisters of Charity of Cincinnati promotion. On May 23, 2014, Sister Judith Metz, then their archivist, posted for the Daughters of Charity Provincial Archives an internet article titled "Servant of God, Sister Blandina Segale, S.C.," stating:

> *At the End of the Santa Fe Trial*, stories of her twenty-one years in the Southwest, makes fascinating reading through her letters [sic] to her sister, Justina, **especially her encounter with Billy the Kid.**

On June 24, 2014, a Sisters of Charity of Cincinnati press release by the Director of Communications, Sister Georgia Kitt, titled "Sisters of Charity Announce Approval of Cause for Canonization of Sister Blandina Segale," proclaimed:

> Her [frontier] adventures have been featured in novels, television programs, histories, and even a comic book. **These often focus in her fearless befriending of Billy the Kid and his gang.**

A July 19, 2014 *DailyMail.com* Associated Press article was titled " 'Fastest Nun in the West' Sister Blandina Segale who stopped Billy the Kid may become a saint." Flashing a huge picture of Billy Bonney's tintype - almost as big as Blandina's portrait - it stated:

> A nun who intervened to stop **Billy the Kid** murdering four doctors could be made a saint to honor her work in setting up hospitals and schools in New Mexico ...
> **Her encounters with Billy the Kid remain among her most popular and well-known Western frontier adventures.**

On August 26, 2015, *The Washington* Post reporter, Sarah Kaplan, wrote: " 'The fastest nun in the West,' who took on Billy the Kid, is on the road to sainthood." Kaplan wrote: "The case for canonizing the 19th century Italian-born nun, **whose run-in with Old West outlaw Billy the Kid is the stuff of legend**, was presented at a ceremonial 'first inquiry' in Albuquerque." As usual, Kaplan rolled out Blandina's tale of her "saving the Trinidad doctors," stating:

> Nearly four years into her time in Trinidad, Segale had her **famous encounter with "Billy the Kid"** – who, at 17, was already leader of a gang with a price on his head … [After she convinces him to cancel his plan to scalp the doctors], the outlaw and the nun shook hands.

Also on August 26, 2015, Associated Press reporter, Russell Contreras, was quoted in the *Albuquerque Journal* for " ' The Fastest Nun in the West' " faces first test in sainthood push: Vatican to investigate the work of Sister Blandina Segale." His article's lead-in called Blandina, "An Italian-born nun who challenged Billy the Kid." Contreras wrote:

> **[H]er encounters with Billy the Kid remain among her most popular and well-known Western Frontier adventures.**
>
> According to one story, she received a tip that the Kid was coming to her town to scalp the four doctors who had refused to treat his friend's gunshot wound. Segale nursed the friend to health and when Billy came to Trinidad, Colo. to thank her, she asked him to abandon his violent plan. He agreed.

On August 29, 2015, Associated Press reporter, Russell Contreras, was used again, now for the Dayton, Ohio, *Journal* for "Nun who Stood Up to Billy the Kid: Catholic Church considering her case for sainthood." It repeated the lead-in of Blandina and Billy the Kid, and her tale of her doctor-saving encounter with him in Trinidad, Colorado.

On August 31, 2015, Blandina's honorable sainthood Petitioner, Allen Sánchez apparently had some sobering effect with Catholic News Agency's Albuquerque reporter, Mary Rezac, who wrote "Nuns, guns and the Wild West – the extraordinary tale of Sr. Blandina." The tried-and-true Billy the Kid hook was used, but Rezac threw in ambiguously: "**Billy the Kid (William LeRoy)** was still unhappy. Word got out that the outlaw was coming to town to scalp the four doctors of Trinidad." Rezac thereby side-stepped that Blandina never knew the famous and actual Billy the Kid.

The November 13, 2015 Associated Press article, "Nun who stood up to Billy the Kid moves toward sainthood," that first caught my attention, simply ignored Allen Sánchez's Billy-the-Kid-as-Billy-LeRoy disclaimer, to make it seem as if Sánchez personally validated Blandina's claims, when, in fact, he and his researcher, Peso Chavez, had validated other Blandina claims, and had *denied* her claim of Billy the Kid being "William H. Bonney." The reporter blithely wrote:

> **Billy the Kid and his gang once found Segale in a covered wagon they attempted to rob. The nun had previously convinced the "Kid" not to scalp four doctors so he recognized her and abandoned his holdup.**
>
> Sanchez said church investigators were able to find a descendant of a passenger in the covered wagon who confirmed the story.
>
> **"I think we've proven that we can trust the stories in (her) book because we've verified the stories,"** Sanchez said.

A December, 2015 *People of God's* article titled: "Servant of God, Rosa Maria Segale (Sr. Blandina Segale, SC) Moves Closer to Sainthood AKA The Fastest Nun in the West Who Stood Up to Billy the Kid" tried to reflect Allen Sánchez's efforts - even giving his contact information at the end - but fell far short of clarity - or of abandoning the powerful Billy the Kid hook - by writing:

> There is public corroborating literature about Sr. Blandina Segale, SC standing up to and befriending **Billy the Kid "William LeRoy."**

On July 16, 2016, the *Calgary Herald* printed Associated Press reporter, Russell Contreras's article as: "Old West nun stood up to Billy the Kid: Sister Segale, who will be subject of TV series, considered for sainthood." Contreras reported on Albuquerque-based Saint Hood Productions executive producer, Thomas Sanchez's, intent to dramatize her *At the End of the Santa Fe Trail*. The lead-in was the usual: "An Italian-born nun who challenged Billy the Kid;" and it recycled Blandina's outlaw "Billy the Kid" and the Trinidad doctors tale.

EIGHT DECADES OF RISING MEDIA CRESCENDO

DELVING INTO THE PAST

I soon realized that the current press was just the tip of the iceberg of almost nine decades of media hoopla about the tales of Blandina Segale and Billy the Kid.

When Blandina's future *At the End of the Santa Fe Trail* book was still in serial form in the Santa Maria Institute's magazine, the *Santa Fe New Mexican* sent her a copy of its article in a letter dated April 7, 1930. The article stated:

SISTER BLANDINA DEFIED OUTLAWS, SAVED ONE ARCHBISHOP, ALSO VISITED BILLY THE KID

The STORY of Santa Fe has received no more thrilling contribution than the journal of Sister Blandina, "At the End of the Santa Fe Trail" kept during her Mission in the Southwest. Running in serial form for the past two years in "Veritas," a Catholic magazine for the Italians published in Cincinnati, it is still continuing, a story of heroism, self-sacrifice, determination, devotion, unsurpassed. On every page is a stirring tale, back of it all one feels the dominating force of character, overcoming all obstacles; the delicious sense of humor, the dogged persistence, the brilliant personality of a extraordinary woman ...

VISITS BILLY IN JAIL
In Santa Fe she visited Billy the Kid in jail, and as he lay shackled

hand and foot and chained to a ring in the floor, he politely excused his inability to offer her a chair while she consoled with him. Accurately she gauged the character of this debonair young murderer and longed for a chance to see his feet back on the right path.

On November 17, 1933, for *The Commonweal*, Eugene P. Murphy wrote "Keeping the Record" about Blandina Segale's recent book, *At the End of the Santa Fe Trail*. But he focused largely on Billy the Kid, his garbled misinformation and own fantasies adding to Blandina's fables. Murphy wrote:

Billy the Kid was an outlaw whose name cast terror along the Santa Fe trail for many a year. What our grandfathers and fathers have told us, and what the penny-dreadfuls of our youth supplied, gave this terrorist a character that is completely savage. However he was not that. Young and of striking appearance, as were most of his confederates, he had many traits which compelled admiration. Sister Blandina saw the unrealized possibilities for good that lay in his untamed soul. Like a true teaching nun she wondered what the result might have been had some good influence reached him in time. Could it not have stilled the hate rising in the heart of the lad of twelve and prevented him from starting on his career of killing ...

Today William H. Bonney lies buried on the site of old Fort Sumner, New Mexico. At his side are two of his comrades of the gang, Charlie Bowdre and Tom O'Folliard. Old friends and others fascinated by the memory of the slightly built, boy-faced Robin Hood of the plains have built a marker around his grave. It indicates almost the exact spot where Sheriff Pat Garret [sic] shot him to death, July 14, 1881 ... Peace prevails where the Kid knew only bloody strife.

Trumping other Billy the Kid fakery was a June 15, 1949 *Topix* comic book titled "Sister Blandina meets Billy the Kid." Its cover had the black-habited sister and a man on a rearing horse dressed like a Mexican dandy.

TOPIX, June 15, 1949. Vol. 7, No. 20. Published semi-monthly, September through June, by CATECHETICAL GUILD Educational Society, 145-147 East 5th St., St. Paul, Minnesota. Yearly subscription (U.S. and foreign): $2.00; entered as second class matter November 27, 1942, at the post office at St. Paul, Minnesota, under the Act of March 3, 1879. Copyright 1949. Catechetical Guild Educational Society. Printed in U.S.A.

TOPIX, June 15, 1949. Vol. 7, No. 20. Published semi-monthly, September through June, by CATECHETICAL GUILD Educational Society, 145-147 East 5th St., St. Paul, Minnesota. Yearly subscription (U.S. and foreign): $2.00; entered as second class matter November 27, 1942, at the post office at St. Paul, Minnesota, under the Act of March 3, 1879. Copyright 1949. Catechetical Guild Educational Society. Printed in U.S.A.

It was published by Catechetical Guild Educational Society of St. Paul, Minnesota. The comic book's text began:

> In 1876, Sister Blandina Segale, S.C., was teaching school in the Town of Trinidad, Colorado. The notorious Billy the Kid was at the height of his power and everyone feared him – everyone but Sister Blandina.

The comic illustrated Blandina's tale of caring for "gang member Schneider," meeting "Billy the Kid," then encountering him again on the Staab trip and getting a friendly response.

The September, 1953 edition of *The Irish Digest* had an article by a L.G. O'Carroll titled "The Nun and Billy the Kid: How timid, inexperienced little sister Blandina earned the respect of the bad men of the wild and wooly West." As usual, bad "Billy the Kid" was the foil for good Blandina. O'Carroll, indulging in his own fantasy embellishments to Blandina's existing fables, wrote:

Perhaps the influence of Sister Blandina with hardened men is best illustrated by **her meeting with Billy the Kid**. Billy was the most daring of the South-West desperados. He was young, debonair, fiercely loyal to his friends, yet one of the cruelest and most ruthless killers of those lawless times – he would put a bullet through a man as nonchalantly as he would light a cigarette. He died at twenty-one, fair-haired, slim, boyish in appearance, yet he had killed a man for every year of his life ...

But it seems certain that the notorious outlaw had a special reverence for the little nun, and in time her gentle sympathy might have softened the core of hardness in him.

The two met in this way [by her nursing his injured gang member]...

Billy had heard of his follower's plight. Coldly angry, he decided he would ride into Trinidad and scalp the four doctors in the town for not helping his pard ... On his way he called to see the wounded outlaw, found Sister Blandina at the bed side and promised he would grant her any favor in his power ... [So she asked for the doctors to be spared.]

The Kid's eyes flashed coldly. But after a moment he said: "I granted the favor before I knew it. But my word stands. And if at any time, Sister, my pards and I can help you, you will always find us willing."

A big favor that certainly was, granted by an outlaw so relentlessly vindictive and so feared. Once, ... Sister Blandina visited him in the goal. The Kid was chained hand and foot to the ground, guarded by three men ... "Wish I could place a chair for you, Sister," he said...

The last meeting of the nun and the gun-swinging desperado brought a striking display of homage to the little Sister of Charity. [Encountering her in a carriage traveling on the plains, he did not conduct an intended hold-up.] ... The Kid lifted his sombrero in a sweeping obeisance. He wheeled his mount, darted back a little distance, wheeled again ... At last horse and daredevil rider raced towards the Sister, shot into the air, and then swept the ground in final tribute ...

Billy the Kid had seen little in life but evil ... But that day he paid homage to virtue in the only way he knew – to virtue as he saw it in the life of the softly-spoken, unassuming and courageous nun.

The November 11, 1957 *Rocky Mountain News* had an article by a Jack Foster titled "How Colo. Nun Saved 4 From Killer!" It covered Hollywood producer, Sam Engel's, film plan about Blandina saving the four Trinidad doctors from scalping by Billy the Kid, and topped off with her tale of her next encounter with him in her carriage ride across the plains.

In a September 7, 1958, *The American Weekly*, published under "New True Tales of the Old West," an article by an Warren Hall titled: "Sister Blandina and Billy the Kid: A Young nun's letters, written more than 80 years ago, reveal an incredible friendship." It had a slick full-page illustration of "Billy the Kid," on horseback, doffing his hat to Sister Blandina, who stood next to a stage coach. Histrionic Warren Hall also added a garbled biography for Billy, writing:

Sister Blandina's first encounter with Billy the Kid completely upset the odds, for in that vastness of mountains and plains it seemed unlikely that the two would meet – the Old West's most spectacular juvenile delinquent and the little Italian-born nun who hated violence. [The tale of meeting Billy the Kid because of the wounded gang member followed.] ...

[He] was a product of New York City. His widowed tubercular mother, Catherine McCarty, moved west for her health, married a roving odd-job man named William H. Antrim, and died in Silver City, New Mexico in 1881. Her son, Henry McCarty, occasionally used the name of Antrim but eventually, for reasons unknown, called himself William H. Bonney, which his friends shortened to Billy the Kid ...

The length of the Kid's lifetime was also the number of years Sister Blandina spent in the West ... She never forgot him.

Writer, Warren Hall, then wrote a June, 1959 article in *The Irish Digest* titled: "The Favor is Granted," said Billy the Kid: A nun foiled his plan to murder four men."

The *Victorian* magazine, for January, 1961, ran a story by a Louise Parnell titled: 'The Nun who knew Billy the Kid: Throughout her years in the West Sister Blandina continued to be the friend of Billy the Kid. Though she did not succeed in converting him, her influence on Billy showed the pioneer world the power of a nun's prayerful courage." Parnell fictionalized Blandina's fiction, writing:

Word was spreading FAST. Billy the Kid was out to kill. One of his gang had been refused help by the people of the town and the doctors ... [H]e threatened to shoot every doctor he could find ...

Sister Blandina ... went to him. It wasn't the first time she had done this.

She remembered the time she had visited him in jail and found him sitting on the floor like a beleaguered animal, cuffs and chains on his hands and legs ...

Sister Blandina had tried to comfort him as she had comforted so many other prisoners. But Billy the Kid was a problem. He was the meanest and most feared gunman of the West.

There were times she had felt like giving up on him, but she had continued to talk top him and pray for him. At least her prayers had been answered inasmuch as he treated her with courtesy and respect ...

[When she asked him to spare the doctors] the lawless man, who obeyed neither written nor unwritten code, gave Sister Blandina his word that he would respect her wishes.

Throughout her years in the West, Sister Blandina continued to be the friend of Billy the Kid.

In 1963, columnist, Louella O. Parsons, wrote an article titled "Life of a Colorado Nun," about actress, Susan Hayward, being in talks with producer, Sam Engel, about playing Blandina in a movie titled "One Foot in Hell." Parson's wrote:

The movie producers are very interested in the **incident of Sister Blandina and Billy the Kid**. Four Trinidad physicians refused to treat gunshot wounds of one of the outlaw's henchmen, and Billy was determined to wipe out the mining town's medics. Sister Blandina warned the doctors and then stopped Billy from taking drastic action.

By November 28, 1963, a TV program on the same subject was announced in *The Denver Catholic Register* under "Sister Blandina Story on TV." It stated:

The story of Sister Blandina Segale, early pioneer nun who helped bring civilization and law and order to the wild frontier, and **her encounter with the notorious outlaw Billy the Kid** ... will form the basis of a drama, "The Outlaw and the Nun" ... on CBS' "The Great Adventure."

On August 3, 1973, for *The Cincinnati Enquirer*, its Women's Editor, Rosemary Davis, wrote "Santa Maria's Founder Nun Who Tamed Billy the Kid." Davis wrote:

Sister Blandina kept a careful journal throughout her long career, in it recording some stranger-than-fiction incidents. One was her **meeting with and "taming" of Billy the Kid**.

HER CANDID ACCOUNTS of this and other exploits have been used as the basis of stories and television shows. One TV show portrayed her first meeting with Billy:

"I understand," Sister Blandina said, "that you have come to scalp our Trinidad physicians, which act I ask you to cancel."

It seems that these physicians had refused to take a bullet out of the leg of one of Billy's gang. Billy was "out to get them." The nun, who heard of his plot, sought him out and extracted his promise not to kill them.

And he is reported to have added: "You're game. Any time my pals and I can serve you, you will find me ready."

High-sounding for an outlaw, but **the gist of the story is true.**

On May 19, 1974, an Anne Tansey wrote "She Faced Down Billy the Kid" for *Catholic Family Weekly*. Unlike most reporters, Tansey focused more on Blandina than Billy. But she wrote: "She faced the famous outlaw across the bed of the sick man [gang member] and asked that he spare the lives of the three [sic] physicians. Her request was granted."

A June 6, 1974 supplement to the *Denver Catholic Register* for the Pike's Peak area by a Sisters of Charity nun, Ellen Rita Rawley, was titled: "She Knew Billy the Kid." It further garbled Blandina's own "Billy the Kid" fable, stating:

> One day **Billy the Kid** passed the school mounted on a spirited stallion dressed in Toreodores. A figure of six feet three on a beautiful animal, made restless by a tight bit, drew sister Blandina's attention. This, of course, was what Billy wanted.

With a possible date of 1974, and in the Sisters of Charity of Cincinnati archives, is a parish bulletin addressed to the Youth of St. Mary's (and there were five such parishes in the country, so the precise location is uncertain). With hyperbolic fervor about Trinidad being "one of the wickedest cities in the West," it was titled: "Sister Blandina and Billy the Kid: A Footnote in American History." It stated:

> If the role of pioneer women is given little attention in the history of the American West, even less is passed down about the Catholic Sisters who went West ...
>
> One of these valiant ladies was Sister Blandina Segale. In 1872, at the age of 22, this Sister of Charity ... was assigned to the mission in Trinidad ... Colorado, at the time one of the wickedest cities in the West, a meeting-place for outlaws and all kinds of bad men ...
>
> **She was protected by Billy the Kid** after she treated one of his band who had been shot, and whom no one else would help. When Billy entered Trinidad to kill the town's doctors because they had refused to aid his companion, Sister Blandina faced the outlaw and talked him out of his revenge.

Ignorance about the real Billy the Kid at the Sisters of Charity of Cincinnati archives was epitomized by its saving an article about none other than long dead, old-timer, imposter, Oliver "Brushy Bill" Roberts for their Blandina Segale files! Dated April 13, 1987 and from *The Cincinnati Post*, it was titled "Has Billy the Kid been unmasked?" From Hico, Texas - where there is a minor tourist industry for "Brushy's" duped true-believers - it was an Associated Press story about some of those true-believers placing a plaque for "Brushy" as being Billy the Kid.

On July 21, 1991, a Lucie E. Mayeux reported from Albuquerque for *Our Sunday Visitor* with the title: "When Billy the Kid met the cowboy nun: The adventures of Sister Blandina reads like a pulp Western - except they are all true." It reproduced the bad illustration of Billy the Kid's tintype from the 1948 edition of *At the End of the Santa Fe Trail.* Mayeux's unsurprising lead-in was Billy the Kid, quoting Blandina's apocryphal tale:

> Taking her hand, [Billy the Kid] added: "Sister, any time my pals and I can serve you, you will find us ready."

Ranks were broken on August 30, 1991 in the Trinidad, Colorado, *Chronicle,* by reporter Richard Louden in his "Local legend about Sister Blandina and Billy the Kid is a case of mistaken ID: Creative exaggerations of his violent life created such myths as the one that by the time he was killed at age 21, he had killed that many men." Louden's intent was to use the Billy LeRoy excuse to rationalize Blandina's false Billy the Kid claims. Though the biography of Billy LeRoy, titled *Bandit Years,* by Mark Dugan, had come out four years earlier, in 1987, Richard Louden appeared unaware of it; and he was likely relying on an apocryphal 1986 book by a Donald Cline titled *Alias Billy the Kid.* (See Pages 343-350) Louden consequently contrived a match by misstating LeRoy's aliases to include "Billy the Kid," and misstating the dating of his outlawry to overlap with Blandina's tales. So he inadvertently publicized a new myth: the "two Billy the Kids" (as debunked here with regard to LeRoy; see Pages 320-343). Nevertheless, Louden joined those denying Blandina's claims. So he was subsequently ignored by the media. Louden wrote:

> [After nursing the gang member, Sister Blandina met his leader, whom she talked out of killing Trinidad's four doctors.] Sister Blandina knew of no name for this youthful gang leader other than Billy the Kid. She did not know **he was, in fact, Billy LeRoy – with aliases of Billy the Kid**, William Pond, among various others. Although he had the same fair complexion, blue eyes, and youthful look as William Bonney, LeRoy was a bit older than the other youth – who hadn't yet come to be known by his infamous title.
>
> The escapades of LeRoy, including his brother Sam, were well recorded in the area. They were notorious for holding up stages and other travelers along the routes of southern Colorado and Northern New Mexico. His exploits are reasonably well documented, including

an account in the "Trinidad Enterprise" newspaper of a raid made on Trinidad by the gang as an alternative revenge to retribution against the doctors.

This "Billy the Kid" was the subject of a creative pulp magazine story which purportedly outlined his life ...

In June, 1877, Sister Blandina had her second encounter with a "Billy the Kid" ... when a stagecoach on which she was a passenger was stopped by the outlaw she knew as Billy the Kid.

It was undoubtedly LeRoy – stage robbing was his specialty ...

Sister Blandina's final encounter with her friend Billy seems to have been in the Santa Fe jail some time between her letters of April 24 and May 16, 1881. It could not have been William Bonney [since he was already in Mesilla for trial, and then escaped from Lincoln's jail] ...

The fact that Sister Blandina was understandably confused by the identity of the two Billy the Kids should not detract from the valuable contributions she made to the area's knowledge.

She has merely given some insights into the real story of Trinidad's own Billy the Kid.

A March 17, 1996 article in *The Cincinnati Enquirer* by a Owen Findsen, blithely returned to Billy the Kid claims with "Sister Blandina faced down The Kid." The well-worn Trinidad doctors tale is told with added punch line: "**Sister Blandina had faced down Billy the Kid.**" Reporter Findsen continued: "And although she judged him to be "the greatest murderer in the Southwest," she always referred to him as "my old acquaintance" in letters [sic - one journal entry] to her sister."

In 2000, *Catholic Heritage Curricula*, a home-schooling vehicle, published its online "The Nun Who Took on Billy the Kid" by a Katie O'Brien. Elaborating on and garbling Blandina's own tales, O'Brien wrote:

> Did you know that one of the most dangerous outlaws of the West was convinced not to murder four doctors by none other than a Catholic nun? ...

Throughout Sister Blandina's years in the wild western town of Trinidad, she had heard many stories of the murders committed by well-known and feared outlaws. One outlaw that she heard so much about was **"Billy the Kid," whom she was soon to meet in person** ...

[She nursed one of his gang members who] told Sister Blandina that Billy and the gang would be arriving in Trinidad at 2 p.m. on Saturday to scalp the four doctors in the town that refused to treat his injury, just because he was an outlaw. Sister Blandina decided that no such thing was going to happen. On that Saturday at 2 p.m., Sister Blandina was waiting to meet one of the most feared outlaws in the West ... He said to her ... "I want to say, it would give me great pleasure to be able to do you a favor." ... At that offer, Sister Blandina told him that she did have a favor to ask him. He replied, "The favor is granted." [She asked him to spare the doctors.] Reluctantly he agreed ...

Later on, Sister Blandina was transferred to Santa Fe ... While there she visited her old acquaintance "Billy the Kid who had been captured and put in jail, only to escape shortly after. On one of her trips on a stagecoach, her companions had heard that Billy was nearby ... [Billy rode up to the stagecoach.] Sister Blandina shifted her bonnet ... Their eyes met, [he] raised his hat and bowed ... and rode away ... The men [with her] believed he was just a cowboy riding on the plains, but Sister Blandina knew better, it was "Billy the Kid."

For the August, 2006 edition of *Catholic Digest,* an article called "Sister Blandina Meets Billy the Kid," merely excerpted Blandina's own Billy the Kid tales from *At the End of the Santa Fe Trail.*

TV, FILM, AND BLANDINA

In 1966, was a CBS special called "The Fastest Nun in the West," about Blandina's stopping a Trinidad, Colorado, lynch mob - and astoundingly not relying on Billy the Kid.

On May 10th and 18th, 2017, I met, in Albuquerque, with Thomas Sanchez of Fort Hood Productions about their planned TV series on Blandina Segale's frontier adventures. For the second meeting, Sanchez's script writer joined in from Los Angeles by Skype. I explained to them that there was no chance that Blandina knew the real Billy the Kid. And a program that presented her antique outlaw myth of him would do great harm to his true history. I offered to consult. I never heard from them again. They, like all other media types, were facing the temptation of a great hook - and the downside of relinquishing it. I could not predict the outcome.

SMOKING GUNS FOR A HOAX: Though Blandina's claims of knowing Billy the Kid were debunked by the 1980's, and an outlaw named Billy LeRoy was postulated as another "Billy the Kid" whom she had actually encountered, the media never relinquished the sure hook of the real Billy Bonney; and it merely segued into using "Billy the Kid LeRoy, the original Billy the Kid" if pressed. But that excuse relied on Billy LeRoy matching-up with Blandina's "Billy the Kid." And the real outcome of Blandina's media thrusts was that the 20th and 21st century public remained duped into believing that a doughty Old West nun had been a pal of the horrendous and famous outlaw named "Billy the Kid."

4

THE REAL BILLY THE KID

THE HISTORY OF BILLY BONNEY

SLEUTHING HOAXBUSTING CLUES: Since Blandina Segale's published journal makes dated first-person claims about interacting with "Billy the Kid" and his "gang members," and also makes dated second-hand claims reporting on his supposed historical events, it is important to present his actual biography to demonstrate that none of her claims remotely relate to the actual Billy Bonney. Furthermore, the reality of Billy Bonney's life as an anti-Santa Fe Ring freedom fighter makes clear the great injustice of her published fables of him as a depraved outlaw youth.

SUMMARY: Billy Bonney, born illegitimately on November 23, 1859, in New York City, as William Henry McCarty, spent his childhood in Indiana; possibly Kansas; and Silver City, New Mexico Territory. There, his stepfather abandoned him and his brother after their mother's 1874 tuberculosis death when he was 14½. He became a local petty thief. And, when jailed there in September of 1875 at 15½, he escaped and fled across the border to Bonita, Arizona, where he became a cook and petty horse thief. On August 17, 1877, he killed a local bullying blacksmith, and escaped back to New Mexico Territory. He was hired as a ranch hand in October of 1877 by British merchant-rancher, John Tunstall in Lincoln County. The Territory was then wracked by regional uprisings against the land-grabbing politically corrupt Santa Fe Ring, headed by Thomas Benton Catron. Inspired by Ring-opponent Tunstall, and Tunstall's attorney friend, Alexander McSween, Billy abandoned delinquent ways. Tunstall's murder by the Ring in February of 1878, made Billy fight the Ring along with other self-named Regulators and Hispanic farmers. Escalating Ring outrages led to Regulator killings of two of Tunstall's murderers; then the

Ringite Lincoln County Sheriff, his deputy, and one of his possemen. The culmination was the six day Lincoln County War Battle in July of 1878. Billy's side was crushed, and McSween was murdered by the Ring's illegal use of troops. But 18 year old Billy emerged as a hero. For the remainder of his short life, he pursued an anti-Ring course. He gave a deposition in June of 1978 about Tunstall's murder to a presidential investigator; in February of 1879, after witnessing the Ring murder of anti-Ring lawyer, Huston Chapman, he offered Governor Lew Wallace his testimony against the killers in exchange for a pardon for his three Lincoln County War murder indictments; in May of 1879, at 19, he testified in a military court against the treasonous military commander in the Lincoln County War; and he conducted his own petty guerilla rustling against Ringites. Because the Ring feared that he could lead a future Hispanic uprising, they began a campaign to outlaw him, and, thus, to block any Lew Wallace pardon. Billy was called a counterfeiter, murderer, and rustler to bring in a Secret Service Agent with resources to terminate him. A press campaign advertised him as the outlaw Billy the Kid. That Agent assisted in the election of Pat Garrett as Lincoln County Sheriff, as well as sponsoring posses to achieve Billy's capture on December 22, 1880. Billy was held in the Santa Fe jail from December 27, 1880 to March 28, 1881 - and in solitary confinement after a failed jailbreak on February 28th - while the Ring awaited the completion of railroad tracks, because they feared his rescue by partisans from a coach. His hanging trials were under a Ringite judge in the Doña County town of Mesilla, his venue having been changed from Lincoln County to prevent a favorable jury. His trials were from March 30, 1881 to April 13, 1881, when he was sentenced to hang on May 13, 1881. He was transferred to jail in Lincoln on April 21, 1881, and escaped on April 28, 1881 by killing his two guards. Refusing to leave the Territory, he hid near Fort Sumner until he was killed in ambush by Pat Garrett on July 14, 1881 at the age of 21. He had killed nine men: the blacksmith, five in encounters during the Lincoln County War, one bounty hunter in self-defense, and his two deputy guards. And Lew Wallace, having betrayed his pardon promise, spent the remainder of his life covering up his guilty conscience by writing articles creating the outlaw myth of Billy the Kid.

****

    In a hot, full-mooned, New Mexico Territory night as bright as day, the 21 year old, homeless youth, Billy Bonney, with trusting stockinged feet, approached the porticoed, two story, Fort Sumner mansion of the Maxwell family, at about a quarter to mid-night.

    That day, July 14, 1881, was the third anniversary of the Lincoln County War's start, which had left him branded as the outlaw, "Billy the Kid;" though, to himself, he was a freedom fighter: the last Regulator and that War's only participant to be convicted and sentenced. His April 13, 1881, first degree murder sentence was death by hanging.

    That July night, Billy intended to cut a dinner steak from the side of beef hanging - at the patrón's generosity - on the mansion's north porch. But first he would check in, as requested, with that patrón and town owner, Peter Maxwell, at the man's south porch's corner bedroom.

    Asleep in that mansion was Billy's secret lover, Maxwell's sister, Paulita, seventeen, and just pregnant with Billy's child. Also there, lived a never-emancipated Navajo slave, Deluvina; purchased, as a child, by Peter's and Paulita's fabulously wealthy, deceased father, Lucien Bonaparte Maxwell. Then, the family lived in Cimarron, a New Mexico Territory town in Colfax County, which Lucien had created on his and his wife's almost two million acre land grant, later named after himself.

    That was before Lucien was cheated in the sale of that Maxwell Land Grant by lawyers, Thomas Benton Catron and Stephen Benton Elkins, whose profits propelled their Santa Fe Ring. As Billy knew, that corrupt collusion of politicians, attorneys, lawmen, and judges still held New Mexico Territory in a stranglehold. As a hero in the failed Lincoln County War of 1878, Billy had fought that Ring. The year before, had been the anti-Ring Colfax County War on that Maxwell Grant land. The year before that, Grant County's citizens had threatened secession to Arizona Territory to escape Ring clutches.

    If Billy thought about his danger, he knew its source was the Ring. If he thought about injustice, its focus would have been his justified pardon withheld by Governor Lew Wallace, now departed from the Territory.

That July of 1881 day was 2½ months since Billy's jailbreak escape from his scheduled hanging on May 13th. He knew that Lincoln County Sheriff Pat Garrett would be in pursuit. Garrett had captured him on December 22, 1880 at Stinking Springs for his hanging trial. And in Billy's April 28, 1881 escape from Garrett's Lincoln jail, he had shot dead his deputy guards: James Bell and Robert Olinger. Garrett would kill him on sight.

When first tracking Billy in late 1880, Garrett had killed Billy's friends, Tom O'Folliard and Charlie Bowdre - missing Billy only by accident in two consecutive ambushes: at Fort Sumner and Stinking Springs. In fact, at the Stinking Springs capture of Billy and his companions, Garrett had killed Bowdre by mistaking him for Billy: the prize for which the Ring had made Garrett a Sheriff.

Billy, to be near Paulita Maxwell, had recklessly chosen return to Fort Sumner, instead of fleeing to Old Mexico, the natural choice given his bi-culturalism and accentlss mastery of Spanish. But he relied on the Maxwell family's protection, as well the affection of the townspeople, who had known him since late 1877. And optimism and uncanny ability to escape danger characterized him. It would take unfathomable betrayal to bring about his death.

Billy's entire life had been traumatic. Illegitimate, he was a second son, born on November 23, 1859, in New York City, as William Henry McCarty. Raised in Indiana with his older brother, Josie, by his mother, Catherine, he became "Henry Antrim" after she married an Indiana man, William Henry Harrison Antrim, in 1873, after the family relocated to New Mexico Territory. Antrim became a miner; and the family lived in Silver City. But Antrim evicted Billy at 14½ to homelessness when Catherine died of tuberculosis in 1874. By 1879, Billy wrote coldly to Lew Wallace: *"Antrim is my stepfather's name."* But Billy's longing for a father remained. He even sometimes used the painful name "Antrim" for himself.

In Silver City's school, 13 year old Billy likely learned excellent Spencerian cursive script, which he later used for his articulate pardon request to Lew Wallace. He also became fluent in Spanish; and, atypically, was equally comfortable in Anglo and Hispanic sub-cultures in those racist times.

By 1975, 15½ year old Billy spent his last year in Silver City doing petty thievery, and butcher shop and hotel work; while altercations with local boys revealed his violent temperament. By September, Silver City Sheriff, Harvey Whitehill, arrested him for burglary, and laundry and revolver robbery; his adult accomplice having escaped. Facing 10 years hard labor - the Territorial statutes making no provision for juveniles - he achieved his first dramatic escape: through the jail's chimney. He fled across the border to Arizona Territory's little town of Bonita.

In Arizona, as Henry Antrim, Billy again combined work - as a cook at a small hotel - with crime: stealing military blankets, saddles, and horses; while ominously developing shootist skills. In 1876, incarcerated at local Fort Grant's guardhouse with his older accomplice, John Mackie, he escaped through a roof ventilation space. But he stayed defiantly in Bonita, relying on his rustling charges being dropped on a technicality, and first demonstrating risky behavior for his unconscious wish to have a "home."

On August 17, 1877, three months before turning 18, Billy's life again changed horrifically. His argument at Bonita's Atkins Cantina with a bullying blacksmith, Frank "Windy" Cahill, escalated to Billy's fatally shooting that unknowably unarmed man. Billy escaped on a stolen horse. The Coroner's Jury declared him - as Henry Antrim - guilty of homicide, though in absentia; ignoring self-defense. So, when 17, Billy was almost hanged for murder. Billy fled back to New Mexico Territory with a self-created alias: William Henry Bonney - Billy Bonney. "Bonney" was likely his mother's maiden name.

In New Mexico Territory, by the next month of September, 1877, Billy again attached himself to sociopaths in Jessie Evans's murderous and rustling Santa Fe Ring-affiliated gang. And since Ringites ended up immune to prosecution and profited financially, intelligent and energetic Billy, unknown to history, would have likely had a wealthy and long life.

But Billy had a conversion. He met kind, wealthy Englishman, John Henry Tunstall, a Ring competitor. By the next month, October of 1877, Billy left Jessie Evans's gang to become a Tunstall ranch hand. Soon Tunstall's men affectionately nick-named him "Kid." Tunstall was the lost father found; even gifting him, under the Homestead Act, a ranch on the Peñasco River in partnership with another employee, half-Chickasaw Fred Waite. That was likely Billy's proudest and most optimistic moment.

Billy had stumbled into a noble cause: ending Ring oppression. His gunman skill now elevated him as a protector of the good. His hair-trigger temper became vehemence for justice. And the town of Lincoln, as well as Tunstall's ranch on the Feliz River, became home. But Billy's tragic destiny was unrelenting. After only 4½ months, this idyllic time ended with Tunstall's Ring murder.

Lincoln, site of the future Lincoln County War, had already sustained Ring abuses through mercantile monopoly of "the House": a huge, two-story adobe, general store run by its local Ring bosses, Emil Fritz, Lawrence Murphy, James Dolan, and John Riley for secret partner Thomas Benton Catron. They bled cash-poor Mexicans and Anglo homesteaders with usurious credit. Redress was impossible, since law enforcement and courts were Ring-controlled. Terror reigned. In 1875, when rancher, Robert Casey, defeated Murphy in a Lincoln election, he was assassinated the same day. Three weeks later, Lincoln's anti-Ring, Mexican community leader, Juan Patrón, was shot by Riley; though accidentally surviving as a limping cripple.

Hope for change began in late 1876 with arrival in Lincoln of English merchant, John Henry Tunstall; persuaded to settle there by a resident attorney, Alexander McSween; a Ring opponent, but once legal counsel to "the House." Tunstall and McSween planned to defeat the Ring by fair mercantile and ranching competition.

By 1877, Tunstall had built - just a quarter mile northeast of "the House" - his own general store and bank. And he started two cattle ranches to wrest from "the House" its beef and flour traderships to local Fort Stanton and the nearby Mescalaro Indian Reservation. He even exposed to the press Lincoln County Sheriff William Brady's abuse of taxpayer money to pay for Ring cattle. So he and McSween were on the Ring's hit list.

Ringmen preferred to kill with guise of legality. So they entangled Tunstall in fabricated criminality, starting with false prosecution of McSween, who was then attorney for the estate of the House's founding partner, Emil Fritz, who died intestate in 1874, but left two local siblings and a life insurance policy.

The Ring seized on that life insurance policy. In 1877, McSween had successfully litigated to get its $10,000 proceeds from its withholding New York City insurance company, minus $3,000 to the collections firm - leaving $7,000. Knowing that the House faced bankruptcy from Tunstall's competition, and would extort that sum from Fritz's local heirs, McSween retained it while seeking possible heirs in Germany. He underestimated Ring evil.

In December of 1877, McSween left on business to St. Louis with his wife and with Tunstall's business associate, the cattle king, John Chisum, then also president of the bank in Tunstall's store. The Ring pounced, declaring McSween an absconding embezzler of the Fritz insurance money. Ring boss Catron, then U.S. Attorney, issued his arrest warrant for capture. Chisum was also jailed in retaliation for backing Tunstall. On February 4, 1878, McSween had his hearing in Mesilla under Ringite District Judge Warren Bristol (later Billy's hanging judge), who indicted McSween for embezzling, intending his incarceration and killing in Lincoln by its Ringite Sheriff, William Brady. McSween was saved by the honest Deputy Sheriff, Adolph Barrier, from his Las Vegas, New Mexico, arrest site, who kept him in personal custody.

But Judge Bristol had set the Ring's desired traps to enable assassination of McSween and Tunstall. When he indicted McSween, he did two things. First, he set the bail at $8,000, with approval only by Ringite District Attorney William Rynerson; who refused all bondsmen to leave McSween open to Sheriff Brady's fatal custody at any time.

Bristol's second stipulation was Tunstall's trap. Bristol attached McSween's property to the sum of $10,000 - falsely deemed the embezzled total - to satisfy any judgment against him at that April's Grand Jury. Then he declared falsely that Tunstall was in a business partnership with McSween, to enable attachment of Tunstall's property also. And Bristol empowered Sheriff Brady and his deputies to do attachment inventories at both men's properties. That harassment was intended to provoke Tunstall and his men to violence to justify his killing. But Tunstall merely said that any man's life was worth more than all he owned. Billy, with Tunstall just three months, must have been overwhelmed by this novel idealism.

But Tunstall protectively sought to transfer his fine horses, which were immune to the attachment, from his Feliz River Ranch. On February 18, 1878, Brady used that stock movement back toward Lincoln to assassinate Tunstall. He sent his large posse (including Jessie Evans and his boys) in pursuit of Tunstall and his men, including Billy, for alleged theft of attached property. Tunstall, becoming isolated, was murdered, his horse slain; and both corpses were mutilated. This martyrdom, coupled with more Ring outrages, triggered the Lincoln County War.

Lincoln County Justice of the Peace John "Squire" Wilson issued murder warrants for James Dolan, Jessie Evans, and other possemen. For service, Wilson appointed, as Deputy Constables under Town Constable Atanacio Martinez, Billy and Fred Waite. And Billy had already volunteered himself by giving an affidavit for the Coroner's jury as to first-hand knowledge of the murderers.

But Brady shielded the murderers by brief illegal incarceration of Billy, Waite, and Martinez in Lincoln's pit jail. And he confiscated Billy's Winchester '73 carbine - likely a gift from Tunstall.

Next, "Squire" Wilson defied the Ring by deputizing Tunstall's foreman, Dick Brewer; who, in turn, made Tunstall's men, including now-released Billy, his possemen to serve those murder warrants. Billy, then 18, was still a lawman.

Meanwhile, Attorney Alexander McSween, certain of mortal risk from Brady, went into hiding with Deputy Sheriff Barrier; mostly in the nearby Hispanic town of San Patricio.

By March of 1878, Dick Brewer's posse had captured Tunstall murder possemen, William "Buck" Morton and Frank Baker, who were shot by the possemen while attempting escape. Billy was in the firing group.

At that point, adding Frank "Windy" Cahill to William "Buck" Morton and Frank Baker, Billy Bonney was involved in three killings.

The Ring retaliated. Ringite Governor Samuel Beach Axtell, by illegal proclamation, removed Wilson's Justice of the Peace powers to retroactively outlaw Brewer's posse; then declared Sheriff Brady to be Lincoln County's only law enforcer.

Enraged, Tunstall's men named themselves "Regulators" after pre-Revolutionary War freedom fighters. Included were Tunstall men - Billy; Fred Waite; John Middleton; Jim "Frenchie" French; farmer cousins, George and Frank Coe; and homesteader, Charlie Bowdre - and a John Chisum cattle detective, Frank MacNab. Dick Brewer was chosen as leader. Only one month after Tunstall died, Billy was being schooled in politics of revolution.

The Ring's next chance to assassinate McSween was April 1, 1878, when he left hiding to return to Lincoln for his Grand Jury embezzlement trial. That morning, to save him, Regulators with carbines, and Billy with only a revolver, ambushed Brady and his three deputies from behind an adobe corral wall at Tunstall's store. Brady and his Deputy, George Hindman, died. Recklessly, Billy, with Jim French, ran out to retrieve his confiscated, Winchester '73 carbine from Brady's body. Both got leg wounds from firing surviving deputy, Jacob Basil "Billy" Matthews. But Billy regained his symbol of father-figure Tunstall. (It is likely the carbine Billy held in his famous tintype two years hence.)

Three days later, on April 4, 1878, Deputy Dick Brewer, seeking stolen Tunstall horses, led Billy, John Middleton, Fred Waite, Frank Coe, George Coe, and Charlie Bowdre to Blazer's Mill - a privately owned, way station and grist mill within the Mescalaro Indian Reservation. There, they encountered bounty-hunter and Tunstall murder posseman, Andrew "Buckshot" Roberts, for whom they had a warrant. With Roberts firing his Winchester carbine at them, Bowdre shot him in the belly. Roberts's bullet hit Bowdre's belt buckle, ricocheted, and wrenched George Coe's revolver, mutilating his trigger finger. Another Roberts shot hit Middleton in the chest, though Middleton survived. Then Roberts killed Brewer, later dying himself from Bowdre's wound. Billy had not fired a shot. Roberts had demonstrably resisted arrest murderously, while necessitating a self defense response. But Catron, as U.S. Attorney, seized on this killing to file his federal indictment against the Regulators, including Billy, claiming the murder site was the Mescalaro Reservation, which was under federal control and, thus, under his jurisdiction.

Billy's murder involvement now totaled six men; though only Frank "Windy" Cahill was demonstrably by his hand, since the others occurred in Regulator groups.

At the April, 1878, Lincoln County Grand Jury, McSween was declared innocent of embezzling. He continued his anti-Ring fight backed by the Regulators, though they had never been paid; John Chisum having dishonestly reneged on his promise to provide salaries. Revolutionary fervor sufficed. And Billy, their hot-headed fearless zealot, was becoming an inspiration - with McSween as his new father substitute.

McSween's tactic was seeking high-level intervention. Knowing that murder of a foreign citizen could elicit a Washington D.C. investigation, he filed a complaint to the British ambassador and to President Rutherford B. Hayes, accusing U.S. officials of murdering Tunstall. In response, investigating attorney, Frank Warner Angel, was sent by the Departments of the Interior and Justice. Arriving May 4, 1878, Angel took over a hundred depositions. Billy, volunteering for one, entered the national stage.

Public optimism of Ring defeat further grew when the Lincoln County Commissioners' appointed neutral John Copeland as Sheriff, replacing Brady. And "Squire" Wilson, ignoring Axtell's proclamation, continued to function as Justice of the Peace.

Optimism was short-lived. New Regulator leader, Frank MacNab, was killed in ambush on April 28th by Ringite Seven Rivers cattle rustlers. By May 28th, because new Sheriff Copeland forgot to post his tax collecting bond, Governor Axtell, by proclamation, removed him and appointed as Sheriff, George Peppin, Brady's deputy, present at Brady's killing.

War fervor built, with furious Regulators and Mexicans calling themselves "McSweens." Billy's affiliation with local, firebrand youth, Yginio Salazar, and Billy's closeness to Hispanic residents of nearby San Patricio and Picacho, had arguably brought them into the McSween alliance. By April 30,

1878, McSweens were skirmishing with Ring partisans, known as "Murphy-Dolans;" though Lawrence Murphy was then dying of alcoholism. And Catron took over his ranch. McSween again hid, often in San Patricio. In revenge, Sheriff George Peppin, with John Kinney's Ring-rustler gang from Mesilla, on July 8th massacred residents and destroyed property there. On July 13th, the defiant "Regulator Manifesto" was sent to Catron's brother-in-law, then managing Catron's ranch, threatening retaliation against Catron himself. Signed only "Regulator," it was likely by Billy.

The Lincoln County War's culminating battle began the next day: July 14, 1878. McSween, with 60 men - Regulators and Hispanic residents of San Patricio and Picacho - occupied Lincoln. Reflecting McSween's intended peaceful victory was that his wife, Susan, and her sister with five children remained in his double-winged house there; along with the sister's attorney husband's law intern, Harvey Morris.

McSween's men took strategic positions in houses throughout the mile-long town, most of whose inhabitants had fled. When Seven Rivers and John Kinney outlaws joined James Dolan and Sheriff George Peppin, Billy; his friends, Yginio Salazar and Tom O'Folliard; and San Patricio men - José Chávez y Chávez, Ignacio Gonzales, Florencio Chávez, Francisco Zamora, and Vincente Romero - rushed to McSween's house, joining the Regulator guard already there: Jim French.

Though Murphy-Dolan men occupied foothills south of Lincoln, they were held at bay for five days by shooting McSweens. Regulators were about to win. But McSween did not realize that Fort Stanton's new commander, Lieutenant Colonel N.A.M. Dudley, was beholden to the Ring. McSween was also reassured by the Posse Comitatus Act, passed the month before in Washington D.C., baring military intervention in civilian disputes.

On July 16th, Dudley began his invention by sending to Lincoln, for "fact-finding," 9th Cavalry Private Berry Robinson, who was almost hit in the mutual gunfire, but the McSween side was blamed. Next, on July 18th, James Dolan documented for Dudley that women and children were at supposed risk at the Lincoln home of Ring-loyalist, Saturnino Baca.

The next day, July 19th, violating the Posse Comitatus Act, Dudley marched on Lincoln with 60 troops - white infantry, black 9th Cavalry, and white officers - two ambulances; a mountain howitzer cannon; and a Gatling machine-gun, that period's most awesome weapon of war. Panicked McSweens - except for those trapped in his besieged house - fled north across the nearby Bonito River. Dudley himself threatened McSween that if any soldier was shot, he would raze his house. He then left three soldiers on McSween's property to inhibit shooting, and left three more to shield Sheriff Peppin. Next, by death threats, Dudley forced Justice of the Peace Wilson to write arrest warrants for McSween and his men as attempted murderers of Private Robinson. Next, feigning non-intervention, Dudley encamped with the rest of his troops at the east side of Lincoln.

Backed by military presence, Sheriff Peppin's outlaw posseman surrounded McSween's house and set fire to its west wing. Eventually evacuated were McSween's family, after Dudley had refused Susan McSween's personal plea for him to save her husband. The obvious intent was to kill McSween and his men.

By nightfall, the McSween house conflagration - worsened by an exploding keg of gunpowder for bullet-making - left all trapped in the east wing. At about 9 p.m., escape was attempted into fire-lit shooting Ringites. With Billy was law intern, Harvey Morris, whom he saw fatally shot. And before Billy escaped across the Bonito River at the property's rear - to rescue by fellow Regulators - he witnessed Dudley's treasonous crime: three of his white soldiers, imbedded with the assailants, fired a volley at those escaping. Arguably, they had killed Harvey Morris.

The Murphy-Dolans shot dead McSween, Francisco Zamora, and Vincente Romero. Yginio Salazar survived with two bullets in his back. The Ring won. Symbolizing horror, McSween's starving, yard chickens ate his corpse's eyeballs. Again was Ring murder and mutilation in Lincoln County.

No one had realized that Ring influence extended to Washington, D.C. Investigator Frank Warner Angel, after documenting crimes of Governor Axtell, U.S. Attorney Catron, and Sheriff Brady's posse, nevertheless concluded in his report - likely under duress - that no U.S. officials were involved in Tunstall's murder. In the cover-up, Catron resigned as U.S. Attorney. And President Hayes removed expendable Governor Axtell, replacing him with Civil War General Lew Wallace. So, by the end of 1878, citizens again had hope; though Lincoln men like Juan Patrón and Justice of the Peace "Squire" Wilson were left at risk after demonstrating Regulator sympathies. But Frank Warner Angel secretly tried to help - again implying his forced cover-up reports - by writing for Lew Wallace a notebook listing Ringites, and sending him an exposé on the Santa Fe Ring printed in Colfax County's Cimarron in 1877.

Though most Regulators fled the Territory, Billy refused to leave and engaged in the "Regulator Manifesto's" guerilla stock rustling with Tom O'Folliard and Charlie Bowdre - who had relocated to Fort Sumner with his wife Manuela. For his stolen stock, Billy used non-Ring outlets: Pat Coghlan in the western part of the Territory; and Dan Dedrick. Dedrick was a counterfeiter and rustler owner of Bosque Grande, a ranch 12 miles south of Fort Sumner, who, with his two brothers, also owned a livery stable in White Oaks, a town about 45 miles northwest of Lincoln. Those brothers were another stock outlet for Billy. Billy also sold rustled horses in Tascosa, Texas; where he wrote a subsequently famous, bill of sale to friendly a doctor, Henry Hoyt, for an expensive sorrel horse - a likely gift to a father-figure, since it had been Sheriff Brady's. Billy bolstered this petty rustling with gambling. He was again a homeless drifter. That would now be permanent.

Amidst public hope, on October 1, 1878, new Governor, Lew Wallace took office. A high-achieving elitist, he was the son of an Indiana governor; a Civil War Major General; an Abraham Lincoln murder trial prosecutor; author of best-selling novel, *The Fair God*; and was writing *Ben-Hur A Tale of the Christ*. He had sought exotic ambassadorship, like to Turkey, not governorship of backwater New Mexico Territory. So, to dispatch quickly with Lincoln County "troubles" without confronting the Santa Fe Ring, a month after arriving he issued an Amnesty Proclamation; though excluding those already indicted. Billy had been indicted for the Brady, Hindman, and Roberts murders.

There were more sources of hope. The new Sheriff, George Kimbrell - having been appointed to replace Sheriff George Peppin who resigned - was anti-Ring. And McSween's intrepid widow, Susan, had brought to Lincoln an attorney from Las Vegas, Huston Chapman, to charge Commander N.A.M. Dudley with the Lincoln County War Battle's murder of her husband and the arson of her home.

In that atmosphere of legal scrutiny and Ring caution, James Dolan made peace overtures, first to Susan McSween, then to Billy - a proof of that teenager's Ring threat. Bi-lingual Billy's bond to Hispanic people had arguably contributed to their joining the War; and could yield another uprising - as Catron feared.

The Billy-Dolan peace meeting was fatefully scheduled on the February 18, 1879 anniversary of Tunstall's murder. It ended in calamity. As James Dolan; Catron's brother-in-law, Edgar Walz; Billy; Jessie Evans and his new gang member, Billy Campbell; and Billy's Regulator friends, Tom O'Folliard and Josiah "Doc" Scurlock, walked Lincoln's dark street after the meeting, they encountered Huston Chapman. Dolan and Campbell fired at point-blank range, killing him, then ignited his clothing. Billy was again an eye-witness. And again there was murder and mutilation in Lincoln County.

Huston Chapman's murder forced Governor Wallace to go to Lincoln - a task he had delayed for five months after arriving. Once there, however, he still avoided Ring confrontation, presenting instead a quixotic plan to eliminate vague "outlaws and rustlers." The Ring had already named Regulators as "outlaws;" with Billy on their list as "the Kid."

Focus on Billy - likely through Dolan - made Wallace put the astronomical reward of $1,000 on his head. Billy responded with his pardon plea, writing on March 13, 1879, to offer Wallace his eye-witness testimony against Chapman's murderers in exchange for annulling his Lincoln County War indictments. It was Billy's bold and calculated risk to negate Ring power over himself.

Billy's articulate letter, in his fine Spencerian handwriting, led to his March 17, 1879, nighttime meeting with Wallace in Justice of the Peace "Squire" Wilson's Lincoln house. Evidence indicates, furthermore, that Wilson covertly backed Billy's plea. There, Billy believed Wallace agreed to his pardon bargain. And Billy subsequently clung to it, and to Wallace, with tragic results.

To prevent Ring assassination before testifying, Billy requested, in writing, from Wallace a sham arrest (He had already lived through Ring assassinations of John Tunstall, Alexander McSween, Harvey Morris, Francisco Zamora, Vincente Romero, and Huston Chapman.) Billy was kept in the home of his Lincoln friend and Regulator partisan, Juan Patrón, the town jailer; where Wallace, housed next door, interviewed him and received an additional letter from Billy about Lincoln County War issues.

Billy fulfilled his pardon bargain the next month by testifying in the April Lincoln County Grand jury. He achieved indictment of Chapman's killers, with James Dolan and Billy Campbell for first degree murder, and Jessie Evans as accessory. But with Billy's being in custody, Ringite District Attorney William Rynerson, in collusion with District Judge Warren Bristol, had his trial venue for his indictments switched from Lincoln to Doña Ana County to guarantee a hanging verdict. Still Wallace issued no pardon.

By that April of 1879, Alexander McSween's widow, Susan, retained Attorney Ira Leonard, dead Attorney Huston Chapman's office-mate from Las Vegas, to prosecute Dudley. In response, under advisement of Catron's law firm, where Catron himself had defended him for two prior court martials, Dudley got defamatory affidavits about her from Ring partisans to diminish her credibility; and requested a military Court of Inquiry, where judges would be biased, and where he would be defended by Catron's law firm member, Henry Waldo. Furthermore, on April 25th, Ira Leonard's assassination was attempted.

Wallace had already removed Dudley. Wallace testified against him in the Court of Inquiry, and was viciously and humiliatingly attacked by Waldo. Though testifying against

Dudley was not part of Billy's own pardon bargain, he too testified in that Court of Inquiry with his own anti-Ring agenda on May 28th and 29th of 1879, devastatingly reporting the three white soldiers firing a volley at him and others - meaning officers; meaning under Dudley's orders; meaning violating the Posse Comitatus Act and justifying court martial and hanging. Billy's courage made Attorney Leonard take him as client.

By July of 1879, the biased Court of Inquiry exonerated Dudley. And Billy, with no pardon and imminent transport to Mesilla for a hanging trial, exited his bogus jailing.

The Ring recouped. By October of 1879, Susan McSween lost her civil trial against Dudley in Mesilla - to which her venue had been changed by Judge Warren Bristol. That month, Judge Bristol also voided James Dolan's Chapman murder indictment based on no witnesses daring to appear for a trial. Dolan, certain of immunity, had even purchased Tunstall's store, while Catron had taken over "the House;" thus continuing the local Ring mercantile monopoly. Tunstall's ranch property was seized illegally; and Billy's Peñasco River ranch was gifted to Jacob Basil "Billy" Matthews, head posseman for Tunstall's murder. And there was a more subtle Ring victory: Lew Wallace's humiliation in the Court of Inquiry made him shun Lincoln County "troubles" and Billy's pardon.

Billy's future killer, Patrick "Pat" Floyd Garrett, had arrived in New Mexico Territory's Fort Sumner the year before. Born to an Alabama plantation family, relocated to Claiborne Parrish, Louisiana, when 9½ - and Billy was just born - young Garrett had even been willed a slave. After his family lost everything in the Civil War, he drifted westward to Texas, where he possibly murdered a black man, before becoming a buffalo hunter from 1876 to 1878 with two partners and a kid named Joe Briscoe. Garrett murdered Briscoe in apparent cold-blood, but claimed self-defense. Garrett had never met fellow buffalo hunter, John William Poe; but later, his, Poe's, and Billy's histories would merge on the night of July 14, 1881.

In Fort Sumner, tall Garrett met transient kid, Billy Bonney, gambling at Hargrove's or Beaver Smith's Saloons. They were given townspeople's nicknames, "Big Casino" and

"Little Casino," for their poker playing and height discrepancies.

The original Fort Sumner was built in 1865 by the U.S. government on desert flatlands east of the Pecos River for soldiers guarding Bosque Redondo: a concentration camp for 3,500 Navajos and 400 Apaches, until their scandalous starvation caused release of the Navajos to their homeland in 1868; the Apaches having already escaped. In 1870, Fort Sumner was purchased by Lucien Bonaparte Maxwell, one of New Mexico Territory's richest men. Converting it into a town around its parade ground, and using the surrounding thousands of acres for sheep raising, he settled there with his wife, Luz Beaubien; daughters, including Paulita; and only son, Peter. Retained was the military cemetery for his family. Eventually it received Billy's body, to lie beside Pat Garrett's earlier shooting victims: Billy's Regulator pals, Tom O'Folliard and Charlie Bowdre. Maxwell died in 1875, leaving the town to his wife and son, Peter; who became the family's ruin through mismanagement. But when Pat Garrett and Billy Bonney gambled there, Fort Sumner was still thriving.

Before buying Fort Sumner, Lucien Maxwell's wealth came from his marriage to Luz Beaubien, an heiress of the almost two million acre Beaubien-Miranda Land Grant, followed by his purchase of that Grant's shares from her siblings. He then sold it as the Maxwell Land Grant. But he was cheated by his robber baron attorneys and politicians, Thomas Benton Catron and Steven Benton Elkins, who resold it for double the money. Their profit and land grab scheme fortified their Santa Fe Ring, whose monopolistic goals and crimes were abetted by other public officials, lawmen, and the military. Catron and Elkins profited immensely in land, railroads, banks, and mines. Catron eventually owned six million acres - more than anyone in U.S. history. And in the Lincoln County War period, Catron held the Territory's highest legal position: U.S. Attorney. By 1912's New Mexico statehood, he became one of the two first senators.

By 1878, before the Lincoln County War, Pat Garrett and Billy Bonney led separate lives, though connected by Fort Sumner's Gutierrez sisters: Juanita, Apolinaria, and Celsa.

Billy befriended Celsa, married to her cousin, Saval Gutierrez, a Maxwell sheep herder. Billy's July 14, 1881 death walk would start at their house. Garrett married Juanita, who died soon after of a possible miscarriage. Two years later, in 1880, Garrett married Apolinaria, with whom he would father eight children. It was a double marriage with his Fort Sumner, best friend, Maxwell's foreman, Barney Mason, later a spy assisting Garrett's capture of Billy.

In 1878, Pat Garrett had been desperate for employment. At Fort Sumner, he drove a wagon for Peter Maxwell; helped a local hog raiser, Thomas "Kip" McKinney; and bartended at Hargrove's Saloon. He would have had no exposure to Lincoln County War issues. Then came 1880 and the opportunity of his life. Lincoln County - the largest county in America; almost a quarter of New Mexico Territory, and big enough to fit Massachusetts, Connecticut, Vermont, Rhode Island, and Delaware - needed a new sheriff for its November election, one compatible with Santa Fe Ring interests. To qualify, Garrett moved with his wife, Apolinaria, to that county's town of Roswell; adding, as a boarder, an unemployed journalist named Ashmun "Ash" Upson. In 1882, Upson would ghostwrite Garrett's book about killing Billy the Kid, with its fanciful, dime novel, life history of Billy Bonney.

By 1880, the Ring's outlaw myth propaganda was advertising Billy's gunman reputation. That almost succeeded in his killing on January 3, 1880 at Fort Sumner's Hargrove's Saloon. A Texan bounty hunter named Joe Grant tried to shoot him in the back. Grant's gun's misfired. Billy retaliated fatally. Obvious self-defense, that killing was not legally pursued.

Billy was now linked to murders of seven men: Frank "Windy" Cahill, William Brady, George Hindman, Andrew "Buckshot" Roberts, William "Buck" Morton, Frank Baker, and Joe Grant.

That 1880, when his now-famous tintype photograph was taken, Billy may have heard first mythological whispers of his having killed a man for each year of his life. The Ring was setting its legal trap for capturing and killing him. In addition to murderer and rustler, he would be declared a counterfeiter to bring in the Secret Service, a branch of the U.S. Treasury Department, with enough funding to track him down. Catron's Lincoln County agent, James Dolan, initiated it by reporting receipt of a counterfeit $100 bill in his Lincoln store. And Catron or Elkins were the likely contact to Secret Service Chief, James Brooks.

By September 11, 1880, Secret Service Special Operative Azariah Wild was sent to Lincoln. Dolan's counterfeit bill, falsely linked to Billy, actually came from two youths, Billy Wilson and Tom Cooper, employed by the real counterfeiter, Dan Dedrick. But they occasionally rustled with Billy and his regulars: Tom O'Folliard, Charlie Bowdre, and a "Dirty Dave" Rudabaugh. Billy himself used Dedrick as an outlet for rustled stock, along with Dedrick's brothers at their White Oaks livery.

Gullible Operative Azariah Wild was led to believe by James Dolan and Catron's brother-in-law, Edgar Walz - then managing Catron's Lincoln County cattle ranch - that Billy was in the country's largest counterfeiting and rustling gang. In December of 1880, the *New York Sun* featured Billy in "Outlaws of New Mexico. The Exploits of a band headed by a New York Youth, War Against a Gang of Cattle Thieves, Murderers, and Counterfeiters." Billy was alias "the Kid." The Ring had launched his national fame.

The Ring's plot almost backfired when Azariah Wild was told by Attorney Ira Leonard that his client, Billy Bonney, would testify against the counterfeiters. On October 8, 1880, Wild wrote in his daily report to Chief James Brooks that he himself would arrange a pardon for Billy in exchange for that testimony. And there is no reason that Lew Wallace would have blocked that pardon, since it removed his own confrontation with the Ring. But Wild confided that pardon plan to his Ringite informers, who convinced him that Billy, staying in Fort Sumner, was the gang's leader! In his report for October 14, 1880, Wild wrote that he intended to arrest those Fort Sumner desperados in Fort Sumner. By then, Billy was cautious. He held up the stagecoach with Operative Wild's mail, read that report, and avoided apprehension by avoiding the meeting with Leonard and Wild. But another pardon was lost.

The Ring still needed to eliminate Billy. The next option was getting a Lincoln County Sheriff willing do it. The current Sheriff, George Kimbrell, who had assisted in Billy's sham arrest, was a McSween-side sympathizer. The Ring chose Pat Garrett. Secretly, Wild worked with Garrett to form a dragnet to capture Billy and his "rustler-counterfeiter gang;" while, for the upcoming sheriff's election, Garrett was advertised as a law-and-order man to new gold-rush settlers in White Oaks, unaware of Lincoln County War issues, but representing a third of Lincoln County's voters.

In the November 2, 1880 sheriff's election, Pat Garrett got 358 votes to George Kimbrell's 141. Azariah Wild, convinced by his Ringite contacts that Kimbrell protected the "Kid gang," also gave Garrett immediate Territorial power for capturing Billy by appointing him Deputy U.S. Marshall before he became Sheriff in January of 1881. Unaware, Billy would have wrongly thought that Garrett's lawman authority was limited to Lincoln County, not Fort Sumner's San Miguel County where he stayed.

Also, unaware of his locally publicized "outlawry," Billy still brought stolen horses to the Dedrick's White Oaks livery. On November 22, 1880, a White Oaks posse ambushed him, Tom O'Folliard, Billy Wilson, Tom Pickett, and "Dirty" Dave Rudabaugh at nearby Coyote Spring, shooting dead two of their horses before Billy's group escaped. Five days later, that posse attacked them again at the way station ranch of "Whiskey" Jim Greathouse, 45 miles northeast of White Oaks; accidentally killing one of their own men, Jim Carlyle, but blaming Billy.

That accusation prompted Billy's only letter of 1880 to Governor Lew Wallace. On December 12th, he wrote, aware that he was then called Billy the Kid, and denying his outlawry and murdering of Jim Carlyle. He made clear that he had no gang. He even described his Robin Hood role of seeking justice for the downtrodden. Wallace never answered. Instead, on December 22nd, Wallace placed a Las Vegas *Daily Gazette* notice: "Billy the Kid: $500 Reward." He would repeat that reward notice in the *Daily New Mexican* on May 3, 1881, after Billy's jailbreak. Wallace's betrayal of the pardon bargain was complete.

By December of 1880, dreadful days began for Billy. As Deputy U.S. Marshall, Pat Garrett, coordinating with Azariah Wild, had assembled posses to ride after Billy; using Texans, since New Mexicans, to whom Billy was a freedom fighting hero, refused. Garrett's first ambush was on December 19, 1880, when Billy, Tom O'Folliard, Charlie Bowdre, Billy Wilson, Tom Pickett, and Dave Rudabaugh rode into Fort Sumner in a snowstorm. O'Folliard was shot dead by Garrett. The rest escaped.

Billy's group tried to flee the Territory in another snowstorm; but stopped, about 16 miles from Fort Sumner, on December 21, 1880, at a rock-walled, windowless, shepherds' line cabin at Stinking Springs. There Garrett ambushed them the next morning, killing Charlie Bowdre, whom he mistook for Billy, his intended victim. The rest surrendered. It would be seven months before Garrett succeeded in his mission to kill Billy.

Garrett transported his prisoners by train - with an overnight stay in the Las Vegas jail - to the Santa Fe jail. Billy was there from December 27, 1880 to March 28, 1881 as the Ring awaited completion of the railroad to Mesilla to impede any rescue. But Billy almost escaped by tunneling out with fellow prisoners. That resulted in his being placed in solitary confinement from February 28th to March 28, 1881.

From his cell, Billy wrote four unanswered letters to Wallace, in 1881, pleading for his pardon: writing on March 4th: *"I have done everything that I promised you I would, and you have done nothing that you promised me."* On March 2nd, he threatened: *"I have some letters which date back two years and there are Parties who are very anxious to get them but I will not dispose of them until I see you."* Wallace never got over that audacity or his own guilt, reworking the pardon promise obsessively till the end of his life in vindictive fictionalized writings on "the outlaw Billy the Kid;" always making himself the hero, and reversing his own sadism to claim falsely that Billy Bonney had sworn a vendetta against himself.

Billy's Mesilla murder trial, under Judge Warren Bristol, began on March 30, 1881, with jurors unaware of Lincoln County War's issues, and without any Lincolnites daring to be witnesses for his defense. Attorney Ira Leonard represented Billy for past U.S. Attorney Catron's 1878 federal indictment, Case Number 411, the United States versus Charles Bowdre, Josiah Scurlock, Henry Brown, William Bonney alias Henry Antrim alias the Kid, John Middleton, Frederick Waite, Jim French, and George Coe for the murder of Andrew "Buckshot" Roberts. Surprising everyone, Leonard got it quashed as invalid, because the federal government had no jurisdiction over Blazer's Mill, the murder site; since private property, like it, was under Territorial jurisdiction; and its being in the Mescalaro Reservation's perimeter was irrelevant.

Remaining were only the Brady and Hindman Territorial indictments; and, though Billy been in the firing group of Regulators, he had only a revolver lacking accurate range. He could not have been their killer. But suddenly, Leonard withdrew, likely after a Ring threat. That was disastrous for Billy. He got Ring-biased, court appointed attorney, Albert Jennings Fountain, who considered him an outlaw. And Fountain's co-counsel was Ring-biased John D. Bail.

On April 8th and 9th of 1881, was Billy's Brady murder trial. His Spanish-speaking jury, given no translator, heard only prosecution witnesses - including James Dolan. After Judge Bristol's biased instructions (with translator) made Billy's mere presence equivalent to firing the fatal shot, the jury found Billy guilty of first degree murder; its sole punishment being hanging. On April 13th, Judge Bristol set Billy's hanging date for May 13th, insuring insufficient time for appeal. Billy was to be hanged in Lincoln by its Sheriff: Pat Garrett.

From the Mesilla jail, Billy wrote to Attorney Edgar Caypless - then conducting his replevin case against Stinking Springs posseman, Frank Stewart for stealing his horse at the capture - hoping to get money from sale of that bay mare to pay for an appeal. Billy did not plead again with Wallace for the pardon. Unbeknownst to him, Lew Wallace had even taken the precaution of writing his death warrant for Pat Garrett.

Ironically, the new Lincoln jail, where Billy was incarcerated to await hanging, was in the past "House," which Thomas Benton Catron had taken over by mortgaging, and then sold to Lincoln County for conversion to its courthouse with second floor jail.

On April 21, 1881, Billy arrived to Sheriff Garrett's custody. For his 24 hour guard, Garrett deputized a White Oaks man, James Bell, and a Seven Rivers man, Bob Olinger. Garrett's further precaution was shackling Billy at wrists and ankles, with securing to a floor ring - all to guarantee Billy's hanging death.

But on April 28th, with Garrett away collecting White Oaks's taxes, Billy escaped using a gun left in the outhouse by an accomplice, or by wresting away Deputy James Bell's revolver. For providing an outhouse gun, the likely person was the building's caretaker, Gottfried Gauss, Tunstall's past cook, who had been at the ranch on Tunstall's murder day, and present during the Ring's Lincoln County War outrages. With the revolver, Billy shot Bell dead as the man fled down the jail's stairway to sound alarm.

Deputy Bob Olinger, across the street at the Wortley Hotel at lunch with jail prisoners, either heard the shot or was directed to the ambush. Billy waited at the second-floor window, and killed him with his own Whitney double-barrel shotgun.

Billy then spent hours using a miner's pick, supplied by Gauss, to break his leg chain to enable riding; while gathered Lincoln townspeople, in passive resistance, did nothing to stop him. He finally rode away on a pony supplied by Gauss.

As of that April 28, 1881 escape, Billy was involved in the murder of nine men; James Bell and Robert Olinger adding to Frank "Windy" Cahill and Joe Grant as Billy's only provable killings.

Of the dead, Billy would have said that that Cahill's and Grant's killings were in self-defense; that he was a legal posseman at the group shooting of escaping arrested Tunstall murderers, William "Buck" Morton and Frank Baker; that his gun lacked range to hit Sheriff William Brady or Deputy George Hindman, and their killings by the Regulators were to save Alexander McSween from them; that he had not shot Andrew "Buckshot" Roberts, a Tunstall murderer and murderer of Dick Brewer firing at his group, and killed solely by Charlie Bowdre in self defense; and that Deputy James

Bell, after refusing to be tied, had tried to run for help, so was killed to save himself from unjust hanging (and Bell had been in the White Oaks posse which killed Jim Carlyle and falsely accused him).

Only Seven Rivers rustler, Bob Olinger, would have been admittedly hated as being in each Lincoln County War period crime - Tunstall's murder, Frank MacNab's ambush murder, and the War's skirmishes and battle. Billy's rage was so great, that, after firing both barrels at him, he smashed apart Olinger's shotgun to throw it on his corpse, delaying his own escape.

That count of nine killed men - with only four certain - remained as Billy's final true tally.

Billy's escape route was across the Capitan Mountains to the Las Tablas home of his friend, Yginio Salazar; then to Fort Sumner and Paulita Maxwell, where he hid in the Maxwell's sheep camps, confident of protection by that family and townspeople. He was unaware that Pat Garrett was paying Maxwell's foreman, Barney Mason, through Secret Service Agent Azariah Wild, as a spy.

Garrett's two deputies for the pursuit of Billy to Fort Sumner - John William Poe and Thomas "Kip" McKinney - did not know Billy. Poe, a buffalo hunter, past Deputy U.S. Marshall in Texas, cattle detective, and recent White Oaks settler, had met Garrett during the Wild-assisted tracking of the "Kid gang." McKinney knew Garrett from their 1878, hog farming days.

Once in Fort Sumner, Garrett, doubting Billy's presence, was urged by Poe to stay. On July 14, 1881, Poe searched the town and also checked with Sunnyside postmaster, Milnor Rudolph, seven miles to its north. That night, convinced Billy was nearby, he, Garrett, and McKinney planned an ambush in Peter Maxwell's bedroom, with Maxwell playing a traitorous decoy. Unknown accomplices likely directed Billy to Maxwell's bedroom at the unusually late hour, where Garrett waited, with Poe and McKinney posted outside on the surrounding porches to kill Billy if he escaped.

Near midnight, Billy proceeded from the converted barracks house of Celsa and Saval Gutierrez, carrying their butcher knife across the parade ground to cut a dinner steak in light of the almost-full, huge, moon-illusion moon. He first went toward Maxwell's bedroom; but seeing Poe, asked in Spanish who he was, then entered. Inside, to Maxwell in bed, Billy asked again in Spanish who was there, possibly sensing Garrett in the darkness.

Garrett then shot Billy. Poe, McKinney, and townspeople heard that shot. Next, Garrett fired wild. But Billy was already dead.

The townspeople held a night vigil for Billy in their carpenter's shop. The Coroner's Jury, the next day on July 15, 1881, had as President, Ringite Postmaster Milnor Rudolph. The terrified juryman had no alternative but to sign his concluding statement:

> [O]ur verdict is that the deed of said Garrett was justifiable homicide and we are unanimous in the opinion that the gratitude of all the community is due to the said Garrett for his deed and is worthy of being rewarded.

Ring terrorism was now complete. A generation of silence ensued before any of Billy Bonney's friends and sympathizers dared contradict the Santa Fe Ring's outlaw mythology of Billy the Kid by alluding to his bi-cultural brilliance, heroism, and the lost freedom fight.

Meanwhile, Pat Garrett, with motive of profiting from successfully killing Billy, with ghostwriter Ash Upson, had immediately sought to perpetuate the self-serving outlaw falsehoods himself. That enabled the establishment of Billy the Kid misinformation in the public mind, and distorted the work of the earliest 20th century Billy the Kid history writers.

Unforeseen, however, was insatiable public fascination with Billy the Kid, and unexpected intuition that he was actually a "Robin Hood" figure. Though the dangerous Santa Fe Ring survived, it could not stop the flood of books by emboldened old-timers that peaked in the 1930's. Then, the mere mention of a relationship with Billy the Kid guaranteed publication. That was the wave Blandina Segale had ridden for her own tales of "Billy the Kid."

BILLY BONNEY'S CONTEMPORARY FRIENDS

SUMMARY: Books contradicting Billy Bonney's Santa Fe Ring outlaw mythology began in the 20th century, when his aging past associates felt safe enough to praise him in autobiographies riding on coattails of his growing posthumous fame.

Compared to Billy Bonney's recorded, 19th century, Santa Fe Ring outlaw mythology in his lifetime, exacerbated by Pat Garrett's outlaw myth book, *Authentic Life of Billy the Kid*, published in 1882, the year after he killed him, Billy's contemporary friends and fellow freedom fighters were self-protectively silent. The few who did write, waited until old age. And they recorded his charismatic, bi-cultural, brilliance. But none dared mention the still existing, dangerous Santa Fe Ring.

FRANK AND GEORGE COE

John Tunstall's employees, local Homestead Act farmers, like cousins Frank and George Coe, affectionately nick-named new ranch hand, teenaged Billy Bonney, as "Kid." Frank and George were 26 and 21 respectively when Billy met them in late 1877, when he was 17. By 1878, after Tunstall's murder, the Coes became his fellow anti-Santa Fe Ring Regulators. After the lost Lincoln County War, the Coes fled to northwest New Mexico Territory, near Farmington, not returning to Lincoln County until 1884.

In 1878, George Coe had been federally indicted by U.S. Attorney Thomas Benton Catron, along with Billy and other Regulators, for the April 4, 1878 murder of Andrew "Buckshot" Roberts at Blazer's Mill. And Frank and George were both indicted Territorially in 1878 by the Lincoln County Grand Jury for the murders of William Brady and George Hindman. They were never prosecuted.

FRANK COE

As an old-timer, Frank Coe wrote about Billy in an unpublished letter to a William Steele Dean, dated August 3, 1926. He emphasized Billy's multiculturalism, and above-average height (5'6" was average), belying his mythologized "shortness":

[He was] 5ft 8in, weight 138 lb stood straight as an Indian, fine looking a lad as I ever met. He was a lady's man, the Mex girls were all crazy about him. He spoke their language well. He was a fine dancer, could go all their gaits and was one of them. **He was a wonder, you would have been proud to know him.**

On September 16, 1923, Frank Coe - like Billy, considering himself a Regulator soldier - gave a quote to the *El Paso Times*:

[Billy] was brave and reliable, one of the best soldiers we had. He never pushed his advice or opinions, but he had a wonderful presence of mind; the tighter the place the more he showed his cool nerve and quick brain.

Frank Coe also related Billy's shootist preoccupation:

He never seemed to care for money, except to buy cartridges with; then he would much prefer to gamble for them straight. Cartridges were scarce, and he always used about 10 times as many as any one else.

GEORGE COE

In 1934, George Coe published *Frontier Fighter: The Autobiography of George Coe Who Fought and Rode With Billy the Kid*. He confirmed Sheriff William Brady as dangerously brutal - even before John Tunstall's arrival - abusing him and fellow farmer and future Regulator, Josiah "Doc" Scurlock, by false arrest. And he described Tunstall's paternal affection for Billy:

> Tunstall seemed really devoted to the Kid. One day I was in Lincoln and I asked him about Billy.
> "George, that's the finest lad I ever met," he said. "He's a revelation to me every day and would do anything to please me. I'm going to make a man out of that boy yet. He has it in him."

George Coe also emphasized Billy's charisma:

> Billy came down to the Dick Brewer Ranch on the Ruidoso. He was the center of interest everywhere he went, and though heavily armed, he seemed as gentlemanly as a college-bred youth. He quickly became acquainted with everybody, and because of his humorous and pleasing personality grew to be a community favorite. In fact, Billy was so popular there wasn't enough of him to go around. He had a beautiful voice and sang like a bird. One of our special amusements was to get together every few nights and have singing. The thrill of those happy evenings still lingers – a pleasant memory – and tonight I would give a lot to live through one again. Frank Coe and I played the fiddles, and all of us danced, and here Billy, too, was in demand.

About Lincoln County War fighting, George Coe quoted Billy to show the boy's militant fervor in the Lincoln County War; writing:

> "As for ... giving up to that outfit, we'll die first."

Billy himself had exhibited that same brave bellicosity in his March 20, 1879 pardon bargain letter to Governor Lew Wallace:

"I am not afraid to die like a man fighting but I would not like to be killed like a dog unarmed."

George Coe gave a telling anecdote about Billy's teasing bravado which occurred around April 3, 1878 in the lead-up to the Lincoln County War. It shows how this teenager inspired grown men, and foreshadowed Billy's undaunted and ironic press interviews after his capture and after his hanging trial:

> We made a big bonfire, and sat around swapping lies and bragging ... Then we talked about riding into Lincoln and setting in short order all the difficulties that were troubling the people there. We were a brave band as we told it.
>
> Our guns, which formed the most important part of our possessions, had been placed carelessly around against nearby trees. **Billy sized up the situation and, looking for a little fun and excitement with an inexperienced bunch of greenhorns, he slipped about five or six cartridges out of his belt and tossed them into the fire. In less than a minute they began to go off, and such a mad dash for tall timber you have never seen ... I looked back as I ran, and there stood the Kid with his arms folded, perfectly unconcerned ...**
>
> "Well, you're a damn fine bunch of soldiers. Run like a bunch of coyotes and forget to take your guns. I just wanted to break you in a little before we met the enemy, and, boys, I'm sure proud of your nerve."

GOTTFRIED GAUSS

German-born Gottfried Gauss was 56 at Billy's April 28, 1881 great escape from Lincoln's courthouse-jail, and had been part of Billy's Lincoln County history from that teenager's October of 1877 arrival as a John Tunstall ranch hand - when Gauss was Tunstall's cook - through the Lincoln County War period; and to Billy's jailbreak, when Gauss was the Lincoln courthouse-jail's caretaker and likely supplier of Billy's escape revolver. Gauss's anti-Ring stance went back to 1876 when he was employed in Lincoln in "the House's" L.G. Murphy and Company incarnation, and was cheated out of his wages and profits from its brewery, which he ran.

On March 1, 1890, in an interview with the *Lincoln County Leader* about Billy's famous jailbreak from the Lincoln's courthouse-jail, Gauss implied enabling by non-intervening sympathetic Lincolnites, as well as his own sympathy for Billy. Gauss may even have directed Deputy Bob Olinger to the courthouse's east side, where Billy waited in ambush at the second floor window. Gauss stated:

> I was crossing the yard behind the courthouse, when I heard a shot fired then a tussle upstairs in the courthouse, somebody hurrying downstairs, and deputy sheriff Bell emerging from the door running toward me. He ran right into my arms, expired the same moment, and I laid him down, dead. That I was in a hurry to secure assistance, or perhaps to save myself, everybody will believe.
>
> When I arrived at the garden gate leading to the street, in front of the courthouse, I saw the other deputy sheriff Olinger, coming out of the hotel opposite, with the four or five other county prisoners, where they had taken their dinner. I called to him to come quick. He did so, leaving his prisoners in front of the hotel. When he had come up close to me, and while I was standing not a yard apart, I told him that I was just after laying Bell dead on the ground in

the yard behind. Before he could reply, he was struck by a well-directed shot fired from a window above us, and fell dead at my feet. I ran for my life to reach my room and safety, when Billy the Kid called to me: "Don't run, I wouldn't hurt you – I am alone, and master not only of the courthouse, but also of the town, for I will allow nobody to come near us." "You go," he said, "and saddle one of Judge (Ira) Leonard's horses, and I will clear out as soon as I have the shackles loosened from my legs." With a little prospecting pick I had thrown to him through the window he was working for at least an hour, and could not accomplish more than to free one leg. He came to the conclusion to wait a better chance, tie one shackle to his waistbelt, and start out. Meanwhile I had saddled a small skittish pony belonging to Billy Burt (the county clerk), as there was no other horse available, and had also, by Billy's command, tied a pair of red blankets behind the saddle ...

When Billy went down the stairs at last, on passing the body of Bell he said, "I'm sorry I had to kill him but I couldn't help it."

On passing the body of Olinger he gave him a tip with his boot, saying, "You are not going to round me up again." And so Billy the Kid started out that evening, after he had shaken hands with everybody around and after having a little difficulty in mounting on account of the shackle on his leg, he went on his way rejoicing.

IRA LEONARD

Billy's best friend in a high place, New York-born Attorney Ira Leonard, bravely took Susan McSween's case against Commander N.A.M. Dudley right after the Ring murdered his office-mate predecessor: Attorney Huston Chapman. Leonard was 46 when he met Billy in Lincoln in 1879, when the boy was risking his life to testify against Chapman's killers in Lincoln County's April Grand Jury; followed by the boy's assisting the prosecution by testifying in Dudley's military Court of Inquiry the next month.

Leonard appears to have known about Lew Wallace's bargain to grant the boy pardons for his Lincoln County War indictments in exchange for his eye-witness testifying against Attorney Huston Chapman's Ring murderers. Leonard kept Wallace informed about Billy's Lincoln County Grand Jury testimony: that bargain's crux. In an April 20, 1879 letter to Wallace, Leonard wrote sympathetically about Billy's courtroom pressure:

> *I will tell you Gov. that the prosecuting officer of this Dist. [William Rynerson] is no friend to the enforcement of the law. He is bent on going for the Kid & ... is proposed to destroy his testimony & influence. He is bent on pushing him to the wall. He is a Dolan [Santa Fe Ring] man and is defending him by his conduct all he can.*

HENRY HOYT

Henry Hoyt was a 24 year old medical doctor, working as a mail rider, when he met Billy Bonney in Tascosa, Texas, three months after the lost Lincoln County War. Billy and fellow Regulators, Charlie Bowdre and Tom O'Folliard, were selling horses, rustled retaliatively from Ringmen, as forewarned in Billy's "Regulator Manifesto" letter of July 13, 1878 to Catron's Carrizozo Cattle Ranch manager and brother-in-law, Edgar Walz.

Billy became attached to intellectual Hoyt as another father-figure, and gifted him with a sorrel horse. Apparently, to avoid suspicion - and with likelihood that the horse, Dandy Dick, had belonged to killed Sheriff William Brady, and may have been stolen from Ringmen, Charles Fritz or Edgar Walz - Billy created an elaborate bill of sale for Hoyt.

Dated October 24, 1878, written in Spencerian penmanship, it used correct legalese and was properly signed by witnesses. Teenaged Billy, then 18, impressed Hoyt enough to save it.

Henry Hoyt, like the Coe cousins, Frank and George, admired Billy's intelligence and bi-culturalism. In his autobiographical, 1829 book, *A Frontier Doctor*, Hoyt wrote about Billy:

> After learning his history directly from himself and recognizing his many superior natural qualifications, I often urged him, while he was free and the going was good, to leave the country, settle in Mexico or South America, and begin all over again. He spoke Spanish like a native and although only a beardless boy was nevertheless a natural leader of men. With his poise, iron nerve, and all-around efficiency properly applied, he could have made a success anywhere.

JOHN P. MEADOWS

A cattle rancher living in New Mexico from early 1880, John P. Meadows, when an old-timer, gave interviews to historians about having known Billy, and performed about it in an historical pageant called "Days of Billy the Kid in Story, Song and Dance" on February 26, 1931 in Roswell, New Mexico. It was also serialized in 1931 in the *Roswell Daily Record*. That year also, Meadows wrote a 78 page manuscript about Billy. And from August 8, 1935 to June 25, 1936, the *Alamogordo News* printed Meadows's reminiscence articles, which were later published in a 2004 book titled *Pat Garrett and Billy the Kid as I Knew Them*. It gives insight into how Billy inspired the older men to risk their lives to fight for freedom in the Lincoln County War. Meadows stated:

> When he was rough, he was as rough as men ever get to be, yet he had a good streak in him.

E.C. "TEDDY BLUE" ABBOTT

E.C. "Teddy Blue" Abbott, a cowboy about Billy's age, roving through New Mexico Territory in 1878, and having merely heard of him, recorded Billy's atypical multiculturalism. That implied Billy could instigate a Hispanic revolt against the land-grabbing, Anglo, Santa Fe Ring minority.

In 1955, as an old-timer, "Teddy Blue" Abbott published *We Pointed Them North: Recollections of a Cowpuncher*. Open about his own racism, Abbott reported, as common knowledge, the existence of two sides, with Billy as the Mexican's hero, writing:

> The Lincoln County troubles was still going on, and you had to be either for Billy the Kid or against him. It wasn't my fight ... it was the Mexicans that made a hero of him.

A TERRITORY IN REBELLION

Unknown to Blandina Segale was the political climate she entered upon coming to New Mexico Territory in the 1870's. People were in a cataclysmic clash with the rapidly and rapaciously growing despotic Santa Fe Ring, which was started in 1866 by relocated Missouri lawyers, Thomas Benton Catron and Stephen Benton Elkins. The Ring began as a land-grab scheme to cheat Mexican and Spanish grant holders of vast tracts whose ownership had been protected by the Mexican-American War's 1848 Treaty of Guadalupe Hidalgo. But legal technicalities in the granting of titles allowed Catron and Elkins to acquire the lands for themselves or compatriots, and to become fabulously rich. Their endeavors soon spread to banks, money-lending, railroads, monopolistic mercantile control of Lincoln County, cattle ranching, and mining. They cemented their power and protection from prosecution by political offices of Attorney General and U.S. Attorney; with Catron controlling the Territory through corrupt governors, judges, lawmen, and legislators, while Elkins served in Washington, D.C. as a Senator and as Secretary of War.

Popular uprisings against the Ring resulted. The 1878 Lincoln County War was the culmination of anti-Ring rebellions of the 1872 Legislature Revolt, the 1876 Grant County Rebellion with "Declaration of Independence" intending secession to Arizona, and the 1877 Colfax County War. The Santa Fe Ring's retaliations progressed in those years from malicious prosecutions of opponents to terrorist atrocities, assassinations, and inducing military treason to kill civilians.

And 19 year old Billy Bonney was the people's hero who emerged from the six day, July 1878, Lincoln County War Battle, pitting Anglo Homestead Act farmers and poor Hispanic residents against Santa Fe Ring forces. So he was outlawed by Ring propaganda with the moniker "Billy the Kid," with the intent of eliminating him and future opposition.

Blandina Segale was present throughout this period - apparently unaware of the desperate and lost fights for freedom. In fact, her own attorney in Santa Fe was Thomas Benton Catron himself. And her chosen symbol for depraved criminality was Billy the Kid. Thus, she contributed, in her writings, to the obscuring fog of misinformation from complicit press and cowardly historians that enabled the colluding corruption of the Santa Fe Ring to prosper in her day, and to continue unabated to the present in New Mexico.

BILLY BONNEY'S "REGULATOR MANIFESTO"

Highly literate, articulate, and inspired by Lincoln County's anti-Santa Fe Ring cause, and by the escalating Ring atrocities since its assassination of John Tunstall on February 18, 1878, Billy Bonney likely authored a letter sent one day before the start of the Lincoln County War Battle to the brother-in-law of the Ring's head: Thomas Benton Catron. I named it the "Regulator Manifesto;" and it sealed Billy's freedom fighter stance and later guerilla rustling against Ringites, stating fervently: *"Steal from the poorest or richest American or Mexican, and the full measure of the injury you do, shall be visited upon the property of Mr. Catron."*

Billy wrote:

In Camp, July 13, 1878.

Mr. Walz. Sir: - We are all aware that your brother-in-law, T.B. Catron sustains the Murphy-Kinney party, and take this method of informing you that if any property belonging to the residents of this county is stolen or destroyed, Mr. Catron's property will be dealt with as nearly as can be in the way in which the party he sustains deals with the property stolen or destroyed by them.

We returned Mr. Thornton the horses we took for the purpose of keeping the Murphy crowd from pursuing us with the promise that these horses should not again be used for that purpose. Now we know that the Tunstall estate cattle are pledged to Kinney and party. If they are taken, a similar number will be taken from your brother [sic – brother-in-law]. It is our object and efforts to protect property, but the man who plans destruction shall have destruction measured on him. **Steal from the poorest or richest American or Mexican, and the full measure of the injury you do, shall be visited upon the property of Mr. Catron.** *This murderous band is harbored by you as your guest, and with the consent of Catron occupies your property.*

Regulator

BLANDINA'S GREAT INJUSTICE

The measure of Blandina's injustice to the real Billy Bonney is obvious. For "Feast of All Saints, 1876" - when he was 16 and in Arizona - she wrote: "**Billy and his gang are terrorizing the country.**" For "March, 1881" - when he was either in the Santa Fe jail or facing his Ringite judge in his hanging trial - she claimed: "**His marauding has drawn the attention of the whole Territory.**" For "May 16, 1881," fabricating a visit to him in the Santa Fe jail - when he was first in his hanging trial and then had escaped the jail in Lincoln - she moralized:

Finding himself captain and dictator, with no religious principles to check him, he became what he is – **the greatest murderer of the Southwest.**

And the lying insults reached back to his childhood with her "September 8, 1881" entry, stating:

"Billy the Kid," was shot by Sheriff Patrick F. Garrett ... That ends the career of one who **began his downward course at the age of twelve years by taking revenge for the insult that had been offered to his mother.** (1948, Page 186)

And since Blandina never knew Billy Bonney, her "Billy the Kid" entries stand in malicious contrast to legitimate writings of the Coes, Henry Hoyt, Gottfried Gauss, and John Meadows, who respected his bi-culturalism, intelligence, and freedom fighting.

BLANDINA'S MAKE-BELIEVE WORLD

The real history of Billy Bonney was unavailable in Blandina Segale's day. Her ignorance and prejudices in creating her "Billy the Kid" fables can be put in perspective by the content of a 1946, pirated, dime novel-style edition of Pat Garrett's 1882 book, *The Authentic Life of Billy the Kid*, published 14 years after her own book, *At the End of the Santa Fe Trail*. This version garbled Pat Garrett's book's title as: *Billy the Kid: The Outlaw, Authentic Story of Billy the Kid by Pat F. Garrett, Greatest Sheriff of the Old Southwest*.

Its "Foreword," written by a John M. Scanland, makes clear that Blandina had been true to her period's accepted "Billy the Kid" stories. Scanland set the tone with his Billy the Kid song; writing:

"Ballad of Billy the Kid"

Listen to the song of Billy the Kid
To all the horrible deeds he did
Down in Lincoln a long time ago
When a man lived and died by his forty fo.

When Billy was a very small lad
He killed a man and went very bad.
Way out West with a gun in his hand
He shot up Lincoln, he and his band.

All the fair maidens strum and they sing
The only true song of Billy, their king,
Who killed twenty-one before he got through
And he swore he'd get Pat Garrett too.

Now listen and hear how Billy met his fate,
One moony night, the hour was late,
Shot in the back by Garrett his friend
And Billy the Kid came to his end.

Scanland's entirely fictionalized introductory text, gave the accepted history. He wrote:

> The "Dark Age" of southeastern New Mexico covers the period in the local history from about 1878 to 1882. That is, this is the historic Dark Age. Before that time little is known, as records of crimes were imperfectly kept, or rather not kept ... As each section of the United States became settled and orderly, the "bad men" sought new and unprotected fields where they could rob and murder with little fear of punishment ... They fled to this "pocket" on the southwestern frontier ...

The real bad man was of course always armed, and he was quick on the draw ... They craved the excitement of committing a murder, and gloated in the shedding of human blood ...

Perhaps Lincoln County was the bloodiest spot in the United States from 1875 to 1882 ... Lawlessness reigned supreme ... *Billy the Kid* and his gang were rough-riding the country, and he must be put down, or he would soon become powerful enough to dominate the entire country ... During the hottest period of the cattle rustlers' war, in 1879, Patrick F. Garrett ... was offered the position of deputy sheriff. Garrett at once showed his mettle by capturing a number of "bad men" and killing a few others who attempted to get the drop on him. He soon became sheriff, and this was the beginning of the reign of law in Lincoln county.

SMOKING GUNS FOR A HOAX: The real history of Billy Bonney demonstrates that Blandina's published false writings damaged public awareness of the truth of his Lincoln County War freedom fighting against the Santa Fe Ring. But this does not necessarily mean that Blandina was the person who intended a hoax. It still remains to be seen whether her future editors were actually responsible for the "Billy the Kid" journal entries. That conclusion would depend, in part, on which version first presented the tall tales: those from her lifetime, or those after she had died.

5

SLEUTHING BLANDINA'S PUBLISHED "BILLY THE KID" CLAIMS

MEETING BLANDINA'S PETITIONER FOR SAINTHOOD

SLEUTHING HOAXBUSTING CLUES: Blandina Segale's petitioner for sainthood is an honorable man, who studied for the priesthood, and reflects the best in her; making it hard to conceive of her with conniving or self-aggrandizing motivation to perpetrate a Billy the Kid hoax. But had he been misled?

My first phone call exploring the Nun's Tale Hoax was on April 4, 2017 to Santa Fe-based Peso Chavez, who was conducting the investigation for Blandina Segale's Petitioner for Sainthood, Allen Sánchez. Chavez said he just finds information, and his clients make the conclusions. However, he made clear his belief that Blandina did not know Billy Bonney, and had confused him with Billy LeRoy, "another Billy the Kid." He gave me Allen Sánchez's contact information.

On April 27, 2017, I met with Allen Sánchez in the lovely downtown Albuquerque building he had designed and built for Catholic Health Initiative (CHI) St. Joseph's Children, of which he was CEO and President. His organization had developed from the original St Joseph's Hospital founded by Blandina herself. And its progressive social service vision was rooted in her Santa Maria Institute, which she had founded in Cincinnati, Ohio in 1897. There, Blandina innovated a day care and home visiting program for Italian immigrants. Today, Allen Sánchez continues her mission by operating the largest home visiting program in the United States for prenatal to three year olds. The recent newspaper articles about Blandina had focused on him as the Petitioner for her sainthood. He likely knew more about Blandina than anyone on the planet.

Allen Sánchez has degrees from Rome's Pontifical Gregorian University and Aquinas Pontifical University. He had diligently studied Blandina Segale's Sisters of Charity of Cincinnati archives. And he wrote the new "Preface" for the latest edition of *At the End of the Santa Fe Trail*, published in 2014 by the Sisters of Charity of Cincinnati. His focus for it - in contrast to the 1948 edition's Billy the Kid thrust - was to emphasize for readers Blandina's inspirational spirituality and good works. He wrote:

> As you read [*At the End of the Santa Fe Trail*], you will see new and wondrous adventures. Sister Blandina gives her account of them, and her continuing question to us today is "Where do our adventures take us?" Her trail has taken her to the doorstep of sainthood. She invites us down the trail for the sake of encountering those in need and serving them.

In that "Preface," Allen Sánchez admiringly describes Blandina as: "courageous and dauntless, understanding and kind, determined and blunt, with common sense and a sense of humor, dedicated and prayerful;" and states that she became the most recognized name of the Sisters of Charity, especially in the Southwest. He also claims that she "changed the history of the Southwest," and that her writings are now "a window to her heroic virtues," or courageously good acts, fulfilling some of the justification for her attaining sainthood. Not mentioning Billy the Kid, he concluded:

> From her words to innocent children and to guilty outlaws, one can still be advised.

Nevertheless, on page 144b of that edition is a photo of Billy the Kid's tintype, captioned: "William H. Bonney, 'Billy the Kid,' ca. 1879, from tintype. Courtesy Museum of New Mexico, Negative N. 30769." It faces page 145's text of the journal, which states identically to the 1948 edition:

Jan., 1880. My old acquaintance 'Billy the Kid' is using his gun freely. The people of the territory are aroused and demand his capture, dead or alive.

For a reader of that 2014 edition, there is still no doubt raised that Blandina's "Billy the Kid" is Billy Bonney.

But when I told Allen Sánchez that I could not get a copy of the rare 1932 edition of *At the End of the Santa Fe Trail* on internet searches, he scanned his own special copy for me. It was signed: *"God bless you, Sister Blandina."*

His devout idealism had been expressed in the August 31, 2015 article by Catholic News Agency's Albuquerque reporter, Mary Rezac, for her "Nuns, guns and the Wild West – the extraordinary tale of Sr. Blandina." He was quoted:

> "Sainthood isn't about an award, it isn't about honoring, its about helping the faithful know that there is a source of God's grace being worked on Earth."

And to show Blandina's "heroic virtue" - an earthly attribute required for sainthood - Sánchez chose the verified incident of her stopping a lynch mob in Trinidad, Colorado - not her "Billy the Kid" fables. Reporter Mary Rezac quoted him:

> "She must have been charming to them!" he added. "I think they would fall in love with her and do what she would ask them to do, because she cared for them and she honestly was able to see the dignity of every human being from the innocent orphans to the guilty outlaws."

His belief, when we first spoke, was that there were "two Billy the Kids," that "Billy LeRoy was the original Billy the Kid," and that "LeRoy was the "Billy the Kid" Blandina knew." If true, that would save her from being a hoaxer.

SMOKING GUNS FOR A HOAX: It was clear that if a Billy the Kid hoax had occurred with Blandina Segale's journal, her backer for sainthood, Allen Sánchez, was determined to explain it, and certainly not to perpetuate it. His integrity might have reflected her own.

BACK TO THE FIRST EDITION OF 1932

SLEUTHING HOAXBUSTING CLUES: If an editor of the 1948 edition of At the End of the Santa Fe Trail inserted "Billy the Kid" entries to add popular appeal, and if they were not Blandina's own words, they would not be in the 1932 edition, since it was supposedly prepared from her original - though later destroyed - journal. But if entries are identical, the responsibility for the "Billy the Kid" fables would seem to go to Blandina herself for hoaxing.

Thanks to Allen Sánchez, I was able to go back to the *At the End of the Santa Fe Trail* book as it was created in 1932, during Blandina Segale's lifetime. In fact, she had nine more years of life to respond to text errors, if needed. My hope was that it would vindicate Allen Sánchez's heroine of hoaxing.

And that 1932 edition, if different from the 1948 one in terms of "Billy the Kid" claims, could prove that a later editor, after her death - like 1948's Sister Therese Martin - could have embellished the entries. And, at that stage of my thinking, the entries with information on Billy Bonney could have been tacked on to her own 1876 tale about an outlaw she *thought* was Billy the Kid; but was, in fact, Billy LeRoy - as Allen Sánchez believed.

So I compared entry to entry in the 1932 first edition of *At the End of the Santa Fe Trail* with its 1948 counterpart, which had first revealed to me the smoking guns of a Billy the Kid historical hoax.

The 1932 edition had no editorial introductions added to its four parts: "Trinidad," "Santa Fe," "Albuquerque," "Trinidad Again." It also had no footnotes, bibliography, or index. And it lacked any plate picturing Billy Bonney's tintype.

Adding complexity to the evaluation, was Blandina's own demand that her original journal be destroyed as its passages were transcribed for publication. Was that a noble gesture to protect people named therein - as the Sisters of Charity of Cincinnati archivists believe? Or would it prove to be a destruction of evidence of a hoax?

THE BOOK'S COMMENTATOR

The 1932 edition's "Foreword" was written by a Henry J. Grimmesman, on August 10, 1932, and co-signed by John T. McNicholas, Archbishop of Cincinnati - as repeated in the 1948 edition. That was why the 1948 editor, Sister Theresa Martin, titled it *"Original* Foreword." Since Henry J. Grimmesman had been impressed by the "Billy the Kid" tales, both the 1932 and the 1948 editions provided the following lead-in:

[Blandina] is seen fearlessly confronting the notorious outlaw, "Billy the Kid," demanding safety for the physicians of Trinidad, [Colorado,] whose lives he threatened, and not only winning his confidence but inspiring him with respect for every member of the religious garb. Who shall say what effect her ministrations to a neglected member of his band of outlaws may have had on the soul of this misguided youth?

BLANDINA'S INTRODUCTORY NOTE

Present in the 1932 edition, as in the 1948 edition, is Blandina's own "Author's Note." Written when she was alive, and therefore without a doubt by her, it made definite claims about her Old West journal, as follows:

1) That she had originally had no "thought of its publication;"

2) That "[a] short time ago, the editor of THE SANTA MARIA MAGAZINE [Anna Minogue] prevailed upon me to allow its publication in that periodical;"

3) That readers believed it had "historic value in its record of events made by an eye-witness;" and

4) It was not rewritten from the magazine articles for the book because her busy schedule made necessary that a "wish to re-write it must be set aside."

Blandina had written:

Into the keeping of this Journal of my life in the Southwest, there **never entered the thought of its publication.** The reward for the work involved was to come if Sister Justina and myself would meet and read it together.

A short time ago, the editor of THE SANTA MARIA MAGAZINE [Anna Minogue] prevailed upon me to allow its publication in that periodical. After the appearance of a few installments, requests for the Journal in book form began to come from many places in the United States, especially from New Mexico, whose Governor and Secretary of State, with the Archbishop of Santa Fé, found **historic value in its record of events made by an eye-witness.**

[T]he crowded hours that allowed no time for the leisurely writing of my Journal still prevail for me; and I realized if the urgent requests for the book were to be met, **my wish to re-write it must be set aside.**

CLUES: Blandina committed herself in writing to having no original intent to publish her journal; to being persuaded by The Santa Maria magazine's editor to publish her journal there; to the fact that the persuading was "a short time ago" (though it was now 1932 and she had been publishing the articles since 1926); to the magazine having an editor, though she and her sister were its publishers; to her journal entries having convinced readers that they were her real eye-witness historic record; and to her not having rewritten entries from her journal - presumably meaning also from her journal entries published in The Santa Maria magazine. No mention is made of an editor for the 1932 book, even though she claimed no time to rewrite it. Also, there exists no record of Blandina's disclaiming of any of her entries. So on these entries, one can judge her veracity.

BLANDINA'S 1932 "BILLY THE KID" ENTRIES

"Blandina's" "Billy the Kid" journal entries from the 1932 edition are compared to those in the 1948 edition, which was prepared after her death, to check for later alterations or additions to her original text for *At the End of the Santa Fe Trail*.

The 1932 edition is taken to be Blandina's intended writing, based on her 19th century Old West journal. So any misinformation can be called her own. If the text is identical, my hoaxbusting commentaries about the 1948 texts also apply here. (See Pages 36-46) The texts are again provided here, but now as being from Blandina's lifetime.

1932 "BILLY THE KID" ENTRY 1
IDENTICAL DATE AND TEXT TO 1948 VERSION

The 1932 and 1948 editions are dated "September, 1876," from Trinidad, for Blandina's first "Billy the Kid" reference with both "Bill's Gang" and "Billy the Kid's Gang;" as follows:

> My scattered notes on **"Billy the Kid's Gang"** are condensed, and someday you will be thrilled by their perusal.
>
> *The Trinidad Enterprise* – the only paper published here – in its last issue gave an exciting description of how **a member of "Bill's Gang"** painted red the town of Cimarron ...
>
> Yesterday one of the Vigilant Committee came to where I was ... and said: ... "I want you to see one of 'Billy's gang,' the one who caused such fright in Cimarron ...
>
> Billy's accomplice headed toward us ...
>
> He was mounted on a spirited stallion ... and was dressed as the *Torreros* (Bull-Fighters) dress in old Mexico. Cowboy's sombrero, fantastically trimmed, red velvet knee breaches, green velvet short coat, long sharp spurs, gold and green saddle cover. A figure of

six feet three ... The impression made on me was of intense loathing, and I will candidly acknowledge, of fear also. (1932, Pages 72-73)

1932 "BILLY THE KID" ENTRY 2: IDENTICAL DATE AND TEXT TO 1948

The 1932 and 1948 editions' date is "September, 1876." Their text is identical for "gang member Schneider's" confessions, his warning about "Billy the Kid's" scalping intent (1932, Pages 75-77), and Blandina's meeting with "Billy the Kid." She wrote:

> [At another visit, the gang member] lost no time in telling me that Billy and the "gang" are to be here, Saturday at 2 P.M., and I am going to tell you why they are coming ...
>
> "Well, the 'gang' is going to scalp the four of [the town's physicians] ... because not one of them would extract the bullet from my thigh ..."
>
> Saturday, 2 P.M. came, and I went to meet Billy and his gang ... The introduction was given. I can only remember, "Billy, our Captain, and Chism ..."
>
> **The leader, Billy, has steel-blue eyes, peach complexion, is young, one would take him to be seventeen – innocent-looking, save for the corners of his eyes, which tell a set purpose, good or bad** ... My glance took this description in while "Billy" was saying: "We are all glad to see you, Sister, and I want to say, it would give me pleasure to do you a favor ..."
>
> I took the hand saying: "I understand you have come to scalp our Trinidad physicians, which act I ask you to cancel ..."
>
> "Not only [do I grant] that, Sister, but at any time my pals and I can serve you, you will find us ready." (1932, Pages 80-82)

Absent is the footnote from the 1948 edition stating: "Billy was angry because Sister Blandina knew his purpose in coming to Trinidad. He felt that he and his gang had been betrayed by the sick member."

1932 "BILLY THE KID" ENTRY 3:
IDENTICAL DATE AND TEXT TO 1948 VERSION

The 1932 and 1948 editions are dated, from Trinidad, "Feast of All Saints, 1876," with identical text about "Billy the Kid's" then dying "gang member," and his gang, stating:

> This is the ninth month of our work with this patient who now never mentions "the Gang," though Trinidad often hears of **the atrocities committed by it – only say "Billy the Kid" and every individual is at attention** ...
>
> **Billy and his gang are terrorizing the country between this place and La Glorieta**, the historic battleground of Texans and Mexicans. (1932, Page 85-86)

1932 "BILLY THE KID" ENTRY 4:
SLIGHTLY DIFFERENT DATE FROM 1948
IDENTICAL TEXT TO 1948 VERSION

The 1932 date is "**December 16 [1876].**" The 1948 date is just "**December, 1876.**" The text is identical about people's fear of traveling because of "Billy the Kid." Blandina wrote:

> **"Billy's Gang" is quite active on the plains** ...
> When we arrived at Aqua Dulce – Sweet Water – all at the place were **prepared to fight the Gang and leader**, if attacked ... Whatever may have been the thoughts of those prepared to defend their lives, we were not molested. (1932, Pages 87-88)

1932 BILLY THE KID ENTRY 5:
DIFFERENT DATE FROM 1948
IDENTICAL TEXT TO 1948 VERSION

The 1932 date is **"March, 1878."** The 1948 date is **"Fourth week in May, 1877."** The text is identical, from Santa Fe, about Billy the Kid's "gang;" stating:

> Most Rev. Archbishop Lamy wishes me to go with the Staab family to the terminus of the railroad, which is five miles west of Trinidad, Colorado ... Everybody is concerned about our going. Mr. [Adolph] Staab spoke to Sister and myself about the **danger of travel (at the present time) on the Santa Fé Trail, owing to Billy the Kid's gang.** He told us that the gang is attacking every mail coach and private conveyance ... (1932, Pages 109-110)

1932 "BILLY THE KID" ENTRY 6:
DIFFERENT DATE FROM 1948
IDENTICAL TEXT TO 1948 VERSION

The 1932 date is **"June 9" [1878]**. The 1948 date is **"June 9, 1877."** The text is identical about visiting Trinidad, planning a return trip to Santa Fe, and being told of the dangers of "Billy the Kid," then encountering Billy the Kid;" stating:

> "The Kid is attacking the coaches or anything of profit that comes this way," [the man] answered. **The "Kid" means Billy the Kid and gang ... [But I retorted:] "I have no more fear than if the gang did not exist"** ... (1932, Page 111)
>
> [A highwayman approached.] I shifted my big bonnet, so that when he did look [inside the coach], he could see the Sisters. **Our eyes met; he raised his large-brimmed hat with a wave and a bow,** looked his recognition, fairly flew a distance of about three rods,

and then stopped to give us some of his wonderful antics and bronco maneuvers. **The rider was the famous "Billy, the Kid!"** (1932, Page 113)

1932 "BILLY THE KID" ENTRY 7: DIFFERENT DATE FROM 1948 IDENTICAL TEXT TO 1948 VERSION

The 1932 date is **"October 1, 1979."** The 1948 date is "October 1, 1878," from Santa Fe. The texts are identical about "Billy the Kid" and his "gang," along with historical names relevant to Billy Bonney; stating:

> Our new Governor is **General Lewis [sic -Lew] Wallace.** It is difficult to predict anything about him, except that he has a difficult task before him. Not the least of which will be to check the depredations being committed by **Billy and his gang.**
>
> **The work of the "Gang" is arousing the anger of good men. Mr. Tunstall**, a rancher, was brutally murdered by "Cattle King" **Major L.G. Murphy's** men.
>
> "Billy," cowboy for **Tunstall**, witnessed the deed and swore to shoot down like a dog every man he could find who had a part in the murder of his friend. (1932, Page 131)

1932 "BILLY THE KID" ENTRY 8: DIFFERENT DATE FROM 1948 IDENTICAL TEXT TO 1948 VERSION

The 1932 date is **"January, 1881."** The 1948 date is "January, 1880," from Santa Fe. The text is identical about "Billy the Kid" and his sought capture; stating:

> **My old acquaintance, "Billy the Kid," is using his gun freely.** The people of the Territory are aroused and demand his capture, dead or alive. **Rewards have**

been offered for his capture.

Our Governor, Lewis Wallace, has shown heroic bravery by going to Lincoln County to try to pacify the storm. **He had a number of interviews with "Billy," but to no effect. New rewards have been offered** both by the Governor and the people to capture Billy." (1932, Page 174)

1932 "BILLY THE KID" ENTRY 9:
DIFFERENT DATE FROM 1948
IDENTICAL TEXT TO 1948 VERSION

The 1932 date is **"July 23 [1881]."** The 1948 date is **"July 23, 1880."** The text is identical; stating:

"Billy the Kid" is playing high pranks. The Governor and the people in the Territory have **offered big rewards** for his capture, dead or alive. (1932, Page 201)

1932 "BILLY THE KID ENTRY" 10:
DIFFERENT DATE FROM 1948
IDENTICAL TEXT TO 1948 VERSION

The 1932 is **"March, 1882."** The 1948 date is **"March, 1881."** The text is identical; stating:

Unfortunate "Billy the Kid!" His marauding has drawn the attention of the whole Territory, and the "Kid" is as confident of safety as though he had a battalion at his command. It has been bruited about that he intends undoing Governor Wallace. Friends of law and order are on the *qui vive* that no harm come to the author of *Ben Hur*. (1932, Page 207)

1932 "BILLY THE KID" ENTRY 11:
DIFFERENT DATE FROM 1948
IDENTICAL TEXT TO 1948 VERSION

The 1932 date is **"April 24 [1882]."** The 1948 date is **"April 24, 1881."** The text is identical about the murderer of a "tenderfoot patient of Blandina's," who was now in the Santa Fe jail with "Billy the Kid." It stated:

> The murderer [of a "tenderfoot" she had warned about showing off wealth by fancy dressing] was intoxicated and is now **in jail with "Billy the Kid,"** who attempted to carry out his threat against Governor Wallace, but the latter was well guarded by every honest man in the territory – hence Billy's capture. My first free hours will be to visit the prisoners. (1932, Page 208)

1932 "BILLY THE KID" ENTRY 12:
DIFFERENT DATE FROM 1948
IDENTICAL TEXT TO 1948 VERSION

The 1932 date is **"May 16 [1882]."** The 1948 date is **"May 16, 1881."** The text is identical, and is about Blandina's Santa Fe jail visit with "Billy the Kid." It stated:

> I have just returned from the jail. The two prisoners were chained hands and feet, but **the "Kid" besides being cuffed hands and feet, was also fastened to the floor** ... When I got into the prison-cell and "Billy" saw me, he said – **as though we had met yesterday instead of four years ago** – "I wish I could place a chair for you, Sister ..."
> After a few minutes talk, the "Kid" said to me:
> "Do what you can for Kelly [the other prisoner who killed the fancy-dressed "tenderfoot"] ... this is his first offense, and he was not himself when he did

it. I'll get out of this; you will see, Sister."

Think, dear Sister Justina, how many crimes might have been prevented, had someone had influence over "Billy" after his first murder ... Finding himself captain and dictator, with no religious principles to check him, he became what he is – **the greatest murderer of the Southwest.**

I marvel at the assurance of the chained youth. No one can surmise how he can escape punishment this time. Mr. Kelly, his companion prisoner, is much dejected – fully realizing the enormity of his crime. (1932, Pages 208-209)

1932 "BILLY THE KID" ENTRY 13:
DIFFERENT DATE FROM 1948
SLIGHTLY DIFFERENT TEXT TO 1948 VERSION

The 1932 date is **"September 8, 1882."** The 1948 date is **"September 8, 1881."**

The 1932 text is slightly different. It misspells "Garrett" in the name " Patrick Garret." The 1948 version is corrected, and his middle initial is added, to yield: "Patrick F. Garrett."

The text is otherwise identical, and is about the killing of Billy the Kid, along with some childhood history and his "proper name - William H. Bonney" - stating:

> Poor, poor **"Billy the Kid," was shot by Sheriff Patrick Garret [sic]** of Lincoln County. That ends the career of one who **began his downward course at the age of twelve years by taking revenge for the insult that had been offered to his mother.**
>
> Only now have I learned his proper name – **William H. Bonney.** (1932, Pages 224-225)

1932 "BILLY THE KID" ENTRY 14: IDENTICAL DATES AND TEXT

The 1932 and 1948 editions are both dated "August 1889. " The text is identical about "Billy the Kid," stating:

> Trinidad has lost its frontier aspect. The jail is [now] built to hold its inmates. **Billy the Kid's gang is dissolved.** (1932, Page 341)

WHAT THE 1932 EDITION REVEALS

Since the texts are identical in the 1932 and 1948 editions of *At the End of the Santa Fe Trail*, the global criticism that Blandina's entries have nothing to do with the historical Billy Bonney stands. (See Pages 36-46)

Even more serious, is the 1932 dating, which is a year *later* than in the 1948 edition. That means that someone recognized the preposterousness of the dates after Blandina's death, and attempted to correct them to match Billy the Kid history for the 1948 edition. That implies a willful attempt to dupe readers as to Blandina's accuracy, since there was no disclaimer about the date changing or about erroneous dating.

Worse, the original 1932 dating, supposedly from Blandina's own master copy journal - or its published version from the Santa Maria Institute's magazine - shows no possibility of Blandina's keeping a real journal of "Billy the Kid" events or of her knowing the real "Billy the Kid."

Worse, the wildly wrong dates and date altering, point to historical hoaxing. But, with Blandina's "Author's Note" disclaimer of not being hands-on for re-writing the book, there was a chance of an unknown editor's erroneous interventions even for the 1932 book in her lifetime.

So the next attempt to vindicate Blandina would be to go back to her 1926 to 1931 articles in The Santa Maria Institute's magazine - called *Veritas*, and renamed as *The Santa Maria* - which were allegedly created by Blandina directly from her own 19th century journal.

SMOKING GUNS FOR A HOAX: Changes in the 1948 book to fix-up dating in the 1932 book imply a willful attempt to conceal its wildly erroneous dating of alleged journal entries about "Billy the Kid." More important is that the concept of an authentic dated journal is now ended, since correct dates characterize a real diary-style journal like Blandina's. And the 1932 book was allegedly its true reproduction. Altered dating, a feigned journal, and false "Billy the Kid" claims point to historical hoaxing. But the magazine articles preceding the book might provide unforeseen answers as to responsibility.

BLANDINA'S 1932 REFERENCES RELEVANT TO BILLY THE KID'S HISTORICAL PERIOD:

SLEUTHING HOAXBUSTING CLUES: Since the 1932 book's journal entries also reference historical figures relevant to Billy the Kid history, they must be compared to the 1948 edition of At the End of the Santa Fe Trail.

As noted in the "1932 "Billy the Kid" Entry 7" above, John Tunstall, Lawrence Murphy, and Lew Wallace, key figures in Billy Bonney's history, were cited when mentioning "Billy the Kid." Other historical figures relevant to Billy Bonney's historical period are also used by Blandina in the 1932 edition's entries. All are identically worded to the 1848 version. They are as follows:

LEW WALLACE

New Mexico Territorial Governor Lew Wallace is frequently mentioned, though without awareness of his betrayed pardon promise to Billy Bonney.

1932 LEW WALLACE ENTRY 1:
DIFFERENT DATE FROM 1948
IDENTICAL TEXT TO 1948

The 1932 date, from Santa Fe, is **"October 1, 1879."** The 1948 date is **"October 1, 1878."** The 1948 footnote, not present in 1932, had stated: "Appointed by president Hayes, he was inaugurated on October 1, 1878 at Santa Fe."

The identical text stated:

> Our new Governor is General **Lewis [sic - Lew] Wallace.** It is difficult to predict anything about him, except that he has a difficult task before him. Not the least of which will be to check the depredations being committed by Billy and his gang. (1932, Page 113)

1932 LEW WALLACE ENTRY 2:
DIFFERENT DATE FROM 1948
IDENTICAL TEXT TO 1948

Dated for 1932 as **"January, 1881,"** and for 1948 as **"January, 1880,"** the identically worded text states:

> Our Governor, **Lewis [sic - Lew] Wallace**, has shown heroic bravery by going to Lincoln County to try to pacify the storm. He had a number of interviews with "Billy," but to no effect. New rewards have been offered both by the Governor and the people to capture Billy. (1932, Page 145)

1932 LEW WALLACE ENTRY 3:
DIFFERENT DATE FROM 1948
IDENTICAL TEXT TO 1948

Dated **"March, 1882"** for 1932, and **"March, 1881"** for 1948, the identically worded entry states:

> [Billy the Kid's] marauding has drawn the attention of the whole Territory ... It has been bruited about that he intends undoing Governor **Wallace.** Friends of law and order are on the *qui vive* that no harm come to the author of *Ben Hur*. (1932, Page 172)

1932 LEW WALLACE ENTRY 4:
DIFFERENT DATE FROM 1948
IDENTICAL TEXT TO 1948

The 1932 date is **"April 24 [1882],"** with 1948's being **"April 24, 1881."** The text is identical, stating:

The murderer was intoxicated and is now in jail with "Billy the Kid," who attempted to carry out his threat against **Governor Wallace**, but the latter was well guarded by every honest man in the Territory – hence Billy's capture. (1932, Page 173)

THOMAS BENTON CATRON

Blandina cites her lawyer, Thomas Benton Catron, without apparent awareness that he was head of the deadly land-grabbing Santa Fe Ring against which Billy Bonney and the Regulators fought in the Lincoln County War.

1932 THOMAS BENTON CATRON ENTRY 1:
DIFFERENT DATE FROM 1948
IDENTICAL TEXT TO 1948

The 1932 date is **"September 21, 1882."** The 1948 date is **"September 21, 1881."** The text is identical, stating:

The capital [of the Territory] will never be moved from Santa Fe while Mr. Thomas B. Catron lives. (1932, Page 227)

1932 THOMAS BENTON CATRON ENTRY 2:
SLIGHTLY DIFFERENT DATE FROM 1948
IDENTICAL TEXT TO 1948

The 1932 date is **"November [1886]."** The 1948 date is just **"1886."** The text is identical; stating:

I consulted with Mr. T.B. Catron, who has been from the beginning our counselor-in-law, besides being considered the "Legal Light" of our Territory ... (1932, Page 317)

[I]n walked every lawyer in the building ... Mr. [William] Thornton, one of Catron's firm, wanted to know if I had been intimidated by that threatening letter [blocking her school warrants, receipts for paying teachers at the Albuquerque public school she founded]. Mr. [Frank] Clancy [another partner] said: "What are you going to do about it?" All seemed to enjoy the "threat" ...

Mr. Catron [said:] "[N]ow rest assured those school warrants will be legalized." (1932, Page 318)

SANTA FE RING

Blandina cited the Santa Fe Ring, but not its crimes.

1932, SANTA FE RING ENTRY 1: IDENTICAL DATE AND TEXT TO 1948

The 1932 and 1948 editions are dated "July 16, 1879." The identical text states:

One belonging to the "Santa Fe Ring" political, of course – came to ask me to visit "Big Jim" who is in jail for the murder of a policeman. (1932, Page 133)

1932 SANTA FE RING ENTRY 2: IDENTICAL DATE AND TEXT TO 1948

The 1932 and 1948 editions are dated "January, 1880." The identical text states:

There are two political parties here, Republicans and Democrats. The first party goes by the name of the **"Santa Fe Ring."** This party has been doing things to suit themselves, so the Democrats say. (1932, Pages 149-150)

LAND-GRABBERS AND LAND GRANTS:

1932 LAND-GRABBER ENTRY 1:
IDENTICAL DATE AND TEXT TO 1948

The 1932 and 1948 editions are dated "September 21, 1881." The texts are identical, stating:

> I am going to make a further prediction. The "land-grabbers" will do tremendous havoc among our native population, both spiritually and financially ... (1932, Page 188)
>
> When the men from the States come out West to dispossess the poor natives of their lands, they used many subterfuges. (1932, Page 194)

1932 LAND-GRABBER ENTRY 2:
IDENTICAL DATE AND TEXT TO 1948

The 1932 and 1948 editions are dated "May, 1883." The texts are identical, stating:

> Lawyer Catron told me he had a large grant of land. "Select a thousand acres and they are yours in fee simple, for your Industrial School," he said to me. (1932, Page 197)

VICTORIO:
IDENTICAL DATE AND TEXT TO 1948

About Mimbres Apache Chief Victorio, the 1932 and 1948 editions are dated "February 2, 1886." The identical text stated:

> Not only is Gerónimo riding at large, but Victorio and other captains also.
>
> Last week Sister Catherine and myself visited one of the grading camps and stood on a mound where, the day before, Victorio had scalped two of the

working men. Everyone in the camp was as quiet as though nothing had occurred. (1932, Page 244)

SMOKING GUNS FOR A HOAX: The 1932 journal entries here are identically worded to the 1948 edition's entries. So they were written when Blandina was alive, and theoretically responsible for wrong dating. And date changes in 1948 indicate fix-up attempts to hide her wildly wrong dating. But was she the original writer?

CHECKING THE LATER EDITIONS OF *AT THE END OF THE SANTA FE TRAIL*

SLEUTHING HOAXBUSTING CLUES: The question was whether Blandina's "Billy the Kid" misinformation was further corrected in later editions.

Later authorized editions of *At the End of the Santa Fe Trail* appeared in 1996 and 2014. They essentially reprinted the text of the 1948 edition, maintaining "Billy the Kid" errors.

THE 1996 EDITION

The 1996 edition of *At the End of the Santa Fe Trail* was published by the Sisters of Charity of Cincinnati, with a new short "Preface" and added illustrations. The "Preface" makes no mention of Billy the Kid. Retained are Blandina's "Original Author's Note" and the "Original Foreword" citing Blandina's "Billy the Kid" adventures. The text is the same as in the 1948 book. There is a photo on page 178a of the Billy the Kid tintype, demonstrating intent to portray Blandina's "Billy the Kid" as Billy Bonney.

THE 2014 EDITION

The 2014 edition of *At the End of the Santa Fe Trail* was published by the Sisters of Charity of Cincinnati, with a new "Preface" by Allen Sánchez. A short biography cites her encounters with **Billy the Kid,** Geronimo, and "frontier justice." Retained is Blandina's "Original Author's Note." The 1948 introductions are retained with their references to scalper Billy the Kid, and Blandina's visiting him in the Santa Fe jail. Page 144b has an improved photo of the Billy the Kid tintype, making clear that this was the intended Billy the Kid.

SMOKING GUNS FOR A HOAX: Though it is arguable that those involved in the 1996 and 2014 editions knew that Blandina's "Billy the Kid" entries were not about Billy Bonney, this publicity hook was kept without disclaimer.

BACK TO THE FIRST PUBLICATION: "AT THE END OF THE SANTA FE TRAIL" MAGAZINE ARTICLES

SLEUTHING HOAXBUSTING CLUES: From 1926 to 1931, Blandina Segale created magazine articles serializing her journal as "At the End of the Santa Fe Trial." Since she concomitantly destroyed her original journal, those articles now represent her words. Any with "Billy the Kid" would prove she wrote the fables. And changes from them to the 1932 book could show evolution of the hoax.

The Sisters of Charity's Santa Maria Institute in Cincinnati, Ohio, had been founded in 1897 by Blandina and her sister, Justina, to provide multiple services to benefit the local Italian immigrant population.

In February of 1926, Blandina and Justina created that Institute's monthly magazine, which they named *Veritas*, and renamed, in January of 1930, as *The Santa Maria*. The Sisters of Charity Archives at Mount St. Joseph, Ohio, calls the magazine the sisters' `official publication to promote the social work of the Santa Maria Institute.` Blandina also chose its sophisticated printing company: Bruce Publishing Company in Milwaukee, Wisconsin (which also printed her 1948 book's edition).

From October of 1926 to March of 1931, Blandina serialized her Old West journal, under the title "At the End of the Santa Fe Trail." She reasonably sought to capitalize on her interesting Southwest experiences to benefit her Santa Maria Institute, since all profits went there. That might have motivated the audience-seeking, literary license that yielded attention-grabbling "Billy the Kid" fables. She likewise applied later profits from the book version to that religious order.

Her advertising thrust can be seen in a February 1, 1927 article by Blandina's Santa Maria Institute staff member, Michael Girolamo, who wrote on their letterhead, which stated:

Veritas
(Truth)
A Monthly Magazine Devoted to the Interest of Italians
Published by THE SANTA MARIA INSTITUTE
21 West Thirteenth Street
Cincinnati, Ohio

So the magazine's mission was communication with the immigrant population from which the Segale sisters had once come, and which was the target audience for its purchase. Michael Girolamo wrote:

> This is the beginning of the second year of Veritas, the magazine that is published expressly for you. You enjoyed it in 1926. If you have not paid up, send $1.00 for 1926 and $2.00 in advance for 1927.
> Veritas is published in English and Italian, and mailed to every part of the United States. It promotes religion, education, Americanization, and contains articles suitable to every member of the family. Old and new writers will give the news of greatest interest to Italians. The magazine will be enlarged, and new attractions added. If you are in business send your advertisement; it will reach far and near.

Venality was not evidenced. According to the Sisters of Charity archivist:

> Any profits from *Veritas* and *Santa Maria* went directly to the Santa Maria Institute. However, it was a very costly publication and didn't seem to be profitable. That might have been the intent though to promote the cause and encourage more people to interact with the Institute and possibly donate their time or money to its various programs. The Cincinnati Archdiocesan Archives has some correspondence about the publication from 1931 urging Sister Blandina to pursue a simple one-sheet handout rather than the then 24-page long professional publication. Rather than compromising on the quality, it was decided to terminate the publication ...
>
> [A]s far as the At the End of the Santa Fe Trail [book] is concerned ... [for the past 17 years of records-keeping] the Sisters of Charity haven't profited from sales ... The rights to the 1948 edition were somehow given to the Bruce Publishing Company ... So both of these works continue to work in spreading the charism of the Community through its missions and Sisters' works, but are certainly not profitable financially.

Blandina and Justina further contributed to their magazine by running an additional serial on "The Story of an Immigrant Italian Family: The Authentic Early Life of the Segales." Likely written by Blandina, it ran from May 1931 to December 1931. Noteworthy is her putting "Authentic" into the title. That allows one to ponder if she was distinguishing that writing from her more fictionalized frontier adventures in "At the End of the Santa Fe Trail."

Since Blandina began her journal in 1872 with the stated sole intent of sharing it with Justina, one can see its first publication as a coming to full circle with the sisters' now sharing publication of the adventures.

Sister Carmela Cassano and Sister Lucy Comella, writing for the Santa Maria Institute files, possibly in 1957, had been young orphans who worked with Blandina in preparing the original manuscripts for the "At the End of the Santa Fe Trail" magazine articles. They provided insight into the Segale sisters, writing for the record:

Sister Justina Segale was a strong right arm and a loving sister to Sister Blandina. The later [sic] needed her talents to supplement her fiery vigor. Sister Justina was her direct oppistr [sic]: gentle, soft spoken, did the office work, prepared the dummy for the VERITAS or SANTA MARIA MAGAZINE and did the office work. Both did the field work.

Sister Blandina had a beautiful high soprano voice; Sister Justina sounded like a rusty hinge. We always had singing at Mass and Benediction. One day Sister Justina said to Sister Blandina, ''I know you can poke me to keep still in Chapel, but I'll just move over,'' chuckling all the time as she spoke. They were beautiful together.

RESPONSES TO THE "AT THE END OF THE SANTA FE TRAIL" MAGAZINE ARTICLES

The Santa Maria article of May, 1930 titled "Honor for Sister Blandina," praised her journal. Her "Billy the Kid" fictions had passed for fact. But she made no disclaimer that they were fables. The magazine's editor, Anna Minogue, wrote:

> If Sister Blandina, author of "At the End of the Santa Fe Trial," which for some time has been running in the SANTA MARIA, had not been well trained in the school of humility, praise enough has come to her lately to stir a natural pride in her accomplishment. **As it is, she shows only sincere surprise over these unexpected testimonials**, which we have prevailed on her to share with our readers.
>
> There was never any doubt in our mind of the great value of this Journal which Sister Blandina, on being missioned, in her early religious life, to the Southwest, started for Sister Justina. When finally

she consented to publish it in the SANTA MARIA, our readers were not slow in expressing their appreciation.

[Governor of New Mexico R.E. Dillon wrote:]

My Dear Sister Blandina:

My attention has been called to an article "At the End of the Santa Fe Trail" now appearing in Veritas magazine. I find this article intensely interesting as it relates so intimately to the life of New Mexico over half a century ago.

On account of the fact that **this journal is a valuable contribution to the history of the Southwest**, I am now writing to urge that you have it published in book form in order that it may be preserved, not only as a record of your own heroic achievements as a Sister of Charity, **but for the benefit of those interested in the powerful and vivid history of the Southwest which was in the making during the period you write about in this journal** ...

[Archbishop of Santa Fe Albert O. Daeger wrote:]

Well, the thought has occurred – not only to me but to others – that these valuable letters of Sister Blandina ought to be published in book form.

[The Editor of the *Santa Fe New Mexican* E. Dana Johnson wrote:]

I am not a Catholic, but that does not prevent me from congratulating you on this splendid and **invaluable contribution to the history of the Southwest** ... [T]his is the most absorbing chronicle

I have read and a **priceless historical service**. At a time when there is a national vogue for such books, I believe yours would be one of the most popular.

BLANDINA'S "BILLY THE KID" ENTRIES

Ground zero for hoaxbusting were Blandina's monthly magazine articles, published from 1926 to 1931, and allegedly directly reproducing her 19th century journal, which she noted had been stored in a "Saratoga trunk." They were titled "At the End of the Santa Fe Trail: From the Journal Kept by Sister Blandina During Her Mission to the Southwest." The Sisters of Charity archivist provided me with the issues.

The key question was: Were Blandina's "Billy the Kid" tales in those articles? If not, an unknown editor could have added them to the 1932 book without Blandina's knowledge. Or, if the tales were present in the magazine, was there less fabrication? Or, for a worse scenario, were there even more fables?

I did find articles mentioning "Billy the Kid" and related historical figures. Most were identical to the 1932 book. But a few had new information significantly different from that book. And their differences were very revealing.

SEPTEMBER, 1927 *VERITAS* "BILLY THE KID" ENTRY 1: MEETING WITH GANG MEMBER, "SCHNEIDER," IDENTICAL TO 1932 BOOK

For the September, 1927, issue of *Veritas,* Blandina gave her journal entry as "Trinidad, Col., Sept. 1876." The date was the same for 1932. The text is identical, and about having notes on "Billy the Kid's Gang," and then having encounters with "gang member Schneider," as a flamboyant rider, then as a shot and confessing patient.

CLUES: The unchanged date shows Blandina's commitment to it, though it was historically unrelated to the real Billy the Kid. Her first-hand encounters are discussed in Chapter 7.

OCTOBER, 1927 *VERITAS* "BILLY THE KID" ENTRY 2: MEETING "BILLY THE KID," DIFFERENT DATE FOR 1932 BOOK SLIGHT TEXT CHANGE TO 1932 BOOK

The October, 1927, *Veritas* entry is dated **October 5, 1876."** The 1932 book is dated **"September, 1876."** The text is almost identical to 1932's book, about Blandina's meeting with "Schneider," and meeting "Billy the Kid" and stopping the doctors scalpings. But the article first gives a blank instead of the name "Chism;" as follows:

The 1927 *Veritas* states: "I can only remember, "Billy, our Captain, and ----"

The 1932 book states: "I can only remember, "Billy, our Captain, and **Chism.**"

CLUES: The date change indicates that no actual date ever existed from a supposed journal entry, casting doubt on a 19th century source, instead of a 20th century creation. And the two dates used are both historically meaningless. The use of historical names from second-hand sources to feign reality is discussed in Chapter 6.

NOVEMBER, 1927 *VERITAS* "BILLY THE KID" ENTRY 3: TERRORIZING BY THE "BILLY THE KID GANG," IDENTICAL TO 1932 BOOK

For the November, 1927, issue of *Veritas,* Blandina gave her journal entry as "Feast of All Saints - 1876;" the same as used in 1932. The text is identical about "Billy the Kid" and his "gang" terrorizing from Trinidad to La Glorieta.

CLUES: The date, to which Blandina stayed committed for the 1932 book, has no historical connection to Billy the Kid. The use of second-hand sources to construct a "Billy the Kid gang" is discussed in Chapter 6.

NOVEMBER, 1927 *VERITAS* "BILLY THE KID" ENTRY 4: TRAVEL WORRIES BECAUSE OF "BILLY THE KID'S GANG," SLIGHTLY DIFFERENT DATE FROM 1932 BOOK IDENTICAL TEXT TO 1932 BOOK

For the November, 1927, issue of *Veritas,* Blandina gave her journal entry as "**December 16, 1876.**" The 1932 date was "**December, 1876.**" The identical entry was about travel worries because of the "Billy the Kid gang."

CLUES: The date, which Blandina kept for the 1932 book, has no historical connection to Billy the Kid.

FEBRUARY, 1928 *VERITAS* "BILLY THE KID" ENTRY 5: STAAB FAMILY'S FEAR OF "BILLY THE KID'S GANG," DIFFERENT DATE FROM 1932 BOOK IDENTICAL TEXT TO 1932 BOOK

For the February, 1928, issue of *Veritas,* the entry is dated "**Fourth week in May [1877].**" The 1932 book is dated "**March, 1878.**" The text is identical, and is about the Staab family carriage ride between Santa Fe and the railroad station near Trinidad, while fearing the "Billy the Kid gang."

CLUES: The date change indicates that no actual date ever existed from a supposed journal entry, casting doubt on a 19th century source, instead of a 20th century creation. And the date alteration for 1932 further suggests that Blandina herself was fixing-up the book.

FEBRUARY, 1928 *VERITAS* "BILLY THE KID" ENTRY 6: ENCOUNTERING "BILLY THE KID" WITH STAAB GROUP, DIFFERENT DATE FROM 1932 BOOK IDENTICAL TEXT TO 1932 BOOK

For the February, 1928, issue of *Veritas,* the entry is dated **"June 9 [1877]."** The 1932 book is dated **"June 9, 1878."** The text is identical, and is about the returning Staab family carriage ride to Santa Fe and encountering "Billy the Kid," who performed "bronco maneuvers" when he saw Blandina.

CLUES: The date change indicates that no actual date ever existed from a supposed journal entry, casting doubt on a 19th century source, instead of a 20th century creation. The dates have no connection to Billy Bonney.

MAY, 1928 *VERITAS* "BILLY THE KID" ENTRY 7: BACK HISTORY OF "BILLY THE KID," DIFFERENT DATE FROM 1932 BOOK WILDLY DIFFERING TEXT TO 1932 BOOK

For the May, 1928, issue of *Veritas,* Blandina dated her journal entry as **"October 1, 1878."** It was changed to **"October 1, 1879"** in 1932's book.

The text, about the arrival of Lew Wallace as governor, and history of Billy the Kid is very different from the 1932 book's text, and is wildly fabricated. It has Billy's "friend," for whom he swore the revenge, as a shot "Mr. Murphy," instead of the 1932 version's fix-up to "Mr. Tunstall."

For *Veritas,* and not the 1932 book, Blandina wrote that "Mr. McSwain's [sic – McSween's] men" shot "Murphy," and that "Mr. Murphy was brought to our Hospital [in Santa Fe]." She even had "Billy the Kid" visiting "Murphy" there, and swearing revenge against "Murphy's" shooters.

The *Veritas* text, - with the boldfaced words differing from 1932's - stated:

Our new Governor is General Lewis [sic - Lew] Wallace. It is difficult to predict anything about him, except that he has a difficult task before him. Not the least of which will be to check the depredations being committed by Billy and his gang.

The work of the "Gang" is arousing the anger of good men. **Mr. Murphy, one of the "Cattle Kings" of Lincoln county, was shot in a fight between his men and Mr. McSwain's [sic – McSween's] men.**

Mr. Murphy was brought to our Hospital. "Billy" came to see him, when he learned that Mr. Murphy's wound would be fatal. He swore at the bedside of the sick man, "that every one connected with the shooting would 'kiss the ground.'"

Here was a man with qualities to make him great, smothering his best instincts to become a murderer and an outlaw.

The subsequent 1932 book, with fix-up in boldface, stated:

Our new Governor is General Lewis [sic - Lew] Wallace. It is difficult to predict anything about him, except that he has a difficult task before him. Not the least of which will be to check the depredations being committed by Billy and his gang.

The work of the "Gang" is arousing the anger of good men. **Mr. Tunstall, a rancher, was brutally murdered by "Cattle King" Major L.G. Murphy's men.**

"Billy," cowboy for Tunstall, witnessed the deed and swore to shoot down like a dog every man he could find who had a part in the murder of his friend.

> *CLUES: The date change indicates that no actual date ever existed from a supposed journal entry, casting doubt on a 19th century source, instead of a 20th century creation. And the two dates used are both historically meaningless. The article has egregious errors of making "Mr. Murphy" "Billy the Kid's" friend, when, in fact, Ringite Lincoln mercantile boss, Lawrence Murphy, was Billy's and the Regulators' mortal enemy; was dying of alcoholism in the Lincoln County War which ended on July 19, 1878, had died on October 19, 1878, and was never shot. Key for hoaxbusting is that the "Murphy" fabrications are worsened by entries' brazenly converting them into Blandina's own first-hand encounters by having "shot Murphy" taken to her Santa Fe hospital, by having "vengeful Billy the Kid" visiting him there, and by having their words presumably overheard by her. For the 1932 book, Blandina herself, or an editor, recognized the revealingly preposterous lies, and fixed-up by switching "Tunstall" for "Murphy" as Billy the Kid's friend and shot victim, and by cutting out Blandina's first-hand encounter. This editing pin-points when Billy the Kid research sources were used as the interim between the articles' writing and the 1932 book's publication. And the actual sources used will be discussed in Chapter 6.*

OCTOBER, 1928 *VERITAS* "BILLY THE KID" ENTRY 8: BACK-STORY TO "BILLY THE KID'S" LOYALTY TO KILLED "MR. MURPHY" AND THE LINCOLN COUNTY WAR, DIFFERENT DATE TO 1932 BOOK WILDLY DIFFERING TEXT TO 1932 BOOK

For the October, 1928, issue of *Veritas,* the journal entry is **"September, 1879."** But the 1932 book is dated **"January, 1881."** The *Veritas* text shows wild fabrication, with "Billy the Kid" feeling gratitude to his dying friend, "Mr. Murphy," who was shot in a made-up version of the "Lincoln County War," which was ridiculously described as fought between cowboys to win first place at a watering hole!

The *Veritas* article stated:

My old acquaintance, "Billy the Kid," is using his gun freely. The people of the Territory are aroused and demand his capture, dead or alive. Rewards have been offered for his capture.

Few know the reason that started Billy the Kid on his downward course. It was gratitude. Gratitude to Mr. Murphy, one of the cattle bosses of Lincoln County. I will give you the gist of what today is called the "Lincoln County War." At the yearly "round up," the men – "cowboys" working for cattle bosses aim to arrive first with their herds at the best watering place. The first group that reaches the place has the right of possession for that season. Two groups arrived simultaneously, each claiming to be first. And the war began. In the conflict, Mr. Murphy was mortally wounded, though "Billy" exposed his life to save him. It was at Mr. Murphy's dying bed at our hospital that "Billy" took the path, "to make every man kiss the earth who was in any way implicated in Mr. Murphy's death."

Our Governor, Lewis Wallace, has shown heroic bravery by going to Lincoln County to try to pacify the storm. He had a number of interviews with "Billy," but to no effect. New rewards have been offered both by the Governor and the people to capture Billy."

The 1932 book only stated:

My old acquaintance, "Billy the Kid," is using his gun freely. The people of the Territory are aroused and demand his capture, dead or alive. Rewards have been offered for his capture.

Our Governor, Lewis Wallace, has shown heroic bravery by going to Lincoln County to try to pacify the storm. He had a number of interviews with "Billy," but to no effect. New rewards have been offered both by the Governor and the people to capture Billy."

CLUES: The date change indicates that no actual date ever existed from a supposed journal entry, casting doubt on existence of a 19th century source, instead of a 20th century creation for the magazine. And the two dates used are both historically meaningless. The Lincoln County War was in 1878. Governor Lew Wallace went to Lincoln in March of 1879. This tale continues Blandina's May, 1928 magazine's, "friend Murphy" fabrication, and adds a fabrication of the Lincoln County War. Though false, it leaves no doubt that Blandina's entries were intending the famous Billy Bonney of that War to be her "Billy the Kid." But by the 1932 book, Blandina herself, or an editor, recognized the revealingly preposterous lies, and did a fix-up by deleting the entire absurd passage. This editing pin-points the use of Billy the Kid researching to the interim between the articles' writing and the book's 1932 publication. And the sources used will be discussed in Chapter 6.

FEBRUARY, 1929 *VERITAS* "BILLY THE KID" ENTRY 9: HIGH PRANKS BY "BILLY THE KID," BIG REWARDS OFFERED, DIFFERENT DATE FROM 1932 BOOK IDENTICAL TEXT TO 1932 BOOK

For the February, 1929 issue of *Veritas,* the entry date is **"July 23 [1880]."** The 1932 book is dated **"July 23, 1881."** The text is identical about "Billy the Kid's" high pranks causing big rewards offered by Governor Wallace and citizens.

CLUES: The date change indicates that no actual date ever existed from a supposed journal entry, casting doubt on a 19th century source, instead of a 20th century creation. And the two dates used are both historically meaningless.

MARCH, 1929 *VERITAS*
"BILLY THE KID" ENTRY 10:
MARAUDING "BILLY THE KID" GETS TERRITORIAL ATTENTION,
FRIENDS PROTECT WALLACE,
DIFFERENT DATE FROM 1932 BOOK
IDENTICAL TEXT TO 1932 BOOK

For the March, 1929 issue of *Veritas,* the entry date is **"March, 1881."** The 1932 book is dated **"March, 1882."** The text is identical about "Billy the Kid's" marauding making friends protective of the author of *Ben-Hur.*

CLUES: The date change indicates that no actual date existed from a so called journal entry, casting doubt on a 19th century source, instead of a 20th century creation. And the two dates used are historically meaningless.

MARCH, 1929 *VERITAS*
"BILLY THE KID" ENTRIES 11 AND 12:
"BILLY THE KID" AND "KELLY"
IN THE SANTA FE JAIL,
DIFFERENT DATE TO 1932 BOOK
MORE TEXT COMPARED TO 1932 BOOK

For the March, 1929, issue of *Veritas,* Blandina dated her journal entries about learning of, then visiting, "Billy the Kid" and "Kelly" in the Santa Fe jail as **"April, 24 [1881]"** and **"May 16 [1881]"** respectively. For the 1932 book, the year was **changed for both to 1882**.

The text had parts identical to the 1932 book's, and was about her murdered "tenderfoot" patient, then her visit to his murderer, "Kelly," and "Billy the Kid" in the Santa Fe jail.

But just the magazine had a subsequently deleted flash-back about her already told tale of "Billy the Kid" as a scalper, and herself as a savior of his potential Trinidad doctor victims. Blandina wrote:

> Finding himself captain and dictator, with no religious principles to check him, he became what he is – the greatest murderer of the Southwest. **Some day, dear Sister Justina, when you receive this journal, you will see that the first time that I met the subject of these lines was at the bed-side of one of his gang who was marked for death. "Billy" and his pals had a grudge against the four physicians in Trinidad who had not made an effort to extract the bullet from the desperado's thigh and had come with the sole purpose of scalping the doctors. It was at this encounter that "Billy" wanted to show his appreciation of what had been done for the unwanted patient. After an introduction, "Billy" said, "Sister, if there is any favor that I can do for you I am here to do it."**
> **The four physicians were not touched.**
> I marvel at the assurance of the chained youth ...

CLUES: The date change indicates that no actual date ever existed from a supposed journal entry, casting doubt on existence of a 19th century source, instead of a 20th century creation. And all dates used are historically meaningless anyway. The flash-back summarizes Blandina's earlier magazine tales of "Billy the Kid's gang" and meeting with scalper Billy. Here it is a literary vehicle for this magazine series by filling in a new reader on her "Billy the Kid" back-story. However, it is possible that this short version was the original story around which was formed the more extensive fiction of the Trinidad doctors tale. Blandina's claimed first-hand encounter with "Billy the Kid" and "Kelly" is analyzed in Chapter 7, Pages 284-301.

MAY, 1929 *VERITAS*
"BILLY THE KID" ENTRY 13:
KILLING OF "BILLY THE KID,"
DIFFERENT DATE FROM 1932 BOOK
WILDLY DIFFERENT TEXT TO 1932 BOOK

For the May, 1929, *Veritas*, Blandina dated her entry as **"August, 1881."** The 1932 date was **"September 8, 1882."** The text differs, with *Veritas* using the "friend Murphy" fable to explain "Billy the Kid's" criminality. The 1932 book substituted a different fable: that "Billy" was a 12 year old killer avenging an insult to his mother.

The *Veritas* article stated:

> Poor, poor "Billy the Kid," was shot by Sheriff Patrick Garret [sic] of Lincoln County. That ends the career of one who **began his downward course by taking revenge for the death of one who had befriended him [Mr. Murphy] – or so the story goes.**
>
> Only now have I learned his proper name – William H. Bonney.

The 1932 book stated:

> Poor, poor "Billy the Kid," was shot by Sheriff Patrick Garret [sic] of Lincoln County. That ends the career of one who **began his downward course at the age of twelve years by taking revenge for the insult that had been offered to his mother.**
>
> Only now have I learned his proper name – William H. Bonney.

CLUES: The date change indicates that no actual journal date existed for this 20th century creation. And both dates are meaningless. And fix-up for the 1932 book is seen with mid-sentence splicing in of a "Billy the Kid" crime at age 12, instead of the "friend Murphy" claim. This reflects use of sources, as discussed in Chapter 6.

DECEMBER, 1930 *THE SANTA MARIA* "BILLY THE KID" ENTRY 14: "BILLY THE KID GANG" DISSOLVED, DIFFERENT DATE TO 1932 BOOK IDENTICAL TEXT TO 1932 BOOK

The October, 1930, *The Santa Maria* journal entry is dated **"Election time, 1891."** It was changed to **"August, 1889"** for the 1932 book. It was her last Billy the Kid entry. The text was identical, and about Trinidad losing its "frontier aspect" since "Billy the Kid's gang is dissolved."

CLUES: The date change indicates that no actual date ever existed from a supposed journal entry, casting doubt on existence of a 19th century source, instead of a 20th century creation. The use of "Billy the Kid" seems like a literary ploy to maintain his mention in entries, though he was long dead by either date.

BLANDINA'S ENTRIES FOR SOME OTHER RELATED HISTORICAL CHARACTERS

FEBRUARY, 1930 *THE SANTA MARIA*, ENCOUNTER WITH VICTORIO: IDENTICAL DATE AND TEXT TO 1932 BOOK

For the February, 1930, *The Santa Maria* edition, Blandina gave her journal entry as: "Albuquerque, New Mexico, February 2, 1886." The 1932 book used the same date. The texts are identical, with linking of Geronimo and Victorio, and Blandina's alleged encounter with a fresh Victorio attack.

CLUES: The date is unrelated to historical Victorio, and shows that this fable was Blandina's own from the start of her magazine's publication of her journal. This Victorio tale is further discussed in Pages 182-184 and under first-hand encounters in Chapter 7, Page 302.

OCTOBER, 1930 *THE SANTA MARIA*: FLASH-BACK TO NURSING "BILLY THE KID" "GANG MEMBER 'SNYDER' NOT 'SCHNEIDER' ": NOT IN 1932 BOOK

For the October, 1930, *The Santa Maria* edition, Blandina gave her journal entry as: "Albuquerque, New Mexico. (Scraps found in Saratoga trunk.) Cherry season. 1884." It is not in the 1932 book. In it, Blandina repeated her tale of quarreling "Billy the Kid gang" members - though "Schneider" is now spelled "Snyder." It stated:

[It was at Dick Wooten's toll house that] "Happy Jack" and "Snyder" (two of Billy the Kid's gang) from friends became mortal enemies, keeping the "drop" on each other for three days ... At dinner on the third day, both thought the other off guard simultaneously. **Snyder shot "Happy Jack" through the heart; "Happy Jack's" shot caught Snyder in the thigh** ... Mr. Snyder was brought to Trinidad and thrown into an uninhabited adobe. It was in that adobe house that two of my pupils and I brought him daily nourishment, clean bandages, etc. He was ill nine months and, of course, he died because the ball was never extracted from his thigh.

CLUES: The date is historically meaningless. This short version is missing the lengthy "Schneider" nursing and confessing scenes leading to a first-hand meeting with "Billy the Kid" which were present in an earlier magazine article and in the 1932 book. One wonders if this version was original, built around a kernel of truth of Blandina's nursing another shot man. The different spelling of "Schneider" as "Snyder" also implies an underlying different story. This clue was further elucidated by a newspaper article located by the Sisters of Charity archivist, and discussed in Chapter 8, Pages 370-373.

DECEMBER, 1927 *VERITAS* AND MAY, 1930 *THE SANTA MARIA*: ABOUT THE MAXWELLS AND "BILLY THE KID," ONLY PARTLY IN 1932 BOOK

In the December, 1827, edition of *Veritas,* dated "February 3, 1877" in the magazine and 1932 book, from Santa Fe, Blandina recorded her fellow nun, Sister Catherine, describing to her the first journey from Cincinnati, in 1865, of the Sisters of Charity through Colorado to Santa Fe. Recounted is a night stop-over at "Maxwell's ranch in New Mexico," where the Sisters were alarmed to see Indians loitering, and feared an attack had taken place. So they stayed in their coach. (The date would place the location to Cimarron, New Mexico Territory.) Blandina's entry stated:

[Sister Catherine said] Whilst we Sisters were in fear and suspense as to what would happen, Mrs. Maxwell made her appearance. She was inconsolable to find the Sisters had been in the coach during the night, more especially when she learned of their fright. The Maxwell family is noted for its hospitality. There, the American, the native [Mexicans], the Indian, are all made to feel at home. The feeling of "live and let live" permeates the very foundation of the Maxwell Ranch, hence, the Indians as they were seen by our Sisters, were guests on the Ranch.

We reached Santa Fe at nightfall, September 13, 1865.

For the October, 1930 edition of *The Santa Maria,* Blandina presented more about the Maxwell family. It was not in the 1932 book. Her entry dated "Cherry season, 1884," claimed that her Trinidad school had educated the Maxwell's daughter, whom she calls "Paoline." This tale also recycles Blandina's earlier articles about "Billy the Kid's friend "Mr. Murphy."

So Blandina has "Paoline" attempt to stop "Billy the Kid" from avenging the killing of "Mr. Murphy." The entry also implies a first-hand encounter, since Blandina claims that "Paoline" was at her Trinidad school, then quotes "Paoline" about "Billy the Kid," as if told to her by the girl. The entry stated:

> Saint Joseph Academy, Trinidad, Colorado, [which she had founded] has educated a number of young ladies whose families have been and are very much in the public eye for the part taken in the development of our South-western territories ...
>
> [Y]ou had Paoline [sic – Paulita] Maxwell, from "Maxwell Ranch." Nothing can exceed Mr. and Mrs. Maxwell's hospitality. There either Archbishop, priest, the Sisters, the Mexicans, the Americans, the Indians, and yes, the fugitive from justice finds hospitality ...
>
> At this place Billy the Kid often lingered and Miss Paoline Maxwell (who attended our academy in Trinidad) used many persuasive arguments to induce "Billy" to desist from carrying out his oath to "make every man kiss the earth who had anything to do with the killing of my friend [Mr. Murphy].

CLUES: Blandina seems unaware that the Maxwell's left the Cimarron location she was describing in 1870 to move to Fort Sumner, where Billy Bonney did go. And she misstates the daughter's actual name: Paulita. The entry seems to be a ploy to add another "Billy the Kid" mention. And it seems to have been deleted for the 1932 book with the purging of Blandina's other absurd fabrications about "Billy the Kid's friend Murphy." But the entry may also mark the first use of a Billy the Kid history book, as discussed under use of sources in Chapter 6, Pages 199-202. And since it also implies Blandina's first-hand contact with Paulita Maxwell, it is further discussed under first-hand encounters in Chapter 7, Page 305.

THE LOST OCTOBER, 1926 *VERITAS* ISSUE

I had one last hope for exonerating Blandina as the magazine articles gave strong evidence of her willful Billy the Kid hoaxing. There was a missing issue in the Sisters of Charity of Cincinnati archives: tantalizingly the first in Blandina's "At the End of the Santa Fe Trail" series, and dated October, 1926 for *Veritas*.

There was a chance that, at the start, Blandina gave her Italian immigrant readers an introduction to explain the fictional nature of her reporting. Seeking it from Harvard University, the only other site having the Santa Maria Institute's magazine set, made for a suspense-filled wait. The wait ended on July 11, 2017 when I got it from the Sisters of Charity archives when they received it from Harvard.

As I had suspected, there was an introduction to explain the series. It was a "Foreword," signed "Associate Editor;" and her name was listed on the magazine masthead as "Anna C. Minogue." And she was fully aware, as must have been Blandina, of the lure of "western writers." Minogue wrote:

> The lure of the West is as strong to-day as when it first tempted men to blaze a way through its great forests, mark out a trail across its illimitable deserts. The popularity of the novels of western writers, the multiplication of western story magazines, in themselves bear witness to the fact. If circumstances prevent us from rising up and following that lure, we go, in imagination.
>
> Often the writer of this Foreword to what we believe is going to prove to be one of the most interesting of western recitals, listening to Sister Blandina tell some incident of her life in the Southwest, begged her to write an account of the romantic, tragic, historic adventures and events which clustered around those days. The promise was given that some day, perhaps, she would do so.

This is another illustration of the way things work out, that this promise should be fulfilled through the columns of VERITAS, for we believe Sister Blandina could prize no other audience more highly than the readers of this magazine. As will appear from the first installment, Sister Blandina wrote in the form of a journal for her sister, Sister Justina, which further enhances it by giving it an intimate, personal appeal.

We remind the readers to consider the date – 1872 – and try to picture for themselves the West toward which the young nun was traveling ... **As Sister Blandina's journal unfolds, you will be shown the West of olden times, and we promise you thrills that the novelist would not dare to offer, truth being stronger than fiction.**

So Anna Minogue stated, in no uncertain terms, that the entries would have "thrills that the **novelist would not dare to offer.**" And she stated, in no uncertain terms, that the readers would be getting **"truth,"** not **"fiction."** That would translate into Anna Minogue being as duped by the hoaxing as everyone else.

And there was more. Anna Minogue gave another clue that moved the hoaxing back to the interval between the so-called journal entries and the magazine articles: they were first story-telling! Blandina herself would talk to enthralled Anna Minogue about her Old West adventures. It appears that Anna then brought about their publication. As she wrote: "[I] **begged her to write an account of the romantic, tragic, historic adventures and events which clustered around those days.**" In fact, Blandina's originally telling Anna her "Billy the Kid" stories may have inhibited Blandina from later admitting to Anna that they were just tall tales when they were finally put in print. At that juncture, would have solidified the Nun's Tale Hoax, which may have started out as amusement for the two friends: Blandina and Anna. (It is odd that no mention is ever made of Justina herself reading the journal.)

> CLUES: The "Foreword" to the first installment of "At the End of the Santa Fe Trial" advertised Blandina's journal entries as "truth," not fiction. That appeared to end the last chance for Blandina's explaining her "Billy the Kid" tales as taking literary license into fantasy. They were presented as reality to duped readers.

DEMISE OF THE MAGAZINE

By January 24, 1932, Blandina herself wrote a termination letter for her magazine for economic reasons to: "Dear friend and subscriber," stating:

> We regret to inform you that, because of this depression, and the fact that the Institute's funds are limited and must be entirely utilized for the work of the Institute, we are compelled to discontinue publication of the Santa Maria Institute magazine.

By then, her journal in book form, as *At the End of the Santa Fe Trail*, was in process; and its further contribution through sales could reasonably be anticipated. So it appears that this was the logical time for Blandina to decide to let its fabrications remain secret.

By August 4, 1934, Blandina got a letter from an Elizabeth Workman, praising the book, writing:

> Your most interesting book, THE END OF THE SANTA FE TRAIL , was loaned to us by a friend and we have enjoyed reading it so much we want to tell you about it ...
> [B]est of all, dear Sister Blandina, we admire your faith and your zeal for the glory of God. You have given us an example of a life consecrated by love of God.

By then, it was obviously impossible to reveal its fictions. And the Nun's Tale Hoax took on a life of its own.

ANALYSIS OF THE MAGAZINE ARTICLES

Veritas and *The Santa Maria* magazine articles, as allegedly transcribed by Blandina from her actual frontier journal, show telling differences from her 1932 book, *At the End of the Santa Fe Trail*. The differences imply a pattern of reckless fabrication by Blandina, or an editor, as follows:

1) The entries' wildly wrong and non-historical dates - with attempted fix-ups for the 1932 book - belie the reality of 19th century, real journal entries; and point to their creation at the 20th century writing of the articles.

2) The presence in the magazine articles of all the "Billy the Kid" entries - about his Trinidad "gang," with bull-fighter costumed, and later confessing, "Schneider;" about her encounter with potential scalper-murderer "Billy" himself; about her meeting "Billy" as a highwayman on the plains; and about her visiting "Billy" in the Santa Fe jail - prove they were created from the start of publication.

3) The magazine articles' use of "Billy the Kid;" "Chism," as a gang member; "Mr. Murphy;" and "Lincoln County War" indicate willful feigning of reality by borrowed historic names.

4) The magazine articles' global preposterousness of incidents - from meeting the bull-fighter costumed gigantic gang member to the "bronco maneuvers" of "Billy the Kid" encountered during the Staab trip - point to naïve fantasies of the Old West.

5) Ignorance of Billy the Kid history and reliance on fabrication is shown in entries' "friend Murphy" creation to explain "Billy the Kid's" outlawry. In truth, Lawrence Murphy was one of the Santa Fe Ring-affiliated original owners of the mercantile monopoly in Lincoln, "the House," against which Billy Bonney and the Regulators fought in the Lincoln County War. Murphy was Billy's deadly enemy, not friend. Worse for the fabrication, in that 1878 War period, Murphy

was dying of alcoholism at his Lincoln County ranch. The blatancy of entries' premeditated falsehoods in portraying Murphy as a friend, as a cattle king, and as fatally shot in the Lincoln County War are breathtaking. And the addition of "Mr. McSwain's [sic - McSween's] men" as shooting Murphy, reverses that Alexander McSween headed Billy's own Regulator side; and, of course, had nothing to do with "shooting" Murphy, who was never shot by anyone. There was worse. The Billy-Murphy friendship scenario was turned into a first-hand encounter of Blandina's, making shot "Murphy" cared for in her Santa Fe hospital - presumably by her - and even has distraught "Billy the Kid" there too at the bedside, swearing a quoted revenge, as presumably overheard by Blandina herself!

6) Oddly uninhibited while willfully writing fiction as fact, was the entry that audaciously dove into the Lincoln County War with quaint ignorance, making it a competitive quarrel between cowboys for first spot at a water hole, and the site of "Mr. Murphy's" shooting, while Billy the Kid "exposed his life to save him."

7) The apparent realization of the ridiculous Murphy and Lincoln County War errors, led not to an explanatory disclaimer of fictionalizing for entertainment, but to a cover-up attempt by deleting those texts for the 1932 book.

8) The use of source material for fix-ups after the articles and for the 1932 book is traceable, and is discussed in Chapter 6.

9) The magazine entries about the visit to the Santa Fe jail visit stayed intact for the 1932 book, except for the deleted flash-back to "Billy the Kid's" past to further emphasize that he was Blandina's "old acquaintance" as a potentially-doctor-murdering-scalper outlaw. The jail entries are analyzed for their fakery in Chapter 7. But implied is Blandina's - or someone else's - apparent belief that these fables did not risk her exposure as much as the "friend Murphy" ones.

10) The magazine entry claiming first-hand encounter with Victorio stayed intact for the 1932 book, was another fabrication which was apparently thought able to survive scrutiny; and is analyzed in Chapter 7.

11) The magazine entries about Maxwell's ranch and the daughter "Paoline" [sic - Paulita] Maxwell, were an opportunity for another "Billy the Kid" mention, as well as for first-hand insertion of Blandina into the story by having "Paoline" attend her Trinidad school. But the tale may also imply the first use of a Billy the Kid book for the fix-ups that characterized the 1932 book; as discussed in use of sources and first-hand encounters in Chapters 6 and 7.

12) The magazine's back-story text for the death of Billy the Kid was later changed for the 1932 book by use of sources, as will be seen in Chapter 6. But for the magazine, the fabricated killed-friend-Murphy-revenge motive was used to explain Blandina's fabricated "Billy the Kid crimes.

13) The first magazine installment for "At the End of the Santa Fe Trail" offered no explanation for its fictionalizing; thus, willfully misled readers as to its being publication of a real historical journal. And the writer of its "Foreword," Associate Editor Anna Minogue, appears to have been Blandina's true-believer, though she may have assisted in corrections for the 1932 book.

SMOKING GUNS FOR A HOAX: The articles not only contain the same elaborate "Billy the Kid" fabrications published in the 1932 book, At the End of the Santa Fe Trail, but they have additional tall tales. It also appears that the articles' unexpected success - up to New Mexico Governor Richard C. Dillon - may have been a "runaway horse" that could not be stopped without admitting her "Billy the Kid" fictions, and discrediting Blandina's other entries and herself. And cover-up and attempted fix-ups of the 1932 book's text were apparently chosen, instead of confessions. But was there an editor involved?

BACK TO THE ORIGINAL JOURNAL

SLEUTHING HOAXBUSTING CLUES: The document to clarify intent would have been Blandina's original journal. She had retained it from 1872 to 1926. But after allegedly using it as the source for her magazine articles, she destroyed it in entirety.

The obvious solution to attributing entries was to go back to the Blandina's original journal to check its text. That was impossible. According to the Sisters of Charity of Ohio archives, Blandina had destroyed her journal when preparing her magazine articles. Not a single page remains.

Why would Blandina do that? On the surface it is an obvious hoaxer's ploy to destroy evidence of fabricating, in that real entries never existed. On the other hand, Blandina allegedly claimed that she was concerned about confidentiality issues in some of her entries. But why would she then not have merely altered or destroyed those entries, and preserved the entries that she published, and which charmed her audience?

Some comments made by her in published journal entries do give hints about the original journal's true nature. For the October, 1928, *Veritas*, for entry dated "September, 1879, Blandina described merely hoarded notes, writing:

> Dear Sister Justina: Looking over the **scribblings I wrote on scraps** since January, I noticed that they were not entered into this journal which I trust some day you will enjoy. I've condensed the scraps and here is the result.

For the October, 1930, *The Santa Maria* edition, Blandina gave her journal entry as: "Albuquerque, New Mexico. (**Scraps found in Saratoga trunk**.) Cherry season. 1884." Again, "scraps" were noted.

For "Billy the Kid," she had written for "September, 1876":

My **scattered notes on "Billy the Kid's Gang"** are condensed, and someday you [Justina] will be thrilled by their perusal.

Or for "1886" from Albuquerque, she wrote:

From [my] notes taken at different times, you [Justina], may read some facts. Here are some of my findings ...

And that collection of "scraps," "notes," letters, newspaper clippings, and other mementos from her days on the frontier may have been all there was to the "Billy the Kid" parts of her so-called Old West journal.

The big picture is that Blandina's magazine articles are now ground zero for assessing her written claims and intent.

SMOKING GUNS FOR A HOAX: The total destruction of the original journal for confidentiality reasons is belied by the claim that its actual entries had been published as magazine articles, proving no need for destruction of those portions. That makes more likely a cover-up of the fact that no real journal entries for "Billy the Kid" ever existed. And the changed entry dating has already indicated that no true diary-like journal entries had ever existed for "Billy the Kid" and some related historical figures. Additionally, there is no evidence that the writings were ever shared with Justina, that claim being possibly only a literary vehicle for presenting collected reminiscences assembled in the 20th century time of publication. And the origin of the "Billy the Kid" fables may have been in tales told to Western fan Anna Minogue long before any publication took place. That would leave the likely reality that the "Billy the Kid" entries were cobbled together from saved 19th century "notes," jotted "scraps," and memorabilia at the 20th century time of writing. And the changes from magazine to book indicate fix-ups to cover-up the hoax.

SUMMARY OF DATE AND TEXT ALTERATIONS IN PUBLISHED JOURNAL

SLEUTHING HOAXBUSTING CLUES: Summarizing date and text changes demonstrates wild variations in different publications of so-called journal entries.

ENTRY 1: Has notes on BTK gang; "gang member Schneider" paints Cimarron red; sees "Schneider"

    1948: September, 1876
    1932: September, 1876
    September, 1927 *Veritas*: September, 1876

ENTRY 2: Nursing "Schneider;" meeting BTK and stopping scalping of doctors

    1948: September 1876
    1932: September, 1876
    October, 1927 *Veritas*: October 5, 1876

ENTRY 3: BTK gang terrorizing from Trinidad to La Glorieta

    1948: Feast of All Saints, 1876
    1932: Feast of All Saints, 1876
    November, 1927 *Veritas*: Feast of All Saints, 1876

ENTRY 4: Travel worries because of BTK highwaymen

    1948: December 16, 1876
    1932: December, 1876
    November, 1927 *Veritas*: December 16, 1876

ENTRY 5: Lamy requests her to travel with Staabs worried about BTK attacks

    1948: Fourth week in May, 1877
    1932: March, 1878
    February, 1928 *Veritas*: Fourth week in May, 1877

ENTRY 6: Second BTK meeting during Staab carriage ride on plains

    1948: June 9, 1877
    1932: June 9, 1878
    February, 1928 *Veritas*: June 9, 1877

ENTRY 7: Arrival Governor Wallace; depredations BTK gang; back-story for BTK

    1948: October 1, 1878; "friend Tunstall" version
    1932: October 1, 1879;" friend Tunstall" version
    May, 1928 *Veritas*: October 1, 1878; "friend Murphy" version

---

ENTRY 8: BTK as old acquaintance; BTK failed Wallace interviews; rewards offered

    1948: January, 1880
    1932: January, 1881
    October, 1928 Veritas: September, 1879 – with made-up Lincoln County War and "friend Murphy"

ENTRY 9: High pranks by BTK; rewards offered

    1948: July 23, 1880
    1932: July 23, 1881
    February, 1929 *Veritas*: July 23, 1880

ENTRY 10: Marauding by BTK gets attention of territory

    1948: March, 1881
    1932: March, 1882
    March, 1929 *Veritas*: March, 1881

ENTRY 11: Tenderfoot patient murdered by Kelly; with BTK in Santa Fe jail

    1948: April 24, 1881
    1932: April 24, 1882
    March, 1929 *Veritas*: April 24, 1881

ENTRY 12: Visit with BTK and Kelly in Santa Fe jail

    1948: May 16, 1881
    1932: May 16, 1882
    March, 1929 *Veritas*: May 16, 1881 – with flash-back to nursing "Schneider" and stopping BTK's scalping of Trinidad doctors

---

ENTRY 13: Killing of BTK, a murderer since age of 12

    1948: September 8, 1881
    1932: September 8, 1882
    May 1929 *Veritas*: August, 1881 – with "friend Murphy" explanation for BTK's crimes

---

ENTRY 14: BTK gang dissolved

    1948: August, 1889
    1932: August, 1889
    December, 1930, *The Santa Maria*: Election time, 1891

ENTRY ONLY IN MAGAZINE: Omitted in books; about "Paoline" Maxwell and BTK

December, 1927 *The Santa Maria*: February 3, 1877

ENTRY ONLY IN MAGAZINE: Omitted in books; short version of nursing BTK gang member "Snyder"

October, 1930: *The Santa Maria*: Cherry Season, 1884

OVERALL SMOKING GUNS FOR A HOAX: It is clear that the concept of a journal was stretched in the presentation of "At the End of the Santa Fe Trail," with its alterations (and likely fabrications) of dates, and with alleged destruction of the original removing any way to prove that a real journal had ever existed. And it is now also clear that the "Billy the Kid" entries were fabricated and false from its earliest publication as magazine articles. Their descriptions of "Billy the Kid's" depravity in the face of Blandina's holy compassion, and their dramatic spacing throughout the work, point to literary manipulation, not journal-keeping. And the fact that they attracted unexpected attention and prominent true-believers may have inhibited Blandina - or anyone else responsible - from making public confession about their being tall tales; which would have diminished credibility of her whole creation, and even her mission. And after her death, with increased awareness of fabrications, her later editors may have decided not to rock the boat, and to tweak "Billy the Kid" corrections while using him as a selling point - adding the famous tintype and commentaries advertising the connection to him. Of course, that all adds up to willful hoaxing, with all aware participants being fellow hoaxers.

6

SLEUTHING BLANDINA'S SECOND-HAND SOURCES FOR HER "BILLY THE KID" CLAIMS

RESEARCH AND THE NUN

> SLEUTHING HOAXBUSTING CLUES: *In her journal, Blandina recorded that she did research and made notes for some entries - including notes on Billy the Kid. And the wildly erroneous dating of those Billy the Kid entries points to their final writing not being in the 19th century. Finding her secondary sources would demonstrate entries' fabrication; especially if the sources are not from the journal's 19th century period, but are from the 1926 to 1932 period of creating the magazine articles and book for At the End of the Santa Fe Trail.*

When one explores Blandina Segale's use of Billy the Kid sources to flesh-out her tales, one encounters the peculiarity of hoaxes within hoaxes, since the sources themselves were fantastical creations of their writers - be they books or newspaper articles. So if Blandina intended to dupe, she was, in turn, duped herself.

Hoaxing an historical journal requires research to portray experiences with feigned details. The problem encountered by all Billy the Kid hoaxers in the first half of the 20th century, was that scholarly history books on the subject had not yet been written. The existing books, fictionalizing to fill huge gaps in information, ended up in the lurid and camp dime novel tradition. And importantly, since the writers copied each other, they repeated the same tell-tale errors.

The massive amount of Billy the Kid press from 1880 onward was no better. It was propelled by Santa Fe Ring propaganda, which fabricated to cover up the freedom fight of the Lincoln County War by demonizing its hero, Billy Bonney, as the murdering desperado "Billy the Kid," so as to turn that grass roots rebellion into meaningless general outlawry.

A major additional contributor to Billy the Kid press was Lew Wallace. His role in betraying his pardon bargain with Billy Bonney, and his subsequent obsessive creating of Billy the Kid outlaw myth articles till the end of his life, are analyzed in my book: *The Lost Pardon of Billy the Kid: An Analysis Factoring in the Santa Fe Ring, Governor Lew Wallace's Dilemma, and a Territory in Rebellion*. But the gist was that dishonest Wallace's unconscious guilt from betraying the boy caused him to reverse their roles: fabricating Billy as the betrayer of the pardon by being an incorrigible outlaw, and fabricating himself as the wronged savior and object of the boy's murderous vindictive vendetta.

Of course, Blandina, or an editor, would have been unaware of building on sand if these disreputable sources were used. And worse for Blandina, or an editor, they were all traceable to reveal the artificial construction of her frontier tales.

BLANDINA'S RESEARCH ACUMEN

Blandina Segale was a smart and formidable researcher and chronicler, as she documented herself in her journal.

RESEARCHING "BILLY THE KID"

For her "September, 1876" Trinidad entry (the same in 1932 and 1948 editions) - in which she also cites a local newspaper (*The Trinidad Chronicle*) for her information on the "Billy the Kid Gang" - she wrote:

> **My scattered notes on "Billy the Kid's Gang" are condensed**, and someday you [Justina] will be thrilled by their perusal.

One of Blandina's "Billy the Kid" research documents is still in the Sisters of Charity of Cincinnati archives. It is a magazine article from July of 1933 with 82 year old Blandina's neatly penned script above its title, "Buffalo Days: Billy the Kid," declaring:

The most untrue account I've seen of "Billy"
Sister Blandina

That article was authored by J. Wright Mooar (as told to a James Winford Hunt) for Holland's, *The Magazine of the South*. Mooar was a famous buffalo hunter, who, in fact, had no contact with Billy the Kid. But Blandina's comment implies her comparative perusal of other Billy the Kid accounts as well. Noteworthy, is that its big illustration of "Billy the Kid and his gang," is of Mexican vaqueros, costumed in harlequin patterns like Blandina's own version of her "Billy the Kid gang member" from Trinidad - implying it was a popular way of portraying Old West outlaws by naïve press and fabricating writers.

Like Blandina - and many other old-timers in this period - Mooar sought attention by a Billy the Kid hook, writing:

This chronicle would be incomplete without recording the story of my long journey to Arizona, and my final experiences with the buffalo and wilder men, among whom was **none other than the notorious outlaw Billy the Kid.**

Mooar's tall tale was of going to New Mexico Territory's town of Fort Sumner, which he calls "a little adobe village" – unaware of its oddity of converted military buildings still arranged around its original big parade ground from its fort days. He describes encountering "a tough-looking band of men, all heavily armed and accompanied by the outlaw Billy the Kid." That came from fake Santa Fe Ring press which Billy got in the late 1880's; and was likely December 22, 1880's *New York Sun* article: "Outlaws of New Mexico. The Exploits of a Band Headed by a New York Youth. The Mountain Fastness of the Kid and His Followers - War Against a Gang of Cattle Thieves and Murderers." (See Pages 210-216 for article) But, for some reason, Mooar's "Billy the Kid" is controlling vast amounts of flour! So Mooar negotiates to buy some from him. Mooar then meets a man in a "lonely sod claim house" who tells him that Billy the Kid might steal his mules. One can see why even Blandina found it preposterous.

As to Blandina's actual research on Billy the Kid, two key books are presented in the bibliography created by Sister Therese Martin for the 1848 edition of *At the End of the Santa Fe Trail*. Though they were, in fact, used by Blandina (as will be seen below), they are not now in the Sisters of Charity of Cincinnati archives. They are the 1927 edition of Pat Garrett's ghostwritten book, *The Authentic Life of Billy the Kid The Noted Desperado of the Southwest, Whose Deeds of Daring and Blood Made His Name a Terror in New Mexico, Arizona, and Northern Mexico*; and the 1926 edition of Walter Noble Burns's *The Saga of Billy the Kid*. Important to realize is that these were the only "history books" available when Blandina's magazine articles and book were written. But lacking real research, these two books were largely fiction. In addition, Burns relied on Garrett's book from its 1882 first edition.

OTHER BLANDINA RESEARCH

The sophistication of Blandina's research skill can be seen in her elaborate entry of "1886" from Albuquerque. It shows the extent of her researching, the accumulation of notes on her subject, and her use of expert consultants. She wrote:

From [my] notes taken at different times, you [Justina], may read some facts. Here are some of my findings: Rev. Brother Baldwin, Vice-President of St. Michael College, Santa Fé, was a substantial help to me in talking notes.

Education in New Mexico began in 1599 by the Franciscans who had accompanied Onate. The Spaniards were expelled in 1680. The Franciscans had no possibility of continuing this branch of their work until after the reconquest by De Vargas 1692-1693, at which time the Franciscans used educational methods among the Indians, opening every avenue to Spanish children. In 1721, the King of Spain ordered public schools to be established. From 1721 to 1822 many efforts were made to maintain schools, but the results were meager ... A law was passed in 1823 to establish a high school in El Paso del Norte (Juarez). Two colleges, one in Santa Fé, the other in Taos, were established in 1826. This was done by V.G. Fernandez of Santa Fé and Padre Martinez of Taos, who shouldered the expense ... At this time (1826) there were also about seventeen schools scattered here and there. By 1844 schools had been opened in all important places. Governor Mariano Martinez, 1844-1845, had two professors come from Europe and helped with his own money to carry on public schools, adding military instruction in the school at Santa Fé. Governor Francisco Xavier Chavez gave $1000 to help pay the teachers. (1932, Pages 323-324)

In another example of research, for September 21, 1882, from Santa Fe, Blandina wrote:

The Navajo and Apache tribes of Indians kept the natives [Mexicans] in constant turmoil. So in the end the "Gringo" was a welcome intruder. **This is the information I gathered from the oldest inhabitants, many of whom belong to the old school of Spanish aristocracy.** (1932, Page 228)

BEING SMART AND WORLDLY

The complexity of Blandina's achievements in handling teaching, financing, building of schools and hospitals, and founding social service organizations prove her canny skills. And the cleverness of her journal entries and observations proves her intellectual adroitness. She certainly had the ability and creativity to mimic a journal, rather than to actually prepare all entries in real time.

Her own entries demonstrate her formidable skills. For example, concerning contested legal enforceability of school warrants issued to guarantee teachers' salaries in the

Albuquerque public school she was founding - about which she had also aggressively used powerhouse, Thomas Benton Catron, as her attorney - she successfully petitioned and charmed then Governor, Edmund G. Ross, in 1886. Showing off her cocky confidence and historical competence in her "1886" journal entry from Albuquerque, she quoted her savvy conversation with Ross, as follows:

> [I said,] "Have you remarked how uniquely you are taking action in two transition periods?"
>
> "In what way, Sister?" [asked Governor Ross.]
>
> "Did not your vote prevent President Andrew Jackson from impeachment in the Reconstruction period after the Civil War? And now you are doing the act that will prevent a great amount of discontent among the old residents. Yet you will be criticized by the late comers who will not take time to study conditions as they were and as they find them." (1932, Page 320)

And Blandina was nobody's fool. For August 8, 1885 from Albuquerque, she wrote about building an annex to her school there, and her triumphant undoing of a dubious character:

> A gentleman, who holds a responsible position in New Albuquerque, came to me last week and said with apparent anxiety: "Sister, you are building on a public road. I looked at the Armijo plat..."
>
> I remarked: "It is kind of you to take so much interest, but we had the road condemned ...."
>
> He said: "In that case, the land of the road reverts to the original owners and you must clear your title through them."
>
> "That was done before we began to build the adobe," I replied. "The plea, and the proceeding of the grant you will find in the Commissioner's County Records." (1932, Page 294)

And Blandina was a true intellectual, with broad span of interests. Her unnamed biographer in the Sisters of Charity mother house in Cincinnati noted that late in life, beyond her faith-oriented contributions, she was keen-minded; as follows:

> The radio she loved, and the operas, which she knew thoroughly, were her special delight. Political speeches she listened to with avidity. The Rt. Rev. Fulton J. Sheen, speaking over the Catholic Hour, held first place.

WRITING IN JOURNAL STYLE RATHER THAN WRITING A JOURNAL

SLEUTHING HOAXBUSTING CLUES: Since a journal is dated, the fact that Blandina's "Billy the Kid" entry dates are radically wrong - and were changed in the 1932 book - implies their insertion at a later date, not diary-like 19th century recording.

Blandina's threadbare, 14 entry tale of "Billy the Kid" as a gang-leading, serial murderer, sadistically scalping highwayman bears signs of not being the direct experience a journal implies. Not only are the claims about him glaring fabrications, but the dating of supposed events and encounters is wildly off. Implied are later insertions after conducting Billy the Kid "research" to add interest and sparkle to less than riveting renditions of building schools and hospitals, and doing missionary work with the downtrodden.

ANACHRONISTIC JOURNAL ENTRY DATES

A dated journal, like a diary, is its author's recounting of real-time occurrences that they experienced. Dating mistakes cannot be off by months or years. Adding or changing dates at a later time affects the credibility of a journal; yet that was done with Blandina's journal as was seen in the comparison of the magazine articles, and 1932 and 1948 books; with the 1948 edition dialing back dates by a year to make them correspond better to actual Billy the Kid history. That fix-up, however, failed, since the new dates were also incorrect. An example is Governor Lew Wallace's rewards for Billy the Kid. An additional example of the same false dating applies to the alleged marauding of Mimbres Apache Chief, Victorio.

LEW WALLACE'S INCORRECTLY DATED BILLY THE KID REWARD NOTICES

BLANDINA'S CLAIMS ABOUT REWARD NOTICES ARE A YEAR TOO EARLY

Blandina wrote about rewards for capture of "Billy the Kid," though reward notices for hunted outlaws were common knowledge, and, thus, easy to guess. But Blandina was specific, dating them to 1932's "January, 1881" - corrected to 1948's "January, 1880" - in her entry to Justina. She wrote:

> My old acquaintance, "Billy the Kid," is using his gun freely. The people of the Territory are aroused and demand his capture, **dead or alive. Rewards have been offered for his capture.**
> Our Governor, Lewis Wallace, has shown heroic bravery by going to Lincoln County to try to pacify the storm. He had a number of interviews with "Billy," but to no effect. **New rewards have been offered both by the Governor and the people to capture Billy.**"

Even for the "1880" "correction," Blandina would have had to time-travel 11 months into the future to read Governor Lew Wallace's actual December 22, 1880 Las Vegas *Gazette* first reward notice for Billy the Kid.

And for that same entry for "1880," she would have needed to project into the future by almost a year and a half by "seeing" Wallace's "new" "Billy the Kid, $500 Reward" notice in the May 3, 1881 *Daily New Mexican*.

And if any Wallace reward posters were ever posted, Blandina needed even deeper penetration of the future from her January, 1880 entry to get to their possible reality of May 20, 1881 or June 2, 1881.

More important, at January of 1880, no one would have posted any reward for Billy Bonney, since his being publicly outlawed and actively pursued was still almost a year away. And no known personal rewards from citizens exist.

And by alternate date of January of 1881, Billy had been captured by Pat Garrett, and was in the Santa Fe jail.

REALITY ABOUT BILLY THE KID REWARDS

After Governor Lew Wallace betrayed his pardon promise to Billy Bonney in 1879, Billy remained in limbo for most of 1880, doing petty rustling from Ringites and gambling. It was only in September through December of 1880, after the Santa Fe Ring's outlaw myth propaganda, that Billy was pursued by the Secret Service, White Oaks citizens, and Sheriff Pat Garrett.

On December 22, 1880, Lew Wallace published, in the Las Vegas *Gazette*, the first of his two reward notices for Billy the Kid. It was in a front page column, and appears not to have had an additional wanted poster. The notice stated:

BILLY THE KID
$500 REWARD

I will pay $500 reward to any person or persons who will capture William Bonney, alias The Kid, and deliver him to any sheriff of New Mexico. Satisfactory proofs of identity will be required.
   LEW. WALLACE,
   Governor of New Mexico

After Billy's hanging trials in Mesilla, from March 30 to April 13, 1881, and subsequent jailbreak from Lincoln's courthouse-jail on April 28, 1881, Lew Wallace issued his second reward notice, this time on May 3, 1881 in the Santa Fe *Daily New Mexican*, stating:

BILLY THE KID.
$500 REWARD.
I will pay $ 500 reward to any person or persons who Will capture William Bonney, alias The Kid, and deliver him to any sheriff of New Mexico. Satisfactory proofs of identity will be required.
                    LEW. WALLACE,
                    Governor of New Mexico

It is not certain that actual reward posters were printed for Billy Bonney, though possibly spurious ones have been sold to Old West collectors in recent times. However, I discovered, in Lew Wallace's collected papers in the Indiana Historical Society, bills to him from the New Mexico Printing and Publishing Company for posters for "the Kid" dated May 20, 1881 and June 2, 1881. That would date reward posters even later into 1881 than the newspaper reward notices.

APACHE CHIEF VICTORIO

BLANDINA'S CLAIMS ABOUT APACHE CHIEF VICTORIO ARE SIX YEARS TOO LATE

For her "February 2, 1886" entry from Albuquerque, Blandina wrote about Mimbres Apache Chief Victorio, solidifying the date by a first-hand claim; stating:

> Not only is Gerónimo riding at large, but Victorio and other captains also.
> **Last week Sister Catherine and myself visited one of the grading camps and stood on a mound where, the day before, Victorio had scalped two of the working men.** Everyone in the camp was as quiet as though nothing had occurred. (1932, Page 244)

REALITY ABOUT VICTORIO

Victorio was dead six years when Blandina made her alleged journal entry with her alleged direct experience of missing Victorio's scalping atrocity by one day. In fact, rebellious Chief Victorio, fighting illegal confiscations of his tribe's lands, had matched Billy Bonney's lurid press in late 1880, when he was finally slaughtered that October 14, 1880.

Victorio's killing in Old Mexico was reported in the October 20, 1880 Las Cruces *Thirty-Four Newspaper* as: "Glory! Hallelujah!! Victorio Killed." He had been chased into Old Mexico by over 200 American soldiers. From the Mexican side came Joaquín Terrazas, with over 350 men. Victorio was surrounded on a small mountain, and he and his band were killed and scalped for the bounties. The article stated:

GLORY!
Hallelujah!!
VICTORIO KILLED
WAR ENDED!!!
PEACE!

Governor Terrazas telegraphs that the Mexican troops under his brother came up with Victorio at Tres Castillos, near Pino mountains, **on the 14th and killed Victorio and fifty of his warriors and eighteen squaws and children and captured 70 squaws and children and two hundred and fifty head of stock**. The news is official and is telegraphed all over the country for general information.

Gen. Buell was recalled from Mexico just in time to prevent his reaping the full benefit of his chase after the hostiles. He chased them several hundred miles into Mexico and to a point a hundred and fifty miles from Fort Quitman and was on a hot trail when ordered to return. His pursuit of them so far across the line rendered their defeat by the Mexican troops only a question of time, and to him and his command is due a large share of the praise for the ending of this terrible war. But for the meddling which caused his recall, he would not doubt have done just what the Mexicans have done. It is to be regretted that he did not get far enough into the interior to be out of reach of orders. It is now in order for the *New Mexican* to claim that Hatch planned the whole campaign. It is known everywhere on this border that he had nothing to do with it except that he did everything in his power to prevent it becoming a success. That this battle will end the war, there can scarcely be a doubt. Hurrah for Buell and Terrazas.

Blandina may have been relying on secondary sources for her misinformation linking Geronimo and Victorio in time to construct her fable of almost being scalped by Victorio in a mining town she visited a day after his alleged depredation. In her collected papers in the Sisters of Charity of Cincinnati, Ohio, archives is the above-mentioned article titled, "Buffalo Days: Billy the Kid," by the buffalo hunter, J. Wright Mooar, in the July of 1933 Holland's, *The Magazine of the South*. The article appeared a year after Blandina's *At the End of the Santa Fe Trail*. But Mooar, a fabricator himself, may have relied on an earlier source - possibly used by also Blandina - to erroneously link Geronimo and Victorio. Mooar gives the date as October of 1880 for both chiefs being on the warpath. But October of 1880 was actually the date that Victorio was killed after being chased into Old Mexico. Mooar had stated:

> I had been warned that the grim old Apache chiefs Geronimo and Victorio were on the warpath, killing, robbing, and burning.

SMOKING GUNS FOR A HOAX: Since Blandina's journal entries imply personal experiences in real-time, incorrect dating of verifiable events exposes entries' fabrication. Blandina implies seeing or being told about the existence of Billy the Kid reward notices by Governor Lew Wallace and private citizens. She describes a near miss with a scalping rampage by Victorio. But her wildly wrong dates put a lie to her claims, indicating that those entries were fabricated.

USING 20th CENTURY WRITINGS OF PAT GARRETT AND WALTER NOBLE BURNS FOR THE "19th CENTURY JOURNAL"

> *SLEUTHING HOAXBUSTING CLUES: Lack of first-hand knowledge forces historical hoaxers to use secondary sources to build their fables. The only history books existing when Blandina published her journal from 1926 to 1932 were books by Pat Garrett and Walter Noble Burns. Both were highly fictionalized because historical facts were then unknown. So Blandina's repeating of those authors' fictions would prove her use of their books for her entries. That use would also date creation of her so-called 19th century journal entries to after the 1926 and 1927 publication dates of the Burns and Garrett books. That would mean the entries were fabricated.*

So few historical sources existed in Blandina's day, that they can be easily traced by her repeating their misinformation. Pilfered "facts" are a way to spot an historical hoaxer, since they rarely know enough true history to screen out erroneous or fake claims made by other authors. When they use those bloopers for their own tales, they provide smoking guns for their scam. Blandina's book has those bloopers.

Blandina's alleged Old West journal was prepared for publication in the heyday of Billy the Kid identity hoaxes. The burgeoning of Billy Bonney's national popularity, with the guarantee of book publication to any old-timer writer having first-hand contact with him, made Billy tempting prey for profiteering hijacking.

The problem all those hoaxers had was the long delay in creation of valid history books on Billy and the Lincoln County War period. It took till 1957 for publication of amateur historian William Keleher's *Violence in Lincoln County 1869-1881*, which presented his discoveries of documents like Billy Bonney's Coroner's Jury Report.

But it required the more professional and massive research of British historian, Frederick Nolan, for Billy the Kid history to enter the scholarly realm. Nolan began with his 1965 *The Life and Death of John Henry Tunstall*. It was not until the 1990's, however, that he published the foundation history books for Billy the Kid: his 1992 *The Lincoln County War: A Documentary History* and his 1998 *The West of Billy the Kid*. Billy's childhood and early adolescence were unknown until 1993, when Jerry Weddle's *Antrim is My Stepfather's Name: The Boyhood of Billy the Kid* came out. And my own 21st century revisionist history books on William Bonney add perspective to his pardon quest, and his heroic participation in freedom fight uprisings against the Santa Fe Ring.

Blandina's sources were first listed by editor, Therese Martin, in the 1948 edition of *At the End of the Santa Fe Trail's* "Bibliography." They were the 1927 reprint of Pat Garrett's 1882 *The Authentic Life of Billy the Kid The Noted Desperado of the Southwest, Whose Deeds of Daring and Blood Made His Name a Terror in New Mexico, Arizona, and Northern Mexico*; and Walter Noble Burns's 1926 *The Saga of Billy the Kid*.

In Blandina's and Therese Martin's day, it was still too early to realize that Pat Garrett's ghostwritten book substituted dramatic fabrications for historical accuracy, and sprinkled historical names for effect, yielding essentially an expanded dime novel. And journalist, Walter Noble Burns's, book, lacking bibliography or index of a legitimate history text, relied on Garrett's book for information, and likewise rampantly fictionalized. So Garrett and Burns, when surreptitiously cribbed for Blandina's "journal entries," can reveal her smoking gun bloopers for hoaxing - not only for their copied misinformation, but for exposing that the so-called journal was actually manufactured decades later, instead of being written in real-time of its claimed dating.

As has been discussed, for the *Veritas* and *The Santa Maria* magazine articles, Blandina ad-libbed "Billy the Kid" tales so embarrassingly in the "friend Murphy" entries, that she, or an editor, turned to sources for fix-ups for her 1932 book. That allows pin-pointing of her reliance on Garrett and Burns to her 1931 to 1932 preparation of her book.

Below are Blandina's historical claims in the 1932 book, which demonstrate her use of Garrett and Burns as her sources for various topics and entries.

BILLY THE KID'S CHILDHOOD

BLANDINA'S BLOOPER

Blandina used the age of 12 for the start of Billy the Kid's murdering, and used a motive of protecting his mother; writing:

> That ends the career of one who began his downward course at the **age of twelve years by taking revenge for the insult that had been offered to his mother.**

GARRETT'S FABRICATED HISTORY

Since Billy the Kid's early years were then unknown, Pat Garrett and ghostwriter, Ash Upson, made up an elaborate fiction using the age 12 and an insult to Billy's mother to manufacture their outlaw boy character. They wrote:

> **When young Billy was about twelve years of age, he first imbrued his hand in human blood.** This affair, it may be said, was the turning point of his life, for it outlawed him and left him a victim of his worser impulses and passions. **As Billy's mother was passing a knot of idlers on the street, one of the loafers made an insulting remark about her. Billy heard it, and quick as thought, with blazing eyes, he planted a stinging blow on the blackguard's mouth.** Then springing out into the middle of the street, he stooped for a rock. The brute made a rush for the boy, but as he passed Ed Moulton, a well-known citizen of Silver City, he received a stunning blow on the ear which felled him, while Billy was caught and restrained. However, the punishment inflicted on the offender by no means satisfied Billy. Burning for revenge, he visited a miner's cabin, procured a Sharp's rifle, and

started in search of his intended victim. By good fortune, Moulton saw him with the gun and persuaded him to return it.

Some weeks subsequent to this adventure, Moulton ... became involved in a rough-and-tumble bar-room fight at Joe Dyer's saloon ... He had two "shoulder-strikers" to contend with and was getting the best of them [when] the man who had been one of Moulton's "lifters" ... thought he saw an opportunity to take cowardly revenge on Moulton and rushed upon him with a heavy bar-room chair upraised.

Billy ... saw the motion and like lightning darted beneath the chair. Once, twice, thrice, his arm rose and fell. Then rushing through the crowd, his right hand above his head grasping a pocket-knife, its blade dripping with blood, **he went out into the night, and outcast and a wanderer, a murderer self-baptized in blood ... His hand was now against every man, and every man's hand against him.**

BURNS'S PILFERED FABRICATED HISTORY

Knowing no early history for Billy the Kid, Burns merely copied Garrett's version of 12-years-old-and-insulted-mother-causing-murder scenario - inadvertently making it seem a verified fact to a fellow fabricator like Blandina. Burns wrote:

> "**It was at Silver City, when twelve years old, That Billy killed his first man.** His mother with Billy at her side was on her way from home into the business section to do some shopping ... A group of men lounged in front of a saloon, a young blacksmith among them ... As Billy and his mother passed, the smith ... dropped some light remark ... at Mrs. Antrim ... **Billy flamed at once into violent passion and resentment, picked up a stone, hurled it**

with all his might at the head of the insulter of his mother ... Unhurt but blazing with anger, the fellow rushed at Billy ... A man named Moulton ... knocked him down with his fist ... [and] for the time being, closed the incident.

On an evening a few weeks later ... [Moulton became embroiled in a bar room brawl] in Dyer's saloon ... Billy Bonney was ... idly observant ...

The blacksmith saw in the situation an opportunity for revenge ... [H]e sprang from his seat, raised his heavy chair high in the air, aiming it at the back of Moulton's head ... [T]he blow failed on its target ... Billy Bonney ... too, saw an opportunity for revenge and also to render assistance to a friend in distress ... **Whipping out his pocketknife, he rushed upon the blacksmith ... Three times the boy struck with his blade** ... [T]he blacksmith, **staggering back, clutched at his heart, pitched headlong.**

So, for the first time, the wolf cub tasted blood.

[T]he first murder in Billy's long list – was hall-marked by native expertness in deadliness ...

With his victim at his feet, Billy darted out the door ... The boy slipped out into the night.

EVIL NATURE OF BILLY THE KID

BLANDINA'S BLOOPER

In the 19th century and early 20th century period of ascendancy of Billy the Kid's outlaw myth, it was typical to portray him as a demonic uber-outlaw - a gang leader, murderer, stage robber, rustler, and counterfeiter among his dramatized crimes. Blandina followed that trend for her own religiously moralizing impact. And she exceeded fashion, taking parts of Garrett's and Burns's texts to create her "greatest murderer of the Southwest." She wrote:

[H]ow many crimes might have been prevented, had someone had influence over "Billy" after his first murder ... **Finding himself captain and dictator, with no religious principles to check him, he became what he is – the greatest murderer of the Southwest.**

GARRETT'S FABRICATION

The title of Garrett's book was itself used by Blandina for hyperbolic claims of "Billy the Kid's outlawry as : *The Authentic Life of Billy the Kid **The Noted Desperado of the Southwest**, Whose Deeds of Daring and Blood Made His Name a Terror in New Mexico, Arizona, and Northern Mexico.* And Billy Bonney's evil, as portrayed in Garrett's book, was extreme. The book stated:

> "The Kid had **a devil lurking in him**. It was a good-humored jovial imp, or a cruel and bloodthirsty fiend, as circumstances prompted. Circumstances favored the worser angel, and the Kid fell."

BURNS'S FABRICATION

Journalist Burns, relying on Garrett for specifics of outlawry, added his own florid elaborations making his "Billy the Kid" the incarnation of evil; writing:

> **[Billy] placed no value on human life ... He killed a man as nonchalantly as he smoked a cigarette. Murder did not appeal to Billy the Kid as tragedy; it was merely a physical process of pulling a trigger ...** In his murders, he observed no rules of etiquette ... As long as he killed a man he wanted to kill, it made no difference to him how he killed him ...
>
> It is impossible now to name twenty-one men that he killed, though, if Indians be included, it is not difficult to cast up the ghastly total ...

The Lincoln County war and the subsequent reign of terror Billy the Kid had set up had given the territory [of New Mexico] an evil reputation.

APPEARANCE OF BILLY THE KID

BLANDINA'S BLOOPER

When Blandina wrote her tales, people believed in phrenology and other studies of physical characteristics as a measure of character. It was de rigueur to give physical descriptions of criminals to prove their base nature, or to marvel at how youth hid their depravity, which could only be found in their eyes. Blandina also described her "Billy the Kid" as young - not a big leap given the nickname of "the Kid." Blandina wrote:

> The leader, Billy, has steel-blue eyes, peach complexion, is young, one would take him to be seventeen – innocent-looking, **save for the corners of his eyes, which tell a set purpose, good or bad.**

GARRETT'S DRAMATIZATION

> [H]is eyes were a deep blue, dotted with spots of hazel hue, and were very bright, expressive, and intelligent ...
>
> **Those who knew him would always watch his eyes for an exhibition of anger ... One could scarcely believe that those blazing, baleful eyes and that laughing face could be controlled by the same spirit.**

BURNS'S DRAMATIZATION

> His face was long and colorless ... His eyes were gray, clear, and steady ... Many persons, especially women, thought him handsome ... He was ... for ever on guard.

JOHN HENRY TUNSTALL

BLANDINA BLOOPER

Like Garrett and Burns, Blandina was ignorant of the Lincoln County War as a freedom fight, or of the Santa Fe Ring's murder of John Tunstall. They attributed Billy's aggression to avenging his murdered "friend," John Tunstall. After using Garrett and Burns to correct her magazine mistakes of "friend Murphy," Blandina wrote:

> **Mr. Tunstall**, a rancher, was brutally murdered ...
> "Billy," cowboy for Tunstall, witnessed the deed and **swore to shoot down like a dog every man he could find who had a part in the murder of his friend.**

GARRETT'S DRAMATIZATION

> This murder [of Tunstall] occurred on the 18th of February, 1878. **Before night the Kid was appraised of his friend's death. His rage was fearful. Breathing vengeance,** he quitted his herd, mounted his horse, and **from that day to the hour of his death his track was blazed with rapine and blood.**

BURNS'S DRAMATIZATION

> [Tunstall] set off on horseback for town accompanied by two of his men. Dick Brewer ...[and] a quiet, grey-eyed, slender youth ... known as Billy the Kid ... From a distant hillside they witnessed [Tunstall's] murder ...
> Billy the Kid was in the little group that stood beside [Tunstall's] grave ... **Tunstall had been his friend and his employer ... This boy had his own way of paying tribute to a lost friend ...** From the brink of this grave which for him was the brink of a new

career that was to be filled with graves, he turned away.

With the murder of [Tunstall], the Kid threw himself into the feud to avenge his friend's death. There seems no reason to attribute any other motive to him.

LAWRENCE G. MURPHY

BLANDINA'S BLOOPER

With no first-hand knowledge of Billy the Kid history, Blandina first made up her "friend Murphy" tale. Later, using Garrett and Burns, she mixed-up cattle king, John Chisum, with Lincoln County's Ringite merchant, Lawrence Murphy. She wrote:

Mr. Tunstall, a rancher, was brutally **murdered by "Cattle King" Major L.G. Murphy's men.**

GARRETT'S TEXT

John S. Chisum [was] called the **Cattle King of New Mexico** ... (Page 52)
On the other side [of the Lincoln County conflict] were the firm of **Murphy** & Dolan, merchants in Lincoln, the county seat, **backed by nearly every small cattle owner in the Pecos Valley.**

BURNS'S TEXT

[John Chisum] **became a cattle king** ...
Major L.G. Murphy ... developed in time other business interests [in Lincoln County] – a cattle ranch, a flour mill, a hotel, a saloon – and entered politics. He became ... the wealthiest man in the mountains.

JOHN SIMPSON CHISUM

BLANDINA'S BLOOPER

Blandina also seems to have plucked historical names simply to feign history. Real cattle king, John Chisum, ended up as part of "Billy the Kid's gang!" She even finessed by claiming poor "recall" of gang members' names. She wrote:

> I went to meet Billy and his gang ... The introduction was given. I can only remember, "Billy, our Captain, and **Chism.**
>
> I was not prepared to see the men that met me, which must account for my not being able to recall their names.

GARRETT'S DRAMATIZATION

> The principals in the [Lincoln County War] were on one side **John S. Chisum**, called the Cattle King of New Mexico ...

BURNS'S DRAMATIZATION

> **John Chisum** knew cows ... So in the fullness of years he became a cattle king ...

BILLY THE KID'S GANG

A central theme in Billy Bonney's outlaw myth, was his having a gang; which was in keeping with the large-scale criminality fabricated for him by the Santa Fe Ring. That will be further discussed below in relation to Billy's press, and the 1880 reports of Secret Service Agent Azariah Wild.

Billy Bonney himself responded to that press by denying any gang. On December 12, 1880, he wrote to Lew Wallace:

> *I noticed in the Las Vegas Gazette a piece which stated that, Billy "the" Kid, the name by which I am known in the Country was the captain of a Band of Outlaws who hold Forth at the Portales.* **There is no such Organization in Existence.** *So the Gentleman must have drawn very heavily on his Imagination.*

BLANDINA BLOOPER

As discussed below, besides Garrett and Burns, Blandina used newspaper articles for a "Billy the Kid gang." She wrote:

> Lewis [sic - Lew] Wallace ... has a difficult task before him ... to check the depredations being **committed by Billy and his gang.**

GARRETT'S DRAMATIZATION

> [After the ambush murder of Sheriff Brady] **[t]he Kid and his desperate gang were now outlawed in Lincoln**, yet they haunted the plaza by stealth and always found a sure and safe place of concealment at [Alexander] McSweens ...
>
> [After the lost Lincoln County War] **the Kid gathered together such of his gang as were fit for duty** and took to the mountains south of Lincoln.

BURNS'S DRAMATIZATION

> There was no vendetta now [for Tunstall's murder] to give the Kid even a spurious legitimacy ... From now on, he was an outlaw pure and simple ... He was well known everywhere, and those who bought [cattle] from him were under no illusions regarding the transactions ...
>
> Billy the Kid lost three **members of his band** in 1880 at Tascosa and the Canadian River.

GOVERNOR LEW WALLACE'S COMING TO LINCOLN COUNTY

The reasons for Governor Lew Wallace's coming to Lincoln County's town of Lincoln (from March to May of 1879) were beyond the historical knowledge of Garrett and Burns. It was a time of turmoil following the unjust Santa Fe Ring victory in Lincoln County War the year before; now exacerbated by another Ring murder in Lincoln: this time of anti-Ring attorney, Huston Chapman, on February 18, 1879. This forced Wallace's reluctant coming to Lincoln in March of 1879. It was as a testifying eye-witness to this Chapman murder that Billy Bonney proposed his pardon bargain to Lew Wallace that March of 1879.

BLANDINA'S BLOOPER

With 1932 dating of "January 1881," Blandina wrote about Lew Wallace's coming to Lincoln - which actually occurred in March of 1879. She wrote:

> **Our Governor, Lewis Wallace, has shown heroic bravery by going to Lincoln County** to try to pacify the storm. He had a number of interviews with "Billy," but to no effect. New rewards have been offered both by the Governor and the people to capture Billy."

GARRETT'S BOOK'S NOTE BY HISTORIAN-EDITOR, MAURICE GARLAND FULTON

The murder of [lawyer, Huston] Chapman seemed to indicate another outbreak of lawlessness in Lincoln. Governor Wallace, who had tried to terminate the original feud by his proclamation of pardon issued November 13, 1878, **promptly came to Fort Stanton and took personal charge of the efforts to stamp out the new appearance of lawlessness.**

BILLY THE KIDS CAPTURE

BLANDINA'S BLOOPER

Using Lew Wallace as focus, and ignorant of what actually motivated capturing of Billy Bonney on December 22, 1880, neither Blandina nor Garrett nor Burns knew Billy had to be killed because of his political risk to the Santa Fe Ring by leading another popular uprising.

Blandina wrote for 1932's "April 24 [1882]":

> [Governor Wallace] was well guarded by every honest man in the Territory – **hence Billy's capture.**

GARRETT'S DRAMATIZATION

> I told my [posse] companions that I was confident we had [Billy and his companions] trapped [in the rock cabin at Stinking Springs].

BURNS'S DRAMATIZATION

> If this potentially rich territory was to share in the prosperity of the new day that was dawning in the West, the desperado must be exterminated …
>
> It was primarily against lawlessness. Incidentally it was a **war against Billy the Kid as the head and front of lawlessness.**

BILLY THE KID'S THREAT TO LEW WALLACE

BLANDINA'S BLOOPERS

This theme will be discussed more extensively below in the context of its creation by Lew Wallace himself in his newspaper articles from the late 19th to early 20th century for his outlaw myth of Billy the Kid. In fact, there was no such threat. That fable was also used by Walter Noble Burns, who took it from Lew Wallace's 1906 *Autobiography*.

For the 1932 date of "March, 1882," Blandina wrote:

> It has been bruited about that **["Billy the Kid"] intends undoing Governor Wallace.** Friends of law and order are on the *qui vive* that no harm come to the author of Ben Hur ...
>
> [A murderer named Kelly] is now in jail with **"Billy the Kid," who attempted to carry out his threat against Governor Wallace,** but the latter was well guarded by every honest man in the Territory – hence Billy's capture.

BURNS'S DRAMATIZATION

Burns used Lew Wallace's 1906 *Autobiography*, from which he copied Lew Wallace's wife's published May 11, 1879 letter to their son, Henry. It stated:

> "The Lincoln County reign of terror is not over," wrote Mrs. Susan E. Wallace, the governor's wife, in a letter from Fort Stanton, "and we hold our lives at the mercy of desperados and outlaws, chief among them Billy the Kid, whose boast is that he has killed a man for every year of his life. Once he was captured and escaped and now he swears, **when he has killed the sheriff and the judge who passed sentence upon him and Governor Wallace, he will surrender and be hanged.**
>
> " ' I mean to ride into the plaza in Santa Fé, hitch my horse in front of the palace [of the Governors], and put a bullet through Lew Wallace.'
>
> "These are his words. One of my friends warned me to close the shutters in the evening, so the bright light of the student lamp might not make such a shining mark of the governor writing till late upon 'Ben Hur.' "

> SMOKING GUNS FOR A HOAX: *Fictional tales from Pat Garrett's and Walter Noble Burns's books were unwittingly lifted to create Blandina's supposed "Billy the Kid" journal entries. Thus, though dated to the 1880's, their writing can be dated to after the 1926 and 1927 dates of the Garrett and Burns books. And the lack of use of their books for her magazine articles, with later use in her book, dates the creation of those journal entries specifically to the 1931 to 1932 period of correcting her errors in the articles for the book's text. This is shown by the repeating of these men's errors in her book. And using these sources to correct errors - like the "friend Murphy" one - prove that entries were not only willfully fabricated, but had willfully covered-up errors to trick readers into believing that an authentic 19th century journal was presented. And when her "Billy the Kid" tales became popular as fact, Blandina never issued a disclaimer that they were fiction.*

THE MAGAZINE TALE OF "PAOLINE" MAXWELL

There was one magazine article that did suggest Blandina's use of sources back then. About the rich Maxwell family, it was in her October, 1930 edition of *The Santa Maria*, but not in the 1932 book. Dated "Cherry season, 1884," it was a garbling of their daughter, Paulita, called "Paoline," for another "Billy the Kid" tale. My guess is that it marked Blandina's first cursory checking of the Garrett and Burns books.

The facts were that the name "Paulita" was derived from her mother, Doña María de la Luz Beaubien Maxwell's, mother's name: María Paula Lovato. María Paula had been a daughter of the most prominent Spanish family in Taos, which is where Paulita's father, Lucien Maxwell, first met Luz Beaubien. And Paulita was a diminutive of "Paula." Blandina further misunderstood that the "Maxwell Ranch" moved in 1870 from Cimarron, New Mexico to Fort Sumner, New Mexico, after Lucien Maxwell sold his Maxwell Land Grant to Santa Fe Ring attorneys, Thomas Benton Catron and Stephen Benton Elkins. So Blandina's magazine entry stated:

Saint Joseph Academy, Trinidad, Colorado, [which she founded] has educated a number of young ladies whose families have been and are very much in the public eye for the part taken in the development of our South-western territories ...

[Y]ou had Paoline Maxwell, from "Maxwell Ranch." Nothing can exceed Mr. and Mrs. Maxwell's hospitality. There either **Archbishop, priest, the Sisters, the Mexicans, the Americans, the Indians, and yes, the fugitive from justice finds hospitality** ...

At this place Billy the Kid often lingered and Miss Paoline Maxwell (who attended our academy in Trinidad) used many persuasive arguments to induce "Billy" to desist from carrying out his oath to "make every man kiss the earth who had anything to do with the killing of my friend [Mr. Murphy]."

WALTER NOBLE BURNS'S AS THE SOURCE

Blandina's source for her "Paoline" and Billy the Kid anecdote was Walter Noble Burns's *Saga of Billy the Kid*, where a chapter was set aside for Paulita as "The Belle of Old Fort Sumner." Burns personally interviewed Paulita in 1924 in her old age, and stated by letter that he knew that she and Billy were sweethearts, but had concealed that in his book for fear of being sued. But he gave adequate clues, that apparently influenced Blandina's quick and imprecise glance. He wrote:

[Paulita] and Billy the Kid were friends, and the **friendship of this good, pure girl was a gracious influence on his life.** [As to Billy, hate-filled Burns had already hissed:] "On his way to hell, it gave him his one vision of Heaven."

Blandina also copied from Burns about the Maxwell's hospitality for that entry. She listed it as for: "Archbishop, priest, the Sisters, the Mexicans, the Americans, the Indians, and yes, the fugitive from justice." Burns wrote:

> [Lucien] Maxwell [Paulita's father] built a palatial home in Cimarron, where for years he lived in a style of baronial magnificence. Here he dispensed **lavish hospitality, and the guests who came and went in endless procession included travelers of the Santa Fé trail which passed his door, cattle kings, governors, merchants, army officers, and men distinguished in public life and international affairs in Europe and America.**

Blandina's references to "Paoline's" school in Trinidad, and Billy the Kid's avenging a friend, used Burns's interview with Paulita Maxwell, which quoted Paulita, as follows:

> "I have a perfectly clear picture of **Billy the Kid** the first time I ever saw him ... He was eighteen years old and I was fifteen and back home for a vacation from **St. Mary's convent school in Trinidad**. It was the Kid's first visit to Fort Sumner ... [A man who came with Billy the Kid got into a dangerous altercation with another man there.]
>
> "Just then we saw a young man walking rapidly across the road towards us ... [S]omeone in the little crowd that had gathered said, 'Here comes **Billy the Kid** ...'
>
> "The Kid had a hard little smile on his face when he came up to us ...
>
> **"Don't let this man kill my friend,'** my mother begged of him."
>
> "He said something in Spanish [to the man], who at once put his six-shooter back in its holster."

SMOKING GUNS FOR A HOAX: The only evidence in the Santa Maria Institute's magazine articles of the use of either Garrett or Burns, was in the apparent consulting of Burns for a relationship between Paulita Maxwell and Billy Bonney, and for citing the generosity of the Maxwell family that extended to a diverse group - which the entry modified to add clerics and nuns. Since Blandina's article was dated October of 1930, that may have been when the books were first obtained – and later used extensively for the 1932 book's revisions. That indicates that the journal entry was not prepared in the 19th century, but in 1930. Furthermore, Blandina's first-hand encounter was implied, since the entry claimed "Paoline" as going to her Trinidad school - though Burns gives a different school. The whole entry was abandoned for the 1932 book, possibly indicating Blandina's - or an editor's - uncertainty about the information after more thorough use of Burns and Garrett for her book.

ALSO USING EARLY HISTORIAN RALPH EMERSON TWITCHELL

It appears that Blandina also used an early New Mexican historian named Ralph Emerson Twitchell for a Lincoln County War reference. His 1911, five volume *Leading Facts in New Mexico History* is listed in her "Bibliography" for the 1948 edition of *At the End of the Santa Fe Trail* by editor, Therese Martin. There was no way for Sisters Blandina and Therese to know that Twitchell was a lawyer-politician member of the Santa Fe Ring, and close associate of Thomas Benton Catron. Twitchell's writings willfully covered up the existence of the Ring and the Territorial uprisings against it. So, like all Ringites, Twitchell fabricated the history of the Colfax and Lincoln County Wars as depredations of outlaws, and featured the Ring's outlaw myth of "Billy the Kid." (See Page 402 below for Twitchell's full text)

Some *Veritas* articles give clues that Blandina used Twitchell for peculiar misinformation, as follows:

THE "McSWAIN" MISSPELLING

For the May, 1928, *Veritas*, Blandina wrote that the conflict in Lincoln County was with "**Mr. McSwain's men.**" Twitchell wrote that one side in the conflict was the "**party known as the McSwain faction.**" Twitchell's unique misspelling of Alexander McSween's name, was a give-away for her cribbing.

THE "LINCOLN COUNTY WAR"

For the October, 1928, *Veritas,* Blandina gave her ridiculous rendition of the Lincoln County War; stating:

> I will give you the gist of what today is called the "Lincoln County War." At the yearly "round up," the men – "cowboys" working for cattle bosses aim to arrive first with their herds at the best watering place. The first group that reaches the place has the right of possession for that season. **Two groups arrived simultaneously, each claiming to be first. And the war began.**

Ralph Emerson Twitchell, himself fabricating, wrote:

> In [Lincoln County] a feud was begun which, in the annals of New Mexico, is known as the "Lincoln County War." The cause of this trouble and era of crime can be **traced to the rivalry existing between prominent cattlemen at the time living in Lincoln and the Pecos valley, respectively ... This was the basis for the war.**

THE "FRIEND MURPHY" CORRECTION

To correct her outlandish "friend Murphy" creation found in her *Veritas* articles of May, 1928, and October, 1928, Blandina may have also gone back to Twitchell with more careful reading to discover his version of "friend Tunstall."

Blandina had originally written for the May, 1928, magazine her "friend Murphy" creation; stating:

> Mr. Murphy, one of the "Cattle Kings" of Lincoln county, was shot in a fight between his men and Mr. McSwain's [sic – McSween's] men.
> **Mr. Murphy was brought to our Hospital. "Billy" came to see him**, when he learned that Mr. Murphy's wound would be fatal. He swore at the bedside of the sick man, "that every one connected with the shooting would 'kiss the ground.'"

In contrast, Twitchell had written using the notion of "friend Tunstall." In fact, hired hand Billy had no friendship with Tunstall in his mere 4½ month employment before Tunstall's murder by the Santa Fe Ring. Billy, like others, then fought against the Ring, not to avenge Tunstall's killing. Twitchell wrote:

> The beginning of the so-called Lincoln county war occurred when John H. Tunstel [sic] was killed by a sheriff's posse seeking to levy an attachment upon property belonging to Tunstel [sic]. **The latter had a friend and employe [sic], William H. Bonney, later famous as "Billy the Kid"** ... After the killing of Tunstel [sic] his sympathizers organized themselves into a **party known as the McSwain [sic] faction.**

So, for her 1932 book, Blandina had rewritten "friend Murphy" to "friend Tunstall;" stating:

> Mr. Tunstall, a rancher, was brutally murdered by "Cattle King" Major L.G. Murphy's men.
> "Billy," cowboy for **Tunstall**, witnessed the deed and swore to shoot down like a dog every man he could find who had a part in the murder of **his friend**.

SMOKING GUNS FOR A HOAX: Blandina – or an editor – appears to have attempted to decipher complex Lincoln County War history by also using 1911 New Mexico history books by Ringite Ralph Emerson Twitchell, which fabricated the War's issues to hide the Santa Fe Ring. So the repeating of Twitchell's distinctive misspelling of McSween as "McSwain," and his misrepresentation of the Lincoln County War as a cattlemen's conflict, appeared in Blandina's 1928 articles for Veritas magazine. And the switching of the magazine article's "friend Murphy" to "friend Tunstall" for the 1932 book could have also used Twitchell as a source.

USING CONTEMPORARY NEWSPAPERS AS SOURCES FOR "BILLY THE KID'S GANG" AND OUTLAWRY

SLEUTHING HOAXBUSTING CLUES: Another source available to Blandina for "Billy the Kid" outlaw tales was contemporary press. It was a creation of Santa Fe Ring propaganda, with some historical names added. Reproducing of those newspaper claims for alleged journal entries in the 1870's is a tip-off for them as sources. Since the relevant articles range from 1880 to 1902, their use would point to creation of so-called journal entries after their claimed dates of writing.

Blandina's main themes of Billy the Kid having a gang and Billy the Kid being a murderous depraved outlaw can be traced to contemporary newspapers when Billy Bonney's mythology was first being created in the 1880's, and spread nationally from New Mexico Territory. But Blandina's time-frame of her Colorado journal entries from 1876 to 1877 had nothing to do with teenaged Billy Bonney, who was then in Bonita, Arizona, for all of 1876, and departed Arizona only in August of 1877.

BLANDINA ON "BILLY THE KID'S GANG"

Blandina's most dramatic "Billy the Kid" journal entries - besides her visit with "Billy the Kid" in the Santa Fe jail - are her 1870's encounters with "Billy the Kid" and his "gang." It should be noted, however, that one of the crimes she attached to an alleged "Billy the Kid gang member," and a crime planned by "Billy" himself, was murder by scalping. Even Billy Bonney's most lurid press never lapsed into that absurdity.

For the 1932 date of "September, 1876," from Trinidad, Blandina wrote about "Billy the Kid's" wounded but terrifying "gang member," who facilitated her meeting with sadistic scalper "Billy" himself. Blandina wrote:

[O]ur patient lost no time in telling me that **Billy and the "gang" are to be here, Saturday at 2 P.M.**, and I'm going to tell you why they are coming ...

"Well, **the 'gang' is going to scalp the four of [the town's physicians] ... because none of them would extract the bullet from my thigh ...**"

Saturday, 2 P.M. came, and I went to meet **Billy and his gang** ... The introduction was given. I can only remember, **"Billy, our Captain**, and Chism ..."

The leader, Billy, has steel-blue eyes, peach complexion, is young, one would take him to be seventeen – innocent-looking, save for the corners of his eyes, which tell a set purpose, good or bad ... My glance took this description in while "Billy" was saying: "We are all glad to see you, Sister, and I want to say, it would give me pleasure to do you a favor ..."

I took the hand saying: "I understand you have come to scalp our Trinidad physicians, which act I ask you to cancel ..."

"Not only [do I grant] that, Sister, but at any time my pals and I can serve you, you will find us ready."

For a 1932 entry dated "December 16 [1876]." Blandina wrote about her traveling to Las Vegas, New Mexico, and concerns about attacks by "Billy the Kid's gang," stating:

> The Rev. gentleman, having business in Las Vegas, accompanied us to that city. In my opinion, the Las Vegas business was a secondary consideration. **"Billy's Gang" is quite active on the plains** ... The Rev. gentleman wants to be helpful in case of attack ...

With a 1932 date of "March, 1878," Blandina wrote about her traveling with the Staab family, and concerns about "Billy the Kid's gang;" stating:

> Most Rev. Archbishop Lamy wishes me to go with the Staab family to the terminus of the railroad, which is five miles west of Trinidad, Colorado ... Everybody is concerned about our going. Mr. [Adolph] Staab spoke to Sister and myself about the **danger of travel (at the present time) on the Santa Fe Trail, owing to Billy the Kid's gang. He told us that the gang is attacking every mail coach and private conveyance** ...
> If you ever get this journal, you will see how very little fear I have of **Billy's gang.**

For the 1932 date of "October 1, 1979," Blandina wrote again about "Billy the Kid" and his "gang," stating:

> Our new Governor is General Lewis Wallace. It is difficult to predict anything about him, except that he has a difficult task before him. Not the least of which will be to **check the depredations being committed by Billy and his gang.**
> **The work of the "Gang" is arousing the anger of good men** ...

From Santa Fe, for 1932 date of "May 16 [1882]," Blandina called "Billy the Kid" "the greatest murderer of the Southwest," writing:

> Finding himself captain and dictator, with no religious principles to check him, he became what he is – **the greatest murderer of the Southwest.**

Having returned to Trinidad, Colorado, for an "August 1889" date for the 1932 book, Blandina mentioned the civilizing effect of the termination of "Billy the Kid's gang," writing:

> Trinidad has lost its frontier aspect. The jail is built to hold its inmates. **Billy the Kid's gang is dissolved.**

PRESS ON BILLY THE KID'S GANG

On December 3, 1880, the Santa Fe Ring began its newspaper campaign against Billy Bonney, using a leak of Secret Service Agent Azariah Wild's own fabricated reports of that year about the "Kid gang" as being the largest counterfeiting-rustling group in the country. The Las Vegas *Gazette* published an editorial by its Ring-complicit editor-owner, J.H. Koogler, titled "Powerful Gang of Outlaws Harassing the Stockmen." And Billy was now publicly named "Billy the Kid."

It would be in response to this article that Billy wrote to Lew Wallace on December 12, 1880:

> *I noticed in the Las Vegas Gazette a piece which stated that, Billy "the" Kid, the name by which I am known in the Country was the captain of a Band of Outlaws who hold Forth at the Portales.* **There is no such Organization in Existence.** *So the Gentleman must have drawn very heavily on his Imagination.*

The article stated:

> **The gang includes forty to fifty men, all hard characters, the off scouring of society, fugitives from justice, and desperados by profession. Among them are men, with whose names and deeds the people of Las Vegas are perfectly familiar, such as "Billy the Kid,"** Dave Rudabaugh, Charles Bowdre, and others of equally unsavory reputation ...
>
> **The gang is under the leadership of "Billy the Kid," a desperate cuss, who is eligible for the post of captain in any crowd, no matter how mean and lawless.** They spend considerable time in enjoying themselves at the Portales, keeping guards out and scouting the country for miles around before turning in for the night. Whenever there is a good opportunity to make a haul they split up in gangs and scour the country ...
>
> They run stock from the Panhandle country into the White Oaks and from the Pecos country into the Panhandle ...
>
> Are the people of San Miguel county to stand this any longer? Shall we suffer this hoard of outcasts and the scum of society, who are outlawed by a multitude of crimes, to continue their way to the very border of our county?
>
> We believe the citizens of San Miguel county to be order loving people, and call upon them to unite in forever wiping out this band to the east of us.

On December 27, 1880, the Las Vegas *Daily Gazette* published an article by Lucius "Lute" Wilcox about Billy Bonney's capture titled: 'The Kid. Interview with Billy Bonney The Best Known Man in New Mexico."

The same December 22, 1880 that Wallace's $500 reward notice for Billy appeared in the Las Vegas *Gazette*, Billy Bonney gained national fame in a long *New York Sun* "Outlaws of New Mexico" article, along with his fantasy "outlaw gang" and a few names of historical figures and places. It stated:

OUTLAWS OF NEW MEXICO.

THE EXPLOITS OF A BAND HEADED BY A NEW YORK YOUTH.

The Mountain Fastness of the Kid and his Followers— War against a Gang of Cattle Thieves and Murderers — The Frontier Confederates of Brockway, the Counterfeiter.

LAS VEGAS, New Mexico, Dec. 20.—One hundred and twenty-seven miles southeast of Las Vegas, New Mexico, is Fort Sumner, once the base of operations against the Indians who committed depredations against the stockmen. The fort was abandoned some ten or twelve years ago, owing to the removal of troops further south, toward the border of Mexico. The property was condemned and sold to Pete Maxwell, a well-known ranchman of the section. Since then it has been a depot of supplies for stockmen and a stage station on the postal route to the Pecos Valley and Panhandle, Texas.

Until recently, on almost any fair day, there might have been seen lounging about the store or engaged in target practice four men, all of them young, neatly dressed, and of good appearance. A stranger riding in the little hamlet would have taken them to be a party of Eastern gentlemen who had come into that sparsely settled region in search of sport. Many who have gone into that country have struck up an acquaintance with these men and found them agreeable fellows. These men are the worst desperadoes in the West, and large parties of armed men are now scouring the country in pursuit of them.

For a number of years the people of eastern New Mexico and Panhandle, Texas, have been harassed by a gang who have run off stock, burned ranches, and committed acts of violence and murder. It was only recently that the leaders and organization of the band were discovered. The leaders are Billy the Kid, so called from his youth; Dave Rudabaugh, Billy Wilson, and Tom O'Phallier, the four loungers about Fort Sumner. The Kid is the captain of the gang. Their fastness is about thirty-five miles nearly due east from Fort Sumner, on the edge of the great Staked Plain. In that region there is a small lake called Las Portales. It is surrounded by steep hills, from which flow numerous streams that feed the little lake. This place the robbers selected for their resort partly on account of its hiding places, but mainly on account of the opportunities it afforded them for stock thieving. No matter from what direction the storm came, it drove to the lake the herds of cattle which roam at large in the rich grazing country. There the band built for themselves one of those rude dugouts so common on the Western frontier, two sides formed by the side of the hill, the other two constructed of sod and dirt plastered together, and the whole covered by a thatched roof. Stockades or corrals were built near by in which to put stolen stock. During pleasant weather the members of the gang lounged about Fort Sumner or other stations in that section. When the storm sent cattle scudding over the plains to the haven afforded by the hill-protected lake basin, the gang would hurry to their rendezvous and cut out from the herds the best cattle, driving them into their corral, whence they were later sent to market. Their booty was large, for they had a vast stock to select from, the whole country for a distance of one hundred and fifty miles either way being a rich, continuous pasture. Besides the active members of the band, there were many who had apparently some settled occupation and made themselves useful in disposing of the stolen cattle. In every town of any size within a radius of 150 miles there were butchers who dealt regularly in this stolen stock. When supplies from roving herds ran short the desperadoes would make a raid on herds that were guarded, attacking ranches and killing or diving off the inmates. Besides their station at Las Portales, they had one at Bosque Grande, fifty miles to the southwest, and another at Greathouse's rancho, fifty miles to the north. Whenever they were pursued when running of stock, they had the choice of three places to which to resort.

The people of the surrounding country finally found the existence of this band unendurable. After repeated searches, which failed, owing to the smallness of the pursuing parties, it was resolved to organize several bands, who should cooperate in a campaign, which should end only when the outlaws were driven out of the country, or their capture, dead or alive, was effected. **The authorities of the several counties which bordered on the country ranged over by the Kid's gang had been repeatedly petitioned to send out a posse of men to hunt them down,** but, as Las Portales was on disputed territory, the authorities were never able to settle upon any plan of action. At last the ranchmen took the matter into their own hands, and the first party they sent out succeeded in getting on the track of a detachment of the gang who were hauling material to Las Portales, where they were building large stock yards. Although the party was not successful in capturing the outlaws, they made the outlaws flit about the country in a more lively manner than had been their wont. This showed that nothing could be done by a small force. A guard was always kept out on the numerous peaks about Las Portales, from which outlook; the country for twenty miles either way could be scanned by the outlaws, so that they could easily elude a small party!

The Panhandle Transportation Company, an association of stockmen of western Texas, banded together for mutual protection, commissioned their superintendent, Frank Stewart, a brave fellow, who was just the man for such work, to organize an expedition against the outlaws. The White Oaks, a flourishing mining camp, organized a band of rangers. Still another party of picked men, under the lead of Sheriff Pat Garrett of Lincoln County, who is considered one of the bravest and coolest men in the whole region, joined in the campaign. In the latter part of November Garrett, with a force of fourteen men, made a dash for Bosque Grande, riding all night, and there succeeded in capturing five of the outlaws. One of them was a condemned murderer who had escaped from jail; another of them was a murderer for whose arrest $1,500 had been offered. These are the sort of men who reinforce the band. Las Portales has long been an asylum for fugitives from justice. Bosque Grande (Great Forest) is situated in one of the most fertile regions of the West, and as the rich lands bordering on the Pecos River are the objective point of many who intend to settle in the Territory, it was thought best to rid that region of the outlaws first, in order that none might be deterred from settling there. Precautions have been taken which will prevent this refuge of the band from ever sheltering them again.

It was expected that the two other parties would work with Garrett's band, but the Panhandle party were delayed, owing to scarcity of feed, and the White Oaks Rangers had their hands full in another quarter. The latter party had a brush with the Kid, Rudabaugh, Wilson, and several others at Coyote Spring, near the Oaks camp, and the outlaws succeeded in escaping, although two had their horses shot from under them. The rangers started back for reinforcements and supplies, and then pressed on after the outlaws, coming upon them at their other station at Greathouse's ranch. It was night when the rangers reached the ranch. They threw up earthworks a few hundred yards from the stockade of the ranch, and when the outlaws rose up in the morning they found themselves hemmed in. The rangers sent a messenger to Jim Greathouse, the owner of this ranch, demanding the surrender of the outlaws. Greathouse replied in person. He came out to the camp of the rangers and stoutly asserted that the outlaws had taken possession of his ranch and that he had no power over them nor anything to do with them. It was considered best to hold Greathouse as a hostage, while Jim Carlyle, the leader of the rangers, heeded to the Kid's request for a conference. A long time elapsed and Carlyle did not return. His men began to feel uneasy about him, and dispatched a note to the renegade chief saying that unless Carlyle was given up in less than five minutes they would kill Greathouse. No reply was received. Soon after the rangers saw Carlyle leap from the window and dash down the hill toward their entrenchments. He had not gone far, however, when they saw the Kid throw half his body through the window, and, taking deliberate aim, brought down poor Carlyle, killing him instantly. A sharp fight followed, but the outlaws succeeded in making their escape, Greathouse also getting away during the confusion. Before leaving for home with the dead body of their leader, the rangers fired everything about the place, and Greathouse concealed some miles away, saw the smoke of his burning property.

The three parties are now engaged in scouting the country, and will not give up the chase till the country is rid of every one of the outlaws. Money and outfits have been freely offered by men who have large interests in that section. Government officials are now interested in the campaign, for, in addition to their other crimes, the outlaws have put in circulation a large quantity of the counterfeit money manufactured by William Brockway, the forger. The bills were obtained by one of the gang named Doyle who formerly operated in Chicago, and counterfeit $100 bills in large numbers have been put in circulation among the stockmen and merchants in all that region. The information that enabled the Government officers to discover the handling of counterfeit money by the Kid's gang came from a freighter named Smith. Soon afterward, while Smith was on his way from Las Vegas to Fort Sumner with a load of freight, he was waylaid and murdered by some of the gang.

William Bonney, alias the Kid, the leader of the band, is scarcely over 20 years of age. He is handsome and dresses well. He has a fair complexion, smooth face, blue eyes, and light brown hair. He is about six feet tall and deceptively handsome. A beautiful bay mare, that he has carefully trained, is all that he seems to care for, unless he reserves some affection for his brace of six-shooters and Winchester rifle, which have helped him out of many a tight place. His care of the beautiful mare is well deserved, for many a time has her fleetness which surpasses that of any other horse in the Territory, saved his life. The Kid is an admirable rider, and as he is always expected to be obliged to take flight, he usually rides another horse, leading his pet behind, in order to make the best time possible on a fresh horse. He is considered a dead shot and much of his time is spent in target practice. He was born in New York State, but his parents moved to Indiana when he was quite small, and thence to Arizona. There in the Tombstone District the Kid killed his first man when he was only 17 years old, and was obliged to leave the country. He came to New Mexico, where he has since lived.

About three years ago a difficulty arose in Lincoln County, New Mexico, between the stockmen and the

Indian agent on the reservation. The trouble arose in regard to some cattle that had been purchased for the Indians. Nearly every man in the county was under arms, and the troops were called out by Gov. Wallace to quell the disturbance. The Kid was mixed up in the affair, and had some narrow escapes. On one occasion he was hotly pursued and was obliged to take refuge in a house in Lincoln, which was surrounded by sixty solders. To the demand to surrender, he only laughed and shot down a soldier just to show that he was game. The house was set on fire, when the Kid, after loading up his Winchester Rifle, leaped from the burning building and made a dash for liberty. All the while he was running he kept firing from his Winchester, bringing down a number of his pursuers. Bullets whistled over his head, but he made his escape, and leaping on a horse was soon laughing at his pursuers. There is no telling how many men he has killed. He sets no value on human life, and has never hesitated at murder when it would serve his purpose. Gov. **Wallace a few days ago offered a reward of $500 for his capture, and prominent citizens would make up a handsome purse in addition.**

[AUTHOR'S NOTE: Recall Blandina's entry for Wallace and citizens both offering rewards.]

Billy Wilson is much the same sort of good looking fellow as his chief. He is about the same build, with dark hair and a slight moustache. He left the Ohio home where his people, who are all highly esteemed, still reside, several years ago. After being engaged in the cattle business in Texas for some time, he came to New Mexico. When the excitement broke out over the new camp at White Oaks, he went there and was engaged in the butchering business. He was always considered a smart, energetic fellow, and was well thought of. In some way the Kid persuaded him to join his party, and it was by him that much of the forged paper was put into circulation.

Tom O'Phallier is a Texan and is also a man of good appearance. He has a ruddy, face, and can be an exceedingly agreeable companion. He has been with the band from the first, and has committed many crimes.

Dave Rudabaugh is 36 years old, and was born in New York city, where he lived until about eight years ago. He has raided over southern Kansas, the Indian nations, Texas, southern Colorado, and New Mexico. It would not be difficult to establish charges of murder against him in any or all of those States and Territories. In Colorado, a few years ago he ran off some Government stock, and, while pursued by a detachment of soldiers, he killed a Sergeant and two privates. He once headed an attack on the Las Vegas jail, in order to liberate one of his friends, and shot down a guard who interfered. He is a thorough desperado in look, word, and action, ready at all times for a fight. He thinks no more of putting a bullet through a human brain than through the bull's eyes of the target before which he is continually practicing. He is 5 feet 8 inches tall, and weighs about 180 pounds. He has a swarthy complexion, black hair and beard, and hazel eyes, whose cruel, defiant expression has often been noted.

The career of the band is about run, for they are hotly pursued, and the chances are that before long they will be killed or captured. It is not expected that the Kid or Rudabaugh will be taken alive, as they will fight to the last.

Lew Wallace himself used outlaw gang and highwayman themes for his first full-blown Billy the Kid, outlaw myth, newspaper article - written in dime novel style - which appeared on May 16, 1881 in the *St. Louis Daily Globe-Democrat*, titled: "The Thugs Territory, Stage Robbers and Cut-Throats Have Things Their Own Way in New Mexico, Gen. Lew Wallace Anxious to Punish Crime that is So Prevalent - A Chapter About "Billy the Kid" - The Governor has a Narrow Escape from Being Spanked."

Noteworthy for Blandina, are the themes of "Stage Robbers," "Cut Throats," and "Narrow Escape," since she used them all.

This creation - Wallace's first tale of the Old West - portrays "Billy the Kid" as the villain, with himself as hero - as did Blandina herself. The article stated:

The Thugs Territory.

Stage Robbers and Cut-Throats Have Things Their Own Way in New Mexico.

Gen. Lew Wallace Anxious to Punish Crime that is So Prevalent – A Chapter About "Billy the Kid" – The Governor has a Narrow Escape from Being Spanked.

Special correspondence of the Globe-Democrat.

DEMING, N.M. May 9, 1881. – Your correspondent visited ... Santa Fe and had a pleasant talk with Governor Lew Wallace ... [T]he Governor gave a very interesting sketch of the life of

"BILLY THE KID,"

the most noted and desperate character in New Mexico, and who was sentenced to be hanged on the 13th inst., but escaped by killing his guards and defying the entire population of Lincoln to take him, and Governor Wallace has offered a reward of $500 for his recapture, and has a posse consisting of seventy-five men on his trail.

"I deem him," said the Governor, **"the most dangerous man at large, and I hope I will have the pleasure of seeing him meet his just deserts for the many crimes he has committed."**

Billy, he said, was born in the East, and for some years lived in Indianapolis, Ind. He is 21 years of age, and came to New Mexico with his head crammed with dime novel stories. **His ambition was to become one of the most noted outlaws he had read so much of. He settled down in Lincoln, and a splendid field was afforded to make his name in the terror of the inhabitants. He stole, murdered, ravished women, and at one time stole a herd of cattle consisting of 300 head, drove them to a station and sold them. He then pocketed the money and went back to Lincoln and defied the authorities to take him. It is claimed he has killed some forty men, and it is positively known that he killed at least five or six in Mexico alone.** Some two years ago a murder was committed in New Mexico and Governor Wallace was positive that Billy had a hand in the deed, but was unable to discover his whereabouts. Finally he learned that he was in the mountains a short distance from Santa Fe, and sent a messenger with a note to the outlaw, saying that if he knew anything about the matter and was willing to give his evidence before the Grand Jury, he would grant him a pardon, providing he also led a different life. Billy was to meet him at a certain house in Santa Fe at 12 o'clock on a certain night and date, and the matter would be thoroughly discussed. At the appointed time

GOV. WALLACE

was at the house, and exactly at 12 o'clock a knock was heard at the door and in walked "Billy the Kid," A long talk followed, and it was agreed that the Sheriff should arrest him to protect him from the pals of the murderer. The Governor's idea in granting a pardon to Billy was to capture the leader and break up the gang. On the next day the Sheriff with a posse of men captured Billy and he was brought before the Grand Jury, testified, and two of the men were sentenced to be hanged on Billy's evidence. **Since the day Billy received the Governor's letter he has been leading the life of a murderer, stage robber, etc.,** and felt that the letter would forever shield him from the law should he be captured. **At length Billy committed one murder too many, was arrested, and sentenced to be hanged** on the 13th inst. at Santa Fe, but escaped by killing two of the guards. While in jail he wrote two letters to the Governor, demanding a pardon, and threatening to expose him should he not do as requested. The Governor remembered the letter, and sent word to Billy's lawyer that he might do him a favor by publishing it. This was too much for the outlaw, and he by letters and words openly avowed that Lew Wallace would die by his hands before he left the Territory. But the Governor does not fear him, and as soon as the outlaw is within two days ride of Santa Fe Wallace himself will start the pursuit. A hundred other frontiersmen are also on the track of Billy, and will capture him if he is within the Territory.

Governor Wallace, since performing the duties of Chief Executive officer of New Mexico, has done considerable toward

PUTTING DOWN LAWLESSNESS

in the Territory. He is a man of courage, as the people know, and would not hesitate to face and attempt to take the most desperate character in this Territory if it became necessary. **An interesting and ludicrous story is told of a recent meeting which was held by stage robbers and cut-throats of the Territory generally. It was resolved that as Governor Wallace had taken such great care in placing a large number of their crowd under arrest, that he should be assassinated when the first opportunity presented itself.** Each man was sworn to the agreement in a general celebration and jubilee followed at Lincoln over the action of the meeting. The members, some 300 in number paraded through the streets with cocked guns and revolvers, and the citizens deemed it best to look on and not in any way molest the gang. Somehow or other, when the boys got pretty full of whiskey, a streak of goodness entered their hearts, and right in the saloon another meeting was called, and it was resolved that Lew Wallace was a brave man, and only doing his duty. As this was the case, the first resolution was reconsidered, and the following notice was sent to Governor Wallace, which is still in his possession:

"At our first meeting we

resolved that you should die for interfering with our crowd, but as we think you a brave man and one who fought for the same cause that we did during the war, therefore we have resolved that instead of killing you we will, when the first opportunity presents itself, take off your pants and give you the worst spanking you ever had."

The Governor said that he actually believed that they would carry out their intention and he was very careful that they shouldn't get an opportunity

TO SPANK HIM

if he could help it. A short time after receiving the note he had occasion to cross the country, and he felt that the outlaws would attempt the trick. He felt so certain of this that before he started he gave the driver notice that should any person order the coach to halt, the mules should be whipped into a dead run. As the coach was descending a steep ditch a couple of men jumped out, and before they had time to sing out, the driver gave the mules the whip and away they dashed down the declivity. The Governor here jocosely remarked "that he didn't know which was the worst – running the risk of breaking his neck or getting the spanking." Anyhow, they didn't catch him, and if they do, it must be before the new Governor arrives. Governor Wallace will return to the East in a few weeks, settle up his affairs, then return to New Mexico for the purpose of seeing to his mining interests.

The extent of Lew Wallace's obsession with Billy Bonney is shown by his next "Billy the Kid" article: an interview written on June 13, 1881, when he was back home in Crawfordsville, Indiana, for just 11 days after departing his New Mexico Territory governorship. Wallace was still reworking his pardon betrayal to mollify his guilty conscience when interviewed for the Crawfordsville *Saturday Evening Journal*. The article was titled "Billy the Kid, General Wallace Tells Why the Young Desperado of New Mexico Wanted to Kill Him. A Dashing and Daring Career in the Land of the Petulant Pistol." And Wallace was still reversing his destruction of Billy Bonney's life by refusing him an earned pardon, by floating the distracting lie that Billy had wanted to kill him. The article stated:

BILLY THE KID.

General Wallace Tells Why the Young Desperado of New Mexico Wanted to Kill Him.

A Dashing and Daring Career in the Land of the Petulant Pistol.

Late newspaper accounts of the exploits of "Billy the Kid," the New Mexico outlaw, have made him the chief among frontier desperados and familiarized readers with his depredations and murdering. In Crawfordsville additional interest in him is created by the fact that he is the same who swore to kill General Wallace, late Governor of New Mexico. His real name is William Bonne [sic], and he was born in New York, which place he left when a small boy with his widowed mother, for Indiana. He lived for a while in Indianapolis, and then Terre Haute, and four years ago went to the Territory of New Mexico. He had been a close reader of blood-and-thunder literature, and soon succeeded in out doing any of the desperate thugs he had ever read of. He now belongs to Silver City where his mother resides, but lives in the mountains to evade the edicts of the law, he now being under sentence for death for murder. He has killed in all, thirty-nine men, and is still not satisfied. He worked for John Chisum, the cattle dealer, in the late Lincoln county trouble, and claiming he has never received the promised $5 per day for his services, he is hunting down and killing Chisum's herdsmen, and giving their employer credit for $5 for each man killed.

[AUTHOR'S NOTE: Hiding Santa Fe Ring issues, Wallace claims anger at John Chisum as Billy's motive for killings.]

It is only recently that he killed two guards of the Lincoln county jail, compelled one man to file off his irons, and another to furnish him with a horse and rode away before the eyes of the whole town. It was during this confinement that he swore to kill Governor Wallace. Given in the following narrative which a reporter of THE JOURNAL got from General Wallace, last Monday, is the cause of Billy's anger at the Governor: A young lawyer named Chapman was murdered in Lincoln county, and for this were arrested four men, among whom was the notorious Jesse James, under one of his many names. The witnesses against the murderers all lied, and the latter were about to be liberated on a writ of habeas corpus. Governor Wallace heard that the "kid" saw the murder, and finding a man who could find Billy, sent him a note requesting a conference with him at midnight at a certain house which was designated. The note assured the "kid" that if the conference proved that he did not have the necessary information about the murder he would be permitted to leave the city, but if he did and would testify before the grand jury, the note implied that the Governor would pardon him for crimes for which he had been indicted, provided he would leave the Territory for good.

Governor Wallace repaired to the meeting place early, and promptly at midnight, a slight knock was heard at the door and upon response in the inside, "Billy the Kid" opened the door and walked in. The Governor found Billy to be a mild-faced young man, 19 years old, small, slender, sloping shoulders, manly head, and an open expression of the face, and a deliberate and pleasant voice. After taking a cigar apiece, and talking over matters in Indiana, (for Billy was proud to say that he was once a Hoosier), Governor Wallace asked Billy to tell what he knew. He proceeded in good language to slowly tell what he knew, which proved to be what the authorities wanted. The Governor asked him if he would go before the grand jury and tell the same thing. Billy's reply was that he would not dare to do it voluntarily, as the criminals' friends would kill him. The Governor suggested that the difficulty might be surmounted by the "kid" permitting himself to be captured.

[AUTHOR'S NOTE: Lying Wallace, in his decades of reworking this tale, would always undo Billy's courage in contacting him and in suggesting the sham arrest, by claiming he himself instigated both.]

This was agreed upon, and accordingly and by arrangement Billy was surprised at a safe place in the mountains, while asleep, captured, and taken to jail. He went before the grand jury and by his evidence the criminals were indicted for murder. But before the trial in which he was to appear as a witness for the prosecution, he tired of jail life, and one day at dinner, he left his guards and took to the mountains.

[AUTHOR'S NOTE: Lew Wallace, in this jumbled version, admits Billy testified for the pardon bargain. But to hide his own betrayal, he fabricates that Billy absconded before testifying in a another fabricated trial. In later articles, Wallace used the absconding story to make Billy the bargain betrayer. Omitted here, and forever after, is that Billy stayed in jail until June of 1879 to testify in the Dudley Court of Inquiry.]

He then resumed robbing raids and stealing cattle ... until two years later, Pat Garrett, Sheriff of Lincoln County, and the only man now in New Mexico who is not afraid of Billy, got on his track and effected his capture. During this imprisonment the "kid," who had constantly carried the Governor's note about the convicting of Chapman's murderers, wrote twice to Governor Wallace, threatening to publish the proposition to pardon if he was not liberated. No attention was paid to these and Billy's lawyer then came before the Governor with the same threat. The reply from the executive was that Billy might publish as much as he chose, as the matter had been reported in Washington and there approved.

Billy was further informed that he had not complied with all the conditions of the promise. This greatly enraged the young outlaw and he said he would take the life of the Governor. While under sentence of death he swore to kill three men before he died – Governor Wallace, John Chisum, the cattle dealer, and Pat Garrett, the Lincoln County Sheriff. In a short time he gained liberty by killing his two guards as before stated. Although Bonne [sic] was a desperate character, Governor Wallace felt no particular alarm and was more anxious to find Billy than Billy was to find him. He had it so arranged that he would have heard of the young desperado's approach 150 miles from Santa Fe, and other precautions were taken at the Governor's office.

[AUTHOR'S NOTE: This fabricated and obsessively retold tale of Billy's murderous vendetta against him, is Wallace's projection of his murderous feelings

against Billy. It might have also been his real fear of retaliation for his betrayal. For his fiction, "threat" also puts Wallace in the center of the jailbreak, when, in fact, he was irrelevant by then. But Wallace recycled it in all future articles after Billy's death.]

Billy was sentenced to be hung, and took desperate chances to escape. He was successful and was in no hurry to come in the way of the law. His success had in his great amount of nerve. He never allowed himself to become excited, and never missed the object he shot at. Before Billy became involved in so many crimes he had one day showing Governor Wallace a specimen of his workmanship. He explained his perfection thus: He never took aim with the revolver, but placed his index finger along the barrel, and as if pointing at the object pulled the trigger with his second finger ... Nevertheless he is ever on the alert guarding against the other fellows getting the "drop."

There was once a three day siege of a house in which were Billy and a party. General Wallace had a report of the maneuvering on the out-side and when Billy was a prisoner had him to tell of the workings on the inside. The besieging party finally succeeded in firing the house and those inside were driven from room to room, and finally to the kitchen. Then, there was but one door of exit and the outside men kept a continual storm of bullets pouring into it. One by one those attacked "took chances" and ran out the door rather than to be burned. Each fell with from four to fourteen bullets in the bodies until the "kid" who was the last to go rushed out and escaped without a scratch, though his clothing was completely riddled with bullets, and even his necktie was cut at his throat.

The "Kid" is a great favorite with Mexican women and does not want for friends, but as hard, bold, and daring as he is, he will doubtless soon meet death at the rope end of the gun's muzzle.

Lew Wallace obsessed about Billy Bonney for the rest of his life, reworking the outlaw myth he had created to justify his own betrayal of the pardon bargain, and to make himself a victim of terrifying outlaw Billy the Kid. By June 23, 1900, he published in *The Indianapolis Press* "Gen. Wallace's Feud with Billy the Kid, When the General Was Governor of New Mexico and Billy Bonne Was the Most Dangerous Western Outlaw, He Was a Waif and was Reared in Indiana." Like Blandina would do in her journal, Wallace aggrandized Billy Bonney's fame, writing: "Billy the Kid [was] the New Mexican outlaw that attracted the attention of the nation ... [People] were victims of that mysterious something that Billy exerted over men ... Over him, with a majesty, hung the cloak of fearlessness and alertness penetrated only by two eyes that looked deep into every man's intentions." And Wallace created the mystical murder tally: "[H]e killed a man for every one of the twenty-two years he lived." He also continued to fabricate that Billy had a vendetta against him. The article stated:

GEN. WALLACE'S FEUD WITH BILLY THE KID
When the General Was Governor of New Mexico and Billy Bonne Was the Most Dangerous Western Outlaw
HE WAS A WAIF AND WAS REARED IN INDIANA

(By a Staff Correspondent) CRAWFORDSVILLE, Ind., June 23. –

"Yes, he killed a man for every one of the twenty-two years he lived, and died in his stocking feet – a marvelous, far more than marvelous, career his was – a nightmare of existence."

Gen. Lew Wallace's shaggy brows contracted with a frown as he closed his eyes as though to shut out from his memory unpleasant things. There was a pause. He arose from his chair, and after walking up and down his study in silence, finally said:

"So long as I live, I will never lose the image of Billy the Kid, as I saw him that midnight in old Santa Fe, back in 1879. There he stands in the doorway of the little adobe house, form outlined by moonlight at his back, face illuminated by glow of the little lamp. The clock had made its first stroke of the midnight hour, when by appointment to the second there was a knock at the door that I can hear yet. 'Come in,' I said. The door flew open and there stood the most feared, the most adored, the most reverenced man in New Mexico, hunted by every limb of the law as a criminal, and sought by every Spanish senorita as her lover. The room was covered by a Winchester rifle held in one hand. In the other was a Colt's revolver. It was a musical growl that said, "I was to meet the Governor here at midnight. It is midnight: is he here?"

"I asked him to come in for a conference, and told him that I was the Governor of New Mexico.

"Your note gave me the promise of protection," he said.

"There is no one here but us three," replied I, pointing to the owner of the cottage.

"Billy threw his gun over his arm and came straight to the table near which I sat. I looked at him in wonder. This was the man that had killed his scores: the man whom every officer hunted. I was not expecting to see a stripling, with rounded shoulders, slightly stooping stature, slender, effeminate physique. His face was smooth and soft, and yet character and firmness were shown in every line. His voice was as musical as that of a society belle. Over him, with a majesty, hung the cloak of fearlessness and alertness penetrated only by two eyes that looked deep into every man's intentions."

Reared in Indiana.

The General passed from the thoughtful to the narrative and said: "Billy the Kid, the New Mexican outlaw that attracted the attention of a nation, and under whose fearful vendetta I was placed while Governor of New Mexico, was a New York waif whose name was William Bonne.

[AUTHOR'S NOTE: To inflate daring, Wallace makes Billy famous in 1879, and invents the "fearful vendetta."]

He was brought to Indiana when he was a small boy and was reared in Indianapolis and Terre Haute. He was about 17 years old in 1876, when he went West. During his early years he had been a close reader of blood-and-thunder literature. He outdid in reality the lurid pictures of the literature in which he was schooled.

"It was not long until 'Billy the Kid' became the most daring and notori-

ous of desperadoes. Stories of his crimes, his escapes, his fascinating faculties were the nursery tales of the Territory. He started to grow up with the country by taking employment of John Chisum, who was known as the 'Cattle King,' was a hard taskmaster and disputed Billy's account. The latter swore that he would square matters by killing Chisum's herdsmen: that for each man he killed he would credit the cattleman with $5, but if he killed Chisum himself then the whole account would be wiped out.

Midnight Meeting Arranged.

"A young lawyer named Chapman was murdered at Lincoln. Four men were arrested, among them the notorious Jesse James.

[AUTHOR'S NOTE: New Mexico Territory outlaw, Jessie Evans, in this fiction becomes famous Jesse James!]

The witnesses to the killing were filled with terror and fled the country. Because of the lack of evidence the prisoners were about to be released on a writ of habeas corpus. I had been sent to pacify the country and had realized this was an opportunity I could not let slip. At last I heard that Billy the Kid had witnessed the murder.

[AUTHOR'S NOTE: Wallace hides Billy's pardon bargain to make himself the hero.]

In the outskirts of Santa Fe lived an old 'squire,' who was one of Billy's friends.

[AUTHOR'S NOTE: Wallace substitutes Santa Fe for Lincoln.]

I went to him one evening and told him I wanted the young outlaw to meet me promptly at midnight. He professed that he had no connection with the sought-for youth. I ordered pen and ink and wrote a note, and, leaving it, told him that I would expect it to be delivered to Billy. In the note I said I understood he was the only remaining man that had witnessed the murder, and that if he would appear before the Grand Jury and court and convict them I would pardon him for all his crimes.

"The midnight meeting was as I have described. When he heard from my lips my proposition he said: 'My God, Governor, they would kill me.' 'But that can be arranged,' I replied.

[AUTHOR'S NOTE: Wallace lies that he, not Billy, devised the sham imprisonment.]

It was decided that Billy was to be taken the next morning while asleep in a cabin back in the mountain. He picked the men that were to capture him. He required me to keep him in irons during confinement, that his reputation not be marred."

[AUTHOR'S NOTE: Wallace hides the Lincoln location of the jail.]

Billy's Secret in Revolver Shooting.

"It was during this confinement that 'the Kid' gave the most phenomenal exhibition of shooting I have ever witnessed. I sent word to the jail to have him brought to my office.

" 'Billy,' I said, 'I am told you are a phenomenal shot. I wish you would give me an exhibition of your skill.'

" 'With pleasure, Governor. Have my pistols brought.'

" 'Here is a pistol, and a good one.'

" 'A violinist always wants his own bow, though another might be better. I want my own pistol.'

"His pistol was brought and we took him out into the big, open court. I ordered his chains taken from him. The guards whispered to me, 'For God's sake, Governor, do you know that you are giving him your life or his escape?'

[AUTHOR'S NOTE: Wallace omits that the jailing was a sham]

"I know that I was the last man in New Mexico Billy wanted to kill, for I was the only man that could give him a pardon.

"The guards stood with their weapons in their hands, ready to defend themselves from this man with a charmed life. Billy spied a small Boston bean can in the court. He ordered a guard to throw it high as he could. The can sailed in the air. Without taking aim, and seemingly without concern, he fired at it. The bullet passed through the center. As it struck the ground, in the same unconcerned manner, Billy fired at it, and, emptying his revolver, he rolled it along much the same as one can roll a can with the stream from a lawn hose.

" 'Billy,' said I, 'There is a trick in that, and I want to know it.'

" 'Yes,' he replied, 'there is a trick. Ever since you

were a child, Governor, you have been doing it unconsciously, every time you have said 'Look at that you have pointed at it with your index finger. Without knowing it, you have become an expert mark – and so has everyone. I put my index finger along the barrel, catch the trigger with my second finger and say, 'Why look at that, Billy,' and, pointing unconsciously at it, pull the trigger. I am not known as a crack shot, Governor – rather a dead shot.'

"He asked for his horse and gun – his own Winchester. Mounting, he started down the court on a dead run, and as he went he shot with his left hand, emptying his magazine into a four-inch sapling that was 200 yards distant. Back he came on a gallop, shooting with the right hand. Every shot took effect.

" 'And what is the trick about that, Billy?'

" 'Oh, General, there is no trick in that rifle. My horse bounds away, I level, I feel it all over, I pull the trigger and the bullet goes straight.

Was Something of a Hypnotist.

"It was a week before the trial. Billy had been taken to dinner in his chains. After the meal he said: "Well, I wish you would tell the Governor that I am tired. Much obliged boys,' and leaving them as though in a trance, he quietly walked across the street, and, unhitching a horse, dashed out of town. There could be no suspicion that the guards had conspired for his release. They were victims of that mysterious something that Billy exerted over men.

[AUTHOR'S NOTE: Here is Wallace's perfidy: hiding Billy's testimony that fulfilled the pardon bargain, substituting a dream-like escape.]

"Later Billy was arrested for a series of murders.

[AUTHOR'S NOTE: This is a purposeful lie, since Billy's Stinking Springs arrest by Sheriff Pat Garrett was only for the three Lincoln County War indictments for which Billy deserved the pardon, which Wallace betrayed.]

He had kept my note offering pardon in the affair. He had been in jail a week when he addressed me: 'Governor, why haven't you come to see me?' I paid no attention to it. A few days later there was a second note: 'Governor, I have some papers you would not want to see displayed. Come to the jail.' I knew what he meant. I sent a copy of the old note and the story over to the paper and it was published. I sent him a copy of the paper and drew his fire. **It was then that he swore his vendetta on my life and on that of Pat Garrett, the sheriff of Lincoln County.**

[AUTHOR'S NOTE: Wallace is fabricating this "vendetta."]

He was convicted for murder and sentenced to be hanged. When the sentence was read, he arose in court and said:

" 'Judge, that doesn't frighten me the least bit. Billy the Kid was not born to be hung.'

"This young desperado was a thorough fatalist. He believed that for the time he had a charmed life: that he had nothing to fear from the weapons of enemies, and that he would not go 'until his time came,' and the time was not at hand.

"He had gone through many a danger. At one time, surrounded in a Mexican house, 'the Kid' fought nine men. The house was set on fire, and he made a dash for liberty and escaped through all the musketry of the guards. There were a dozen bullet holes in his clothing and his necktie had been cut away at the throat by a bullet, but Billy received not a mark on his skin.

[AUTHOR'S NOTE: This is Wallace's dishonest reducing of the six day Lincoln County War Battle to a "surrounded … Mexican house" and "the Kid" fighting "nine men" to remove his own humiliation of having failed the citizens oppressed by the Santa Fe Ring.]

"From his trial," continued General Wallace, "Billy was taken back to jail. He was in no wise disturbed. A day before the execution nine guards were watching him. At dinner time all but one left. Billy was in chains. The guard on duty received a tray that bore Billy's dinner. As the guard stood to place the tray on the floor, Billy the Kid struck him on the head with the handcuffs, crushing the skull. Then he took the guard's revolver, routed all the other guards that appeared, forced a blacksmith near by to break the handcuffs, mounted a good horse near at hand and rode away. He said as he started: 'Tell the Judge that I said that Billy the Kid was not born to be hung.'"

[AUTHOR'S NOTE: This fake escape, multiplying Billy's guards, reveals Wallace's fantasizing Billy as a super-human.]

End of Billy the Kid.

"It is needless to touch upon my danger under the vendetta," returned Gen. Wallace. Sufficient it is to say that he started for Santa Fe at once, and, determined to have a shot in return, I started out to meet him, but for some reason he never reached the point.

[AUTHOR'S NOTE: Wallace fabricated the vendetta.]

Sheriff Pat Garrett was the only man in New Mexico not afraid of Billy and his charmed life. Garrett started out to make his capture, and it was a scout lasting for weeks, each man waiting to get the drop. All New Mexicans had their eyes on the two, and every morning the general question was, 'Has Pat and the Kid met yet?' It was a long siege, but Billy fell through love.

"Pat received information that Billy had gone back to an old fort in the mountains to see his sweetheart. Garrett journeyed there. He lay in wait in the dooryard of Billy's love, and finally saw the door open one night and a man come out in stocking feet. His hat was off; he wore only shirt and trousers. He passed out into the night. Garrett walked in and covered the girl's father with a gun. 'Not a word,' he whispered, as he passed behind the headboard of the bed with gun in hand. The door opened again. Billy seemed to smell danger, as a camel smells rain. He knew by instinct that something was wrong. He cried to the old man in Spanish, 'Who's there? Who's there?' Garrett raised his revolver. There were two reports. Billy the Kid jumped into the air and fell in his tracks. There were two bullet holes through his heart."

As he concluded the story there was a tremble in Gen. Wallace's voice that indicated that with the horrible picture there was a feeling of admiration for Billy. There was a pause and he said: "And he was only twenty-two."
E.I. LEWIS

On June 8, 1902, twenty-one years after Billy' was killed because he had denied him the deserved pardon, and for the last of his Billy the Kid articles before he died in 1905, Lew Wallace published in *New York World Magazine*, a novella-like article titled: "General Lew Wallace Writes a Romance of 'Billy the Kid' Most Famous Bandit of the Plains, Thrilling Story of the Midnight Meeting Between Gen. Wallace, Then Governor of New Mexico, and the Notorious Outlaw, in a Lonesome Hut at Santa Fe." The article maintained the outlaw myth, guaranteeing its projection for a century of unjust distortions, including Blandina Segale's. The article stated:

GENERAL LEW WALLACE WRITES A ROMANCE OF 'BILLY THE KID' MOST FAMOUS BANDIT OF THE PLAINS

Thrilling Story of the Midnight Meeting Between Gen. Wallace, Then Governor of New Mexico, and the Notorious Outlaw, in a Lonesome Hut at Santa Fe.

Gen. LEW WALLACE, author of "Ben Hur," is completing his autobiography, which will be issued in a few weeks.

The most thrilling chapter in this remarkable personal narrative tells of the midnight meeting in a lonely hut between Gen. Wallace, at the time Governor of the Territory of New Mexico, and **"Billy the Kid," the most notorious outlaw the far West has ever produced.**

From advance sheets of Gen. Wallace's book the following account of this strange rendezvous has been copied and compiled for the Sunday World Magazine. The story has never been printed in any newspaper or magazine before.

The episode occurred in 1879. The outlaw was at the zenith of his wild career. Gen. Wallace conceived the idea that he might gain certain important information by a face-to-face talk with the outlaw. With much difficulty the meeting was finally arranged. It was not without a strong element of danger to both participants, but they trusted each other and the trust was not betrayed.

The Midnight Rendezvous.

On the night of the meeting two men sat,

shortly before midnight, silent and expectant, in the hut which had been chosen for the rendezvous, which was on the outskirts of Santa F, N.M.

Their gaze was fastened on the door, and, as the minutes slipped away the tension grew more severe, the silence more oppressive.

One man was the owner of the rude home that stood desolate in the shifting sands of the great mesa.

The other was Gen. Lew Wallace, Governor of New Mexico.

The hands of the clock pointed to 12.

The hush deepened. Suddenly it was broken by the sound of a resolute knock on the door of the cabin.

"Come in," said the Governor of New Mexico.

The door flew open and, standing with his form outlined by the moonlight behind him, was "Billy the Kid." In his left hand he carried a Winchester rifle. In his right was a revolver. The weapons, quick as a flash, covered the two occupants in the room.

"I was to meet the Governor here at midnight. It is midnight: Is the Governor here?"

The light of the candles flickered against a boyish face, yet the man who stood in the doorway was the most notorious desperado in all the West. He had killed scores of men: he was the quarry of every sheriff from the Rio Grande to the bordering foothills that shut in Death Valley.

The Boy Outlaw.

In facial features "Billy the Kid" was a mere stripling. His narrow shoulders were rounded, his posture slightly stooping, his voice low and effeminate. **But his eyes were cold and piercing, steady, alert, gray like steel.**

Gen. Wallace rose to his feet and held out his hand, inviting the visitor forward for a conference.

"Your note gave the promise of absolute protection," said the outlaw, warily.

"I have been true to my promise," replied the Governor. "This man," pointing to the owner of the cabin, "and myself are the only persons present."

The rifle was slowly lowered, the revolver returned to its leather holster. "Billy" advanced and the two seated themselves at opposite sides of the narrow table.

Gen. Wallace was able to effect an important arrangement with the outlaw, of which he gives the details. In fact, a very friendly understanding was established between the two.

Explaining the purpose of the interview and its result with "Billy," Gen. Wallace says:

"Shortly before I had become Governor of New Mexico, Chapman, a young attorney in Lincoln, had been murdered.

[AUTHOR'S NOTE: This lying date of Chapman's murder is to hide Wallace's blame. It was on February 18, 1879, 4½ months into Wallace's term; and Wallace was blamed for having refused to come earlier to Lincoln County.]

Half a dozen men were arrested, accused of the crime. Among them was Jesse James.

While it was more than probable that one or more of the men charged with the murder were guilty, it was impossible to prove the allegation, for the witnesses, filled with terror, fled the country. When I reached New Mexico it was declared on every hand that "Billy the Kid" had been a witness to the murder. Could he be made to testify?

"That was a question on the tip of every tongue.

"I had been sent to the Southwest to pacify the territory; here was an opportunity I could not afford to pass by. Therefore I arranged the meeting by note deposited with one of the outlaw's friends, and at midnight was ready to receive the desperado should he appear. He was there on time – punctual to the second.

"When 'Billy the Kid' stepped to the chair opposite mine, I lost no time in announcing me proposition.

Agrees to the Plan.

" 'Testify,' I said, 'before the Grand Jury and the trial court and convict the murderer of Chapman and I will let you go scot-free with a pardon in your pocket for all your misdeeds.'

" 'Billy' heard me in silence; he thought several minutes without reply.

" 'Governor,' said he, "if I were to do what you ask they would kill me."

" 'We can prevent that," said I.

"Then I unfolded my plan. 'Billy' was to be seized while he was asleep. To all appearances, his capture was to be genuine. To this he agreed, picking the men who were to effect his capture. He was afraid of hostile bullets and would run no risk. Another stipulation was to the effect that during his confinement he should be kept in irons. 'Billy the Kid' was afraid also of the loss of his reputation as a desperate man."

The plan agreed upon in the cabin on the lonely mesa at midnight was carried out to the letter. "Billy the Kid" was seized the following morning and confined in the Lincoln County jail. It was here that Gen. Wallace, in spite of the fears of the guards, permitted the outlaw to give an exhibition of his skill with the revolver and the rifle. "Billy," standing or riding, using either the one weapon or the other, sent every bullet true to its mark.

"Billy," said the General, "there's some trick to that shooting. How do you do it?"

"Well, General," replied the desperado, "there is a trick to it. When I was a boy I noticed that a man in pointing to anything he wished observed, used his index finger. With long use, unconsciously, the man had learned to point it with unerring aim. When I lift my revolver, I say to myself, 'Point with your finger.' I stretch the finger along the barrel and, unconsciously, it makes the aim certain. There is no failure; I pull the trigger and the bullet goes true to its mark."

"Billy," though at his own request kept in irons, did not remain long confined. One morning the guards led him to breakfast. Returning, the desperado drawled in the feminine voice that was a part and parcel of his character:

"Boys, I'm tired. Tell the Governor I'm tired."

The manacles slipped like magic from his wrists. The guards stood stupefied, and "Billy the Kid," laughing mockingly, walked leisurely from the jail yard, through the gate and across the street. Easily, gracefully, he threw himself into the saddle on the back of a horse standing near at hand and, putting spurs to the animal, dashed away. "Billy" was gone. He had not escaped in the night; he had walked away in the broad light of day, with his guards, heavily armed, standing about him.

[AUTHOR'S NOTE: This hides Billy's testifying, and leaving his sham arrest only after lack of pardon risked his life by being hanged by the Ring.]

"Boys," I'm tired," he said, and looked them straight in the eyes.

They were not in collusion with the desperado; Gen. Wallace satisfied himself of the fact.

But how account for "Billy's" escape?

Hypnotism, some say – hypnotism or that strange something that lurked in the depths of the steel-gray eyes.

The desperado's freedom, however, was not long-lived. **He was arrested soon afterward for a series of murders,** and was brought again to the Lincoln County Jail. Patrick Garrett was Sheriff. He was probably the one man in New Mexico who did not fear "Billy the Kid." He was his match in every respect – as calm, as desperate, as certain.

[**AUTHOR'S** Wallace's **demonizing of Billy continues by fabricating murders.**]

Perhaps "Billy" knew this. At any rate he must have considered himself in desperate straits. He sent for Gen. Wallace. The General refused to respond. Then the outlaw sent him a note. The note said:

"Come to the jail. I have some papers you would not want to see displayed."

"I knew what he meant," said Gen. Wallace, reminiscently. "He referred to the note he received from me in response to which he appeared in the hut on the mesa. He was threatening to publish it if I refused to see him. I thwarted his purpose by giving a copy of the latter and a narrative of the circumstances connected with it to the paper published in the town. It was duly printed and upon its appearance a copy was sent to "Billy" in his cell. He had nothing further to say."

Not Daunted by His Sentence.

In the end the desperado was convicted and sentenced to be hanged. When the sentence was read he stood before the trial judge and said:

"Judge, that doesn't frighten me a bit. 'Billy the Kid' was not born to be hung."

He was a thorough fatalist. He believed he bore a charmed life. He believed he would not die until his "time came," and then death was inevitable.

From the court-room "Billy" was led back to the jail. Nine men were put on guard, and he was never allowed a moment from the sight of one of them.

On the day before that set for his execution one man sat in front of Billy while he ate his dinner. During the meal the guard forgot himself and suddenly stooped. "Billy's" quick eye took in the situation in a glance.

With a leap he sprang upon the bending man and dashed his brains out with his handcuffs. He seized the dead guard's revolver and, his steel-gray eyes gleaming, he walked forward deliberately and routed all the other guards, who ran to the assistance of their comrade.

Once more "Billy the Kid" escaped in the full light of day through the doors of the jail. He forced a blacksmith to break the manacle chains, seized a good horse that stood nearby and rode away.

He called back as he spurred the animal into a gallop:

"Tell the judge that I said 'Billy the Kid' was not born to be hung."

But "Billy" had forgotten one thing; he had not reckoned on the character of the man who was Sheriff of the county. He had forgotten Patrick Garrett. Garrett shut his teeth hard, like a man who is determined to accomplish his purpose, no matter the obstacles presenting themselves. He set out to take "Billy the Kid," dead or alive.

Garrett received information that "Billy" had gone back to an old fort in the mountains to see his sweetheart. Garrett followed. He lay in wait in the dooryard of the home of "Billy's" love, and finally his vigil was rewarded when he saw the door open one night and a man step out into the white light of the moon.

His hat was off, he was in his stocking feet and he wore only shirt and trousers. He passed out into the night.

Garrett crept to the door and passed in.

He covered the girl's father with his gun.

"Not a word," he said, and slid behind the headboard of the bed.

The Death of "Billy the Kid."

The door opened again and "Billy the Kid" entered. He seemed to scent danger as a camel scents rain; instinct taught him that something was wrong. He cried to the cowering old man in Spanish:

"Who's here?" he asked. "Who's here?"

Garrett raised his revolver; two shots rang out on the quiet air and the room filled with smoke. A form tottered, then crashed to the floor. In the nerveless hand was a smoking revolver; for the first and last time the notorious New Mexican outlaw had missed his aim. Garrett escaped unwounded. But there were two bullet wounds in the body of "Billy the Kid" and both pierced the heart. Garrett's aim was unerring.

To-day there is a little lowly heap of earth located in Las Cruces, N.M. [sic – Fort Sumner] To the curious stranger some idle native may, now and again, point out this little grave and explain, with a certain pride, that Las Cruces possesses the final resting place of the **worst bad man that ever infested the Southwestern border.** An ancient Mexican, who sometimes shows this grave to visitors, once made the cautious remark regarding its occupant that, had he lived, he would probably have turned out to be a bad man.

"And how old was 'Billy' when he died?" asked one curious stranger.

"Twenty-one, senor," replied the ancient. "He died, almost one might say, before he fully began to live."

"You say he was bad?" remarked another stranger.

"He is said to have killed many men."

"How many? How many, amigo, had this man killed at the time he himself died?"

"He had killed," replied the ancient Mexican, "twenty-one men, one for each year of his age, may the saints defend us," said the Mexican.

[AUTHOR'S NOTE: Lew Wallace's fabricated 21 men for 21 years is on one of Billy Bonney's gravestones.]

"He was a good man, and very kind to poor people. Yet, had he lived, he might, according to the opinion of some, have turned into a bad man."

Gen. Wallace also tells in his autobiography how and why "Billy the Kid" started on his career of crime:

A Waif of New York City.

"The man whose deeds of blood had drawn upon him the eyes of an entire nation, was born a New York waif. Before he was more than ten years of age he was brought to Indiana, and in Terre Haute and Indianapolis, where he was reared, he was known as William Bonne. In 1876, when he was about seventeen years old, he suddenly left his home, crossed the Mississippi and went to the country of the men of his kind – the frontier of the far West.

"Billy began his career with an oath to kill John Chisum, his first employer when the lad reached the plains. Chisum and the "Kid' had been unable to agree on terms of settlement for a season's work. The result was the lad's fearful vendetta, sworn not only against Chisum, but against all of Chisum's other employees as well.

" 'For each herdsman employed by you whom I kill," Billy sent him word, "I will deduct $5 from our unsquared account. If I kill you,' he added grimly, 'my bill will be receipted in full.'

"Then his bloody career began.

[AUTHOR'S NOTE: Wallace fabricates a Chisum conflict as Billy's killing motive to hide the Lincoln County War.]

It was not long until William Bonne, the waif, reared in the peaceful surroundings of Indiana, **became the most feared man in the Southwest.** At the same time, he was the most revered, the most adored and the most respected man in the Territory.

"It was the kind of good reward that sometimes comes to bad men."

SMOKING GUNS FOR A HOAX: In reality, Billy Bonney had no gang, and his extensive outlawry was fabricated by the press, including Lew Wallace's many outlaw myth articles. Furthermore, Billy Bonney's historical fame began with articles in 1880 and onward. So Blandina's so-called journal entries for 1876 and 1877 about "Billy the Kid" and his blood-thirsty "gang" are fabricated, and can be traced to use of later newspaper articles as sources for a "gang" and for "outlawry." And that points to her journal entries being created far later than their claimed journal dates. And all that points to hoaxing.

INDIRECT USE OF SECRET SERVICE REPORTS FOR "BILLY THE KID'S GANG" AND OUTLAWRY

SLEUTHING HOAXBUSTING CLUES: Unbeknownst to Blandina, was that the fictitious press reports of Billy the Kid's gang were based on equally factitious reports by an incompetent Secret Service Agent brought in by the Santa Fe Ring to capture or kill Billy Bonney.

The Secret Service, a branch of the Treasury Department, was likely enlisted by Santa Fe Ring head, Thomas Benton Catron. The Agent sent in September of 1880 to New Mexico Territory to track Billy down - after all efforts to kill him had failed - was named Azariah Wild. Doing no real investigations, gullible Wild was fed fabrications by his Ringite handlers, and soon mixed-up real counterfeiters with Billy Bonney as leading a fictitious gang of counterfeiters, murderers, and rustlers.

Writing his daily report for his Chief for October 5, 1880, Wild wrote about Billy for the first time, stating:

> *There is an outlaw in the mountains here who came here from Arizona after committing a murder there named* **William Antrom alias W<u>m</u> Bonney alias Billy Kid** *with whom these cattle thieves meet, and by many it is believed that they ... receive the counterfeit money. I have found no evidence so far to support their suspicions.*

Controlled by local Ring boss, James Dolan, and Thomas Benton Catron's brother-in-law, Edgar Walz, Wild focused on Fort Sumner for his report about October 14, 1880. He would later call it the "gang's" headquarters, writing:

> *William Wilson [a real counterfeiter] is at present with eighteen other desperados at Fort Sumner one hundred and sixty miles from here, and 125 miles from Las Vegas.* **He has with him three men [one of whom was Billy Bonney] who were indicted in the U.S. Court.** *They are a terror to the whole country.*

Reporting about October 16, 1880, Wild passed along the outlaw myth he was being fed, writing:

> *These men (outlaws) have centered at and make Fort Sumner their headquarters, and at the present time **there are about eighteen notorious characters there who are engaged in stealing stock, passing counterfeit money, and robbing the mails.***

By his report about October 17, 1880, Wild had added Billy (with garbled history) to the fabricated gang, writing:

> *As I have learned the names of several of the outlaws now congregated at and near Fort Sumner I will give them with their history ....*
> **William Antrom alias Billie Bonnie alias "Billie Kid." Indicted in 3rd District of U.S. Court for the murder of the Indian Agent. Comes from Kansas here.**

For his report about October 20, 1880, Wild described a real mail coach theft by Billy, done to steal Wild's reports to understand his mission. This act would be turned into a career of stage coach robberies for Billy's outlaw press. Wild wrote:

> *In this mail I had several reports ... If this is as I believe it must be the plans of our capture and my mission here is as well known to them as it is to myself ...*
> *The parties **Kid**, Wilson, O'Follier [O'Folliard] and Picket who are undoubtedly the ones who robbed the mail on the 17th [sic - 16th] are out at a ranch twelve miles from Fort Sumner.*

[AUTHOR'S NOTE: That Wild's reports were being leaked to the press can be seen from the December 3, 1880 Las Vegas *Gazette's* "Powerful Gang of Outlaws Harassing the Stockmen." And the December 22, 1880 *New York Sun's* "Outlaws of New Mexico, The Exploits of a Band Headed by a New York Youth" even modified Wild's misspelled name of Billy's friend, Tom O'Folliard, as "O'Phallier."]

By his report for October 28, 1880, Wild was hysterically inflating his phantom gang to his Chief, writing:

> *I am now perfectly confident that there is a counterfeiting gang here who are making counterfeit $100 – and $50 – notes as I am of anything that I do not know absolutely certain, and that I have not seen with my own eyes ...*
>
> The **force of desperados** *now at Fort Sumner the headquarters of the gang numbers twenty six. They openly say that they number sixty two in Lincoln County and defy the authorities.*

By November 6, 1880, duped Wild was terrified of the non-existent "gang," making "Billy Kid" its leader, writing:

> *From every indication there is no scare amongst this gang or they are calculating to make a stand at Fort Sumner and fight. They are known to be twenty nine in number ...*
>
> ***The parties who robbed the mail or who were the leaders of it was William Wilson and William Antrom alias "Billy Bony" alias "Billy Kid."***

Having helped make Pat Garrett Lincoln County Sheriff, and appointing him as a Deputy U.S. Marshal to capture Billy, duped Wild wrote hysterically for November 29, 1880:

> *It is believed that there will be blood shed when ever our men come up with the main gang if ever we are able to do so.*

Of course, no gang was found. But for December 9, 1880, before "escaping" the Territory on December 23rd, Wild wrote:

> *I am very anxious to get away from here ...* ***[T]he "rustlers" a (name given to Wilson and his band) have men on two out of three roads*** *... I am going to leave here for headquarters first occasion that presents itself to get away with safety.*

USING CONTEMPORARY PRESS AS SOURCES FOR BILLY THE KID'S THREAT TO LEW WALLACE

SLEUTHING HOAXBUSTING CLUES: Blandina wrote about "Billy the Kid's" threat to Lew Wallace. But no such threat existed. Wallace himself created it for his articles on Billy the Kid to put the focus on himself; then it was used in his 1906 Autobiography - all available to Blandina. And one entry outstrips Blandina's sources by fabricating an attempted attack by "Billy the Kid" on Lew Wallace as being the reason for Billy's capture.

BLANDINA'S TAKE ON BILLY THE KID'S "THREAT" TO LEW WALLACE

An excellent example of a smoking gun for a hoax, was Blandina's writing in her journal about "Billy the Kid's threat to Lew Wallace." No threat existed in reality. Like Blandina's cribbing from Garrett's and Burns's books, this notion was lifted from Lew Wallace himself, who made it up, and put it in his fictitious articles about Billy the Kid; then added it to his 1906 Autobiography.

Blandina introduced the threat theme for the 1932 book's date of "March, 1882," from Santa Fe, writing:

> Unfortunate "Billy the Kid!" His marauding has drawn the attention of the whole Territory, and the "Kid" is as confident of safety as though he had a battalion at his command. **It has been bruited about that he intends undoing Governor Wallace.** Friends of law and order are on the *qui vive* that no harm come to the author of *Ben Hur*.

From Santa Fe, dated for 1932 edition's "April 24 [1882], Blandina wrote:

> The murderer [of a "tenderfoot" she had warned about showing off wealth by fancy dressing] was intoxicated and is now in jail with **"Billy the Kid," who attempted to carry out his threat against Governor Wallace,** but the latter was well guarded by every honest man in the Territory – hence Billy's capture. My first free hours will be to visit the prisoners.

PRESS USE OF "THREAT" TO LEW WALLACE

To prejudice potential jurymen for Billy Bonney's April 9, 1881 trial in Mesilla - where jurymen were ignorant of Lincoln County War issues - the Ring advertised Billy's danger to Lew Wallace if he was set free by them. On April 2, 1881, *Newman's Semi-Weekly*" ran "The Kid;" stating:

[The Kid] is a notoriously dangerous character, has on several occasions before escaped justice where escape appeared even more improbable than now, and has made his **brags that he only wants to get free in order to kill three men – one of them being Governor Wallace.** Should he break jail now, there is no doubt that he would immediately proceed to execute his threat ... We expect every day to hear of his escape and hope that legal technicalities may not be permitted to render escape more probable.

Lew Wallace's invention of the Billy the Kid threat theme was already seen above in some of his articles. His June 13, 1881 Crawfordsville *Saturday Evening Journal* article was titled: "Billy the Kid, General Wallace Tells **Why the Young Desperado of New Mexico Wanted to Kill Him**. A Dashing and Daring Career in the Land of the Petulant Pistol." It stated:

Billy was further informed that he had not complied with all the conditions of the promise. **This greatly enraged the young outlaw and he said he would take the life of the Governor.**

For Wallace's June 23, 1900 *Indianapolis Press* article titled *The* "Gen. Wallace's Feud with Billy the Kid, When the General Was Governor of New Mexico and Billy Bonne Was the Most Dangerous Western Outlaw," he wrote:

He had been in jail a week when he addressed me: 'Governor, why haven't you come to see me?' I paid no attention to it. A few days later there was a second note: 'Governor, I have some papers you would not want to see displayed. Come to the jail.' I knew what he meant. I sent a copy of the old note and the story over to the paper and it was published. I sent him a copy of the paper and drew his fire. **It was then that he swore his vendetta on my life and on that of Pat Garrett, the sheriff of Lincoln County.**

The theme of Billy the Kid being a threat to him was also featured in Wallace's December 10, 1893 *San Francisco Chronicle* article titled "**Lew Wallace's Foe, Threatened by 'Billy the Kid,'** The Writing of "Ben-Hur" Interrupted, An Incident of the Soldier-Author's Career in New Mexico." Here, after Billy's escape from Lincoln's courthouse-jail, Wallace manufactured that Billy planned to come to Santa Fe to kill him in revenge for not getting the pardon - a projection of Wallace's own guilty conscience at his own betrayal of their pardon bargain, for which Wallace really did deserve punishment! Noteworthy, is that Blandina used for her journal identical themes of "Billy the Kid's" threat to Lew Wallace linked to Wallace's writing of his religious novel: *Ben-Hur: A Tale of the Christ*. In fact, Blandina's journal entry is much like the article, stating: " 'Billy the Kid' ... attempted to carry out his threat against Governor Wallace" [though Wallace was protected by friends]. The article stated similarly:

The news of the escape [of Billy the Kid from Lincoln's jail] quickly reached Santa Fe, and Governor **Wallace's friends became very uneasy lest the "Kid" should carry out his threat.**

Wallace's made-up "Billy the Kid" threat was presented in that article as follows:

"After I have settled accounts with these three men," said the desperado, "I will be willing to surrender and be hanged. When I get out **I will ride into Santa Fe, hitch my horse in front of the Palace, and walk in and put a bullet through Lew Wallace."**

And the article's theme of Billy the Kid's being a "terror on the frontier" was used by Blandina; and was in the article as: "The Governor's enemy was no less a personage than the illustrious "Billy the Kid," than whom no man had ever excited more terror on the frontier or given better ground for the dread in which he was held." The article stated:

LEW WALLACE'S FOE.
Threatened by
"Billy the Kid"
The Writing of "Ben-Hur" Interrupted.
An Incident of the Soldier-Author's Career in New Mexico.

General Lew Wallace, best known to the general public by his two great books, "Ben-Hur" and the "Prince of India," is a man of many roles. He has been successful as a soldier, politician, diplomat and author, and some startling experiences have fallen to his lot. His career on the battlefield, his life in Turkey, When he was Minister to Constantinople, and his later triumphs in the world of literature have all gone to make an eventful record, and they have all been so often recounted in the public prints that it would seem that every incident of his life would be familiar to those who keep themselves posted on the careers of public men. Yet there is one ordeal through which General Wallace has passed, and which he probably will never forget, that has escaped the vigilance of the scribes. It is, probably, not generally remembered that General Wallace was once Governor of the Territory of New Mexico, but it is a fact that in 1880, and for a year or so after that, he occupied the former palace of the Captains-General of Spain, in the historic old town of Santa Fe, N.M. He was the chief executive of the Territory, by appointment of President Garfield [sic-Hayes], and it was during his administration that he fell under the ban of an assassin, and was given very good reason to believe that he would have to look down the ugly barrel of a 45-caliber revolver, and to defend his life as best he might.

The Governor's enemy was no less a personage than the illustrious "Billy the Kid," than whom no man had ever excited more terror on the frontier or given better ground for the dread in which he was held. He had perpetrated murder after murder and there were few crimes of which he was not believed to be capable. He boasted that he had killed more men than he was years of age and would shoot a man if he felt so disposed, "just to see him kick."

After "Billy the Kid" had been carrying things with a high hand for a long time Governor Wallace offered a reward for his capture. It proved a tempting bait to the "gun fighters" and officers of the law in the Territory. There were plenty of men among them who would not shirk from a hunt through the mountain fastnesses, even after such formidable game as this border bully, and the result of the Governor's offer was that after a most exciting pursuit "Billy the Kid" was surrounded by overwhelming numbers and forced to surrender. He was taken to Santa Fe and thence to Lincoln County to answer a charge of murder.

Enraged at having been trapped, the outlaw swore that if he ever regained his liberty he would kill three men. One was a judge who had passed sentence upon him, one was Pat Garrett of Lincoln county, who had been conspicuously active in effecting his capture, and the third was Governor Lew Wallace.

"After I have settled accounts with these three men," said the desperado, "I will be willing to surrender and be hanged. When I get

out I will ride into Santa Fe, hitch my horse in front of the Palace, and walk in and put a bullet through Lew Wallace.

This seemed idle boasting at the time, because there appeared to be not the remotest possibility of the prisoner's escape. He was in the custody of Sheriff Garrett in the County Jail of Lincoln, and the Sheriff, besides being a cool, courageous and reliable man, had every incentive to be watchful of his charge. It was thought a pretty sure thing that Garrett would never let the "Kid" go, and Governor Wallace felt fairly secure in his office away off in Santa Fe.

Garrett appointed as guards over the "Kid" Bob Ollinger [Olinger] and John [James] Bell. They were his personal friends, both big, burley six-footers, who towered over their diminutive prisoner. In addition to this physical superiority over him, they counted themselves as his equals when it came to a fair and square gun-fight. If anyone had told them that the "Kid" would outwit them and escape they would have laughed at the very thought of it.

For months the "Kid" was a docile as a kitten. The guards became used to him, then familiar, and then friendly. He seemed to have forgotten that they had helped to cage him and were his custodians, and as time passed the trio became boon companions. The guards laughed at the "Kid's" stories of his exploits, played cards with him during their long watches and would often remove one of the "cuffs" from his wrist, so that he could manipulate his cards or ply knife and fork at meal times. Whenever this was done both handcuffs were fastened to the right wrist, and thus locked in a cell with one of his stalwart guards the little cutthroat was safe enough.

Ollinger and Bell took turns watching in the jail and relieved each other to go to dinner. One day when Ollinger had gone across the street to a restaurant Bell took the "Kid" from his cell to an up-stairs room in the little two-story adobe jail. He put some food on a table for him and then unfastened the left cuff and locked it on the prisoner's right wrist.

The "Kid" sat down and began to eat without the slightest apparent concern. While he was munching the coarse prison fare Bell strode restlessly up and down the room. He wore no coat and his heavy revolver protruded from the holster attached to his cartridge belt. Each time he walked the room he passed within two feet of where the "Kid" sat, and once when he came within reach the "Kid," with the quickness of a cat, leaped upon his chair and dealt him a rap on the head with the handcuffs. Bell staggered under the blow, and before he could recover the "Kid" has snatched the revolver from the holster and sent a bullet through Bell's body. The guard tottered and fell and in a few moments was dead.

Ollinger was across the street and had, no doubt, heard the shot. The outlaw seized a double-barreled shotgun and ran out on the front balcony. Already Ollinger had crossed the street. He had come on the run, but before his foot struck the steps he fell with a load of buckshot in his heart.

The murderer walked carelessly down the stairs, stepped over Ollinger's prostrate form and strutted down the street with the revolver and shotgun in his hands. A blacksmith was shoeing a horse in a neighboring shop, and "Billy the Kid" easily persuaded him to desist, then mounted and rode out of town at a walk, saying just before he started: **"Now for the Governor."**

The news of the escape quickly reached Santa Fe, and Governor Wallace's friends became very uneasy lest the "Kid" should carry out his threat. The Governor himself was not entirely tranquil in the circumstances. It is one thing to face an enemy in the open field and quite another to have a treacherous one dogging one's footsteps.

Brave as Governor Wallace had shown himself to be, he recognized his danger and prepared to meet it. At that time he had already begun "Ben-Hur," and used to sit for hours in his office each day engaged upon the absorbing work. From the day upon which "Billy the Kid" escaped from the Lincoln County jail a close observer entering the office might have detected lying on the table, partially hidden among papers and scraps of manuscript, the glint of a pistol, for the Governor was never without one while he knew that his arch-enemy was at large.

The people of Santa Fe were well aware that the head of the Territorial Government was preparing for war for every morning about 7 o'clock the sharp crack of a revolver being fired rapidly resounded from the corral in the rear of the gubernatorial residence. It soon became known that it was Governor Wallace improving himself as a pistol shot preparatory to an impromptu duel with "Billy the Kid." A figure had been marked on the adobe wall of the corral, and the Governor filled it full of holes. He became so expert that he could knock an imaginary eye out of the figure at twenty paces. He made no bones of the matter and, in fact, could be easily seen from the adjoining houses.

During the weeks which elapsed before the termination of this period of suspense Pat Garrett was in hot pursuit of "Billy the Kid." It was a most remarkable and exciting chase. The whole Territory was deeply intent upon it, and news of the whereabouts of the two men was eagerly looked for. Governor Wallace repeatedly said to the writer: "When these two men meet one or both of them will bite the dust."

He was right. The announcement finally came from Fort Sumner that Garrett had forever rid the country of the "Kid." He had tracked him to the house of Peter Maxwell, near Fort Sumner, and, concealing himself in one of the rooms, had fired one shot at his man. That shot passed through the desperado's heart and he fell dead in his tracks.

Governor Wallace breathed easier, and the next night a reporter found tall, muscular Pat Garrett waltzing with a four-foot Mexican girl in a dance hall of Santa Fe.

On January 6, 1894, a month after Wallace published his violent Billy the Kid fantasy of "Lew Wallace's Foe," he gave a "Billy the Kid" interview to the Weekly *Crawfordsville Review* as "Street Pickings." For it, Wallace again fabricated himself as the object the Kid's vengeful obsession, as well as Billy the Kid's being a murderous monster. Wallace was quoted: "[Billy the Kid] was wildly enraged at having been trapped and swore that the moment he got free he would ride clear through to Santa Fe, shoot me down and then gladly hang."

The article stated:

Street Pickings

Gen. Lew Wallace is a dead-shot with the pistol. Speaking of how and why he acquired such expert marksmanship, the renowned author-soldier said a few days ago in conversation with a party of friends:

"**When I was governor of New Mexico that territory was and had been for years terrorized by bands of daring and murderous outlaws, at the head of whom was the famous border desperado, "Billy the Kid." By virtue of my office I became this man [sic] deadliest enemy. No man ever excited more terror along the frontier or gave better ground for the dread in which he was held than this man. He perpetrated murder and their [sic] were few crimes of which he was not guilty. He had openly boasted that he killed nearly fifty men and enjoyed shooting a man down 'just to see him kick.'** I determined to rid the territory of this scourge and offered a large reward for his capture. The offer proved to be a great sensation throughout the territory and a tempting bait to ready shooters and officers of the law. There were in the territory hundreds of men who accepted with great delight this opportunity to take a hunt through the mountains after such formidable game. Well, the result was that after a most exciting chase the outlaw was surrounded by overwhelming numbers and compelled to surrender at the point of fifty guns after shooting down three of his pursuers. **He was taken to Lincoln county, away up in the state, to answer an unusually flagrant murder. He was wildly enraged at having been trapped and swore that the moment he got free he would ride clear through to Santa Fe, shoot me down and then gladly hang.**

"I knew the character of the man and while never dreaming that he would ever again be at large, I determined in order to be safer, to begin pistol practice in case an impromptu duel should ever take place between us. I got a brace of the best pistols I could find and every morning spent an hour in the corral firing at a mark. In a few weeks I got so I could hit the figure of a man marked out on the wall at twenty paces about every time. And as I became more and more skillful, I felt correspondingly safer and didn't much dread an open meting even with the caged murderer and with my life for the stake.

"Two months dragged along and one day at Santa Fe we got the alarming news that "**Billy the Kid" had murdered his two jailors, stolen a horse and had started for Santa Fe with the open threat, 'Now for the governor and now hang.'** Then I began practicing several hours every day and for weeks I was in daily expectation of meeting the ruffian. I still went about my duties, but heavily armed with my pistols ever ready. Pat Garrett was the sheriff to whose charge "Billy the Kid" had been entrusted, and when he learned a half-hour afterward and while away from home, that 'Billy the Kid' had escaped, he started in hot pursuit. For weeks there was unbroken suspense during which he heard nothing from the pursuer or pursued. They were both dead shots and there would be killing when they met. It was a most remarkable and exciting chase. The whole territory was deeply intent upon it and news of the whereabouts of both men was eagerly awaited.

"Finally, one day there rode up to my residence a travel-stained six-footer in a wide sombrero hat, mounted on a pony worn out with hard work. He got off, let his pony wander loose and came up to the door. I met him on the front step with my guns ready for instant use and asked him his errand. 'I am Pat Garrett, governor, and have just shot 'Billy the Kid' out here at Ft. Sumner.' And it was true. **He had come up with the desperado heading for Santa Fe to end me, had got the drop on him and without a word shot him through the heart**. I have still kept up my practice somewhat, but not under as thrilling circumstances.'"

SMOKING GUNS FOR A HOAX: The idea that Billy the Kid had a vendetta against Lew Wallace was fabricated by Lew Wallace. Its use in Blandina's journal shows the reliance on sources. And her journal dates it to 1882, when Billy was dead. And the 1948 "correction" to March then April of 1881 was also fake, since on those dates Billy was first in jail in Santa Fe, then jailed in Lincoln. Indicated is the later creation of fabricated entries.

USING CONTEMPORARY PRESS AS SOURCES FOR LEW WALLACE INTERVIEWING BILLY THE KID

SLEUTHING HOAXBUSTING CLUES: By mentioning Lew Wallace's "interviews" of Billy the Kid, Blandina's journal used true information available only in Wallace's own articles, some from the 1900's.

BLANDINA'S REFERENCE TO LEW WALLACE'S BILLY THE KID INTERVIEWS

Though not mentioning Wallace's pardon bargain with Billy Bonney, Blandina cited "interviews" for it which he had with the boy in Lincoln County. For her entry from Santa Fe, dated for 1932 as "January, 1881," Blandina wrote:

> Our Governor, Lewis Wallace, has shown heroic bravery by going to Lincoln County to try to pacify the storm. **He had a number of interviews with "Billy,"** but to no effect.

LEW WALLACE'S OUTLAW MYTH ARTICLES REFERENCE HIS BILLY THE KID INTERVIEW

Because Lew Wallace was unconsciously guilty about betraying his pardon bargain with Billy Bonney, he spent over 20 years writing long articles to reverse his own blame. For these fictions, he devised the outlaw myth of Billy the Kid, with his offering a pardon, and Billy's betraying its conditions. That involved reversing how he and the boy originally made that bargain. Wallace wrote that he - rather than Billy - devised the deal for Billy's testifying against the murderers of Attorney Huston Chapman to get it. And their March 17, 1879 meeting to formalize the bargain was switched by Wallace from the Lincoln County town of Lincoln, to Santa Fe.

Blandina was apparently uninterested in the notion of a pardon. What struck her was that her good guy Wallace met with her bad guy "Billy." And, using Wallace's articles, she determined that, as she wrote, "interviews" were "to no effect."

As can be seen from Blandina's likely source articles below, her using the word "interview" was telling, since Wallace used it only in a 1902 article, when "explaining the purpose of the **interview** and its result with "Billy;" rather than the more accurate word "meeting" for discussing the pardon bargain.

When Billy still alive, Wallace began his outlaw myth articles with the reworked pardon bargain meeting. For the May 16, 1881 *St. Louis Daily Globe-Democrat*, he created "The Thugs Territory, Stage Robbers and Cut-Throats Have Things Their Own Way in New Mexico, Gen. Lew Wallace Anxious to Punish Crime that is So Prevalent - A Chapter About "Billy the Kid," as discussed above. Its version of the meeting is switched it to Santa Fe and the bargain is betrayed by Billy; as follows:

Finally [Wallace] learned that [Billy the Kid] was in the mountains a short distance from Santa Fe, and sent a messenger with a note to the outlaw, saying that if he knew anything about the matter and was willing to give his evidence before the Grand Jury, he would grant him a pardon, providing he also led a different life. **Billy was to meet him at a certain house in Santa Fe at 12 o'clock on a certain night and date, and the matter would be thoroughly discussed.** At the appointed time GOV. WALLACE was at the house, and exactly at 12 o'clock a knock was heard at the door and in walked "Billy the Kid," A long talk followed, and it was agreed that the Sheriff should arrest him to protect him from the pals of the murderer. The Governor's idea in granting a pardon to Billy was to capture the leader and break up the gang. On the next day the Sheriff with a posse of men captured Billy and he was brought before the Grand Jury, testified, and two of the men were sentenced to be hanged on Billy's evidence. Since the day Billy received the Governor's letter he has been leading the life of a murderer, stage robber, etc., and felt that the [pardon promise] letter would forever shield him from the law should he be captured.

On June 13, 1881, back home in Crawfordsville, Indiana, Wallace gave an interview with the Crawfordsville *Saturday Evening Journal*, titled "Billy the Kid, General Wallace Tells Why the Young Desperado of New Mexico Wanted to Kill Him. A Dashing and Daring Career in the Land of the Petulant Pistol," discussed above. It had the pardon meeting, called a "conference," at an unclear location. It stated:

Governor Wallace heard that the "kid" saw the murder, and finding a man who could find Billy, sent him a note **requesting a conference with him at midnight at a certain house which was designated.** The note assured the "kid" that if the conference proved that he did not have the necessary information about the murder he would be permitted to leave the city, but if he did and would testify before the grand jury, the note implied that the Governor would pardon him for crimes for which he had been indicted, provided he would leave the Territory for good.

Governor Wallace repaired to the **meeting place** early, and promptly at midnight, a slight knock was heard at the door and upon response in the inside, "Billy the Kid" opened the door and walked in. The Governor found Billy to be a mild-faced young man, 19 years old, small, slender, sloping shoulders, manly head, and an open expression of the face, and a deliberate and pleasant voice ... The Governor asked him if he would go before the grand jury and tell the same thing [that he had witnesses]. Billy's reply was that he would not dare to do it voluntarily, as the criminals' friends would kill him. The Governor suggested that the difficulty might be surmounted by the "kid" permitting himself to be captured. This was agreed upon, and accordingly and by arrangement Billy was surprised at a safe place in the mountains, while asleep, captured, and taken to jail. He went before the grand jury and by his evidence the criminals were indicted for murder. But before the trial in which he was to appear as a witness for the prosecution, he tired of jail life, and one day at dinner, he left his guards and took to the mountains.

On June 23, 1900, Wallace published in *The Indianapolis Press*: "Gen. Wallace's Feud with Billy the Kid, When the General Was Governor of New Mexico and Billy Bonne Was the Most Dangerous Western Outlaw, He Was a Waif and was Reared in Indiana;" as discussed above. Its rendition of the pardon meeting - with Billy as pardon bargain betrayer - was again called a "conference." The article stated:

'Come in,' I said. The door flew open and there stood the most feared, the most adored, the most reverenced man in New Mexico, hunted by every limb of the law as a criminal, and sought by every Spanish senorita as her lover. The room was covered by a Winchester rifle held in one hand. In the other was a Colt's revolver. It was a musical growl that said, **"I was to meet the Governor here at midnight.** It is midnight: is he here?"

"I asked him to **come in for a conference,** and told him that I was the Governor of New Mexico.

"Your note gave me the promise of protection," he said.

"There is no one here but us three," replied I, pointing to the owner of the cottage.

"Billy threw his gun over his arm and came straight to the table near which I sat ...

[They made the agreement and Billy was jailed] "It was a week before the trial. Billy had been taken to dinner in his chains. After the meal he said: "Well, I wish you would tell the Governor that I am tired. Much obliged boys,' and leaving them as though in a trance, he quietly walked across the street, and, unhitching a horse, dashed out of town.

Wallace only used the word **"interview"** for the pardon meeting in his June 8, 1902 *New York World Magazine* article titled: "General Lew Wallace Writes a Romance of 'Billy the Kid' Most Famous Bandit of the Plains, Thrilling Story of the Midnight Meeting Between Gen. Wallace, Then Governor of New Mexico, and the Notorious Outlaw, in a Lonesome Hut at Santa Fe." This version is set in Santa Fe, with the usual reversal of roles to make Billy the bargain betrayer, stating:

Gen. Wallace was able to effect an important arrangement with the outlaw, of which he gives the details. In fact, a very friendly understanding was established between the two.

Explaining the purpose of the interview and its result with "Billy," Gen. Wallace says:

"Shortly before I had become Governor of New Mexico, Chapman, a young attorney in Lincoln, had been murdered. Half a dozen men were arrested, accused of the crime ...

When I reached New Mexico it was declared on every hand that "Billy the Kid" had been a witness to the murder. Could he be made to testify?

"That was a question on the tip of every tongue.

"I had been sent to the Southwest to pacify the territory; here was an opportunity I could not afford to pass by. Therefore I arranged the meeting [with Billy the Kid] ...

"When 'Billy the Kid' stepped to the chair opposite mine, I lost no time in announcing my proposition.

Agrees to the Plan.

" 'Testify,' I said, 'before the Grand Jury and the trial court and convict the murderer of Chapman and I will let you go scot-free with a pardon in your pocket for all your misdeeds.'

" 'Billy' heard me in silence; he thought several minutes without reply.

" 'Governor,' said he, "if I were to do what you ask they would kill me."

" 'We can prevent that," said I.

"Then I unfolded my plan. 'Billy' was to be seized while he was asleep. To all appearances, his capture was to be genuine ...

The plan agreed upon in the cabin on the lonely mesa at midnight was carried out to the letter. "Billy the Kid" was seized the following morning and confined in the Lincoln County jail ...

"Billy," though at his own request kept in irons, did not remain long confined ...

The manacles slipped like magic from his wrists. The guards stood stupefied, and "Billy the Kid," laughing mockingly, walked leisurely from the jail yard, through the gate and across the street. Easily, gracefully, he threw himself into the saddle on the back of a horse standing near at hand and, putting spurs to the animal, dashed away. "Billy" was gone.

THE REAL LEW WALLACE-BILLY THE KID INTERVIEWS

Illustrative of the destructive quality of Blandina's "Billy the Kid" fables, is her perpetuation of Lew Wallace's own despicable fabrication that Billy Bonney had betrayed their pardon bargain - or as Blandina wrote: "He had a number of interviews with "Billy," but to no effect." The facts make clear the breathtaking injustice done by Lew Wallace, and of Blandina's promotion of that hypocrite.

In fact, after the Lincoln County War's end on July 19, 1878, Billy Bonney, unlike the other primary freedom fighters, refused to be chased from New Mexico Territory by Santa Fe Ring terrorism. He retained the Regulators' idealistic mission of opposing the Ring, which he did by petty guerilla rustling of Ringites' stock for the remainder of 1878.

The arrival of non-Ringite new Governor Lew Wallace on October 1, 1878, brought hope to New Mexico Territory citizens. But on February 18, 1879, anti-Ring attorney, Huston Chapman, was assassinated by Ringites in Lincoln. Billy was an eye-witness. The two events combined in Billy's mind, yielding the pardon plan: to make an alliance with Wallace by offering his testimony against the murderers in exchange for a pardon for his indictments for three murders committed during the Lincoln County War. A pardon would free Billy of the risk of being hanged by the Ring - in fact, his federal indictment had been prepared by Ring head, Thomas Benton Catron, himself. And an alliance with non-Ringite Wallace, could advance Billy's own anti-Ring agenda.

So on March 13, 1878, in his fine Spencerian script, Billy made his surprising proposition to Lew Wallace, who was then staying in Lincoln in the aftermath of the Chapman murder. And what Billy offered was just what Wallace needed. Wallace, more interested in writing *Ben-Hur* and decorating the Palace of the Governors, had done nothing but write a meaningless Amnesty Proclamation for people not already indicted in the War. Citizens were enraged, and Ring injustices were continuing, culminating with Chapman's murder. Billy wrote:

> To his Excellency the Governor
> General Lew Wallace
> Dear Sir I have heard that You will give one thousand $ dollars for my body which as I can understand it means alive as a witness. I know it is as a witness against those that murderd M<u>r</u> Chapman. if it was so as that I could appear at court, I could give the desired information. but I have indictments against me for things that happened in the late Lincoln County War and am afraid to give up because my Enimies would Kill me the day M<u>r</u> Chapman was murderded I was in Lincoln, at the request of good citizens to meet Mr J.J. Dolan to meet as Friends, so as to be able to lay aside our arms and go to Work. I was present when M<u>r</u> Chapman was murderded and know who did it and if it was not for those indictments I would have made it clear before now if it is in your power to Anully those indictments I hope you will do so so a to give me a chance to explain. please send me an annser telling me what you can do You can send annser by bearer
>
> I have no wish to fight any more indeed I have not raised an arm since your proclamation. As to my Character I refer to any of the Citizens. for the majority of them are my Friends and have been helping me all they could. I am called Kid Antrim but Antrim is my stepfathers name.
> Waiting an annser I remain
> Your Obedient Servant
> W.H. Bonney

After their meeting (the "interview" cited by Blandina) on March 17, 1879 in the Lincoln house of Justice of the Peace John Wilson to arrange the pardon terms, Billy devised a sham arrest so his Ringite adversaries would not realize he would be a prosecution witness in the upcoming Grand Jury the following month and kill him. In his confirming letter of March 20, 1879 - just three days after their meeting - Billy made clear to Lew Wallace that he knew he was risking his life; writing:

San Pat<u>ricio</u>

Lincoln <u>County</u>
Thu<u>rsday</u> 20th <u>1879</u>
General. Lew. Wallace:

Sir. I will keep the appointment I made. but be Sure and have men come that You can depend on I am not afraid to die like a man fighting but I would not like to be killed like a dog unarmed. tell Kimbal [sic - Sheriff Kimbrell] to let his men be placed around the house and for him to come in alone: and he can arrest us. all I am afraid of is that in the Fort we might be poisoned or killed through a window at night. but You can arrange that all right. tell the Commanding Officer to watch)Let Goodwin(he would not hesitate to do anything there Will be danger on the road of Somebody Waylaying us to kill us on the road to the Fort. You will never catch those fellows on the road Watch Fritzes Captain Bacas ranch and the Brewery they Will either go to Seven Rivers or to Jicarillo Mountains they will stay around close untill the scouting parties come in. give a spy a pair of glasses and let him get on the mountain back of Fritzes and watch and if they are there there will be provisions carried to them. it is not my place to advise you, but I am anxious to have them caught, and perhaps know how men hide from Soldiers, better than you. please excuse me for having so much to say
and I still remain Yours Truly

W H. Bonney

P.S.
I have changed my mind Send Kimbal to Gutieres just below San Patricio one mile, because Sanger and Ballard are or were great friends of Camels [sic - Billy Campbell's] Ballard told me ~~today~~ yesterday to leave for you were doing everything to catch me. it was a blind to get me to leave tell Kimbal not to come before 3 oclock for I may not be there before

Billy's sham incarceration for the pardon bargain was in the home of his friend, the jailor, Juan Patrón. It was next door to the Lincoln house in which Lew Wallace was staying during his Lincoln County fact-finding visit. Since Billy believed he had forged an alliance with Wallace, he trustingly gave him an actual interview from custody on March 23, 1879 to inform him about the real Santa Fe Ring outlawry of cattle rustling then taking place. Wallace took notes, writing:

William Bonney ("Kid")
relative to arrangement
with him.

Notes:

3-23-1879

<u>Statements by Kid, made Sunday night March 23, 1879</u>

1. There is a cattle trail beginning about 5 miles above Yellow Lake in a cañon, running a little west of north to Cisneza del Matcho (Mule Spring) and continuing around the point of the Capitan Mountains down toward Carrizozo in the direction of the Rio Grande. Frank Wheeler, Jake Owens and Dutch Chris are supposed to have used this trail taking a bunch of cattle over. Vansickle told K. so. They stopped and killed two beavers for Sam Corbett – hush money to Vansickle to whom they gave the beavers. Vansickle also said the Owens-Wheeler outfit mentioning "Chris" Ladbessor using this trail for about a year, but that lately their horses had given out, and of 140 head which they started to work they had only got through with 40. That now they were going to the Reservation to make a raid on the Indian horses to work on.

<u>The Rustlers.</u>

The "Rustlers," Kid says: were organized in Fort Stanton. Before they organized as "Rustlers" they had been with Peppin's posse. They came from Texas. Owens was conspicuous amongst them. They were organized before the burning of McSween's house, and after that they went on their first trip down the county as far as the Coe's ranch and thence to the Feliz where they took the Tunstall cattle. From the Feliz they went to the Pecos, where some of them deserted, Owens amongst them. (Martin, known to Sam Corbett) was in charge of the Tunstall cattle, and was taken prisoner, and saw them kill one of their own party. On the same trip they burnt Lola Wise's house, and took some horses. Coe at the time was ranching at the house. On this trip they moved behind a body of soldiers, one company, and a company of Navajo Scouts. They moved in sight of the soldiers, taking horses, insulting women. Lorenzo Trujillo (Jus. Peder) Juan Trujillo, Jose M. Gutierres, Pancho Sanchez, Santos Tafoya, are witnesses against them. They stopped on Pecos at Seven Rivers. Collins, now at Silver City, was one of the outfit – nick-named the Prowler by the cowboys. At Seven Rivers. There joined them Gus Gildey (wanted at San Antonio for killing Mexicans) Gildey is carrying the mail now from Stockton to Seven Rivers – James Irvin and Reese Gobles, (rumored that their bodies were found in a drift down the Pecos) – Rustling Bob (found dead in the Pecos, killed by his own party) – John Selman (whereabouts unknown) came to Roswell while [Captain] *Carroll was there –*

The R's [Rustlers] *stayed at Seven Rivers; which they left on their second trip via the Berenda for Fort Stanton. On their return back they killed Chavez boys and the crazy boy, Lorenzo – and the Sanchez boy, 14 years old. They also committed many robberies. They broke up after reaching the Pecos, promising to return when some more horses got fat.*

Shedd's Ranch

The trail used going from Seven Rivers to Shedd's was round the S.W. part of the Guadalupe Mts. by a tank on the right hand of trail: from Shedd's the drives would be over to Las Cruces Jesse Evans, Frank Baker (killed) Jim McDaniels (at Cruces, ranging between Cruces and El Paso) Reed at Shedd's bought cattle from them – also sold cattle to E.C. Priest, butcher in Cruces. "Big Mose" (at Cruces last heard from) and [blank], deserter from cavalry – (went to Arizona)

Mimbres

Used to be called Mormon City – situated 30 miles on the road to Cruces from Silver City south. A great many of what are known as "West Harden gang" are there. Among them Joe Olney, known in Mimbres as Joe Hill; he has a ranch in old Mexico somewheres near Coralitos. He makes trips up in this country: was at Penasco not long ago.

San Nicholas Spring

Is about 18 miles from Shedd's Ranch on the road to Tularosa, left hand road. There's a house at the spring and about 4 or 5 miles from it N.W. is another corral of brush and a spring, situated in a cañon. There Jim McDaniels used to keep stolen Indian horses. McD. one of the Rio Grande posse. Kid says the latter is still used.

The Jones Family

Came from Texas. Used to keep saloon at Fort Griffin. The family consists of the father, Jim Jones, John Jones, boy about 10 years old, a girl about 13, and the mother. Marion Turner lives with the family, and he killed a Mexican man at Blazers Mill "just to see him kick." He had no cattle when the War started. The Jones, John and Jim, killed a man named Riley, a partner of theirs, on the Penasco 3 or 4 years ago.

Though Lew Wallace ignored Billy's efforts, and obsessively wrote years of articles to misstate the pardon bargain in attempt to mask the magnitude of his betrayal that caused Billy Bonney's death, he did have a confessional break-through of honesty three years before his own death. In his June 8, 1902 *York World Magazine* article titled: "General Lew Wallace Writes a Romance of 'Billy the Kid' Most Famous Bandit of the Plains;" he admitted:

"Testify," I said, **"before the Grand Jury and the trial court and convict the murderer of Chapman and I will let you go scot-free with a pardon in your pocket for all your misdeeds."**

And Billy had done just that; but no pardon was ever issued by Wallace. That is why captured Billy wrote to Wallace from the Santa Fe jail on March 4, 1881, attempting unsuccessfully to stimulate conscience in him:

I have done everything that I promised you I would, and you have done nothing that you promised me.

SMOKING GUNS FOR A HOAX: Blandina's reference to Lew Wallace's Billy the Kid "interviews" could only be from Wallace's newspaper articles, putting in question any real time journal entry, since Wallace only called his pardon bargain meeting with Billy an "interview" in 1902. Furthermore, Blandina's use of Wallace's misrepresented pardon meetings damages Billy Bonney's real history by her blaming Billy with the false claim that the Wallace "interviews" were to "no effect." The reality was that Billy's complying with all conditions of the pardon bargain was to "no effect" in getting dishonest Wallace to honor their agreement!

USING AN 1881 DIME NOVEL ON "BILLY THE KID"

SLEUTHING HOAXBUSTING CLUES: Besides the fact that Blandina's "Billy the Kid" tales are non-historic, is the peculiarity that they are about a Colorado highwayman. Her source may have been an 1881 dime novel about Billy LeRoy who was falsely called "Billy the Kid" by its hoaxing author. (See also Pages 320-341)

In a mind-boggling possibility of hoaxing within hoaxing within hoaxing, Blandina may have surreptitiously lifted the gist of her "Billy the Kid" fables from an 1881 hoaxing dime novel, which itself plagiarized hoaxed Billy the Kid claims of a Santa Fe Ring *New York Sun* article, as well as hoaxed Billy the Kid mythology of Lew Wallace articles!

The dime novel - discussed below for Billy LeRoy - is titled *Billy LeRoy: The Colorado Bandit*, and is thought to be authored by a Thomas Daggett for the *Police Gazette* series. Key for Blandina's purposes, was Daggett's putting his brutal highwayman named "Billy the Kid" in Colorado.

Daggett had plagiarized the December 20, 1880, *New York Sun* article, "Outlaws of New Mexico, The Exploits of the Kid and His Followers - War Against a Gang of Cattle Thieves and Murderers - The Frontier Confederates of Brockway, the Counterfeiter." (See Pages 210-216 for article) Daggett wrote:

> For a number of years the people of eastern New Mexico and Panhandle, Texas, have been harassed by a gang who have run off stock, burned ranches, and committed acts of violence and murder. <u>In the Winter of '80 their deviltry stirred the law-abiding citizens of New Mexico to take action against them.</u> **[Underlined text was added by Daggett].**

[AUTHOR'S NOTE: Possibly using Daggett or the *New York Sun* for her journal entry of "January, 1880," Blandina wrote; " 'Billy the Kid,' is using his gun freely. The people of the Territory are aroused and demand his capture, dead or alive. Rewards have been offered for his capture." And for her "March, 1881" entry, she wrote: "Billy the Kid['s] marauding has drawn the attention of the whole Territory."]

Daggett, still plagiarizing from the December 20, 1880, *New York Sun* article, wrote:

> Nearly every man in the county was under arms, and the troops were called out by Gov. Wallace to quell the disturbance. The Kid was mixed up in the affair, and had some narrow escapes. On one occasion

he was hotly pursued and was obliged to take refuge in a house in Lincoln, which was surrounded by sixty colored **["colored" added by Daggett]** solders.

To the demand to surrender, he only laughed and shot down a soldier just **to show that he was game.**

[AUTHOR'S NOTE: Possibly using Daggett or the *New York Sun,* Blandina features the word "game" in her "June, 1876" entry about her first meeting with "Billy the Kid." She wrote: " 'I understand that you have come to scalp our Trinidad physicians, which act I ask you to cancel.' Billy looked down at the sick man ["Schneider"] who remarked: 'She is game.' What he meant by that I am yet at a loss to understand."]

Still plagiarizing from the December 20, 1880, *New York Sun* article, Daggett wrote:

A few days afterward Gov. Wallace **[original stated: "Gov. Wallace a few days ago"]** offered a reward of $500 for his capture, and prominent citizens would make up a handsome purse in addition.

[AUTHOR'S NOTE: This reward idea linking Wallace and citizens is repeated by Blandina in her "July 23, 1880" entry as: "The Governor and the people in the Territory have offered big rewards for Billy the Kid's capture, dead or alive."]

Daggett next plagiarized from Lew Wallace's first Billy the Kid outlaw myth article for the May 16, 1881 *St. Louis Daily Globe-Democrat* titled "The Thugs Territory, Stage Robbers and Cut-Throats Have Things Their Own Way in New Mexico, Gen. Lew Wallace Anxious to Punish Crime that is So Prevalent - A Chapter About "Billy the Kid." (See Pages 217-219 for the full article) Daggett used Lew Wallace for a fictionalized rendition about his reward notices causing "detectives" to attempt capture of "murderous Billy."

[AUTHOR'S NOTE: Blandina's also used Wallace's reward notices for her own presentation: "The people of the Territory are aroused and demand ["Billy the Kid's"] capture, dead or alive. Rewards have been offered for his capture ... [After Lew Wallace's interviews with "Billy" had "no effect"] [n]ew rewards have been offered both by the Governor and the people to capture Billy."]

For the capture of Billy LeRoy as "Billy the Kid," Daggett portrayed him as devil-may-care, and his fellow outlaw brother as crestfallen, writing:

> [LeRoy said] "that he would be out of the "quay," as he termed the jail ... before the United States Marshals could arrive ... His brother, on the contrary, seemed to be in depressed spirits."

[AUTHOR'S NOTE: This contrast of LeRoy and another prisoner is like Blandina's May 16, 1881 (or 1882) journal entry about her alleged visit to the Santa Fe jail to see "Billy the Kid," where "Billy" is certain of escape, and his fellow prisoner, "Kelly," is dejected.]

SMOKING GUNS FOR A HOAX: Blandina's journal entries resemble text in the Billy LeRoy as "Billy the Kid" dime novel, which may have been her inspiration to create her "Billy the Kid" as a Colorado highwayman.

USING HOLLYWOOD WESTERNS

SLEUTHING HOAXBUSTING CLUES: Since Blandina's "Billy the Kid" scenes are very visual and action-filled, an inspiration may have been Hollywood Westerns.

A striking feature of Blandina's tales is their extreme visual detail, mad-cap action, and quaint chivalry. Since they appear to have been written in the 20th century, her inspiration may have been early Hollywood Westerns. One can see her cinematic style, reading the following:

[The "Billy the Kid" gang member] was mounted on a spirited stallion ... and was dressed as the *Torreros* (Bull-Fighters) dress in old Mexico. Cowboy's sombrero, fantastically trimmed, red velvet knee breaches, green velvet short coat, long sharp spurs, gold and green saddle cover. A figure of six feet three.

The leader, Billy, has steel-blue eyes, peach complexion, is young, one would take him to be seventeen – innocent-looking, save for the corners of his eyes, which tell a set purpose, good or bad.

[H]e raised his large-brimmed hat with a wave and a bow, looked his recognition, fairly flew a distance of about three rods, and then stopped to give us some of his wonderful antics and bronco maneuvers. The rider was the famous "Billy, the Kid!"

The two prisoners were chained hands and feet, but the "Kid" besides being cuffed hands and feet, was also fastened to the floor ... When I got into the prison-cell and "Billy" saw me, he said – as though we had met yesterday instead of four years ago – "I wish I could place a chair for you, Sister ..."

For a November 10, 2007 internet article titled "Cowboy Business," a Thomas Schatznov pointed out that from earliest films of the silent era of 1894 to 1927, to low budget sound films beginning in 1927 to 1928, the Western comprised nearly a fifth of them. They began with Edwin S. Porter's 1903 "Great Train Robbery," with a dramatic gunfight and outdoor scenes. By the mid-1920's, when Blandina was putting together her "Billy the Kid" journal entries, about half of Universal's 60 films a year were Westerns, most starring Hoot Gibson. Fox Film Corporation's Westerns starred Buck Jones and

Tom Mix, and included the 1924 big-budget "The Iron Horse" by John Ford.

A Tim Dirks of filmsite.org described early Western stars. Gilbert M. "Broncho Billy" Anderson (1881-1971) was the first Western film hero. He made about 400 "Broncho Billy" Westerns, beginning with "Broncho Billy and the Baby" (1910), and finishing his career with "The Son of a Gun" (1919). Noteworthy is the "Broncho Billy" nickname, which brings to mind Blandina's use of "bronco" instead of horse for her "**bronco maneuvers.**" Tom Mix (1880-1940) personified the wholesome hero with fancy costuming. He first appeared as Bronco Buster in Selig Polyscope's "Ranch Life in the Great Southwest" (1910), and then in many others (for Selig and later for Fox). They included "The Man From Texas" (1915); "The Heart of Texas Ryan" (1916); and expensive features like Fox's "Riders of the Purple Sage" (1925), and "The Great K & A Train Robbery" (1926). Noteworthy is that Mix was a rodeo rider who performed his own stunts. And one should recall Blandina's stunt-like riding created for "gang member Schneider" and "Billy the Kid" at the encounter on the plains.

SMOKING GUNS FOR A HOAX: The preposterously camp renditions of "gang member Schneider" and "Billy the Kid" can be understood in the context of their inspiration by early Hollywood Westerns.

OVERALL SMOKING GUNS FOR A SECOND-HAND CLAIMS HOAX: One can trace Blandina's second-hand Billy the Kid claims to books by Pat Garrett, Walter Noble Burns, and Ralph Emerson Twitchell; to newspaper articles dating from the 19th to 20th centuries; to a dime novel from 1881; and to Hollywood Westerns. Most incriminating is the entries' repeating tell-tale mistakes about the history from these later sources, then dating them earlier to feign 19th century journal writing. The outcome was the perpetuation of the entries' damaging fabrications of "Billy the Kid" to the present. And all these factors indicate hoaxing.

7

SLEUTHING BLANDINA'S FIRST-HAND ACCOUNTS OF CONTACTS WITH "BILLY THE KID" AND RELATED OTHERS

A HOAXER'S RISK OF EXPOSURE WITH FIRST-HAND ACCOUNTS

SLEUTHING HOAXBUSTING CLUES: A hoaxer is most vulnerable to exposure when giving alleged first-hand accounts. In her 1932 book, Blandina ventures three meetings with "Billy the Kid," many with his "gang member Schneider," one with inmate "Kelly," and one with Apache Chief Victorio. Her magazine articles add another meeting with "Billy the Kid" and his "friend Murphy," and with a "Paoline" Maxwell as a "Billy the Kid friend" also. All are open to comparison with reality.

After Blandina's magazine articles and 1932 book made readers believe that the her Old West journal entries were real, Blandina could have responded: "I never knew Billy the Kid." She never did. So she can now be judged on the veracity of her alleged first-hand experiences.

Recall that Billy the Kid hoaxer, Oliver "Brushy Bill" Roberts, had described the July 14, 1881 night on which he claimed Pat Garrett did not kill him as Billy the Kid. He said it was dark and moonless. But, not having been there, he was unaware of its giant, moon-illusion, near-full moon, making night as light as day. His lie was exposed by his garrulousness.

Blandina was likewise verbose about "Billy the Kid's gang members" and "Billy" himself - as in the gang member's "bull-fighter" costume, or details of her jail cell meeting with "Billy." If they fail historical scrutiny, each can be Blandina's own "dark and moonless night."

Complicating analysis, is Blandina's demand that her original journal be destroyed after its publication. Was that a noble protection of people's confidentiality - as the Sisters of Charity archivists believe? Or was it destruction of evidence?

MANY ENCOUNTERS WITH "BILLY THE KID'S GANG MEMBER SCHNEIDER"

SLEUTHING HOAXBUSTING CLUES: Blandina's multiple first-hand claims about Trinidad encounters with bull-fighter garbed "gang member Schneider" - including the date of meeting, newspaper reporting, a gang's existence, a connection to "Billy the Kid," and a committed crime of scalping - can be checked for reality.

BLANDINA'S WORDS

With *Veritas* and the 1932 book dated "September, 1876," from Trinidad, Blandina introduces a "Billy the Kid gang," and her meeting with his "gang member accomplice;" writing:

The Trinidad Enterprise – the only paper published here – in its last issue gave an exciting description of how **a member of "Bill's Gang"** painted red the **town of Cimarron** by mounting his stallion and holding two six-shooters aloft while shouting his commands, which everyone obeyed, not knowing when the trigger on either weapon would be lowered. This event has been the town talk, excluding every other subject, for the past week.

Yesterday one of the Vigilant Committee came to where I was on our grounds – acting as umpire for a future ball game - and said: "Sister, please come to the front yard. I want you to see one of **'Billy's gang,' the one who caused such fright in Cimarron week before last** ..."

We stood in our front yard, everyone trying to look indifferent, while **Billy's accomplice** headed toward us.

He was mounted on a spirited stallion of unusually large proportions, and was **dressed as the *Torreros* (Bull-Fighters) dress in old Mexico.** Cowboy's sombrero, fantastically trimmed, red velvet knee breaches, green velvet short coat, long sharp spurs, gold and green saddle cover. A figure of six feet three, on a beautiful animal, made restless by the tight bit – you need not wonder, the rider drew attention. **His intention was to impress you with the idea "I belong to the gang."**

For "September, 1876," Blandina presented other contacts with that flamboyant gang member, now called "Schneider" and nursed by her for his eventually fatal gunshot wound from fellow gang member, "Happy Jack," whom he fatally shot in the same encounter. To Blandina, he confesses his crimes and warns about "Billy the Kid's" intent to scalp Trinidad's doctors for refusing to remove the bullet from his leg. Blandina wrote:

[He said to me] "I have done all that a bad man can do. I have been a decoy on the Santa Fe Trail ... I dressed in my best when I expected to see horsemen or private conveyance take to the Trail. Addressing them politely, I would ask, 'Do you know the road to where you are going?' If they hesitated, I knew they were greenies. I would offer to escort them ... If they possessed money or jewelry, I managed to lose the trail at sunset and make for a camping place. **When they slept, I murdered them** ...

"Another thing I took pleasure in doing was to **shoot cows and steers for their hides** ... [He was apprehended by an old cattle owner from Kansas, and almost lynched, but persuaded the mans herders to let him go. When he returned to he gang, he told them] 'I'll wager ten cents I'll scalp the old man and throw the scalp on this counter'

[Finding the old man with his cattle, he said] **"I slipped up quietly behind him and passed my sharp knife round his head while holding his hair, and carried his scalp on a double run to where I left my bronco ...** [Returning to the gang, he said] "give me my dime."

"Sister, now do you think God can forgive me?"

I answered: "Turn to me in sorrow of heart and I will forgive, saith the Lord."

In the same entry of "September, 1876," Blandina described another visit with "gang member Schneider" in which he warned her about "Billy the Kid's" intent to scalp Trinidad's four doctors for refusing to remove the bullet from his leg. She wrote:

[Schneider] lost no time in telling me that Billy and the "gang" are to be here, Saturday at 2 P.M., and I am going to tell you why they are coming ...

"Well, the 'gang' is going to scalp the four of [the town's physicians] ... because not one of them would extract the bullet from my thigh ..."

I looked at the sick man a few seconds, then said: "Do you believe that with this knowledge I'm going to keep still?"

"What are you going to do about it?"

"Meet your gang at 2 P.M. next Saturday."

Only in the October, 1930, *The Santa Maria* edition, for journal entry "Albuquerque, New Mexico. (Scraps found in Saratoga trunk.) Cherry season. 1884," did Blandina give a short version of the quarreling "Billy the Kid gang" members, but spelled "Schneider" as "Snyder." She wrote:

[It was at Dick Wooten's toll house that] "Happy Jack" and "Snyder" (two of Billy the Kid's gang) from friends became mortal enemies, keeping the "drop" on each other for three days ... At dinner on the third day, both thought the other off guard simultaneously. **Snyder shot "Happy Jack" through the heart; "Happy Jack's" shot caught Snyder in the thigh** ... Mr. Snyder was brought to Trinidad and thrown into an uninhabited adobe. It was in that adobe house that two of my pupils and I brought him daily nourishment, clean bandages, etc. He was ill nine months and, of course, he died because the ball was never extracted from his thigh.

ANALYSIS OF "SCHNEIDER" ENCOUNTERS

There is no verifiable truth in Blandina's "Schneider" encounters as connected to a "Billy the Kid gang." And she gave a different spelling of his name as "Snyder" for the magazine article. The following pertains:

1) The entry's date is "September of 1876" for "Billy the Kid's gang." For that entire year, 16 year old Billy Bonney lived in Bonita, Arizona. And he was never in Colorado.

2) Her alleged newspaper source for gang information - *Trinidad Enterprise* - did not exist in 1876. Trinidad's paper in 1876 was *The Enterprise and Chronicle.*

3) Cimarron was a town in New Mexico Territory, 51 miles from Trinidad, Colorado. For 1876, no incident of "a gang member painting the town red" as described by Blandina occurred in its local *Cimarron News And Press.*

4) As to a "Bill's Gang" or "Billy the Kid Gang," none was reported in Colorado newspapers in the 1872 to 1877 time Blandina lived there.

5) For her first encounter with "Schneider," in Trinidad, she portrays him as dressed like a matador, which is incompatible with 1870's Anglo, outlaw dress, like cowboys.

6) No highwayman gang members named "Schneider" (or "Snyder") - or his murder victim, "Happy Jack" - appeared in Colorado papers in the 1872 to 1877 time Blandina lived there. (But the names alone did appear in different contexts, as is discussed on Pages 365-373)

7) For her nursing encounters with wounded "Schneider," for "September, 1876," he improbably lists his crimes to include scalping. But scalping was associated with Native Americans or with bounty hunters of Native Americans. And no reference is made in the Colorado press in the 1872 to 1877 period of what would have been an attention-grabbing crime like a scalping done by outlaw "Schneider." (Period press on scalping is discussed below for Blandina's first Billy the Kid encounter.)

8) "Billy the Kid" is introduced improbably as planning to scalp local doctors for revenge.

9) For the October, 1930, *The Santa Maria* magazine, Blandina summarized her encounters with gang member "Schneider," but spelled the name as "Snyder."

SMOKING GUNS FOR A HOAX: There exists no verifiable encounter of Blandina with a career criminal and "Billy the Kid" gang member named "Schneider/Snyder." It is Blandina's apparent fiction demonstrating her confession and conversion of a bad person. Nothing in its specifics of date, newspaper report about a Cimarron incident, gang existence, costume, or scalping crime seem real. And Billy the Kid was never in Colorado, and had no gang there - or anywhere else. Noteworthy, however, is that Colorado newspaper reports do exist using the names "Snyder" and "Happy Jack," as discussed below on Pages 365-373, as the entries' likely sources for the names.

FIRST ENCOUNTER WITH ON-THE-LOOSE "BILLY THE KID"

SLEUTHING HOAXBUSTING CLUES: Blandina links "Billy the Kid" to her bad man "Schneider" in Trinidad in 1876. That requires Billy Bonney to have been in Colorado at that time, and to have had a gang.

Though Blandina claimed just two, brief personal encounters with on-the-loose "Billy the Kid," for her 1932 book's "January 1881" entry from Santa Fe, she inflated that by calling him "[m]y old acquaintance," implying a special relationship with that famous personage, along with its attention-grabbing potential for her readers.

BLANDINA'S WORDS

From Trinidad, for the *Veritas* date of "October 5, 1876" or the 1932 book's "June, 1876," Blandina gave her first meeting with "Billy the Kid;" writing:

> Saturday, 2 P.M. came, and **I went to meet Billy and his gang**. When I got to the patient's [Schneider's] room, the men were around his bed. The introduction was given. I can only remember, "Billy, our Captain, and Chism."
>
> I was not prepared to see the men that met me, which must account for my not being able to recall their names.
>
> **The leader, Billy, has steel-blue eyes, peach complexion, is young, one would take him to be seventeen – innocent-looking, save for the corners of his eyes, which tell a set purpose, good or bad** ... My glance took this description in while "Billy" was saying: "We are all glad to see you, Sister, and I want to say, it would give me pleasure to do you a favor."

I answered, "Yes, there is a favor you can grant me." He reached his hand toward me with the words: "The favor is granted."

I took the hand saying: "I understand you have come to scalp our Trinidad physicians, which act I ask you to cancel ..."

Billy then said, "I granted the favor before I knew what it was, and it stands. Not only [do I grant] that, Sister, but at any time my pals and I can serve you, you will find us ready."

I thanked him and left the room ...

Life is a mystery. What of the human heart? A compound of goodness and wickedness. Who has ever solved the secret of its working? I thought: One moment diabolical, the next angelical.

ANALYSIS OF FIRST ENCOUNTER WITH ON-THE-LOOSE "BILLY THE KID"

There is no verifiable truth in Blandina's first "Billy the Kid" encounter. The following pertains:

1) Blandina's date alteration between her magazine and her book indicate no real journal entry, and a mere creation made at the times of their publications.

2) Billy Bonney was never in Colorado, and was in Bonita, Arizona, in 1876 at the year of the alleged meeting.

3) Billy Bonney had no gang.

4) "Billy the Kid's" accompanying gang member, "Chism," appears to be a lifting of cattle king, John Chisum's, name.

5) Billy's description as young is an obvious extrapolation of his "Kid" moniker.

6) "Billy the Kid's" contemplated crime of scalping doctors is implausible, and seems to have been picked as the most repulsively depraved atrocity Blandina could conceive.

SCALPING

Scalping was never attributed to Billy Bonney, even in his most rabidly lurid, fantastical press - except by Blandina. It was associated with Native Americans; or with bounty hunters of Native Americans, using scalps as proof of killings.

But there were Colorado period articles available to Blandina to create her scalping tales; albeit with the perpetrators being Native Americans.

On April 25, 1872, Pueblo, Colorado, *The Colorado Chieftain* reported scalpings in Arizona, with additional crimes resembling Blandina's list for her "Billy the Kid Gang," stating:

By the last number of the Prescott *Miner*, dated the 6th inst., we see that the playful pets of Vincent Colyer, are **still amusing themselves by scalping settlers, burning houses, robbing stages and stealing horses.**

On January 1, 1876 was a Colorado Springs edition of *The Colorado Springs Gazette and El Paso County News*, whose "Personalities" section had a mention of a boy murderer named "Pomeroy," who read dime novels about scalping, and may have inspired Blandina's fictional "Billy" as a young scalping murderer, as follows:

Mr. James T. Fields visited Pomeroy, the boy murderer, in his jail recently, and learned from him that he had been a great reader of blood-and thunder stories. He had **read sixty dime novels, all about scalping** and other bloody performances, and he had no doubt these books had put the horrible thoughts into his mind which led to his murderous acts.

On July 21, 1876, scalping by Native Americans was cited in the Pueblo, Colorado, *Colorado Chieftain*, which stated:

While many of the officers and men of the army are engaged in propping up these miserable burlesques on government [in corrupt states], the **Indians are murdering and scalping the miners** in the Black Hills country and the settlers on the plains.

On August 24, 1876, "scalping" and a "gang" were put together for a tongue-in-cheek article on kidnapping of an unpopular judge for the Pueblo, Colorado, *Colorado Weekly Chieftain* titled "Kidnapping a Judge." It stated:

The telegraph announced on Tuesday evening that a special train carrying Judge Stone, Mr. Moffat and other interested parties to Boulder, where Mr. Moffat was about to qualify as receiver of the [rail]road [through questionable decision of Judge Stone], had been **captured by a gang** of masked men and Judge Stone carried off into the woods. Exactly what was done with the eminent jurist we have not learned, but **no doubt visions of scalping, burning and other savage amusements arose before the judge's eyes** as his masked captors carted him into their mountain fastness. His friends are probably uneasy about him, but we hardly think any permanent damage will be done him.

SMOKING GUNS FOR A HOAX: No facts support Blandina's 1876 meeting with Billy the Kid. The altered dating indicates no real journal entry, and its creation at the time of publication. The contemplated crime of scalping is not only unrelated to Billy Bonney, but is incompatible with its actual use by Native Americans and bounty hunters. Using the misspelled name "Chism" appears a awkward attempt to add a period detail. The "Billy the Kid" scene appears to be an artificial parable to show Blandina's spiritual goodness bringing forth honor in "Billy the Kid," as a very bad person.

SECOND ENCOUNTER WITH ON-THE-LOOSE "BILLY THE KID"

SLEUTHING HOAXBUSTING CLUES: Encountering "Billy the Kid" on the plains when traveling, continued Blandina's fiction of him as a Colorado highwayman. And his and her bizarre behavior in this second meeting lend to the suspicion of its being fiction.

Blandina's dramatically foreshadows her second meeting with on-the-loose "Billy the Kid," by making him a terrifying highwayman, about whom she is warned - without ever revealing to her companions that she knows him. From Santa Fe, with *Veritas* date "Fourth week in May [1877]," and 1932's "March, 1878," she describes her traveling from Santa Fe to the railroad near Trinidad with the Staab family, writing:

> Everybody is concerned about our going. Mr. [Adolph] Staab spoke to Sister [Augustine] and myself about the danger of travel (at the present time) on the Santa Fé Trail, owing to **Billy the Kid's gang**. He told us that the gang is attacking every mail coach and private conveyance ...
> If you ever get this journal [Justina], you will see how little fear I have of Billy the Kid's gang. Even if "Billy" has mustered new pals, I'm marked for protection as well as anyone wearing my garb. So I answered Sister's look by saying to Mr. Staab: "Where could the danger lurk being in the company of so many freight drivers?"

Still foreshadowing danger, for *Veritas's* "June 9 [1877]," and 1932's "June 9 [1878]," Blandina described the return carriage trip to Santa Fe with the Staab group, writing:

> [A member of the traveling group said] "The Kid is attacking the coaches or anything of profit that comes this way" ...
>
> **The "Kid" means Billy the Kid and gang ...** When I told Sister [Augustine] what the [man] said, she asked me how I felt about venturing. **"I have no more fear than if the gang did not exist."** "Well, then, in the name of God, we'll go" ...
>
> It was an understood thing that this return trip was to break the record in time, traveling from Trinidad to Santa Fé ... **We were told that "Billy's gang was dodging around, and we expect they will attack us tonight."**

For the actual second encounter with "Billy the Kid" - dated "June 9 [1877]" for *Veritas* and "June 9 [1878]" for 1932's book - Blandina described "Billy the Kid's" intercepting their carriage. She wrote:

> As the rider came from the rear of the vehicle ... I shifted my big bonnet, so that when he did look, he could see the Sisters [herself and Sister Augustine]. **Our eyes met; he raised his large-brimmed hat with a wave and a bow, looked his recognition, fairly flew a distance of about three rods, and then stopped to give us some of his wonderful antics and bronco maneuvers. The rider was the famous "Billy, the Kid!"**

ANALYSIS OF THE SECOND ENCOUNTER WITH ON-THE-LOOSE "BILLY THE KID"

There is no verifiable truth in the second encounter with on-the-loose "Billy the Kid." The following pertains:

1) The altered datings from magazine to book imply no real journal entry, and creations at the time of publication.

2) For the magazine dating of June 9, 1877, Billy Bonney was still in Bonita, Arizona, and did not return to New Mexico Territory until August 17, 1877. For the 1932 book's dating of June 9, 1878, it was the day after Billy gave his deposition about John Tunstall's murder to President Hayes's investigator in Lincoln County's town of Lincoln. During that month was also the build-up of Regulator activity leading to the July 14, 1878 Lincoln County War Battle.

3) Billy Bonney was not a highwayman. He robbed one mail coach in October of 1880 to steal Secret Service Agent Azariah Wild's reports to determine Wild's risk to him.

4) Blandina's encounter scene is made even more implausible by her peculiar demeanor. First she pretends not to know why other passengers would be afraid - though she knew from "Schneider" the gang's terrible crimes, and knew from "Billy" himself that he was a sadistic scalper. Then, rather than expressing nun-like compassion and reassuring the passengers that "Billy the Kid" had a treaty with her, she acts weirdly coy by keeping that secret - even from her fellow nun, Sister Augustine. And after recognizing her, this "Billy the Kid" likewise keeps secret their connection, but preposterously sticks around to be shot for a presumable bounty to the men in the party by performing "some of his wonderful antics and bronco maneuvers."

SMOKING GUNS FOR A HOAX: No facts support Blandina's 1877 or 1878 second meeting with Billy Bonney. The changed dating from magazine to 1932 book indicates the existence of no real journal entry, but of creations of the entries at the 20th century time of publication. And the odd encounter scene appears written for literary titillation of Blandina's having a special secret relationship with famous "Billy the Kid," instead of describing a real occurrence.

SANTA FE JAIL MEETING WITH "BILLY THE KID"

SLEUTHING HOAXBUSTING CLUES: Blandina ventured into historically well documented territory for her scene of meeting "Billy the Kid" in the Santa Fe jail. Any errors would be a give-away to hoaxing.

Blandina's entry for a third alleged meeting with "Billy the Kid" was set in a cell of the Santa Fe jail. It had a back-story of "Billy the Kid" being in jail with a murderer of a "tenderfoot" patient of hers. So Blandina's subsequent visit to the jail included an encounter with both men.

BLANDINA'S WORDS

BACK-STORY TO SANTA FE JAIL VISIT

Blandina first introduces the fellow inmate of "Billy the Kid" as a murderer of a "tenderfoot" miner who was a past patient of hers. That back-story is in *Veritas* as "April 24, 1881," and in the 1932 book as "April 24, 1882." It presents the victim and the murderer, later named just "Kelly." She wrote:

> We have a patient who is **a real tenderfoot, who came to prospect**. He tells me he is going to Los Corrilos. He is splendidly groomed and wears valuable jewelry. I advised him to leave all the valuables in the bank for safe-keeping and wear miner's clothes in camp. He did not take the precaution necessary. Two weeks later his corpse was consigned to St. Louis, his home city. Sunday he dressed in fine clothes. The miners take off Sunday, not to honor God, but to debauch. **When one of the miners ["Kelly"] saw our patient so well groomed, he said to him, "You have no right to be among us," and with his words went the shot that killed him.**

The murderer was intoxicated and is now **in jail with "Billy the Kid," who attempted to carry out his threat against Governor Wallace**, but the latter was well guarded by every honest man in the territory – hence Billy's capture. My first free hours will be to visit the prisoners.

VISIT TO THE SANTA FE JAIL

Blandina's visit to the Santa Fe jail is for *Veritas* date of "May 16, 1881," and the 1932 book's "May 16, 1882." It is Blandina's most troubling journal entry, pointing to willful hoaxing. It has extensive detail, including furniture and elaborate quoting of "Billy the Kid." "Kelly" seems an afterthought, and no mention is made of her "tenderfoot" patient, his victim. Blandina wrote:

I have just returned from the jail. The two prisoners were chained hands and feet, but **the "Kid" besides being cuffed hands and feet, was also fastened to the floor.** You can imagine the extreme discomfort of the position. When I got into the prison-cell and "Billy" saw me, he said – **as though we had met yesterday instead of four years ago** – "I wish I could place a chair for you, Sister."

At a glance I saw the contents of the prison. Two empty nail kegs, one empty soap box, one backless chair, upon which sat ["Kelly"] the man who shot our patient. After a few minutes talk, the "Kid" said to me:

"Do what you can for **Kelly**," pointing to the chair, "this is his first offense, and he was not himself when he did it. I'll get out of this; you will see, Sister."

Think, dear Sister Justina, how many crimes might have been prevented, had someone had influence over "Billy" after his first murder ... His ascendancy was instantaneous over the minds of our free-lance cowboys, who are spurred on by freedom that is not freedom. Finding himself captain and dictator, with no religious principles to check him, he became what he is – **the greatest murderer of the Southwest.**

I marvel at the assurance of the chained youth. No one can surmise how he can escape punishment this time. **Mr. Kelly,** his companion prisoner, is much dejected – fully realizing the enormity of his crime. Were not the doings of these two captives publicly known, I would not mention them – for what a prisoner says to me remains my property.

So Blandina's entry alleges the following:

1) "Billy the Kid" was captured after attempting "to carry out his threat against Governor Wallace;"

2) "Billy the Kid" was captured because Wallace "was well guarded by every honest man in the territory;"

3) the jail is in Santa Fe;

4) she is allowed entry into the cell to see "Billy the Kid" by herself and without any guard;

5) in the cell is another prisoner, named "Kelly;"

6) "Kelly" was there for murdering her "tenderfoot" patient, a fellow "miner;

7) the murder took place in "Los Corrilos;"

8) she recognizes "Billy the Kid" as the same outlaw she met "four years" ago (presumably in Colorado - making the date 1877 or 1878 depending on magazine dating or book dating, and not 1876 of her original date for meeting scalper "Billy the Kid," and 1877 and 1878 being when she was in Santa Fe, not Trinidad, Colorado of her first entries);

9) "Billy the Kid" likewise recognizes her;

10) "Billy the Kid" is chained hand and foot, and to a floor ring;

11) "Billy the Kid" is polite to her;

12) "Billy the Kid" feels sorry for "Kelly;"

13) "Billy the Kid" is certain of being able to escape himself; and

14) she calls "Billy the Kid" "the greatest murderer of the Southwest."

FOLLOW-UP TO SANTA FE JAIL VISIT

For her 1932 book's date of "June 20, 1882" (and absent from *Veritas*), Blandina wrote:

> On the fifteenth of last month [making it May 15, 1882], Mr. Lionel Sheldon took his place at the Palace as Governor. **A committee of two lawyers have asked me to make an appeal to the new governor in behalf of Mr. Kelly,** the murderer of one of our patients. Mr. Kelly makes no pretense. He is weighed down by the act he did while intoxicated.

ANALYSIS OF THE JAIL ENCOUNTER WITH "BILLY THE KID"

BLANDINA'S GLOBAL FACTUAL ERRORS

The jail encounter could not have happened as Blandina described it for the following reasons:

1) Blandina wrongly claims Billy the Kid was captured for attempting to carry out his "threat" against Lew Wallace. In

fact, Billy was arrested with warrants for his three Lincoln County War indictments of 1878.

2) Billy Bonney was in the Santa Fe jail from December 27, 1880 to March 28, 1881; and was not there for *Veritas's* "May 16, 1881" or the 1932 book's "May 16, 1882."

3) From December 27, 1880 to February 28, 1881, Billy Bonney was held awaiting trial in the same Santa Fe jail cell with two associates, Dave "Dirty Dave" Rudabaugh and Billy Wilson; along with an unrelated inmate named Edward Kelly.

4) Edward Kelly murdered a John Reardon in the Santa Fe County mining town of Carbonateville in the Cerrillos Mining District on October 13, 1880.

5) After the cell's inmates - Billy, Rudabaugh, Wilson, and Kelly - were caught in a tunneling-out jailbreak attempt on February 28, 1881, Billy Bonney was placed in solitary confinement until leaving the jail on March 28, 1881 for transport to Mesilla, New Mexico, for his hanging trial.

6) The only time Blandina could have seen Billy in the cell with Kelly was from December 27, 1880 to February 27, 1881 - not the dates she gave.

7) If Blandina had seen Billy with Kelly, Dave Rudabaugh and Billy Wilson would have been present also. But Blandina lists only a "Kelly" as present.

8) On December 28, 1880, Billy Bonney told a reporter that he was allowed no visitors, and repeated that in a letter to Lew Wallace on March 4, 1881.

9) If they did converse, real Billy Bonney would have made clear to Blandina - like he did with anyone who would listen - the injustice of his case. That is why he stated to a *Mesilla News* reporter on April 15, 1881, after his hanging trial: "I think it hard that I should be the only one to suffer the extreme penalty of the law."

10) Both Blandina and her "Billy the Kid" recognize each other from "four" years earlier. But four years earlier, for *Veritas* dating, is May of 1877, when he was in Arizona; and for the 1932 book's dating of May of 1878, he was in Lincoln County War skirmishes - and not in Colorado.

BLANDINA'S "KELLY" PROBLEM

It appears more than coincidence that Blandina houses a "Kelly" in the same Santa Fe jail cell with her "Billy the Kid." That name "Kelly" was in newspapers after February 28, 1881, when Edward Kelly - along with fellow inmate Billy Bonney - was caught in their attempted tunneling-out jailbreak. Less memorable for a reader like Blandina, would have been their other cellmates, Dave Rudabaugh and Billy Wilson, who were also in the jailbreak attempt. But Rudabaugh and Wilson would have been present for any jail cell meeting with Kelly and Bonney between December 27, 1880 and the attempted escape day of February 28, 1881. And on February 28, 1881, Billy was put in solitary confinement, so was not with Kelly after that. And Billy was removed, on March 28, 1881, for transport to his Mesilla trial, and was not returned to that jail. Kelly and Rudabaugh had been taken from the Santa Fe jail on March 7, 1881 for their trials in Las Vegas. Kelly was subsequently returned to the Santa Fe jail to await another trial. Rudabaugh was not. So Kelly and Billy Bonney could not have been together in the Santa Fe jail on or around the May 16, 1881 (or 1882) for Blandina's alleged visit.

Edward Kelly's biography was published by Philip J. Rasch in 1987 in an article for the *Quarterly of the National Association and Center for Outlaw and Lawman History*, titled "The Curious Case of Edward M. Kelly." Kelly's full name was Edward M. "Choctaw" Kelly. He had murdered a John Reardon on March 13, 1880, in the Santa Fe County mining town of Carbonateville.

For his Las Vegas trial in March of 1881, Kelly's attorney was Edgar Caypless, who also was one of Billy Bonney's lawyers. That same month, Kelly was sentenced to death; but Caypless got it commuted to life imprisonment.

Blandina had detailed Kelly's crime of murder. She had located the miner "tenderfoot" victim of "Kelly" to a "Los Corrilos." There is no such town. But real Edward Kelly's murder of John Reardon took place in Santa Fe County's Cerrillos Mining District, established in 1879. In specific, the murder occurred in the town of Carbonateville, mined for silver carbonate. And Blandina knew about the Cerrillos Mining District, having described a visit to it in a December, 1928, *Veritas* article for "At the End of the Santa Fe trial;" where she wrote about visiting a mine there; stating: "I took a Sister companion and rode to Los Cerrillos where the supposed mine was located."

That leaves Blandina's "Kelly" committing murder in non-existent **Los Corrilos**. And real Edward Kelly's murder was committed in the **Cerrillos Mining District** town of Carbonateville. They may have been different "Kellys." But the real "Kelly" imprisoned with the real Billy the Kid, strains credulity as not being Blandina's source for lifting "Kelly" and misspelled "Los Corrilos" for creating her "jail entry."

As to Kelly's murder victim, he did not correspond to Blandina's "tenderfoot" miner; nor did the murder scene match her creation. Blandina had written:

> We have a patient who is a real tenderfoot, who came to prospect. He tells me he is going to Los Corrilos. He is splendidly groomed and wears valuable jewelry. I advised him to leave all the valuables in the bank for safe-keeping and wear miner's clothes in camp. He did not take the precaution necessary ...Two weeks later his corpse was consigned to St. Louis, his home city. Sunday he dressed in fine clothes. The miners take off Sunday, not to honor God, but to debauch. **When one of the miners ["Kelly"] saw our patient so well groomed, he said to him, "You have no right to be among us," and with his words went the shot that killed him.** The murderer ["Kelly"] was intoxicated and is now in jail with "Billy the Kid."

According to Philip Rasch, Edward Kelly had been a local miner, but his partner was murdered. Kelly had then opened a dance hall in Carbonateville with a partner. On October 13, 1880, Kelly, his new partner, and two men named Jenks and Sullivan, went for drinks to Abbott's saloon. Kelly disputed payment of their bill with diminutive Sullivan. A big-bodied saloon patron named John Reardon took Sullivan's side. Kelly tried unsuccessfully to stab Reardon, left the saloon, returned with his Winchester carbine, and fatally shot Reardon.

Not realizing the extent of Blandina's fabricating, Philip Rasch addressed her journal's claim of her jail visit on May 16, 1881 (meaning that he used the 1948 edition of her book, since the 1932 book used 1882.) Rasch, perplexed, wrote that "[t]his date cannot possibly be correct."

He then addressed her shackling claim. She had written:

> [T]he "Kid" besides being cuffed hands and feet, was also fastened to the floor.

Rasch cited a March 1, 1881 Santa Fe *Daily New Mexican* article to refute her claim - while inadvertently presenting the article from which she likely constructed it - stating:

> Billy the Kid was not secured in this fashion until February 28, 1881, when a fellow prisoner [likely Kelly] informed Sheriff Romulo Martinez that Kelly, the Kid, Rudabaugh, and Wilson were digging their way out of their cell [and Billy was put in solitary confinement, where he was thus chained, but could not have been be seen by her].

Still trying to rationalize Blandina's meaningless May 16, 1881 date, Philip Rasch offered that after Edward Kelly's trial in Las Vegas, he was returned to the Santa Fe jail on about March 23, 1881. And Billy Bonney was not taken to Mesilla for his trial until March 28, 1881. So Rasch wondered if Blandina saw Kelly and Bonney for her jail visit in the last week of March. But this idea misses that Billy Wilson would have been present with Kelly, and Billy Bonney would not - being then in solitary confinement.

There was much press on Edward Kelly available to Blandina. And that would imply sources for her elaborate construction of "Kelly" as the murderer for her jail cell tale.

Philip Rasch stated:

> [Edward Kelly's] case received an enormous amount of attention in the Santa Fe and Las Vegas, New Mexico, newspapers, partly because it established new principles in Federal vs. Territorial relations.
>
> Due to outstanding coverage by the Santa Fe *Daily New Mexican* and the Las Vegas *Daily Optic* we know more about Kelly's life, his personal appearance, the facts of the murder, and the consequent ramifications of the case than is usually true.

For March 8, 1881, the Santa Fe *Daily New Mexican* had reported, under "Rudabaugh's departure," in a manner that may have revealed Blandina's reason for having no first name for "Kelly" for constructing her tale: his first name was not used by the press! The article stated:

> Dave Rudabaugh and **Kelly, who killed Reardon in Carbonateville,** were taken yesterday to Las Vegas to await trial. **Kelly,** it will be remembered, obtained a change of venue at the last term of the court in this city.

The March 22, 1881 edition of the Santa Fe *Daily New Mexican*, still lacking Kelly's first name, reported:

> **Kelly of Carbonateville**, who was accused of killing Reardon at that place some months ago, and who was taken to Las Vegas for trial having secured a change of venue from the court here, was tried on Saturday last and convicted of murder in the first degree ... The accused was remanded to jail, and yesterday he was brought back to Santa Fe and confined to jail here.

On March 23, 1881, the Santa Fe *Daily New Mexican*, still lacking Kelly's first name, stated:

> The Santa Fe jail is about the safest in the territory, and houses most of the desperate characters, murderers, etc. Among the inmates at present are **Billy the Kid**, Dave Rudabaugh, **Kelly,** Gallegos, and Billy Wilson.

BLANDINA'S NO VISITORS PROBLEM

Billy Bonney was a high security prisoner, with extreme risk of rescue by his freedom fighting partisans. He was allowed no visitors after being placed in solitary confinement on February 28, 1881. He was also considered dangerous, and a guard would have been present.

Billy himself documented the prevention of visitors in his letter of March 4, 1881 to Lew Wallace, writing:

> *Santa Fe. In jail.*
> *March 4th 1881*
>
> *Gov. Lew Wallace*
> *Dear Sir*
> *I wrote You a little note the day before yesterday but have received no annser. I Expect you have forgotten what you promised me, this Month two Years ago. but I have not, and I think You had ought to have come and seen me as I requested you to. I have done everything that I promised you I would, and You have done nothing that You promised me.*
>
> *I think when You think the matter over, You will come down and See me, and I can then Explain Everything to You.*
>
> *Judge Leonard, Passed through here on his way East, in January and promised to come and See me on his way back. but he did not fulfill his Promise. it looks to me like* **I am getting left in the Cold. I am not treated right by [U.S. Marshal John] Sherman. he lets Every Stranger that comes to See me through Curiosity in to See me, but will not let a Single one of my friends in, not Even an Attorney.**

ARTICLES AS SOURCES FOR THE JAILING

The jailing in Santa Fe of Billy Bonney as Billy the Kid was big news. Blandina, then living in Santa Fe, would have had many sources of information.

On December 28, 1880, the day after Billy's jailing, the Santa Fe *Daily New Mexican* announced his presence in "Behind the Bars, 'The Kid' and Two of His Gang in Limbo, They Now Roost in Santa Fe Jail." Blandina had written: "My first free hours will be to visit the prisoners."

In the jail, Blandina describes a brash "Billy the Kid" and a subdued "Kelly." This contrast was used similarly in a December 28, 1880 Las Vegas *Gazette* article, written six days after Billy's Stinking Springs capture, and, after he was held for a day in the Las Vegas jail. Billy spoke to Lucius "Lute" Wilcox, city editor for J.H. Koogler's Las Vegas *Gazette*, for an article to be called "The Kid. Interview with Billy Bonney The Best Known Man in New Mexico." In the cell were also Dave Rudabaugh and Billy Wilson. It stated:

Wilson scarcely raised his eyes, and spoke but once or twice to his compadres. Bonney on the other hand was light and chipper, and was very communicative ... "You appear to take it easy," the reporter said. "Yes! What's the use of looking on the gloomy side of everything. The laugh's on me this time," he said.

On December 30, 1880, the Santa Fe *Daily New Mexican* reported:

The custodians of the Santa Fe jail are apparently determined that The Kid shall have no opportunity to escape this time. He is shut up in a stone cell to which even the light of day is denied admittance, and only when some of the jailors or officers enter can he be seen at all. **He is nevertheless cheerful and hopes to escape even under the present circumstances. At least this is the supposition, for it cannot fairly be presumed that he hopes to be acquitted of all his crimes.**

Blandina had written:

I marvel at the assurance of the chained youth. No one can surmise how he can escape punishment this time.

HOAXBUSTING ANNOTATION OF BLANDINA'S SANTA FE JAIL SCENE TEXT

The extent of Blandina's misstatements can be revealed by their annotation, as follows:

Her entry for *Veritas* was dated "April 24, 1881," and for her 1932 book was dated "April 24, 1882."

[AUTHOR'S NOTE: This changed dating, incompatible with keeping a real journal, points to fix-up attempts to make the entry correspond to Billy the Kid history. It failed. Both dates are wrong for the jail scene. In April of 1881, captive Billy Bonney was in Mesilla, standing trial for his Lincoln County War indictments. In 1882, he was dead.

[AUTHOR'S NOTE: And if Billy LeRoy was Blandina's "Billy the Kid" (as will be debunked below), his dates do not correspond either. For March of 1881, he was first jailed in Pueblo, Colorado, then was escaping arrest during his transport to the House of Correction in Detroit, Michigan, to serve his 10 year sentence. On the run, he was in Kansas City in April; then home in West Liberty, Iowa, to recruit his brother as a fellow bandit. By May 13, 1881, he and his brother were in Colorado holding up stages, until they were captured and lynched on May 23, 1881. Thus, for any 1881 date, LeRoy was not in the Santa Fe jail. And for an 1882 date, he was dead.]

Blandina's entry dated for *Veritas* as "April 24, 1881," or the 1932 book's "April 24, 1882," is about her murdered "tenderfoot" patient. She wrote:

We have a patient who is a real tenderfoot, who came to prospect. He tells me he is going to Los Corrilos.

[AUTHOR'S NOTE: There is no town called "Los Corrilos." The name may be Blandina's corruption of "Cerrillos," from the Cerrillos Mining District where the real Edward Kelly murdered a John Reardon. This may be a researched attempt to insert her possibly fictional "tenderfoot" patient into her "Billy the Kid" tale, and to get herself into the jail scene.]

[The patient] is splendidly groomed and wears valuable jewelry. I advised him to leave all the valuables in the bank for safe-keeping and wear miner's clothes in camp. He did not take the precaution necessary. Two weeks later his corpse was consigned to St. Louis, his home city. Sunday he dressed in fine clothes. The miners take off Sunday, not to honor God, but to debauch. When one of the miners ["Kelly"] saw our patient so well groomed, he said to him, "You have no right to be among us," and with his words went the shot that killed him.

[AUTHOR'S NOTE: Blandina does not reveal how she knew the murderer's exact words, and it points to over-elaboration of fabrication.]

The murderer was intoxicated and is now in jail with "Billy the Kid,"

[AUTHOR'S NOTE: "The murderer" is later called "Kelly." This sets up Blandina's jail meeting with "Billy the Kid," though it is not explained why she wanted to meet the murderer of her "tenderfoot" patient.]

who attempted to carry out his threat against Governor Wallace,

[AUTHOR'S NOTE: As discussed above, this falsity of a Billy the Kid threat to Lew Wallace is taken from press fabrications - mostly written by self-aggrandizing Wallace himself. No such threat existed.]

but the latter was well guarded by every honest man in the territory – hence Billy's capture.

[AUTHOR'S NOTE: This fabricates that Wallace had a guard against Billy the Kid, and that his being guarded or allegedly threatened by Billy the Kid had anything to do with "Billy's capture." This is manufactured because Blandina obviously had no idea why real Billy Bonney was pursued for capture.]

My first free hours will be to visit the prisoners.

[AUTHOR'S NOTE: This masterfully sets up dramatic anticipation for her upcoming Santa Fe jail meeting.]

The Santa Fe jail encounter is dated for *Veritas* as "May 16, 1881" or for the 1932 book as "May 16, 1882."

[AUTHOR'S NOTE: Neither Billy the Kid, nor Billy LeRoy, were in the Santa Fe jail at either date. The manipulated dating indicates no real journal entry, and its creation at the 20th century time of publication.]

I have just returned from the [Santa Fe] jail. The two prisoners were chained hands and feet, but **the "Kid" besides being cuffed hands and feet, was also fastened to the floor.** You can imagine the extreme discomfort of the position.

[AUTHOR'S NOTE: This shacking description may have been gained from press reports of Billy Bonney's chaining in solitary confinement in the Santa Fe jail, or of his famous chaining in this manner in the Lincoln courthouse-jail from April 21, 1881 to April 28, 1881, while he awaited hanging, and then escaped anyway.]

When I got into the prison-cell

[AUTHOR'S NOTE: Billy the Kid was allowed no visitors. Even if Blandina had been allowed to visit, a guard would have been present because of the high security risk.]

and "Billy" saw me, he said – as though we had met yesterday instead of four years ago –

[AUTHOR'S NOTE: The fact that Blandina's "Billy the Kid" recognizes her, and she him, from "four years ago" is her attempted confirmation that he is one-and-the-same with her Trinidad, Colorado, "Billy the Kid" scalper highwayman from the 1870's (though four years back does not correspond to her original 1876 date). But this back-dating removes both the real Billy the Kid and Billy LeRoy from the running as her "Billy the Kid" character.]

"I wish I could place a chair for you, Sister."

[AUTHOR'S NOTE: This excessive detailing by dialogue is compatible with lying by confabulation or hoaxing.]

At a glance I saw the contents of the prison. Two empty nail kegs, one empty soap box, one backless chair,

[AUTHOR'S NOTE: Beds are oddly omitted; but this excessive and irrelevant detailing implies willful faking of a real experience.]

upon which sat ["Kelly"] the man who shot our patient.

[AUTHOR'S NOTE: This is an apparent ploy of inserting an actual cell-mate of real Billy the Kid in the Santa Fe jail scene: Edward Kelly. But real Kelly was transferred from the Santa Fe jail on March 7, 1881. He was returned on March 23, 1881, but Billy Bonney was then in solitary confinement before his transfer to Mesilla on March 28,

1881. And in 1882, Billy was dead. So, in Blandina's claimed May 16, 1881 or 1882, the combination of Kelly and Billy alone in a cell could not have occurred. So using Kelly indicates merely trying to make fable meet fact.]

[AUTHOR'S NOTE: But if Billy and Kelly were in the same cell at any time, a Dave Rudabaugh and a Billy Wilson would also have been present. Those two were there in real Billy the Kid's Santa Fe jail stay from December 27, 1880 to February 28, 1881, along with Edward Kelly. Omission of Rudabaugh and Wilson points to Blandina's fabrication of the scene.]

After a few minutes talk, the "Kid" said to me:

"Do what you can for Kelly," pointing to the chair, "this is his first offense, and he was not himself when he did it. I'll get out of this; you will see, Sister."

[AUTHOR'S NOTE: Though Blandina had allegedly come to see "Kelly," no contact or motive was described. And she (like everyone else in the Territory) presumably knew enough about Billy's famous Lincoln jailbreak on April 28, 1881 to add literary spice of prescience to her entry actually written later than its claimed date.]

Think, dear Sister Justina, how many crimes might have been prevented, had someone had influence over "Billy" after his first murder ... His ascendancy was instantaneous over the minds of our free-lance cowboys, who are spurred on by freedom that is not freedom. Finding himself captain and dictator, with no religious principles to check him, he became what he is – **the greatest murderer of the Southwest.**

[AUTHOR'S NOTE: This "greatest murderer of the Southwest" references Billy Bonney's outlaw myth press. The alternative, Billy LeRoy, was known as a highwayman and a road agent, not a murderer.]

I marvel at the assurance of the chained youth. No one can surmise how he can escape punishment this time.

[AUTHOR'S NOTE: Again, this may be a literary ploy to foreshadow Billy the Kid's subsequent Lincoln jailbreak (though the date of Blandina's visit was after it occurred on April 28, 1881).]

Mr. Kelly, his companion prisoner, is much dejected – fully realizing the enormity of his crime.

[AUTHOR'S NOTE: This contrast of brash Billy and subdued "Kelly," may have been inspired by a similar image of captured Billy and his captured companions from available press: A December 28, 1880 Las Vegas *Gazette* article by Lucius "Lute" Wilcox, titled "The Kid. Interview with Billy Bonney The Best Known Man in New Mexico," stated: "Wilson scarcely raised his eyes, and spoke but once or twice to his compadres. Bonney on the other hand was light and chipper, and was very communicative."]

Were not the doings of these two captives **publicly known**, I would not mention them – for what a prisoner says to me remains my property.

[AUTHOR'S NOTE: This reference may further confirm Blandina's use of "publicly known" press to get information for her tale.]

To follow-up on the "Kelly" theme, for her entry dated for the 1932 book's "June 20, 1882" (and not in *Veritas*), Blandina wrote:

On the fifteenth of last month, Mr. Lionel Sheldon took his place at the Palace as Governor.

[AUTHOR'S NOTE: Lionel Sheldon became New Mexico Territory Governor after Lew Wallace departed his incomplete term on May 28, 1881. This confirms that the 1882 dating for the 1932 book was made up, since that wrong date would have been obvious to any contemporary diarist or journal-keeper.]

A committee of two lawyers have asked me to make an appeal to the new governor in behalf of Mr. Kelly, the murderer of one of our patients. Mr. Kelly makes no pretense. He is weighed down by the act he did while intoxicated.

[AUTHOR'S NOTE: The real Edward Kelly did appeal the death sentence he got in Las Vegas, New Mexico, in March of 1881. If Blandina was later involved with Kelly's lawyer, Edgar Caypless, in getting that sentence commuted to life in prison, she might have obtained the kernel for her tale for her alleged Santa Fe jail visit. But such an extensive, successful, and precedent-making plea about a Territorial death penalty was something she likely would have put in her journal as a separate anecdote and achievement. And she certainly would have known "Kelly's" first name.]

SMOKING GUNS FOR A HOAX: No facts support Blandina's 1881 Santa Fe jail encounter with either Billy Bonney, or Edward Kelly as being present with him, at the same time. The journal entry merely used available historical information like the name "Kelly" and the fact that Billy the Kid had been in the Santa Fe jail. Later fix-up of the date for the book's subsequent editions implies that no real journal entry ever existed before creation for 20th century publication. And no match occurs for the necessary corollary of any gang-leading highwayman outlaw called "Billy the Kid" for her to recognize from four years earlier in Colorado. And Billy LeRoy's dates cancel him out. This appears to be brazen hoaxing. But was Blandina the actual author?

FIRST-HAND ENCOUNTER WITH VICTORIO

It should be recalled, as discussed above, that Blandina similarly fabricated a first-person insertion of herself into her entry about famous Mimbres Apache Chief Victorio, for an entry that had a give-away date six years after Victorio's killing - thus, revealing her lie.

That entry, from Albuquerque, dated identically for *The Santa Maria* magazine and the 1832 book as "February 2, 1886," referenced Victorio by her alleged personal encounter with his depredations at a mining camp the "day before" her journal's entry date. But Victorio had been killed in Old Mexico in October of 1880, six years earlier. Blandina had written:

> Not only is Gerónimo riding at large, but Victorio and other captains also.
>
> Last week Sister Catherine and myself visited one of the grading camps and stood on a mound **where, the day before, Victorio had scalped two of the working men.** Everyone in the camp was as quiet as though nothing had occurred.

SMOKING GUNS FOR A HOAX: Reality does not support an 1886 near-encounter with Victorio, who was dead.

OVERALL SMOKING GUNS FOR HOAXED FIRST-HAND CLAIMS IN THE 1932 BOOK: There is no historical support for any of Blandina's first-hand claims of being involved with a "Billy the Kid gang member;" encountering "Billy the Kid" in Trinidad, Colorado; meeting with "Billy the Kid" in the Santa Fe jail; or being at a location a day after a Victorio attack. But these false entries, with their impossible dating ruling out real journal entries, contain details, names, and events added to feign historical reporting, leaving only willful fabrication as a possible explanation.

FIRST-HAND ENCOUNTERS JUST IN *VERITAS* MAGAZINE ARTICLES

> *SLEUTHING HOAXBUSTING CLUES: Preposterously fabricated first-hand entries, written for Veritas, were later recognized and replaced by Blandina or an editor with corrected versions for her 1932 book.*

There were also first-hand encounters presented by Blandina in her Santa Maria Institute's *Veritas* magazine that were so embarrassingly ridiculous, that she herself apparently kept them out of her 1932 book, *At the End of the Santa Fe Trail*, in fix-ups that also involved changing entries' dates. It should not be missed that second-hand accounts can be rationalized as mistaken information, but first-hand is supposed to be lived by their narrator!

"BILLY THE KID" AND HIS "FRIEND MURPHY" IN BLANDINA'S SANTA FE HOSPITAL

For the May, 1928, issue of *Veritas,* Blandina gave her journal entry as "October 1, 1878," then changed it to "October 1, 1879" for 1932's book.

The *Veritas* text - about the arrival of Lew Wallace as Territorial Governor, and about the back history of "Billy the Kid"- is dramatically different from the 1932 book's text, and is wildly fabricated. It has Billy's murdered "friend" - for whom Billy swore revenge - as "**Mr. Murphy.**" Recognizing that faux pas for the 1932 book, Blandina substituted "Tunstall" for "Murphy," then claimed *Tunstall* was murdered by "Murphy."

Even worse, for that *Veritas* article, Blandina put herself into the action by a first-hand encounter. She stated that "Mr. McSwain's men" shot "Murphy," and that he "was brought to our Hospital [in Santa Fe]." Then "Billy the Kid" visited "Murphy" there, swearing revenge. So implied is that she was present at her hospital to witness "Billy" at the bedside of his "friend Murphy," and to overhear "Billy's" vindictive oath. She wrote:

> Mr. Murphy, one of the "Cattle Kings" of Lincoln county, was shot in a fight between his men and Mr. McSwain's [sic – McSween] men.
>
> **Mr. Murphy was brought to our Hospital.** "Billy" came to see him, when he learned that Mr. Murphy's wound would be fatal. He swore at the bedside of the sick man, "that every one connected with the shooting would 'kiss the ground.'"

For her 1932 book, Blandina did a desperate fix-up, writing:

> **Mr. Tunstall, a rancher, was brutally murdered by "Cattle King" Major L.G. Murphy's men.**
>
> "Billy," cowboy for Tunstall, witnessed the deed and swore to shoot down like a dog every man he could find who had a part in the murder of his friend.

The October, 1928, issue of *Veritas,* with date "January, 1880," continued the wild fabrication, in which the "Billy the Kid"-and-"friend-Murphy" fable was elaborated by a made-up "Lincoln County War" in which "Murphy" was shot during cowboy competition for a cattle watering hole! The 1932 book eliminated that silly lying, and changed the entry date to "January, 1881." For *Veritas,* Blandina had written:

> **Few know the reason that started Billy the Kid on his downward course. It was gratitude. Gratitude to Mr. Murphy, one of the cattle bosses of Lincoln County. I will give you the gist of what today is called the Lincoln County War."** At the yearly "round up," the men – "cowboys" working for cattle bosses aim to arrive first with their herds at the best watering place. The first group that reaches the place has the right of possession for that season. Two groups arrived simultaneously, each claiming to be first. And the war began. In the conflict, Mr. Murphy was mortally wounded, though "Billy" exposed his

life to save him. It was at Mr. Murphy's dying bed at our hospital that "Billy" took the path, "to make every man kiss the earth who was in any way implicated in Mr. Murphy's death."

"PAOLINE" MAXWELL'S MISSION TO SAVE "BILLY THE KID" AS TOLD TO BLANDINA

Another magazine entry that was kept from the 1932 book, was in the October, 1930 *The Santa Maria*. It continued the "friend Murphy" fable to include the rich Maxwell family. Unaware that the daughter's name was Paulita, and that the family had relocated to Fort Sumner in 1870 from Cimarron, where Blandina placed their "Maxwell ranch," she threw in "Billy the Kid" as a Cimarron visitor. But Blandina turned her creation into her first-hand experience by having that daughter, whom she misnames "Paoline," attend her Trinidad school and apparently tell her a "Billy the Kid"-killed-friend-"Murphy"-revenge anecdote. Blandina wrote:

> At this place [Maxwell ranch in Cimarron] Billy the Kid often lingered and **Miss Paoline [sic] Maxwell (who attended our academy in Trinidad)** used many persuasive arguments to induce "Billy" to desist from carrying out his oath to "make every man kiss the earth who had anything to do with the killing of my friend [Murphy]."

SMOKING GUNS FOR A HOAX: Blandina's magazine's ridiculously wrong Santa Fe hospital scene with her overhearing vengeful "Billy the Kid" with his dying "friend Murphy," along with its removal for her 1932 book, point to willful cover-up of incriminating prevarication. And the comparable first-hand claim of "Paoline" Maxwell telling her another "Billy the Kid" "friend Murphy" anecdote, also appears ablated for the book after recognizing its as a give-away for fabrication. These cover-ups and fix-ups imply unsavory intent to deceive readers about made-up first hand encounters.

OVERALL SMOKING GUNS FOR FIRST-HAND ENCOUNTERS HOAXES: There is no support in reality for Blandina's first-hand encounters with Billy the Kid, Victorio, Lawrence Murphy, or Paulita Maxwell. In addition, the false dating indicates that the so-called journal entries were not written at their alleged dates 19th century dates, but were created in the 20th century. All this places Blandina's entries into the most serious category of exposed willful hoaxing, comparable to Billy the Kid imposter, "Brushy Bill" Roberts's, "dark and moonless night" error. But the uncertainty of someone else embellishing the entries remained.

8

BLANDINA'S BACKERS' "TWO BILLY THE KIDS" THEORY

RATIONALIZING BLANDINA'S "BILLY THE KID" CLAIMS

SLEUTHING HOAXBUSTING CLUES: Blandina's apologists and backers sought to side-step the possibility of her hoaxing by claiming that there were "two Billy the Kids," and she referred to one named Billy LeRoy. That would obviously require Billy LeRoy to be in Colorado when she was, and to be called "Billy the Kid."

To exonerate Blandina from hoaxing, her backers claimed she was referring to another outlaw named both Billy LeRoy and "Billy the Kid," who was in Colorado in 1876 and 1877, and in the Santa Fe jail in 1881. Of course, this belies the fact that Blandina was quite clear that she was referring to the famous Billy Bonney; writing a journal entry from Albuquerque for her 1932 book with date of "September 8, 1881": "Only now have I learned his proper name – William H. Bonney."

Unfazed by Blandina's providing his name and Lincoln County War history, her backers claim she merely heard the moniker "Billy the Kid," and, in confusion, attached Billy Bonney's history to her different, "original," "Billy the Kid" outlaw. Noteworthy, however, is that Blandina had no doubt about her "Billy the Kid's" fame, writing for her 1932 book for "April 24, 1882": [he was] "the greatest murderer of the Southwest." Furthermore, Billy Bonney himself had made the moniker widely famous only after 1880, which then caused others to adopt it for reflected glory.

So clarifying the identity of Blandina's "Billy the Kid" is important for deciding between the possibilities of her excusable confusion or inexcusable hoaxing. And Billy LeRoy was an obvious contender to examine.

THE "BILLY THE KID" MONIKER

SLEUTHING HOAXBUSTING CLUES: Dating of Billy Bonney's "Billy the Kid" moniker by contemporary sources would show if it was in use in Blandina's 1876 to 1877 Colorado period, or if it only appeared later and after his 1878 Lincoln County War fame began.

Billy Bonney's "Billy the Kid" moniker was not used until May of 1879, considerably later than Blandina's first 1876 and 1877 "Billy the Kid" Colorado journal entries. Its roots went back to when Billy came to Lincoln County in October of 1877 to work as a ranch hand for John Henry Tunstall, and was just 17; so was nicknamed simply "Kid."

That partial moniker was first used pejoratively by Lew Wallace in a March 31, 1879 letter to Secretary of the Interior Carl Schurz, to denigrate Billy during his secret sham arrest for their pardon bargain. Wallace reported from Lincoln:

A precious specimen nick-named "The Kid," whom the Sheriff is holding here in the Plaza, as it is called, is an object of tender regard. I heard singing and music the other night; going to the door, I found the minstrels of the village actually serenading the fellow in his prison.

The complete moniker appeared for the first time on in the Fort Stanton military Court of Inquiry for potential court martial of Commander Nathan Augustus Monroe Dudley for treasonously supporting the Santa Fe Ring side in the Lincoln County War to enable murder of its freedom fighters. Billy was a key prosecution witness, presenting his eye-witness account of seeing Dudley's soldiers firing a volley at him and others fleeing for their lives.

The moniker was presented in that court on May 23, 1879 by the witness, Susan McSween, whose husband, Alexander, had been killed because of Dudley's action. She heard Dudley use the name. It represented the Ring side's start of Billy's outlaw myth. She was testifying about pleading with Dudley to protect her, her sister, and her sister's children; as follows:

> [Dudley] then got very angry and said it was none of my business, that he would send his soldiers where he pleased, that I have no such business to have **such men as Billy the Kid,** Jim French, and others of like character in my house.

Testifying himself in that Court of Inquiry on May 28, 1879, Billy Bonney responded about the forming moniker, which still confused him, as follows:

> Q. by Recorder [Prosecutor]. What is your name and place of residence?
> Answer. My name is William Bonney. I reside in Lincoln.
> Q. by Recorder. Are you known or called Billy Kidd, also Antrim?
> Answer. Yes Sir ...
> Q. By Col. Dudley [Attorney for Defense]. In addition to the names you have given, are you also known as the "Kid?"
> Answer. I have already answered that question, Yes Sir, I am, but not "Billy Kid" that I know of.

On December 3, 1880, the Santa Fe Ring began its press campaign against Billy using a leak of Secret Service Agent Azariah Wild's fabricated reports about a counterfeiting and rustling "Kid gang," with Fort Sumner as its headquarters. That day, the Las Vegas *Gazette* published an editorial by editor-owner J.H. Koogler titled "Powerful Gang of Outlaws Harassing the Stockmen," which stated:

> The gang includes forty to fifty men, all hard characters, the off scouring of society, fugitives from justice, and desperados by profession. Among them are men, with whose names and deeds the people of Las Vegas are perfectly familiar, such as **"Billy the Kid,"** Dave Rudabaugh, Charles Bowdre, and others of equally unsavory reputation ... **The gang is under the leadership of "Billy the Kid," a desperate cuss, who is eligible for the post of captain in any crowd, no matter how mean and lawless.**

By his December 12, 1880 letter to Governor Lew Wallace to deny the Ring's press attempt to frame him, Billy was fully aware of the moniker, writing:

> *I noticed in the Las Vegas Gazette a piece which stated that,* ***Billy "the" Kid, the name by which I am known in the Country*** *was the captain of a Band of Outlaws who hold Forth at the Portales. There is no such Organization in Existence. So the Gentleman must have drawn very heavily on his Imagination.*

When Lew Wallace placed his first reward notice on December 22, 1880, in the Las Vegas *Daily Gazette*, it was for "Billy the Kid," proving the moniker's assumed universal recognition by then. Wallace wrote:

BILLY THE KID
$500 REWARD

I will pay $500 reward to any person or persons who will capture William Bonney, alias The Kid, and deliver him to any sheriff of New Mexico. Satisfactory proofs of identity will be required.
   LEW. WALLACE,
Governor of New Mexico

On the same December 22, 1880 day that Lew Wallace's $500 reward notice for Billy appeared, Billy Bonney gained national fame as Billy the Kid in a long *New York Sun* article titled "Outlaws of New Mexico, The Exploits of a Band Headed by a New York Youth, The Mountain Fastness of the Kid and his followers." With text arguably provided to the paper by the Santa Fe Ring, it stated:

> The leaders are **Billy the Kid,** so called from his youth; Dave Rudabaugh, Billy Wilson, and Tom O'Phallier, the four loungers about Fort Sumner. The Kid is the captain of the gang ...
> **William Bonney, alias the Kid**, the leader of the band, is scarcely over 20 years of age. He is handsome and dresses well. He has a fair complexion, smooth face, blue eyes, and light brown hair. He is about six feet tall and deceptively handsome. A beautiful bay mare, that he has carefully trained, is all that he seems to care for, unless he reserves some affection for his brace of six-shooters and Winchester rifle, which have helped him out of many a tight place.

On December 27, 1880, the *Las Vegas Daily Gazette*, published an article by Lucius "Lute" Wilcox about Billy's Stinking Springs capture, titled 'The Kid. Interview with Billy Bonney The Best Known Man in New Mexico, The greatest excitement prevailed yesterday when the news was abroad that Pat Garrett and Frank Stewart had arrived in town bringing with them Billy 'the Kid.' " It stated:

> With its customary enterprise, the *Gazette* was the first paper to give the story of the capture of **Billy Bonney, who has risen to notoriety under the sobriquet of "the Kid"** ... **"Billy the Kid,"** and Billy Wilson who were shackled together stood patiently while a blacksmith took off their shackles and bracelets to allow them an opportunity to make a change of clothing.

Describing Billy's transport from the Santa Fe jail to Mesilla, on April 3, 1881 the Santa Fe *Daily New Mexican* in "Something About the Kid," stated:

> Tony Neis and Francisco Chaves, deputy U.S. Marshals, arrived Thursday night with **Billy, the Kid,** and Billy Wilson ... At Las Cruces an impulsive mob gathered around the coach and someone asked which is **"Billy the Kid."** The Kid himself answered by placing his hand on [his attorney] Judge Leonard's shoulder and saying "this is the man."

On May 3, 1881, after Billy's April 28, 1881 jailbreak, Lew Wallace repeated his Billy the Kid reward notice in the *Santa Fe Daily New Mexican*; writing:

> **BILLY THE KID.**
> **$500 REWARD.**
> I will pay $ 500 reward to any person or persons who will capture William Bonney, alias The Kid, and deliver him to any sheriff of New Mexico. Satisfactory proofs of identity will be required.
> LEW. WALLACE,
> Governor of New Mexico

On May 4, 1881, the day after Wallace's second notice, *Santa Fe Daily New Mexican* reported Billy's jailbreak:

> The above is the record of as bold a deed as those versed in the annals of crime can recall. It surpasses anything of which **the Kid** had been guilty, so far that his past offences lose much of their heinousness in comparison with it.

By May 16, 1881, Lew Wallace published his *St. Louis Daily Globe-Democrat* article: "The Thugs Territory, Stage Robbers and Cut-Throats Have Things Their Own Way in New Mexico, Gen. Lew Wallace Anxious to Punish Crime that is So Prevalent - A Chapter About "Billy the Kid;" writing:

> [T]he Governor gave a very interesting sketch of the life of **"BILLY THE KID,"** the most noted and desperate character in New Mexico, and who was sentenced to be hanged on the 13th inst., but escaped by killing his guards and defying the entire population of Lincoln to take him ... At the appointed time [for their meeting] GOV. WALLACE was at the house, and exactly at 12 o'clock a knock was heard at the door and in walked **"Billy the Kid."**

On June 18, 1881, Wallace published in the Crawfordsville *Saturday Evening Journal* his article titled "**Billy the Kid**, General Wallace Tells Why the Young Desperado of New Mexico Wanted to Kill Him. A Dashing and Daring Career in the Land of the Petulant Pistol;" writing:

Late newspaper accounts of the exploits of **"Billy the Kid,"** the New Mexico outlaw, have made him the chief among frontier desperados and familiarized readers with his depredations and murdering ...

Governor Wallace repaired to the meeting place early, and promptly at midnight, a slight knock was heard at the door and upon response in the inside, **"Billy the Kid"** opened the door and walked in.

Billy's July 15, 1881 Coroner's Jury Report alluded to his moniker as follows:

> On this 15th day of July, A.D. 1881, I, the undersigned, Justice of the Peace of the above named precinct, received information that a murder had taken place in Fort Sumner, in said precinct, and immediately upon receiving said information I proceeded to the said place and named Milnor Rudolph, Jose Silva, Antonio Sevedra, Pedro Antonio Lucero, Lorenzo Jaramillo and Sabal Gutierres a jury to investigate the case and the above jury convened in the home of Luz B. Maxwell and proceeded to a room in the said house where they found the body of **William Bonney alias "Kid"** with a shot in the left breast

Billy Bonney's killer, Pat Garrett, featured the by now famous moniker to sell his 1882 book: ***The Authentic Life of Billy the Kid:*** *The Noted Desperado of the Southwest, Whose Deeds of Daring and Blood Made His Name a Terror in New Mexico, Arizona, and Northern Mexico.*

A March 1, 1890, *Lincoln County Leader* interview about Billy's 1881 escape from the Lincoln County courthouse-jail, by Gottfried Gauss - Billy's possible jailbreak accomplice - stated:

And so **Billy the Kid** started out that evening, after he had shaken hands with everybody around and after having a little difficulty in mounting on account of the shackle on his leg, he went on his way rejoicing.

The December 10, 1893 *San Francisco Chronicle* carried "Lew Wallace's Foe, Threatened by 'Billy the Kid,' The Writing of "Ben-Hur" Interrupted," which stated:

The Governor's enemy was no less a personage than the illustrious **"Billy the Kid,"** than whom no man had ever excited more terror on the frontier or given better ground for the dread in which he was held.

On January 6, 1894, Lew Wallace gave a "Billy the Kid" interview to the Weekly *Crawfordsville Review* as "Street Pickings;" stating:

"When I was governor of New Mexico that territory was and had been for years terrorized by bands of daring and murderous outlaws, at the head of whom was the famous border desperado, **"Billy the Kid"** ... "Two months dragged along and one day at Santa Fe we got the alarming news that **"Billy the Kid"** had murdered his two jailors, stolen a horse and had started for Santa Fe with the open threat, 'Now for the governor and now hang.'

For *The Indianapolis Press* on June 23, 1900, Lew Wallace presented "Gen. Wallace's Feud with Billy the Kid, When the General Was Governor of New Mexico and Billy Bonne Was the Most Dangerous Western Outlaw, He Was a Waif and was Reared in Indiana." Wallace stated:

So long as I live, I will never lose the image of **Billy the Kid,** as I saw him that midnight in old Santa Fe, back in 1879. There he stands in the doorway of the little adobe house, form outlined by moonlight at his back, face illuminated by glow of the little lamp ... "It was not long until **'Billy the Kid'** became the most daring and notorious of desperadoes.

For *New York World Magazine* on June 8, 1902, Wallace presented a long article as "General Lew Wallace Writes a Romance of 'Billy the Kid' Most Famous Bandit of the Plains, Thrilling Story of the Midnight Meeting Between Gen. Wallace, Then Governor of New Mexico, and the Notorious Outlaw, in a Lonesome Hut at Santa Fe;" stating:

> Gen. LEW WALLACE, author of "Ben Hur," is completing his autobiography, which will be issued in a few weeks.
>
> The most thrilling chapter in this remarkable personal narrative tells of the midnight meeting in a lonely hut between Gen. Wallace, at the time Governor of the Territory of New Mexico, and **"Billy the Kid,"** the most notorious outlaw the far West has ever produced ...
>
> In facial features **"Billy the Kid"** was a mere stripling. His narrow shoulders were rounded, his posture slightly stooping, his voice low and effeminate. But his eyes were cold and piercing, steady, alert, gray like steel.

In 1906 Billy appeared in Wallace's late-life *Autobiography*, completed by his wife Susan after he died in 1905. She inserted her above-mentioned May 11, 1879 letter to her son Henry to parrot Lew Wallace's outlaw myth of Billy the Kid, writing:

> [W]e hold our lives at the mercy of desperados and outlaws, **chief among them Billy the Kid**, whose boast is that he has killed a man fore every year of his life. Once he was captured and escaped and now he swears, when he has killed the sheriff and the judge who passed sentence upon him and Governor Wallace, he will surrender and be hanged.

In the 1930's, old-timer, John P. Meadows, a cattle rancher living in New Mexico from early 1880, gave interviews to historians about having known Billy Bonney, and performed about it on February 26, 1931 in Roswell, New Mexico, in an historical pageant he named "Days of Billy the Kid in Story,

Song and Dance." Subsequently, Meadows used his "Days of Billy the Kid" act for serialized newspaper accounts in the *Roswell Daily Record* on March 2nd, 3rd, and 4th of 1931. That year, Meadows also typed a 78 page manuscript with information about Billy the Kid. And from August 8, 1935 to June 25, 1936, the *Alamogordo News* printed almost forty of Meadows's reminiscence articles.

In 1934, George Coe published *Frontier Fighter: The Autobiography of George Coe Who **Fought and Rode With Billy the Kid***.

In 1955, as an old-timer, "Teddy Blue" Abbott published *We Pointed Them North: Recollections of a Cowpuncher*. Open about his own racism, Abbott reported, as common knowledge, the existence of two sides, with Billy Bonney as the Mexican's hero, writing:

> The Lincoln County troubles was still going on, and you **had to be either for Billy the Kid or against him.** It wasn't my fight ... it was the Mexicans that made a hero of him.

SMOKING GUNS FOR A HOAX: *Blandina's journal entries not only use the name "Billy the Kid" for the dates of 1876 and 1877, but claim it was by then well known and feared by people in Colorado and northern New Mexico, and was being reported in the press along with his "Billy the Kid" gang. And Blandina recounts meeting a youth in Trinidad in 1876 whose alleged accomplice, "Schneider," introduces as "Billy the Kid." In fact, the Billy the Kid moniker attained wide public fame only in late 1880; and, as shown below, it appears in no Colorado press of those dates. But Blandina's backers postulated another "Billy the Kid," named Billy LeRoy, to whom she was referring, to negate her entries' hoaxed addition of the moniker retroactively for feigning a relationship. And this possibility is examined below.*

PAT GARRETT'S DENIAL OF OTHER "BILLY THE KIDS"

SLEUTHING HOAXBUSTING CLUES: Pat Garrett, responsible for capturing Billy Bonney, denied other "Billy the Kids" in that period.

After killing Billy Bonney in 1881, Pat Garrett, in his 1882 book, *The Authentic Life of Billy the Kid*, appears to have chosen that title to address the glut of inauthentic others trying to cash in on the famous "Billy the Kid" moniker by adding it to their own unknown outlaw, or for pure fantasy, in articles and dime novels. In his "Introductory," (with ghostwriter Ash Upson) Garrett stated:

> I am incited to this labor [of writing this book] in a measure by an impulse to correct the thousand false statements which have appeared in newspapers and in yellow-covered cheap novels. Of the latter no less than three have been foisted upon the public, any one of which might have been the history of any other outlaw who ever lived, but which was miles from correct as applied to the Kid. These pretend to disclose his name, the place of his nativity, the particulars of his career, the circumstances which drove him to his desperate life, detailing a hundred deeds of reckless crime of which he was never guilty and in localities which he never visited. I would dissever the Kid's memory from that of meaner villains whose deeds have been attributed to him.

SMOKING GUNS FOR A HOAX: Pat Garrett himself was aware that the "Billy the Kid" moniker was being used in hoaxed history of Billy Bonney.

DIME NOVEL FABRICATION OF BILLY LEROY AS "BILLY THE KID"

SLEUTHING HOAXBUSTING CLUES: For their claim of "two Billy the Kid's," Blandina's backers were relying on an 1881 dime novel which claimed that a Colorado highwayman named Billy LeRoy also used the moniker "Billy the Kid." But this dime novel also plagiarized real newspaper articles on Billy Bonney to claim them as history for Billy LeRoy. Importantly, it is the only contemporary source in existence claiming that Billy LeRoy used that moniker.

By objecting to inauthentic use of the Billy the Kid moniker, Pat Garrett may have been angrily referring to a dime novel outlaw written up in 1881, the year before he published his *Authentic Life of Billy the Kid*. And it turns out that Blandina Segale's backers were relying indirectly on that same, largely fictitious, dime novel about Billy LeRoy, to argue for "two Billy the Kids" to get Blandina off the hoaxing hook.

Likely written by a Thomas F. Daggett, it was rushed out in 1881 by Richard K. Fox, the publisher of the popular dime novel *Police Gazette Series of Famous Criminals*, to cash in on Billy Bonney's killing and his famous moniker. It was titled *Billy LeRoy, the Colorado Bandit; or, The King of American Highwaymen. A Complete and Authentic History of This Famous Young Desperado, His Crimes and Adventures*.

As discussed above, Blandina Segale, or an editor, may even have used Daggett's creation as a source themselves, since his largely fictional bandit, Billy LeRoy, resembles her brutal Colorado highwayman, whom she too called "Billy the Kid" in her entries. And her pseudo-historical references to Lew Wallace are in Daggett's book too. But Daggett had a secret that would have tricked her. He was a plagiarist, copying real Billy the Kid's press for his narrative. Possibly conscience inhibited his full naming of his dark highwayman hero "Billy the Kid," because Daggett used a tell-tale give-away of a comma separating his "Billy" from "the Kid" as "Billy, the Kid."

Courtesy of The Newberry Library, Chicago. Call No. Graff 968

For the caption of his frontispiece's etched portrait of old-looking clean-shaven Billy LeRoy, Daggett wrote, "William Pond, alias Billy LeRoy, alias **Billy 'the Kid,'** the celebrated Colorado highwayman."

THOMAS DAGGETT'S FABLE

Thomas Daggett introduces his 66 page, "little biography" of Billy LeRoy as a "thrilling drama of outlaw life."

Chapter I describes Billy LeRoy as being born Arthur Pond in Indianapolis, Indiana, of "poor but honest" parents. He showed "evidences of a devil" at ten years old as a "ring-leader in schemes where 'pure cussedness' and audacity were the essentials to a successful prosecution." Daggett immediately added the money-making moniker:

> The devil, it is affirmed, takes care of his own, and Arthur Pond, **alias Billy, the Kid**, was recognized by his cloven-footed, long-tailed majesty as a very promising lieutenant, who, as he progressed in life, would certainly be an effective aid in working out his scheme to hither mankind to Hades.

Daggett's "Billy, the Kid" becomes a thief, who leaves home as a youth, carrying a "seven-shooter" in hopes of becoming "King of American Bandits." Immediately, he becomes, at 18, a "highwayman," and holds up a wealthy cattle "drover" whom he meets on the road and shoots in cold blood because "his soul was dead to remorse."

For Chapter II, in salacious, dream-like, dime novel-style, Daggett's "Billy, the Kid" becomes a performer in a "temple of pleasure saloon" as "Billy LeRoy, The Greatest Female Impersonator of the Age," along with "voluptuous May Vivian," a singer, who "would have made Venus jealous." As a raucous crowd waits, Daggett introduces his "female" "Billy LeRoy dressed in the costume of a society belle" and singing "in the most bird-like manner."

Billy's liaison with May Vivian angers "Dead-Shot Charlie, a famous Indian scout and sharp-shooter; but, in their confrontation, Billy LeRoy showed his terrifying side (though still dressed as a lady) and "Dead-Shot Charlie" backed off. But May Vivian fanned the fires of jealousy. Daggett wrote:

There was trouble in store for Billy LeRoy, although it lay some time in the future.
And Dead-Shot Charlie was to bear a very prominent part in it.

Into the saloon came a little man (a sheriff in disguise) who confided in "Dead-Shot Charlie" that "Billy LeRoy is a murderer and a thief," and he has a "requisition" for him from "the Governor of Indiana." But when they tried to shoot Billy LeRoy, he shot them both, killing the sheriff. So "[o]ut into the night went Billy LeRoy, the revengeful shouts of the revelers in his ears ... He had become an outlaw in earnest, and he mustered up all the villainy in his nature for the profession."

Chapter III sees Billy LeRoy - for unstated reason keeping his female impersonator name - stealing a horse to escape Leadville for prairie land. There he meets real highwaymen, who are impressed that he is a "plucky" kid. They turn out to be "Dave Rudabaugh" and "Tom O'Phallier, one of the most notorious desperados in the West."

[AUTHOR'S NOTE: What has occurred is author Daggett's cross-over into Billy Bonney's history, since, in 1880, Billy Bonney, the real Billy the Kid, used Dave Rudabaugh and Tom O'Folliard for his petty rustling. And Daggett's likely source is revealed: a December 22, 1880, *New York Sun* article: "Outlaws of New Mexico, The Exploits of the Kid and His Followers – War Against a Gang of Cattle Thieves and Murderers – The Frontier Confederates of Brockway, the Counterfeiter." Tell-tale is Daggett's misspelling of "O'Folliard" like the article's "O'Phallier."(See Pages 210-216 for full article.)]

So Billy LeRoy, asserting that he was as bad as the highwaymen, joins them and is taken to their hide-out cave. There Tom O'Phallier introduces Billy LeRoy to the compatriots as: "Don't you make any mistake in him lads ... Although he is a kid he has got just the stuff we want."

LeRoy was then subjected to a bizarre initiation inside the cave involving drinking from a skull full of liquor - which he enjoyed. Then all sang a highwayman's song:

> The hirelings and minions of the law we defy,
>   We scorn Death and his six-foot abode;
> Our motto is, "plunder, boys, never say die."
>   Hurrah, hurrah, three cheers for the road!

Author Daggett concludes that "many a poor traveler's untimely grave" would testify to Billy LeRoy's success as a highwayman "on the plains of Colorado and New Mexico."

In Chapter IV, masked Billy LeRoy proves himself to the highwaymen by a mail-coach robbery, and inside is May Vivian herself as passenger; though her face is concealed.

[AUTHOR'S NOTE: Do not miss the similarity of coach passenger, May Vivian, with face concealed from her Billy LeRoy, and Blandina's Staab carriage scene with her face concealed by her bonnet from *her* highwayman, "Billy the Kid."]

During the robbery, Billy LeRoy kills one male passenger, wounds the other two, and takes the woman prisoner. At that point he recognizes her and takes off his mask, exclaiming:

> "I'm Billy LeRoy, ex-female impersonator and professional highwayman. You said you would stick by me, May ... Let me see now if you're as good as your word."

May Vivian willingly joins him, as author Daggett declares: "He had captured a wealthy mail-bag and his sweet-heart!"

Chapter 5 has successful coach robber Billy LeRoy made Chief of the highwaymen's gang. And May Vivian's swigging of whiskey leads Tom O'Phallier to declare her a "brick" as she too joins the gang.

LeRoy's murder of the sheriff, the attempted murders, and the mail robbery bring pursuit by Leadville's two bravest detectives. But they encounter May Vivian in a boat. So she fires her gun at them, and is soon joined by Billy LeRoy who fatally shoots both. The gang decides to leave the area, but fearless Billy LeRoy first intends to return May Vivian to Leadville.

Author Thomas Daggett notes that:

> [F]rom his earliest experiences in crime, the consequences of his deeds never troubled him ... As an example of this spirit of recklessness which ruled his life and actions, it is stated that when **confined in jail in Santa Fe, New Mexico under a sentence of death**, he regaled his keepers with ribald songs, of which the following is a specimen:
>
> > ... Then hurrah for a funeral revel,
> > Hurrah for the coffin and pall,
> > Old Death is the friend of the Devil,
> > And both of them go for us all.

Back in Leadville, and with May Vivian's help, Billy LeRoy is back in female disguise as a saloon waitress, "Miss Flora Mason," "a damsel of free and easy virtue." There he tricked Dead-Shot Charlie for a week, but the man became suspicious and apprehended him in bed with May Vivian.

Taken to jail, Billy LeRoy faced only the crime of mail robbery, being sentenced to hard labor in a Detroit, Michigan, prison. Then, for LeRoy's train ride to prison, a gang member disguised himself as women, and, accompanied by May Vivian, planned to free him. They spiked the public water cooler with a chemical which the deputy guard drank and cause a bathroom emergency. In that brief time, they dressed Billy LeRoy the same as May Vivian - who departed to another car. When the guard returned, he could not recognize Billy LeRoy, dressed as May Vivian, in the company of the likewise cross-dressed gang member. At Kansas City, LeRoy and his accomplice got off the train, and LeRoy, a free man, bid farewell to May Vivian, who had joined them.

Chapter VI is pivotal, in that author Daggett now hijacked the press of the real Billy the Kid - Billy Bonney - to hoax his Billy LeRoy as "Billy the Kid" history. First, however, Daggett has Billy LeRoy return home to Indiana. There his parents protect him, and he convinces his brother, "Sam [sic - Silas] Pond, alias Potter" to join his outlawry.

Then Daggett's wholesale plagiarism begins by poaching, in near-entirety, the long December 22, 1880 *New York Sun* article: "Outlaws of New Mexico, The Exploits of the Kid and His Followers." (See Pages 210-216 for entire article)

[AUTHOR'S NOTE: For clarity, Daggett's minimal rewordings or insertions into the article's text of Billy LeRoy fabrications are underlined, and any of the article's original deleted text is supplied in brackets. And Daggett's more extensive deletions of the article's Billy Bonney text are restored in Author's Notes.]

Daggett wrote, plagiarizing in near entirety, as follows:

> One hundred and twenty-seven miles southeast of Las Vegas, New Mexico, is Fort Sumner, once the base of operations against the Indians who committed depredations against the stockmen.
>
> The fort was abandoned some ten or twelve years ago, owing to the removal of troops further south, toward the border of Mexico. The property was condemned and sold to Pete Maxwell, a well-known ranchman of the section.
>
> Since then it has been a depot of supplies for stockmen and a stage station on the postal route to the Pecos Valley and Panhandle, Texas.
>
> <u>Until recently,</u>

[AUTHOR'S NOTE: Original states, "During the fall of 1880 and the winter of 1881"]

on almost any fair day, there might have been seen lounging about the store or engaged in target practice five

[AUTHOR'S NOTE: Original states, "four"]

men, all of them young, neatly dressed, and of good appearance. A stranger riding in the little hamlet would have taken them to be a party of Eastern gentlemen who had come into that sparsely settled region in search of sport. Many who have gone into that country have struck up an acquaintance with these men and found them agreeable fellows. <u>Appearances were woefully deceiving, however. Agreeable and mild-mannered as they appeared, not one in the five but would have cut a throat, rob a stage coach, shoot on the slightest provocation, or steal a drove of cattle, with as little hesitation or compunction as they would tackle a meal when hungry.</u>

[AUTHOR'S NOTE: Deleted here from the original article is: "These men are the worst desperadoes in the West, and large parties of armed men are now scouring the country in pursuit of them. For a number of years the people of eastern New Mexico and Panhandle, Texas, have been harassed by a gang who have run off stock, burned ranches, and committed acts of violence and murder. (This sentence was inserted later by Daggett into his plagiarized text.) It was only recently that the leaders and organization of the band were discovered."]

The leader of this interesting party was Billy LeRoy, and his lieutenants were Tom O'Phallier, Jim Wilson, Dave Rudabaugh, and Sam [sic – Silas] Pond, alias Potter, alias LeRoy, the second.

[AUTHOR'S NOTE: Deleted from original article is: "The leaders are Billy the Kid, so called from his youth; Dave Rudabaugh, Billy Wilson, and Tom O'Phallier, the four loungers about Fort Sumner. The Kid is the captain of the gang."]

<u>They had all drifted together after quitting Colorado, and had eclipsed all their former deeds of villainy in the state.</u>

For a number of years the people of eastern New Mexico and Panhandle, Texas, have been harassed by a gang who have run off stock, burned ranches, and committed acts of violence and murder. <u>In the Winter of '80 their deviltry stirred the law-abiding citizens of New Mexico to take action against them.</u>

[AUTHOR'S NOTE: This last sentence, added by Daggett, is important to note, since Blandina's journal repeats the tale for "January, 1880" as: "Billy the Kid," is using his gun freely. The people of the Territory are aroused and demand his capture, dead or alive;" and for her "March, 1881" entry she wrote: "Billy the Kid['s] marauding has drawn the attention of the whole Territory."]

Their fastness <u>was</u> [original used "is"] about thirty-five miles nearly due east from Fort Sumner, on the edge of the great Staked Plain.

In that region there is a small lake called Las Portales. It is surrounded by steep hills, from which flow numerous streams that feed the little lake. This place the robbers selected for their resort partly on account of its hiding places, but mainly on account of the opportunities it afforded them for stock thieving.

No matter from what direction the storm came, it drove to the lake the herds of cattle which roam at large in the rich grazing country. There the band built for themselves one of those rude dugouts so common on the Western frontier, two sides formed by the side of the hill, the other two constructed of sod and dirt plastered together, and the whole covered by a thatched roof. Stockades or corrals were built near by in which to put stolen stock.

During pleasant weather the members of the gang lounged about Fort Sumner or other stations in that section. When the storm sent cattle scudding over the plains to the haven afforded by the hill-protected lake basin, the gang would hurry to their rendezvous and cut out from the herds the best cattle, driving them into their corral, whence they were later sent to market.

Their booty was large, for they had a vast stock to select from, the whole country for a distance of one hundred and fifty miles either way being a rich, continuous pasture.

Besides the active members of the band, there were many who had apparently some settled occupation and made themselves useful in disposing of the stolen cattle.

In every town of any size within a radius of 150 miles there were butchers who dealt regularly in this stolen stock.

When supplies from roving herds ran short the desperadoes would make a raid on herds that were guarded, attacking ranches and killing or diving off the inmates.

Besides their station at Las Portales, they had one at Bosque Grande, fifty miles to the southwest, and another at Greathouse's rancho, fifty miles to the north. Whenever they were pursued when running of stock, they had the choice of three places to which to resort.

The people of the surrounding country finally found the existence of this band unendurable. After repeated searches, which failed, owing to the smallness of the pursuing parties, it was resolved to organize several bands, who should cooperate in a campaign, which should end only when the outlaws were driven out of the country, or their capture, dead or alive, was effected.

The authorities of the several counties which bordered on the country ranged over by **the Kid's gang** had been repeatedly petitioned to send out a posse of men to hunt them down, but, as Las Portales was on disputed territory, the authorities were never able to settle upon any plan of action.

At last the ranchmen took the matter into their own hands, and the first party they sent out succeeded in getting on the track of a detachment of the gang who were hauling material to Las Portales, where they were building large stock yards. Although the party was not successful in capturing the outlaws, they made the outlaws flit about the country in a more lively manner than had been their wont.

This showed that nothing could be done by a small force. A guard was always kept out on the numerous peaks about Las Portales, from which outlook; the country for twenty miles either way could be scanned by the outlaws, so that they could easily elude a small party!

The Panhandle Transportation Company, an association of stockmen of western Texas, banded together for mutual protection, commissioned their superintendent, Frank Stewart, a brave fellow, who was just the man for such work, to organize an expedition against the outlaws.

The White Oaks, a flourishing mining camp, organized a band of rangers.

Still another party of picked men, under the lead of Sheriff Pat Garrett of Lincoln County, who is considered one of the bravest and coolest men in the whole region, joined in the campaign.

In the latter part of November Garrett, with a force of fourteen men, made a dash for Bosque Grande, riding all night, and there succeeded in capturing five of the outlaws. One of them was a condemned murderer who had escaped from jail; another of them was a murderer for whose arrest $1,500 had been offered.

These are the sort of men who reinforce the band. Las Portales has long been an asylum for fugitives from justice.

Bosque Grande (Great Forest) is situated in one of the most fertile regions of the West, and as the rich lands bordering on the Pecos River are the objective point of many who intend to settle in the Territory, it was thought best to rid that region of the outlaws first, in order that none might be deterred from settling there. Precautions have been taken which will prevent this refuge of the band from ever sheltering them again.

It was expected that the two other parties would work with Garrett's band, but the Panhandle party were delayed, owing to scarcity of feed, and the White Oaks Rangers had their hands full in another quarter.

The latter party had a brush with **the Kid**, Rudabaugh, Wilson, and several others at Coyote Springs [**original was "Spring"**], near the Oaks camp, and the outlaws succeeded in escaping, although two had their horses shot from under them.

The rangers started back for reinforcements and supplies, and then pressed on after the outlaws, coming upon them at their other station at Greathouse's ranch.

It was night when the rangers reached the ranch. They threw up earthworks a few hundred yards from the stockade of the ranch, and when the outlaws rose up in the morning they found themselves hemmed in.

The rangers sent a messenger to Jim Greathouse, the owner of this ranch, demanding the surrender of the outlaws. Greathouse replied in person.

He came out to the camp of the rangers and stoutly asserted that the outlaws had taken possession of his ranch and that he had no power over them nor anything to do with them.

It was considered best to hold Greathouse as a hostage, while Jim Carlyle, the leader of the rangers, heeded to the Kid's request for a conference.

A long time elapsed and Carlyle did not return. His men began to feel uneasy about him, and dispatched a note to the renegade chief saying that unless Carlyle was given up in less than five minutes they would kill Greathouse.

[AUTHOR'S NOTE: Omitted after "would kill Greathouse," possibly by accident of Daggett's plagiaristic recopying, is: "No reply was received."]

Soon after the rangers saw Carlyle leap from the window and dash down the hill toward their entrenchments. He had not gone far, however, when they saw **the Kid** throw half his body through the window, and, taking deliberate aim, brought down poor Carlyle, killing him instantly.

A sharp fight followed, but the outlaws succeeded in making their escape, Greathouse also getting away during the confusion.

Before leaving for home with the dead body of their leader, the rangers fired everything about the place, and Greathouse concealed some miles away, saw the smoke of his burning property.

The three parties <u>then began</u> **[original was: "are now engaged in]** scouting the country, and <u>determined to continue the chase</u> **[original was: "will not give up the chase"]** till the country is rid of every one of the outlaws.

Money and outfits have been freely offered by men who have large interests in that section. Government officials are now interested in the campaign, for, in addition to their other crimes, the outlaws have put in circulation a large quantity of the counterfeit money manufactured by William Brockway, the forger.

The bills were obtained by one of the gang named Doyle who formerly operated in Chicago, and counterfeit $100 bills in large numbers have been put in circulation among the stockmen and merchants in all that region.

The information that enabled the Government officers to discover the handling of counterfeit money by the Kid's gang came from a freighter named Smith. Soon afterward, while Smith was on his way from Las Vegas to Fort Sumner with a load of freight, he was waylaid and murdered by some of the gang.

[AUTHOR'S NOTE: For his plagiaristic scam, Daggett then deletes the article's following reference to Billy Bonney: "William Bonney, alias the Kid, the leader of the band, is scarcely over 20 years of age. He is handsome and dresses well. He has a fair complexion, smooth face, blue

eyes, and light brown hair. He is about six feet tall and deceptively handsome. A beautiful bay mare, that he has carefully trained, is all that he seems to care for, unless he reserves some affection for his brace of six-shooters and Winchester rifle, which have helped him out of many a tight place. His care of the beautiful mare is well deserved, for many a time has her fleetness which surpasses that of any other horse in the Territory, saved his life. The Kid is an admirable rider, and as he is always expected to be obliged to take flight, he usually rides another horse, leading his pet behind, in order to make the best time possible on a fresh horse. He is considered a dead shot and much of his time is spent in target practice. He was born in New York State, but his parents moved to Indiana when he was quite small, and thence to Arizona. There in the Tombstone District the Kid killed his first man when he was only 17 years old, and was obliged to leave the country. He came to New Mexico, where he has since lived."]

About three years ago a difficulty arose in Lincoln County, New Mexico, between the stockmen and the Indian agent on the reservation. The trouble arose in regard to some cattle that had been purchased for the Indians.

Nearly every man in the county was under arms, and the troops were called out by Gov. Wallace to quell the disturbance. **The Kid** was mixed up in the affair, and had some narrow escapes. On one occasion he was hotly pursued and was obliged to take refuge in a house in Lincoln, which was surrounded by sixty <u>colored</u> **[original lacks "colored"]** solders.

To the demand to surrender, he only laughed and shot down a soldier just **to show that he was game.**

[AUTHOR'S NOTE: Blandina also toys coyly with the word "game" in her 1932 book's "Billy the Kid" entry of "June, 1876" for her first meeting with him. She wrote: " 'I understand that you have come to scalp our Trinidad physicians, which act I ask you to cancel.' Billy looked

down at the sick man ["Schneider"] who remarked: 'She is game.' What he meant by that I am yet at a loss to understand."]

The house was set on fire, when the Kid, after loading up his Winchester Rifle, leaped from the burning building and made a dash for liberty.

All the while he was running he kept firing from his Winchester, bringing down a number of his pursuers. Bullets whistled over his head, but he made his escape, and leaping on a horse was soon laughing at his pursuers.

[AUTHOR'S NOTE: Daggett deletes the following here: "There is no telling how many men he has killed. He sets no value on human life, and has never hesitated at murder when it would serve his purpose."]

<u>A few days afterward Gov. Wallace</u> [original stated: "Gov. Wallace a few days ago"] offered a reward of $500 for his capture, and prominent citizens would make up a handsome purse in addition.

[AUTHOR'S NOTE: This non-historical reward concept linking Wallace and citizens is repeated by Blandina in her journal for "July 23, 1880" as: "The Governor and the people in the Territory have offered big rewards for Billy the Kid's capture, dead or alive."]

[AUTHOR'S NOTE: The rest of the article is deleted.]

Chapter VII continues Thomas Daggett's plagiarism of real Billy the Kid press, now by copying Lew Wallace's first article, in which Wallace began his own literary fabrication to create the outlaw myth of Billy the Kid. That article came out May 16, 1881, in the *St. Louis Daily Globe-Democrat* as "The Thugs Territory, Stage Robbers and Cut-Throats Have Things Their Own Way in New Mexico, Gen. Lew Wallace Anxious to Punish Crime that is So Prevalent - A Chapter

About "Billy the Kid." (See Pages 217-219 for article) Since the article had no historical dates, Daggett had to invent them.

For his fraudulent rendition, Daggett inserts Lew Wallace into his own convoluted concoction of Wallace's reward notices motivating "detectives" to attempt capture of "murderous Billy," along with "Billy's" killing more people and facing a failed capture attempt on a non-historical April 18, 1881 near Lincoln, New Mexico, with murder of the two reward-seekers.

[AUTHOR'S NOTE: Recall Blandina's use of Wallace's reward notices for her own presentation.]

Then Daggett switches for script to Wallace's "The Thugs Territory," after his Billy LeRoy returns to live in Lincoln, and Daggett copies: "He stole, murdered, ravished women, and at one time stole a herd of cattle consisting of 300 head."

Daggett then continued with verbatim plagiarism, adding his minor variations to the text of the article - as underlined and highlighted here - as follows:

> <u>During this time</u> [original states: "Some two years ago"] a murder was committed in New Mexico, and Governor Wallace was positive that Billy had a hand in the deed, but was unable to discover his whereabouts. Finally he learned that he was in the mountains a short distance from Santa Fe, and sent a messenger with a note to the outlaw, saying that if he knew anything about the matter and was willing to give his evidence before the Grand Jury, he would grant him a pardon, providing he also led a different life.
>
> Billy was to meet him at a certain house in Santa Fe at 12 o'clock on a certain night and date, and the matter would be thoroughly discussed.
>
> At the appointed time Gov. Wallace was at the house, and exactly at 12 o'clock a knock was heard at the door and in walked **"Billy the Kid."**

[AUTHOR'S NOTE: In his plagiarizing, Daggett here forgot his fake Billy LeRoy punctuation of "Billy, the Kid," and simply lifted "Billy the Kid."]

A long talk followed, and it was agreed that the sheriff should arrest him to protect him from the pals of the murderer. The Governor's idea in granting a pardon to Billy was to capture the leader and break up the gang.

On the next day the Sheriff with a posse of men captured Billy and he was brought before the Grand Jury, testified, and two of the men were sentenced to be hanged on Billy's evidence.

From [original article says "since"] the day Billy received the Governor's letter he has been leading the life of a murderer, stage robber, etc., and felt that the letter would forever shield him from the law should he be captured.

At length Billy committed one murder too many, was arrested, and sentenced to be hanged on the 13th inst. [original article says 13th of June, 1881] at Santa Fe.

[AUTHOR'S NOTE: At this point, Daggett adds some text of his own before returning to lifting from the article.]

Daggett then inserted his own compilation of publicly known Billy Bonney history, by having his Billy LeRoy transferred to jail in Lincoln, making his jailbreak by killing his two guards, and demanding a horse for his escape.

Daggett then wrote that his Billy LeRoy had "a gang in the southern part of New Mexico" and "organized a mass meeting of outlaws to protest against the vigilance of Gov. Wallace in hunting them down." That literary ploy enabled Daggett to segue back to plagiarizing from Lew Wallace's "The Thugs Territory" article, which had stated: "An interesting and ludicrous story is told of a recent meeting which was held by stage robbers and cut-throats of the Territory generally."

So Daggett then continued his plagiarizing; writing:

<u>At the meeting over which Billy LeRoy presided, it was decided</u> [the original stated only: "It was resolved"] that as Governor Wallace had taken such great care in placing a large number of their crowd under arrest, that he should be assassinated when the first opportunity presented itself.

Each man was sworn to the agreement in a general celebration and jubilee followed at Lincoln over the action of the meeting. The members, some 300 in number paraded through the streets with cocked guns and revolvers, and the citizens <u>deemed</u> [original states: "thought"] it best to look on and not in any way molest the gang.

Somehow or other, when the boys got pretty full of whiskey, a streak of goodness entered their hearts, and right in the saloon another meeting was called, and it was resolved that Lew Wallace was a brave man, and only doing his duty. As this was the case, the first resolution was reconsidered, and the following notice was sent to Governor Wallace, which is still in his possession:

"At our first meeting we resolved that you should die for interfering with our crowd, but as we think you a brave man and one who fought for the same cause that we did during the war, therefore we have resolved that instead of killing you we will, when the first opportunity presents itself, take off your pants and give you the worst spanking you ever had."

The Governor said that he actually believed that they would carry out their intention and he was very careful that they shouldn't get an opportunity to spank him if he could help it. A short time after receiving the note he had occasion to cross the country, and he felt that the outlaws would attempt the trick. He felt so certain of this that before he started he gave the driver notice that should any person order the coach to halt, the mules should be whipped into a dead run.

As the coach was descending a steep ditch a couple of men jumped out, and before they had time to sing out, the driver gave the mules the whip and away they dashed down the declivity. The Governor here jocosely remarked "that he didn't know which was the worst – running the risk of breaking his neck or getting the spanking." Anyhow, they didn't catch him.

[AUTHOR'S NOTE: The rest of the article is omitted.]

Daggett continued with his Billy LeRoy fused with Billy Bonney history by plagiarizing from another Lew Wallace article. It was from the Crawfordsville *Saturday Evening Journal* of June 18, 1881, and titled "Billy the Kid, General Wallace Tells Why the Young Desperado of New Mexico Wanted to Kill Him. A Dashing and Daring Career in the Land of the Petulant Pistol." It gave Wallace's own fabrications vilifying Billy Bonney by a fabricated vendetta against John Chisum. Wallace had written:

> [Billy Bonney] worked for John Chisum, the cattle dealer, in the late Lincoln county trouble, and claiming he has never received the promised $5 per day for his services, he is hunting down and killing Chisum's herdsmen, and giving their employer credit for $5 for each man killed.

Paraphrasing that for plagiarizing, Daggett created:

> A month after getting his liberty, [Billy LeRoy] rode up to a cow camp of John Chisum's, the well-known cattle man, in the Panhandle, in which there were four cowboys

Riding up to [one of them], "Kid" inquired, "Are you working for old John Chisum" "Yes," was the reply.

"Then here's your pay," a bullet from the "Kid's" pistol piercing his brain at the same time ..."Now," continued Billy [to the remaining cowboys], "I want you to take a message to old John Chisum from me. Tell him that during the war he promised to pay me $5 a day for fighting for him. I fought for him and never got a cent. Now I intend to kill his men whenever I meet them, giving him credit for $5 every time I drop one."

[AUTHOR'S NOTE: Blandina similarly garbled a few factual names with her fiction when she converted an historical L.G. Murphy into a made-up Lincoln County cattle king in the Lincoln County War, and elsewhere made a "Chism" one of her "Billy the Kid's" gang instead of the historical, real cattle king, John Chisum.]

Then Thomas Daggett, writing in 1881, ran out of real Billy the Kid articles. So for Chapter VIII, he reverted to his Billy LeRoy story, bringing LeRoy back to Del Norte in Colorado. There, in Daggett's fiction, LeRoy's reuniting with May Vivian, leads to his capture. And his brother - now carelessly called Arthur instead of Sam - is captured at the same time. Daggett has his always nonchalant LeRoy betting with the capturing sheriff, stating "that he would be out of the 'quay,' as he termed the jail ... before the United States Marshals could arrive from Denver." Daggett adds that "His brother, on the contrary, seemed to be in depressed spirits."

[AUTHOR'S NOTE: This contrast of LeRoy and another prisoner is like Blandina's journal entry about her alleged visit to the Santa Fe jail to see "Billy the Kid," where he is certain of escape, but his fellow prisoner, "Kelly," is dejected.]

Daggett brings his creation to completion with real Billy LeRoy history. He has the LeRoy brothers placed in the Del Norte, Colorado, jail, from which vigilantes seize and lynch them. A note pinned to their corpses stated: "Road Agents, Bunko Steerers and Horse Thieves, Beware!!" Then Daggett reverted to Billy Bonney-related historical names, and had gang members, Jim [sic - Billy] Wilson and Tom O'Phallier [sic - O'Folliard] killed during a stage robbery.

Daggett presents the real coroner's jury report for "Arthur Pond, alias Billy LeRoy" and "Sam Potter" dated May 23, 1881. The Sheriff in charge is listed as L.M. Armstrong.

[AUTHOR'S NOTE: Since LeRoy's Coroner's Jury Report was real and printed in the press, Daggett apparently felt inhibited about attaching his fake "Billy, the Kid" moniker into it, because, of course, the real document did not name LeRoy as "Billy the Kid," since it was never his moniker.]

Daggett concludes his scammed book by referencing the actual photograph of the dead Pond brothers, rendered as an etching for his dime novel, and writes:

> The day following the hanging, the corpses, stiff as crowbars, in Zulu costume, were balanced against the outside of the jail and photographed as they appear in this book.
> Adios –
> BILLY LEROY, THE KING OF AMERICAN HIGHWAYMEN.

SMOKING GUNS FOR A HOAX: Since Billy LeRoy was only given the moniker "Billy the Kid" in one dime novel that plagiarized Billy Bonney's own history for it, there existed no "two Billy the Kid's" to excuse the use of that moniker in Blandina's entries. Nevertheless, some similarities to her "Billy the Kid gang" tales may imply that this dime novel was used as her source for them.

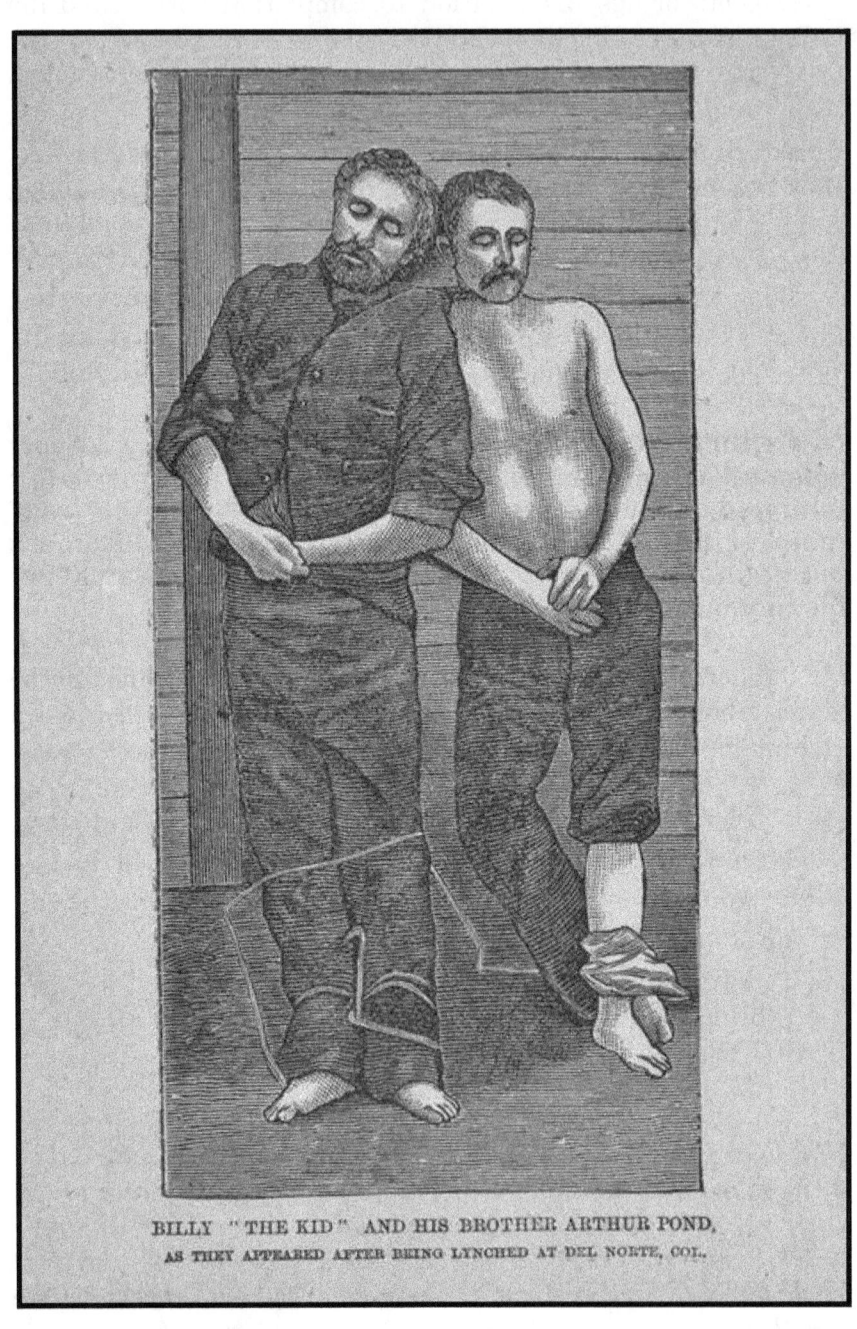

BILLY "THE KID" AND HIS BROTHER ARTHUR POND,
AS THEY APPEARED AFTER BEING LYNCHED AT DEL NORTE, COL.

Courtesy of The Newberry Library, Chicago. Call No. Graff 968

MODERN THROWBACK TO DAGGETT'S DIME NOVEL FAKERY OF "TWO BILLY THE KIDS"

SLEUTHING HOAXBUSTING CLUES: The book on which Blandina's backers relied was written in 1986 and used the Thomas Daggett dime novel to claim "two Billy the Kids" as confusing Blandina into writing her entries.

In a peculiar and misguided 1986 book titled *Alias Billy the Kid: The Man Behind the Legend*, its author, Donald Cline, argues for "two Billy the Kids" by meaningless reliances on Thomas Daggett's 1881 fictionalized dime novel, *Billy LeRoy, the Colorado Bandit*; on Blandina Segale's "Billy the Kid" journal fictions in *At the End of the Santa Fe Trail*, and on his own misstatements of both. Cline's flawed book was, however, used in naïve good faith by Blandina's Petitioner for her sainthood, Allen Sánchez, and by the Sisters of Charity of Cincinnati, Ohio, to excuse Blandina's false references to Billy the Kid by thinking there were "two Billy the Kids," with Billy LeRoy being "the original Billy the Kid" she had intended.

Donald Cline cites two irrelevant newspapers citing Billy LeRoy in 1881 in his bibliography, but gives no earlier articles to prove that his escapades went back to the 1870's to correspond with Blandina's "Billy the Kid" in 1876 and 1877, or to indicate that LeRoy was in the Santa Fe jail in 1881 (instead of Billy Bonney), enabling her to visit LeRoy, instead of Bonney. And he has no sources linking the "Billy the Kid" moniker to LeRoy. Despite proving nothing, Cline placed the photo of hanged Billy LeRoy and his brother, Sam, on page 100, with caption: "Billy LeRoy ... the original Billy the Kid."

Cline's apology for Blandina's obviously false Billy Bonney as "Billy the Kid" claims was that she was mixed-up. This does her a disservice, since she was sharp as a tack, successfully built schools and hospitals, established social service programs, was politically adept, did historical research, and was fully functioned into late life.

Nonetheless, Cline builds his fallacious case for "two Billy the Kids" by the following false statements:

1) [Cline's "Foreword" states:] "William Bonney was not the first person to use the sobriquet of Billy the Kid – he was the second. (Page 8)

[AUTHOR'S NOTE: This presents Cline's false claims for his "two Billy the Kids" argument. In fact, Billy Bonney never used "the sobriquet of Billy the Kid." It was devised by his enemies. His friends called him "Kid," because he was one. And Cline misleadingly treats as a given, his book's false premise of there being "two Billy the Kids," with Billy LeRoy using the moniker it first.]

2) [Cline introduces Billy LeRoy, stating:] "The first, and original, Billy the Kid was known as Billy LeRoy although some said his real name was Arthur Pond or Potter. He operated in southern Colorado and northeastern New Mexico from 1876-1881 in conjunction with his brother Sam who sometimes went by the name of Silas Potter. (Page 122)

[AUTHOR'S NOTE: Writing a year before LeRoy's biographer Mark Dugan's *Bandit Years* (see below), Cline makes up LeRoy's history by fusing Thomas Daggett's, Richard K. Fox dime novel with Blandina's use of the 1876 date for her "Billy the Kid" meeting. In fact, LeRoy was a highwayman from mid-1880 to 1881. And he was never called "Billy the Kid" except by dime-novelist Daggett, who plagiarized Billy Bonney's history and moniker. Cline even knew that Daggett "was mixing LeRoy with Bonney" (Page 123), but ignored it. In fact, Cline presented Daggett's fantasized early history as historical LeRoy's actual background. And LeRoy's brother was actually Silas Pond, aka Sam Potter.]

3) In December of 1874 a Catholic nun named Sister Blandina arrived in Trinidad, Colorado. By that time LeRoy was a household name and his name was said to have appeared frequently in the newspapers concerning his depredations. (Page 123)

[AUTHOR'S NOTE: With typical misinformation, Cline dates Blandina's arrival to 1874, not 1872; and fabricates that LeRoy was a "household name." He is relying on Blandina's unsubstantiated reporting of newspaper articles on "Billy the Kid" and his "gang," while doing no verifying research of his own.]

4) [Blandina] often heard the name Billy the Kid around [Trinidad] town as local citizens were afraid of him and news of his robberies were in the local papers. (Page 124)

[AUTHOR'S NOTE: There is no evidence that the name "Billy the Kid" was used by any Trinidad area outlaw gang in Blandina's day - 1872 to 1877. Cline - without telling the reader - is just paraphrasing Blandina's entry dated "September, 1876" from Trinidad about "Bill's gang." This sets up Cline's straw-man argument for "two Billy the Kid's," which also relies on his using Blandina's irrelevant early dates for LeRoy's activities.]

5) [Blandina] never knew [her outlaw] by any other name than Billy the Kid and it was not until she had been transferred to Santa Fe that she read the name of Billy the Kid involved in the Lincoln County War and thought it was the same person. (Page 124)

[AUTHOR'S NOTE: Cline portrays Blandina as a confused person who could not tell one outlaw from another, because "she led the cloistered, secluded life of a nun who was normally out of touch with the times and the real world" (Page 124), and was therefore unaware, according to Cline, of "two Billy the Kids." In fact, she was not a "cloistered nun," and was very much in touch.]

6) In September of 1876 [Blandina] was contacted by a member of the LeRoy gang to ...give medical aid to one of the outlaws ... None of the local Trinidad doctors would administer to the outlaw identified only as "Happy Jack."

[sic – "Schneider" was the name Blandina gave, and her "Schneider" had murdered fellow gang member, "Happy Jack."] (Page 124)

[AUTHOR'S NOTE: Without ever establishing that LeRoy was actually Blandina's "Billy the Kid" - which he was not - Cline uses it as fact, claiming she was contacted by "a member of the LeRoy gang." Continuing with his typical misinformation, Cline garbles Blandina herself, by calling her shot gang member patient "Happy Jack," instead of "Schneider," having carelessly substituted "Schneider's" murder victim's name in his place.]

7) [The injured gang member asked Blandina] whether she would like to meet the famous Billy the Kid. [She did want that.] At two o'clock that afternoon LeRoy rode up and was introduced to Sister Blandina only as Billy the Kid. [He soon agreed to her wishes not to kill Trinidad's doctors.] (Page 124)

[AUTHOR'S NOTE: Cline both garbles and relies on Blandina for his "Billy the Kid" meeting, himself inserting "LeRoy" as being the one to meet her as "Billy the Kid."]

8) Though LeRoy kept his word concerning the doctors he made a raid upon the town instead and was duly reported in the Trinidad Enterprise. (Page 125)

[AUTHOR'S NOTE: Cline garbles Blandina's book to portray a raid on Trinidad as reported in the *Trinidad Enterprise*. In fact, Blandina had reported gang activity in New Mexico Territory's Cimarron as the subject of a *Trinidad Enterprise* article - and occurring *before* her meeting her "Billy the Kid." And Blandina reported no reactive raid after the no scalping promise.]

9) Not long afterwards LeRoy's brother Sam was captured and incarcerated in Trinidad's jail. A member of the Trinidad Vigilante Club escorted the nun to the jail to

meet Sam whom the nun reported in her letters was a "partner" of Billy the Kid. (Page 125)

[AUTHOR'S NOTE: "Not long afterwards" would mean 1876 or 1877. This Blandina visit to Sam in the Trinidad jail is fabricated by Cline. Sam was not in the Southwest until mid-1880; and Blandina never claimed a "Billy the Kid"-related visit to a Trinidad jail anyway.]

10) In June of 1877 [Blandina, when riding in a carriage to] St. Vincent's Hospital and Asylum in Santa Fe, along with nuns and the Staab brothers [they encountered Billy the Kid.] Billy the Kid upon recognizing the nun in the carriage allowed them to pass unmolested. (Page 125)

[AUTHOR'S NOTE: Cline merely paraphrases Blandina's own false claims of a "Billy the Kid" encounter, without doing independent verification.]

11) The following year [1878] the Lincoln County War exploded ... and Sister Blandina came to hear the name Billy the Kid in association with it and falsely concluded that it was the same man she had known in Colorado. This is an example of her lack of knowledge of what went on about her for William Bonney's name appeared in the Santa Fe newspapers. (Page 125)

[AUTHOR'S NOTE: This is Cline's "confused nun" rationalization. It, however, relies on his fabricated notion of the existence of "two Billy the Kids" to "confuse" her. And it is belied by all the entries in her journal demonstrating a sharp-as-a-tack lady.]

12) On April 24, 1881, Sister Blandina wrote a letter to Sister Justina in Trinidad that one of her patients had been murdered by a man named Edward Kelly, a bartender in nearby Cerrillos. [And that Kelly was] in the Santa Fe jail along with her old friend Billy the Kid [and she would visit them]. (Page 125)

[AUTHOR'S NOTE: In fact, Blandina named the location of her patient as "Los Corillos," not Cerrillos, and never claimed that her "Kelly's" name was "Edward," or that his job was "bartender." And Cline also appears unaware of Blandina's own garbling of Billy Bonney's Santa Fe jail history to create her own tale of a visit, as he fills in details himself.]

13) A month following, on May 16, [Blandina] again wrote Sister Justina and said she had gone to the jail where she had a chance to talk to Edward Kelly and Billy the Kid was lodged in the same cell. [Her scene of talking to chained Billy, who wanted to offer a chair, is quoted in full.] (Pages 125-126)

[AUTHOR'S NOTE: In fact, Blandina used only the name "Kelly," not Edward Kelly in her journal entry for May 16, 1882 (changed for 1948 edition to 1881) as a cell-mate of "Billy the Kid." But real Billy the Kid cellmate, Edward Kelly, could not have been with Billy the Kid at Blandina's date of May 16, 1881 (or 1882), since Billy was removed on March 28th. In 1987, a year after Cline's book, an article by Philip J. Rasch was published in the *Quarterly of the National Association and Center for Outlaw and Lawman History* titled "The Curious Case of Edward M. Kelly," which gave Edward Kelly's history.]

14) [Cline states that William Bonney was not in the jail at that time.] If [Sister Blandina] had asked for Billy the Kid the jailer would have informed her that he was not there [since March 28, 1881] but, instead, she asked to see Edward Kelly and LeRoy happened to be in the same cell with him. (Page 126)

[AUTHOR'S NOTE: Cline's problem for his fantasized explanation is that there is no evidence that Billy LeRoy was ever in the Santa Fe jail - and Blandina makes clear that it was the same "Billy" she knew from Trinidad days. So the jail scene remains unexplained as corresponding to any reality. Historian Philip Rasch addressed Donald Cline's Billy LeRoy claim in his 1987 article, "The Curious Case of Edward M. Kelly," writing: "Some writers have endeavored to solve Blandina's jail visit date contradiction by assuming that Billy LeRoy, aka Arthur Pond, was the inmate visited by Sister Blandina, but this theory falls afoul of the fact that he was in jail in Colorado at the time."]

15) There is also some question about the May 16 [1881] date ... On the day [of Sister Blandina's] letter ... LeRoy, Sam, and an unidentified bandit held up the Del Norte-Lake City stage. (Page 126)

[AUTHOR'S NOTE: There are more problems to Cline's LeRoy as Billy the Kid concoction beyond Blandina's May 16, 1881 date! In fact, Cline did nothing to establish LeRoy's outlaw presence in Colorado in the 1870's, or his ever having the moniker "Billy the Kid!"]

16) [The tracking and capture of LeRoy and Sam after the May 16, 1881 stage robbery, followed by their lynching, are described in verbatim detail from the newspapers cited in the bibliography.] (Pages 126-130) Only two articles have ever been discovered in New Mexico newspapers concerning the two men. [*The New Southwest & Grant County Herald* of June 4, 1881, is quoted:]

> Billy LeRoy, the stage robber of southern Colorado and an accomplice who is believed to have been his brother, paid the extreme penalty for crime in Del Norte on Sunday night. The executioners were an enraged, outraged people.

The second and final 1881 article was originally printed in the *Denver Republican* and reprinted in the *New Southwest & [Grant County] Herald.*

The tragic end of Billy LeRoy, the stage robber, brings to mind a joke perpetrated at his expense by Judge Hallett. [Saying his age was 23, the judge said he would be 33 when released from prison and] "young enough to become a member of congress or an indian agent."

[AUTHOR'S NOTE: These 1881 articles add nothing to Cline's claim of Billy LeRoy's outlawry in the 1870's or of LeRoy's ever having the moniker "Billy the Kid."]

17) The first and original Billy the Kid (LeRoy) was dead and his successor (Bonney) had but a month and a half yet to live. (Page 130)

[AUTHOR'S NOTE: Cline is doing a straw-man argument: pretending Billy Bonney was the "successor" to the name "Billy the Kid" without having offered any valid evidence that LeRoy was ever known as "Billy the Kid." Instead, Cline relied solely on fraudulent author Thomas Daggett's plagiarized Billy Bonney history and "Billy the Kid" moniker in Daggett's fake Billy LeRoy biography; and on Blandina's published "Billy the Kid" fables.]

18) Though LeRoy operated over a seven year period and gained much notoriety in Colorado, William Bonney had a shorter span of three and a half years [yet] future writers and historians would single Bonney out for immortality. (Page 130)

[AUTHOR'S NOTE: Cline provides no basis for claiming Billy LeRoy's seven year highwayman career, beyond parroting Blandina's tales. LeRoy's outlawry was actually about eight months in the 1880's, according to LeRoy's biographer, Mark Dugan, as will be seen below.]

SMOKING GUNS FOR A HOAX: The Donald Cline book fails to establish "two Billy the Kid's," since it uses only the fake Daggett dime novel and Blandina's fake entries.

BIOGRAPHY OF THE REAL ARTHUR POND, ALIAS BILLY LeROY

SLEUTHING HOAXBUSTING CLUES: Billy LeRoy's biographer dates his brief outlaw career to 1880-1881, and confirms he had no "Billy the Kid" moniker.

Billy LeRoy's biographer is Mark Dugan. His 1987 book, *Bandit Years: A Gathering of Wolves* makes clear that LeRoy did not have the moniker "Billy the Kid," writing:

> Throughout the years Billy LeRoy has remained one of the most elusive figures in the annals of outlaws of the Old West. At least one noted historian and author, Burton Roscoe, claimed in error that LeRoy was just a figment of the imagination devised by early pulp publisher Richard K. Fox. The reason for Roscoe's claim was that Fox integrated LeRoy's career with that of Henry McCarty/Billy Bonney, the famous Billy the Kid, and claimed they were one and the same. Fox was able to do this as his book was written before **the real Billy the Kid** was killed on July of 1881. (Page 26)

The Billy LeRoy that Dugan documents cannot be Blandina's "Billy the Kid," because his Colorado crime spree was under eight months long - from 1880 to 1881; he was not in the Santa Fe jail; and he was not called "Billy the Kid."

"Billy LeRoy" was an alias of Arthur Pond, who was born in Ohio in 1857, and had two older brothers: Silas and Charles, younger brothers, Levi, Willie, and Harry, and a sister, Sarah. With his family, he lived variously in Indiana, Iowa, and Nebraska. Dugan states: "Nothing is known of Arthur Pond's early life prior to the summer of 1880."

In mid 1880, Pond left West Liberty, Iowa, for Colorado - so was not in Trinidad in 1876 as Blandina's "Billy the Kid." And by 1880, when he was in Colorado, she was in Santa Fe.

By mid-September of 1880, Arthur Pond met stage robber, Bill Milner aka William A. Morgan or "California Bill." And Pond assumed the alias "Billy LeRoy" when he joined Milner.

On September 23, 1880, LeRoy's first robbery was of the Barlow and Sanderson stage near Ohio City, Colorado, with accomplice Milner. They did two more stage robberies. On October 7, 1880, was one near Lake City, Colorado. On October 14, 1880, near Alamosa, Colorado, was another, with a haul of $4,000. Then LeRoy returned home to Iowa, claiming mining earnings; though he squandered all that stolen money.

On January 1, 1881, LeRoy was in Denver, but was arrested 13 days later. *The Denver Tribune* reported him as "a distinguished desperado, who robs the United States mail by profession," describing him as follows:

> He is a light complexioned man, with smooth face, rather sharp featured with a large mouth. He is about five feet seven or eight inches high, weighs 135 pounds, and may be anywhere from twenty-two to twenty-eight years old. (Page 30)

LeRoy was placed in the Arapahoe County jail. On January 26, 1881, he made an unsuccessful escape attempt. He then confessed to the robberies. He was transferred to Pueblo, Colorado, for his district court trial on March 1, 1881, and was sentenced to 10 years in the House of Correction in Detroit, Michigan. He escaped during the train ride to prison.

Billy LeRoy ended up in Kansas City, Missouri, where on April 3, he wrote an illiterate letter to his father asking for money and stating: "*i am a Robber And i am a good one.*" He then showed up at home in West Liberty, Iowa.

LeRoy then persuaded his 32 year old brother, Silas, to join him; and Silas took the alias "Sam Potter."

Returning to Colorado, by May 13, 1881, they were joined by a Frank Clark, and made a failed attempt to hold up a stage. On May 18, 1881, near Clear Creek, Colorado, they successfully robbed a stage, and wounded a passenger. (But May 16, 1881 was when Blandina Segale claimed to meet with her "Billy the Kid" in the Santa Fe jail, showing how implausible LeRoy was as her contact.)

Finally, Del Norte, Colorado, citizens, angered by the LeRoy's repeated stage robberies, offered a capture reward and organized a posse under Sheriff Lew M. Armstrong. It was joined by Max Frost, General Superintendant of the victimized Sanderson and Company Stage Lines.

On May 20, 1881, they apprehended Silas Pond (Sam Potter) first. Chasing LeRoy, they shot him in the leg, before his capture. LeRoy and his brother were then transported to Del Norte, after being warned by the lawmen that there was a lynch mob there. LeRoy confessed to the robberies, and Dugan stated that LeRoy added that he had killed no one.

On May 22, 1881, they were placed in the Del Norte jail by Sheriff Armstrong. That night, at 9 p.m., a vigilante mob forced Armstrong to hand over the jail keys. In the early morning of May 23, 1881, the mob seized LeRoy and his brother, and hanged them from a cottonwood tree. A note saying "Road agents, Bunko Steerers and Horse Thieves, BEWARE" was attached to Billy LeRoy's corpse. Later that day, the bodies were propped up and photographed. And the Coroner's Jury report was prepared - as quoted by the Fox Publishing Company's dime novel: *Billy LeRoy: The Colorado Bandit.* They were buried in the Del Norte cemetery.

Author Dugan stated that there was much press on the lynching. *The San Juan Prospector's* headline was: "BUZZARD MEAT, They register at the Del Norte Jail, are taken out by masked men, and 'Fixed' for the coyotes, Broken Necks are Trumps, and Billy and Sammy Ornament the Lower Pits of Hades."

Obviously, in Mark Dugan's biography of Billy LeRoy, there was nary a mention of "Billy the Kid" the "Billy the Kid Gang," or even a gang to provide a foothold for Billy LeRoy as being Blandina's "Billy" for her "Billy the Kid" tales.

But even with Mark Dugan's clear rebuttal, Billy LeRoy continued to get misleading press as being Blandina's "original Billy the Kid" to give some legitimacy to her tall tales.

SMOKING GUNS FOR A HOAX: Billy LeRoy's crime spree from 1880-1881 and lack of a "Billy the Kid" moniker, cancel him out as Blandina's "Billy the Kid."

REAL BILLY LeROY'S CONTEMPORARY PRESS

SLEUTHING HOAXBUSTING CLUES: There are no mentions in Colorado newspapers about a Billy LeRoy or an Arthur Pond or a Billy the Kid from 1872 to 1877. And by 1876 the Trinidad Enterprise was renamed as The Enterprise and Chronicle. These facts are incompatible with Blandina's claim of reading about a Billy the Kid gang in The Trinidad Enterprise in 1876.

SEARCHING 1870's COLORADO NEWSPAPERS

Blandina claimed that she first read about the "Billy the Kid gang" in September of 1876. She wrote:

> The Trinidad Enterprise – the only paper published here – in its last issue gave an exciting description of how **a member of "Bill's Gang"** painted red the town of Cimarron.

First of all, *The Trinidad Enterprise* did not exist in 1876, when she claimed to read about the "Billy the Kid Gang" in it. *The Trinidad Enterprise* (weekly) began in September of 1870. It merged with the *Colorado Chronicle* to become *Trinidad Enterprise and Chronicle* on March 19, 1875. It changed title again on April 2, 1876 to become *The Enterprise and Chronicle*. So there was no *Trinidad Enterprise* in 1876, just *The Enterprise and Chronicle*!

Nevertheless, could Billy LeRoy's biographer, Mark Dugan, have overlooked earlier Billy LeRoy press - meaning LeRoy came to Colorado before 1880? Easy vindication of Blandina hinged on Billy LeRoy's press dates, which could make her *"Billy"* possibly Billy LeRoy - as her backers hoped.

Antique Colorado newspapers have been digitized for the Colorado Historic Newspapers Collection. And the Denver, Colorado, History Colorado Center, Library and Collections' microfilms cover some relevant newspaper issues not in the Colorado Historic Newspapers Collection, namely:

Colorado Chronicle (that merged with *The Trinidad Enterprise* in 1875): 3/21/1874, 10/3/1874, 10/14/1874, 12/25/1874, 1/7/1875, 2/11/1875-2/25/1875, 3/4/1875-3/11/1875; *Colorado Pioneer*: 2/6/1875-4/15/1875, 8/19/1875, 1/4/1877; and *Trinidadian*: 2/10/1875, 2/17/1875, 2/24/1875, 3/10/1875.

A search of both collections, yielded no results in Blandina's Trinidad residency period of 1872 to 1877 for topics: Billy LeRoy, Arthur Pond, Billy the Kid, gang, stage coach robbers, or scalping. And from 1872 to 1877, in Colorado papers, there was only one mention of a highwayman robbery. It was in the Saturday, March 13, 1875 *The Colorado Chieftain* for Trinidad. In a column summarizing news items, it stated in entirety:

> A highwayman recently went through the agent of the Denver and South Park railroad for twenty dollars.

Billy LeRoy is only mentioned in 1881, for his outlawry, escape, recapture, and lynching. And, even then, LeRoy got no mention of having the moniker "Billy the Kid" or of having a "Billy the Kid Gang;" though he is described as having accomplices and a gang.

And Colorado newspapers did not mention real Billy the Kid's "gang" until the *New York Sun's* December 22, 1880 article titled: "Outlaws of New Mexico, The Exploits of a Band Headed by a new York Youth, The Mountain fastness of the Kid and his Followers - War against a Gang of Cattle Thieves and Murderers - The Frontier Confederates of Brockway, the Counterfeiter." That was four years after Blandina had left Colorado and her supposed "Billy the Kid gang."

And from 1880 onward, there were obviously hundreds of Colorado articles about Billy Bonney as Billy the Kid.

SEARCHING BILLY LeROY'S 1880's PRESS

Billy LeRoy's press corresponded to his presence in Colorado only in the 1880's, as his biographer, Mark Dugan, had presented. The Pueblo, Colorado, *Colorado Daily Chieftain* reported for March 2, 1881 that he was in jail in Pueblo. To be noted is that this eliminates him as being in the Santa Fe jail during the incarceration of Billy Bonney there. The article, furthermore, does not call him "Billy the Kid," or claim that he had a widely ranging highwayman gang; and merely calls him "the San Juan stage robber." The article stated:

> **LeRoy, the San Juan stage robber**, was brought to this city [Pueblo] on Monday last from Denver, and is now lodged in the county jail. Yesterday his trial came up before Judge Hallett in the United States district court, and he pleaded guilty to one indictment, there being three or four charges against him, and was recommitted to jail to await the decision of the judge, who has taken the matter under advisement. He pleased hard for leniency. He will probably be sentenced to-day. From here he will probably go to the United States prison at Detroit, Michigan.

The Daily News: Denver of Saturday, April 9, 1881, reported LeRoy's escape during transport to the Detroit, Michigan, prison. The article was titled "Billy Le Roy, The Story of His Escape From Cantril, Detailed Minutely to a Reporter of the News, by the 'Solid Pard' of the Bold Stage Robber, Who Put Up the Job and Successfully Executed It, Billy's Girl, Who Loves Him Most Devotedly, Lends a Helping Hand to the Scheme, The Deputy's Fatal Drink of Water at the Tank, Which Had Been Dosed With Croton Oil, While Cantril Was in the Toilet Room, Billy Le Roy in a Twinkling Don's Women's Attire, And Settles into The Arms of His Pard, The Cleverest Piece of Work in the Annals of Crime." The reporter stated that "Billy LeRoy" was the alias of Arthur Pond. Nowhere is LeRoy called "Billy the Kid." The article stated:

> Deputy United States Marshal Cantril returned to Denver on last Monday with tidings that **William Le Roy, the dashing road agent and prince of mail robbers, had made his escape** while en route to the government prison at Detroit ... Le Roy frequently made the announcement that he would bid the marshals good-bye before Chicago was gained on their eastern journey ... [Cantril] told his story about how Le Roy had taken the advantage of a favorable moment when the guard was asleep and Cantril in

the toilet room, to throw off his handcuffs and shackles and leap from the swift running train ...

Cantril ... furnished the following circular letter of description, which had been mailed to a number of states:

> Two Hundred Dollars Reward – For the capture and detention until I come for him, of **Arthur Pond, alias William Le Roy**. He was five feet four and a half inches high, had light hazel eyes, light chestnut brown hair, fair complexion, twenty-three years old, but looks to be about eighteen. He is very quick in all his movements. Road agent by occupation. He jumped from Kansas Pacific passenger train five miles west of Hayes City, Kansas, March 28, 1881, while running at full speed, and may be crippled ... face clean shaven. Address
> SIM W. CANTRIL, Deputy U.S. Marshal, Denver, Colorado

[An informer then gives the reporter "The True Story of Le Roy's Escape."] As planned by **Billy**, it was to bring [his old girl] up to town, and get two suits of clothes for her just exactly alike ... Then we were to get a suit of clothes, man's clothes, for Billy ... [She would ride the train. When Le Roy had the chance, after the accomplice informer had drugged the guard's water cooler drink, he would change into the extra clothes, she would leave, and he would "disappear" in the disguise as her.] ... On arriving in Kansas City we were driven to a hotel ... Billy changed clothes ... [His girl] got in on the next train, joined us and we went out from town about seven miles, and there bid Billy Le Roy good-bye.

The Daily News: Denver of Tuesday, April 12, 1881, reported on escapee Billy LeRoy in "Le Roy's Luck, Colorado's Stage Robber and Road Agent, Goes Through a Kansas City Pawn Shop, Securing Several Thousand Dollars Worth of Jewelry, And Returns to Denver With His Booty, How He Spent Last Sabbath Day in Our Midst." The article called him: "Billy Le Roy, the fearless road agent, the prince of stage robbers." There was no "Billy the Kid" moniker. And while it reported that searches were conducted for him in "Iowa, Illinois, Missouri, Kansas, Nebraska and New Mexico," he was actually in Kansas City, Missouri, robbing a pawn shop, returning to Denver, disposing of stolen jewelry, and being recognized by "former confederate" "who had known Le Roy three years ago."

An article dated April 6, 1881 about his pawn shop burglary called him a "thief named Arthur Pond, alias William Le Roy" and "prince of the road;" and said that he "left Kansas City for Denver, accompanied by one or more persons in his gang." The article surmised:

> Le Roy's future intentions are difficult even to predict. It is thought that he and Frank Younger have formed an alliance, and will either take the road in New Mexico and Arizona and continue Le Roy's favorite game of holding up stages ... It is a well-known fact that Le Roy and California Bill were planning a train wrecking expedition when the former was captured ... Now that Le Roy has associated with him Frank Younger and another Missouri train wrecker especially bold and desperate, the public may soon expect to hear from this prince of the road in a new role.

The Daily News: Denver of Monday, May 23, 1881, reported: "Le Roy is Dead, He Falls Victim to Del Norte's Hemp ... Lynched at Del Norte." Reporting from Del Norte, the unnamed reporter wrote:

> The Le Roy brothers, the mail robbers recently captured by Sheriff Armstrong and his posse from this place, reached here last night about 8 o'clock and were placed in jail. [They were later removed from jail and hanged.] **The shooting and robbing [by the brothers] was done within twenty-five miles of Lake City** ... The universal opinion here justifies their fate.

The headline for a editorial in *The Daily News: Denver* of Wednesday, May 24, 1881, was: "Billy Le Roy, The Last Act in the Drama of His Life, Captured by the Sheriff of Rio Grande County, He is Conveyed With His Brother to the County Jail in the Town of Del Norte, From Thence They are Taken By the Lynchers, Who Hang Them on the Banks of the River, A Terrible End to a Career of Outrageous Crime." The lynching was described; and no mention was made of the moniker "Billy the Kid." The editorial stated:

Billy Le Roy, the notorious outlaw and stage robber, whose dare-devil deeds during the past two or three years kept his name so prominently before the country [meaning local area], and who recently escaped from the custody of Deputy Sheriff Sim Cantril, of Denver, while being conveyed to the Detroit penitentiary, to fill out a sentence of ten years' penal servitude, has at last paid the penalty of his crimes, having been hung by a vigilance committee at Del Norte on the evening of the 22d [sic – 23rd] instant.

The Daily News: Denver of Wednesday, May 25, 1881, reported: "Lynched, The Story of Le Roy's Capture Saturday, After a Tedious Trail Through the Mountains ... Details of the Scenes at Del Norte When the Prisoners Were Hung to a Tree." The article, by an unnamed reporter, makes no mention of an incarceration in the Santa Fe jail earlier that month - or ever - to correspond with Blandina's May 16, 1881 [or 1882] visit to see her "Billy the Kid" in the Santa Fe jail. The dating after LeRoy's escape from lawman Cantril on the transport train, puts him in Pueblo, Colorado, at about May 12th. Just before that he was spotted in Missouri with his brother. On the night of May 13th, they did an unsuccessful stage robbery. On the 15th, they passed through Del Norte to Wagon Wheel Gap. On the 18th, they robbed a stage near Antelope Springs, and shot the engineer's leg. This last crime enraged Del Norte citizens, who offered a large reward; and whose Sheriff, Armstrong, pursued, shot LeRoy in the leg, and then captured and jailed the brothers on May 23rd. That night, the lynch mob seized and killed them. The coroner's jury report was printed in full. LeRoy was called "the notorious road agent Arthur Pond alias Billy Le Roy" - not "Billy the Kid." A compatriot in the May 18th stage robbery, still on the loose, was named as Frank Clark.

SMOKING GUNS FOR A HOAX: Evidence from his biographer and contemporary press refutes Billy LeRoy as Blandina's "Billy." He was not in Colorado in her time-frame, and was never called "Billy the Kid," except in a fraudulent 1881 dime novel. Furthermore, there was no mention of any "Billy the Kid" in the press during her Colorado residency. Her tales appear to be hoaxed.

SEEKING OTHER OUTLAWS IN THE NEWS FOR BLANDINA

SLEUTHING HOAXBUSTING CLUES: The possibility that Blandina, or an editor, was referencing another highwayman named Billy, or that different "gang members" were in the press was explored as another explanation for the aberrant journal entries. The less palatable alternative was that she, or an editor, used newspapers as sources to lift names and stories to cobble together to manufacture her "Billy the Kid and gang" tales, and to write her into the action.

Since it was now clear that Blandina never knew Billy Bonney, to avoid naming her a hoaxer, her backers hoped that she wrote about another Colorado outlaw she knew in the 1870's. So one can give her the benefit of the doubt by searching Colorado newspapers for a despicable outlaw and highwayman in the Colorado area from 1872 to early 1877 who met her descriptions of depravity; and, ideally, had the name "Billy" and was pleasant-looking and young. Such searches yielded unconvincing possibilities. But revealed was another clue about the constructing of the Nun's Tale Hoax.

A "BILL" FOR BLANDINA

An ideal "Billy" for Blandina would be a William or a Bill. There was one in her Colorado time-frame: "Persimmon Bill." That Bill made the news in Thursday's, May 11, 1876, Boulder, Colorado, *The Colorado Banner* as: " 'Persimmon Bill,' Otherwise Known as William T. Chambers, the North Carolina Outlaw, Interesting Chat with the notorious Black Hills Horse Thief and Desperado."

The article describes the unnamed reporter's wagon train encounter and kidnapping by looting Indian highwaymen and their white cohort. On questioning, the white man says:

"I am **Persimmon Bill**; some call me Soger-killing Bill; while those who desire to be polite call me Government William."

Our party did not desire to hear any more. If they had been miserable and disconsolate a moment before, the announced presence of **this notorious cut-throat and outlaw** did not contribute to their happiness. There is an old saying that "the devil is not so bad as he is painted;" and certainly **Persimmon Bill, with all of his bloody crimes upon his hands**, is not a bad man to look upon ...

[He gave his history:] Early in 1867, Chambers made his way to Cheyenne, where he became associated with a crowd of roughs, who, just prior to the completion of the Union Pacific to Cheyenne, made the region anything but a pleasant resort ...

[In late 1870, in Sioux City] [w]hile in a drunken frenzy he shot his horse [then shot the Deputy Sheriff] through the arm ... He was arrested ... but succeeded in working his way out of jail ...

[After stealing a horse] he was met by the Sheriff, who requested him to surrender ... Bill immediately shot him down ... and dashed away and escaped.

[H]e went to Sherman, on the line of the Union Pacific, where in company with two or three others, he became **a "road agent" or robber** ...

On the sixth of March [1876] ... "Persimmon Bill" walked boldly into the sutler's store [at Fort Fetterman] ... [A]fter pocketing a bottle of whiskey and some cigars ... half-frenzied with whiskey, he rode along the road [where he encountered a Sergeant Sullivan] "and then," said this **cool-blooded murderer**, "I remember seeing that Sergeant have some money ... so I just ... plugged him in the back." **... He laughed merrily while he recited this last murder**, and closed by saying, "I'm death on soldiers and Government property, and that's why the call me Government Bill." ...

These continued outrages perpetrated by this ubiquitous desperado has prompted the Government to offer a reward of $1,000 in addition to the $1,000 offered in Sioux City for the arrest of **"Persimmon Bill."** ...

He acknowledged that he expected to be hung when caught, but reiterated in his long conversation his determination to die before taken.

A "YOUNG AND DASHING HIGHWAYMAN" FOR BLANDINA

An highwayman in the news fitted the bill for youth. He was reported in Thursday's, August 24, 1876, Boulder, Colorado, *The Colorado Banner* as "Adventures of a Young and Dashing Highwayman." It reported:

During the past week or two, says the St. Joseph (Mo.) *Gazette*, the eastern portion of Jackson County has been somewhat excited over the **daring and dashing operations of a youthful highwayman**, who has cried "Stand and deliver" to several worthy citizens ... His operations have been of the boldest ... He did not appear to fear creature, or care for identification ... He was, in fact, a bold highwayman of the foolhardy sort ...

[He was captured.] The prisoner is a young man, evidently not more than 22 years of age. He has a smooth, beardless face, has dark hair and dark eyes, the latter bright and restless ... he is not heavily built, and is not more than five feet eight or nine inches high. **He gave his name as George Demasters.**

A CIMARRON BADMAN FOR BLANDINA

Blandina's first reference to "Billy the Kid" is from an alleged September of 1876 *The Trinidad Enterprise* article about "an exciting description of how a member of 'Bill's Gang' **painted red the town of Cimarron.**"

Leaving out that there was no Colorado paper of that name in 1876, notorious Colfax County, New Mexico Territory, hell-raiser and Maxwell Land Grant settler, Clay Allison, habitually made trouble in Cimarron, which was just 51 miles from Trinidad. Clay Allison's siding with Colfax County's anti-Santa Fe Ring faction, from 1875 onwards, generated much biased outlaw press against him as a desperado; and his drunken, violent, exhibitionistic nature helped that image.

Historian, Norman Cleaveland, in his 1971 book titled *The Morleys – Young Upstarts on the Southwest Frontier*, quoted Cimarron businessman, Henry M. Porter, about young Clay Allison as follows:

> **The younger set ... would frequently come to Cimarron, get full, and as they called it shoot up the town;** that is shoot at men, chickens, dogs, pigs, and at the pictures on the walls of the bar rooms, make men they did not fancy dance at the point of their guns ... for their amusement. During these escapades the stores and houses would be closed and the streets deserted.

A *Colorado Chieftain* article about Clay Allison from Pueblo, Colorado, on Thursday, December 28, 1876, was titled: "Murder in Las Animas: The Allison Desperados Make a Raid on West Las Animas." It was repeated in *The Colorado Miner* for Georgetown on Saturday, December 30, 1876. It stated:

> It is our sorrowful duty to record the death of another officer – one highly esteemed in the community. Last night about twelve o'clock, or a few minutes later (railroad time) Constable Charles Faber, in attempting to disarm John and Clay Allison, at the Olympic dance hall, was fired upon by both of them and fell at the first shot.

By January 21, 1977, the Pueblo, Colorado, *Colorado Chieftain* made a correction, repeated on Thursday, January 25, 1877, titled "The Allison Case" by Colfax County resident, Dr. W.L. South, claiming the Allisons were actually attacked by Constable Faber first. South wrote:

> What crime did John Allison commit that he should be made a target for a policeman's murderous gun-shot, and can any man honestly attach much blame to Clay Allison's act in defending his own brother?

And the Pueblo, Colorado, *Colorado Chieftain* for March 30, 1877 and for April 5, 1877, reported that Clay Alison was acquitted by self-defense.

But nothing stopped Clay Allison's outlaw myth. By October 16, 1894, *The Salida Mail* of Salida, Colorado, manufactured the following:

> **RECORD OF A TEXAS DESPERADO: The graves of His Victims Were Scattered From Dodge City to Santa Fe**
>
> The man who told the story between puffs of his cigar was from Texas.
>
> "Clay Alison's life was a tragic romance," he began. "**Clay Allison was a desperado.** He lived in the Red river country in the Panhandle. **His trigger finger was the busiest in the early eighties. His record was 21. He boasted of it. Twenty-one dead men, whose graves were scattered from Dodge City to Santa Fe!**"

One can see in Clay Allison's fantastical press the counterpart of Blandina's yarns. An example comes from an April 3, 1906 Eagle, Colorado, *The Eagle Valley Enterprise* article titled "The Duel that Failed;" stated:

> **The Duel That Failed**
> O.S. Clark of Attica, Ind., went to the Texas Panhandle when it was wild and wooley. There he met **Clay Allison, a famous gunfighter** who told him about the strangest duel he'd ever seen. It was between two frontiersmen who didn't like the color of each other's hair. So they agreed to fight it out with long rifles – stand back to back, then each take ten long steps, turn and begin firing.
>
> The duel began ... They fired at the same instant but neither bullet took effect.
>
> They fired a second time – a third – a fourth – and a fifth. In fact they kept shooting until each man had used up 20 cartridges. "There's something spooky about this," said one. "Shore is!" said the other. "Maybe we ain't supposed to kill each other." ...
>
> They started towards each other .... As they met and clasped hands, one exclaimed "Ouch!" Something's burnin' through my boot!"
>
> They looked down. There on the ground was a

pile of melted lead ... So accurate had been their aim that their bullets had met halfway with such terrific force that they melted each other and dropped to the ground ... Clay said this was true because he saw the place on the ground were the melted lead had been and there wasn't a speck of grass growing there.

"HAPPY JACKS" AND A "SNYDER" BECOME HOAXBUSTING CLUES FOR BLANDINA

Blandina's longest "Billy the Kid" tale features his "gang members Schneider and Happy Jack" - without full names.

BLANDINA'S TALES OF "SCHNEIDER"/"SNYDER," "HAPPY JACK," AND TRINIDAD DOCTORS

For "September, 1876," "Schneider" appears as a bull-fighter clad rider in Trinidad. His fatal fight with "Happy Jack" was in *Veritas* and the 1932 book:

> ["Schneider"] and Happy Jack, his partner, got into a quarrel, and each got the drop on the other. They continued eyeing and following each other for three days ...
>
> The tragedy took place when they were eating dinner. Each thought the other off guard, both fired simultaneously. **Happy Jack was shot through the breast.** He was put in a dug-out 3x6 ft. **Schneider received a bullet in his thigh**, and has been brought to Trinidad. (1932, Page 73)

In that entry, Blandina also called "Schneider" "Billy the Kid's partner." (1932, Page 79) She recorded nursing him, his confessing heinous crimes, his warning that "Billy the Kid" would scalp Trinidad's four doctors for not removing the bullet from his thigh, and her meeting "Billy the Kid" to stop those scalpings. She listed the Trinidad doctors; writing:

Here are the names of the physicians who were doomed to be scalped:

Dr. **Michael Beshoar**, our Convent and Academy physician; the two **Menger brothers**. The elder has a large family; the younger is a bachelor. The fourth is **Dr. Palmer**, whom I know by reputation. (1932, Page 82)

She also mentioned Dr. Beshoar in her March, 1929 *Veritas* article for entry of March 1881; writing:

Dr. Michael Beshoar, of Trinidad, Colorado, who is a scientist as well as a physician, claims that at one time tropical fruits grew at this latitude.

"September, 1876's" entry ended with dying "Schneider's" mother taking over his care:

Another month passed by and the patient was visibly losing strength. I managed to get his mother's address. She lives in California ... (1932, Page 80)

The patient's mother is going to have her son removed to a private facility ... I judge she has a high opinion of herself ... She is a Methodist. Hereafter our visits will be friendly ones, no relief, whatever. The mother has taken full responsibility. (1932, Page 83)

For "Feast of All Saints, 1876," Blandina wrote:

Our poor desperado is fast approaching the shores of eternity ... [H]e never mentions "the Gang," though Trinidad often hears the atrocities committed by it – only say "Billy the Kid" and every individual is at attention ...

When we entered the patient's room we saw plainly that he could not survive many hours.

Kneeling, we said prayers, which included an act of contrition, he repeated them, then said "good bye." **We felt this was the end of our services to the tiger desperado. We left him to the mercy of God.** (1932, Page 86)

But, as mentioned above, there was a strange clue about "Schneider": Blandina originally spelled it as "Snyder" for her article in the October, 1930 *The Santa Maria*, for entry dated "Cherry season, 1884," which abbreviated her "Schneider" and "Happy Jack" shootings tale. And "Billy the Kid's gang" is added in parentheses, as if in an afterthought or editing. This version was eliminated from the 1932 book. Blandina wrote:

[It was at Dick Wooten's toll house that] **"Happy Jack" and "Snyder" (two of Billy the Kid's gang) from friends became mortal enemies**, keeping the "drop" on each other for three days ... At dinner on the third day, both thought the other off guard simultaneously. **Snyder shot "Happy Jack" through the heart; "Happy Jack's" shot caught Snyder in the thigh** ... Mr. Snyder was brought to Trinidad and thrown into an uninhabited adobe. It was in that adobe house that two of my pupils and I brought him daily nourishment, clean bandages, etc. **He was ill nine months and, of course, he died because the ball was never extracted from his thigh.**

PRESS WITH "HAPPY JACKS"

In this case, one can trace the newspaper sources for creating the "Schneider/Snyder-Happy Jack" names and tales.

"Happy Jack" first appears as a Jack McManus in a March 23, 1873 *Daily Rocky Mountain News* article titled "Recapture and Escape of a Horse Thief." It stated:

Recapture and Escape of a Horse Thief.

We published in the NEWS, about a month ago, an account of the capture of James McManus, at Fort Collins, his being taken out of the hands of Deputy Sheriff Follett, of Larimer county, and being hung up some seven times by vigilantes ... now we have a continuation of the story.

It seems that the jailor at Boulder has not a very high appreciation of the uses of a jail, and allows his prisoners the liberty of the town. **This horse thief, McManus – or "Happy Jack," as he is called** – was allowed to perambulate around Boulder as he pleased, until Tuesday night of last week, when he broke into a jewelry store, stole two pistols and a small amount of money, and quietly took his departure on a horse furnished by an accomplice ... [Deputy Sheriff Allen,] [u]pon getting the assistance of Sheriff Mason [of Larimer county] ... recaptured the prisoner way up on Lone Pine creek.

When found, McManus was asleep, and had with him a rifle and lots of ammunition, a large revolver and a bowie knife, all of which he had stolen. There was found on him also a bunch of keys, one of which belonged to the valiant Bounder jailor.

Among the other crimes committed by this desperado since leaving Boulder ... was knocking down and grossly assaulting Mrs. W.F. Day, of Lone Pine ...

McManus was taken to Fort Collins on Wednesday evening, and kept there securely ironed until Thursday evening, locked up in the court house ... in about ten minutes after he was taken back to the court house, the report was heralded that the prisoner had jumped out of the window, some fourteen feet from the ground, and made his escape ... Two suspicious characters were around town all afternoon, and were not seen afterwards, and they undoubtedly planned and aided his escape ...

From the reports we hear of the temper of the people of Larimer county, we feel sure if this reckless criminal is ever found within her limits again it will be but a very short time before he is seen ornamenting a cottonwood tree.

The saga of this horse thief and petty robber named "Happy Jack" was completed in the *Daily Rocky Mountain News* of April 1, 1873 in " 'Happy Jack,' the Horse Thief," which reported his vigilante killing by shooting; stating:

"Happy Jack," the Horse Thief"

The Evans *Journal* of Saturday contains the particulars of "Happy Jack's" movements:

" 'Happy Jack,' the desperado and horse thief, whose escape we recorded last week, is still at large ... [H]e was in company with a tall man, who is evidentially an accomplice of his ... A reward of $250 is offered for the arrest of Jack by the sheriff of Larimer county, besides some smaller amounts by citizens amounting to $500 ...

[W]hen "Happy Jack" was [originally] arrested in Lone Pine ... he was taken to Fort Collins where he was heavily ironed and locked up. His keepers then left him ... and when they returned their prisoner was gone ...

Last evening we learned, upon most reliable authority, that **"Happy Jack" has paid the debt of his deviltries.** Upon his escape from Fort Collins jail he was overhauled by a party of men who commanded him to halt. **He refused to comply, when a bullet from a carbine brought him down. He died shortly after, and his body was thrown into the creek.**

Three years after these James McManus aka "Happy Jack" articles, and near the time of Blandina's "September, 1876" journal entry, there was a Thursday, December 7, 1876, Pueblo, Colorado, *Colorado Chieftain* article titled "San Juan: Few Notes by Hol. Gorden." It was about a "Happy Jack," who was not killed, and did not appear to be an escapee horse thief. This new "Happy Jack" seems to have been an affable regular citizen and friend of the author, and an Oak Creek resident. But it kept the "Happy Jack" nick-name in public view for Blandina's entries' potential using. Gorden wrote:

[In Lake City] we met a good many old friends, and among them **Happy Jack**, an old Oak creek friend ... The conversation with him ran as follows:

"Hello! Isn't your name **Happy Jack**, whom they reported killed last winter, and who used to hang up with Sam on Oak creek," we asked him.

"You are right," he said.

PRESS WITH BOTH "SNYDER" AND "HAPPY JACK"

On July 11, 2017, Sisters of Charity archivist, Veronica Buchanan, located an obituary of a John M. Snyder from the January 10, 1877, El Moro, Colorado, *The Enterprise and Chronicle*. And it had yet another "Happy Jack;" this one named R.I. Donnlson. And neither this Snyder nor this "Happy Jack" were outlaws. But importantly, this Snyder was shot in the thigh by this "Happy Jack!" Even though it was an accident, and "Happy Jack" was not shot at all – like Blandina's "Happy Jack" The obituary stated:

Death of John M. Snyder

Mr. John M. Snyder, who was accidentally shot last July by **R.I. Donnlson, familiarly known as "Happy Jack,**: died on Monday morning. The circumstances of the shooting are familiar to our readers. We understand Snyder fully exonerated Donnlson from any blame in the matter.

At one time Snyder was in a fair way of recovery, and was able to get up and walk about the house, but getting a fall one day, the wounded part was injured again and abscesses formed which probably terminated his life. **Dr. Rogers, assisted by Drs. Cushing and Beshoar, made an ante-mortem amputation of the thigh bone and found that the rifle ball had entered the surgical neck of the femur and passing through lodged in the muscles**.

Snyder was about 32 years of age. He came from Ohio. **His mother, sister and brother were present at this death.**

HOAXBUSTING CLUES OF
"SNYDER" AND "HAPPY JACK"

Just like with Blandina's entries' tell-tale lifting from Pat Garrett's, Walter Noble Burns's, And Ralph Emerson Twitchell's books to create her so-called "Billy the Kid" journal entries after 1926, we can see the same technique here. Newspaper articles from her Trinidad period with names "Happy Jack" and "Snyder," and a shooting incident between them, as well as a different "Happy Jack" who was fatally shot, were lifted for her overheated "Billy the Kid" fable with Trinidad's doctors refusing to treat her shot "Schneider/Snyder" and incurring "Billy the Kid's" revenge scalping plan. And she may have even participated in nursing real John M. Snyder.

That would also show that articles might have been saved by her in the 1870's, and later used to create her magazine's journal entries during 1926 to 1931 by her or an editor. Or she may have written her fantasy sketches in their 19th century time-frame, like the short version above from the October, 1930 *The Santa Maria*, about the "Snyder" and "Happy Jack" shootings, which later grew to "Billy the Kid" fables.

But such repurposing to feign historic legitimacy is hoaxing. Here is the incriminatory result showing both lifted details and fantasy alterations from the "Happy Jack" and "Snyder" articles. And, of course, there was no mention of a "Billy the Kid gang" related to real "Happy Jacks" or "Snyder."

1) **James McManus aka "Happy Jack" was a minor Colorado outlaw, with crimes of horse thieving and robberies, who was killed by vigilantes in 1873.**

But Blandina's "Happy Jack" was a highwayman member of "Billy the Kid's" rapacious and terrifying gang, who was fatally shot by "gang member Schneider."

2) **"Happy Jack," as a Colorado non-outlaw friend of Hol. Gorden, and apparently not James McManus, was an affable local, falsely rumored as killed.**

But Blandina's tale has "Happy Jack" murdered by "Schneider/Snyder."

3) John M. Snyder" and R.I. Donnlson aka "Happy Jack" were not outlaws.
But Blandina's tale called them part of "Billy the Kid's gang," and claimed atrocious crimes committed by "Schneider."

4) R.I. "Happy Jack" Donnlson shot John M. Snyder by accident.
But Blandina's tale said "Happy Jack's" willful shooting of Snyder occurred after a hostile stand-off lasting days.

5) R.I. "Happy Jack" Donnlson was not shot at all.
But Blandina's tale said that "Schneider/Snyder" willfully shot "Happy Jack" fatally through the heart.

6) John M. Snyder was shot in the thigh.
Blandina's "Schneider/Snyder" was shot in the thigh.

7) John M. Snyder was, in fact, treated [ante-mortem means before death] by the local doctors, named as Rogers, Cushing, and Beshoar.
But Blandina's tale claimed that "Schneider/Snyder" was refused treatment by Trinidad's doctors, whom she named as Michael Beshoar, two Menger brothers, and Dr. Palmer. One can wonder if the article's "ante-mortem" was misread by her as "post-mortem," giving rise to her wild creation of doctors refusing to treat "Schneider," which segued into her even wilder creation of "Billy the Kid's" intended scalping revenge, and of different doctors than named in the Snyder obituary.

8) Drs. Rogers, Cushing, and Beshoar found the bullet lodged in Snyder's muscles after it damaged his femur.
But Blandina denied that Trinidad's doctors had treatment contact with "Schneider/Snyder."

9) John M. Snyder first rallied and went home, then died there of infection following a fall.
But Blandina's "Schneider/Snyder" is abandoned in a random Trinidad house and failed progressively over nine months of her nursing care.

10) **John M. Snyder's mother, sister and brother were present at his death**.
But in Blandina's version, only the mother is present.

SMOKING GUNS FOR A HOAX: Colorado newspapers from Blandina's Trinidad period were used to lift details and names - like "Snyder" and "Happy Jack" and shootings - to manufacture her entries' fictional accounts of a "Billy the Kid" outlaw gang. But no single outlaw yet discovered matches her Colorado highwayman-murderer gang leader in the 1870's. And period newspapers would have covered a gang of the magnitude described in her entries. And that omission also removes a Colorado outlaw for Blandina to encounter in the Santa Fe jail "four years" later in May of 1881.

OVERALL SMOKING GUNS FOR FIRST-HAND ENCOUNTERS HOAXES: Blandina's entries' first-hand accounts of encounters with "Billy the Kid," "Schneider/Snyder," Victorio, "Mr. Murphy" and "Paoline" Maxwell are revealed as fictional by their non-historic dates, fatal flaws of misinformation, and their components being demonstrably lifted from sources like 19th century articles and 20th century books. And the possibility of a match with Billy LeRoy for "two Billy the Kid's" to create Blandina's "confusion" is removed by LeRoy's late dating and lack of "Billy the Kid" moniker. Revealed is hoaxing, pure and simple, with the pernicious implication of Blandina being fraudulently written, by herself or an editor, into Billy the Kid's history as a participant.

9

CRACKING THE NUN'S TALE HOAX

CRACKING THE NUN'S TALE HOAX

SLEUTHING HOAXBUSTING CLUES: Though it is now clear that Blandina's "Billy the Kid" Old West journal entries were fabricated, it was still uncertain if she was their author. Then a document was found which described just how the original "journal" was transformed into its first publication as "At the End of the Santa Fe Trail" articles; and who did it.

THE COMELLA-CASSANO PAPER

With the original frontier journal destroyed by Blandina Segale, it seemed impossible to know how, and by whom, her journal was created for publication in the Santa Maria Institute's magazine from 1926 to 1931 as "At the End of the Santa Fe Trail." As was seen above, the fabricated entries for "Billy the Kid" and related figures were largely written in the 20th century, and not at their claimed 19th, century dates. Key for deciding responsibility for that Nun's Tale Hoax was determining Blandina's role in creating those articles which subsequently gave rise to her 1932 book, *At the End of the Santa Fe Trail*.

I had asked the Sisters of Charity archivist, Veronica Buchanan to search for any documents related to the process of publishing the magazine articles. That led, by chance, to the paper that helped to crack the Nun's Tale Hoax.

On May 18th, 2017, I was speaking by phone with Veronica, and she mentioned a single typed page which was all that remained of a letter written by Blandina's original typists, Sisters Lucy Comella and Carmela Cassano, to record for archival history how Blandina prepared her journal articles for publication! Veronica thought it had already been e-mailed to me. It had not. The possibility of knowing exactly what had occurred was breathtaking.

The page was dated approximately to 1932. Veronica read it to me. It cracked the Nun's Tale Hoax. It stated the following:

<u>It is recorded</u> in her journal ... Billy the Kid and the Gang were going to kill the doctors who neglected to take care of his wounded pal. Sister Blandina approached Billy the Kid to spare the life of the doctors.

Traveling by stagecoach, Billy the Kid and his gang were about to attack the coach. When he came near enough S. Blandina leaned forward so she could be seen and recognized. Billy the Kid saw her, doffed his hat gallantly, wheeled around and left.

There were many other instances in her hand written journal which have either been lost or destroyed. When these article [sic] were being prepared for publication in the magazine, (Veritas) I worked with S. Blandina In her office. Reams of paper rolled and packed in boxes (her daily journal kept for her sister, S. Justina) were taken out, inspected and either handed to me to be typed or thrown into the basket. **Often as she read these silently before she handed them to me to be typed or throw [sic] in the basket, Sister would add comments to what she had written. Had a tape recorder been available at this time, a wealth of history, both of the west and the community would have been preserved.**

       Sister Lucy Comella
       Sister Carmela Cassano

I named it the Comella-Cassano paper. It proved that Blandina was the articles' hands-on author, fashioning her tales out-loud at their typing, as she perused her saved reams of rolled papers, stored more than 50 years. Some she had Lucy Comella and Carmela Cassano copy, some she kept secret by destroying without copying, and, most importantly, she "would add comments to what she had written." And some tales Blandina may have created de novo, as implied by the transcriptionists' statement: "There were many other instances in her hand written journal which have either been lost or destroyed" – as if Blandina ad-libbed to Comella and Cassano with the claim that those particular entries had been "lost or destroyed."

So the notion of having written her original journal to share with her sister, Justina, seems more like a literary device for the articles' presentation, since there is no mention by the transcriptionists that the stored papers had previously been unpacked. And, by 1926, Blandina had been back in Cincinnati with Justina for 29 years!

Also, since Lucy Comella and Carmela Cassano noted that it was "recorded in Blandina's journal" about "Billy the Kid and the Gang's" plan to kill the doctors and about her "Billy the Kid" encounter on the plains, it can be concluded that the basic fables were formulated by Blandina in the 19th century, then elaborated by her for her magazine articles.

In fact, Blandina had described in entries in what form she accumulated her data: writing that she kept "notes," "scribblings," and "scraps" to "condense." She stated:

[For "September, 1876" for *Veritas*] **My scattered notes on "Billy the Kid's Gang" are condensed**, and someday you [Justina] will be thrilled by their perusal.

[For "October, 1930" for *The Santa Maria* the entry was dated as] "Albuquerque, New Mexico. (**Scraps found in Saratoga trunk**) Cherry season. 1884."

[The entry for "1886" stated] **From [my] notes taken at different times**, you [Justina], may read some facts. Here are some of my findings.

Blandina also interviewed people to research entries, writing:

[The entry for "1886" also stated] **Rev. Brother Baldwin, Vice-President of St. Michael College, Santa Fé, was a substantial help to me in talking notes.**

One now sees that Blandina had even revealed her technique of building her tales on her "notes," albeit without admitting that those tales were not put into "journal form" until the 20th century for the articles, or that the "Billy the Kid" ones were fables. For the October, 1928, *Veritas*, Blandina spelled it out for the entry dated "September, 1879;" writing:

Dear Sister Justina: Looking over the scribblings I wrote on scraps since January, **I noticed that they were not entered into this journal** which I trust some day you will enjoy. **I've condensed the scraps and here is the result.**

Now that the Nun's Tale Hoax was revealed as being by Blandina, the other pieces of its puzzle fit together, permitting a hypothetical reconstruction of its creation. Here it is:

During her 19th century time in the Old West, Blandina Segale collected items of interest to her: some were her own fictional tales, some were descriptions of real incidents or interviews, some were newspaper clippings, and some recorded her historical research. These were unpacked years after her return to Cincinnati to create magazine articles which were written in a literary vehicle of a journal from frontier days for her fellow nun and sister, Justina. Such

was Blandina's writing skill, that she could devise her tales off-the-cuff around the "scraps" she handed to Lucy Comella and Carmela Cassano, as well as creating some de novo while claiming their "original notes" had been lost. And Comella and Cassano typed her dictation innocently; adding with awe: "Had a tape recorder been available at this time, a wealth of history ... of the west ... would have been preserved." By the 1932 book, Blandina used 20th century history books to correct her "Billy the Kid" errors in the magazines, and also moved dates a year forward in a failed attempt to mimic historical events.

That conclusion left two unanswered questions. Why did Blandina publish her journal after so many years? And why did she tell "Billy the Kid" fables?

The second question was the most baffling, since conceiving of this high-achieving and religiously devout woman as a willful and reckless hoaxer strained belief. And her Petitioner for her sainthood, Allen Sánchez, had already claimed to have verified non-Billy the Kid dramatic incidents described in her entries - like her stopping a lynch mob. Called for was more consideration before accusation. But the Nun's Tale Hoax was nevertheless the creation of Blandina Segale.

SMOKING GUNS FOR A HOAX: It was now certain that Blandina Segale created the "Billy the Kid" journal fables, first published as magazine articles. At that juncture, their preparation came not from recopying a real journal, but from assembling her old hoarded notes and materials of interest to elaborate them as a facsimile of journal entries, or from simply making up entries with the claim that the originals had been lost. That explains their surmised and incorrect dating, and their embellishments from her imagination, from newspaper articles, and from that stage's bit of book research, as her transcriptionists, Lucy Comella and Carmela Cassano, took her dictation. All that made her "Billy the Kid" entries a premeditated hoax for which she was responsible, and never disclaimed.

WEIGHING IN
BLANDINA'S HOAXING INTENT

SLEUTHING HOAXBUSTING CLUES: Intrinsic to hoaxing is the intent to deceive. Could Blandina Segale have had other reasons for her "Billy the Kid" misinformation which would mitigate her culpability?

Blandina Segale was without a doubt a brilliant, complex, and high-achieving renaissance-style woman with unshakable religious faith and the admiration of all who knew her. She in no way conformed to a typical historical hoaxer, who is usually a sociopathic loser, attempting to feign achievement to get fame or fortune. There can be no better example than the unsavory New Mexico governor, lawmen, and rogue history professor I exposed for their Billy the Kid DNA hoax in my 2014 book, *Cracking the Billy the Kid Case Hoax.*

But there is no doubt that Blandina's alleged "Billy the Kid" 19th century journal entries were her largely 20th century creation, born of her collected sources and story-telling skills, with its fictional character of "Billy the Kid" being used for drama. And their basic tall tales went back to her youthful days in the Southwest, since Lucy Comella and Carmela Cassano saw her notes on "Billy the Kid," and confirmed two of her fables as being "recorded in her journal," writing:

> **It is recorded in her journal** ... Billy the Kid and the Gang were going to kill the doctors who neglected to take care of his wounded pal. Sister Blandina approached Billy the Kid to spare the life of the doctors.
>
> Traveling by stagecoach, Billy the Kid and his gang were about to attack the coach. When he came near enough S. Blandina leaned forward so she could be seen and recognized. Billy the Kid saw her, doffed his hat gallantly, wheeled around and left.

With made-up dates and events from the start, the journal entries were willful fabrication for the magazine articles. Then followed additional 20th century interventions for its 1932 book - only a year after the articles ended - by use of books and newspaper articles to fix-up glaring errors and to make the tales better match that period's known Billy the Kid history. All that looks like Blandina's intent to deceive her readers, since she had to know that she never had a relationship with a monstrous outlaw-highwayman-murderer named "Billy the Kid." And in the nine years left of her long life after the publication of *At the End of the Santa Fe Trail*, with her readers obviously believing she had published a real journal of real experiences, Blandina never said otherwise.

This astounded me. At the start of my investigation, I had expected to find the simple solution of an over-zealous editor - like an earlier example of 1948's Therese Martin - who inserted the "Billy the Kid" fables without even telling busy Blandina; who, during the publication period, was running her Santa Maria Institute of Cincinnati on her energy, labor, creativity, charisma, and faith. But no such editor emerged. Then it became clear from the Comella-Cassano paper that the creation of the "Billy the Kid" tales was by Blandina herself.

With Blandina on the firing line for a hoax, my further contemplation of her motive was required. Before I was comfortable categorizing her with the conscienceless self-serving charlatans I had already exposed for the Billy the Kid Case Hoax and the "Brushy Bill" Billy the Kid Pretender Hoax, I wanted to see if her tall-tales could be mitigated by good, or at least explicable, intents. That meant exploring other aspects of her personality that were known, and which were reflected in her journal.

SMOKING GUNS FOR A HOAX: With no doubt of a "Billy the Kid" hoax existing, or of Blandina being its creator, all that remained was to seek mitigating factors to explain her dishonest portrayals in her so-called journal entries, and to explain why she never issued a disclaimer for her duped readers.

JUST PARABLES FOR ENRICHMENT?

SLEUTHING HOAXBUSTING CLUES: Possibly Blandina's "Billy the Kid" tales were parables, with her religious intent being to save any lost youth's soul - and to likewise inspire her readers with the power of her religion. That kind of spiritual mission was also the intent of the Santa Maria Institute's magazine in which she first published her Old West journal.

The first *Veritas* magazine was in February of 1926. Its goals, assumedly written by founder, Blandina Segale, stated:

> The Santa Maria Institute is undertaking the publication of the monthly magazine VERITAS with the object of uniting still more firmly the Italians of Cincinnati and nearby cities in the bond of friendship. **We need to stimulate one another in fidelity to the Holy Mother Church; in obedience to the Constitution of the government under which we live; in the striving after the highest education which our schools offer us; in the interchange of ideas as the means of greater progress; in bringing to light the latent talent of young people.** What can do this more effectually than a magazine which will express all this in a friendly monthly visit?

By the May, 1927 *Veritas* magazine, the cover listed a three word intent as: "Religion, Education, Americanization." The January, 1931, issue of *The Santa Maria* gave its mission statement, which certainly was not scholarly. That would have been absurd for its readership of needy Italian immigrants, some with limited English language skills. It stated:

> The Santa Maria Institute was founded by the Sisters of Charity in 1897. The object is religious, benevolent and educational work among the poor, and

Americanization among foreigners. In the attainment of this, it conducts a social center, night school, kindergarten, day nursery and various clubs.

The Santa Maria is an extension of the work. It counteracts proselytism, and gives religious instruction. **It replaces pernicious reading by supplying interesting articles and good fiction.** Some of the best known Catholic writers are among its contributors. Its surplus fund is devoted to the education of worthy boys for the priesthood.

Every month, beginning on the first day and ending on the ninth, a novena is made by the Sisters and children for the intentions of all subscribers. Those wishing to do so, may send in their intentions, which will be placed near the statue of the Blessed Virgin.

On the First Friday of every month, the Holy Sacrifice of the Mass will be offered for the intentions of subscribers.

Teaching and inspiring by parables would have been a compatible goal. A parable, according to *Webster's Dictionary*, is "a short fictitious story that illustrates a moral attitude or religious principle." Blandina's "Billy the Kid" tales, with their transformative goodness of a holy practitioner, do seem like parables.

BLANDINA'S PARABLES

With obvious didactic intent, Blandina had written:

[For 1932 date "September, 1876"] I took ["Billy the Kid's"] hand saying: "I understand you have come to scalp our Trinidad physicians, **which act I ask you to cancel.**" ...

"**Not only [do I grant] that, Sister, but at any time my pals and I can serve you, you will find us ready.**"

[For 1932 date "Feast of All Saints, 1876"] Our poor desperado ["Billy the Kid gang member Schneider"] is fast approaching the shores of eternity ... When we entered the patient's room we saw plainly that he could not survive many hours. **Kneeling, we said prayers, which included an act of contrition, he repeated them, then said "good bye." We felt this was the end of our services to the tiger desperado. We left him to the mercy of God.**

[For 1932 date "May 16 [1882]"] **Think, dear Sister Justina, how many crimes might have been prevented, had someone had influence over "Billy" after his first murder** ... Finding himself captain and dictator, **with no religious principles to check him,** he became what he is – the greatest murderer of the Southwest.

Blandina's tales were, indeed, appreciated for their moral value. Her posthumous editor, Sister Therese Martin, was obviously moved by her message, even contemplating "Billy the Kid's" soul's salvation through Blandina's efforts; writing:

[Blandina] is seen [in her journal entries] fearlessly confronting the notorious outlaw, "Billy the Kid," demanding safety for the physicians of Trinidad, whose lives he threatened, and **not only winning his confidence but inspiring him with respect for every member of the religious garb. Who shall say what effect her ministrations to a neglected member of his band of outlaws may have had on the soul of this misguided youth?**

One can cite again the November 17, 1933 article titled "Keeping the Record" for *The Commonweal,* by Eugene P. Murphy. Murphy wrote:

> Billy the Kid was an outlaw whose name cast terror along the Santa Fe trail for many a year ... **Sister Blandina saw the unrealized possibilities for good that lay in his untamed soul. Like a true teaching nun she wondered what the result might have been had some good influence reached him in time. Could it not have stilled the hate rising in the heart of the lad of twelve and prevented him from starting on his career of killing.**

Likewise, the September, 1953 edition of *The Irish Digest's* article by L.G. O'Carroll titled "The Nun and Billy the Kid: How timid, inexperienced little sister Blandina earned the respect of the bad men of the wild and wooly West," stated:

> **Perhaps the influence of Sister Blandina with hardened men is best illustrated by her meeting with Billy the Kid**. Billy was the most daring of the South-West desperados. **He was** young, debonair, fiercely loyal to his friends, yet **one of the cruelest and most ruthless killers of those lawless times – he would put a bullet through a man as nonchalantly as he would light a cigarette**. He died at twenty-one, fair-haired, slim, boyish in appearance, yet he had killed a man for every year of his life ...
>
> **But it seems certain that the notorious outlaw had a special reverence for the little nun, and in time her gentle sympathy might have softened the core of hardness in him.**

Blandina may have agreed with L.G. O'Carrol that she showed the power of faith on "hardened men." And mythic "Billy the Kid" was her time's example of that. So her motive might have been the message, not the historical accuracy.

SMOKING GUNS FOR A HOAX: Since Blandina had unshakable religious faith, her acts must be seen in that context. Her story-telling skill may have been for parables to elevate readers, making "Billy the Kid" more of a symbol than a real person. But that does not remove her obligation to disclose, when people confused her fiction for fact. Hoaxing remains, but with mitigation.

JUST A FOLIE À DEUX?

Another mitigating possibility is psychological: that Blandina came to believe her long-told fantasy tales.

Billy the Kid imposter, "Brushy Bill" Roberts, certainly believed his stories. He was a confabulator, with at least 12 aliases and life stories, all of famous characters - Billy the Kid being just one. "Brushy" claimed also to be a member of the Jesse James gang and of Roosevelt's Rough Riders, a participant in Buffalo Bill Cody's Wild West Show, a Pinkerton Detective, a bronco rider, a friend of Bell Starr, a Deputy U.S. Marshall, a rancher in Old Mexico, and an associate of Pancho Villa. For his audience of one - his future author, William V. Morrison - he featured himself as Billy the Kid.

That brings to mind Blandina's original audience: Anna Minogue, Associate Editor of her magazine. (And since the journal was allegedly prepared for her sister, Justina herself might have been also been her audience for verbal story-telling in the years after 1897, when they were reunited in Cincinnati.) As discussed above, Anna Minogue was Blandina's motivator for publishing her so-called journal in the Santa Maria Institute's magazine. As Minogue had written in the articles' *Veritas* "Foreword": "[I] **begged her to write an account of the romantic, tragic, historic adventures and events which clustered around those days.**"

As an aside, I briefly considered Anna Minogue as the secret editor who created the "Billy the Kid" entries, but there was no evidence for her in the Sisters of Charity archives. Minogue was, however, a published author, even having a 1922 book titled *The Blind Priest: A Thrilling Story of the West*. But it was set in Oklahoma, had no "Billy the Kid" or outlaws, was a romance around early oil drilling, and had a writing style different from Blandina's.

That left the search for a psychological clue to Blandina's relationship with Anna Minogue, since it appears that Anna was the recipient, for years, of Blandina's oral "Billy the Kid" stories. She was Blandina's first true-believer. And the tales - going back to young Blandina's Trinidad fantasies - by then, may have seemed true to Blandina also. That peculiar loss of reality is called folie à deux, where one person's false belief or delusion is transmitted to another, who believes it also; and the belief strengthens in their mutuality.

A clue about Blandina's story-telling relationship with Anna Minogue is in a November, 1927 *Veritas* article titled "The West Revisited," about Blandina's return, in 1927, to the Southwest. Blandina shared her impressions with loyal Anna in a letter dated "September 23, 1927," which Anna reprinted in the magazine, while noting by way of its explanation, that Blandina recognized her own "intense love for the West." Anna wrote about herself:

> Knowing the Associate Editor's **[Anna Minogue's] intense love for the West and all things pertaining thereto,** Sister Blandina took the time to write her of the ever-alluring land, and the changes Sister found.

And Blandina's letter to Anna had an eye-opening clue. In its 707 words summarizing her memories of her 21 years on the frontier, she devoted 54 to a yet another "Billy the Kid" fable! It was a tale about Pat Garrett (whom she still misspelled as "Garret," like in her article and 1932 book): stating:

> In my time **Gallup was particularly noted as the place where Mr. Patrick Garret [sic] lived when rewards were offered from many places in New Mexico for the capture of the notorious "Billy the Kid," dead or alive.** Mr. Garret [sic] followed "Billy the Kid's" trail to Maxwell's ranch, New Mexico, where he shot him dead.

[AUTHOR'S NOTE: Pat Garrett lived in Roswell, not Gallup. She makes up that, in her time in the West, he lived there. Her misspelling as "Garret" was also in her entries for *Veritas* of "August, 1881" and for the 1932 book's "September 8, 1882" about the killing of "Billy the Kid." And rewards were not offered in many places in New Mexico for Billy's capture. And she continued her misconception that the Maxwells were in Cimarron - not Fort Sumner - when Billy was shot at their mansion.]

So it seems that Blandina felt no inhibition in spinning "Billy the Kid" yarns - and overlapping them with her own time in the West - and certainly not as if burdened by guilt at their fabricating. In fact, Allen Sánchez told me that when she was 90, and living in the Sisters of Charity of Cincinnati Mother House a year before she died, she told a visitor, whom he interviewed years later, her tales of "Billy the Kid" - as well as saying prayers with her!

Using this explanation of a folie à deux relationship between Blandina and Anna Minogue, that involved Blandina's peculiar conviction that she was telling the truth, is not likely to be embraced by her advocates or the press. "Nutty Nun Hallucinates Billy the Kid" will not gain the mileage of "The Fastest Nun in the West Tames Billy the Kid."

> **SMOKING GUNS FOR A HOAX:** *Blandina's "Billy the Kid" fables are so out of touch with reality that one can contemplate delusions. If she thought they had happened, it would explain her not making a disclaimer to Anna Minogue or her readers. Though she evidenced no obvious mental problems, people do have isolated delusions. That would not negate hoaxing, but it would mitigate criticism for its creation.*

JUST IN JEST?

> **SLEUTHING HOAXBUSTING CLUES:** *The literary quality of Blandina's published journal must be considered. She never claimed it as scholarly research; and its audience was the Cincinnati, Ohio, Italian immigrant population served by her Santa Maria Institute, where her intent was maintaining their faith and providing entertainment.*

One of Blandina's traits was her playful sense of humor. Was it a clue to her "Billy the Kid" tales? In looking over unrelated articles in Blandina Segale's *Veritas* and *The Santa Maria* magazines, I noticed that she used the words "fancies" and "imaginary occurrences" lightheartedly. Could her imaginary friend, "Billy the Kid," have been intended as no more than that?

To contemplate that possibility, one has to acknowledge that Blandina's first public audience for "At the End of the Santa Fe Trail" was the downtrodden Italian immigrant population served by her Santa Maria Institute in Cincinnati, Ohio. Many read her 20 to 24 page publication, in its duration from 1926 to 1931, to learn English or to gain religiously uplifting stories. There was clearly no intent or logic to publish scholarly works in this venue.

And, as can be seen from her journal entries, Blandina was a natural story-teller and entertainer, in control of her medium with suspenseful build-ups, emotional catharses, moral lessons contrasting good and evil, attention-grabbing adventures, colorful dialogue, psychological introspection, and research into her topics. She emerges from her writings with the infectious exuberance that fueled her for 91 years. *At the End of the Santa Fe Trail* reads like a series of delightful anecdotes expressing her sense of fun, her rollicking hyperboles, and her observations of humanity's foibles. All that was the flip side of her courage, which drew on her unshakable faith for tests of hardship and evil in frontier life.

One can recall the above-mentioned *Santa Fe New Mexican* article of about 1930, sent to Blandina herself and titled "Sister Blandina Defied Outlaws, Saved One Archbishop, Also Visited Billy the Kid." It stated that she had a "**delicious sense of humor.**" One can see that in her journal entries. For her entry under "1886," she summed up that tone and intent of her journal to her sister, Justina, writing:

> If ever we meet and have time to review the many serious, humorous and ludicrous situations I have found myself in, our health will receive 100% to its credit by laughter.

Examples abound in her entries of her playful, philosophical, pervasive, and exuberantly ironic humor. They prove that part of her teaching skill was her ability to see the light side, to laugh at herself, and to entertain her audience. Here are examples.

GENERAL HUMOR

When only 22, and sent to Trinidad by her Sisters of Charity Mother-superior, Josephine, Blandina merrily recorded in her first journal entry to her sister, Justina:

> Neither of us could find Trinidad on the map **except in the island of Cuba**.

Next, two men tell her that Trinidad was a "little mining town in Southwestern Colorado," and try to scare her. She deadpanned them, as she reported:

> "Sister, you may be snow-bound while on the plains." I looked my assent, I knew I could not stop the snow ...
> "This though is not the greatest danger to you."
> **Mentally I was wishing the gentlemen were somewhere else.**
> "Your real danger is from cowboys." I looked at the speakers. "You do not seem to grasp our meaning. No virtuous woman is safe near a cowboy."

Blandina bided her time with novelist's skill to give her punch line on virtue, snow and outlaws.

For her initially solitary stagecoach ride to Trinidad, Colorado, she relates:

> Oh, the lonely, fearful feeling! The night was dark. No passengers to allay my turbulent thoughts. Footsteps near the stage. My heart was thumping. The driver opened the stage door and said:
> "You will have a traveling companion for some miles."
> In the open door, by the light of the lantern, I saw a tall, lanky, hoosier-like man, wearing a broad brimmed hat ... [He] sat beside me on the rear seat.

The driver closed the door and we were in utter darkness ... **I knew he was a cowboy!** ... **I expected he would speak – I answer – he fire.**

[But his innocent talk led to her chiding herself.] To think that this lubbery, good-natured cowboy had made me undergo such mortal anguish. He got off on the outskirts of Trinidad where the driver stopped to point out to me dugouts at the side of the foothills.

She completed her tale of the miniscule primitive town with her driver announcing: "**This, lady, is Trinidad.**"

Blandina laconically summarized Trinidadians for Justina:

Keep in mind that the **only three aims** I can read in the minds of those who, at present, live in Trinidad, and its surroundings are:

1. Health for invalids.

2. Strenuous efforts at money making.

3. Jesuits and Sisters of Charity trying to stem the undesirable conditions. **For the last named, their effort is like trying to stop an avalanche.**

From Trinidad, Blandina wrote how she had told a fellow Sisters of Charity nun, Eulalia, her idea for getting a new school building, after Eulalia bemoaned lack of money; writing:

Here is my plan, Sister [Eulalia]. **Borrow a crowbar, get on the roof of the [old] schoolhouse and begin to detach the adobes.** The first Mexican who sees me will ask, "What are you doing, Sister?" I will answer, "Tumbling down this structure to rebuild it before the opening of the fall term of school." You should have seen Eulalia laugh!

When the time came to plaster the interiors of the new schoolhouse, Blandina had to cajole the plasterer into using her

"American" style lime, sand and hair formula. But his workmen had already left. Blandina told the outcome:

> [T]here was not a man to carry the mortar to the plasterer, so I got a bucket and supplied a man's place. **The comedy follows ...**
> On this day of my hod-carrying, the Rt. Rev. Bishop Machebeuf of Denver, Colorado, arrived [with Pastor Charles Pinto] on his visitation. The first place to which he was taken was the schoolhouse being built without money. Bishop and Pastor had just turned the kitchen corner when the three of us came face to face. Both gentlemen stood amazed ... **The Bishop remarked: "I see how you manage to build without money."**

From Santa Fe, Blandina described her turn to prepare Sunday dinner for the other Sisters; writing:

> I went over the grounds to the place called a hothouse [on Archbishop Lamy's private property] ... and there, to my surprise, I found strawberries! I picked them more quickly than the miners out here dig for gold ... When Sister Louise saw the strawberries she laughed aloud and said, "You certainly were brave to pick the strawberries!" ...
> **I wanted my dinner to be a complete surprise, which it was, as far as I am concerned.**

Later, she repeated that trick when her infirmary ran out of food for its indigent patients, 35 orphans and 16 Sisters. She wrote:

> I went to the rear of our empty vegetable garden and looked over the adobe wall into the Archbishop's [Lamy's] garden. There I saw an abundance of cabbage, turnips, carrots, and what not ... I made one

athletic spring (old habits die slowly) and landed near the cabbage patch. Throwing over into our vacant garden at least two dozen cabbage heads, I did the same with each of the other vegetables ... Then I went to His Grace's door and rapped.

"Come in." ...

"I have come to make a confession out of the confessional." ...

"My little Sister, what have you been doing?" ...

"Stealing, Your Grace ... I dug up enough vegetables from your garden to last us three days." ...

"Tell Louis to give you all there are."

From Santa Fe, Blandina described excitement about the opportunity to ride a ferry boat across the Rio Grande; writing:

What do you think is the greatest pleasure I anticipate? Crossing the river in a ferry boat!

I've been told the river is crossed at Albuquerque on a ferry boat. Even to see a boat's smokestack will give me a thrill ...

[Her business near Albuquerque was completed, and the traveling resumed.] **We crossed the Rio.** I remember the blank looks of a child of six when he discovered that Santa Claus was not Santa Claus. Picture me with that look when the driver pointed to some heavy planks nailed together ...

Man power is used to propel the raft from the river bank as far as it is safe for the men to wade. They then got on the "ferry boat" until we were near the opposite bank of the river, when they jumped in the water again and used their physical engines to land us.

From Santa Fe, she recounted discovering a fire on the roof of her just-built infirmary there; writing:

> The thought uppermost in my mind was that the last patients will be cremated ...
>
> I went to the roof of the first story. From here I looked at the roof of the second story. There a blaze was issuing from the chimney ... **I touched the three-inch drainer tin spout and soliloquized: "I cannot ascend on that." My next act from the hospital roof was to say: "You two men stand and let the third man on your shoulders to hand me the bucket of salt."** ... Water was handed to me in the same manner. I poured one bucket down the chimney and nothing came out but black smoke; the fire was extinguished! ...
>
> **[Then someone asked] "[H]ow did Sister get up there?"**
>
> **This question made me think ... Diving quickly into psychic phenomena I knew I had been the subject of mind over matter ... I doubt not the men think I'm either a saint or a witch.**

From Santa Fe, Blandina told of inadequate funds to bury deceased indigent patients in her hospital, and how she took action with a recalcitrant County Commissioner; writing:

> On arriving at the hospital I was informed that the moribund patient had passed away.
>
> I returned to the Commissioner ... and said ... "Will you allow $15.00 for his burial;?"
>
> "Now, Sister, you must help me economize. Bury him for ... $8.00."
>
> **I made answer, "In fifteen minutes the corpse will be brought to your office. You can economize as you wish. Good-bye."**
>
> I had walked about forty steps when the Commissioner's voice said ... "We will allow you $15.00 for the burial of each poor patient."

From Santa Fe, Blandina teased herself about fear of a corpse in the infirmary she had constructed; writing:

> I noticed that the dissecting room door was ajar ... I looked in and saw the corpse and where the cuttings around the heart had been made ... I began to tremble with an indefinable fear and an ungovernable impulse to run away, which I did ... **I said to myself: "Sister Blandina, walk back and look at the corpse until you have conquered yourself."**
> Slowly walking where a few moments before I had run, I reached the mortuary room ... I commanded myself and said" "Walk in and stand near the corpse until fear leaves you." I went and stood and looked, but the impulse to run was strong.
> "Are you afraid now, Sister Blandina?"
> "Yes, I am."
> "Well, stand until you have conquered."
> "Now, will you walk out slowly?"
> "Yes." ...
> After this soliloquy ... I had conquered at last!

"BILLY THE KID" HUMOR

Blandina's "Billy the Kid" tales can be read as entertainment too. In her prelude to meeting him, she told about his flamboyant "gang member Schneider," whom she and other Trinidad residents watched approaching as a 6'3" giant, murdering, outlaw monster, writing:

> **We stood in our front yard, everyone trying to look indifferent,** while Billy's accomplice headed toward us.

Blandina magnified "Schneider" to an entire Hispanic festival; writing with giddy silliness:

He was mounted on a spirited stallion of unusually large proportions, and was dressed as the *Torreros* (Bull-Fighters) dress in old Mexico. Cowboy's sombrero, fantastically trimmed, red velvet knee breaches, green velvet short coat, long sharp spurs, gold and green saddle cover. A figure of six feet three, on a beautiful animal ... you need not wonder, the rider drew attention. **His intention was to impress you with the idea "I belong to the gang."**

Starting to nurse "Schneider" after he was shot, she joked with him; writing:

I exclaimed, "I see that nothing but a bullet through your brain will finish you!"
I saw a quivering smile pass over his face, and his tiger eyes gleamed. My words seemed heartless ...
After a few days of retrospection, I concluded it was not I who had spoken, but Fear, so psychologists say.

Blandina makes fun of herself when she meets "Billy the Kid" by emphasizing her quaintness:

I took his hand saying: "I understand you have come to scalp our Trinidad physicians, which act I ask you to cancel." Billy looked down at the sick man ["Schneider"] who remarked: **"She is game."**
What he meant by that I am yet at a loss to understand.

Blandina teases others as playfully. Being sure that "Billy the Kid" will not hurt her during her plains carriage ride since she is "marked for protection" by his vow from Trinidad, she tells the Staab group instead: **"Where could the danger lurk, being in the company of so many freight drivers?"** And she tells her nun companion, Sister Augustine, in a take-off on bravery: "**I have no more fear than if the gang did not exist.**" And when her "Billy the Kid" does approach, and recognizes her, his response is more than somber honoring of his vow: it is a madcap manic comic rendition. She writes:

> **[He] fairly flew a distance of about three rods [16.5 yards], and then stopped to give us some of his wonderful antics and bronco maneuvers.**

Keeping the private joke with her readers, she lets them know there is no danger, but tells no one in the Staab group, letting them stew. She write:

> Naturally, [Sister Augustine] cannot understand why I had no fears of "Billy's Gang" – nor does she know who the cowboy is who frightened our party, **for she has not asked.**

Irony is her strong suit. She adds up comments: "My old acquaintance, "Billy the Kid," is **using his gun freely.**" ... "Billy the Kid is **playing high pranks** ..."[T]he "Kid" is as **confident of safety as though he had a battalion at his command.**"

In the Santa Fe jail scene, she has her hand, leg, and floor-fastened "Billy the Kid" say to her with absurdity calculated for a laugh: **"I wish I could place a chair for you, Sister."**

Her salutation to the Old West, in contrast to modern civilization, was tongue-in-cheek;

> Trinidad has lost its frontier aspect. The jail is [now] built to hold its inmates. Billy the Kid's gang is dissolved ... The remaining men who were ready at the least provocation or no provocation (except that of strong drink) to raise the trigger **have settled down to domestic infelicity.** Few of the latecomers would

venture to read on the faces of men who at present **aim at being peaceful citizens** – the freaks performed in other days. Those who know **thank God that conditions are partly adjusted.**

> **SMOKING GUNS FOR A HOAX:** *Blandina's innate sense of humor kept her from dwelling on grim realities or from swaying from her mission of religious service. Her absurd "Billy the Kid" tales can be seen as so exaggerated as to depart reality for her message of good triumphing over evil. As her "Schneider" character said - and as she intended for her readers - "[W]hat strength and courage those words put into me." Beyond that, she may have had no interest in their historical validity. If people read history into them, she may have felt no obligation to set them straight. Nevertheless, her attitude does not make her tall tales less of a hoax, though the intent to entertain might be mitigating.*

JUST BLIND-SPOT PREJUDICES OF THE DAY?

> **SLEUTHING HOAXBUSTING CLUES:** *One needs to consider that, in Blandina's lifetime, the real Billy the Kid was like a fictional character anyway; with fabricated press, falsely attributed crimes, and enemies generating propaganda to get him killed. And by the early 20th century, he was part of outlaw mythology and early Hollywood movies. His unreal presentation may have inspired Blandina's own literary license.*

There is another facet to consider in Blandina's "Billy the Kid" tales. That is to see Billy Bonney through her eyes and those of her contemporaries. Her fabrications merely mirrored the 19th and 20th century national prejudices about Billy the Kid. One can see them in a July 28, 1881 Pueblo, Colorado, *Colorado Daily Chieftain* article four days after Billy Bonney's killing. It stated:

The New York *Tribune* shows a delicate appreciation of the situation of affairs on the frontier hardly to be expected of a newspaper published so far east. Speaking of the killing of the **death-dealing outlaw and tiger in human form known as "Billy the Kid,"** it says:

"The inhabitants of New Mexico do not stand upon technicalities of the law in dealing with desperados. A certain Mr. McCarthy, formerly of New York, and better known as **"Billy the Kid," a promising young man of twenty-one, whose proud boast was that he killed a man for every year of his life,** has lately been pursued and shot dead on sight, by a sheriff near Las Vegas. The coroner's jury which sat on the body thus energetically furnished for its use tendered a verdict of justifiable homicide, and passed a vote of thanks to the sheriff for ridding the community of this remarkable young man, who seems to have made himself **a terror in the region.** Furthermore, the sheriff will receive a handsome reward ... In all of which there is more of justice, rude as it is, than in many of the decisions of the courts, aided, as they are, by all the machinery of civilization.

And Blandina, though open-minded and egalitarian for her day, expressed other period prejudices and biases. She championed those in need, but sided with the rich and powerful to enable her "building without money" and maneuvering through political minefields. For her, Santa Fe Ringites Thomas Benton Catron; his law partners, William Thornton and Frank Clancy; and Dr. Robert Longwill were the good guys; as was hypocrite, Lew Wallace. Their outlaws were her outlaws. And Billy the Kid was on the top of their list.

Blandina's 20th century sources that reinforced her Billy the Kid prejudices were listed in the 1948 edition of *At the End of the Santa Fe Trail*'s bibliography by editor, Therese Martin. For overview, was used Ralph Emerson Twitchell's 1911, five volume *Leading Facts in New Mexico History*, without apparent awareness that he was a lawyer-politician member of the Santa Fe Ring, and associate of Thomas Benton Catron. His books covered up the existence of the Ring and the Territorial uprisings against it. So he fabricated the history of the Colfax and Lincoln County Wars accordingly, and blamed "Billy the Kid;" writing:

> At this period in the history of New Mexico the territory was the asylum of all the desperate men on the southwestern frontier. Colfax county on the north ... Lincoln county in the southeast, were the catch-basins for the reckless and criminal element. In the last named county a feud was begun which, in the annals of New Mexico, is known as the "Lincoln County War." The cause of this trouble and era of crime can be traced to the rivalry existing between prominent cattlemen at the time living in Lincoln and the Pecos valley, respectively. Both were furnishing cattle to the Mescalaro Indian agent and each accused the other of stealing from their respective herds. This was the basis for the war, although the acts and depredations in which the sympathizers of these two principals were involved may have brought on the crisis. Others believe, and not without reason, that **the turbulence that terrorized the entire community, was the result of the outlawry established by such desperadoes as Billy the Kid** ... (Pages 418-419)
>
> The beginning of the so-called Lincoln County War occurred when John H. Tunstel [sic - Tunstall] was killed by a sheriff's posse seeking to levy an attachment upon property belonging to Tunstel [sic]. **The latter had a friend and employe [sic], William H. Bonney, later famous as "Billy the Kid"** ... After the killing of Tunstel [sic] his sympathizers organized themselves into a **party known as the McSwain [sic] faction** and a sort of guerilla warfare continued for the following eighteen months until finally broken up by the civil authorities with the aid of the military. (Pages 422-423)

And, as has been mentioned, Blandina also lifted prejudicial misinformation for her entries from Walter Noble Burn's *Saga of Billy the Kid*, from Pat Garrett's *Authentic Life of Billy the Kid*, and from contemporary press.

SMOKING GUNS FOR A HOAX: *There existed no publications in Blandina's day to dissuade her from presenting her "Billy the Kid" creation as a depraved outlaw-murderer. That prejudice may have been her blind-spot, removing her guilt at fabricating entries about a generic bad man. Nevertheless, the result was a hoax, though mitigated by her contemporary milieu.*

JUST GULLIBILITY?

SLEUTHING HOAXBUSTING CLUES: *Blandina's backers contributed their own creative mitigating factors to her hoaxed entries.*

I kept Blandina's Petitioner for her sainthood, Allen Sánchez, informed of the progress of my investigation. When I told him that the Snyder-Happy Jack obituary (See Pages 370-373) demonstrated Blandina's lifting names and events from newspapers to construct her tales, he had a different thought: What if shot John M. Snyder had been Blandina's patient, and had taken advantage of her youthful gullibility (at 26) and had pulled her leg with fantastical tales of his "crimes," of shooting "Happy Jack," and of both being in a "Billy the Kid gang!" So she merely wrote what she was told.

That grasping-at-straws scenario demonstrates Allen Sánchez's well-meaning attempt to protect a woman be believes is a saint. But the gullibility scenario has the same problems that Blandina's "Schneider-"Billy the Kid" entries had: their 1876 date, which preceded Billy Bonney's "outlaw" history and moniker. If anything, the real Snyder's obituary pins down that date. Also Blandina created the tales as her own first-hand encounters, not hearsay. And it goes without saying, that Blandina did not seem gullible anyway.

> **SMOKING GUNS FOR A HOAX:** *If someone else, like John M. Snyder, told Blandina tall tales which she repeated, it would remove her blameworthiness for falsities. But the early dates of Snyder's succumbing to his bullet wound cancel out his even knowing about a "Billy the Kid." Also, there was no one telling Blandina her fabrications of the "Billy the Kid" Santa Fe jail scene or the near encounter with Victorio six years after he was dead. The hoaxed entries cannot be mitigated by a third party telling them to a gullible Blandina.*

JUST AN ADDLED LADY?

> **SLEUTHING HOAXBUSTING CLUES:** *Blandina's backers could not visualize her as a willful hoaxer, though it was irrefutable that she never knew Billy Bonney. So I postulated for them a scenario to vaguely match her tales. It involved another "Billy," but only one degree of separation from the real Billy the Kid: Billy Wilson. But Blandina would have needed to be addled to confuse those two youths, and Billy Wilson would have needed to be in Colorado in the 1870's.*

Just when I was ready to go to press with this book, with the Nun's Tale Hoax as being barely mitigated fabrications, I had a July 17, 2017 meeting with Allen Sánchez and his investigator, Peso Chavez, in Santa Fe's La Fonda Hotel.

As originally the Exchange Hotel at the end of the Santa Fe Trail, La Fonda was fitting as to Blandina's journal's title. And it was also where Billy the Kid's famous story began. In late 1876, visiting British merchant, John Tunstall, met there with Lincoln County lawyer, Alexander McSween, and was convinced by McSween to settle in the town of Lincoln to invest his family's fortune. If not for that meeting, Billy Bonney's famous and tragic history would not have unfolded.

In our meeting I was again impressed by both men's candor, but also by their dismay at the hoax as I presented it - though they could not deny it. I shared my own perplexity that Blandina simply did not seem like a typical hoaxer. A piece of the puzzle seemed missing. During my long drive home, a possible solution came to me. I realized that there might have been a "Billy" in the Santa Fe jail alone in a cell with a "Kelly" for Blandina to visit. It was *Billy Wilson* with Edward Kelly! Once home, I rushed to research Wilson. I was right.

ABOUT BILLY WILSON AND BILLY THE KID

Billy Wilson was a young man working to pass counterfeit bills for New Mexico Territory counterfeiter, Dan Dedrick, from Dedrick's Bosque Grande ranch, 12 miles south of Fort Sumner. And Billy Bonney used Billy Wilson for his petty rustling against Ringites, as well as using Dedrick to buy some of his rustled stock.

Secret Service Special Agent Azariah Wild had written reports in 1880 to his Chief about Wilson when in New Mexico investigating counterfeiting. On October 6, 1880, Wild wrote:

> *In tracing the history and character of William Wilson known here as Billy Wilson I find he is an American **who has been here in Lincoln County for several years, and has the name of being engaged with others of his kind in stealing horses and cattle**.*

On October 10, 1880, Wild wrote:

> *William Wilson is reported to be at Bosque Grande at Dedrick's ranch. Dedrick is reported as being one of the leaders of the clan [gang], and partners with [W.H.] West on the coral [sic - corral] at White Oaks [livery stable].*

Wild was eventually duped into believing that Billy Wilson and Billy the Kid led a huge counterfeiting, rustling, mail coach robbing gang, which he called the Kid-Wilson gang or Kid gang. Wild's leaked reports made local and national 1880 press - available to Blandina - about a "Billy the Kid gang."

From Wild's leaked reports, was written the December 22, 1880 *New York Sun* "Outlaws of New Mexico, The Exploits of a Band Headed by a New York youth, The Mountain Fastness of the Kid and his Followers – War Against a Gang of Cattle

Thieves and Murderers – The Frontier Confederates of Brockway, the Counterfeiter." About Billy Wilson, it stated:

> Billy Wilson is much the same sort of good looking fellow as his chief [Billy the Kid]. **He is about the same build, with dark hair and a slight moustache.** He left the Ohio home where his people, who are all highly esteemed, still reside, several years ago. After being engaged in the cattle business in Texas for some time, he came to New Mexico. When the excitement broke out over the new camp at White Oaks, he went there and was engaged in the butchering business. He was always considered a smart, energetic fellow, and was well thought of. In some way the Kid persuaded him to join his party, and it was by him that much of the forged paper was put into circulation.

Wilson was captured by Pat Garrett along with Billy Bonney, Dave Rudabaugh, and Tom Pickett at Stinking Springs on December 22, 1880. With them, Wilson spent a night in the Las Vegas jail. There Pickett was released for lack of an arrest warrant. Billy Bonney, Rudabaugh, and Wilson were then taken to their destination, the Santa Fe jail, with arrival on December 27, 1880. They were placed in a cell with a murderer, Edward "Choctaw" Kelly.

As discussed above, there were no times in which Billy Bonney could have been in that cell alone with Edward Kelly for Blandina to visit in 1881. (See Pages 287-289; 295-301)

But early Billy the Kid historian, William Keleher, also wrote about Billy Wilson in his 1957 book, *Violence in Lincoln County*. His information provided a time frame for an Edward Kelly and Billy Wilson presence in the Santa Fe jail, without Dave Rudabaugh and Billy Bonney being with them; as follows:

1) Blandina claimed a meeting with a "Billy the Kid" and a "Kelly" at or around May 16, 1881 (though also called 1882 in some of her published versions).

2) The scene is apocryphal for the real Billy Bonney. There is no time frame in which Blandina could have seen him alone

with Edward "Choctaw" Kelly. Billy Bonney was with Kelly, Rudabaugh, and Wilson from December 27, 1880 to February 28, 1881, when they were all caught in a tunneling-out jailbreak attempt. **After that, Billy Bonney was in solitary confinement without visitors from February 28, 1881 to March 28, 1881, when he was transported to his hanging trial in Mesilla – and never returned. And in the December 27, 1880 to February 28, 1881 period, he would have always been with Dave Rudabaugh and Billy Wilson, besides Kelly**. So Blandina could not have had a solely Billy-Kelly meeting.

3) Edward Kelly was removed from the cell on March 7, 1881, along with Dave Rudabaugh, for transport to their trials in Las Vegas, New Mexico. **Kelly was returned to the Santa Fe jail on March 23, 1881.** Rudabaugh was not returned to that jail again.

4) Billy Wilson had remained in the Santa Fe jail (and not in solitary confinement) until being removed with Billy Bonney, on March 28, 1881. for their trials in Mesilla; with Wilson's lawyer being Edgar Caypless.

5) **So from Kelly's March 23, 1881 return, to the March 28th removal of Wilson, Kelly could have been alone in a Santa Fe jail cell with Billy Wilson.**

6) Then, after their Mesilla trials, Billy Bonney was transported for hanging to the Lincoln County courthouse-jail. **But Billy Wilson was returned to the Santa Fe jail on March 30, 1881.**

7) **So from March 30, 1881, Wilson and Kelly were, for a second time, possibly alone together for an extended period awaiting the progression of their cases.** And Wilson might even have been arm and leg shackled as a high risk prisoner who had already attempted escape.

8) **So one can have a potential Billy-Kelly Santa Fe jail meeting for Blandina if her "Billy" was Wilson.**

FURTHER REQUIREMENTS FOR
BILLY WILSON TO BE BLANDINA'S "BILLY"

WAS WILSON IN COLORADO IN THE 1870's?

The key to Billy Wilson actually being Blandina's "Billy" is the claimed mutual recognition in the jail scene after "four years." As Blandina wrote:

> When I got into the prison-cell and "Billy" saw me, he said – **as though we had met yesterday instead of four years ago** – "I wish I could place a chair for you, Sister ..."

So was Billy Wilson an outlaw in Colorado in the 1870's for Blandina to meet in her first encounters?

Azariah Wild had described *"several years"* of Wilson's criminal activities. Since counterfeiter, Dan Dedrick, sent his men great distances (like to Old Mexico) to buy cattle in exchange for his counterfeit bills, Wilson might have been in Colorado in Blandina's time. She had claimed that "Bill's gang" was known in the press and by residents in 1876, writing:

> *The Trinidad Enterprise* – the only paper published here – in its last issue gave an exciting description of how **a member of "Bill's Gang"** painted red the town of Cimarron ...

> Trinidad often hears of the atrocities committed by it – **only say "Billy the Kid" and every individual is at attention** ...

So it was logical to search for an outlaw Billy Wilson in Colorado press from Blandina's stay of 1872 to 1877. And historian, William Keleher, noted that later in life Wilson used the alias David L. Anderson. So that name had to be sought also. In Blandina's period, there was just one mention in a September 18, 1873 *Daily Rocky Mountain News* of a murderer named Billy Wilson, who escaped from the Cañon City county jail. Since William Keleher listed the real Billy Wilson as 18 in 1880 (though providing no source), the age canceled out this murderer, even if Wilson was somewhat older in 1880.

And Colorado papers from 1872 to 1877 had no other outlaw named Billy Wilson or D.L. Anderson that matched Blandina's description of her "Billy the Kid." And, as already discussed, there was also no press mention of any "Billy the Kid" highwayman gang in Colorado in that period.

DID THE PHYSICAL DESCRIPTION MATCH?:

Blandina gave a physical description of the "Billy the Kid" she had met in Trinidad as a fair complected; writing:

> The leader, Billy, has **steel-blue eyes, peach complexion, is young**, one would take him to be seventeen – innocent-looking, save for the corners of his eyes, which tell a set purpose, good or bad

The above December 22, 1880 *New York Sun* article painted Wilson as dark; stating he had "dark hair and a slight moustache."

SMOKING GUNS FOR A HOAX: Though Blandina could have encountered Billy Wilson with a "Kelly" in the Santa Fe jail in the first half of 1881, there is no evidence that Wilson was additionally a Colorado outlaw in the 1870's, or that Blandina met him as such when she was in Trinidad. So Billy Wilson could not also have been known to Blandina from "four years" earlier. And if she had merely encountered Wilson in some other context four years earlier, he did not match her entries' physical description of a fair "Billy the Kid." Thus, there is no evidence that Blandina was writing about Billy Wilson, not Billy Bonney, in her "Billy the Kid" entries. So confusion of the two youths cannot be a mitigating factor for her hoaxed entries about an outlaw named "Billy."

JUST BLAME BILLY THE KID?

> *SLEUTHING HOAXBUSTING CLUES: Another creative thought by Blandina's backers was that Billy the Kid was in Colorado in her period, but all historians missed that fact. So there was no hoaxing on her part.*

Reluctant to admit Blandina's hoaxing, Allen Sánchez and Peso Chavez provided another angle: What if Billy Bonney had been in Blandina's area in 1876 as she reported, but all historians missed that fact? As "proof," Peso Chavez showed me an ad related to Cimarron's St. James Hotel, which listed its alleged outlaw visitors, and included "Billy the Kid." And Allen Sánchez also wondered if Billy Bonney had traveled in 1876 from Arizona to Trinidad, Colorado, for Blandina to meet him.

These sincere men inadvertently encountered the problem in dealing with Billy the Kid history: the profusion of apocryphal tales about him.

The idea that in 1876, at 16, Billy Bonney, who was just a cook at the little Hotel de Luna in Bonita, Arizona, and a petty thief of military horses and saddles from local Fort Grant, traveled 442 miles to Trinidad, Colorado, where he transformed, in September of 1876, into a murderous, highwayman, scalping, gang leader and met Sister Blandina - then high tailed back to Bonita in time to be locked up in Fort Grant's jail in March of 1877 as a juvenile delinquent stealing their horses - then, in June 9, 1877, returned to Colorado or northern New Mexico to attack the Staab traveling group as a lone robber - before returning to Bonita, Arizona, to kill "Windy" Cahill on August 17, 1877 is like science fiction (or Blandina's backers' wishful thinking), not fact.

And there is no evidence that Billy Bonney was ever at the St. James Hotel, a distance of about 210 miles from his Lincoln base, and 145 miles to his Fort Sumner base, from mid-1877 to his death in mid-1881.

But the fatal flaw is no 1872 to 1877 press with Blandina's horrible Colorado highwayman named "Billy the Kid."

> *SMOKING GUNS FOR A HOAX: Postulating apocryphal Billy the Kid history does not undo Blandina's hoax.*

JUST YIELDING TO TEMPTATION?

SLEUTHING HOAXBUSTING CLUES: Knowing all along that people thought her published "Billy the Kid" fables were true, Blandina never denied them.

The simplest explanation of the Nun's Tale Hoax is that Blandina made up her tales for the fun of shocking people when they thought she had been pals with famous and scary Billy Bonney. One may not picture a possible saint as riding on Billy the Kid's coat-tails, but Blandina was no conformist.

She never denied her human foibles, and may have felt that her tales helped her to save people. And her she probably did want to save her fantasized "Billy the Kid" when she wrote: "[H]ow many crimes might have been prevented, had someone had influence over "Billy" after his first murder."

Her temptation may have been trying too hard. As she wrote in an entry: "I wish I had many hands and feet, and a world full of hearts to place in the service of the Eternal."

And her feigned friendship hinted at secret wildness absent from her chaste life. Her mischievousness may have had no more guilt that her stealing vegetables from Archbishop Lamy:

> "I have come to make a confession out of the confessional." ...
>
> "My little Sister, what have you been doing?" ...
>
> "Stealing, Your Grace ... I dug up enough vegetables from your garden to last us three days."

SMOKING GUNS FOR A HOAX: Playful and wild, Blandina likely enjoyed shocking people as a nun palling with "the greatest murderer of the Southwest." That still leaves her a hoaxer, though unrepentant.

OVERALL SMOKING GUNS FOR HOAX INTENT: Blandina likely created "Billy the Kid" fiction to inspire religiosity, while enjoying glamorous secondary gains of writing herself into his famous life in her fables.

THE REAL BILLY THE KID IN SIMPATICO

Blandina Segale would have been shocked at her similarities with the real Billy the Kid. As bright, as dedicated to a cause, as subjected to hardships, like her, Billy Bonney faced life courageously by defying its "gloomy side." His insouciance was documented in my 2011 book, *Billy the Kid's Writings, Words, and Wit.*

On December 28, 1880, after his Stinking Springs capture, and in the Las Vegas jail on the way to the Santa Fe jail and an eventual hanging trial, he spoke to Lucius "Lute" Wilcox, city editor for J.H. Koogler's Las Vegas *Gazette*, for "The Kid. Interview with Billy Bonney The Best Known Man in New Mexico." He teased and taunted any future hangman and his own fate. The reporter recorded:

> Bonney ... was light and chipper, and was very communicative, laughing, joking and chatting with bystanders.
>
> "You appear to take it easy," the reporter said.
>
> "Yes! **What's the use of looking on the gloomy side of everything. The laugh's on me this time**," he said.

With similar irony, Billy had written, on December 12, 1880, to Lew Wallace about the fabricated "Billy the Kid gang":

> *I noticed in the Las Vegas Gazette a piece which stated that, Billy "the" Kid, the name by which I am known in the Country was the captain of a Band of Outlaws who hold Forth at the Portales.* **There is no such Organization in Existence. So the Gentleman must have drawn very heavily on his Imagination.**

Had Billy Bonney read Blandina's preposterous "Billy the Kid" journal entries, he might well have shrugged his shoulders at life's strange turns, and repeated for her: "The laugh's on me this time."

SURPRISING SHOWDOWN ON SEPTEMBER 30, 2017

SLEUTHING HOAXBUSTING CLUES: Blandina Segale's backers set up a meeting with me to coordinate findings. Their response would determine how they would present Blandina's "Billy the Kid" entries in the future.

When Allen Sánchez set up a September 30, 2017 meeting at his Albuquerque office for me; Sisters of Charity archivist, Veronica Buchanan (whom he flew in from Cincinnati); and investigator, Peso Chavez (coming from Santa Fe), I assumed it was for us to decipher Blandina's motive for hoaxing her Billy the Kid entries; since Veronica had located no explanatory disclaimer from Blandina, and Peso had found no evidence that Billy Wilson was Blandina's Colorado "Billy."

The actual agenda took me by surprise. As Allen said in the meeting, "No author has the credibility of my Blandina. I can't see her as a liar. And Billy Bonney did commit bad crimes."

I should have known better. Investigator Peso, denying bias, nevertheless called Blandina his client through her entries' "testimony," which he was investigating to validate. Allen, from his New Mexico childhood, had heard about amazing Sister Blandina, and was certain she was a saint. Veronica loyally represented the Sister's of Charity.

My thoughts returned to other true-believers I had encountered in hoaxbusting: "Brushy Bill's" modern followers. I could identify them by their certainty that the July 14, 1881 night of Pat Garrett's shooting of Billy the Kid was "dark and moonless" - despite eye-witness accounts of its daylight-bright full moon. "Brushy" was ground zero for their "truth." Capitalizing on that mind-set, the true hoaxers of the Billy the Kid Case intoned: "History is not what's written."

So my friendly adversaries in this show-down to determine Blandina's veracity in her "At the End of the Santa Fe Trail" writings - or lack of it - had come to the meeting with creatively developed scenarios to justify her "Billy the Kid" tales as having happened; i.e., there existed no hoax.

Their paraphrased ideas, with my responses, follow:

- **Blandina did so much good and was so religious that she could not have lied and created a hoax.**

My response is that she was indeed an unexpected hoaxer, and otherwise admirable person, but that did not negate hoaxing.

- **There is no dispute that Blandina destroyed the original "journal," but that was to maintain confidentiality for people she had written about.**

My response is that publishing her journal demonstrated lack of confidentiality concern, but those published entries were destroyed too. And for confidentiality, needed only was to black-out information or expurgate certain entries. But not a single page remains. To me that indicates concealing that it was never a real, 19th century, diary-like journal, as claimed.

- **There is no dispute that Blandina wrote her entries, according to the Comella-Cassano paper; or that no editor wrote her "Billy the Kid" text, or that she made no known disclaimer. But she was not a hoaxer.**

My response is that confirming her as the author was key to proving her as a hoaxer - once the entries were analyzed.

- **It is accepted, but irrelevant, that Blandina's journal entries were created in the 20th century, rather than the claimed 19th century.**

My response was that faking a "frontier journal" for publication was a slippery slope for dishonesty, since readers were misled. A pretend journal was a short step to giving pretend events.

- **It is accepted that Blandina used sources for her "Billy the Kid" second-hand entries, but that means those authors should be blamed for errors. Furthermore, including those entries means that she had an abiding interest in "Billy the Kid."**

My response is that source use for content and fix-ups was part of her using famous "Billy the Kid" for drama throughout her articles and book; and it bolstered the insertion of herself into fabricated first-hand encounters with him.

- **If Blandina used sources for a hoax, she would have made the dates correct - which she did not.**

My response is that she did research, but was not a real historian. And her approximated dates do show her attempts to match sources. Furthermore, the Garrett and Burns books provided minimal dating.

- **Blandina *helped* Billy Bonney's reputation by showing he had good-hearted concern for "Kelly" in the Santa Fe jail scene. And he also was courteous in the Trinidad patient bedside scene and in the Staab carriage encounter scene.**

My response is that this odd claim was an apparent attempt to placate me about her "Billy the Kid" tales damaging Billy Bonney's true history. Omitted are her punch lines that her "Billy" was about to do a terrorist atrocity of murder by scalping in Trinidad, was about to hold up carriage riders on the road to Santa Fe, and was, as she states, "the greatest murderer in the Southwest" for her jail scene. Overall, her "Billy" is the outlaw myth caricature of her times, created by the Santa Fe Ring and Lew Wallace. Perpetuating her hoax, perpetuates this damage to his actual freedom fighter role.

- **My claims for her hoaxing are unsupported. They are just assumptions.**

My response is that I had only told these backers the issues as they emerged. They had not seen the completed book. But authoring a fabricated journal; contradicting known Billy Bonney history in first hand accounts, and using press and 20th century books for second-hand accounts and fix-ups between magazine articles and book point to willful hoaxing.

- **Because I had exposed other Billy the Kid hoaxes, I was predisposed to seeing them; and this prejudiced me against Blandina.**

My response is that they well knew that, rather than condemning her, I had sought every possible explanation other than her being a hoaxer: that an editor wrote Billy the Kid passages, that her earliest published versions might lack hoaxed entries, that her disclaimers for fictionalizing might be in the magazine articles' or book's introductions or the Sisters of Charity Archives, and that she may have confused Billy Wilson for a "Billy the Kid." Only after all these possibilities failed, and evidence proved that she wrote the fables herself, did I accuse her of hoaxing.

- **There is no doubt of the truth of Blandina's first-hand accounts of meeting "Schneider" and "Billy the Kid," of meeting "Billy the Kid" during the Staab carriage ride, and of visiting "Billy the Kid" in the Santa Fe jail.**

My response is that the issue of veracity of her first-hand accounts is the subject of this book, in which their veracity is denied as hoaxing.

- **Historians of Billy the Kid disagree and make mistakes, so none can be trusted to contradict Blandina's "Billy the Kid" entries. Investigation should focus on validating her claims, since historians could have missed her truths.**

My response is that there is no documentation that Billy Bonney was in Trinidad, he was not a highwayman, he had no gang, and he was not in the Santa Fe jail in dates and circumstances she claimed. And saying that the only accurate recorder ever of Billy the Kid history was Blandina is absurd. And no documentation has been found to confirm her claims.

- **But no historians stated Billy was *not* in Trinidad, Colorado. So Blandina could have been right.**

My response is that arguing by negatives is meaningless: Billy was also not documented in Alaska. The burden of proof is giving real evidence that he was there. That does not exist.

- **Blandina is not accountable for entries that are not first-hand, since they are hearsay, which is barred from courtroom testimony.**

My response is that her writings were not courtroom testimony, but were willful insertion by her into a text to create a facsimile of her historical participation in the 19th century frontier, while concealing their 20th century creation from sources. Her purpose was to convince naïve readers that, as a 19th century journal writer, she kept track of her "old acquaintance Billy the Kid."

- Billy Bonney must have been in Trinidad, Colorado, because there was a 1929 article about a no longer existent Kit Carson Museum there, which had a knife labeled as belonging to Billy the Kid.

My response is that apocryphal claims about famous Billy Bonney abound. This is apparently one, and proves nothing. There is a joke about a Texas saloon which had a single-action revolver hung above the bar with a sign: "This is the only gun in the West that did not kill Billy the Kid."

- Blandina's "gang member Schneider" entry must be true since there was an obituary of a shot John M. Snyder in the January 10, 1877, El Moro, Colorado, *The Enterprise and Chronicle.* And it had an R.L. Donnlson "Happy Jack" too. So this Snyder must be the "Schneider" Blandina nursed in Trinidad. And its dating confirms the date of her Trinidad "Billy the Kid" meeting involving "Schneider."

My response is that this obituary does the opposite, by demonstrating her use of sources to get names and kernels of events for fabricated entries. In fact, in her entry she ended up spelling "Snyder" as "Schneider," transforming the two regular citizen victims of an accidental shooting into "Billy the Kid" gang members willfully shooting each other, and repurposed non-shot R.I. Donnlson into "Schneider's" fatally shot "Happy Jack." Furthermore, in her Trinidad period from 1876 to early 1877, the "Billy the Kid" moniker and outlaw gang myth did not yet exist. So, of course, the article - like all others of the period - has no mention of John Snyder or R.L. Donnlson "Happy Jack" being involved with a young highwayman outlaw named "Billy the Kid."

- The scalping threat connected to "Billy the Kid" in Trinidad is credible, because white men did scalpings, as evidenced by an article about Native Americans scalped by them.

My response is that the red flag peculiarity of Blandina's claim is that scalping was being used by her "Billy the Kid" to murder Anglos. It was undisputedly an atrocity of Native Americans against whites, and of white bounty hunters against Native Americans - which this irrelevant article indicates.

- In those days, young men were very athletic, and could cover great distances on horse-back. So Billy could have ridden back and forth between Bonita, Arizona, and Trinidad, Colorado. And he was a criminal in Arizona, so could be a criminal in Colorado.

My response is that Billy might have been able to do the riding, but there was no reason for it, nor record of it. And his stealing a few military horses, and military saddles and blankets in the Bonita area, has nothing to do with the sadistic, highwayman, gang leader of Blandina's Trinidad fantasies.

- What if Schneider was a relative of Billy the Kid, which explains Billy's going to Trinidad to visit him, because Silver City investigation showed a resident named "Snyder?" And a "gang" may have just been a group of Billy's associates in Trinidad.

My response is that arguing based on an unsupported postulate is merely false logic. Billy Bonney had no known relative named "Schneider," was never in Trinidad, and had no gang.

- What if John M. Snyder was pulling Blandina's leg, and made up tales of a "Billy the Kid gang" as her "Schneider" because she was naïve and young and he was teasing. And parroting *his* fables created her entries.

My response is that this construction of a hoax once-removed denigrates Blandina's own tale of "Schneider's" religious confessions - making them just a made-up joke. Also, she gives other "evidence" for "the gang," as follows: "Trinidad often hears of the atrocities committed by [the "Billy the Kid gang"] – only say "Billy the Kid" and every individual is at attention ... Billy and his gang are terrorizing the country between this place and La Glorieta."

- **If "Schneider" was a joker, he may have taken "Billy the Kid" in on his joke about scalping Trinidad doctors. That is proved by "Billy's" turning to "Schneider" and saying, "She is game." So "game" means they were playing a game with Blandina, and were not a real gang.**

My response is that this is again fallacious logic of using an unsubstantiated premise of "joker Schneider" to build others. Furthermore, the period meaning of "game" is misconstrued to back the made-up notion of playing a game with Blandina. For example, the above December 22, 1880 *New York Sun* "Outlaws of New Mexico" article stated: "To the demand to surrender,[Billy] only laughed and shot down a soldier **just to show that he was game**." The meaning is tough, and is also used to describe fighting dogs and cocks which continue fighting when ordinary ones would give up. This offering does nothing to contradict the hoaxed Trinidad entry about Billy.

- **Investigation located an December 7, 1881 article from the *Santa Fe Daily New Mexican* stating that Billy Bonney's brother, Joseph Antrim, was then living in Trinidad, Colorado. This is evidence that Billy Bonney traveled from Bonita, Arizona, to visit him there in the 1876 to 1877 period, since they came from a close-knit family because Catherine Antrim was their good mother.**

My response is that, like claiming "Schneider" was a visited relative, this one also has zero evidence. In fact, according to Richard Weddle, an expert on Billy's Arizona period in his 1993 book, *Antrim is My Stepfather's Name*, Joseph "Josie" Antrim was in school in Silver City, New Mexico Territory, through 1876; and from 1877 to 1879 lived in Silver City's Grant County, where Billy met with him in August or September of

1877 when escaping from Arizona into New Mexico Territory. Josie only moved to Colorado in the 1880's.

- **When Blandina said that the *Trinidad Enterprise* reported that "a member of "Bill's Gang" painted red the town of Cimarron," she meant Clay Allison, a Cimarron troublemaker.**

My response is that she may have been inspired to create her "Billy the Kid" gang tales, in part, by Clay Allison's press; but Clay had no connection to Billy the Kid history.

- **When Billy went to Trinidad or Cimarron, like other bad men, he went under an assumed name. So he could have been there without being recorded as Billy Bonney during 1876 to 1877.**

My response is that the point of Blandina's tales is that he was known and feared by everyone in the area under the name "Billy the Kid." It was no secret. The bigger problem with this notion is that, in the 1876-1877 period, the Billy the Kid moniker did not exist, and his name was Henry Antrim until he returned to New Mexico Territory in August of 1877 as a wanted killer of "Windy" Cahill, so made-up the alias of Billy Bonney.

- **As to the hold-up of the Staab carriage ride, "Billy the Kid's" antics and "bronco maneuvers" were not preposterous, but were typical of a young boy of the times showing off for a girl.**

My response is that Blandina was a nun, not a girl being courted by Billy Bonney - though the scene is peculiarly coquettish as written. But Billy Bonney was never in the area, making the point moot.

- **The apparent first-hand claim that "Billy the Kid's" shot friend Murphy" stayed in Blandina's Santa Fe hospital, with Billy at his bedside swearing revenge, was not really first-hand, but was told to Blandina by other nuns. So she just recorded *their* misinformation.**

My response is that this is an attempt at putting the hoax one degree removed. And it is preposterous to think that random Sisters of Charity nuns would or could make up bizarre fabrications of Billy the Kid history to tell Blandina.

- **The apparent first-hand claim that "Paoline" Maxwell attended her Trinidad school and told her that she had tried to stop "Billy the Kid" from revenging his shot "friend Murphy," was not really first-hand, but was related to Blandina by other nuns. So she just recorded misinformation.**

My response is that this is an attempt at putting the hoax one degree removed. And it is preposterous to think that random Sisters of Charity nuns would or could conceive this elaborate, fabricated, and historically false scenario for Blandina.

- **Blandina's Santa Fe jail scene for Billy Bonney and "Kelly" cannot be discredited by lack of presence in the cell of Dave Rudabaugh and Billy Wilson. She may just have left them out.**

My response is that, even disregarding her non-historical May 16, 1881 (or 1882) date, her hoaxing style is characterized by over-elaboration. Thus, for the visit, she even adds: "At a glance I saw the contents of the prison [cell]. Two empty nail kegs, one empty soap box, one backless chair, upon which sat the man who shot our patient." It is not credible that she would omit two additional men.

- **To date, there was no finding that Billy Wilson - the possible "Billy" I thought up as a mitigating explanation for the "Billy the Kid" meetings - was ever in Colorado, for her to meet "four years" before the Santa Fe jail encounter. And no other youth has been found for Blandina's three slots of the same outlaw in Trinidad, the Staab carriage ride, and the Santa Fe jail.**

My response is that finding a substitute "Billy" for the "addled nun" theory is unlikely; but I would add any such information post-publication to this book.

- Allen Sánchez concluded that: "no author has the credibility of my Blandina;" "I can't see her as a liar;" and "Billy Bonney did commit bad crimes."

My response is that after abandoning their Billy LeRoy excuse, the backers had reverted to using Billy Bonney, with bizarre notions to match his history to Blandina's fables.

SUMMARY OF THE BACKERS' TALE: Added to the Nun's Tale Hoax are her backers' new tales that unbeknownst to historians, or contemporary records and press, by the age of 16, in 1876, athletic Billy Bonney led a double life of a hotel cook and thief of occasional military horses and saddles in Bonita, Arizona, while frequently commuting by horse about a thousand miles round-trip, around and over mountain ranges through Arizona, New Mexico, and Colorado, to get to Trinidad to visit hypothetical relatives and to lead a sadistic, scalping, highwayman gang. Sister Blandina encountered him, in his super-villain persona, in Trinidad and on a trip to Santa Fe where she brought out his good side by stopping one of his scalping atrocities and one of his carriage robberies. When she later saw him in his Santa Fe jail cell - and later recorded one out of three of his fellow inmates - he was polite. And this is the only true history of Billy the Kid, since Blandina would not lie; though she did use 20th century sources for her 19th century journal.

After the meeting, when I phoned Billy the Kid historian, Richard Weddle, to check the backers' claims for Billy's Arizona period, he said Veronica Buchanan of the Sisters of Charity had contacted him about Billy the Kid's tintype for a new edition of *At the End of the Santa Fe Trail*. I got the chilling feeling that the backers had no intent to abandon Blandina's "Billy the Kid" tales for her book or the Saint Hood TV series - which had first motivated me to expose her Nun's Tale Hoax.

SMOKING GUNS FOR A HOAX: Hoaxes exist in two phases: by the creator, followed by true-believers and/or opportunistic hoaxers. There was a risk that Blandina's hoax would now live on through either of them.

SUMMARY OF THE NUN'S TALE HOAX

> *OVERVIEW OF THE NUN'S TALE HOAX: Blandina Segale fabricated tales of "Billy the Kid" and his "gang" in fictional 19th century journal entries claiming personal encounters, but actually composed them in the 20th century by cobbling together her fantasies, and information from old newspaper articles and books on Billy Bonney and related others. Her motives were boosting her religious message and her reputation.*

The features of Blandina Segale's Nun's Tale Hoax are as follows:

- Blandina Segale authored the "At the End of the Santa Fe Trail" magazine and book journal entries which fabricated her relationship with Billy Bonney as Billy the Kid, and fabricated her recording of the related events in a 19th century.
- She destroyed her original collected papers to conceal that the 19th century journal entries never existed.
- She mimicked real journal entries for her journal's publications from 1926 to 1932 by fabricating 19th century dates and events.
- She fixed-up entries' dates and information from her magazine articles to her 1932 book in attempt to hide errors in her faked entries.
- She never knew Billy Bonney aka Billy the Kid.
- She never met with a "Billy the Kid gang."
- She never knew "Billy the Kid gang member Schneider."
- She never knew any other outlaw named "Billy the Kid."
- She wrote herself into the history by fabricating that she stopped "Billy the Kid" from scalping Trinidad's doctors.

- She wrote herself into the history by fabricating that "Billy the Kid" was a highwayman who spared robbing her carriage companions when he saw her with them.

- She wrote herself into the history by fabricating to have nursed Billy the Kid's alleged Lincoln County, shot "friend," Lawrence Murphy, while hearing Billy the Kid, at his bedside, swearing revenge for Murphy's shooting.

- She wrote herself into the history by fabricating that she heard a "Paoline" Maxwell of Cimarron talk about a relationship with Billy the Kid as "Murphy's friend."

- She wrote herself into the history by fabricating a visit with Billy the Kid in the Santa Fe jail.

- She wrote herself into the history by fabricating a one day miss of a scalping atrocity by Apache Chief Victorio.

- She constructed her tales by lifting from contemporary press, 20th century books, and possibly a Billy LeRoy dime novel, to present Billy the Kid "history" and related period names, like Victorio.

- She constructed her tales by lifting random names and events from newspapers like non-outlaw John M. Snyder being shot by a man nick-named "Happy Jack" to create her "gang member Schneider" fable.

- She used possible kernels of real experience - like maybe nursing John M. Snyder, knowing some Trinidad doctors, riding in a carriage with the Staab family, or visiting other Santa Fe jail prisoners - to construct her fictitious tales.

- Her blameworthiness for hoaxing is mitigated by her spiritual goals, lighthearted intent, and conformity with contemporary prejudice about Billy the Kid's outlaw mythology.

- Her blameworthiness for hoaxing is aggravated by her self-aggrandizing riding on famous Billy the Kid's coat-tails, by never admitting to fabricating her Billy the Kid fables, and by her ongoing legacy of damage to real history of Billy Bonney as a freedom fighter.

RESPONSIBILITY FOR THE NUN'S TALE HOAX

The Nun's Tale Hoax may have been authored by Blandina Segale, but it has been promulgated by her supporters for almost eight decades after her death - even after it was clear that she never knew Billy the Kid. One can recall that the "Billy the Kid" relationship was an ongoing theme in Sisters of Charity of Cincinnati promotion to the present. On May 23, 2014, archivist, Sister Judith Metz, posted for the Daughters of Charity Provincial Archives an internet article titled "Servant of God, Sister Blandina Segale, S.C.," stating:

> *At the End of the Santa Fe Trial*, stories of her twenty-one years in the Southwest, makes fascinating reading through her letters [sic] to her sister, Justina, **especially her encounter with Billy the Kid.**

And on June 24, 2014, a Sisters of Charity of Cincinnati press release by the Director of Communications, Sister Georgia Kitt, titled "Sisters of Charity Announce Approval of Cause for Canonization of Sister Blandina Segale," proclaimed:

> Her [frontier] adventures have been featured in novels, television programs, histories, and even a comic book. **These often focus in her fearless befriending of Billy the Kid and his gang.**

Efforts for public clarification by the honest Petitioner for Blandina's sainthood, Allen Sánchez, had been impaired by his incorrect claim that she had known another "Billy the Kid" named Billy LeRoy. With Billy LeRoy debunked, it remains to be seen if he will return to favoring Billy Bonney as her "Kid."

And Saint Hood Productions allowed the "Billy the Kid" relationship to be used in press promotion for their future TV series on Blandina's life. It is unknown if they will feature her "Billy the Kid" character.

And the press has clung to its fabulous hook of an all-good nun who took on an all-bad famous Billy the Kid.

CONCLUSION:
"POPCORN HOAXING" AND
"THE MARIA PROBLEM"

Blandina Segale's' true motives may never be known, but it is certain that she fabricated her "Billy the Kid" tales. She was a "popcorn hoaxer": puffing kernels of information into fables to ride on Billy Bonney's fame. And her hoax was perpetuated through the 20th and 21st centuries by her backers and the press. That makes her so-called journal an unfortunate preservation of archaic outlaw propaganda about Billy Bonney.

It is hoped that her honorable, latest backers will admit to her Nun's Tale Hoax, and end its perpetuation in future editions of her *At the End of the Santa Fe Trail*, in the press, and in their Saint Hood Productions TV series. Then Blandina Segale's legacy will, at last, be set right.

As to that talented and free-spirited lady herself, I leave it to her backers to deal with their "Blandina problem" by adapting Oscar Hammerstein's "Maria" lyrics from "The Sound of Music," about another exasperating nun:

> How do you solve a problem like Blandina?
> How do you catch a cloud and pin it down?
> How do you find the word that means Blandina?
> A flibbertijibbet! A will-o'-the wisp! A clown!

POSTSCRIPT: 2018

It is now a year since this book's release. Alan Sanchez, Blandina's backer for sainthood, had promised me a press conference to present the truth. I never heard from him again. Her documentary-maker, Thomas Sanchez, returned this boxed book unopened, and told me he did not want to read it. The Sisters of Charity of Cincinnati never responded. As Blandina's role model, Jesus Christ, stated in his "Sermon on the Mount": "Ye shall know them by their fruits." Her honorable backers had retreated into silence of secrecy on her behalf, fulfilling the sermon's wisdom: "A good tree cannot bring forth evil fruit, neither can a corrupt tree bring forth good fruit."

SOURCES AND INDEX

ANNOTATED BIBLIOGRAPHY

SOURCES FOR BLANDINA (ROSA MARIA) SEGALE

AUTOBIOGRAPHICAL WRITINGS OF (CHRONOLOGICAL)
BY OR ABOUT
"AT THE END OF THE SANTA FE TRAIL"
VERITAS AND *THE SANTA MARIA* MAGAZINE ARTICLES

Segale, Blandina. Founder. Mission statement. *Veritas* magazine. **February, 1926.** Volume 1. Number 1. Sisters of Charity of Cincinnati Archives, Mount Saint Joseph, Ohio. Sisters of Charity of Cincinnati Archives, Mount Saint Joseph, Ohio. Santa Maria Institute Collection. (**First of the magazines**)

Minogue, Anna C. "Foreword to 'At the End of the Santa Fe Trail: From the Journal Kept by Sister Blandina during her mission to the Southwest.'" *Veritas* magazine. **October, 1926.** Volume 1. Number 9. Sisters of Charity of Cincinnati Archives, Mount Saint Joseph, Ohio. Santa Maria Institute Collection as obtained from Harvard University collection. (**First of the journal series articles, and giving their introduction**)

Girolamo, Michael. "This is the beginning of the second year of Veritas ..." **February 1, 1927.** Letter to subscribers. Sisters of Charity of Cincinnati Archives, Mount Saint Joseph, Ohio. Santa Maria Institute Collection. (**About Veritas being for the Italian community**)

Segale, Blandina. Founder. Cover text. *Veritas* magazine. **May, 1927.** Volume 2. Number 4. Sisters of Charity of Cincinnati Archives, Mount Saint Joseph, Ohio. Santa Maria Institute Collection. (**Goals listed of "Religion, Education, Americanization"**)

_____. "At the End of the Santa Fe Trail: From the Journal Kept by Sister Blandina during her mission to the Southwest." *Veritas* magazine. **September, 1927.** Volume 2. Number 8. Sisters of Charity of Cincinnati Archives, Mount Saint Joseph, Ohio. Santa Maria Institute Collection. (**About notes on Billy the Kid and meeting gang member**)

_____. "At the End of the Santa Fe Trail: From the Journal Kept by Sister Blandina during her mission to the Southwest." *Veritas* magazine. **October, 1927.** Volume 2. Number 9. Sisters of Charity of Cincinnati Archives, Mount Saint Joseph, Ohio. Santa Maria Institute Collection. (**About meeting Billy the Kid**)

_____. "At the End of the Santa Fe Trail: From the Journal Kept by Sister Blandina during her mission to the Southwest." *Veritas* magazine. **November, 1927.** Volume 2. Number 10. Sisters of Charity of Cincinnati Archives, Mount Saint Joseph, Ohio. Santa Maria Institute Collection. (**About Billy the Kid gang terrorizing**)

_____. "The West Revisited." *Veritas* magazine. **November, 1927.** Volume 2. Number 10. Sisters of Charity of Cincinnati Archives, Mount Saint Joseph, Ohio. Santa Maria Institute Collection. (**About a return visit in 1927, with another "Billy the Kid" fable, with introduction by Anna Minogue**)

Minogue, Anna. Introduction to "The West Revisited." *Veritas* magazine. **November, 1927.** Volume 2. Number 10. Sisters of Charity of Cincinnati Archives, Mount Saint Joseph, Ohio. Santa Maria Institute Collection. (**About Minogue's intense love of the Old West**)

Segale, Blandina. "At the End of the Santa Fe Trail: From the Journal Kept by Sister Blandina during her mission to the Southwest." *Veritas* magazine. **December, 1927.** Volume 2. Number 11. Sisters of Charity of Cincinnati Archives, Mount Saint Joseph, Ohio. Santa Maria Institute Collection. (**About Maxwell's ranch**)

_____. "At the End of the Santa Fe Trail: From the Journal Kept by Sister Blandina during her mission to the Southwest." *Veritas* magazine. **February, 1928.** Volume 3. Number 1. Sisters of Charity of Cincinnati Archives, Mount Saint Joseph, Ohio. Santa Maria Institute Collection. (**About Staab family and Billy the Kid encounter**)

_____. "At the End of the Santa Fe Trail: From the Journal Kept by Sister Blandina during her mission to the Southwest." *Veritas* magazine. **May, 1928.** Volume 3. Number 4. Sisters of Charity of Cincinnati Archives, Mount Saint Joseph, Ohio. Santa Maria Institute Collection. (**About Billy the Kid being friend's with "Mr. Murphy" and wanting to revenge his death**)

_____. "At the End of the Santa Fe Trail: From the Journal Kept by Sister Blandina during her mission to the Southwest." *Veritas* magazine. **May, 1928.** Volume 3. Number 4. Sisters of Charity of Cincinnati Archives, Mount Saint Joseph, Ohio. Santa Maria Institute Collection. (**About Billy the Kid being friend's with "Mr. Murphy" and wanting to revenge his death**)

_____. "At the End of the Santa Fe Trail: From the Journal Kept by Sister Blandina during her mission to the Southwest." *Veritas* magazine. **October, 1928.** Volume 3. Number 9. Sisters of Charity of Cincinnati Archives, Mount Saint Joseph, Ohio. Santa Maria Institute Collection. (**About Lincoln County War and Billy the Kid revenging "Mr. Murphy's" death**)

_____. "At the End of the Santa Fe Trail: From the Journal Kept by Sister Blandina during her mission to the Southwest." *Veritas* magazine. **December, 1928.** Volume 3. Number 9. Sisters of Charity of Cincinnati Archives, Mount Saint Joseph, Ohio. Santa Maria Institute Collection. (**About visiting a Los Cerrillos mine**)

_____. "At the End of the Santa Fe Trail: From the Journal Kept by Sister Blandina during her mission to the Southwest." *Veritas* magazine. **March, 1929.** Volume 4. Number 3. Sisters of Charity of Cincinnati Archives, Mount Saint Joseph, Ohio. Santa Maria Institute Collection. (**About jail visit with Billy the Kid and flash-back to his being a scalper**)

_____. "At the End of the Santa Fe Trail: From the Journal Kept by Sister Blandina during her mission to the Southwest." *The Santa Maria* magazine. **May, 1929.** Volume 4. Number 5. Sisters of Charity of Cincinnati Archives, Mount Saint Joseph, Ohio. Santa Maria Institute Collection. (**About death of Billy the Kid**)

_____. "At the End of the Santa Fe Trail: From the Journal Kept by Sister Blandina during her mission to the Southwest." *The Santa Maria* magazine. **February, 1930.** Volume 5. Number 2. Sisters of Charity of Cincinnati Archives, Mount Saint Joseph, Ohio. Santa Maria Institute Collection. (**About near encounter with Victorio**)

_____. "At the End of the Santa Fe Trail: From the Journal Kept by Sister Blandina during her mission to the Southwest." *The Santa Maria* magazine. **May, 1930.** Volume 5. Number 5. Sisters of Charity of Cincinnati Archives, Mount Saint Joseph, Ohio. Santa Maria Institute Collection. (**About herself and Justina laughing about journal entries**)

No Author. "Honor for Sister Blandina." Santa Maria Institute *The Santa Maria* magazine. **May, 1930.** Volume 5. Number 5. Sisters of Charity of Cincinnati Archives, Mount Saint Joseph, Ohio. Santa Maria Institute Collection. (**Possibly by Blandina about encouragement to publish articles as a book**)

Segale, Blandina. "At the End of the Santa Fe Trail: From the Journal Kept by Sister Blandina during her mission to the Southwest." *The Santa Maria* magazine. **July, 1930.** Volume 5. Number 7. Sisters of Charity of Cincinnati Archives, Mount Saint Joseph, Ohio. Santa Maria Institute Collection. (**About writing the journal from her jotted scraps**)

_____. "At the End of the Santa Fe Trail: From the Journal Kept by Sister Blandina during her mission to the Southwest." *The Santa Maria* magazine. **September, 1930.** Volume 5. Number 9. Sisters of Charity of Cincinnati Archives, Mount Saint Joseph, Ohio. Santa Maria Institute Collection. (**About writing the journal from her jotted scraps**)

_____. "At the End of the Santa Fe Trail: From the Journal Kept by Sister Blandina during her mission to the Southwest." *The Santa Maria* magazine. **October, 1930.** Volume 5. Number 10. Sisters of Charity of Cincinnati Archives, Mount Saint Joseph, Ohio. Santa Maria Institute Collection. (**Summary of Happy Jack and "Snyder" gang members tale; and about the Maxwell family's 'Paoline" knowing Billy the Kid**)

_____. "At the End of the Santa Fe Trail: From the Journal Kept by Sister Blandina during her mission to the Southwest." *The Santa Maria* magazine. **December, 1930.** Volume 5. Number 12. Sisters of Charity of Cincinnati Archives, Mount Saint Joseph, Ohio. Santa Maria Institute Collection. (**About Billy the Kid gang being dissolved in Trinidad**)

_____. "At the End of the Santa Fe Trail: From the Journal Kept by Sister Blandina during her mission to the Southwest." *The Santa Maria* magazine. **January, 1931.** Volume 6. Number 1. Sisters of Charity of Cincinnati Archives, Mount Saint Joseph, Ohio. Santa Maria Institute Collection. (**Last magazine**)

No Author. Mission statement of *The Santa Maria* magazine. **January, 1931.** Volume 6. Number 1. Sisters of Charity of Cincinnati Archives, Mount Saint Joseph, Ohio. Santa Maria Institute Collection. (**About religious and educational goals for articles**)

Segale, Blandina. "Dear friend and subscriber: We regret to inform you ..." **January 24, 1932.** Letter to subscribers. Sisters of Charity of Cincinnati Archives, Mount Saint Joseph, Ohio. Santa Maria Institute Collection. (**About financial necessity of ending *Santa Maria* magazine**)

No Author. "Research Work Done at Santa Maria." **August, 1957.** Sisters of Charity of Cincinnati Archives, Mount Saint Joseph, Ohio. Santa Maria Institute Collection. (**History of the Santa Maria Institute's magazine**)

BY OR ABOUT
AT THE END OF THE SANTA FE TRAIL
BOOK

Segale, Blandina. *At the End of the Santa Fe Trail*. Columbus, Ohio: The Columbian Press. **1932.**

Workman, Elizabeth. "Your most interesting book ..." **August 4, 1934.** Letter to Blandina Segale. Sisters of Charity of Cincinnati Archives, Mount Saint Joseph, Ohio. Santa Maria Institute Collection. (**About praising Blandina's book**)

Segale, Blandina. *At the End of the Santa Fe Trail*. Milwaukee, Wisconsin: The Bruce Publishing Company. **1948.**

_____. *At the End of the Santa Fe Trail*. Mount St. Joseph, Ohio: Sisters of Charity of Cincinnati. **1996.**

_____. *At the End of the Santa Fe Trail*. Mount St. Joseph, Ohio: Sisters of Charity of Cincinnati. **2014.**

BLANDINA'S ACTUAL AND POSSIBLE SOURCES FOR HER "BILLY THE KID" AND GANG CREATIONS (CHRONOLOGICAL)

No Author. No title. **April 25, 1872.** The Pueblo, Colorado, *The Colorado Chieftain.* www.coloradohistoricnewspapers.org. **(About Native Americans doing scalping and robbing stages)**

No Author. "Recapture and Escape of a Horse Thief." **Sunday Morning, March 23, 1873.** *Daily Rocky Mountain News.* History Colorado. Stephen H. Hart Library and Research Center. Newsbank database. **(A "Happy Jack" outlaw named James McManus)**

No Author. "Recapture and Escape of a Horse Thief." **Tuesday Morning, April 1, 1873.** *Daily Rocky Mountain News.* History Colorado. Stephen H. Hart Library and Research Center. Newsbank database. **(James McManus aka "Happy Jack" killed by vigilantes)**

No Author. No title. **Saturday, March 13, 1875.** *The Colorado Pioneer.* Denver, Colorado, History Colorado Center, Collections and Library. **(single newspaper mention of any Colorado highwayman from 1872 to 1877)**

No Author. "Personalities." **January 1, 1876.** Colorado Springs, *The Colorado Springs Gazette and El Paso County News.* www.coloradohistoricnewspapers.org. **(About boy murderer named Pomeroy, who was inspired by scalping in dime novels)**

No Author. " 'Persimmon Bill,' Otherwise Known as William T. Chambers, the North Carolina Outlaw, Interesting Chat with the notorious Black Hills Horse Thief and Desperado." **Thursday, May 11, 1876.** Boulder, Colorado, *The Colorado Banner.* www.coloradohistoricnewspapers.org.

No Author. No title. **July 21, 1876.** Pueblo, Colorado, *Colorado Chieftain.* www.coloradohistoricnewspapers.org.

No Author. "Adventures of a Young and Dashing Highwayman." **Thursday, August 24, 1876.** Boulder, Colorado, *The Colorado Banner.* www.coloradohistoricnewspapers.org.

No Author. "Kidnapping a Judge. **August 24, 1876.** Pueblo, Colorado, *Colorado Weekly Chieftain.* www.coloradohistoricnewspapers.org **(Scalping and a gang were put together for a tongue-in-cheek article on kidnapping an unpopular judge.)**

No Author. "San Juan: Few Notes by Hol. Gorden." **Thursday, December 7, 1876.** Pueblo, Colorado, *Colorado Chieftain.* www.coloradohistoricnewspapers.org. **(About non-outlaw "Happy Jack")**

No Author. "Murder in Las Animas: The Allison Desperados Make a Raid on West Las Animas." **Thursday, December 28, 1876.** Pueblo, Colorado, *Colorado Chieftain.* www.coloradohistoricnewspapers.org.

No Author. "The Leader records another murder in Las Animas." **Saturday, December 30, 1876.** Pueblo, Colorado, *Colorado Chieftain.* www.coloradohistoricnewspapers.org.

No Author. "Death of John M. Snyder." (Obituary). **January 10, 1877.** El Moro, Colorado, *The Enterprise and Chronicle.* **(With names "Snyder" and "Happy Jack" likely used by Blandina Segale for her "Billy the Kid gang member" tale, and used as a hoax cracking clue)**

South, W.L. "The Allison Case." **Sunday, January 21, 1877 and Thursday, January 25, 1877.** Pueblo, Colorado, *Colorado Chieftain.* www.coloradohistoricnewspapers.org.

No Author. No title. **March 30, 1877 and April 5, 1877.** Pueblo, Colorado, *Colorado Chieftain.* www.coloradohistoricnewspapers.org. **(Clay Allison acquitted of murder)**

No Author. Editorial. "Powerful Gang of Outlaws Harassing the Stockman." Las Vegas *Gazette.* **December 3, 1880. (Condemnation of William Bonney as an outlaw leader; and resulting in Bonney's response letter of December 12, 1880 to Governor Lew Wallace.)**

No Author. "Outlaws of New Mexico. The Exploits of a Band Headed by a New York Youth. The Mountain Fastness of the Kid and His Followers - War Against a Gang of Cattle Thieves and Murderers - The Frontier Confederates of Brockway, the Counterfeiter." *The Sun.* New York. **December 22, 1880.** Vol. XLVIII, No. 118, Page 3, Columns 1-2.

Wallace, Lew. "Billy the Kid: $500 Reward." Las Vegas *Gazette.* **December 22, 1880.**

No Author. "A Big Haul! Billy Kid, Dave Rudabaugh, Billy Wilson and Tom Pickett in the Clutches of the Law." *The Las Vegas Daily Optic.* Monday, **December 27, 1880.** Vol. 2, No. 45. Page 4, Column 2.

Wilcox, Lucius "Lute" M. " 'The Kid. Interview with Billy Bonney The Best Known Man in New Mexico, The greatest excitement prevailed yesterday when the news was abroad that Pat Garrett and Frank Stewart had arrived in town bringing with them Billy 'the Kid.' " Las Vegas *Gazette.* **December 27, 1880. (With "laugh's on me" quote)**

_____. "Interview With The Kid." Las Vegas *Gazette.* **December 28, 1880.**(From "Billy the Kid: Las Vegas Newspaper Accounts of His Career, 1880-1881." W.M. Morrison, Waco, Texas. 1958.)

No Author. "Behind the Bars, 'The Kid' and Two of His Gang in Limbo, They Now Roost in Santa Fe Jail." **December 28, 1880.** Santa Fe *Daily New Mexican.* Collection of New Mexico State Library, Santa Fe. **(Capture and jailing of Billy the Kid)**

No Author. **December 30, 1880.** Santa Fe *Daily New Mexican.* Collection of New Mexico State Library, Santa Fe. **(Provisions to prevent Billy the Kid's escape from Santa Fe jail, but his cheerfulness remains)**

No Author. "Rudabaugh's Departure." **March 8, 1881.** Santa Fe *Daily New Mexican.* Collection of New Mexico State Library, Santa Fe. **(An article mentioning Kelly without a first name of Edward)**

No Author. "The Kid. Billy 'the Kid' and Billy Wilson were on Monday taken to Mesilla for Trial." *Las Vegas Morning Gazette.* Tuesday, **March 15, 1881.**

No Author. **March 23, 1881.** Santa Fe *Daily New Mexican.* Collection of New Mexico State Library, Santa Fe. **(Reporting of Kelly being in the Santa Fe jail with Billy the Kid, which would be when Kelly was returned from Las Vegas)**

No Author. No title. **March 22, 1881.** Santa Fe *Daily New Mexican.* Collection of New Mexico State Library, Santa Fe. **(About sentencing of Kelly, without giving his first name of Edward)**

No Author. No title. **March 23, 1881.** Santa Fe *Daily New Mexican.* Collection of New Mexico State Library, Santa Fe. **(About a Kelly - without first name - being in the Santa Fe jail with Billy the Kid)**

Newman, Simon. "In the Name of Justice! In the Case of Billy Kid." *Newman's Semi-Weekly.* Saturday, **April 2, 1881.**

Koogler, J. H. "Interview with Governor Lew Wallace on 'The Kid.'" *Las Vegas Gazette.* **April 28, 1881.**

No Author. "The Kid." *Santa Fe Daily New Mexican.* **May 1, 1881.** Vol. X, No. 32, Page 1, Column 2.

No Author. "Billy Bonney. Advices from Lincoln bring the intelligence of the escape of 'Billy the Kid.' " *Las Vegas Daily Optic.* Monday, **May 2, 1881.**

No Author. "The Kid's Escape." *Santa Fe Daily New Mexican.* Tuesday Morning, **May 3, 1881.** Vol. X, No. 33, Page 1, Column 2.

Wallace, Lew. "Billy the Kid. $500 Reward." *Daily New Mexican.* **May 3, 1881.** Vol. X, No. 33, Page 1, Column 3.

No Author. "Dare Devil Desperado. Pursuit of 'Billy the Kid' has been abandoned." *Las Vegas Daily Optic.* **May 4, 1881.**

No Author. "More Killing by Kid." Editorial. *Santa Fe Daily New Mexican.* Wednesday Morning, **May 4, 1881**. Vol. X, No. 34, Page 1, Column 2.

No Author. "Kid was then in Albuquerque ..." *Santa Fe Daily New Mexican.* **May 5, 1881**. p.4. c. 1.

No Author. "Richard Dunham's May 2, 1881 encounter with Billy the Kid.", *Santa Fe Daily New Mexican,* **May 5, 1881**, Page 4, Column 3. (private collection)

No Author. "The question if how to deal with desperados who commit murder has but one solution - kill them." *Las Vegas Daily Optic.* Tuesday, **May 10, 1881**.

No Author. "Billy 'the Kid.' " Las Vegas *Gazette.* Thursday, **May 12, 1881**.

No Author. "The Kid was in Chloride City ..." *Santa Fe Daily New Mexican.* **May 13, 1881**. p.4. c. 3.

No Author. "Billy 'the Kid' is in the vicinity of Sumner." Las Vegas *Gazette.* Sunday, **May 15, 1881**.

No Author. "The Thug's Territory. Stage Robbers and Cut-Throats Have Things Their Own Way in New Mexico. Gen. Lew Wallace Anxious to Punish the Crime That is So Prevalent – A Chapter About 'Billy the Kid' – The Governor has a Narrow Escape From Being Spanked." *St. Louis Daily Globe-Democrat.* Monday Morning, **May 16, 1881**. Page 2, Columns 5 and 6. (private collection)

No Author. "The Kid is believed to be in the Black Range ..." *Santa Fe Daily New Mexican.* **May 19, 1881**. p.4. c. 1.

No Author. "Billy the Kid was last seen in Lincoln County ..." *Santa Fe Daily New Mexican.* **May 19, 1881**. p.4. c. 1.

No Author. " 'Billy the Kid' has been heard from again." *Las Vegas Daily Optic.* Friday, **June 10, 1881**.

No Author. " 'Billy the Kid.' He is Reported to Have Been Seen on Our Streets Saturday Night." *Las Vegas Daily Optic.* Monday Evening, **June 13, 1881**. Vol. 2, No. 188, Page 4, Column 2.

Wilcox, Lute, Ed. "Billy the Kid would make an ideal newspaper-man in that he always endeavors to 'get even' with his enemies." *Las Vegas Daily Optic.* Monday Evening, **June 13, 1881**. Vol. 2, No. 188, Page 4, Column 1.

No Author. "Land of the Petulant Pistol. 'Billy the Kid' as a Killer." *Las Vegas Daily Optic.* Wednesday Evening, **June 15, 1881**. Vol. 2, No. 190.

No Author. "Barney Mason at Fort Sumner states the 'Kid' is in Local Sheep Camps." *Las Vegas Morning Gazette.* **June 16, 1881**.

No Author. "The Kid." *Santa Fe Daily New Mexican.* **June 16, 1881**. Vol. X, No. 90, Page 4, Column 2.

No Author. "Billy the Kid. General Wallace Tells Why the Young Desperado of New Mexico Wanted to Kill Him." (Lew Wallace interviewed on June 13, 1881), Crawfordsville *Saturday Evening Journal,* **June 18, 1881**. Indiana Historical Society. The Papers of Lew and Susan Wallace. Microfilm Edition. Indianapolis, Indiana: Indiana Historical Society Press. 2008.

No Author. " 'The Kid' Killed." *Las Vegas Daily Optic.* **July 18. 1881**.

No Author. "Billy the Kid." *Las Vegas Daily Optic.* Thursday, **June 28, 1881**.

No Author. No title. **Thursday, July 28, 1881**. Pueblo, Colorado, Colo*rado Chieftain.* www.coloradohistoricnewspapers.org. **(Quoting from the New York** *Tribune* **on killing of "Tiger in human form known as "Billy the Kid")**

No Author. "Lew Wallace's Foe. Threatened by 'Billy the Kid.' The Writing of 'Ben Hur' Interrupted. An Incident of the Soldier-Author's Career in New Mexico. *San Francisco Chronicle.* **December 10, 1893**. Indiana Historical Society. Lew Wallace Collection. M0292. Box 14. Folder 11. **(Lew Wallace creating outlaw myth of outlaw Billy the Kid")**

No Author. "Street Pickings," Weekly *Crawfordsville Review – Saturday Edition,* **January 6, 1894**. Indiana Historical Society. The Papers of Lew and Susan Wallace. Microfilm Edition. Series I. Reel 27. Indianapolis, Indiana: Indiana Historical Society Press. 2008. **(Lew Wallace on Billy the Kid)**

No Author. "Record of a Texas Desperado: The graves of His Victims Were Scattered From Dodge City to Santa Fe." **October 16, 1894.** Salida , Colorado *The Salida Mail. Colorado Chieftain.* www.coloradohistoricnewspapers.org. (**Cimarron's Clay Allison's outlaw myth**)

Lewis, E.I. "Gen. Wallace's Feud with Billy the Kid, When the General Was Governor of New Mexico and Billy Bonne Was the Most Dangerous Western Outlaw. He Was a Waif and Was Reared in Indiana. *The Indianapolis Press.* Saturday, **June 23, 1900.** Page 7. Lew Wallace Collection. Indiana Historical Society. M0292. Box 14. Folder 11. (photocopy) (Original article is in OMB 23, Box 1. Folder 5) (**Lew Wallace creating self-serving myth of outlaw Billy the Kid"**)

No Author. "An Old Incident Recalled." Crawfordsville *Weekly News-Review.* **December 20, 1901.** Indiana Historical Society. The Papers of Lew and Susan Wallace. Microfilm Edition. Series I. Reel 27. Indianapolis, Indiana: Indiana Historical Society Press. 2008.

Wallace, Lew. "General Lew Wallace Writes a Romance of 'Billy the Kid' Most Famous Bandit of the Plains: Thrilling Story of the Midnight Meeting Between Gen Wallace, Then Governor of New Mexico, and the Notorious Outlaw, in a Lonesome Hut in Santa Fe." *New York World Magazine.* Sunday, **June 8, 1902.** Lew Wallace Collection. Indiana Historical Society. M0292. Box 14. Folder 11.

No Author. "The Duel That Failed." **April 3, 1906.** Eagle, Colorado. *The Eagle Valley Enterprise.* www.coloradohistoricnewspapers.org.

Twitchell, Ralph Emerson. *The Leading Facts of New Mexico History.* Vol. I-II. Santa Fe: Sunstone Press. 2007. (Reprinted from a 1912 edition) (**Reputed Santa Fe Ringman and its cover-up historian**)

Mooar, J. Wright (as told to James Winford Hunt). "Buffalo Days: Billy the Kid." Holland's, *The Magazine of the South.* July, 1933. Sisters of Charity of Cincinnati Archives, Mount Saint Joseph, Ohio. Blandina Segale Collection. Box 5, Folder 10. (**Annotated by Blandina Segale as "untrue account" about Billy the Kid; also has the same information she used of linking Geronimo and Victorio in time**)

Burns, Walter Noble. *The Saga of Billy the Kid.* Stamford, Connecticut: Longmeadow Press. 1992. (Original printing: **1926**, Doubleday.)

Garrett, Pat F. *The Authentic Life of Billy the Kid The Noted Desperado of the Southwest, Whose Deeds of Daring and Blood Made His Name a Terror in New Mexico, Arizona, and Northern Mexico.* Santa Fe, New Mexico: New Mexico Printing and Publishing Co. **1882.** (Reprint used: New York: Indian Head Books. 1994.)

Scanland, John M. (Foreword) using Patrick F. Garrett, Patrick F. *Billy the Kid: The Outlaw. Authentic Story of Billy the Kid by Pat F. Garrett. Greatest Sheriff of the Old Southwest.* New York: Atomic Books Inc. **1946.** Oberlin College Library Special Collections, Pop Culture. Walter F. Tunks Collection. Number 2344. (**Pirated edition of Pat Garrett's *Authentic Life of Billy the Kid* featuring outlawry of Billy the Kid**)

Schatznov, Thomas. "Cowboy Business." **November 10, 2007.** Internet article. (**About original Hollywood Westerns**)

Dirks, Tom. filmsite.org. No date. (**About original Hollywood Westerns**)

LETTER ABOUT WRITINGS OF

Comella, Lucy and Carmela Cassano. "1. It is recorded in her journal ... Billy the Kid and the Gang were going to kill ..." ___ **1932(?).** Letter fragment. Sisters of Charity of Cincinnati Archives, Mount Saint Joseph, Ohio. Santa Maria Institute Collection. Box 3, Folder 3. (**About Blandina's writing of the magazine articles that helped to crack the Nun's Tale Hoax**)

ABOUT HISTORY OF SANTA MARIA INSTITUTE OF

Cassano, Carmela and Lucy Comella. "Activities [of Santa Maria Institute] in Sister Blandina's Time." [**August, 1957 ?**] Sisters of Charity of Cincinnati Archives, Mount Saint Joseph, Ohio. Santa Maria Institute Collection. (**History of the Santa Maria Institute's magazine**)

Minogue, Anna C. *The Santa Maria Institute.* New York: The America Press. 1922. (**The Assistant Editor who got Blandina to publish her journal in the Santa Maria Institute's magazine**)

BOOK BY ANNA MINOGUE

Minogue, Anna C. *The Blind Priest: A Thrilling Story of the West.* Cincinnati, Ohio: St Anthony Messenger. 1922. (**Researched to explore if Minogue was an editor for Blandina's "Billy the Kid" tales, but no evidence found**)

BIOGRAPHICAL

Cassano, Carmela and Lucy Comella. "Activities [of Santa Maria Institute] in Sister Blandina's Time." [**August, 1957 ?**] Sisters of Charity of Cincinnati Archives, Mount Saint Joseph, Ohio. Santa Maria Institute Collection. (**About relationship of Blandina with her sister**)

Cline, Donald. *Alias Billy the Kid: The Man Behind the Legend.* Santa Fe, New Mexico: Sunstone Press. 1986. (**Using Blandina Segale's *At the End of the Santa Fe Trail* in a failed attempt to portray "two Billy the Kids," with Billy LeRoy as preceding Billy Bonney and confusing Blandina**)

ARTICLES ABOUT (CHRONOLOGICAL)

No Author. "Sister Blandina Defied Outlaws, Saved One Archbishop, Also Visited Billy the Kid." **April – (?), 1930**. *The Santa Fe New Mexican.* Sisters of Charity of Cincinnati Archives, Mount Saint Joseph, Ohio. Blandina Segale Collection. Box 8, Folder 1b.

Murphy, Eugene P. "Keeping the Record." **November 17, 1933**. *The Commonweal.* Sisters of Charity of Cincinnati Archives, Mount Saint Joseph, Ohio. .Blandina Segale Collection. Box 5, Folder 11.

O'Carroll, L.G. "The Nun and Billy the Kid: How timid, inexperienced little sister Blandina earned the respect of the bad men of the wild and wooley West." **September, 1953**. *The Irish Digest.* Sisters of Charity of Cincinnati Archives, Mount Saint Joseph, Ohio. Blandina Segale Collection. Box 5, Folder 19.

Foster, Jack. "How Colo. Nun Saved 4 From Killer!" **November 11, 1957**. *Rocky Mountain News.* Sisters of Charity of Cincinnati Archives, Mount Saint Joseph, Ohio. .Blandina Segale Collection. Box 5, Folder 24b. (**About a movie on Blandina featuring Billy the Kid**)

Hall, Warren. "New True Tales of the Old West" "Sister Blandina and Billy the Kid: A Young nun's letters, written more than 80 years ago, reveal an incredible friendship." **September 7, 1958**. *The American Weekly.* . Sisters of Charity of Cincinnati Archives, Mount Saint Joseph, Ohio. .Blandina Segale Collection. Box 5, Folder 28- (**With garbled biography of William H. Bonney as Billy the Kid**)

_____. "The Favor is Granted," said Billy the Kid: A nun foiled his plan to murder four men." **June, 1959**. *The Irish Digest.* Sisters of Charity of Cincinnati Archives, Mount Saint Joseph, Ohio. .Blandina Segale Collection. Box 5, Folder 30.

Parnell, Louise. 'The Nun who knew Billy the Kid: Throughout her years in the West Sister Blandina continued to be the friend of Billy the Kid. Though she did not succeed in converting him, her influence on Billy showed the pioneer world the power of a nun's prayerful courage." **January, 1961**. *Victorian.* Sisters of Charity of Cincinnati Archives, Mount Saint Joseph, Ohio. Blandina Segale Collection. Box 5, Folder 32. (**Fabricating ongoing contact with Billy the Kid**)

Parsons, Louella O. "Life of a Colorado Nun." **1963**. Clipping from unknown publication. Sisters of Charity of Cincinnati Archives, Mount Saint Joseph, Ohio. .Blandina Segale Collection. Box 8, Folder 7. (**About a movie on Blandina featuring Billy the Kid**)

No Author. "Sister Blandina Story on TV." **November 28, 1963**. *The Denver Catholic Register*. Page 9. Sisters of Charity of Cincinnati Blandina Segale Collection. Box 8, Folder 7. (**Publicizing by using Billy the Kid**)

Davis, Rosemary. "Santa Maria's Founder Nun Who Tamed Billy the Kid." **August 3, 1973**. *The Cincinnati Enquirer*. Sisters of Charity of Cincinnati Archives, Mount St. Joseph, Ohio. Blandina Segale Collection. Box 5, Folder 48. (**Publicizing by using Billy the Kid**)

Tansey, Anne. "She Faced Down Billy the Kid." **May 19, 1974**. *Catholic Family Weekly*. Sisters of Charity of Cincinnati Archives, Mount St. Joseph, Ohio. Blandina Segale Collection. Box 5, Folder 44. (**About Billy the Kid not killing the Trinidad doctors**)

Rawley, Ellen Rita. "She Knew Billy the Kid." **June 6, 1974**. Supplement to the *Denver Catholic Register* for the Pike's Peak area. Sisters of Charity of Cincinnati Archives, Mount St. Joseph, Ohio. Blandina Segale Collection. Box 5, Folder 45. (**Further garbles Blandina's Billy the Kid fables**)

No Author. Associated Press. "Has Billy the Kid been unmasked?" **April 13, 1987**. *The Cincinnati Post*. Sisters of Charity of Cincinnati Archives, Mount St. Joseph, Ohio. Blandina Segale Collection. Box 6, Folder 29. (**Saved in Sisters of Charity Archives as about Billy the Kid, but about "Brushy Bill" Roberts**)

Mayeux, Lucie E. "When Billy the Kid met the cowboy nun: The adventures of Sister Blandina reads like a pulp Western – except they are all true." **July 21, 1991**. *Our Sunday Visitor*. Sisters of Charity of Cincinnati Archives, Mount Saint Joseph, Ohio. Blandina Segale Collection Box 5, Folder 72. (**Publicizing Blandina by using Billy the Kid**)

Louden, Richard. "Local legend about Sister Blandina and Billy the Kid is a case of mistaken ID: Creative exaggerations of his violent life created such myths as the one that by the time he was killed at age 21, he had killed that many men." **August 30, 1991**. Trinidad, Colorado, *Chronicle*. Sisters of Charity of Cincinnati Archives, Mount Saint Joseph, Ohio. Blandina Segale Collection. Box 5, Folder 73. (**Explaining the Billy the Kid fabrications as really being about a second Billy the Kid: Billy LeRoy**)

Findsen, Owen. "Sister Blandina faced down The Kid." **March 17, 1996**. *The Cincinnati Enquirer*. Sisters of Charity of Cincinnati Archives, Mount Saint Joseph, Ohio. Blandina Segale Collection. Box 6, Folder 8.

O'Brien, Katie "The Nun Who Took on Billy the Kid." Irving, Texas: *Catholic Heritage Curricula*. (Internet publication) **2000**. (**Portrays Blandina as knowing Billy Bonney**)

Segale, Blandina. "Sister Blandina Meets Billy the Kid." **August, 2006**. *Catholic Digest*. Sisters of Charity of Cincinnati Archives, Mount Saint Joseph, Ohio. Blandina Segale Collection. Box 6, Folder 16e. (**Excerpted Billy the Kid tales from *At the End of the Santa Fe Trail***)

McClarey, Donald R. "Sister Blandina and the Original Billy the Kid." **October 12, 2012**. *The American Catholic*. (**States that Blandina's "Billy the Kid" was William LeRoy as the "original" Billy the Kid**)

Metz, Judith. "Servant of God, Sister Blandina Segale, S.C." **May 23, 2014**. Posting for the Daughters of Charity Provincial Archives. Sisters of Charity of Cincinnati Archive. Blandina Segale Collection. Box 15, Folder 1. (**States highpoint of Blandina's book is relationship with Billy the Kid**)

Kitt, Georgia. "Sisters of Charity Announce Approval of Cause for Canonization of Sister Blandina Segale." **June 24, 2014**. Sisters of Charity of Cincinnati press release. Sisters of Charity of Cincinnati Blandina Segale Collection. Box 15, Folder 1. **(Uses Billy the Kid relationship to announce sainthood cause)**

No Author. Associated Press. " 'Fastest Nun in the West' Sister Blandina Segale who stopped Billy the Kid may become a saint." **July 19, 2014.** *DailyMail.com*.

Contreras, Russell. "Old West nun stood up to Billy the Kid: Sister Segale, who will be subject of TV series, considered for sainthood." **July 16, 2016**. *Calgary Herald*. Sisters of Charity of Cincinnati Blandina Segale Collection. Box 16, Folder 4. **(About Saint Hood Productions TV series using Billy the Kid relationship)**

_____. " ' The Fastest Nun in the West' " faces first test in sainthood push: Vatican to investigate the work of Sister Blandina Segale." **August 26, 2015**. *Albuquerque Journal*. Sisters of Charity of Cincinnati Blandina Segale Collection. Box 15, Folder 7a. **(Publicizing by using Billy the Kid)**

Kaplan, Sarah. " 'The fastest nun in the West,' who took on Billy the Kid, is on the road to sainthood." **August 26, 2015**. *The Washington* Post. Sisters of Charity of Cincinnati Blandina Segale Collection. Box 16, Folder 2. **(Publicizing by using Billy the Kid)**

Contreras, Russell. Nun who Stood Up to Billy the Kid: Catholic Church considering her case for sainthood." **August 29, 2015**. Dayton, Ohio, *Journal*. Sisters of Charity of Cincinnati Blandina Segale Collection. Box 15, Folder 7a. **(Publicizing by using Billy the Kid)**

Rezac, Mary. "Nuns, guns and the Wild West – the extraordinary tale of Sr. Blandina." **August 31, 2015**. Catholic News Agency. Sisters of Charity of Cincinnati Archives, Mount Saint Joseph, Ohio. Blandina Segale Collection. Box 16, Folder 2. **(Calling Billy Bonney, William LeRoy as Billy the Kid)**

No Author. "Nun who stood up to Billy the Kid moves closer to sainthood." Associated Press News on internet. **November 13, 2015**. Sisters of Charity of Cincinnati Archives, Mount Saint Joseph, Ohio. Blandina Segale Collection. Box 15, Folder 8- - **(Ignoring Allen Sánchez's statement that Blandina did not know William Bonney, instead saying everything in her book has been verified)**

No Author. " 'The Fastest Nun in the West': Nun who got Billy the Kid to back down and then became his friend moves up sainthood path." **November 13, 2015**. *Dailymail.com* (with Associated Press) **(Assumes Blandina knew William Bonney)**

No Author. "Servant of God, Rosa Maria Segale (Sr. Blandina Segale, SC) Moves Closer to Sainthood AKA The Fastest Nun in the West Who Stood Up to Billy the Kid." **December, 2015**. *People of God*. Sisters of Charity of Cincinnati Archives, Mount Saint Joseph, Ohio. Blandina Segale Collection. Box 15, Folder 8. **(Reflecting Allen Sánchez's attempted Billy the Kid clarification by using "William LeRoy")**

Nordhaus, Hannah. "Making the Case for the Next American Saint: Sister Blandina Segale showed true grit while caring for orphans and outlaws in New Mexico." **November, 2016**. *Smithsonian Magazine*. **(States that Blandina's "Billy the Kid" was William LeRoy)**

Gomez, Adrian. "Sister Blandina TV pilot filming in New Mexico." **March 22, 2017**. *Albuquerque Journal* (abqjournal.com) **(Assumes Blandina knew William Bonney)**

No Author. Associated Press. "Nun who Stopped Billy the Kid from scalping 4 doctors to become subject of new TV series." **Tuesday, June 6, 2017**. *DailyMail.com*. **(Article on TV series that started my hoaxbusting)**

COMIC BOOK ABOUT

No Author. "Sister Blandina Meets Billy the Kid." **June 15, 1949**. *Topix*. St. Paul, Minnesota: Catechical Guild Educational Society. Volume 7, Number 20. Sisters of Charity of Cincinnati Blandina Segale Collection. Box 5, Folder 17.

MOVIES AND TV ABOUT (CHRONOLOGICAL)

Foster, Jack. "How Colo. Nun Saved 4 From Killer!" **November 11, 1957.** *Rocky Mountain News.* Sisters of Charity of Cincinnati Archives, Mount Saint Joseph, Ohio. .Blandina Segale Collection. Box 5, Folder 24b. (**About a movie on Blandina featuring Billy the Kid**)

Parsons, Louella O. "Life of a Colorado Nun." **1963.** Clipping from unknown publication. Sisters of Charity of Cincinnati Archives, Mount Saint Joseph, Ohio. .Blandina Segale Collection. Box 8, Folder 7. (**About a movie on Blandina featuring Billy the Kid**)

No Author. "Sister Blandina Story on TV." **November 28, 1963.** *The Denver Catholic Register.* Page 9. Sisters of Charity of Cincinnati Blandina Segale Collection. Box 8, Folder 7. (**Publicizing by using Billy the Kid**)

(SEE: William Henry Bonney aka Billy the Kid; Arthur Pond aka Billy LeRoy; Edward "Choctaw" Kelly)

SOURCES FOR OTHER BILLY THE KID HOAXES

BOOKS

Airy, Helen L. *Whatever Happened to Billy the Kid?* Santa Fe, New Mexico: Sunstone Press. 1993. (**John Miller as Billy the Kid hoax**)

Cooper, Gale. *Billy the Kid's Pretenders: Brushy Bill and John Miller.* Gelcour Books: Albuquerque: New Mexico. 2010.

_____. *Cracking the Billy the Kid Case Hoax: The Strange Plot to Exhume Billy the Kid, Convict Sheriff Pat Garrett of Murder, and Become President of the United States.* Albuquerque, New Mexico: Gelcour Books. 2014.

Garcia, Elbert A. *Billy the Kid's Kid. 1875-1964. The Hispanic Connection.* Santa Rosa, New Mexico: Los Products Press. 1999. (**Unsubstantiated claim of being Billy the Kid's grandson**)

Jameson, W.C. and Frederic Bean. *The Return of the Outlaw Billy the Kid.* Plano, Texas: Republic of Texas Press. 1997. ("**Brushy Bill" Roberts as Billy the Kid hoax**)

Sonnichsen, C.L. and William V. Morrison. *Alias Billy the Kid.* Albuquerque, New Mexico: University of New Mexico Press. 1955. (**Oliver "Brushy Bill" Roberts as Billy the Kid hoax**)

LETTER

Pittmon, Geneva. December 16, 1987 letter to Joe Bowlin with copy of Roberts family Bible genealogy page. (private collection) (**"Brushy Bill" as not being Billy the Kid**)

GENERAL HISTORICAL REFERENCES FOR WILLIAM BONNEY AKA BILLY THE KID AND THE LINCOLN COUNTY WAR PERIOD

Nolan, Frederick W. *The Life and Death of John Henry Tunstall.* Albuquerque, New Mexico: The University of New Mexico Press. 1965.

_____. *The Lincoln County War: A Documentary History.* Norman: University of Oklahoma Press. 1992.

_____. *The West of Billy the Kid.* Norman: University of Oklahoma Press. 1998.

HISTORICAL ORGANIZATIONS (PERIOD)

NORTH CAROLINA REGULATORS, 18th CENTURY

HISTORY OF 18th CENTURY REGULATORS

Hudson, Arthur Palmer . "Songs of the Carolina Regulators." *William and Mary Quarterly*. 4. No. 4 (1947): Page 146.

Kars, Marjoline. *Breaking Loose Together: The Regulator Rebellion in Pre-Revolutionary North Carolina*. Chapel Hill and London: The University of North Carolina Press. 2002.

Maier, Pauline. *From Resistance to Revolution: Colonial radicals and the development of American opposition to Britain, 1765-1776*. New York and London: W.W. Norton & Company. 1991.

LINCOLN COUNTY REGULATORS, 19th CENTURY

DIME NOVELS ON REGULATORS (CONTEMPORARY)

Lody, William F. "Gold Bullet Sport; The Knights of the Overland". *Beadle's Dime New York Library*. 7(83). New York: Beadle & Adams, Publishers. December 17, 1874.

Cooms, Oll. "The Boy Ranger: or, The Heiress of the Golden Horn." *Pocket Series*. No. 11. New York: Beadle & Adams, Publishers. 1874.

Wheeler, Edward L. *The Deadwood Dick Library*. "A Tale of the Regulators and Road-Agents of the Black Hills. The Double Daggers; or, Deadwood Dick's Defiance." Beadles Half Dime Library. No. 20. Cleveland, Ohio: Arthur Westbrook Co. 1877.

_____. "Deadwood Dick, The Prince of the Road: or The Black Rider of the Black Hills". *The Deadwood Dick Library*. 1(1). Cleveland, Ohio: The Arthur Westbrook Co. 1877.

No Author. "The Rover of the Forest." *Munro's Ten Cent Novels*. No. 42. New York: George Munro & Co. 1864.

"REGULATOR MANIFESTO" (BY BILLY BONNEY)

Regulator. "Mr. Walz. Sir ..." Letter to Edgar Walz. July 13, 1878. Adjutant General's Office. File 1405 AGO 1878. (Quoted in Maurice Garland Fulton, *History of the Lincoln County War*. Tucson: University of Arizona Press. 1975. pages 246-247, and Frederick Nolan, *The Lincoln County War: A Documentary History*, page 310.)

SANTA FE RING, 19th CENTURY

MODERN SOURCES ON SANTA FE RING

Caffey, David L. *Chasing the Santa Fe Ring: Power and Privilege in Territorial New Mexico*. Albuquerque, New Mexico: University of New Mexico Press. 2014.

_____. *Frank Springer and New Mexico: From the Colfax County War to the Emergence of Modern Santa Fe*. Texas A and M. University Press. 2007.

Cleaveland, Agnes Morley. *No Life for a Lady*. Boston: Houghton Mifflin. 1941.

_____. *Satan's Paradise: From Lucien Maxwell to Fred Lambert*. Boston: Houghton Mifflin Company. 1952.

Cleaveland, Norman, *Colfax County's Chronic Murder Mystery*. Santa Fe: New Mexico. The Rydel Press. 1977.

_____. *A Synopsis of the Great New Mexico Cover-up*. Self-printed. 1989.

_____. *Some Comments Norman Cleveland May Make to the Huntington Westerners on Sept. 19, 1987*. Unpublished.

_____. *Some Highlights of William R. Morley's Contribution to the Pioneer Development of the Southwest*. Self-printed. No Date.

_____. *The Great Santa Fe Cover-up*. Based on a Talk given Before the Santa Fe Historical Society on November 1, 1978. Self-printed. 1982.

_____. *The Morleys - Young Upstarts on the Southwest Frontier*. Albuquerque, New Mexico: Calvin Horn Publisher, Inc. 1971.

Cooper, Gale. *The Lost Pardon of Billy the Kid: An Analysis Factoring in the Santa Fe Ring, Governor Lew Wallace's Dilemma, and a Territory in Rebellion*. Albuquerque, New Mexico: Gelcour Books. 2017.

Keleher, William A. *The Maxwell Land Grant. A New Mexico Item*. Albuquerque, New Mexico: University of New Mexico Press. 1964.

Lamar, Howard Robert N. *The Far Southwest 1846 – 1912: A Territorial History*. New Haven and London: Yale University Press. 1966. (**Chapter 6 covers the Santa Fe Ring**))

Meinig, D. W. *The Shaping of America. A Geographical Perspective on 500 Years of History. Vol. 3. Transcontinental America 1850 - 1915*. New Haven and London: Yale University Press. 1998. (**Pages 127 and 132 are on the Santa Fe Ring.**)

Milner, Clyde A. II, Carol A. O'Connor, Martha Sandweiss. Eds. *The Oxford History of the American West*. New York and Oxford: Oxford University Press. 1994.

Montoya, María E. Translating Property. The Maxwell Land Grant and the Conflict Over Land in the American West, 1840-1900. Berkeley and Los Angeles: University of California Press. 2002.

Naegle, Conrad Keeler. *The History of Silver City, New Mexico 1870-1886*. University of New Mexico Bachelor of Arts thesis. Pages 30-60. Unpublished. 1943. Collection of the Silver City Museum, Silver City, New Mexico. (**Grant County rebellion against Santa Fe Ring**)

_____. "The Rebellion of Grant County, New Mexico in 1876." *Arizona and the West: A Quarterly Journal of History*. Autumn, 1968. Volume 10. Number 3. Tucson, Arizona: The University of Arizona Press. 1968. Pages 225-240. (**Grant County rebellion against Santa Fe Ring**)

Newman, Simeon Harrison III. "The Santa Fe Ring." *Arizona and the West*. Volume 12. Autumn 1970. Pages 269-288.

Otero, Miguel A. *My Life on the Frontier, 1882-1897: Incidents and Characters of the period when Kansas, Colorado, and New Mexico were Passing Through the Last of their Wild and Romantic Years*. New York: The Press of the Pioneers. 1935. Pages 232-233. (Quoted by Victor Westphall, *Thomas Benton Catron and His Era*. Page 188*)* (**Quote: "the 'Santa Fe Ring,' the real machine controlling the political situation in New Mexico."**)

Pearson, Jim Berry. *The Maxwell Land Grant*. Norman: University of Oklahoma Press. 1961.

Taylor, Morris F. *O.P. McMains and the Maxwell Land Grant Conflict*. Tucson, Arizona: The University of Arizona Press. 1979. (**Traces origins of the Santa Fe Ring**)

Theisen, Lee Scott. "Frank Warner Angel's Notes on New Mexico Territory, 1878." *Arizona and the West: A Quarterly Journal of History*. Winter 1976. Volume 18. Number 4. Pages 333-370. (**About the Angel notebook**)

Twitchell, Ralph Emerson. *The Leading Facts of New Mexico History*. Vol. I-II. Santa Fe: Sunstone Press. 2007. (Reprinted from a 1912 edition) (**Reputed Santa Fe Ringman and its cover-up historian**)

Westphall, Victor. *Thomas Benton Catron and His Era*. Tucson, Arizona: University of Arizona Press. 1973. (**Ring-denier biographer**)

CONTEMPORARY SOURCES ON SANTA FE RING
(CHRONOLOGICAL)

No Author. *Diario del Consejo der Territorio de Neuvo Mejico, Session de 1871-1872.* Santa Fe New Mexican. **January 8, 1872.** Santa Fe: A.P. Sullivan. 1872. Pages 144-154. New Mexico Supreme Court Library. Santa Fe, New Mexico. (**A Ring expurgated document, with copy found in 1942 by Conrad Naegle; confirms troops used by Ring to suppress 1872 Legislature Revolt**)

No Author. *Diario del Consejo der Territorio de Neuvo Mejico, Session de 1871-1872.* Las Cruces *Borderer.* **January 24, 1872.** Pages 110-113. (**President of the Council Don Diego Archuleta objects to troops in legislature**)

No Author. *Journal of the House of Representatives of the Territory of New Mexico, Session of 1871-1872.* Santa Fe: A.P. Sullivan. **1872.** Pages 144-154. (**Confirms troops used by Ring to suppress the Legislature Revolt of 1872**)

Mills, Melvin W. "Thought I would write you how things are running." Letter to Robert H. Longwill. **December 5, 1873.** "Exhibit A" in the August 9, 1878 deposition of Frank Springer to Investigator Frank Warner Angel. Frank Warner Angel report titled *In the Matter of the Investigation of the Charges Against S.B. Axtell Governor of New Mexico.* October 3, 1878. Interior Department Papers 1850-1907; Appointments Division and Subsequent Actions. Microfilm Case File No. 44-4-8-3. Record Group 48. Microfilm Roll M750. National Archives and Records Administration. U.S. Department of Interior. Washington, D.C. (**About Catron and Ring empowerment**)

Bristol Warren. "From sources of information that I deem perfectly reliable I am satisfied that there are public disorders in Lincoln County ..." Letter to Governor Marsh Giddings. **January 10, 1874.** Herman B. Weisner Papers, ca. 1957-1992. New Mexico State University Library at Las Cruces. Rio Grande Historical Collections. Accession No. Weisner Ms 0249. Box 4/39. Folder D-4. Folder Name: "Judge Bristol's letter." (**Santa Fe Ring's outlaw myth and proposed use of military intervention**)

No Author. "Ring influence [in the Territorial legislature is] being actively used against every measure that tends to do justice" [in Grant and Doña Counties]." Grant County *Herald.* **August 8, 1875.** Quoted by Conrad Keeler Naegle in *The History of Silver City, New Mexico 1870-1886,* doctoral thesis. Page 39.

Morley, William Raymond and Frank Springer. On Oscar McMains's citizen's Meeting. *Cimarron News and Press.* **November 10, 1875.** In Mary McPherson, Letters and Petitions to President Rutherford B. Hayes re: Removal Governor Axtell and the Santa Fe Ring. 1977. Interior Department Papers 1850-1907; Appointments Division and Subsequent Actions. Microfilm File Case Number 44-4-8-3. **Record Group 48.** Microfilm Roll M750. National Archives and Records Administration. (**Colfax County citizens meeting on F.J. Tolby murder by Santa Fe Ring.**)

_____. " 'The Territory of Elkins.' Assassination of Supposed Sun Correspondent. The Murder of the Rev. F.J. Tolby in New Mexico. A Probate Judge Accused of Complicity in the Crime. Indignation Meeting." *New York Weekly Sun.* **December 22, 1875.** Interior Department Papers 1850-1907; Appointments Division and Subsequent Actions. Microfilm Roll M750. National Archives and Records Administration. Record Group 48. Microfilm Case File Number 44-4-8-3. U.S. Department of Interior. Washington, D. C. (**From May 1, 1877 submission to President Rutherford B. Hates as "Mary E. McPherson and W.B. Matchett 'Make certain charges against the U.S. Officials in the Territory of New Mexico.' "**)

Middaugh, Asa F. Deposition. **March 31, 1876.** "Exhibit B" in the August 9, 1878 deposition of Frank Springer to Investigator Frank Warner Angel. Frank Warner Angel report titled *In the Matter of the Investigation of the Charges Against S.B. Axtell Governor of New Mexico.* October 3, 1878. Interior Department Papers 1850-1907; Appointments Division and Subsequent Actions. Microfilm Case File No. 44-

4-8-3. Record Group 48. Microfilm Roll M750. National Archives and Records Administration. U.S. Department of Interior. Washington, D.C. (**About Catron's malicious prosecution of Ada McPherson Morley**)

No Author. "A Contemplated Political Change." Grant County *Herald*. **September 16, 1876**. Quoted by Conrad Keeler Naegle in *The History of Silver City, New Mexico 1870-1886* doctoral thesis. Pages 39-40. (**Listing reasons to escape the Ring by annexing to Arizona Territory**)

No Author. [Grant County should not] "sort o' wait and hear from Santa Fe ... before taking action." Tucson *Arizona Citizen*. **September 23, 1876**. Quoted by Conrad Keeler Naegle in *The History of Silver City, New Mexico 1870-1886* doctoral thesis. Page 41. (**Arizona encourages escape from Santa Fe Ring**)

No Author. Grant County *Herald*. **September 30, 1876**. (**"Annexation Meeting" announced**)

No Author. "Proceedings of Grant County Annexation Meeting." Grant County *Herald*. **Saturday October 7, 1876**. Page 2. Columns 1 and 2. Collection of the Silver City, New Mexico, Museum. (**Anti-Santa Fe Ring "Grant County Declaration of Independence" published**)

No Author. Grant County *Herald*. " 'Petition to Remove Judge Bristol. We the undersigned citizens of the Third Judicial District of the Territory of New Mexico, without regard to party, would respectfully request and petition for the removal of Judge Warren Bristol ...' " No date. **1876 or 1877**.(Quoted in "W.B. Matchett and Mary E. McPherson 'Make certain charges against the U.S. Officials in the Territory of New Mexico.' " Letter to President Rutherford B. Hayes. Received and filed May 1, 1877. Interior Department Papers 1850-1907; Appointments Division and Subsequent Actions. Microfilm File Case Number 44-4-8-3. Record Group 48. Microfilm No. M750. Roll 1. National Archives and Records Administration. U.S. Department of Justice. Washington, D.C.) (**Anti-Santa Fe Ring article**)

No Author. Report on murder trial for Franklin Tolby. Pueblo, *Colorado Chieftain*. **May 25, 1876**. Quoting *Daily New Mexican*, May 1, 1876. From Morris F. Taylor. *O.P. McMains and the Maxwell Land Grant Conflict*. Tucson, Arizona: The University of Arizona Press. 1979. Page 49. (**Ring-biased jury instructions by Judge Henry Waldo to protect Ring murderers of Tolby**)

McPherson, Mary. "Charges against Thomas B. Catron, U.S. Attorney, and Others." **February 7, 1877**. Letter to Attorney General Alphonso Taft. Interior Department Papers 1850-1907; Appointments Division and Subsequent Actions. Microfilm File Case Number 44-4-8-3. Record Group 48. Microfilm Roll M750. National Archives and Records Administration. U.S. Department of Justice. Washington, D.C.

Catron, Thomas Benton. "Answering Charges of Mary E. McPherson." **February 24, 1877**. Letter to Attorney General Alphonso Taft. Interior Department Papers 1850-1907; Appointments Division and Subsequent Actions. Microfilm File Case Number 44-4-8-3. Record Group 48. Microfilm Roll M750. National Archives and Records Administration. U.S. Department of Justice. Washington, D.C.

Morley William Raymond. "I was astonished beyond measure at your proceedings, and have fears as to the result ..." Letter to Mary McPherson. **March 6, 1877**. McPherson, Mary E. Letters and Petitions to President Rutherford B. Hayes re: Removal Governor Axtell and the Santa Fe Ring. Interior Department Papers 1850-1907; Appointments Division and Subsequent Actions. File Case Number 44-4-8-3. Record Group 48. Microfilm Roll M750. National Archives and Records Administration. U.S. Department of Justice. Washington, D. C. (**Hopes she can help fight against Santa Fe Ring; enclosed in Mary McPherson's addendum to her "Certain Charges against U.S. Officials in the Territory of New Mexico."**)

Morley William Raymond. "I was astonished beyond measure at your proceedings, and have fears as to the result ..." Letter to Mary McPherson. **March 6, 1877**. McPherson, Mary E. Letters and Petitions to President Rutherford B. Hayes re:

Removal Governor Axtell and the Santa Fe Ring. Interior Department Papers 1850-1907; Appointments Division and Subsequent Actions. Microfilm File Case Number 44-4-8-3. Record Group 48. Microfilm Roll M750. National Archives and Records Administration. U.S. Department of Justice. Washington, D. C. (**Hopes she can help fight against Santa Fe Ring; enclosed in Mary McPherson's "Charges Against U.S. Officials in the Territory of New Mexico."**)

Morley, Ada. "Yes, we have received all your letters at Vermejo here but we have hesitated about replying ..." Letter to Mary McPherson. **March 7, 1877**. McPherson, Mary E. Letters and Petitions to President Rutherford B. Hayes re: Removal Governor Axtell and the Santa Fe Ring. Interior Department Papers 1850-1907; Appointments Division and Subsequent Actions. Microfilm File Case Number 44-4-8-3. Record Group 48. Microfilm Roll M750. National Archives and Records Administration. U.S. Department of Justice. Washington, D. C. (**Fears about her fight against Santa Fe Ring; oddly this private letter was in her mother's governmental file**)

Lambert, J.J. "At It Again." Pueblo, Colorado, *Enterprise and Chronicle*. **April 21, 1877**. Interior Department Papers 1850-1907; Appointments Division and Subsequent Actions. Microfilm File Case Number 44-4-8-3. Record Group 48. Microfilm No. M750. Roll 1. National Archives and Records Administration. U.S. Department of Justice. Washington, D.C. (**Description of Santa Fe Ring control of courts and malicious prosecution of opponents like Oscar McMains in the Franklin Tolby murder; used in: "W.B. Matchett and Mary E. McPherson 'Make Certain Charges Against the U.S. Officials in the Territory of New Mexico.' " Letter to President Rutherford B. Hayes. Received and filed May 1, 1877. Interior Department Papers 1850-1907; Appointments Division and Subsequent Actions. Microfilm File Case Number 44-4-8-3. Record Group 48. Microfilm No. M750. Roll 1. National Archives and Records Administration. U.S. Department of Justice. Washington, D.C.**)

Matchett, W.B. and Mary E. McPherson. "W.B. Matchett and Mary E. McPherson 'Make Certain Charges Against the U.S. Officials in the Territory of New Mexico.' " Letter to President Rutherford B. Hayes. Received and filed **May 1, 1877**. Interior Department Papers 1850-1907; Appointments Division and Subsequent Actions. Microfilm File Case Number 44-4-8-3. Record Group 48. Microfilm No. M750. Roll 1. National Archives and Records Administration. U. S. Department of Justice. Washington, D.C. (**Sent to President Rutherford B. Hayes and Secretary of the Interior Carl Schurz 141 pages of letters, affidavits, petitions, newspaper articles, itemized requests for removal of Governor Samuel Beach Axtell and District Judge Warren Bristol, documentation of use of the military against civilians, documentation of the Ring murder of Ring opponent Reverend F.J. Tolby, and identification of the Santa Fe Ring and Elkins and Catron as its leaders.**)

McPherson, Mary and W.B. Matchett. "To the President. Please make the enclosed a part of the evidence in the case of "Charges Against New Mexican Officials" Letter to President Rutherford B. Hayes. **May 3, 1877**. McPherson, Mary E. Letters and Petitions to President Rutherford B. Hayes re: Removal Governor Axtell and the Santa Fe Ring. Interior Department Papers 1850-1907; Appointments Division and Subsequent Actions. Microfilm File Case Number 44-4-8-3. Record Group 48. Microfilm Roll M750. National Archives and Records Administration. U.S. Department of Justice. Washington, D.C. (**Addendum to their May, 1877 "Certain Charges Against U.S. Officials in New Mexico Territory."**)

McPherson, Mary and W.B. Matchett. "The Secretary of the Interior, Sir - Accompanying please find copy of charges, &c., against S.B. Axtell, Governor, and other New Mexican Officials ..." "Charges Against New Mexican Officials." Letter to Secretary of the Interior Carl Schurz. **May 5, 1877**. McPherson, Mary E. Letters and Petitions to President Rutherford B. Hayes re: Removal Governor

Axtell and the Santa Fe Ring. Interior Department Papers 1850-1907; Appointments Division and Subsequent Actions. Microfilm File Case Number 44-4-8-3. Record Group 48. Microfilm Roll M750. National Archives and Records Administration. U.S. Department of Justice. Washington, D. C.

McPherson, Mary E. Letters and Petitions to President Rutherford B. Hayes re: Removal Governor Axtell and the Santa Fe Ring. **1977.** Interior Department Papers 1850-1907; Appointments Division and Subsequent Actions. Microfilm File Case Number 44-4-8-3. Record Group 48. Microfilm Roll M750. National Archives and Records Administration.

McPherson, Mary and W.B. Matchett. "We have respectfully to request that the following named records, documents, papers, communications and correspondence be supplied ..." Records Request to Secretary of the Interior Carl Schurz. **July 26, 1877.** Interior Department Papers 1850-1907; Appointments Division and Subsequent Actions. Microfilm File Case Number 44-4-8-3. Record Group 48. Microfilm No. M750. Roll 1. National Archives and Records Administration. U. S. Department of Justice. Washington, D.C. (**Requesting records of the Santa Fe Ring, Catron, Elkins, and Axtell**)

McPherson, Mary. "Please place before the Attorney General ..." Letter to President Rutherford B. Hayes. **August 23, 1877.** Interior Department Papers 1850-1907; Appointments Division and Subsequent Actions. Microfilm File Case Number 44-4-8-3. Record Group 48. Microfilm No. M750. Roll 1. National Archives and Records Administration. U.S. Department of Justice. Washington, D.C. (**Requesting that her "Charges vs. New Mexico Officials" go to the Attorney General.**)

McPherson, Mary and W.B. Matchett. *"In the Matter of Charges vs. Gov. S.B. Axtell and Other New Mexico Officials. Submitted to the Departments of the Interior and Justice.* **August, 1877.** Printed as a 31 page booklet. No publisher listed. Indiana Historical Society. Lew Wallace Collection. M0292. Box 3. Folder 20. (**Exposé of Santa Fe Ring, Catron, and Elkins; in Lew Wallace's possession**)

McPherson, Mary. "I desire to know when I can be heard ..." Letter to Secretary of Interior Carl Schurz. **September 30, 1977.** Interior Department Papers 1850-1907; Appointments Division and Subsequent Actions. Microfilm File Case Number 44-4-8-3. Record Group 48. Microfilm No. M750. Roll 1. National Archives and Records Administration. U. S. Department of Justice. Washington, D.C. (**Requesting to be heard in person on her charges against officials and Governor Axtell.**)

Angel, Frank Warner. "To Gov. Lew Wallace, Santa Fe, N. M., 1878." Notebook. **1878.** Indiana Historical Society. Lew Wallace Collection. M0292. Microfilm No. F372. (**Original missing, copy on microfilm; Notebook prepared for Lew Wallace listing names in Lincoln County and the Santa Fe Ring**)

Tunstall, John Henry. "A Taxpayer's Complaint ... January 18, 1878." Mesilla *Independent.* **January 26, 1878.** (**Exposé of William Brady, James Dolan, and John Riley for tax fraud and use of public money to purchase cattle; and T.B. Catron then paid that bill**)

Dolan, James J. "Answer to A Taxpayer's Complaint." Mesilla *Independent.* **January 29, 1878.** (**Response to J.H. Tunstall's exposé of him, William Brady, and John Riley for tax fraud and use of public money to purchase cattle; and T.B. Catron then paid that bill**)

Springer, Frank. "I hope you have received a full account of the Troubles in Lincoln County from your nephew ..." Letter to Senator Rush Clark. **April 9, 1878.** Herman B. Weisner Papers, ca. 1957-1992. New Mexico State University Library at Las Cruces. Rio Grande Historical Collections. Accession No. Weisner Ms 0249. Box 4/39. Folder D-6. Folder Name "Frank Springer Letter to Rush Clark." (**Links Santa Fe Ring to murder of J.H. Tunstall**)

Leonard, Ira. "When you left here I promised to write you concerning events transpiring here ..." Letter to Lew Wallace. **May 20, 1878 [sic - 79].** Indiana

Historical Society. Lew Wallace Collection. M0292. Box 4. Folder 10. (**With quote: "the Santa Fe Ring that has been so long an incubus on the government of this territory"**)

Morley, William Raymond. "Your letter of the 7th came last night and it was a good long newsy letter ..." Letter to wife, Ada McPherson Morley. **August 15, 1878**. Collection of Norman Cleaveland. Quoted in Norman Cleaveland, *The Morleys: Young Upstarts in the Southwest*. Albuquerque, New Mexico: Calvin Horn Publisher, Inc. 1971. Pages 152-155. (**About possible betrayal by Angel's reports; about the Santa Fe Ring, T.B. Catron, S.B. Elkins, S.B. Axtell, and Henry Waldo; and the Lincoln County War**)

Angel, Frank Warner. *Examination of Charges Against F. C. Godfroy, Indian Agent, Mescalero, N. M.* **October 2, 1878**. (Report 1981, Inspector E. C. Watkins; Cited as Watkins Report). M 319-20 and L147-44-4-8. Record Group 075. National Archives and Records Administration. U.S. Department of Justice. Washington, D.C.

Morley, William Raymond. Deposition to Investigator Frank Warner Angel. August 9, 1878. Frank Warner Angel report titled *In the Matter of the Investigation of the Charges Against S.B. Axtell Governor of New Mexico*. **October 3, 1878**. Interior Department Papers 1850-1907; Appointments Division and Subsequent Actions. Microfilm Case File No. 44-4-8-3. Record Group 48. Microfilm Roll M750. National Archives and Records Administration. U.S. Department of Interior. Washington, D.C. (**Mentions Catron, Elkins, and the Santa Fe Ring, and provided Exhibits of letters exposing Catron's evil.**)

Angel, Frank Warner. *In the Matter of the Investigation of the Charges Against S.B. Axtell Governor of New Mexico*. **October 3, 1878**. Frank Warner Angel report. Interior Department Papers 1850-1907; Appointments Division and Subsequent Actions. Microfilm Case File No. 44-4-8-3. Record Group 48. Microfilm Roll M750. National Archives and Records Administration. U.S. Department of Interior. Washington, D.C. (**Mentions Santa Fe Ring**)

_____. *In the Matter of the Investigation of the Charges Against S. B. Axtell Governor of New Mexico*. **October 3, 1878**. Angel Report. Microfilm File No. 44-4-8-3. Record Group 48. Roll M750. National Archives. U.S. Department of Interior. Washington, D.C.

_____. *In the Matter of the Examination of the Causes and Circumstances of the Death of John H. Tunstall a British Subject*. **October 4, 1878**. Angel Report. Microfilm File Case Number 44-4-8-3. Record Group 48. Microfilm No. M750. Roll 1. National Archives and Records Administration. U.S. Department of Justice. Washington, D.C.

_____. *In the Matter of the Lincoln County Troubles. To the Honorable Charles Devens, Attorney General*. **October 4, 1878**. Angel Report. Microfilm Case File No. 44-4-8-3. Record Group 48. Microfilm Roll M750. National Archives and Records Administration. U.S. Department of Justice. Washington, D.C.

Wallace, Lew. "Our mutual friend, M. Hinds, who will hand you this ..." Letter to A.H. Markland. **November 14, 1878**. Indiana Historical Society. Lew Wallace Collection. M0292. Box 3. Folder 17. (**Aware of the Santa Fe Ring and its attempt to remove him as governor**)

No Author. *Proceedings of a Court of Inquiry in the Case of Lt. Col. N.A.M. Dudley*. **May 2, 1879 – July 5, 1879**. File No. QQ1284. (Boxes 3304, 3305, 3305A); Court Martial Files 1809-1894. Records of the Office of the Judge Advocate General – Army. Record Group 153. Old Military and Civil Branch. National Archives and Records Administration. Washington, D.C.

Leonard, Ira E. "When you left here I promised to write you concerning events transpiring here ..." Letter to Lew Wallace. **May 20, 1878 [sic - 79]**. Indiana Historical Society. Lew Wallace Collection. M0292. Box 4. Folder 10. (**Has quote on the Murphy-Dolan party as: "part and parcel of the Santa Fe ring that has been so long an incubus on the government of this territory."**)

_____. "I write to you with pencil because I am laboring for breath ..." Letter to Lew Wallace. **May 23, 1879**. Indiana Historical Society. Lew Wallace Collection. M0292. Box 4. Folder 11. (**With quote "we are pouring the 'hot shot' into Dudley." With enclosed letter of May 20, 1879**)

_____. "Yours of the 7th inst reached me ..." Letter to Lew Wallace. **June 13, 1879**. Indiana Historical Society. Lew Wallace Collection. M0292. Box 4. Folder 11. (**Important quotes: "... they would not enter our objections ..." "... would not allow us to show the conspiracy formed with Dolan beforehand ..." "I tell you Governor as long as the present incumbent occupies the bench all that Grand Juries may do to bring to justice these men every effort will be thwarted by him and the sympathizers of that side."**)

Elkins, Stephen Benton. "I have waited some time to reply to your lengthy letter ..." Letter to T.B. Catron. **August 15, 1879**. West Virginia & Regional History Center. West Virginia University Libraries, Morgantown, W. Va. Stephen B. Elkins Papers (A&M 53). Box 1. Folder 1. (**Reveals he prevented Catron's dismissal and indictment from Angel's report**)

Wallace, Lew. "I have the honor to inform you that the Legislature of this Territory adjourned ..." **February 16, 1880**. Letter to Carl Schurz. Indiana Historical Society. Lew Wallace Collection. M0292. Box 4. Folder 14. (**Important documentation of Catron as head of the Santa Fe Ring, and Wallace's Ring opposition**)

No Author. "The Santa Fe Ring is the most corrupt combination that ever cursed any country or community." Las Cruces *Thirty-Four Newspaper*. **October 27, 1880**. From Victor Westphall, *Thomas Benton Catron and His Era*. Page 186. (**Article on Santa Fe Ring abuses urging voters to oppose Ring candidates**)

No Author. "A man named Springer is in Washington trying to defeat the nomination of Governor Axtell. Springer is a friend of the thugs and thieves of Colfax County." *Santa Fe New Mexican*. **July 6, 1882**. (**Santa Fe Ring re-instatement of S.B. Axtell to public office**)

No Author. " 'Chief Justice Axtell' is a bitter pill for the Raton *News and Press*." *Santa Fe New Mexican*. **July 18, 1882**. (**Santa Fe Ring re-instatement of S.B. Axtell as Chief Justice**)

No Author. "The Ring must soon discover that the time has passed in New Mexico when men can be herded like so many sheep ..." *Albuquerque Daily Democrat*. **March 4, 1884**. Quoted by Victor Westphall, *Thomas Benton Catron and His Era*. Page 191. (**About Santa Fe Ring control of appointments to legislature**)

Thornton, W.T. "Your favors received. We will try and have the matter of Mrs. Wilson's estate at Albuquerque attended to for your Bates County friends." Letter to John J. Cockrell, Esq. **January 16, 1886**. Herman B. Weisner Papers, ca. 1957-1992. New Mexico State University Library at Las Cruces. Rio Grande Historical Collections. Accession No. Weisner Ms 0249. Box 12. Folder S-5. Folder Name: "Catron, Thornton, & Clancy Letterhead." (**Catron's law partner discloses Ring planned malicious prosecution in Lincoln County**)

Borrego, Francisco Gonzales y. "dear Sir I have the honor to report to you that I have two men that they have agreed to come to the Republican party ... they want $10.00 each ..." **July 23, 1890**. Letter to Thomas Benton Catron. Catron Papers 102, Box 8. (**Revealing Catron's vote-buying by Ring agents**)

Chavez, Juliana V. "Mr. Catron, you are not above suspicion of knowing more about the assassination of my son than you have found it convenient to reveal ..." Letter of Juliana Chavez to T.B. Catron. Reprinted in *Santa Fe Weekly New Mexican*. **March 8, 1894**. Quoted in Victor Westphall, *Thomas Benton Catron and his Era*. Page 226. (**Accusing Catron as accomplice to murder of Francisco Chavez, with implication of Santa Fe Ring**)

No author. "T.B. Catron's reputation now being "smirched" by evidence that he was a briber and too dishonest even to practice law ..." *Las Vegas Independent*

Democrat. **1895**; quoting from *Las Vegas Optic*. **September 2, 1884**. From Victor Westphall. *Thomas Benton Catron and His Era*. Pages 105-106. **(About Catron's and Elkins's dishonesty, the Santa Fe Ring, and disbarring Catron from law practice in New Mexico)**

Catron, Thomas Benton (As "Anonymous"). "Is it honesty or partisanship?" Letter to the Editor, Thomas Hughes. *Albuquerque Daily Citizen*. **October 9, 1895**. **(Defamation of his disbarment Judge Thomas J. Smith)** Cited by Victor Westphall, *Thomas Benton Catron and His Era*. Page 246. Thomas B. Catron Papers. University of New Mexico Center for Southwest Studies. University Library. MSS 29 BC.

_____. "[Y]ou must absolutely stand pat and not give away any information that will injure me ..." Letter to Editor of the *Albuquerque Daily Citizen* Thomas Hughes. **October 10, 1895**. Catron Papers. 801. Box 1. Quoted by Victor Westphall, *Thomas Benton Catron and His Era*. Page 247. **(Catron influencing the Ringite newspaper editor to prevent his own disbarment by the New Mexico Supreme Court)**

_____. "Editor of the Citizen: I have noticed an article in the Citizen of the 9th inst., which seems to reflect on Chief Justice Smith ..." Letter to Editor of the *Albuquerque Daily Citizen* Thomas Hughes. **October 10, 1895**. Catron Papers 801. Box 1. Quoted by Victor Westphall, *Thomas Benton Catron and His Era*. (page 248) **(Catron lying in letter to complicit Ringite editor to conceal his own authorship of the newspaper's article accusing his Supreme Court disbarment judge of bias)**

_____. "[Chief Justice] Tom Smith, son of "Extra Billy" Smith, brother of ... the embezzler, who fled from justice in Arizona, and brother of the other Smith who took a prominent part in the murder of Dave Broderick ..." "[Judge] Hamilton should ... see that the decision is an absolute, complete, unconditional vindication. This is what I ask him. He can afford to give it." Letter to *Socorro Chieftain* publisher S.W. Williams. **October 25, 1895**. Catron Papers. 105. Vol. 13. Quoted by Victor Westphall, *Thomas Benton Catron and His Era*. Page 251. **(Example of Catron's vicious defamation of his Supreme Court disbarment Chief Judge Thomas Smith in Ringite collusion with the press, and use of illegal influence on another judge)**

Hamilton, Humphrey. *Majority Opinion* in disbarment case against Thomas Benton Catron. "[T]he low moral character and poor reputation for veracity of the prosecution witnesses rendered their testimony beyond belief." **October 25, 1895**. Catron Papers. 801. Box 1. Quoted by Victor Westphall, *Thomas Benton Catron and His Era*. Page 251. **(Ring colluding judge vindicating Catron from disbarment by blocking prosecution evidence)**

Catron, Thomas Benton. "His [Chief Justice Thomas Smith] skin is so thin that the slightest attack punctures him. I think the papers should now puncture him so much ..." Letter to T.W. Collier. **November 11, 1895**. Catron Papers. 105. Vol. 13. Quoted by Victor Westphall, *Thomas Benton Catron and His Era*. Page 249. **(Example of Catron's vicious Ringite harassment of an opponent)**

_____. "The letter of Gov. Thornton [in the September 11, 1896 of the *Santa Fe Daily New Mexican* and exposing his defamation plot] is regarded here by all good citizens as being ... calculated to bring about a state of unrest and possible bloodshed." **September 16, 1896**. Letter to President Grover Cleveland. Catron Papers 801, Box 1. Quoted by Victor Westphall, *Thomas Benton Catron and His Era*. Pages 269-270. **(Catron's paranoid accusations against Thornton)**

Wallace, Lew. "I have your several letters, including the last one of the 3rd inst." Letter to Eugene Fiske. **November 6, 1897**. Indiana Historical Society. Lew Wallace Collection. AC233. Box 1. Folder 7. (part of 1981 addition) **(About T.B. Catron's control over New Mexicans)**

No Author. *Los Angeles Times.* **1899**. Undated clipping, Laughlin Papers, State Records Center, Santa Fe, New Mexico. Quoted by Victor Westphall, *Thomas Benton Catron and His Era.* Page 285. (**Joking article about the Santa Fe Ring**)

Catron, Thomas Benton. "[Otero backers] have made a very villainous, mean ugly fight against me." **September 20, 1902**. Letter to Dave Winters. Catron Papers 105, Volume 20. Quoted by Victor Westphall, *Thomas Benton Catron and His Era.* Pages 291. (**Catron's accusing of rival, Governor Miguel Otero, of his own ring-style criminality**)

Cutting, Bronson. "Catron was the boss of the Territory ..." Letter to James Roger Addison. **December 11, 1911**. Cited by Victor Westphall in *Thomas Benton Catron and His Era* from his citation: Lincoln County Manuscripts Division. Box 12. Courtesy of David Stratton. (**Catron as head of the Santa Fe Ring**)

Johnson, E. Dana. "[H]e ruled with a rod of iron ..." Editorial. *Santa Fe New Mexican.* **May 16, 1921**. Catron Papers 801, Box 1. Quoted by Victor Westphall, *Thomas Benton Catron and His Era.* Pages 394-395. (**Santa Fe Ring tactics of "boss" Catron without using the words Santa Fe Ring**)

Pritchard, George W. "Eulogy." **May 17, 1921**. Catron Papers 801, Box 1. Quoted by Victor Westphall, *Thomas Benton Catron and His Era.* Pages 393-394. (**Cover-up of Santa Fe Ring atrocities for Catron's death eulogy**)

Mabry, Thomas Jewett. "New Mexico's Constitution in the Making." *New Mexico Historical Review.* **1943**. Volume 19, Issue 170. Quoted by Victor Westphall, *Thomas Benton Catron and His Era.* Page 341. (**Revealing that future Governor Mabry was Ring biased, calling T.B. Catron an "able delegate" to New Mexico's 1912 constitutional convention**)

SEE ALSO: Thomas Benton Catron; Stephen Benton Elkins

NEW MEXICO TERRITORY REBELLIONS AGAINST THE SANTA FE RING (CHRONOLOGICAL)

GENERAL SOURCE

Cooper, Gale. *The Lost Pardon of Billy the Kid: An Analysis Factoring in the Santa Fe Ring, Governor Lew Wallace's Dilemma, and a Territory in Rebellion.* Albuquerque, New Mexico: Gelcour Books. 2017.

LEGISLATURE REVOLT (1872)

No Author. *Las Vegas Optic.* **September 2, 1884**. (**About the anti-Ring Legislature revolt and Catron's alliance with corrupt Judge Joseph Palen**)

GRANT COUNTY REBELLION (1876)

MODERN HISTORICAL SOURCES

Naegle, Conrad Keeler. *The History of Silver City, New Mexico 1870-1886.* University of New Mexico Bachelor of Arts thesis. Pages 30-60. Unpublished. 1943. Collection of the Silver City Museum, Silver City, New Mexico.

_____. "The Rebellion of Grant County, New Mexico in 1876." *Arizona and the West: A Quarterly Journal of History.* Autumn, 1968. Volume 10. Number 3. Tucson, Arizona: The University of Arizona Press. 1968. Pages 225-240. (**Rebellion against Santa Fe Ring**)

CONTEMPORARY SOURCES (CHRONOLOGICAL)

No Author. "Diario del Consejo der Territorio de Neuvo Mejico, Session de 1871-1872." *Santa Fe New Mexican.* **January 8, 1872.** Santa Fe: A.P. Sullivan. 1872. Pages 144-154. New Mexico Supreme Court Library. Santa Fe, New Mexico. (**A Ring expurgated document, with a copy found in 1942 by Conrad Naegle; confirming troops used by Ring to suppress Territorial legislature**)

No Author. "Diario del Consejo der Territorio de Neuvo Mejico, Session de 1871-1872. Las Cruces *Borderer.* **January 24, 1872.** Pages 110-113. (**Don Diego Archuleta, President of the Council, gives speech objecting to troops in legislature**)

No Author. "Ring influence [in the Territorial legislature is] being actively used against every measure that tends to do justice" [in Grant and Doña Counties]." Grant County *Herald.* **August 8, 1875.** Quoted by Conrad Keeler Naegle in *The History of Silver City, New Mexico 1870-1886,* doctoral thesis. Page 39.

No Author. "A Contemplated Political Change." Grant County *Herald.* **September 16, 1876.** Quoted by Conrad Keeler Naegle in *The History of Silver City, New Mexico 1870-1886* doctoral thesis. Pages 39-40. (**Listing reasons to escape the Ring by annexing to Arizona Territory**)

No Author. Grant County *Herald.* **September 23, 1876.** (**Need for school system stressed.**)

No Author. Grant County *Herald.* **September 30, 1876.** (**"Annexation Meeting" announced**)

No Author. "Proceedings of Grant County Annexation Meeting." Grant County *Herald.* **Saturday October 7, 1876.** Page 2. Columns 1 and 2. Collection of the Silver City, New Mexico, Museum. (**Anti-Santa Fe Ring "Grant County Declaration of Independence" published**)

No Author. Grant County *Herald.* " 'Petition to Remove Judge Bristol. We the undersigned citizens of the Third Judicial District of the Territory of New Mexico, without regard to party, would respectfully request and petition for the removal of Judge Warren Bristol ...' " No date. **1876 or 1877.**(Quoted in "W.B. Matchett and Mary E. McPherson 'Make certain charges against the U.S. Officials in the Territory of New Mexico.' " Letter to President Rutherford B. Hayes. Received and filed May 1, 1877. Interior Department Papers 1850-1907; Appointments Division and Subsequent Actions. Microfilm File Case Number 44-4-8-3. Record Group 48. Microfilm No. M750. Roll 1. National Archives and Records Administration. U.S. Department of Justice. Washington, D.C.)

SEE ALSO: Santa Fe Ring; Thomas Benton Catron; Stephen Benton Elkins

COLFAX COUNTY WAR (1877)

MODERN SOURCES

Caffey, David L. *Frank Springer and New Mexico: From the Colfax County War to the Emergence of Modern Santa Fe.* Texas A and M. University Press. 2007.

Cleaveland, Norman. *The Morleys - Young Upstarts on the Southwest Frontier.* Albuquerque, New Mexico: Calvin Horn Publisher, Inc. 1971.

Dunham, Harold H. "New Mexican Land Grants with Special Reference to the Title Papers of the Maxwell Grant." *New Mexico Historical Review.* (January 1955) Vol. 30, No. 1. pp. 1 - 23.

Keleher, William A. *The Maxwell Land Grant. A New Mexico Item.* Albuquerque, New Mexico: University of New Mexico Press. 1964.

Lamar, Howard Roberts. *The Far Southwest 1846 - 1912. A Territorial History.* New Haven and London: Yale University Press. 1966.

Montoya, María E. *Translating Property. The Maxwell Land Grant and the Conflict Over Land in the American West, 1840-1900.* Berkeley and Los Angeles, California: University of California Press. 2002.

Murphy, Lawrence R. *Lucien Bonaparte Maxwell. Napoleon of the Southwest.* Norman: University of Oklahoma Press. 1983.

Pearson, Jim Berry. *The Maxwell Land Grant.* Norman: University of Oklahoma Press. 1961.

Poe, Sophie. *Buckboard Days.* Albuquerque, New Mexico: University of New Mexico Press. 1964.

Taylor, Morris F. *O.P. McMains and the Maxwell Land Grant Conflict.* Tucson, Arizona: The University of Arizona Press. 1979.

CONTEMPORARY SOURCES (CHRONOLOGICAL)

Morley, William Raymond and Frank Springer. On Oscar McMains's citizen's Meeting. *Cimarron News and Press.* **November 10, 1875**. In Mary McPherson, Letters and Petitions to President Rutherford B. Hayes re: Removal Governor Axtell and the Santa Fe Ring. 1977. Interior Department Papers 1850-1907; Appointments Division and Subsequent Actions. Microfilm File Case Number 44-4-8-3. Record Group 48. Microfilm Roll M750. National Archives and Records Administration. (**Colfax County citizens meeting on F.J. Tolby murder by Santa Fe Ring.**)

No author. "Anarchy at Cimarron." *Santa Fe Weekly New Mexican.* **November 16, 1875**. (**Ringite backing of Axtell's use of troops in the Colfax County War**)

Morley, William Raymond and Frank Springer. " 'The Territory of Elkins.' Assassination of Supposed Sun Correspondent. The Murder of the Rev. F.J. Tolby in New Mexico. A Probate Judge Accused of Complicity in the Crime. Indignation Meeting." *New York Weekly Sun.* **December 22, 1875**. Interior Department Papers 1850-1907; Appointments Division and Subsequent Actions. Microfilm Roll M750. National Archives and Records Administration. Record Group 48. Microfilm Case File Number 44-4-8-3. U. S. Department of Interior. Washington, D. C.(**From May 1, 1877 complaint to President Rutherford B. Hayes as "Mary E. McPherson and W.B. Matchett 'Make certain charges against the U.S. Officials in the Territory of New Mexico.' "**)

Dawson, Will. Editorial. *Cimarron News and Press.* **December 31, 1875**. (**Ring-biased editorial by temporary editor blaming citizens for unrest**)

Morley William Raymond. "I was astonished beyond measure at your proceedings, and have fears as to the result ..." Letter to Mary McPherson. **March 6, 1877**. McPherson, Mary E. Letters and Petitions to President Rutherford B. Hayes re: Removal Governor Axtell and the Santa Fe Ring. Interior Department Papers 1850-1907; Appointments Division and Subsequent Actions. Microfilm File Case Number 44-4-8-3. Record Group 48. Microfilm Roll M750. National Archives and Records Administration. U.S. Department of Justice. Washington, D. C. (**Hopes she can help fight against Santa Fe Ring; enclosed in Mary McPherson's "Charges Against U.S. Officials in the Territory of New Mexico."**)

Lambert, J.J. "At It Again." Pueblo, Colorado, *Enterprise and Chronicle.* **April 21, 1877**. Interior Department Papers 1850-1907; Appointments Division and Subsequent Actions. Microfilm File Case Number 44-4-8-3. Record Group 48. Microfilm No. M750. Roll 1. National Archives and Records Administration. U.S. Department of Justice. Washington, D.C. (**Description of Santa Fe Ring control of courts and malicious prosecution of opponents like Oscar McMains in the Franklin Tolby murder; used in: "W.B. Matchett and Mary E. McPherson 'Make Certain Charges Against the U.S. Officials in the Territory of New Mexico.' " Letter to President Rutherford B. Hayes. Received and filed May 1, 1877. Interior Department Papers 1850-1907; Appointments Division and Subsequent Actions. Microfilm File Case Number 44-4-8-3. Record Group 48. Microfilm No. M750. Roll 1. National**

Archives and Records Administration. U. S. Department of Justice. Washington, D.C.)

Matchett, W.B. and Mary E. McPherson. "Make Certain Charges Against the U.S. Officials in the Territory of New Mexico." To the President. **April, 1877.** Microfilm File Case Number 44-4-8-3. Record Group 48. Microfilm No. M750. Roll 1. National Archives and Records Administration. U. S. Department of Justice. Washington, D.C. **(Sent to President Rutherford B. Hayes and Secretary of the Interior Carl Schurz 141 pages of letters, affidavits, petitions, newspaper articles, itemized requests for removal of Governor Samuel Beach Axtell and District Judge Warren Bristol, documentation of use of the military against civilians, documentation of the Ring murder of Ring opponent Reverend F.J. Tolby, and identification of the Santa Fe Ring.)**

McPherson, Mary and W.B. Matchett. "To the President. Please make the enclosed a part of the evidence in the case of "Charges Against New Mexican Officials" Letter to President Rutherford B. Hayes. **May 3, 1877.** McPherson, Mary E. Letters and Petitions to President Rutherford B. Hayes re: Removal Governor Axtell and the Santa Fe Ring. Interior Department Papers 1850-1907; Appointments Division and Subsequent Actions. Microfilm File Case Number 44-4-8-3. Record Group 48. Microfilm Roll M750. National Archives and Records Administration. U.S. Department of Justice. Washington, D.C. **(Addendum to their May, 1877 "Certain Charges Against U.S. Officials in New Mexico Territory.")**

McPherson, Mary and W.B. Matchett. "The Secretary of the Interior, Sir - Accompanying please find copy of charges, &c., against S.B. Axtell, Governor, and other New Mexican Officials ..." "Charges Against New Mexican Officials." Letter to Secretary of the Interior Carl Schurz. **May 5, 1877.** McPherson, Mary E. Letters and Petitions to President Rutherford B. Hayes re: Removal Governor Axtell and the Santa Fe Ring. Interior Department Papers 1850-1907; Appointments Division and Subsequent Actions. Microfilm File Case Number 44-4-8-3. Record Group 48. Microfilm Roll M750. National Archives and Records Administration. U.S. Department of Justice. Washington, D. C.

McPherson, Mary and W.B. Matchett. "We have respectfully to request that the following named records, documents, papers, communications and correspondence be supplied ..." Records Request to Secretary of the Interior Carl Schurz. **July 26, 1877.** Interior Department Papers 1850-1907; Appointments Division and Subsequent Actions. Microfilm File Case Number 44-4-8-3. Record Group 48. Microfilm No. M750. Roll 1. National Archives and Records Administration. U.S. Department of Justice. Washington, D.C. **(Requesting records of the Santa Fe Ring, Catron, Elkins, and Axtell)**

McPherson, Mary E. and W.B. Matchett. "In the Matter of the Charges vs. Gov. S. B. Axtell and Other New Mexico Officials; Submitted to the Departments of the Interior and of Justice. Governor of New Mexico." **August, 1877.** Printed as a 31 page booklet. No publisher listed. Indiana Historical Society. Lew Wallace Collection. M0292. Box 3. Folder 20. **(Focus on the Santa Fe Ring)**

McPherson, Mary. "I desire to know when I can be heard ..." Letter to Secretary of Interior Carl Schurz. **September 30, 1977.** Interior Department Papers 1850-1907; Appointments Division and Subsequent Actions. Microfilm File Case Number 44-4-8-3. Record Group 48. Microfilm No. M750. Roll 1. National Archives and Records Administration. U. S. Department of Justice. Washington, D.C. **(Requesting audience on charges against Ring officials)**

Springer, Frank. "I endorse herewith, directed to the President ..." Letter to Secretary of the Interior Carl Schurz. **June 10, 1878.** Microfilm File Case Number 44-4-8-3. Record Group 48. Microfilm No. M750. Roll 1. National Archives and Records Administration. U.S. Department of Justice. Washington, D.C.

_____. "The undersigned, a citizen of the County of Colfax ..." To His Excellency, the President of the United States. Enclosed in letter to Secretary of the Interior Carl Schurz. **June 10, 1878.** Microfilm File Case Number 44-4-8-3. Record Group

48. Microfilm No. M750. Roll 1. National Archives and Records Administration. U.S. Department of Justice. Washington, D.C.

Morley, William Raymond. "Your letter of the 7th came last night and it was a good long newsy letter ..." Letter to wife, Ada McPherson Morley. **August 15, 1878.** Collection of Norman Cleaveland. Quoted in Norman Cleaveland, *The Morleys: Young Upstarts in the Southwest.* Albuquerque, New Mexico: Calvin Horn Publisher, Inc. 1971. Pages 152-155. **(About possible betrayal by Angel's reports; about the Santa Fe Ring, T.B. Catron, S.B. Elkins, S.B. Axtell, and Henry Waldo; and the Lincoln County War)**

No Author. "Rejoicing at Cimarron," "Axtell's Head Falls at Last," "General Lew. Wallace Appointed Governor." *Cimarron News and Press.* **September 6, 1878.**

No Author. *Santa Fe Weekly New Mexican.* **September 21, 1878 and October 19, 1878. (Ring-biased accolades for removed Gov. Axtell)**

SEE ALSO: Regulators, Santa Fe Ring; Thomas Benton Catron; Stephen Benton Elkins

LINCOLN COUNTY WAR (1878)

MODERN HISTORICAL SOURCES

Cooper, Gale. *The Lost Pardon of Billy the Kid: An Analysis Factoring in the Santa Fe Ring, Governor Lew Wallace's Dilemma, and a Territory in Rebellion.* Albuquerque, New Mexico: Gelcour Books. 2017.

Cramer, T. Dudley. *The Pecos Ranchers in the Lincoln County War.* Orinda, California: Branding Iron Press. 1996.

Fulton, Maurice Garland. Robert N. Mullin. Ed. *History of the Lincoln County War.* Tucson, Arizona: The University of Arizona Press. 1997.

Jacobson, Joel. *Such Men as Billy the Kid. The Lincoln County War Reconsidered.* Lincoln and London: University of Nebraska Press. 1994.

Keleher, William A. *The Fabulous Frontier: Twelve New Mexico Items.* Albuquerque, New Mexico: The University of New Mexico Press. 1962.

_____.*Violence in Lincoln County 1869-1881.* Albuquerque, New Mexico: University of New Mexico Press. 1957. **(Las Vegas *Gazette* article of December 28, 1880, "The Kid. Interview with Billy Bonney. Pages 293-295; Las Vegas *Gazette* article of December 28, 1880. Untitled. Pages 296-297)**

Mullin, Robert N. Re: Frank Warner Angel Meeting with President Hayes. August, 1878. Binder RNM, VI, M. Midland, Texas: Nita Stewart Haley Memorial Library and J. Everet Haley History Center. (Unpublished).

Nolan, Frederick W. *The Life and Death of John Henry Tunstall.* Albuquerque, New Mexico: The University of New Mexico Press. 1965.

_____. *The Lincoln County War: A Documentary History.* Norman: University of Oklahoma Press. 1992.

_____. *The West of Billy the Kid.* Norman: University of Oklahoma Press. 1998.

Rasch, Philip J. *Gunsmoke in Lincoln County.* Laramie, Wyoming: National Association for Outlaw and Lawmen History, Inc. with University of Wyoming. 1997.

_____. Robert K. DeArment. Ed. *Warriors of Lincoln County.* Laramie: National Association for Outlaw and Lawmen History, Inc. with University of Wyoming. 1998.

Utley, Robert M. *High Noon in Lincoln. Violence on the Western Frontier.* Albuquerque, New Mexico: University of New Mexico Press. 1987.

Wilson, John P. *Merchants, Guns, and Money: The Story of Lincoln County and Its Wars.* Santa Fe, New Mexico: Museum of New Mexico Press. 1987.

No Author. "Disturbances in the Territories, 1878 - 1894. Lawlessness in New Mexico." Senate Documents. 67th Congress. 2nd Session. December 5, 1921 - September 22, 1922. pp. 176 - 187. Washington, D.C.: Government Printing Office. 1922.

CONTEMPORARY DOCUMENTS (CHRONOLOGICAL)

No Author. "Brady Inventory McSween Property." **February, 1878.** Herman B. Weisner Papers, ca. 1957-1992. New Mexico State University Library at Las Cruses. Rio Grande Historical Collections. Accession No. Weisner Ms 0249. Box 10. Folder M15. Folder Name. "Will and Testament A. McSween."

Angel, Frank Warner. *Examination of charges against F. C. Godfroy, Indian Agent, Mescalero, N. M.* **October 2, 1878.** (Report 1981, Inspector E. C. Watkins; Cited as Watkins Report). M 319-20 and L147, 44-4-8. Record Group 075. National Archives and Records Administration. U.S. Department of Justice. Washington, D.C.

_____. *In the Matter of the Investigation of the Charges Against S. B. Axtell Governor of New Mexico. Report and Testimony.* **October 3, 1878.** Angel Report. Microfilm Case File No. 44-4-8-3. Record Group 48. Microfilm Roll M750. National Archives and Records Administration. U.S. Department of Interior. Washington, D.C.

_____. *In the Matter of the Examination of the Causes and Circumstances of the Death of John H. Tunstall a British Subject.* **October 4, 1878.** Angel Report. Microfilm File Case Number 44-4-8-3. Record Group 48. Microfilm No. M750. Roll 1. National Archives and Records Administration. U.S. Department of Justice. Washington, D.C.

_____. *In the Matter of the Lincoln County Troubles. To the Honorable Charles Devens, Attorney General.* **October 4, 1878.** Angel Report. Microfilm Case File No. 44-4-8-3. Record Group 48. Microfilm Roll M750. National Archives and Records Administration. U.S. Department of Justice. Washington, D.C.

No Author. "Amnesty for Matthews and Long in the Third Judicial Court April Term 1879." **April, 1879.** Herman B. Weisner Papers, ca. 1957-1992. New Mexico State University Library at Las Cruces. Rio Grande Historical Collections. Accession No. Ms 0249. Box 1. Folder 4. Folder Name. "Amnesty."

No Author. "Charges against Jessie Evans and John Kinney." Doña Ana County Civil and Criminal Docket Book. **August 18, 1875 to November 7, 1878.** Herman B. Weisner Papers, ca. 1957-1992. New Mexico State University Library at Las Cruces. Rio Grande Historical Collections. Accession No. Ms 0249. Box 13. Folder V 3. Folder Name. "Venue, Change Of."

No Author. "Dismissal of Cases Against Dolan, Matthews, Peppin, October 1879 District Court." **October, 1879.** Herman B. Weisner Papers, ca. 1957-1992. New Mexico State University Library at Las Cruces. Rio Grande Historical Collections. Accession No. Ms 0249. Box 13. Folder V3. Folder Name: "Venue, Change Of."

No Author. *Proceedings of a Court of Inquiry in the Case of Lt. Col. N.A.M. Dudley.* **May 2,1879 – July 5, 1879.** File No. QQ1284. (Boxes 3304, 3305, 3305A); Court Martial Files 1809-1894. Records of the Office of the Judge Advocate General – Army. Record Group 153. Old Military and Civil Branch. National Archives and Records Administration. Washington, D.C. (**Commander tried for Lincoln County War role**)

No Author. "Killers of Tunstall. February 18, 1879." Herman B. Weisner Papers, ca. 1957-1992. New Mexico State University Library at Las Cruces. Rio Grande Historical Collections. Accession No. Ms 0249. Box 12. Folder T1. Folder Name: "Tunstall, John H."

No Author. "Lincoln County Indictments July 1872 - 1881." Herman B. Weisner Papers, ca. 1957-1992. New Mexico State University Library at Las Cruces. Rio Grande Historical Collections. Accession No. Ms 0249. Box 8. Folder L11. Folder Name. "Lincoln Co. Indictments."

ARTICLES (CHRONOLOGICAL)

Tunstall, John Henry. "A Taxpayer's Complaint ... January 18, 1878." Mesilla *Independent*. **January 26, 1878. (Exposé of William Brady, James Dolan,** and John Riley for using tax money to buy cattle; and Catron's paying that bill)

Dolan, James J. "Answer to A Taxpayer's Complaint." Mesilla *Independent*. **January 29, 1878.** (Response to J.H. Tunstall's exposé of him, William Brady, and John Riley for tax fraud and use of public money to purchase cattle; and T.B. Catron then paid that bill)

No author. "Why Axtell Wanted Troops." **July 31, 1878.** Santa Fe. Newspaper unknown. Enclosed in report of Frank Warner Angel: *In the Matter of the Examination of the Causes and Circumstances of the Death of John H. Tunstall a British Subject*. Report filed October 4, 1878. Interior Department Papers 1850-1907; Appointments Division and Subsequent Actions. Microfilm File Case Number 44-4-8-3. Record Group 48. Microfilm No. M750. Roll 1. National Archives and Records Administration. U.S. Department of Justice. Washington, D.C. **(Enclosed with letter to the President, from a John G. Hubbard of August 1, 1878.).**

LETTERS (CHRONOLOGICAL)

Elkins, Stephen Benton. "Axtell Gov. New Mexico: A strong protest against his removal by S.B. Elkins who says the charges against him are vague & irresponsible." To the President. **June 11, 1877.** Microfilm File Case Number 44-4-8-3. Record Group 48. Microfilm No. M750. Roll 1. National Archives and Records Administration. U.S. Department of Justice. Washington, D.C. **(Referred by President to the Secretary of the Interior on June 13, 1877.)**

McSween, A.A. and B.H. Ellis. Secretaries. "To his Excellency Rutherford B. Hayes, President of the United States of America." With attached proceedings of the April 1878 Lincoln Grand Jury. **April 26, 1878.** Microfilm File Case Number 44-4-8-3. Record Group 48.. Microfilm No. M750. Roll 1. National Archives and Records Administration. U.S. Department of Justice. Washington, D.C.

Isaacs, I. and G.N. Coe. "Charges Against S.B. Axtell, Governor of New Mexico." To President Rutherford B. Hayes. **June 22, 1878.** Microfilm File Case Number 44-4-8-3. Record Group 48. Microfilm No. M750. Roll 1. National Archives and Records Administration. U.S. Department of Justice. Washington, D.C.

Morley, William Raymond. "Your letter of the 7th came last night and it was a good long newsy letter ..." Letter to wife, Ada McPherson Morley. **August 15, 1878.** Collection of Norman Cleaveland. Quoted in Norman Cleaveland, *The Morleys: Young Upstarts in the Southwest*. Albuquerque, New Mexico: Calvin Horn Publisher, Inc. 1971. Pages 152-155. **(About possible betrayal by Angel's reports; about the Santa Fe Ring, T.B. Catron, S.B. Elkins, S.B. Axtell, and Henry Waldo; and the Lincoln County War)**

Angel, Frank Warner. "I enclose copies of letters received by me from Gov Axtell ..." Letter to Secretary of the Interior Carl Schurz. **August 24, 1878.** (Including copy of letter to him from Governor Axtell of August 12, 1878; and his response to Axtell of August 13, 1878.) Microfilm File Case Number 44-4-8-3. Record Group 48. Microfilm No. M750. Roll 1. National Archives and Records Administration. U.S. Department of Justice. Washington, D.C.

_____. "I have just been favored by a call from W.L. Rynerson ..." To Secretary of Interior Carl Schurz. **September 6, 1878.** Microfilm File Case Number 44-4-8-3. Record Group 48. Microfilm No. M750. Roll 1. National Archives and Records Administration. U.S. Department of Justice. Washington, D.C.

Elkins, Stephen Benton. "To the President. Referring to a conversation had with you last week ... Hon. S. B. Elkins favors appointment Axtell, ExGov. as Gov'r of New Mexico." Letter to President Rutherford B. Hayes. **March 17, 1881.** (Received Executive Mansion April 6, 1881). Microfilm Roll M750. National Archives and Records Administration. Record Group 48. Microfilm Case File Number 44-4-8-3. U.S. Department of Interior. Washington, D. C.

Bradstreet, George P. Chairman Judiciary Committee of U.S. Senate. "Asking for papers in the matter of charges against Sam'l B. Axtell late Governor of New Mexico." (For appointment as Chief Justice of New Mexico Supreme Court). **June 22, 1882.** Microfilm File Case Number 44-4-8-3. Record Group 48. Microfilm No. M750. Roll 1. National Archives and Records Administration. U.S. Department of Justice. Washington, D.C.

SEE ALSO: Santa Fe Ring; Thomas Benton Catron; Stephen Benton Elkins

HISTORICAL FIGURES (PERIOD)

ALLISON, CLAY

No Author. "Murder in Las Animas: The Allison Desperados Make a Raid on West Las Animas." **Thursday, December 28, 1876.** Pueblo, Colorado, *Colorado Chieftain.* www.coloradohistoricnewspapers.org.

No Author. "The Leader records another murder in Las Animas." **Saturday, December 30, 1876.** Pueblo, Colorado, *Colorado Chieftain.* www.coloradohistoricnewspapers.org.

South, W.L. "The Allison Case." **Sunday, January 21, 1877 and Thursday, January 25, 1877.** Pueblo, Colorado, *Colorado Chieftain.* www.coloradohistoricnewspapers.org.

No Author. No title. **March 30, 1877 and April 5, 1877.** Pueblo, Colorado, *Colorado Chieftain.* www.coloradohistoricnewspapers.org. (**Clay Allison acquitted of murder**)

No Author. "Record of a Texas Desperado: The graves of His Victims Were Scattered From Dodge City to Santa Fe." **October 16, 1894.** Salida, Colorado *The Salida Mail. Colorado Chieftain.* www.coloradohistoricnewspapers.org. (**Clay Allison's outlaw myth**)

No Author. "The Duel That Failed." **April 3, 1906.** Eagle, Colorado *The Eagle Valley Enterprise.* www.coloradohistoricnewspapers.org.

Cleaveland, Norman. *The Morleys - Young Upstarts on the Southwest Frontier.* Albuquerque, New Mexico: Calvin Horn Publisher, Inc. 1971.

ANGEL, FRANK WARNER

PRESIDENT HAYES MEETING

Mullin, Robert N. Re: Frank Warner Angel Meeting With President Hayes August, 1878. Binder RNM, VI, M. (Unpublished). Midland, Texas: Nita Stewart Haley Memorial Library and J. Evert Haley History Center. (Undated).

LETTERS BY FRANK WARNER ANGEL

Angel, Frank Warner. "I enclose copies of letters received by me from Gov Axtell ..." Letter to Secretary of the Interior Carl Schurz. **August 24, 1878.** (Enclosing copy of letter to him from Governor S.B. Axtell of August 12, 1878; and Angel's response to Axtell of August 13, 1878.) Microfilm File Case Number 44-4-8-3. Record Group 48. Microfilm No. M750. Roll 1. National Archives and Records Administration. U.S. Department of Justice. Washington, D.C.

Angel, Frank Warner. "I have just been favored by a call from W.L. Rynerson ..." Letter to Secretary of Interior Carl Schurz. **September 6, 1878.** Microfilm File Case Number 44-4-8-3. Record Group 48. Microfilm No. M750. Roll 1. National Archives and Records Administration. U.S. Department of Justice. Washington, D.C.

_____. "I am in receipt of a copy of a letter sent you by one Wm McMullen ..." Letter to Carl Schurz. **September 9, 1878.** The Papers of Carl Schurz 1842 -

1906 in 165 Volumes. Library of Congress 1935. General Correspondence July 26, 1878 - October 7, 1878. Shelf Accession No. 14,803. Container 45.

LETTER ABOUT FRANK WARNER ANGEL

Morley, William Raymond. "Your letter of the 7th came last night and it was a good long newsy letter ..." Letter to wife, Ada McPherson Morley. **August 15, 1878.** Collection of Norman Cleaveland. Quoted in Norman Cleaveland, *The Morleys: Young Upstarts in the Southwest.* Albuquerque, New Mexico: Calvin Horn Publisher, Inc. 1971. Pages 152-155. (**About possible betrayal by Angel's reports; about the Santa Fe Ring, T.B. Catron, S.B. Elkins, S.B. Axtell, and Henry Waldo; and the Lincoln County War**)

PAPERS OF FRANK WARNER ANGEL

McMullen, William. "In view of the existing troubles in our territory I appeal ..." Letter to Carl Schurz. **August 24, 1878.** The Papers of Carl Schurz 1842 - 1906 in 165 Volumes. Library of Congress 1935. General Correspondence. July 26, 1878 - October 7, 1878. Shelf Accession No. 14,803. Container 45.

McPherson, Mary E. Letters and Petitions to President Rutherford B. Hayes re: Removal Governor Axtell and the Santa Fe Ring. Interior Department Papers 1850-1907; Appointments Division and Subsequent Actions. Microfilm File Case Number 44-4-8-3. Record Group 48. Microfilm Roll M750. National Archives and Records Administration. U.S. Department of Justice. Washington, D. C.

REPORTS BY FRANK WARNER ANGEL

Angel, Frank Warner. *Examination of charges against F. C. Godfroy, Indian Agent, Mescalero, N. M.* **October 2, 1878**. (Report 1981, Inspector E.C. Watkins; Cited as Watkins Report). M319-20 and L147, 44-4-8. Record Group 075. National Archives and Records Administration. U.S. Department of Justice. Washington, D. C.

_____. *In the Matter of the Investigation of the Charges Against S.B. Axtell Governor of New Mexico. Report and Testimony.* **October 3, 1878.** Angel Report. Interior Department Papers 1850-1907; Appointments Division and Subsequent Actions. Microfilm Case File No. 44-4-8-3. Record Group 48. Microfilm Roll M750. National Archives and Records Administration. U.S. Department of Interior. Washington, D.C.

_____. *In the Matter of the Lincoln County Troubles. To the Honorable Charles Devens, Attorney General.* **October 4, 1878**. Angel Report. Microfilm Case File No. 44-4-8-3. Record Group 48. Microfilm Roll M750. National Archives and Records Administration. U.S. Department of Justice. Washington, D.C.

_____. *In the Matter of the Examination of the Causes and Circumstances of the Death of John H. Tunstall a British Subject.* Report filed **October 4, 1878**. Angel Report. Interior Department Papers 1850-1907; Appointments Division and Subsequent Actions. Microfilm File Case Number 44-4-8-3. Record Group 48. Microfilm No. M750. Roll 1. National Archives and Records Administration. U.S. Department of Justice. Washington, D.C.

NOTEBOOK BY FRANK WARNER ANGEL

Angel, Frank Warner. "Gov. Lew. Wallace / Santa Fe, N.M." **1878**. Indiana Historical Society. Lew Wallace Collection. Microfilm No. F372. (**Original missing, copy on microfilm; Notebook prepared for Lew Wallace on Lincoln County and the Santa Fe Ring**)

Theisen, Lee Scott. "Frank Warner Angel's Notes on New Mexico Territory, 1878." *Arizona and the West: A Quarterly Journal of History.* Winter 1976. Volume 18. Number 4. Pages 333-370. (**About the Angel notebook**)

ANTRIM, JOSEPH "JOSIE" McCARTY

Weddle, Jerry. *Antrim is My Stepfather's Name. The Boyhood of Billy the Kid.* Monograph 9, Globe, Arizona: Arizona Historical Society. 1993.

_____. Personal Communication about Joseph Antrim's whereabouts in 1876 and 1877. August 30, 2017 to October 2, 2017.

AXTELL, SAMUEL BEACH

CONTEMPORARY SOURCES (CHRONOLOGICAL)

No author. "Anarchy at Cimarron." *Santa Fe Weekly New Mexico.* **November 16, 1875.** (**Ring-biased article justifying Governor S.B. Axtell calling in troops in the Colfax County War after murder of Reverend Franklin Tolby**)

Axtell, Samuel B. "The Legislature to Assess Property. *Message of Gov. Samuel B. Axtell to the Legislative Assembly of New Mexico, Twenty-second Session.* Page 4. Manderfield & Tucker, Public Printers: Santa Fe, New Mexico. **1875 or 1876.** Interior Department Papers 1850-1907; Appointments Division and Subsequent Actions. Microfilm File Case Number 44-4-8-3. Record Group 48. Microfilm No. M750. Roll 1. National Archives and Records Administration. U.S. Department of Justice. Washington, D.C.

Morley William Raymond. "I was astonished beyond measure at your proceedings, and have fears as to the result ..." Letter to Mary McPherson. **March 6, 1877.** McPherson, Mary E. Letters and Petitions to President Rutherford B. Hayes re: Removal Governor Axtell and the Santa Fe Ring. Interior Department Papers 1850-1907; Appointments Division and Subsequent Actions. Microfilm File Case Number 44-4-8-3. Record Group 48. Microfilm Roll M750. National Archives and Records Administration. U.S. Department of Justice. Washington, D. C. (**Hopes she can help fight against Santa Fe Ring; enclosed in Mary McPherson's "Charges Against U.S. Officials in the Territory of New Mexico."**)

McPherson, Mary and W.B. Matchett. "To The President. Please make the enclosed a part of the evidence in the case of "Charges Against New Mexican Officials." Letter to President Rutherford B. Hayes. **May 3, 1877.** McPherson, Mary E. Letters and Petitions to President Rutherford B. Hayes re: Removal Governor Axtell and the Santa Fe Ring. Interior Department Papers 1850-1907; Appointments Division and Subsequent Actions. Microfilm File Case Number 44-4-8-3. Record Group 48. Microfilm Roll M750. National Archives and Records Administration. U.S. Department of Justice. Washington, D.C. (**Addendum to their May, 1877 "Certain Charges Against U.S. Officials in New Mexico Territory."**)

McPherson, Mary and W.B. Matchett. "The Secretary of the Interior, Sir - Accompanying please find copy of charges, &c., against S.B. Axtell, Governor, and other New Mexico Officials ..." Letter to Secretary of the Interior Carl Schurz. **May 5, 1877.** McPherson, Mary E. Letters and Petitions to President Rutherford B. Hayes re: Removal Governor Axtell and the Santa Fe Ring. Interior Department Papers 1850-1907; Appointments Division and Subsequent Actions. Microfilm File Case Number 44-4-8-3. Record Group 48. Microfilm Roll M750. National Archives and Records Administration. U.S. Department of Justice. Washington, D. C.

Elkins, Stephen B. "I trouble you to say a word in behalf of Gov. Axtell ..." Letter to President Rutherford B. Hayes. **June 11, 1877.** Interior Department Papers 1850-1907; Appointments Division and Subsequent Actions. Microfilm Roll M750. National Archives and Records Administration Record Group 48. Microfilm Case Number 44-4-8-3. U. S. Department of Interior. Washington D. C.

Axtell, Samuel B. "I have today mailed to you a reply to the charges on file in your Dept against me." Letter to Secretary of the Interior Carl Schurz. **June 15, 1877.** Interior Department Papers 1850-1907; Appointments Division and Subsequent

Actions. Microfilm Roll M750. National Archives and Records Administration Record Group 48. Microfilm Case Number 44-4-8-3 U.S. Department of Interior. Washington D.C. (**Refuting charges made in Colfax County**).

McPherson, Mary and W.B. Matchett. "We have respectfully to request that the following named records, documents, papers, communications and correspondence be supplied ..." Records Request to Secretary of the Interior Carl Schurz. **July 26, 1877.** Interior Department Papers 1850-1907; Appointments Division and Subsequent Actions. Microfilm File Case Number 44-4-8-3. Record Group 48. Microfilm No. M750. Roll 1. National Archives and Records Administration. U. S. Department of Justice. Washington, D.C. (**Requesting records of the Santa Fe Ring, Catron, Elkins, and Axtell**)

_____. *In the Matter of Charges vs. Gov. S.B. Axtell and Other New Mexico Officials. Submitted to the Departments of the Interior and Justice.* **August, 1877.** Printed as a 31 page booklet. No publisher listed. Indiana Historical Society. Lew Wallace Collection. M0292. Box 3. Folder 20. (**Major exposé about the Santa Fe Ring, Catron, and Elkins; in Lew Wallace's personal possession**)

_____. "To the President. I am unable to enforce the law ..." (Telegram). **March 3, 1878.** Interior Department Papers 1850-1907; Appointments Division and Subsequent Actions. Microfilm Roll M750. National Archives and Records Administration Record Group 48. Microfilm Case File Number 44-4-8-3. U.S. Department of Interior. Washington D.C.

_____. "I respectfully request leave of absence for ninety days ..." Letter to President Rutherford B. Hayes. **March 3, 1878.** Interior Department Papers 1850-1907; Appointments Division and Subsequent Actions. Microfilm Roll M750. National Archives and Records Administration Record Group 48. Microfilm Case File Number 44-4-8-3. U.S. Department of Interior. Washington D.C.

McPherson, Mary E. and W.B. Matchett. "In the Matter of the Charges vs. Gov. S.B. Axtell and Other New Mexico Officials; Submitted to the Departments of the Interior and of Justice. Governor of New Mexico." **August, 1877.** Printed as a 31 page booklet. No publisher listed. Indiana Historical Society. Lew Wallace Collection. M0292. Box 3. Folder 20. (**Focus on the Santa Fe Ring**)

Springer, Frank. "Hon Carl Schurz, Secretary of the Interior. Sir: I endorse herewith, directed to the President charges against S.B. Axtell Governor of New Mexico ..." Letter to Carl Schurz. **June 10, 1878.** Interior Department Papers 1850-1907; Appointments Division and Subsequent Actions. Microfilm Roll M750. National Archives and Records Administration Record Group 48. Microfilm Case Number 44-4-8-3. U.S. Department of Interior. Washington D.C.

_____. "The undersigned, a citizen of the County of Colfax ..." Letter to Rutherford B. Hayes enclosed in letter to Secretary of the Interior Carl Schurz. **June 10, 1878.** Interior Department Papers 1850-1907; Appointments Division and Subsequent Actions. Microfilm File Case Number 44-4-8-3. Record Group 48. Microfilm No. M750. Roll 1. National Archives and Records Administration. U.S. Department of Justice. Washington, D.C.

Isaacs, I. and G.N. Coe. "Charges Against S.B. Axtell, Governor of New Mexico." **June 22, 1878.** Interior Department Papers 1850-1907; Appointments Division and Subsequent Actions. Microfilm File Case Number 44-4-8-3. Microfilm No. M750. Roll 1. National Archives and Records Administration. Record Group 48. U.S. Department of Justice. Washington, D.C.

Angel, Frank Warner. "I am in receipt of your favor of the 12th ..." Letter to Samuel Beach Axtell. **August 13, 1878.** Interior Department Papers 1850-1907; Appointments Division and Subsequent Actions. Microfilm Roll M750. National Archives and Records Administration Record Group 48. Microfilm Case Number 44-4-8-3. U.S. Department of Interior. Washington D.C.

Morley, William Raymond. "Your letter of the 7th came last night and it was a good long newsy letter ..." Letter to wife, Ada McPherson Morley. **August 15, 1878.** Collection of Norman Cleaveland. Quoted in Norman Cleaveland, *The Morleys:*

Young Upstarts in the Southwest. Albuquerque, New Mexico: Calvin Horn Publisher, Inc. 1971. Pages 152-155. (**About possible cover-up by Angel's reports; about the Santa Fe Ring, T.B. Catron, S.B. Elkins, S.B. Axtell, and Henry Waldo; and the Lincoln County War**)

McPherson, Mary. "Please place before the Attorney General ..." Letter to President Rutherford B. Hayes. **August 23, 1877**. Interior Department Papers 1850-1907; Appointments Division and Subsequent Actions. Microfilm File Case Number 44-4-8-3. Record Group 48. Microfilm No. M750. Roll 1. National Archives and Records Administration. U.S. Department of Justice. Washington, D.C. (**Requesting that her "Charges vs. New Mexico Officials" go to the Attorney General.**)

McPherson, Mary. "I desire to know when I can be heard ..." Letter to Secretary of Interior Carl Schurz. **September 30, 1977**. Interior Department Papers 1850-1907; Appointments Division and Subsequent Actions. Microfilm File Case Number 44-4-8-3. Record Group 48. Microfilm No. M750. Roll 1. National Archives and Records Administration. U. S. Department of Justice. Washington, D.C. (**Requesting to be heard in person on her charges against officials and Governor Axtell.**)

Angel, Frank Warner. "The Honorable C. Schurz ... I enclose copies of letter received by me from Gov. Axtell (marked A) and my reply there to (marked B)." **August 24, 1878**. Frank Warner Angel reports. Interior Department Papers 1850-1907; Appointments Division and Subsequent Actions. Microfilm Roll M750. National Archives and Records Administration Record Group 48. Microfilm Case Number 44-4-8-3. U.S. Department of Interior. Washington D.C.

Routt, John C. "I am here on a visit to my daughter and have more by accident than otherwise heard statements ..." Letter to President Rutherford B. Hayes. **August 29, 1878**. Interior Department Papers 1850-1907; Appointments Division and Subsequent Actions. Microfilm File Case Number 44-4-8-3. Microfilm No. M750. Roll 1. National Archives and Records Administration. U.S. Department of Justice. Washington, D.C. (**Possibly fraudulent letter, but in opposition to the removal of Governor Axtell and U.S. Attorney Thomas Benton Catron.**)

Schurz, Carl. "I transmit herewith an order from the President ..." **September 4, 1878**. Letter to Lew Wallace. Indiana Historical Society. Lew Wallace Collection. M0292. Box 3. Folder 14. (**Suspension of Governor S.B. Axtell and Wallace's appointment as new Governor**)

Angel, Frank Warner. "The Hon. C. Schurz, Secretary of the Interior, Sir: I have just been favored by a call from W. L. Rynerson Territorial Dist. Attorney 3rd District New Mexico - in the interest of Gov. Axtell." (Letter) **September 6, 1878**. Microfilm M750. National Archives and Records Administration Record Group 48. Microfilm Case Number 44-4-8-3. U.S. Department of Interior. Washington D. C.

Wallace, Lew. "I have the honor to inform you ..." Letter to Carl Schurz. **October 1, 1878**. Indiana Historical Society. Lew Wallace Collection. M0292. Box 3. Folder 15. (**Informing Schurz that he informed Axtell of suspension and that he now qualified as Governor**)

Angel, Frank Warner. *In the Matter of the Investigation of the Charges Against S.B. Axtell Governor of New Mexico.* **October 3, 1878**. Frank Warner Angel report. Interior Department Papers 1850-1907; Appointments Division and Subsequent Actions. Microfilm Case File No. 44-4-8-3. Record Group 48. Microfilm Roll M750. National Archives and Records Administration. U.S. Department of Interior. Washington, D.C. (**Mentions Santa Fe Ring**)

Elkins, Stephen Benton. "To the President. Referring to a conversation had with you last week ... Hon S. Elkins favors appointment Axtell, Ex Gov. as Gov'r of New Mexico". Letter to President James Abram Garfield. **March 17, 1881**. (Received Executive Mansion April 6, 1881). Interior Department Papers 1850-1907; Appointments Division and Subsequent Actions. Microfilm Roll M750.

National Archives and Records Administration Microfilm Roll M750. National Archives and Records Administration Record Group 48. Microfilm Case Number 44-4-8-3. U.S. Department of Interior. Washington D.C. Microfilm Case Number 44-4-8-3. U.S. Department of Interior. Washington D.C. (**Request for re-appointment of Axtell as Territorial New Mexico Governor**)

Bradstreet, George P. "Referring to the nomination of Sam'l B. Axtell of Ohio to be Chief Justice of the Supreme Court of New Mexico ... he is alleged to have been removed by President Hayes ..." Letter to Judiciary Committee of the U.S. Senate. **June 22, 1882.** Interior Department Papers 1850-1907; Appointments Division and Subsequent Actions. Microfilm Roll M750. National Archives and Records Administration Microfilm Roll M750. National Archives and Records Administration Record Group 48. Microfilm Case Number 44-4-8-3. U.S. Department of Interior. Washington D.C.

No Author. "A man named Springer is in Washington trying to defeat the nomination of Governor Axtell. Springer is a friend of the thugs and thieves of Colfax County." *Santa Fe New Mexican.* **July 6, 1882.** (**Santa Fe Ring re-instatement of S.B. Axtell to public office**)

No Author. " 'Chief Justice Axtell' is a bitter pill for the Raton *News and Press.*" *Santa Fe New Mexican.* **July 18, 1882.** (**Santa Fe Ring instatement of S.B. Axtell as Chief Justice**)

WILLIAM HENRY BONNEY ("BILLY THE KID")

WORDS OF WILLIAM HENRY BONNEY (CHRONOLOGICAL)

SOURCES

Cooper, Gale. Billy the Kid's Writings, Words, and Wit. Albuquerque, New Mexico: Gelcour Books. 2017.

_____. *The Lost Pardon of Billy the Kid: An Analysis Factoring in the Santa Fe Ring, Governor Lew Wallace's Dilemma, and a Territory in Rebellion.* Albuquerque, New Mexico: Gelcour Books. 2017.

HOYT BILL OF SALE

Bonney, W H. "Know all persons by these presents ..." Thursday, **October 24, 1878.** Collection of Panhandle-Plains Historical Museum, Canyon, Texas. Item No. X1974-98/1. (**Hoyt Bill of Sale**)

Tilloston, Thomas. "One Gray Horse ..." March, 1879. Indiana Historical Society. Lew Wallace Collection. M0292. Box 4. Folder 7. (**Sample period Bill of Sale**)

LETTERS TO LEW WALLACE

Bonney, W H. "I have heard you will give one thousand $ dollars for my body which as I see it means alive ..." **March 13(?), 1879.** Fray Angélico Chávez Historical Library, Santa Fe, New Mexico. Lincoln County Heritage Trust Collection. (AC481).

_____. "I will keep the keep the appointment ..." **March 20, 1879.** Indiana Historical Society. M0292.

_____. "... on the Pecos." ("Billie" letter fragment). **March 24(?), 1879.** Indiana Historical Society. Lew Wallace Collection. M0292. Box 4. Folder 7.

_____. "I noticed in the Las Vegas Gazette a piece which stated that 'Billy the Kid' ..." **December 12, 1880.** Indiana Historical Society. Lew Wallace Collection. M0292.

_____. "I would like to see you ..." **January 1, 1881.** Indiana Historical Society. Lew Wallace Collection. M0292.

_____. "I wish you would come down to the jail and see me ..." **March 2, 1881.** Fray Angélico Chávez Historical Library, Santa Fe, New Mexico. Lincoln County Heritage Trust Collection. (AC481).

_____. "I wrote you a little note day before yesterday ..." **March 4, 1881.** Indiana Historical Society. Lew Wallace Collection. M0292.

_____. "For the last time I ask ..." **March 27, 1881.** Indiana Historical Society. Lew Wallace Collection. M0292.

LETTER TO SQUIRE WILSON

Bonney, W H. "Friend Wilson ..." **March 18, 1879.** Indiana Historical Society. Lew Wallace Collection. M0292.

LETTER TO EDGAR CAYPLESS

Bonney, W H. "I would have written before ..." **April 15, 1881.** Copy in William Keleher's *Violence in Lincoln County;* originally reproduced in Griggs *History of the Mesilla Valley.* (**Original lost**)

"REGULATOR MANIFESTO" LETTER

Regulator. "Mr. Walz. Sir ..." Letter to Edgar Walz. **July 13, 1878.** Adjutant General's Office. File 1405 AGO 1878. (Quoted in Maurice Garland Fulton, *History of the Lincoln County War.* Tucson: University of Arizona Press. 1975. pages 246-247.)

DEPOSITION

Bonney, William Henry. Deposition to Frank Warner Angel. **June 8, 1878.** Frank Warner Angel report, Pages 314-319 from *In the Matter of the Examination of the Causes and Circumstances of the Death of John H. Tunstall a British Subject.* Report filed October 4, 1878. Angel Report. Records of the Justice Department. Record Group 60. Class 44 Litigation Files. Container 21. National Archives and Records Administration. U.S. Department of Justice. Washington, D.C. or Angel Report in Interior Department Papers 1850-1907; Appointments Division and Subsequent Actions. Microfilm File Case Number 44-4-8-3. Record Group 48. Microfilm No. M750. Roll 1. National Archives and Records Administration. U.S. Department of Justice. Washington, D.C.

COURT TESTIMONY

Rynerson, William. "The Grand Jurors for the Territory of New Mexico taken from the body of the good and lawful men of the County of Lincoln ..." Indictments of the April, Lincoln County Grand Jury. **April 28, 1879.** Herman B. Weisner Papers, ca. 1957-1992. New Mexico State University Library at Las Cruces. Rio Grande Historical Collection. Accession No. Ms 0249. Box 4/39. Folder E-Z. Folder Name: "Jessie Evans Accessory to Murder." (**Billy's testimony indicts J.J. Dolan, Billy Campbell, and Jessie Evans for his pardon bargain**)

Bonney, William Henry. Testimony in Court of Inquiry for N.A.M. Dudley. **May 28-29, 1879.** *Proceedings of a Court of Inquiry in the Case of Lt. Col. N.A.M. Dudley (May 2,1879 – July 5, 1879).* File No. QQ1284. (Boxes 3304, 3305, 3305A); Court Martial Files 1809-1894. Records of the Office of the Judge Advocate General - Army. Record Group 153. Old Military and Civil Branch. National Archives and Records Administration. Washington, D. C.

Waldo, Henry. "Then was brought forward William Bonney, alias "Antrim," alias "the Kid," a known criminal of the worst type ..." Closing argument on Billy Bonney's testimony in Court of Inquiry for N.A.M. Dudley. **July 5, 1879.** *Proceedings of a Court of Inquiry in the Case of Lt. Col. N.A.M. Dudley (May 2,1879 – July 5, 1879).* File No. QQ1284. (Boxes 3304, 3305, 3305A); Court Martial Files 1809-1894. Records of the Office of the Judge Advocate General – Army. Record Group

153. Old Military and Civil Branch. National Archives and Records Administration. Washington, D. C.

INTERVIEW WITH LEW WALLACE

Wallace, Lew. "Statements by Kid, made Sunday night **March 23, 1879.**" March 23, 1879. Indiana Historical Society. Lew Wallace Collection. M0922. Box 4. Folder 6.

NEWSPAPER INTERVIEWS (CHRONOLOGICAL)

Wilcox, Lucius "Lute" M. (city editor, owner, J.H. Koogler). "The Kid. Interview with Billy Bonney The Best Known Man in New Mexico." Las Vegas *Gazette*. **December 28, 1880.** (**Has Billy Bonney's quote that "the laugh's on me this time"**)

_____. Interview, at train depot. Las Vegas *Gazette*. **December 28, 1880.** (**Has Billy Bonney's "adios" quote.**)

No Author. "At least two hundred men have been killed in Lincoln County during the past three years ..." Santa Fe *Daily New Mexican*. **March 28, 1881.**

No Author. "Something About the Kid." Santa Fe *Daily New Mexican*. **April 3, 1881.** (**With quotes Billy Bonney's "this is the man" and "two hundred men have been killed ... he did not kill all of them."**)

No Author. "I got a rough deal ..." *Mesilla News*. **April 15, 1881.**

Newman, Simon N. Ed. Interview with "The Kid." *Newman's Semi-Weekly*. **April 15, 1881.**

_____. Departure from Mesilla. *Newman's Semi-Weekly*. **April 15, 1881.**

No Author. "Advise persons never to engage in killing." *Mesilla News*. **April 16, 1881.** (**Billy Bonney's quote**)

BIOGRAPHICAL SOURCES

Abbott, E.C. ("Teddy Blue") and Helena Huntington Smith. *We Pointed Them North: Recollections of a Cowpuncher.* Norman, Oklahoma: University of Oklahoma Press. 1955. (**Billy the Kid's multiculturalism, page 47.**)

Anaya, Paco. *I Buried Billy.* College Station, Texas: Creative Publishing Company. 1991.

Ball, Eve. *Ma'am Jones of the Pecos.* Tucson, Arizona: The University of Arizona Press. 1969.

Bell, Bob Boze. *The Illustrated Life and Times of Billy the Kid.* Cave Creek, Arizona: Boze Books. 1992. (Frank Coe quote about the Kid's cartridge use, page 45.)

Bell, Bob Boze. *The Illustrated Life and Times of Billy the Kid.* Second Edition. Phoenix, Arizona: Tri Star-Boze Publications, Inc. 1996.

Burns, Walter Noble. *The Saga of Billy the Kid.* Stamford, Connecticut: Longmeadow Press. 1992. (Original printing: 1926, Doubleday.)

_____. *"I also know that the Kid and Paulita were sweethearts."* Unpublished letter to Jim East. June 3, 1926. Robert N. Mullin Collection. File RNM, IV, NM, 116-117. Nita Stewart Haley Memorial Museum, Haley Library. Midland, Texas.

Coe, George. Doyce B. Nunis, Jr. Ed. *Frontier Fighter. The Autobiography of George Coe Who Fought and Rode With Billy the Kid.* Chicago: R. R. Donnelley and Sons Company. 1984.

Cooper, Gale. *Billy the Kid's Writings, Words, and Wit.* Gelcour Books: Albuquerque: New Mexico. 2012.

_____. *Billy and Paulita: A Novel.* Gelcour Books: Albuquerque: New Mexico. 2012.

_____. *The Lost Pardon of Billy the Kid: An Analysis Factoring in the Santa Fe Ring, Governor Lew Wallace's Dilemma, and a Territory in Rebellion.* Gelcour Books: Albuquerque: New Mexico. 2017.

Garrett, Pat F. *The Authentic Life of Billy the Kid The Noted Desperado of the Southwest, Whose Deeds of Daring and Blood Made His Name a Terror in New*

Mexico, Arizona, and Northern Mexico. Santa Fe, New Mexico: New Mexico Printing and Publishing Co. 1882. (Reprint New York: Indian Head Books. 1994.)

Hendron, J. W. *The Story of Billy the Kid. New Mexico's Number One Desperado.* New York: Indian Head Books. 1994.

Hoyt, Henry. *A Frontier Doctor.* Boston and New York: Houghton Mifflin Company. 1929. **(Describes Billy's superior abilities. Pages 93-94.)**

Jacobsen, Joel. *Such Men as Billy the Kid. The Lincoln County War Reconsidered.* Lincoln and London: University of Nebraska Press. 1994.

Kadlec, Robert F. *They "Knew" Billy the Kid. Interviews with Old-Time New Mexicans.* Santa Fe, New Mexico: Ancient City Press. 1987.

Keleher, William A. *The Fabulous Frontier: Twelve New Mexico Items.* Albuquerque, New Mexico: The University of New Mexico Press. 1962.

_____.*Violence in Lincoln County 1869-1881.* Albuquerque, New Mexico: University of New Mexico Press. 1957. **(Las Vegas *Gazette* article of December 28, 1880, "The Kid. Interview with Billy Bonney The Best Known Man in New Mexico": pages 293-295; Las Vegas *Gazette* article of December 28, 1880. Untitled - at train station. Pages 296-297)**

McFarland, David F. Reverend. *Ledger: Session Records 1867-1874. Marriages in Santa Fe New Mexico. "Mr. William H. Antrim and Mrs. Catherine McCarty." March 1, 1873.* (Unpublished). Santa Fe, New Mexico: First Presbyterian Church of Santa Fe.

Meadows, John P. "Billy the Kid to John P. Meadows on the Peñasco, May 1-2, 1881." *Roswell Daily Record.* February 16, 1931. Page 6.

_____. Ed. John P. Wilson. *Pat Garrett and Billy the Kid as I Knew Them: Reminiscences of John P. Meadows.* Albuquerque: University of New Mexico Press. 2004.

Mullin, Robert N. *The Boyhood of Billy the Kid.* Monograph 17, Southwestern Studies 5(1). El Paso, Texas: Texas Western Press. University of Texas at El Paso. 1967.

Poe, John W. *The Death of Billy the Kid.* (Introduction by Maurice Garland Fulton). Boston and New York: Houghton Mifflin Company. 1933.

_____. "The Killing of Billy the Kid." (a personal letter written at Roswell, New Mexico to Mr. Charles Goodnight, Goodnight P.C., Texas) July 10, 1917. Earle Vandale Collection. 1813-946. No. 2H475. Center for American History. University of Texas at Austin.

Rakocy, Bill. *Billy the Kid.* El Paso, Texas: Bravo Press. 1985.

Rasch, Phillip J. *Trailing Billy the Kid.* Laramie, Wyoming: National Association for Outlaw and Lawman History, Inc. with University of Wyoming. 1995.

Russell, Randy. *Billy the Kid. The Story - The Trial.* Lincoln, New Mexico: The Crystal Press. 1994.

Siringo, Charles A. *The History of Billy the Kid.* Santa Fe: New Mexico. Privately Printed. 1920.

Tuska, Jon. *Billy the Kid. His Life and Legend.* Westport, Connecticut: Greenwood Press. 1983.

Utley, Robert M. *Billy the Kid. A Short and Violent Life.* Lincoln and London: University of Nebraska Press. 1989.

Weddle, Jerry. *Antrim is My Stepfather's Name. The Boyhood of Billy the Kid.* Monograph 9, Globe, Arizona: Arizona Historical Society. 1993.

No Author. "The Prisoners Who Saw the Kid Kill Olinger." April 28, 1881. Herman B. Weisner Papers, ca. 1957-1992. New Mexico State University Library at Las Cruces. Rio Grande Historical Collections. Accession No. Ms 0249. Box 30 T. Folder 8.

SECRET SERVICE REPORTS ABOUT

Wild, Azariah F. "Daily Reports of U. S. Secret Service Agents, Azariah F. Wild." Microfilm T-915. Record Group 87. Rolls 306 (June 15, 1877 - December 31, 1877),

307 (January 1,1878 - June 30, 1879), 308 (July 1, 1879 - June 30, 1881), 309 (July 1, 1881 - September 30, 1883), 310 (October 1, 1883 - July 31, 1886). National Archives and Records Department. Department of the Treasury. United States Secret Service. Washington, D. C.

NEWSPAPER ARTICLES ABOUT (CHRONOLOGICAL)

No Author. Grant County *Herald*. **May 10, 1879**. Results of the Lincoln County Grand Jury. (**Also published in the Mesilla** *Thirty Four*. **Confirmation of the William Bonney testimony and James Dolan and Billy Campbell murder indictments, from page 224 of William Keleher,** *Violence in Lincoln County*.)

No Author. Editorial. "Powerful Gang of Outlaws Harassing the Stockman." Las Vegas *Gazette*. **December 3, 1880**. (**Condemnation of William Bonney as an outlaw leader; and resulting in Bonney's response letter of December 12, 1880 to Governor Lew Wallace.**)

No Author. "Outlaws of New Mexico. The Exploits of a Band Headed by a New York Youth. The Mountain Fastness of the Kid and His Followers - War Against a Gang of Cattle Thieves and Murderers - The Frontier Confederates of Brockway, the Counterfeiter." *The Sun*. New York. **December 22, 1880**. Vol. XLVIII, No. 118, Page 3, Columns 1-2.

Wallace, Lew. "Billy the Kid: $500 Reward." Las Vegas *Gazette*. **December 22, 1880**.

No Author. "A Big Haul! Billy Kid, Dave Rudabaugh, Billy Wilson and Tom Pickett in the Clutches of the Law." *The Las Vegas Daily Optic*. Monday, **December 27, 1880**. Vol. 2, No. 45. Page 4, Column 2.

Wilcox, Lucius "Lute" M. " 'The Kid. Interview with Billy Bonney The Best Known Man in New Mexico, The greatest excitement prevailed yesterday when the news was abroad that Pat Garrett and Frank Stewart had arrived in town bringing with them Billy 'the Kid.' " Las Vegas *Gazette*. **December 27, 1880**. (**With "laugh's on me" quote**)

_____. "Interview With The Kid." Las Vegas *Gazette*. **December 28, 1880**.(From "Billy the Kid: Las Vegas Newspaper Accounts of His Career, 1880-1881." W.M. Morrison, Waco, Texas. 1958.)

No Author. "A Bay-Mare. Everyone who has heard of Billy 'the kid' has heard of his beautiful bay mare." *Las Vegas Morning Gazette*. Tuesday, **January 4, 1881**.

No Author. "The Kid. Billy 'the Kid' and Billy Wilson were on Monday taken to Mesilla for Trial." *Las Vegas Morning Gazette*. Tuesday, **March 15, 1881**.

Newman, Simon. "In the Name of Justice! In the Case of Billy Kid." *Newman's Semi-Weekly*. Saturday, **April 2, 1881**.

No Author. "Billy the Kid. Seems to be having a stormy journey on his trip Southward." *Las Vegas Morning Gazette*. Tuesday, **April 5, 1881**.

Koogler, J. H. "Interview with Governor Lew Wallace on 'The Kid.'" *Las Vegas Gazette*. April 28, 1881.

No Author. "The Kid." *Santa Fe Daily New Mexican*. **May 1, 1881**. Vol. X, No. 32, Page 1, Column 2.

No Author. "Billy Bonney. Advices from Lincoln bring the intelligence of the escape of 'Billy the Kid.' " *Las Vegas Daily Optic*. Monday, **May 2, 1881**.

No Author. "The Kid's Escape." *Santa Fe Daily New Mexican*. Tuesday Morning, **May 3, 1881**. Vol. X, No. 33, Page 1, Column 2.

Wallace, Lew. "Billy the Kid. $500 Reward." *Daily New Mexican*. **May 3, 1881**. Vol. X, No. 33, Page 1, Column 3.

No Author. "Dare Devil Desperado. Pursuit of 'Billy the Kid' has been abandoned." *Las Vegas Daily Optic*. **May 4, 1881**.

No Author. "More Killing by Kid." Editorial. *Santa Fe Daily New Mexican*. Wednesday Morning, **May 4, 1881**. Vol. X, No. 34, Page 1, Column 2.

No Author. "Kid was then in Albuquerque ..." *Santa Fe Daily New Mexican*. **May 5, 1881**. p.4. c. 1.

No Author. "Richard Dunham's May 2, 1881 encounter with Billy the Kid.", *Santa Fe Daily New Mexican*, **May 5, 1881**, Page 4, Column 3. (private collection)

No Author. "The question if how to deal with desperados who commit murder has but one solution - kill them." *Las Vegas Daily Optic*. Tuesday, **May 10, 1881**.

No Author. "Billy 'the Kid.' " Las Vegas *Gazette*. Thursday, **May 12, 1881**.

No Author. "The Kid was in Chloride City ..." *Santa Fe Daily New Mexican*. **May 13, 1881**. p.4. c. 3.

No Author. "Billy 'the Kid' is in the vicinity of Sumner." Las Vegas *Gazette*. Sunday, **May 15, 1881**.

No Author. "The Thug's Territory. Stage Robbers and Cut-Throats Have Things Their Own Way in New Mexico. Gen. Lew Wallace Anxious to Punish the Crime That is So Prevalent – A Chapter About 'Billy the Kid' – The Governor has a Narrow Escape From Being Spanked." *St. Louis Daily Globe-Democrat*. Monday Morning, **May 16, 1881**. Page 2, Columns 5 and 6. (private collection)

No Author. "The Kid is believed to be in the Black Range ..." *Santa Fe Daily New Mexican*. **May 19, 1881**. p.4. c. 1.

No Author. "Billy the Kid was last seen in Lincoln County ..." *Santa Fe Daily New Mexican*. **May 19, 1881**. p.4. c. 1.

No Author. " 'Billy the Kid' has been heard from again." *Las Vegas Daily Optic*. Friday, **June 10, 1881**.

No Author. " 'Billy the Kid.' He is Reported to Have Been Seen on Our Streets Saturday Night." *Las Vegas Daily Optic*. Monday Evening, **June 13, 1881**. Vol. 2, No. 188, Page 4, Column 2.

Wilcox, Lute, Ed. "Billy the Kid would make an ideal newspaper-man in that he always endeavors to 'get even' with his enemies." *Las Vegas Daily Optic*. Monday Evening, **June 13, 1881**. Vol. 2, No. 188, Page 4, Column 1.

No Author. "Land of the Petulant Pistol. 'Billy the Kid' as a Killer." *Las Vegas Daily Optic*. Wednesday Evening, **June 15, 1881**. Vol. 2, No. 190.

No Author. "Barney Mason at Fort Sumner states the 'Kid' is in Local Sheep Camps." *Las Vegas Morning Gazette*. **June 16, 1881**.

No Author. "The Kid." *Santa Fe Daily New Mexican*. **June 16, 1881**. Vol. X, No. 90, Page 4, Column 2.

No Author. "Billy the Kid. General Wallace Tells Why the Young Desperado of New Mexico Wanted to Kill Him." (Lew Wallace interviewed on June 13, 1881), Crawfordsville *Saturday Evening Journal*, **June 18, 1881**. Indiana Historical Society. The Papers of Lew and Susan Wallace. Microfilm Edition. Indianapolis, Indiana: Indiana Historical Society Press. 2008.

No Author. "Billy the Kid." *Las Vegas Daily Optic*. Thursday, June 28, 1881.

No Author. " 'The Kid' Killed." *Las Vegas Daily Optic*. **July 18. 1881**.

No Author. "Lew Wallace's Foe. Threatened by 'Billy the Kid.' The Writing of 'Ben Hur' Interrupted. An Incident of the Soldier-Author's Career in New Mexico. *San Francisco Chronicle*. **December 10, 1893**. Indiana Historical Society. Lew Wallace Collection. M0292. Box 14. Folder 11. (**Lew Wallace creating outlaw myth of outlaw Billy the Kid**")

No Author. "Street Pickings," Weekly *Crawfordsville Review – Saturday Edition*, **January 6, 1894**. Indiana Historical Society. The Papers of Lew and Susan Wallace. Microfilm Edition. Series I. Reel 27. Indianapolis, Indiana: Indiana Historical Society Press. 2008.

Lewis, E.I. "Gen. Wallace's Feud with Billy the Kid, When the General Was Governor of New Mexico and Billy Bonne Was the Most Dangerous Western Outlaw. He Was a Waif and Was Reared in Indiana. *The Indianapolis Press*. Saturday, **June 23, 1900**. Page 7. Lew Wallace Collection. Indiana Historical Society. M0292. Box 14. Folder 11. (photocopy) (Original article is in OMB 23, Box 1. Folder 5) (**Lew Wallace creating self-serving myth of outlaw Billy the Kid**")

No Author. "An Old Incident Recalled." Crawfordsville *Weekly News-Review.* **December 20, 1901**. Indiana Historical Society. The Papers of Lew and Susan Wallace. Microfilm Edition. Series I. Reel 27. Indianapolis, Indiana: Indiana Historical Society Press. 2008.

Wallace, Lew. "General Lew Wallace Writes a Romance of 'Billy the Kid' Most Famous Bandit of the Plains: Thrilling Story of the Midnight Meeting Between Gen Wallace, Then Governor of New Mexico, and the Notorious Outlaw, in a Lonesome Hut in Santa Fe." *New York World Magazine.* Sunday, **June 8, 1902**. Lew Wallace Collection. Indiana Historical Society. M0292. . Box 14. Folder 11.

LETTERS MENTIONING BILLY BONNEY

Kimbrell, George. "I have the honor to request that you will furnish me a posse ..." Letter to Lieutenant Millard Filmore Goodwin. **February 20, 1879**. Indiana Historical Society. Lew Wallace Collection. Box 4, Folder 3. (**For pursuit of William Bonney and Yginio Salazar**)

Goodwin, Millard Filmore. ""I have the honor to submit the following report regarding my duties performed ..." Letter to Fort Stanton Post Adjutant John Loud. **February 23, 1879**. Indiana Historical Society. Lew Wallace Collection. Box 4. Folder 3. (**Assisting pursuit of William Bonney and Yginio Salazar**)

Dudley, Nathan Augustus Monroe. "I enclose herewith report of 2nd Lieut. M.F. Goodwin ..." Letter to Acting Assistant Adjutant General at Headquarters. **February 24, 1879**. Indiana Historical Society. Lew Wallace Collection. M0292. Box 4, Folder 3. (**Documents military pursuit of William Bonney**)

Wallace, Lew. "I have just ascertained that 'The Kid' is at a place called Las Tablas ..." Letter to Edward Hatch. **March 6, 1879**. Indiana Historical Society. Lew Wallace Collection. Box 9, Folder 10. (**Written on dead John Tunstall's stationery**)

_____. "I beg to submit to you a list of persons whom it is necessary, in my judgment, to arrest ..." Letter to Henry Carroll. **March 11, 1879**. Indiana Historical Society. Lew Wallace Collection. M0292. Box 4. Folder 5. (**Lists as 14, "The Kid" – William Bonney; also lists Jessie Evans, Yginio Salazar, James Dolan**)

_____. "I enclose a note for Bonney." Letter to John "Squire" Wilson. **March 20, 1879**. Indiana Historical Society. Lew Wallace Collection. M0292. Box 4. Folder 6.

_____. "My time has been so constantly occupied in getting my work into operation ..." Letter to Carl Schurz. **March 21, 1879**. Indiana Historical Society. Lew Wallace Collection. M0292. Box 4. Folder 7. (**Progress report with multiple enclosures; one listing "The Kid -William Bonney in anti-outlaw campaign of "taking the head off the evil."**)

_____. "To day I forwarded a telegram to you, with another to the President ..." Letter to Carl Schurz. **March 31, 1879**. Indiana Historical Society. Lew Wallace Collection. M0292. Box 4. Folder 7. (**Mention of "precious specimen nicknamed 'The Kid' "**)

Leonard, Ira. "The air is filled tonight with 'rumors of wars ... Letter to Lew Wallace. **April 20, 1879**. Indiana Historical Society. Lew Wallace Collection. M0292. Box 4. Folder 9. (**About District Attorney Rynerson: "He is bent on going for the Kid"**)

Hoyt, Henry F. "This time it is me who is apologizing for the long delay in answering ..." (Letter to Lew Wallace Jr.) **April 27, 1927**. Indiana Historical Society. Lew Wallace Collection. M0292. Box 14, Folder 11.

_____. "Copy of a bill of sale written by W[m] H. Bonney ..." Letter to Lew Wallace Jr. **April 27, 1927**. Indiana Historical Society. Lew Wallace Collection. M0292. Box 14, Folder 11. (**Calls Billy Bonney "a natural leader of men"**)

OWNERSHIP FILING ON CARRIZOZO CATTLE COMPANY

Catron, Thomas Benton.. Statement of Sole ownership of Carrizozo Ranch in Tax Dispute Case. No date. Herman B. Weisner Papers, ca. 1957-1992. New Mexico State University Library at Las Cruces. Rio Grande Historical Collections. Accession No. Ms 0249. Box. 2. Folder C-8. Folder Name "T.B. Catron Tax Troubles."

ARTICLES ABOUT AND BY (CHRONOLOGICAL)

Morley, William Raymond and Frank Springer. On Oscar McMains's citizen's Meeting. *Cimarron News and Press.* **November 10, 1875. (Colfax County citizens meeting on F.J. Tolby murder by Santa Fe Ring.)**

_____. " 'The Territory of Elkins.' Assassination of Supposed Sun Correspondent. The Murder of the Rev. F.J. Tolby in New Mexico. A Probate Judge Accused of Complicity in the Crime. Indignation Meeting." *New York Weekly Sun.* **December 22, 1875.** Interior Department Papers 1850-1907; Appointments Division and Subsequent Actions. Microfilm Roll M750. National Archives and Records Administration. Record Group 48. Microfilm Case File Number 44-4-8-3. U.S. Department of Interior. Washington, D. C.**(Submitted on May 1, 1877 to President Rutherford B. Hayes by Mary McPherson and W.B. Matchett)**

Lambert, J.J. "At It Again." Pueblo, Colorado, *Enterprise and Chronicle.* **April 21, 1877.** Interior Department Papers 1850-1907; Appointments Division and Subsequent Actions. Microfilm File Case Number 44-4-8-3. Record Group 48. Microfilm No. M750. Roll 1. National Archives and Records Administration. U.S. Department of Justice. Washington, D.C. **(About Ring control of courts and malicious prosecution of opponents and Franklin Tolby murder)**

Tunstall, John Henry. "A Taxpayer's Complaint ... January 18, 1878." Mesilla *Independent.* **January 26, 1878. (Exposé of William Brady, James Dolan, and John Riley for tax fraud and use of public money to purchase cattle; and Catron then paid that bill)**

Dolan, James J. "Answer to A Taxpayer's Complaint." Mesilla *Independent.* **January 29, 1878. (Response to J.H. Tunstall's exposé)**

No Author. "White Cap's Proclamation." *Las Vegas Optic.* **March 12, 1880. (Manifesto against land-grabbing Catron and the Ring)**

No Author. Las Cruces *Thirty-Four Newspaper.* **October 27, 1880. (Urging voters to overthrow Catron's Santa Fe Ring-backed candidate)**

No Author. *Albuquerque Daily Democrat.* **March 4, 1884. (Time is past for Ring herding men)**

No Author. *Santa Fe Weekly New Mexican Review.* **March 13, 1884.** *Santa Fe Weekly New Mexican Review.* **(Accusation of Catron and the Ring of controlling grand juries and bribery)**

No Author. *Albuquerque Daily Democrat.* **March 15, 1884. (Oscar P. McMains "Memorial" against land-grabbing Ring)**

No Author. *Las Vegas Optic.* **September 2, 1884. (About the anti-Ring Legislature revolt and Catron's alliance with corrupt Judge Joseph Palen)**

Chavez, No First Name. *Santa Fe Weekly New Mexican.* **March 8, 1894. (Open letter from mother of Francisco Chavez implicating Catron in his murder)** Cited by Victor Westphall, *Thomas Benton Catron and His Era.* Page 226.

No author. *Las Vegas Independent Democrat.* ___ **1895**; based on *Las Vegas Optic.* September 2, 1884. **(About disbarring Catron)**

Catron, Thomas Benton (As "Anonymous"). "Is it honesty or partisanship?" Letter to the Editor, Thomas Hughes. *Albuquerque Daily Citizen.* **October 9, 1895. (Defamation of his disbarment Judge Thomas J. Smith)** Cited by Victor Westphall, *Thomas Benton Catron and His Era.* Page 246. Thomas B. Catron Papers. University of New Mexico Center for Southwest Studies. University Library. MSS 29 BC.

_____. "To day I forwarded a telegram to you, with another to the President ..." Letter to Carl Schurz. **March 31, 1879.** Indiana Historical Society. Lew Wallace Collection. M0292. Box 4. Folder 7. (**Quote: "precious specimen nicknamed 'The Kid' "**)

_____. "Be good enough to prepare a draft of proclamation of reward $500 for the capture and delivery of William Bonney, alias the Kid ..." Letter to Territorial Secretary William Ritch. **December 13, 1880.** Herman B. Weisner Papers, ca. 1957-1992. New Mexico State University Library at Las Cruces. Rio Grande Historical Collections. Accession No. Ms 0249. Box W3. Folder 13. Folder Name: "Wallace, Gov. N.M." From Lew Wallace Papers. New Mexico State Records Center. Santa Fe, New Mexico. (**Wallace's first reward for Billy the Kid**)

INTERVIEW BY LEW WALLACE

Wallace, Lew. "Statements by Kid, made Sunday night March 23, 1879." **March 23, 1879.** Indiana Historical Society. Lew Wallace Collection. M0922. Box 4. Folder 6.

ARTICLES (CHRONOLOGICAL)

"Wallace, Lew. "Wallace's Words ..." (interview with Lew Wallace conducted in Washington, D.C. on January 3, 1881), Chicago *The Daily Inter Ocean.* **January 4, 1881.** Indiana Historical Society. The Papers of Lew and Susan Wallace. Microfilm Edition. Indianapolis, Indiana: Indiana Historical Society Press. 2008.

No Author. "Richard Dunham's May 2, 1881 encounter with Billy the Kid.", *Santa Fe Daily New Mexican,* **May 5, 1881,** Page 4, Column 3. (private collection)

No Author. "The Thug's Territory. Stage Robbers and Cut-Throats Have Things Their Own Way in New Mexico. Gen. Lew Wallace Anxious to Punish the Crime That is So Prevalent – A Chapter About 'Billy the Kid' – The Governor has a Narrow Escape From Being Spanked." *St. Louis Daily Globe-Democrat.* Monday Morning, **May 16, 1881.** Page 2, Columns 5 and 6. (private collection)

No Author. (O.L. Houghton's Conversation with Lew Wallace, before May 26, 1881), *The Las Vegas Daily Optic,* **May 26, 1881,** p.4, c.4. Indiana Historical Society. Lew Wallace Collection. M0292.

No Author. "Billy the Kid, General Wallace Tells Why the Young Desperado of New Mexico Wanted to Kill Him." (Lew Wallace interviewed on June 13, 1881), Crawfordsville *Saturday Evening Journal,* **June 18, 1881.** Indiana Historical Society. The Papers of Lew and Susan Wallace. Microfilm Edition. Indianapolis, Indiana: Indiana Historical Society Press. 2008.

No Author. "Street Pickings," Weekly *Crawfordsville Review - Saturday Edition,* **January 6, 1894.** Indiana Historical Society. The Papers of Lew and Susan Wallace. Microfilm Edition. Series I. Reel 27. Indianapolis, Indiana: Indiana Historical Society Press. 2008.

No Author. "An Old Incident Recalled." Crawfordsville *Weekly News-Review.* **December 20, 1901.** Indiana Historical Society. The Papers of Lew and Susan Wallace. Microfilm Edition. Series I. Reel 27. Indianapolis, Indiana: Indiana Historical Society Press. 2008.

Lewis, E.I. "Gen. Wallace's Feud with Billy the Kid, When the General Was Governor of New Mexico and Billy Bonne Was the Most Dangerous Western Outlaw. He Was a Waif and Was Reared in Indiana. *The Indianapolis Press.* Saturday, **June 23, 1900.** Page 7. Lew Wallace Collection. Indiana Historical Society. M0292. Box 14. Folder 11. (photocopy) (Original article is in OMB 23, Box 1. Folder 5)

Wallace, Lew. "Indiana is Now Literary Center, General Lew Wallace Gives His Views on Present Day Writers, Is Working on New Book." Cincinnati *Commercial Tribune* reprinted in Crawfordsville *Weekly News-Review.* **April 15, 1902.** Indiana Historical Society. The Papers of Lew and Susan Wallace. Microfilm

Edition. Series I. Reel 27. Indianapolis, Indiana: Indiana Historical Society Press. 2008.

_____. "General Lew Wallace Writes a Romance of 'Billy the Kid' Most Famous Bandit of the Plains: Thrilling Story of the Midnight Meeting Between Gen Wallace, Then Governor of New Mexico, and the Notorious Outlaw, in a Lonesome Hut in Santa Fe." *New York World Magazine.* Sunday, **June 8, 1902.** Lew Wallace Collection. Indiana Historical Society. M0292. . Box 14. Folder 11.

BOWDRE, CHARLES "CHARLIE"

CONTEMPORARY SOURCES (CHRONOLOGICAL)

Regulator. "Mr. Walz. Sir ..." Letter to Edgar Walz. **July 13, 1878.** Adjutant General's Office. File 1405 AGO 1878. (Attributed to Charles Bowdre in Maurice Garland Fulton, *History of the Lincoln County War.* Tucson: University of Arizona Press. 1975. pages 246-247, and Frederick Nolan, *The Lincoln County War: A Documentary History,* page 310.) **(Possibly dictated to him by Billy Bonney)**

Wallace, Lew. "Please select ten of your Rangers ..." Letter to Juan Patrón. **March 3, 1879.** Indiana Historical Society. Lew Wallace Collection. M0292. Box 4. Folder 4. **(To arrest "Scurlock and Bowdrey")**

_____. Lew. "I have reliable information that J.G. Scurlock and Charles Bowdre are now at a ranch called Taiban ..." Letter to Edward Hatch. **March 6, 1879.** Indiana Historical Society. Lew Wallace Collection. Box 4, Folder 4.

BRADY, WILLIAM

BIOGRAPHICAL SOURCES

Lavash, Donald R. *Sheriff William Brady. Tragic Hero of the Lincoln County War.* Santa Fe, New Mexico: Sunstone Press. 1986.

CONTEMPORARY SOURCES (CHRONOLOGICAL)

Brady, William. Affidavit of **July 2, 1876** concerning appointment as Administrator for the Emil Fritz Estate. Copied from the original District Court Record. (private collection)

_____. Affidavit of **August 22, 1876** documenting business debts to L. G. Murphy and Co. pertaining to the Emil Fritz Estate. Copied from the original District Court Record. (private collection)

_____. Affidavit of **July _, 1876** of Resignation as Emil Fritz Estate Administrator. Copied from the original District Court Record. (private collection.)

_____. Affidavit of **August 22, 1876** confirming giving Alexander McSween the books of the L.G. Murphy Company for the purpose of making business debt collections. Copied from the original District Court Record. (private collection)

Tunstall, John Henry. "A Taxpayer's Complaint ... January 18, 1878." Mesilla *Independent.* **January 26, 1878. (Exposé of William Brady, James Dolan, and John Riley for tax fraud and use of public money to purchase cattle; and Catron then paid that bill)**

Dolan, James J. "Answer to A Taxpayer's Complaint." Mesilla *Independent.* **January 29, 1878. (Response to J.H. Tunstall's exposé of him, William Brady, and John Riley for tax fraud and use of public money to purchase cattle; and T.B. Catron then paid that bill)**

Bristol, Warren. "Action of Assumpsit to command Sheriff Brady of Lincoln County to attach goods of Alexander A. McSween." **February 7, 1878.** District Court Record. (private collection).

_____. Preprinted form for "Writ of Attachment" (Printed and sold at the office of the Mesilla News) filled out to command the Sheriff of Lincoln County to attach goods of Alexander McSween for a suit of damages for ten thousand dollars. **February 7, 1878.** District Court Record. (private collection).

Brady, William. "List of Articles Inventoried by Wm Brady sheriff in the suit of Charles Fritz & Emilie Scholand vs A.A. McSween now in the dwelling house belonging to A.A. McSween." (undated, but in **February of 1878**) (private collection)

BRISTOL, WARREN
CONTEMPORARY SOURCES (CHRONOLOGICAL)

Bristol Warren. "From sources of information that I deem perfectly reliable I am satisfied that there are public disorders in Lincoln County ..." Letter to Governor Marsh Giddings. **January 10, 1874.** Herman B. Weisner Papers, ca. 1957-1992. New Mexico State University Library at Las Cruces. Rio Grande Historical Collections. Accession No. Ms 0249. Box 4/39. Folder D-4. Folder Name. "Judge Bristol's letter." **(Start of Santa Fe Ring's outlaw myth and use of military)**

_____. "Writ of Embezzlement." **December 21, 1877.** Herman B. Weisner Papers, ca. 1957-1992. New Mexico State University Library at Las Cruces. Rio Grande Historical Collections. Accession No. Ms 0249. Box 10. Folder M-13. Folder Name. "Will and Testament A. McSween." **(Emilie Fritz Scholand's sworn complaint against Alexander McSween)**

_____. "Action of Assumpsit to command Sheriff Brady of Lincoln County to attach goods of Alexander A. McSween." **February 7, 1878.** District Court Record. (private collection).

_____. Preprinted form for "Writ of Attachment" (Printed and sold at the office of the Mesilla News) filled out to command the Sheriff of Lincoln County to attach goods of Alexander McSween for a suit of damages for ten thousand dollars. **February 7, 1878.** District Court Record. (private collection).

_____. "My reasons for not holding October term of Court ..." Telegram to U.S. Marshal John Sherman. **October 4, 1878.** Indiana Historical Society. Lew Wallace Collection. M0292. Box 3. Folder 15.

No Author. "For Delegate Benito Baca. County Ticket Juan C. Armijo." *Albuquerque Review*. **October 5, 1878.** Indiana Historical Society. The Papers of Lew and Susan Wallace. Microfilm Edition. Indianapolis, Indiana: Indiana Historical Society Press. 2008. **(About Lew Wallace's arrival in New Mexico Territory and swearing in by Warren Bristol)**

Bristol, Warren. *Instructions to the Jury*. District Court 3rd Judicial. District Doña Ana. Filed **April 9, 1881.** Writ of Embezzlement. New Mexico State University Library at Las Cruces. Rio Grande Historical Collection. Accession No. Ms 0249. Box 1. Folder 14C. Folder Name: "Billy the Kid Legal Documents."

CATRON, THOMAS BENTON
BIBLIOGRAPHICAL

Cleaveland, Norman, *A Synopsis of the Great New Mexico Cover-up*. Self-printed. 1989.

_____. *The Great Santa Fe Cover-up. Based on a Talk given Before the Santa Fe Historical Society on November 1, 1978*. Self-printed. 1982.

_____. *The Morleys - Young Upstarts on the Southwest Frontier*. Albuquerque, New Mexico: Calvin Horn Publisher, Inc. 1971. **(Page 93 gives Catron's vindictive indictment of Cleaveland's grandmother, Ada Morley, for mail theft as revenge denying him use of a Maxwell Land Grant buggy.**

Cooper, Gale. *The Lost Pardon of Billy the Kid: An Analysis Factoring in the Santa Fe Ring, Governor Lew Wallace's Dilemma, and a Territory in Rebellion*. Albuquerque, New Mexico: Gelcour Books. 2017.

Dunham, Harold H. "New Mexican Land Grants with Special Reference to the Title Papers of the Maxwell Grant." *New Mexico Historical Review*. (January, 1955) Vol. 70. No. 1. pp. 1 - 23.

Hefferan, Vioalle Clark. *Thomas Benton Catron*. Albuquerque, New Mexico: University of New Mexico. Zimmerman Library. Unpublished Thesis for the Degree of Master of Arts. 1940. .(**In praise of Catron; includes railroad involvement, Page 35; First National Bank stockholder from 1871 to 1907, Page 28**)

Keleher, William A. *The Maxwell Land Grant. A New Mexico Item*. Albuquerque, New Mexico: University of New Mexico Press. 1964.

Lamar, Howard Robert N. *The Far Southwest 1846 - 1912: A Territorial History*. New Haven and London: Yale University Press. 1966. (**Chapter 6 covers the Santa Fe Ring**))

Montoya, María E. *Translating Property. The Maxwell Land Grant and the Conflict Over Land in the American West, 1840-1900*. Berkeley and Los Angeles: University of California Press. 2002.

Mullin, Robert N. "A Specimen of Catron's Dirty Work. Sworn Affidavit of Samuel Davis." October 1, 1878. Binder RNM IV, EE. (Unpublished). Midland, Texas: Nita Stewart Haley Memorial Library and J. Everts Haley Historical Center.

_____. "Catron Embarrassed Throughout His Life by an Affliction." (Date Unknown). Binder RNM, IV, M. (Unpublished). Midland, Texas: Nita Stewart Haley Memorial Library and J. Everts Haley Historical Center. Robert Mullin Papers. Binder RNM IV, EE (Unpublished).

_____. "Prior to Lincoln County War Catron Had Defended Colonel Dudley." (No Date). Notes from "Lincoln County War Cast of Characters." Midland, Texas: Nita Stewart Haley Memorial Library and J. Everts Haley Historical Center.

Murphy, Lawrence R. *Lucien Bonaparte Maxwell. Napoleon of the Southwest*. Norman: University of Oklahoma Press. 1983.

Otero, Miguel A. *My Life on the Frontier, 1882-1897: Incidents and Characters of the period when Kansas, Colorado, and New Mexico were passing through the last of their Wild and Romantic Years*. New York: The Press of the Pioneers. 1935. Pages 232-233. (Quoted by Victor Westphall, *Thomas Benton Catron and His Era*. Page 188*)* (**About the 'Santa Fe Ring controlling New Mexico."**)

Pearson, Jim Berry. *The Maxwell Land Grant*. Norman: University of Oklahoma Press. 1961.

Routt, John C. "I am here on a visit to my daughter and have more by accident than otherwise heard statements ..." Letter to President Rutherford B. Hayes. August 29, 1878. Interior Department Papers 1850-1907; Appointments Division and Subsequent Actions. Microfilm File Case Number 44-4-8-3. Microfilm Roll M750. National Archives and Records Administration Record Group 48. U.S. Department of Interior. Washington D.C. (**In opposition to removal of Governor Axtell and U.S. Attorney Thomas Benton Catron.**)

Sluga, Mary Elizabeth. *Political Life of Thomas Benton Catron 1896-1912*. Albuquerque, New Mexico: University of New Mexico. Zimmerman Library. Unpublished Thesis for the Degree of Master of Arts. 1941. (**Thesis in praise of Catron for an M.A.**)

Taylor, Morris F. *O.P. McMains and the Maxwell Land Grant Conflict*. Tucson, Arizona: The University of Arizona Press. 1979. (**Traces origins of the Santa Fe Ring with T.B. Catron and S.B. Elkins**)

Westphall, Victor. *Thomas Benton Catron and His Era*. Tucson, Arizona: University of Arizona Press. 1973.

_____. "Fraud and Implications of Fraud in the Land Grants of New Mexico." *New Mexico Historical Review*. 1974. Vol. XLIX, No. 3. 189 - 218.

Wooden, John Paul. *Thomas Benton Catron and New Mexico Politics 1866-1921*. Albuquerque, New Mexico: University of New Mexico. Zimmerman Library. Unpublished Thesis for the Degree of Master of Arts. 1959. (**Thesis in praise of Catron for an M.A.**)

LETTERS BY, TO, ABOUT (CHRONOLOGICAL)
GENERAL

Catron, Thomas Benton. Letters 1866-1921. Coronado Collection. University of New Mexico Library. Albuquerque, New Mexico.

LETTERS (CHRONOLOGICAL)

Giddings, Marsh. "To defeat Catron's confirmation [as U.S. Attorney] a grossly false affidavit [by August Kirchner] has been sent to Senator [Lyman Trumbull]." **Month (?) 1872.** Telegram from Governor Marsh Giddings to Washington, D.C. Attorney General George H. Williams. From Victor Westphall. *Thomas Benton Catron and His Era.* Page 107. (**About the 1872 legislature's actions against Palen and Catron**)

Catron, Thomas Benton. "Answering Charges of Mary E. McPherson." **February 24, 1877.** Letter to Attorney General Alphonso Taft. Interior Department Papers 1850-1907; Appointments Division and Subsequent Actions. Microfilm File Case Number 44-4-8-3. Record Group 48. Microfilm Roll M750. National Archives and Records Administration. U.S. Department of Justice. Washington, D.C.

Riley, John. Letter to N.A.M. Dudley. **May 19, 1878.** (**Fabricated Regulator theft of Catron's cattle from the Dolan Pecos Cow Camp**) Cited by Victor Westphall, Page 87.

Catron, Thomas Benton. Catron letter to Governor S. B. Axtell to intervene in Lincoln County. **May 30, 1878.** Midland, Texas: Nita Stewart Haley Memorial Library and J. Everts Haley Historical Center. Robert Mullin Papers. Binder RNM IV, EE (Unpublished). (**Fabricated attack of Regulators on his cow camp workers**) Cited by Victor Westphall, Page 89-90.

Elkins, Stephen Benton. "I have waited some time to reply to your lengthy letter ..." Letter to T.B. Catron. **August 15, 1879.** West Virginia & Regional History Center. West Virginia University Libraries, Morgantown, W. Va. Stephen B. Elkins Papers (A&M 53). Box 1. Folder 1. (**Reveals he prevented Catron's dismissal and indictment from Angel's report**)

Gonzales y Borrego, Francisco. "dear Sir I have the honor to report to you that I have two men that they have agreed to come to the Republican party ... they want $10.00 each ..." **July 23, 1890.** Letter to Thomas Benton Catron. Catron Papers 102, Box 8. Quoted by Victor Westphall, *Thomas Benton Catron and His Era.* Page 268. (**Revealing Catron's Ringite vote-buying**)

Chavez, Juliana V. "Mr. Catron, you are not above suspicion of knowing more about the assassination of my son than you have found it convenient to reveal ..." Letter of Juliana Chavez to T.B. Catron. Reprinted in *Santa Fe Weekly New Mexican.* **March 8, 1894.** Quoted in Victor Westphall, *Thomas Benton Catron and his Era.* Page 226. (**Accusing Catron as accomplice to murder of Francisco Chavez, with implication of Santa Fe Ring**)

Catron, Thomas Benton. "[The Francisco Chavez murder case] has left me more prostrated than any case I have ever had." Letter to wife, Julia Catron. **June 1, 1895.** C.P. 105, Vol. 12. Quoted in Victor Westphall, *Thomas Benton Catron and His Era.* Page 228. (**Catron implicated in political murder**)

_____. "[Y]ou must absolutely stand pat and not give away any information that will injure me ..." Letter to Editor of the *Albuquerque Daily Citizen* Thomas Hughes. **October 10, 1895.** C.P. 801. Box 1. Quoted by Victor Westphall, *Thomas Benton Catron and His Era.* Page 247. (**Promising payback for secrecy**)

_____. "Editor of the Citizen: I have noticed an article in the Citizen of the 9th inst., which seems to reflect on Chief Justice Smith ..." Letter to Editor of the *Albuquerque Daily Citizen* Thomas Hughes. **October 10, 1895.** C.P. 801. Box 1. Quoted by Victor Westphall, *Thomas Benton Catron and His Era.* (Page 248) (**Defaming his Supreme Court disbarment judge, Thomas Smith**)

Catron, Thomas Benton. "The editorial in your paper came to hand today and the democrats and members of the supreme court are very indignant." Letter to *Albuquerque Daily Citizen's* editor, Thomas Hughes. **October 10, 1895.** (**Secret bribe for the Hughes press plot**) Quoted by Victor Westphall, *Thomas Benton Catron and His Era.* Pages 247-248.

_____. "Tom Smith, son of "Extra Billy" Smith, brother of ... the embezzler, who fled from justice in Arizona ..." "[Judge] Hamilton should ... see that the decision is an absolute, complete, unconditional vindication. This is what I ask him." Letter to *Socorro Chieftain* publisher S.W. Williams. **October 25, 1895.** Catron Papers. 105. Vol. 13. Quoted by Victor Westphall, *Thomas Benton Catron and His Era.* Pages 251-254. (**Defamation of his disbarment Chief Judge Thomas Smith; and illegal influence on another judge**)

_____. "[Smith], thank heaven, took the diarrhoea from the article published in the 'Citizen' and was soon after thrown into a congestive chill ..." Letter to Walter C. Hadley. **October 29, 1895.** (**Gloating over his sadistic attack on his disbarment judge, Thomas Smith**) Quoted by Victor Westphall, *Thomas Benton Catron and His Era.* Page 259.

_____. "His skin is so thin that the slightest attack punctures him. I think the papers should now puncture him ..." Letter to T.W. Collier. **November 11, 1895.** Catron Papers. 105. Vol. 13. (**Sadistic attack on his disbarment judge, Thomas Smith**) Quoted by Victor Westphall, *Thomas Benton Catron and His Era.* Page 249.

_____. "This man [Judge] Laughlin ... tried to disbar me and when he could not do it he wrote a filthy, dirty, dissenting opinion ..." Letter to William J. Mills. **July 18, 1896.** Catron Papers. 105. Vol. 13. Quoted by Victor Westphall, *Thomas Benton Catron and His Era.* Page 258. (**Trying to destroy reputation of disbarment judge, Napoleon B. Laughlin**)

_____. Letter to a Don Matais Contreras. **July 30, 1896.** (**On acquiring land grants by bartering attorney's fees**) Cited in John Paul Wooden's unpublished masters thesis, Page 11.

_____. "Poker Bill" is now engaged in playing a game in which the lives of four men are at stake ..." *Albuquerque Daily Citizen.* **September 11, 1896.** Reprinted September 11, 1896 in the *Santa Fe Daily New Mexican.* Quoted by Victor Westphall, *Thomas Benton Catron and His Era.* Page 262. (**Catron's anonymous defamatory letter about William Thornton**)

Thornton, William T. "This communication to the *Citizen* was prepared in your office, and at your dictation." *Santa Fe Daily New Mexican.* **September 11, 1896.** Reprinting and debunking T.B. Catron's anonymous letter of September 11, 1896 to the *Albuquerque Daily Citizen* of September 11, 1896. Quoted by Victor Westphall, *Thomas Benton Catron and His Era.* Page 262. (**Thornton confronts Catron's anonymous defamatory letter about him**)

Catron, Thomas Benton. "[Your letter] has the appearance of being designed to provoke me to some act of violence, which might give your adherents an opportunity to injure me physically..." **September 16, 1896.** Letter to William T. Thornton. Catron Papers 801, Box 1. Quoted by Victor Westphall, *Thomas Benton Catron and His Era.* Page 263. (**Catron's violent and insanely paranoid accusations of Thornton for exposing his criminality**)

_____. "The letter of Gov. Thornton is regarded here by all good citizens as being ... calculated to bring about a state of unrest and possible blood-shed." Letter to President Grover Cleveland. **September 16, 1896.** Quoted by Victor Westphall, *Thomas Benton Catron and His Era.* Pages 269-270.

_____. "The letter of Gov. Thornton is regarded here by all good citizens as being calculated to bring about a state of unrest and possible blood-shed." **September 16, 1896.** Letter to President Grover Cleveland. Catron Papers 801, Box 1. Quoted by Victor Westphall, *Thomas Benton Catron and His Era.* Pages 269-270. (**Attempted revenge on Governor William Thornton**)

Field, Neill B. "I am exceedingly sick of your method of doing business ..." Letter to Thomas Benton Catron. **December 28, 1896.** C.P. 106, Box 1, quoted in Victor Westphall, *Thomas Benton Catron and His Era.* Page 165. (**Catron accused of attempting to pocket stock of deceased partner**)

Elkins, Stephen Benton. "Mr. Catron's prominence in the capital territory and his leadership ..." Letter to Gideon B. Bantz. **September 9, 1897.** (**Improper influence of Catron's disbarment judge**) Quoted in John Paul Wooden's unpublished thesis, Page 32.

Catron, Thomas Benton. "He [Lew Wallace] and I were not on friendly terms while he was governor." Letter to Stephen Benton Elkins. **August 4, 1897.** (**About Wallace's opposition to his reappointment as U.S. Attorney**) Quoted in Mary Elizabeth Sluga's masters thesis, Page 50.

_____. "I am entitled to same from a political standpoint ... having made the race paying all the expenses ..." Letter to Joshua S. Reynolds. **December 16, 1897.** Quoted in Mary Elizabeth Sluga's masters thesis, Page 53.

_____."His administration has been guilty of the most wholesale plunder of the resources of this territory ..." Letter to Richard C. Kerens. **April 4, 1901.** (**Revenge defamation of Governor Miguel A. Otero**) Quoted in Mary Elizabeth Sluga's masters thesis, Pages 66-69.

_____."You must see that Otero is not reappointed ..." Letter to Stephen Benton Elkins. **November 11, 1901.** Quoted in Mary Elizabeth Sluga's masters thesis, Page 79.

_____. "[Otero backers] have made a very villainous, mean ugly fight against me." **September 20, 1902.** Letter to Dave Winters. Catron Papers 105, Volume 20. Quoted by Victor Westphall, *Thomas Benton Catron and His Era.* Pages 291. (**Accusing Governor Otero of his own Ring-style criminality**)

Catron, Thomas Benton. "[If your son] is to be appointed, I shall be very pleased ... if he will take immediate steps to have the "Augean stables" cleaned ..." Letter to James J. Hagerman. **November 22, 1905.** (**Wanting appointment as Attorney General to maliciously prosecute opponents**) Quoted in Mary Elizabeth Sluga's masters thesis, Pages 87-88.

_____. If I can get New Mexico a state ... my property will be doubled in value." Letter to Richard C. Kerens. **February 3, 1894.** Quoted by Victor Westphall, *Thomas Benton Catron and His Era.* Page 312.

Mills, Melvin W. "There are a few men who are candidates [for Senator] that I guess have some money ..." Letter to Thomas Benton Catron. **September 12, 1911.** Catron Papers 103, Box 37. Quoted by Victor Westphall, *Thomas Benton Catron and His Era.* Page 350. (**Revealing possible bribery for legislators' vote**)

Cutting, Bronson. "Catron was the boss of the Territory ..." Letter to James Roger Addison. **December 11, 1911.** Cited by Victor Westphall in *Thomas Benton Catron and His Era,* Page 98, from his citation: Lincoln County Manuscripts Division. Box 12. Courtesy of David Stratton.

Catron, Charles C. "My father probably spent over a million dollars in following up his hobby [of politics]." Letter to Major Harry F. Cameron. **June 3, 1921.** Catron Papers 101, Box 29. Quoted by Victor Westphall, *Thomas Benton Catron and His Era.* Page 387. (**Revealing possible political bribery**)

FEDERAL INDICTMENT OF BILLY BONNEY AND REGULATORS BY

Catron, Thomas Benton. "Case No. 411. The United States vs. Charles Bowdry [Bowdre], Doc Scurlock, Henry Brown, Henry Antrim alias "Kid," John Middleton, Stephen Stevens, John Scroggins, George Coe and Frederick Waite." **June 21, 1878.** Herman B. Weisner Papers, ca. 1957-1992. New Mexico State University Library at Las Cruces. Rio Grande Historical Collections. Accession No. Ms 0249. Box 1. Folder B-4. Folder Name: Andrew Roberts Indictment. (**Federal murder indictment of Billy Bonney by U.S. Attorney T.B. Catron; made a**

Territorial pardon impossible until quashed on March 30, 1881 by the District Court in Mesilla.)

OWNERSHIP FILING ON CARRIZOZO CATTLE COMPANY

Catron, Thomas Benton.. Statement of Sole ownership of Carrizozo Ranch in Tax Dispute Case. No date. Herman B. Weisner Papers, ca. 1957-1992. New Mexico State University Library at Las Cruces. Rio Grande Historical Collections. Accession No. Ms 0249. Box. 2. Folder C-8. Folder Name "T.B. Catron Tax Troubles."

ARTICLES ABOUT AND BY (CHRONOLOGICAL)

Morley, William Raymond and Frank Springer. On Oscar McMains's citizen's Meeting. *Cimarron News and Press.* **November 10, 1875. (Colfax County citizens meeting on F.J. Tolby murder by Santa Fe Ring.)**

_____. " 'The Territory of Elkins.' Assassination of Supposed Sun Correspondent. The Murder of the Rev. F.J. Tolby in New Mexico. A Probate Judge Accused of Complicity in the Crime. Indignation Meeting." *New York Weekly Sun.* **December 22, 1875.** Interior Department Papers 1850-1907; Appointments Division and Subsequent Actions. Microfilm Roll M750. National Archives and Records Administration. Record Group 48. Microfilm Case File Number 44-4-8-3. U.S. Department of Interior. Washington, D. C.(**Submitted on May 1, 1877 to President Rutherford B. Hayes by Mary McPherson and W.B. Matchett**)

Lambert, J.J. "At It Again." Pueblo, Colorado, *Enterprise and Chronicle.* **April 21, 1877.** Interior Department Papers 1850-1907; Appointments Division and Subsequent Actions. Microfilm File Case Number 44-4-8-3. Record Group 48. Microfilm No. M750. Roll 1. National Archives and Records Administration. U.S. Department of Justice. Washington, D.C. (**About Ring control of courts and malicious prosecution of opponents and Franklin Tolby murder**)

Tunstall, John Henry. "A Taxpayer's Complaint ... January 18, 1878." Mesilla *Independent.* **January 26, 1878. (Exposé of William Brady, James Dolan, and John Riley for tax fraud and use of public money to purchase cattle; and Catron then paid that bill)**

Dolan, James J. "Answer to A Taxpayer's Complaint." Mesilla *Independent.* **January 29, 1878. (Response to J.H. Tunstall's exposé)**

No Author. "White Cap's Proclamation." *Las Vegas Optic.* **March 12, 1880. (Manifesto against land-grabbing Catron and the Ring)**

No Author. Las Cruces *Thirty-Four Newspaper.* **October 27, 1880. (Urging voters to overthrow Catron's Santa Fe Ring-backed candidate)**

No Author. *Albuquerque Daily Democrat.* **March 4, 1884. (Time is past for Ring herding men)**

No Author. *Santa Fe Weekly New Mexican Review.* **March 13, 1884.** *Santa Fe Weekly New Mexican Review.* **(Accusation of Catron and the Ring of controlling grand juries and** bribery)

No Author. *Albuquerque Daily Democrat.* **March 15, 1884. (Oscar P. McMains "Memorial" against land-grabbing Ring)**

No Author. *Las Vegas Optic.* **September 2, 1884. (About the anti-Ring Legislature revolt and Catron's alliance with corrupt Judge Joseph Palen)**

Chavez, No First Name. *Santa Fe Weekly New Mexican.* **March 8, 1894. (Open letter from mother of Francisco Chavez implicating Catron in his murder)** Cited by Victor Westphall, *Thomas Benton Catron and His Era.* Page 226.

No author. *Las Vegas Independent Democrat.* ___ 1895; based on *Las Vegas Optic.* September 2, 1884. (**About disbarring Catron**)

Catron, Thomas Benton (As "Anonymous"). "Is it honesty or partisanship?" Letter to the Editor, Thomas Hughes. *Albuquerque Daily Citizen.* **October 9, 1895. (Defamation of his disbarment Judge Thomas J. Smith**) Cited by Victor

Westphall, *Thomas Benton Catron and His Era.* Page 246. Thomas B. Catron Papers. University of New Mexico Center for Southwest Studies. University Library. MSS 29 BC.

_____. Published letter to the Editor, Thomas Hughes. *Albuquerque Daily Citizen.* **October 10, 1895. (Pretended response to his own anonymous letter, given in Editor Thomas Hughes's perjured editorial)** Cited by Victor Westphall, *Thomas Benton Catron and His Era.* Page 248.

No Author. *Las Vegas Daily Optic* . **September 30, 1896. (Stating Catron had been an incompetent Delegate to Congress)**

Catron, Thomas Benton (As "Anonymous"). *Albuquerque Daily Citizen.* **September 11, 1896. ("Poker Bill" defamatory attack on Governor William Thornton)**

Thornton, William T. *Santa Fe Daily New Mexican.* **September 11, 1896. (Exposing Catron's "Poker Bill" plot)**

No Author. *Los Angeles Times.* **1899.** Undated clipping, Laughlin Papers, State Records Center, Santa Fe, New Mexico. Quoted by Victor Westphall, *Thomas Benton Catron and His Era.* Page 285. **(Joking article about the Santa Fe Ring)**

Johnson, E. Dana. "Editorial." *Santa Fe New Mexican.* **May 16, 1921.** Catron Papers 801, Box 1. Quoted by Victor Westphall, *Thomas Benton Catron and His Era.* Pages 394-395. **(Catron as "boss")**

EXPOSÉS OF (CHRONOLOGICAL)

Mills, Melvin W. "Thought I would write you how things are running." Letter to Robert H. Longwill. **December 5, 1873.** "Exhibit A" in the August 9, 1878 deposition of Frank Springer to Investigator Frank Warner Angel. Frank Warner Angel report titled *In the Matter of the Investigation of the Charges Against S.B. Axtell Governor of New Mexico.* October 3, 1878. Interior Department Papers 1850-1907; Appointments Division and Subsequent Actions. Microfilm Case File No. 44-4-8-3. Record Group 48. Microfilm Roll M750. National Archives and Records Administration. U.S. Department of Interior. Washington, D.C. **(About Catron and Ring empowerment)**

Morley, William Raymond and Frank Springer. On Oscar McMains's citizen's Meeting. *Cimarron News and Press.* **November 10, 1875.** In Mary McPherson, Letters and Petitions to President Rutherford B. Hayes re: Removal Governor Axtell and the Santa Fe Ring. 1977. Interior Department Papers 1850-1907; Appointments Division and Subsequent Actions. Microfilm File Case Number 44-4-8-3. Record Group 48. Microfilm Roll M750. National Archives and Records Administration. **(Colfax County citizens meeting on F.J. Tolby murder by Santa Fe Ring.)**

_____. " 'The Territory of Elkins.' Assassination of Supposed Sun Correspondent. The Murder of the Rev. F.J. Tolby in New Mexico. A Probate Judge Accused of Complicity in the Crime. Indignation Meeting." *New York Weekly Sun.* **December 22, 1875.** Interior Department Papers 1850-1907; Appointments Division and Subsequent Actions. Microfilm Roll M750. National Archives and Records Administration. Record Group 48. Microfilm Case File Number 44-4-8-3. U.S. Department of Interior. Washington, D. C.(**In May 1, 1877 submission to President Hayes as "Mary E. McPherson and W.B. Matchett 'Make certain charges against the U.S. Officials in the Territory of New Mexico.' "**)

Middaugh, Asa F. Deposition. **March 31, 1876.** "Exhibit B" in the August 9, 1878 deposition of Frank Springer to Investigator Frank Warner Angel. Frank Warner Angel report titled *In the Matter of the Investigation of the Charges Against S.B. Axtell Governor of New Mexico.* October 3, 1878. Interior Department Papers 1850-1907; Appointments Division and Subsequent Actions. Microfilm Case File No. 44-4-8-3. Record Group 48. Microfilm Roll M750. National Archives and Records Administration. U.S. Department of Interior. Washington, D.C. **(About Catron's malicious prosecution of Ada McPherson Morley)**

McPherson, Mary. "Charges against Thomas B. Catron, U.S. Attorney, and Others." **February 7, 1877.** Letter to Attorney General Alphonso Taft. Interior Department Papers 1850-1907; Appointments Division and Subsequent Actions. Microfilm File Case Number 44-4-8-3. Record Group 48. Microfilm Roll M750. National Archives and Records Administration. U.S. Department of Justice. Washington, D.C.

Catron, Thomas Benton. "Answering Charges of Mary E. McPherson." **February 24, 1877.** Letter to Attorney General Alphonso Taft. Interior Department Papers 1850-1907; Appointments Division and Subsequent Actions. Microfilm File Case Number 44-4-8-3. Record Group 48. Microfilm Roll M750. National Archives and Records Administration. U.S. Department of Justice. Washington, D.C.

Morley William Raymond. "I was astonished beyond measure at your proceedings, and have fears as to the result ..." Letter to Mary McPherson. **March 6, 1877.** McPherson, Mary E. Letters and Petitions to President Rutherford B. Hayes re: Removal Governor Axtell and the Santa Fe Ring. Interior Department Papers 1850-1907; Appointments Division and Subsequent Actions. Microfilm File Case Number 44-4-8-3. Record Group 48. Microfilm Roll M750. National Archives and Records Administration. U.S. Department of Justice. Washington, D. C. (**Hopes she can help fight against Santa Fe Ring; enclosed in Mary McPherson's "Charges Against U.S. Officials in the Territory of New Mexico."**)

Lambert, J.J. "At It Again." Pueblo, Colorado, *Enterprise and Chronicle*. **April 21, 1877.** Interior Department Papers 1850-1907; Appointments Division and Subsequent Actions. Microfilm File Case Number 44-4-8-3. Record Group 48. Microfilm No. M750. Roll 1. National Archives and Records Administration. U.S. Department of Justice. Washington, D.C. (**Description of Santa Fe Ring control of courts and malicious prosecution of opponents like Oscar McMains in the Franklin Tolby murder; used in: "W.B. Matchett and Mary E. McPherson 'Make Certain Charges Against the U.S. Officials in the Territory of New Mexico.' " Letter to President Rutherford B. Hayes. Received and filed May 1, 1877. Interior Department Papers 1850-1907; Appointments Division and Subsequent Actions. Microfilm File Case Number 44-4-8-3. Record Group 48. Microfilm No. M750. Roll 1. National Archives and Records Administration. U. S. Department of Justice. Washington, D.C.**)

Matchett, W.B. and Mary E. McPherson. "W.B. Matchett and Mary E. McPherson 'Make Certain Charges Against the U.S. Officials in the Territory of New Mexico, Together With Corroboration Evidence.' " Letter to President Rutherford B. Hayes. Received and filed **May 1, 1877.** Interior Department Papers 1850-1907; Appointments Division and Subsequent Actions. Microfilm File Case Number 44-4-8-3. Record Group 48. Microfilm No. M750. Roll 1. National Archives and Records Administration. U. S. Department of Justice. Washington, D.C.

McPherson, Mary and W.B. Matchett. "To The President. Please make the enclosed a part of the evidence in the case of "Charges Against New Mexican Officials" Letter to President Rutherford B. Hayes. **May 3, 1877.** McPherson, Mary E. Letters and Petitions to President Rutherford B. Hayes re: Removal Governor Axtell and the Santa Fe Ring. Interior Department Papers 1850-1907; Appointments Division and Subsequent Actions. Microfilm File Case Number 44-4-8-3. Record Group 48. Microfilm Roll M750. National Archives and Records Administration. U.S. Department of Justice. Washington, D. C. (**Addendum to their May, 1877 "Certain Charges Against U.S. Officials in New Mexico Territory."**)

McPherson, Mary and W.B. Matchett. "The Secretary of the Interior, Sir - Accompanying please find copy of charges, &c., against S.B. Axtell, Governor and other New Mexico Officials ..." "Charges Against New Mexican Officials." Letter to Secretary of the Interior Carl Schurz. **May 5, 1877.** McPherson, Mary E. Letters and Petitions to President Rutherford B. Hayes re: Removal Governor Axtell and the Santa Fe Ring. Interior Department Papers 1850-1907;

Appointments Division and Subsequent Actions. Microfilm File Case Number 44-4-8-3. Record Group 48. Microfilm Roll M750. National Archives and Records Administration. U.S. Department of Justice. Washington, D. C.

McPherson, Mary and W.B. Matchett. "We have respectfully to request that the following named records, documents, papers, communications and correspondence be supplied ..." Records Request to Secretary of the Interior Carl Schurz. **July 26, 1877.** Interior Department Papers 1850-1907; Appointments Division and Subsequent Actions. Microfilm File Case Number 44-4-8-3. Record Group 48. Microfilm No. M750. Roll 1. National Archives and Records Administration. U. S. Department of Justice. Washington, D.C. (**Requesting records of the Santa Fe Ring, Catron, Elkins, and Axtell**)

McPherson, Mary. "Please place before the Attorney General ..." Letter to President Rutherford B. Hayes. **August 23, 1877.** Interior Department Papers 1850-1907; Appointments Division and Subsequent Actions. Microfilm File Case Number 44-4-8-3. Record Group 48. Microfilm No. M750. Roll 1. National Archives and Records Administration. U. S. Department of Justice. Washington, D.C. (**Requesting that her "Charges" go to the Attorney General.**)

McPherson, Mary and W.B. Matchett. *"In the Matter of Charges vs. Gov. S.B. Axtell and Other New Mexico Officials. Submitted to the Departments of the Interior and Justice.* **August, 1877.** Printed as a 31 page booklet. No publisher listed. Indiana Historical Society. Lew Wallace Collection. M0292. Box 3. Folder 20.

McPherson, Mary. "I desire to know when I can be heard ..." Letter to Secretary of Interior Carl Schurz. **September 30, 1977.** Interior Department Papers 1850-1907; Appointments Division and Subsequent Actions. Microfilm File Case Number 44-4-8-3. Record Group 48. Microfilm No. M750. Roll 1. National Archives and Records Administration. U. S. Department of Justice. Washington, D.C.

Tunstall, John Henry. "A Taxpayer's Complaint ... January 18, 1878." Mesilla *Independent.* January 26, 1878. (**Exposé of William Brady, James Dolan, and John Riley for tax fraud and use of public money to purchase cattle; and Catron then paid that bill**)

Dolan, James J. "Answer to A Taxpayer's Complaint." Mesilla *Independent.* January 29, 1878. (**Response to J.H. Tunstall's exposé**)

Springer, Frank. Deposition to Investigator Frank Warner Angel. **August 9, 1878.** Frank Warner Angel report titled *In the Matter of the Investigation of the Charges Against S.B. Axtell Governor of New Mexico.* October 3, 1878. Interior Department Papers 1850-1907; Appointments Division and Subsequent Actions. Microfilm Case File No. 44-4-8-3. Record Group 48. Microfilm Roll M750. National Archives and Records Administration. U.S. Department of Interior. Washington, D.C. (**Mentions Catron, Elkins, and the Santa Fe Ring, and provided Exhibits of letters exposing Catron's evil.**)

Morley, William Raymond. "Your letter of the 7th came last night and it was a good long newsy letter ..." Letter to wife, Ada McPherson Morley. **August 15, 1878.** Collection of Norman Cleaveland. Quoted in Norman Cleaveland, *The Morleys: Young Upstarts in the Southwest.* Albuquerque, New Mexico: Calvin Horn Publisher, Inc. 1971. Pages 152-155. (**About possible cover-up by Angel's reports; about the Santa Fe Ring, T.B. Catron, S.B. Elkins, S.B. Axtell, and Henry Waldo; and the Lincoln County War**)

No Author. "The Santa Fe Ring is the most corrupt combination that ever cursed any country or community." Las Cruces *Thirty-Four Newspaper.* **October 27, 1880.** From Victor Westphall, *Thomas Benton Catron and His Era.* Page 186. (**Article summarizing Ring abuses in urging voters to oppose Ring candidates**)

No Author. "The Ring must soon discover that the time has passed in New Mexico when men can be herded like so many sheep ..." *Albuquerque Daily Democrat.* **March 4, 1884.** Quoted by Victor Westphall, *Thomas Benton Catron and His Era.* Page 191. (**About Santa Fe Ring control of appointments to legislature**)

Thornton, W.T. "Your favors received. We will try and have the matter of Mrs. Wilson's estate at Albuquerque attended to for your Bates County friends." Letter to John J. Cockrell, Esq. **January 16, 1886.** Herman B. Weisner Papers, ca. 1957-1992. New Mexico State University Library at Las Cruces. Rio Grande Historical Collections. Accession No. Ms 0249. Box 12. Folder S-5. Folder Name "Catron, Thornton, & Clancy Letterhead." (**T.B. Catron's law partner discloses Ring planned malicious prosecution in Lincoln County**)

No author. "T.B. Catron's reputation now being "smirched" by evidence that he was a briber and too dishonest even to practice law ..." *Las Vegas Independent Democrat*. ? month, ? day, **1895**; based on *Las Vegas Optic*. September 2, 1884. From Victor Westphall. *Thomas Benton Catron and His Era*. Pages 105-106. (**About disbarring Catron from law practice in New Mexico**)

Hamilton, Humphrey. *Majority Opinion* in disbarment case against Thomas Benton Catron. "[T]he low moral character and poor reputation for veracity of the prosecution witnesses rendered their testimony beyond belief." **October 25, 1895.** Catron Papers. 801. Box 1. Quoted by Victor Westphall, *Thomas Benton Catron and His Era*. Page 251. (**Ring colluding judge vindicating Catron from disbarment by discrediting prosecution evidence**)

Catron, Thomas Benton. "Poker Bill" is now engaged in playing a game in which the lives of four men are at stake ..." *Albuquerque Daily Citizen*. **September 11, 1896.** Reprinted September 11, 1896 in the *Santa Fe Daily New Mexican*. Quoted by Victor Westphall, *Thomas Benton Catron and His Era*. Page 262. (**Catron's anonymous defamatory letter about past partner, William Thornton**)

Thornton, William T. "This communication to the *Citizen* was prepared in your office, and at your dictation." *Santa Fe Daily New Mexican*. **September 11, 1896.** Reprinting and debunking T.B. Catron's anonymous letter of September 11, 1896 to the *Albuquerque Daily Citizen* of September 11, 1896. Quoted by Victor Westphall, *Thomas Benton Catron and His Era*. Page 262. (**Thornton confronts Catron's anonymous defamatory letter about him**)

Wallace, Lew. "I have your several letters, including the last one of the 3rd inst." Letter to Eugene Fiske. **November 6, 1897.** Indiana Historical Society. Lew Wallace Collection. AC233. Box 1. Folder 7. (part of 1981 addition) (**About T.B. Catron's control over New Mexicans**)

Johnson, E. Dana. "[H]e ruled with a rod of iron ..." Editorial. *Santa Fe New Mexican*. **May 16, 1921.** Catron Papers 801, Box 1. Quoted by Victor Westphall, *Thomas Benton Catron and His Era*. Pages 394-395. (**Santa Fe Ring tactics of "boss" Catron without using the words Santa Fe Ring**)

Pritchard, George W. "Eulogy." **May 17, 1921.** Catron Papers 801, Box 1. Quoted by Victor Westphall, *Thomas Benton Catron and His Era*. Pages 393-394.

Mabry, Thomas Jewett. "New Mexico's Constitution in the Making." *New Mexico Historical Review*. **1943.** Volume 19, Issue 170. Quoted by Victor Westphall, *Thomas Benton Catron and His Era*. Page 341. (**Revealing that future Governor Mabry was Ring-biased, calling T.B. Catron an "able delegate" to New Mexico's 1912 constitutional convention**)

SEE ALSO: Stephen Benton Elkins; Santa Fe Ring

CAYPLESS, EDGAR

Keleher, William A. *Violence in Lincoln County 1869-1881*. Albuquerque, New Mexico: University of New Mexico Press. 1957. (**Pages 320-321, the lost William Bonney letter of April 15, 1881 to Attorney Edgar Caypless is presented crediting the original letter to the Billy the Kid Museum in Mesilla as published by its founder, George Griggs, in *History of the Mesilla Valley*. On page 320 is also the *La Vegas Gazette* article of March 12, 1881 about Billy's replevin case with Caypless for his mare.**)

CHAPMAN, HUSTON
CONTEMPORARY SOURCES (CHRONOLOGICAL)

Wallace, Lew. "I enclose you a copy of a letter from Las Vegas ..." Letter to Edward Hatch. **October 28, 1878**. Indiana Historical Society. Lew Wallace Collection. M0292. Box 3. Folder 16. (**Forwards Chapman's letter to Hatch**)

_____. "In a communication, dated October 28. inst., I requested, for reasons stated, a safe-guard for Mrs. McSween ..." Letter to Edward Hatch. **November 9, 1878**. Indiana Historical Society. Lew Wallace Collection. M0292. Box 3. Folder 17.

No Author. (signed E.). "DEATH OF CHAPMAN. The people of Las Vegas were greatly shocked on Sunday last to hear of the cold blooded murder, in Lincoln County ..." *Las Vegas Gazette*. **March 1, 1879**. From *Proceedings of a Court of Inquiry in the Case of Lt. Col. N.A.M. Dudley (May 2,1879 – July 5, 1879)*. File No. QQ1284. (Boxes 3304, 3305, 3305A); Court Martial Files 1809-1894. Records of the Office of the Judge Advocate General – Army. Record Group 153. Old Military and Civil Branch. National Archives and Records Administration. Washington, D. C.

No Author. "Wallace and Lincoln County." Grant County *Herald*. **March 1, 1879**. Indiana Historical Society. The Papers of Lew and Susan Wallace. Microfilm Edition. Indianapolis, Indiana: Indiana Historical Society Press. 2008. (**Ridicule about Huston Chapman's murder**)

Chapman, W.W. "Yours of the 1st inst. came ..." Letter to Ira E. Leonard. **March 20, 1879**. Indiana Historical Society. Lew Wallace Collection. M0292. Box 4. Folder 6.

Rynerson, William. "The Grand Jurors for the Territory of New Mexico taken from the body of the good and lawful men of the County of Lincoln ..." Indictments of the April, Lincoln County Grand Jury. **April 28, 1879**. Herman B. Weisner Papers, ca. 1957-1992. New Mexico State University Library at Las Cruces. Rio Grande Historical Collection. Accession No. Ms 0249. Box 4/39. Folder E-Z. Folder Name: "Jessie Evans Accessory to Murder." (**Billy's testimony indicts J.J. Dolan, Billy Campbell, and Jessie Evans fulfilling his pardon bargain**)

Chapman, W.W. "Since receiving yours of the 1st March ..." Letter to Ira Leonard. **May 8, 1879**. Indiana Historical Society. Lew Wallace Collection. M0292. Box 4. Folder 10.

LETTERS

Chapman, Huston I. "You will please pardon me for presuming so much upon your kindness ..." Letter to Lew Wallace. **October 24, 1878**. Indiana Historical Society. Lew Wallace Collection. M0292. Box 3. Folder 16. (**Makes clear N.A.M. Dudley's danger to Susan McSween**)

_____. 'You attach much importance to the awe-inspiring influence of the military ..." Letter to Lew Wallace. **November 25, 1878**. From Frederick Nolan, *The Lincoln County War*, p. 359.

_____. "You must pardon me for so often presuming upon your kindness ..." Letter to Lew Wallace. **November 29, 1878**. Indiana Historical Society. Lew Wallace Collection. M0292. Box 3. Folder 18.

CHISUM, JOHN SIMPSON

Hinton, Harwood P., Jr. "John Simpson Chisum, 1877-84." *New Mexico Historical Review* 31(3) (July 1956): 177 - 205; 31(4) (October 1956): 310 - 337; 32(1) (January 1957): 53 - 65.

Klasner, Lilly. Eve Ball. Ed. *My Girlhood Among Outlaws*. Tucson, Arizona: The University of Arizona Press. 1988.

COE FAMILY

BIOGRAPHICAL SOURCES

Coe, George. Doyce B. Nunis, Jr. Ed. *Frontier Fighter. The Autobiography of George Coe Who Fought and Rode With Billy the Kid.* Chicago: R. R. Donnelley and Sons Company. 1984.

Coe, Wilbur. *Ranch on the Ruidoso. The Story of a Pioneer Family in New Mexico, 1871 - 1968.* New York: Alfred A. Knopf. 1968.

CONTEMPORARY SOURCE

Coe, George. "We are two residents of Lincoln County ..." Letter written with Isaac Ellis to President Rutherford B. Hayes. **June 22, 1878.** In Angel Report papers. Microfilm File Case Number 44-4-8-3. Record Group 48. Microfilm No. M750. Roll 1. National Archives and Records Administration. U.S. Department of Justice. Washington, D.C.

DEDRICK BROTHERS

BIOGRAPHICAL SOURCES

Upham, Elizabeth. (Related by marriage to Daniel Dedrick). Personal interviews. 1998.
Upham, Marquita. (Relative by marriage to Daniel Dedrick). Personal interview. 1998.

CONTEMPORARY SOURCES (CHRONOLOGICAL)

Dedrick, Dan. "I have been under an arrest for six days ..." **April 5, 1879.** Letter to Lew Wallace. Indiana Historical Society. Lew Wallace Collection. M0292. Box 4. Folder 8. **(Says he was not told his arrest charges)**

No Author. "Arrests of Dedricks. Legal Documents." Herman B. Weisner Papers, ca. 1957-1992. New Mexico State University Library at Las Cruces. Rio Grande Historical Collections. Accession No. Ms 0249. Box 1. Folder B-8. Folder Name: "Lincoln County Bonds."

DOLAN, JAMES J.

CONTEMPORARY SOURCES (CHRONOLOGICAL)

Tunstall, John Henry. "A Taxpayer's Complaint ... January 18, 1878." Mesilla *Independent.* **January 26, 1878. (Exposé of William Brady, James Dolan, and John Riley for tax fraud and use of public money to purchase cattle; and T.B. Catron then paid that bill)**

Dolan, James J. "Answer to A Taxpayer's Complaint." Mesilla *Independent.* **January 29, 1878. (Response to J.H. Tunstall's exposé of him, William Brady, and John Riley for tax fraud and use of public money to purchase cattle; and T.B. Catron then paid that bill)**

McSween, Alexander. "It looks as though the agent were the property of J.J. Dolan & J.H. Riley, known here as Dolan & Co." Letter to Secretary of Interior Carl Schurz. **February 11, 1878.** From Frederick Nolan. *The Life and Death of John Henry Tunstall.* Albuquerque, New Mexico: The University of New Mexico Press. 1965. Page 266.

Rynerson, William. "Friends Riley & Dolan, Lincoln N.M. I have just received letters from you mailed 10th inst." **February 14, 1878.** Letter to James Dolan and John Riley. Copy as Exhibit B in June 6, 1878 deposition of Alexander McSween. Frank Warner Angel report. *In the Matter of the Examination of the Causes and Circumstances of the Death of John H. Tunstall a British Subject.* Report filed October 4, 1878. Frank Warner Angel report. Interior Department Papers 1850-1907; Appointments Division and Subsequent Actions. Microfilm File Case

Number 44-4-8-3. Record Group 48. Microfilm No. M750. Roll 1. National Archives and Records Administration. U.S. Department of Justice. Washington, D.C. (James J. Dolan Deposition. June 20, 1878. Pages 235-247.) (**Implying planned killing of J.H. Tunstall**)

Wilson, John, George B. Barker, Robert M. Gilbert, John Newcomb, Samuel Smith, Benjamin Ellis. "We the undersigned Justice of the Peace and Coroners Jury who sat upon the inquest held this 19th day of February 1878 on the body of John H. Tunstall ..." Coroner's Jury Report for John Tunstall. **February 19, 1878.** (**Naming as murderers, among others, James Dolan, Frank Baker, Jessie Evans, William Morton, and George Hindman**)

Dolan, James J. Deposition to Frank Warner Angel. **June 20, 1878.** Frank Warner Angel Report. *In the Matter of the Examination of the Causes and Circumstances of the Death of John H. Tunstall a British Subject.* Pages 235-247. Report filed October 4, 1878. Angel Report. Microfilm File Case Number 44-4-8-3. Record Group 48. Microfilm No. M750. Roll 1. National Archives and Records Administration. U. S. Department of Justice. Washington, D.C.

Dolan, James. "On my arrival at Fort Stanton, I repeated Your Explanation &c to the Comd'g Officer (Gen'l Dudley) ..." Letter to Lew Wallace. **December 31, 1878.** Indiana Historical Society. Lew Wallace Collection. M0292. Box 3. Folder 19.

_____. "Attorney Wilson told me yesterday that 'your life was threatened' ..." Letter to Lew Wallace. **December 31, 1878.** Indiana Historical Society. Lew Wallace Collection. M0292. Box 4. Folder 7.

Wallace, Lew. "J.J. Dolan was down here tonight. Arrest him upon his return ..." Letter to Henry Carroll. **March 10, 1879.** Indiana Historical Society. Lew Wallace Collection. M0292. Box 4. Folder 4.

_____. "I beg to submit to you a list of persons whom it is necessary, in my judgment, to arrest speedily ..." Letter to Henry Carroll. **March 11, 1879.** Indiana Historical Society. Lew Wallace Collection. M0292. Box 4. Folder 5. (**Lists James Dolan, "The Kid" – William Bonney, Jessie Evans, Yginio Salazar**)

_____. "Upon reflection, I am of opinion that if Col. Dudley is really going to Fort Union ..." Letter to Henry Carroll. **March 11, 1879.** Indiana Historical Society. Lew Wallace Collection. M0292. Box 4. Folder 5. (**Advises not to send prisoners Evans, Campbell, Matthews, and Dolan to Fort Union because of N.A.M. Dudley being there**)

Dolan, James. "I hear from reliable authority that it has been reported to you that I was one of a party ..." Letter to Lew Wallace. **March 14, 1879.** Indiana Historical Society. Lew Wallace Collection. M0292. Box 4. Folder 5.

Rynerson, William. "The Grand Jurors for the Territory of New Mexico taken from the body of the good and lawful men of the County of Lincoln ..." Indictments of the April, Lincoln County Grand Jury. **April 28, 1879.** Herman B. Weisner Papers, ca. 1957-1992. New Mexico State University Library at Las Cruces. Rio Grande Historical Collection. Accession No. Weisner MS 249. Box 4/39. Folder E-Z. Folder Name: "Jessie Evans Accessory to Murder." (**Billy Bonney's testimony indicts J.J. Dolan, Billy Campbell, and Jessie Evans for pardon bargain**)

Purlington, George. "The District Court adjourned on Thursday ..." **May 3, 1879.** Indiana Historical Society. Lew Wallace Collection. M0292. Box 4. Folder 10. (**Letter to Adjutant General on indictments of the Murphy-Dolans - including Dolan for the H.I. Chapman murder - and N.A.M. Dudley; copy sent to Lew Wallace**)

Dolan, James. Testimony in Court of Inquiry for Lieutenant Colonel N.A.M. Dudley. **June 5, 1879.** in Court of Inquiry for N.A.M. Dudley. *Proceedings of a Court of Inquiry in the Case of Col. N.A.M. Dudley (May 2, 1879-July 5, 1879).* File Number QQ1284. (Boxes 3304, 3305, 3305A). Court Martial Case Files 1809-1894. Records of the Office of the Judge Advocate General – Army. Record Group 153. National Archives and Records Administration. Old Military and Civil Branch. Washington, D.C.

Wild, Azariah F. "Daily Reports of U. S. Secret Service Agents, Azariah F. Wild." Microfilm T-915. Record Group 87. Rolls 307 (January 1,1878 - June 30, 1879) and 308 (**July 1, 1879 - June 30, 1881**). National Archives and Records Department. Department of the Treasury. United States Secret Service. Washington, D. C. (**Dolan as an informer against "the Kid gang"**)

DUDLEY, NATHAN AUGUSTUS MONROE

BIOGRAPHICAL SOURCES

Heitman, Francis B. *Historical Register and Dictionary of the United States Army, From Its Organization, September 29, 1789, to March 2, 1903*. (Entry for Galusha Pennypacker, Pages 782-7830.) Washington, D.C.: Government Printing Office. 1903.

Kaye, E. Donald. *Nathan Augustus Monroe Dudley: Rogue, Hero, or Both?* Parker, Colorado: Outskirts Press, Inc. 2007.

Oliva, Leo E., *Fort Union and the Frontier Army in the Southwest*. Southwest Cultural Resource Center, Professional Papers No. 41, National Park Service, 1993, Pages 488-489, 550, 574, 624-626, 656-659 are on Dudley. (**Quoted to E. Donald Kaye from the now-lost letter of Amos Kimball: "I guess you heard that Dudley made Colonel. The army bureaucracy is like a giant cesspool, where the biggest chunks rise to the top."**)

MILITARY COURT OF INQUIRY FOR

Leonard, Ira E. "*Charges and specifications against Lieutenant Colonel N.A.M. Dudley, Commander at Fort Stanton, New Mexico.*" **March 4, 1879**. *Proceedings of a Court of Inquiry in the Case of Lt. Col. N.A.M. Dudley (May 2,1879 - July 5, 1879)*. File No. QQ1284. (Boxes 3304, 3305, 3305A); Court Martial Files 1809-1894. Records of the Office of the Judge Advocate General - Army. Record Group 153. Old Military and Civil Branch. National Archives and Records Administration. Washington, D. C.

Dudley, Nathan Augustus Monroe. Testimony in Court of Inquiry. **June 28 and 30, 1879**. *Proceedings of a Court of Inquiry in the Case of Lt. Col. N.A.M. Dudley (May 2,1879 – July 5, 1879)*. File No. QQ1284. (Boxes 3304, 3305, 3305A); Court Martial Files 1809-1894. Records of the Office of the Judge Advocate General – Army. Record Group 153. Old Military and Civil Branch. National Archives and Records Administration. Washington, D. C.

No Author. *Proceedings of a Court of Inquiry in the Case of Lt. Col. N.A.M. Dudley (May 2,1879 – July 5, 1879)*. File No. QQ1284. (Boxes 3304, 3305, 3305A); Court Martial Files 1809-1894. Records of the Office of the Judge Advocate General - Army. Record Group 153. Old Military and Civil Branch. National Archives and Records Administration. Washington, D. C.

OTHER CONTEMPORARY SOURCES (CHRONOLOGICAL)

Dudley, Nathan Augustus Monroe. "I avail myself of the opportunity to send this in advance of the next mail by Mr. Dolan ..." Letter to Assistant Adjutant General of New Mexico. **September 29, 1878**. Indiana Historical Society. Lew Wallace Collection. M0292. Box 3. Folder 14. (**Outlaw propaganda to distract from Ring activity in Lincoln County**)

Loud, John S. "In compliance with instructions of the General Commanding ..." **October 27, 1878**. Letter to N.A.M. Dudley. Indiana Historical Society. Lew Wallace Collection. M0292. Box 3. Folder 16. (**Order for troops to arrest outlaws and seize their stolen property as per the request of the Secretary of War**)

Dudley, Nathan Augustus Monroe. "I am in receipt of a copy of letter written by one H.I. Chapman, calling himself the Attorney ..." **November 9, 1878**. Letter to Lew

Wallace. From *Proceedings of a Court of Inquiry in the Case of Lt. Col. N.A.M. Dudley (May 2,1879 – July 5, 1879)*. File No. QQ1284. (Boxes 3304, 3305, 3305A); Court Martial Files 1809-1894. Records of the Office of the Judge Advocate General – Army. Record Group 153. Old Military and Civil Branch. National Archives and Records Administration. Washington, D.C. (**Forwarding the Susan McSween affidavits in answer to the charges made by Chapman**)

Wallace, Lew. "I am in receipt of Col. Dudley's reply to the charges against him ..." Letter to Edward Hatch. **November 14, 1878**. Indiana Historical Society. Lew Wallace Collection. M0292. Box 3. Folder 17. (**Has quote: "the "reply is perfectly satisfactory"**)

_____. "Your favor containing the duplicate accounts of the messenger who posted the President's Proclamation ..." Letter to N.A.M. Dudley. **November 30, 1878**. Indiana Historical Society. Lew Wallace Collection. M0292. Box 3. Folder 18.

_____. "I am constrained to request that Lieut Col. N.A.M. Dudley, Commanding at Fort Stanton, be relieved ..." Letter to Edward Hatch. **December 7, 1878**. Indiana Historical Society. Lew Wallace Collection. M0292. Box 3. Folder 18. (**Removal of Dudley requested**)

Dudley, Nathan Augustus Monroe. "An Open Letter, By Lieut. Col. N.A.M. Dudley, 9th Cavalry, to His Excellency Governor Lew Wallace." Letter to Lew Wallace. Santa Fe *Weekly New Mexican*. **December 14, 1878**. Reprinted in *Mesilla News*. December 21, 1878. As Exhibit 13 from *Proceedings of a Court of Inquiry in the Case of Lt. Col. N.A.M. Dudley (May 2,1879 – July 5, 1879)*. File No. QQ1284. (Boxes 3304, 3305, 3305A); Court Martial Files 1809-1894. Records of the Office of the Judge Advocate General – Army. Record Group 153. Old Military and Civil Branch. National Archives and Records Administration. Washington, D.C. (**Attacks Wallace's Amnesty Proclamation as applying to the military**)

Wallace, Lew. "The public interests with which I am officially charged make it in my judgment ..." **December 16, 1878**. Letter to N.A.M. Dudley and other Fort Stanton officers. Indiana Historical Society. Lew Wallace Collection. M0292. Box 3. Folder 19.

_____. "I have the honor to report that affairs of the Territory are moving on quietly ..." Letter to Carl Schurz. **December 21, 1878**. Indiana Historical Society. Lew Wallace Collection. M0292. Box 3, Folder 19. (**N.A.M. Dudley's indignation about the Amnesty Proclamation**)

Shield, David. "It is rumored that 'Eight long Affidavits' are in your possession ..." **February 11, 1879**. Letter to Lew Wallace. Indiana Historical Society. Lew Wallace Collection. M0292. Box 4. Folder 2. (**Commander Dudley's defamatory affidavits about Susan McSween**)

Dudley, Nathan Augustus Monroe. "I enclose herewith report of 2nd Lieut. M.F. Goodwin ..." Letter to Acting Assistant Adjutant General at Headquarters. **February 24, 1879**. Indiana Historical Society. Lew Wallace Collection. M0292. Box 4, Folder 3. (**Documents military pursuit of William Bonney**)

Leonard, Ira E. "You are perhaps fully aware of the outrages that have been perpetrated in Lincoln County ..." Letter to Secretary of War George McCrary. **March 4, 1879**. From *Proceedings of a Court of Inquiry in the Case of Lt. Col. N.A.M. Dudley (May 2,1879 – July 5, 1879)*. File No. QQ1284. (Boxes 3304, 3305, 3305A); Court Martial Files 1809-1894. Records of the Office of the Judge Advocate General – Army. Record Group 153. Old Military and Civil Branch. National Archives and Records Administration. Washington, D.C. (**Accusing N.A.M. Dudley of murders of A.A. McSween and H.I. Chapman and arson of McSween house**)

Wallace, Lew. "I have the honor to repeat the request made on a former occasion that Lt. Col. N.A.M. Dudley be relieved of the command ..." Letter to Edward Hatch. **March 7, 1879**. Indiana Historical Society. Lew Wallace Collection. M0292. Box 4, Folder 4.

Hatch, Edward. "Lieutenant Colonel N.A.M. Dudley is hereby relieved from command and duty ..." Special Field Order 2. **March 8, 1879**. Indiana Historical Society. Lew Wallace Collection. M0292. Box 4, Folder 4. **(Wallace succeeds in removing Dudley)**

_____. "Col. Dudley has received his order and disobeys the order ..." **March 11, 1879**. Indiana Historical Society. Lew Wallace Collection. M0292. Box 4, Folder 5.

Wallace, Lew. "I have official information that a court of inquiry for Col. Dudley has been ordered ..." Letter to Carl Schurz. **April 4, 1879**. Indiana Historical Society. Lew Wallace Collection. M0292. Box 4. Folder 8.

Purlington, George. "The District Court adjourned on Thursday ..." **May 3, 1879**. Indiana Historical Society. Lew Wallace Collection. M0292. Box 4. Folder 10. **(Letter to Adjutant General on indictments of the Murphy-Dolans and N.A.M. Dudley; copy sent to Lew Wallace)**

Waldo, Henry. "Nothing has been accomplished in the least that connects Col. Dudley with anything which transpired in the town of Lincoln on the occasion of his presence there on the 19th..." Closing argument for Dudley Court of Inquiry. **July 5, 1879**. *Proceedings of a Court of Inquiry in the Case of Lt. Col. N.A.M. Dudley (May 2,1879 – July 5, 1879)*. File No. QQ1284. (Boxes 3304, 3305, 3305A); Court Martial Files 1809-1894. Records of the Office of the Judge Advocate General – Army. Record Group 153. Old Military and Civil Branch. National Archives and Records Administration. Washington, D. C.

No Author. Verdict on Civil Cause 298 for arson of Susan McSween's house. *Mesilla News*. **December 6, 1879**. Unpublished. personal communication from Frederick Nolan. July 29, 2005. **(Dudley exonerated)**

ELKINS, STEPHEN BENTON

BIOGRAPHICAL SOURCES

Cleaveland, Norman, *A Synopsis of the Great New Mexico Cover-up*. Self-printed. 1989.

_____. *The Great Santa Fe Cover-up. Based on a Talk given Before the Santa Fe Historical Society on November 1, 1978*. Self-printed. 1982.

_____. *The Morleys - Young Upstarts on the Southwest Frontier*. Albuquerque, New Mexico: Calvin Horn Publisher, Inc. 1971.

Lamar, Howard Robert N. *The Far Southwest 1846 – 1912: A Territorial History*. New Haven and London: Yale University Press. 1966. **(Chapter 6 on Santa Fe Ring)**

Lambert, Oscar Doane. *Stephen Benton Elkins. American Foursquare*. Pittsburgh, Pennsylvania: University of Pittsburg Press. 1955.

Montoya, María E. *Translating Property. The Maxwell Land Grant and the Conflict Over Land in the American West, 1840-1900*. Berkeley and Los Angeles: University of California Press. 2002.

Taylor, Morris F. *O.P. McMains and the Maxwell Land Grant Conflict*. Tucson, Arizona: The University of Arizona Press. 1979. **(Traces origins of the Santa Fe Ring with T.B. Catron and S.B. Elkins)**

Westphall, Victor. *Thomas Benton Catron and His Era*. Tucson, Arizona: University of Arizona Press. 1973.

LETTERS FROM, TO, ABOUT (CHRONOLOGICAL)

Morley William Raymond. "I was astonished beyond measure at your proceedings, and have fears as to the result ..." Letter to Mary McPherson. **March 6, 1877**.

McPherson, Mary E. Letters and Petitions to President Rutherford B. Hayes re: Removal Governor Axtell and the Santa Fe Ring. Interior Department Papers 1850-1907; Appointments Division and Subsequent Actions. Microfilm File Case Number 44-4-8-3. Record Group 48. Microfilm Roll M750. National Archives and Records Administration. U.S. Department of Justice. Washington, D. C. **(Hopes** she can help fight against Santa Fe Ring; enclosed in Mary McPherson's "**Charges Against U.S. Officials in the Territory of New Mexico.**")

Elkins, Stephen B. "I trouble you to say a word in behalf of Gov. Axtell ..." Letter to President Rutherford B. Hayes. **June 11, 1877.** (Referred by direction of President to the Secretary of the Interior June 13, 1877.) Interior Department Papers 1850-1907; Appointments Division and Subsequent Actions. Microfilm File Case No. 44-4-8-3. Record Group 48. National Records and Archives Administration. Microfilm No. M750. Roll 1. U.S. Department of Justice. Washington, D. C.

McPherson, Mary. "Please place before the Attorney General ..." Letter to President Rutherford B. Hayes. **August 23, 1877.** Interior Department Papers 1850-1907; Appointments Division and Subsequent Actions. Microfilm File Case Number 44-4-8-3. Record Group 48. Microfilm No. M750. Roll 1. National Archives and Records Administration. U.S. Department of Justice. Washington, D.C. (**Requesting that her "Charges vs. New Mexico Officials" go to the Attorney General.**)

Morley, William Raymond. "Your letter of the 7th came last night and it was a good long newsy letter ..." Letter to wife, Ada McPherson Morley. **August 15, 1878.** Collection of Norman Cleaveland. Quoted in Norman Cleaveland, *The Morleys: Young Upstarts in the Southwest*. Albuquerque, New Mexico: Calvin Horn Publisher, Inc. 1971. Pages 152-155. (**About possible betrayal by Angel's reports; about the Santa Fe Ring, T.B. Catron, S.B. Elkins, S.B. Axtell, and Henry Waldo; and the Lincoln County War**)

Elkins, Stephen B. "Asking delay of action upon charges against U.S. Atty. Catron ..." **September 24, 1878.** Angel Report. Microfilm File Case No. 44-4-8-3. Record Group 48. National Records and Archives Administration. Microfilm No. M750. Roll 1. U.S. Department of Justice. Washington, D. C.

_____. "Regarding Attorney General's decision on T.B. Catron." Letter. **September___, 1878.** Angel Report. Microfilm File Case No. 44-4-8-3. Record Group 48. National Records and Archives Administration. Microfilm No. M750. Roll 1. U.S. Department of Justice. Washington, D.C.

_____. "Relative to resignation of T. B. Catron U. S. Attorney." Letter. **November 10, 1878.** Angel Report. Microfilm File Case No. 44-4-8-3. Record Group 48. National Records and Archives Administration. Microfilm No. M750. Roll 1. U.S. Department of Justice. Washington, D. C.

Devens, Charles. "To honorable S. B. Elkins re. T. B. Catron continuing to act as U.S. Attorney." Letter to Stephen B. Elkins. **November 12, 1878.** Angel Report. Microfilm File Case No. 44-4-8-3. Record Group 48. National Records and Archives Administration. Microfilm No. M750. Roll 1. U.S. Department of Justice. Washington, D. C.

Elkins, Stephen Benton. "I have waited some time to reply to your lengthy letter ..." Letter to T.B. Catron. **August 15, 1879.** West Virginia & Regional History Center. West Virginia University Libraries, Morgantown, W. Va. Stephen B. Elkins Papers (A&M 53). Box 1. Folder 1. (**Reveals he prevented Catron's dismissal and indictment from Angel's report**)

_____. "To the President. Referring to a conversation had with you last week ... Hon S. Elkins favors appointment Axtell, Ex Gov. as Gov'r of New Mexico". Letter to President James Abram Garfield. **March 17, 1881.** (Received Executive Mansion April 6, 1881). Interior Department Papers 1850-1907; Appointments Division and Subsequent Actions. Microfilm Roll M750. National Archives and Records Administration Record Group 48. Microfilm Case Number 44-4-8-3. U.S. Department of Interior. Washington D. C. (**Requesting S.B. Axtell reappointment as Territorial New Mexico Governor**)

Elkins, Stephen Benton. "Mr. Catron's prominence in the capital territory and his leadership ..." Letter to Gideon B. Bantz. **September 9, 1897.** (**Backing Catron**) Quoted in John Paul Wooden's unpublished masters thesis, Page 32.

EXPOSÉS OF (CONTEMPORARY)
COMPLAINT ABOUT TO PRESIDENT RUTHERFORD B. HAYES

Matchett, W.B. and Mary E. McPherson. " W.B. Matchett and Mary E. McPherson 'Make certain charges against the U.S. Officials in the Territory of New Mexico.' " Letter to President Rutherford B. Hayes. Received and filed **May 1, 1877**. Interior Department Papers 1850-1907; Appointments Division and Subsequent Actions. Microfilm File Case Number 44-4-8-3. Record Group 48. Microfilm No. M750. Roll 1. National Archives and Records Administration. U. S. Department of Justice. Washington, D.C. (**Sent to President Rutherford B. Hayes and Secretary of the Interior Carl Schurz 141 pages of letters, affidavits, petitions, newspaper articles, itemized requests for removal of Governor Samuel Beach Axtell and District Judge Warren Bristol, documentation of use of the military against civilians, documentation of the Ring murder of Ring opponent Reverend F.J. Tolby, and identification of the Santa Fe Ring and Elkins and Catron as its leaders.**)

McPherson, Mary and W.B. Matchett. "To the President. Please make the enclosed a part of the evidence in the case of "Charges Against New Mexican Officials" Letter to President Rutherford B. Hayes. **May 3, 1877**. McPherson, Mary E. Letters and Petitions to President Rutherford B. Hayes re: Removal Governor Axtell and the Santa Fe Ring. Interior Department Papers 1850-1907; Appointments Division and Subsequent Actions. Microfilm File Case Number 44-4-8-3. Record Group 48. Microfilm Roll M750. National Archives and Records Administration. U.S. Department of Justice. Washington, D.C. (**Addendum to their May, 1877 "Certain Charges Against U.S. Officials in New Mexico Territory."**)

McPherson, Mary and W.B. Matchett. "The Secretary of the Interior, Sir – Accompanying please find copy of charges, &c., against S.B. Axtell, Governor, and Other New Mexican Officials ..." "Charges Against New Mexican Officials." Letter to Secretary of the Interior Carl Schurz. **May 5, 1877**. McPherson, Mary E. Letters and Petitions to President Rutherford B. Hayes re: Removal Governor Axtell and the Santa Fe Ring. Interior Department Papers 1850-1907; Appointments Division and Subsequent Actions. Microfilm File Case Number 44-4-8-3. Record Group 48. Microfilm Roll M750. National Archives and Records Administration. U.S. Department of Justice. Washington, D. C.

McPherson, Mary. "Please place before the Attorney General ..." Letter to President Rutherford B. Hayes. **August 23, 1877**. Interior Department Papers 1850-1907; Appointments Division and Subsequent Actions. Microfilm File Case Number 44-4-8-3. Record Group 48. Microfilm No. M750. Roll 1. National Archives and Records Administration. U. S. Department of Justice. Washington, D.C. (**Requesting that her "Charges vs. New Mexico Officials" go to the Attorney General.**)

COMPLAINT ABOUT TO DEPARTMENTS OF INTERIOR AND JUSTICE

McPherson, Mary and W.B. Matchett. *"In the Matter of Charges vs. Gov. S.B. Axtell and Other New Mexico Officials. Submitted to the Departments of the Interior and Justice.* **August, 1877**. Printed as a 31 page booklet. No publisher listed. Indiana Historical Society. Lew Wallace Collection. M0292. Box 3. Folder 20. (**About the Santa Fe Ring, Catron, and Elkins; in Lew Wallace's personal possession**)

Springer, Frank. Deposition to Investigator Frank Warner Angel for the Departments of Justice and the Interior. **August 9, 1878**. Frank Warner Angel report titled *In the Matter of the Investigation of the Charges Against S.B. Axtell Governor of New Mexico*. October 3, 1878. Interior Department Papers 1850-1907; Appointments Division and Subsequent Actions. Microfilm Case File No. 44-4-8-3. Record Group 48. Microfilm Roll M750. National Archives and Records Administration. U.S.

Department of Interior. Washington, D.C. (**Mentions Catron, Elkins, and the Santa Fe Ring, and provided Exhibits of letters exposing Catron's evil.**)

PUBLIC RECORDS REQUEST ABOUT

McPherson, Mary and W.B. Matchett. "We have respectfully to request that the following named records, documents, papers, communications and correspondence be supplied ..." Records Request to Secretary of the Interior Carl Schurz. **July 26, 1877**. Interior Department Papers 1850-1907; Appointments Division and Subsequent Actions. Microfilm File Case Number 44-4-8-3. Record Group 48. Microfilm No. M750. Roll 1. National Archives and Records Administration. U. S. Department of Justice. Washington, D.C. (**Requesting records of the Santa Fe Ring, Catron, Elkins, and Axtell**)

ARTICLES ABOUT (CHRONOLOGICAL)

Morley, William Raymond and Frank Springer. On Oscar McMains's citizen's Meeting. *Cimarron News and Press.* **November 10, 1875**. In Mary McPherson, Letters and Petitions to President Rutherford B. Hayes re: Removal Governor Axtell and the Santa Fe Ring. 1977. Interior Department Papers 1850-1907; Appointments Division and Subsequent Actions. Microfilm File Case Number 44-4-8-3. **Record Group 48**. Microfilm Roll M750. National Archives and Records Administration. (**Colfax County citizens meeting on F.J. Tolby murder by Santa Fe Ring.**)

No Author. " 'The Territory of Elkins.' Assassination of Supposed Sun Correspondent. The Murder of the Rev. F.J. Tolby in New Mexico. A Probate Judge Accused of Complicity in the Crime. Indignation Meeting." *New York Weekly Sun.* **December 22, 1875**. Interior Department Papers 1850-1907; Appointments Division and Subsequent Actions. Microfilm Roll M750. National Archives and Records Administration. Record Group 48. Microfilm Case File Number 44-4-8-3. U. S. Department of Interior. Washington, D.C. (**In May 1, 1877 complaint to President Hayes as "Mary E. McPherson and W.B. Matchett 'Make certain charges against the U.S. Officials in the Territory of New Mexico.' "**)

No Author. "Elkins would probably have been Garfield's Secretary of the Interior ..." *New York Sun.* **June 13, 1881**. Quoted by Oscar Doane Lambert. *Stephen Benton Elkins: American Foursquare.* Page 89. (**Political influence of**)

Faulkner, C.J. "I will tell you the secret of Elkins' political as well as business success." Baltimore, Maryland *The Sun.* **December 17, 1891**. Quoted by Oscar Doane Lambert. *Stephen Benton Elkins: American Foursquare.* Page 141. (**Elkins's success from loyalty to friends**)

No Author. "T.B. Catron's reputation now being "smirched" by evidence that he was a briber and too dishonest even to practice law ..." *Las Vegas Independent Democrat.* **1895**; quoting from *Las Vegas Optic.* September 2, 1884. From Victor Westphall. *Thomas Benton Catron and His Era.* Pages 105-106. (**About Catron's and Elkins's dishonesty, the Ring, and disbarring Catron**)

No Author. "He is the biggest man ... the State of West Virginia has ever had in the Senate of the United States." West Virginia *St. Mary's Journal.* **June 22, 1906**. From Oscar Doane Lambert. *Stephen Benton Elkins.* Page 286.

EVANS, JESSIE

BIOGRAPHICAL SOURCES

McCright, Grady E. and James H. Powell. *Jessie Evans: Lincoln County Badman.* College Station, Texas: Creative Publishing Company. 1983.

CONTEMPORARY SOURCES (CHRONOLOGICAL)

Wilson, John, George B. Barker, Robert M. Gilbert, John Newcomb, Samuel Smith, Benjamin Ellis. "We the undersigned Justice of the Peace and Coroners Jury who sat upon the inquest held this 19th day of February 1878 on the body of John H. Tunstall ..." Coroner's Jury Report for John Tunstall. **February 19, 1878**. (**Naming as murderers, among others, James Dolan, Frank Baker, Jessie Evans, William Morton, and George Hindman**)

Wallace, Lew. "I have information that William Campbell, J.B. Matthews, and Jesse Evans were of the party engaged in the killing ..." Letter to Edward Hatch. **March 5, 1879**. Indiana Historical Society. Lew Wallace Collection. M0292. Box 4, Folder 4. (**Murder of Huston Chapman**)

_____. "Under the circumstances, particularly in the absence here of suitable cells for safekeeping of Jesse Evans, Jacob B. Matthews and William Campbell ..." Letter to Henry Carroll. **March 10, 1879**. Indiana Historical Society. Lew Wallace Collection. M0292. Box 4. Folder 4.

_____. "Upon reflection, I am of opinion that if Col. Dudley is really going to Fort Union ..." Letter to Henry Carroll. **March 11, 1879**. Indiana Historical Society. Lew Wallace Collection. M0292. Box 4. Folder 5. (**Advises not to send Evans, Campbell, Matthews, and Dolan to Fort Union because of N.A.M. Dudley being there**)

_____. "I beg to submit to you a list of persons whom it is necessary, in my judgment, to arrest ..." Letter to Henry Carroll. **March 11, 1879**. Indiana Historical Society. Lew Wallace Collection. M0292. Box 4. Folder 5. (**Lists Jessie Evans, "The Kid" – William Bonney, Yginio Salazar**)

_____. "Be good enough to send word to all your men to turn out soon as possible ..." Letter to Juan Patrón. **March 19, 1879**. Indiana Historical Society. Lew Wallace Collection. M0292. Box 4. Folder 6. (**Reports escape of Jessie Evans and Billy Campbell from Fort Stanton; $1000 reward**)

_____. "With Evans and Campbell at large ..." Letter to Henry Carroll. **March 19, 1879**. Indiana Historical Society. Lew Wallace Collection. M0292. Box 4. Folder 6.

Rynerson, William. "Indictments of the April, Lincoln County Grand Jury." **April 28, 1879**. Herman B. Weisner Papers, ca. 1957-1992. New Mexico State University Library at Las Cruces. Rio Grande Historical Society Collection. Accession No. Ms 0249. Box 4/39. Folder E-Z. Folder Name: "Jessie Evans Accessory to Murder." (**Billy's testimony indicts J.J. Dolan, Billy Campbell, and Jessie Evans fulfilling his pardon bargain**)

Purlington, George. "The District Court adjourned on Thursday ..." **May 3, 1879**. Indiana Historical Society. Lew Wallace Collection. M0292. Box 4. Folder 10. (**Letter to Adjutant General on indictments of the Murphy-Dolans - including Evans for the H.I. Chapman murder - and N.A.M. Dudley; copy sent to Lew Wallace**)

No Author. "Charges against Jessie Evans and John Kinney." Doña Ana County Criminal Docket Book. **August 18, 1875 to November 7, 1878**. Herman B. Weisner Papers, ca. 1957-1992. New Mexico State University Library at Las Cruces. Rio Grande Historical Collections. Accession No. Ms 0249. Box No. 13. Folder V3. Folder Name: "Venue, Change of."

FRITZ FAMILY (EMIL AND CHARLES FRITZ AND EMILIE FRITZ SCHOLAND)

Fritz, Charles. Affidavit of **September 18, 1876** claiming that Emil Fritz had a will. Probate Court Record. (private collection)

_____. Affidavit of **September 26, 1876** Authorizing Alexander McSween to Receive Payments for the Fritz Estate. Probate Court Record. (private collection)

Scholand, Emilie and Charles Fritz. Affidavit of **September 26, 1876** appointing McSween to collect debts for the Emil Fritz Estate. Copied from the original District Court Record. (private collection)

Fritz, Charles. Affidavit of **December 7, 1877** to order Alexander McSween to pay the Emil Fritz insurance policy money. Probate Court Record. (private collection)

Scholand, Emilie. Affidavit of **December 21, 1877** Accusing Alexander McSween of Embezzlement. Copied from the original District Court Record. (private collection)

Bristol Warren. "Writ of Embezzlement." **December 21, 1877**. Herman B. Weisner Papers, ca. 1957-1992. New Mexico State University Library at Las Cruces. Rio Grande Historical Collections. Accession No. Ms 0249. Box 10. Folder M-13. Folder Name. "Will and Testament A. McSween." **(Emilie Fritz Scholand's sworn complaint against Alexander McSween)**

Fritz, Charles. Affidavit sworn before John Crouch, Clerk of Doña Ana District Court, for Writ of Attachment issued against property of Alexander A. McSween. Probate Court Record. **February 6, 1878**. (private collection)

_____ and Emilie Scholand. Attachment Bond sworn before John Crouch, Clerk of Doña Ana District Court, against Alexander A. McSween for indebtedness to them. **February 6, 1878**. (private collection).

No Author. Diagram showing parcels of land to each of the heirs of Emil Fritz. Herman B. Weisner Papers, ca. 1957-1992. New Mexico State University Library at Las Cruces. Rio Grande Historical Collections. Accession No. Ms 0249. Box P1. Folder 11. Folder Name. "Charles Fritz Estate."

GARRETT, PATRICK FLOYD

BIBLIOGRAPHICAL SOURCES

Garrett, Pat F. *The Authentic Life of Billy the Kid The Noted Desperado of the Southwest, Whose Deeds of Daring and Blood Made His Name a Terror in New Mexico, Arizona, and Northern Mexico.* Santa Fe, New Mexico: New Mexico Printing and Publishing Co. 1882.

Metz, Leon C. *Pat Garrett. The Story of a Western Lawman.* Norman: University of Oklahoma Press. 1974.

Mullin, Robert N. "Killing of Joe Briscoe." Letter to Eve Ball. January 31, 1964. (Unpublished). Binder RNM, VI, H. Nita Stewart Haley Memorial Museum. Haley Library. Midland, Texas.

_____. "Pat Garrett. Two Forgotten Killings." *Password.* X(2) (Summer 1965). pp. 57 - 65.

_____. "Skelton Glen's Manuscript Entitled 'Pat Garrett As I Knew Him on the Buffalo Ranges.'" (Unpublished). Binder RNM, III B, 20. Nita Stewart Haley Memorial Museum. Haley Library. Midland, Texas.

CONTEMPORARY SOURCES (CHRONOLOGICAL)

Upson, Ash. Letter from Garrett's Ranch to Upson's Nephew, Frank S. Downs, Esq. re. "His Drawers and pigeon holes of his desk were full of letters, deeds, bills, notes, agreements, & C. I have burned bushels of them and am not through yet." **October 20, 1888**. (Unpublished). Binder RNM, V1-MM. Nita Stewart Haley Memorial Museum. Haley Library. Midland, Texas.

Wild, Azariah F. "Daily Reports of U. S. Secret Service Agents, Azariah F. Wild." Microfilm T-915. Record Group 87. Rolls 306 (June 15, 1877 - December 31, 1877), 307 (January 1,1878 - June 30, 1879), 308 (**July 1, 1879 - June 30, 1881**), 309 (July 1, 1881 - September 30, 1883), 310 (October 1, 1883 - July 31, 1886). National Archives and Records Department. Department of the Treasury. United States Secret Service. Washington, D. C. (**Aiding Garrett's capture of William Bonney**)

ARTICLE ABOUT

No Author. Lew Wallace Collection. Indiana Historical Society) "[Pat F. Garrett] Recommended by Gen. Wallace," *The* (Crawfordsville) *Weekly News-Review*, **December 20, 1901.** Indiana Historical Society. The Papers of Lew and Susan Wallace. Microfilm Edition. Indianapolis, Indiana: Indiana Historical Society Press. 2008.

HAYES, RUTHERFORD BIRCHARD

BIOGRAPHICAL SOURCES

Davison, Kenneth E. *The Presidency of Rutherford B. Hayes.* Westport, Connecticut: Greenwood Press, Inc. 1972.

Hoogenboom, Ari. *Rutherford B. Hayes. Warrior and President.* Lawrence, Kansas: University Press of Kansas. 1995.

Mullin, Robert N. Re: Frank Warner Angel Meeting With President Hayes August, 1878. Binder RNM, VI, M. (Unpublished). Midland, Texas: Nita Stewart Haley Memorial Library and J. Evert Haley History Center. (Undated).

Williams, Charles Richard. *The Life of Rutherford Birchard Hayes. Nineteenth President of the United States. Vol. I.* Boston and New York: Houghton Mifflin Co. 1914.

_____. The Life of Rutherford Birchard Hayes. Nineteenth President of the United States. Vol. II. Boston and New York: Houghton Mifflin Co. 1914.

CONTEMPORARY SOURCES (CHRONOLOGICAL)

PROCLAMATION

Hayes, Rutherford B. "By the President of the United States of America: A Proclamation." **October 7, 1878.** Indiana Historical Society. Lew Wallace Collection. OMB 0023. Box 1. Folder 1; and Senate Documents. 67th Congress. 2nd Session. December 5, 1921 - September 22, 1922. Washington: Government Printing Office. 1922.

LETTERS TO

Leverson, Montague R. "His Excellency Rutherford B. Hayes. President of the United States. Excellency! Since my last letter to your Excellency on the state of affairs in this Territory ..." Letter to Rutherford B. Hayes. **March 16, 1878.** Microfilm Roll M750. National Archives and Records Administration. Record Group 60. Microfilm Case No. 44-4-8-3. U.S. Department of Interior. Washington, D.C

Isaacs, J. and J. N. Coe. "We are two residents of Lincoln Co. who after incurring the greatest peril at the hands of thieves and murderers when the Governor and the U.S. troops aided ..." Letter to Rutherford B. Hayes. **June 22, 1878.** Frank Warner Angel File. Microfilm Roll M750. National Archives and Records Administration. Record Group 60. Microfilm Case Number 44-4-8-3. U.S. Department of Interior. Washington, D.C.

McSween, A. A. "The undersigned have the Honor of transmitting you as requested a copy of the proceeds of a meeting held by the Citizens of Lincoln County, N. Mex. relative to the late troubles ..." Letter to Rutherford B. Hayes. **April 26,1878.** Frank Warner Angel File. Microfilm Roll M750. National Archives and Records Administration. Record Group 060. Microfilm Case Number 44-4-8-3. U.S. Department of Interior. Washington, D.C.

Elkins, Stephen B. "To the President referring to a conversation had with you ..." Letter titled "Hon. S. R. Elkins favors appointment Axtell, ExGov. as Gov'r of New Mexico. **March 23, 1881.** (Received Executive Mansion April 6, 1881) Microfilm Roll M750. National Archives and Records Administration. Record Group 60.

Microfilm Case File Number 44-4-8-3. U.S. Department of Interior. Washington, D.C.

LETTERS TO AND FROM LEW WALLACE

Wallace, Lew. "I avail myself of your request this morning. It is hardly necessary to give reasons for a preference of the Italian mission ..." Letter to Rutherford B. Hayes. **March 9, 1877.** Indiana Historical Society. Lew Wallace Collection. M0292. Box 3. Folder 13. (**Desired ambassadorships**)

_____. "The feuds recently in Lincoln county, New Mexico, left a large many thieves and murderers, who, with others of like class since added to their number, are now confederated for plunder." Letter to Rutherford B. Hayes. **March 31, 1879.** Indiana Historical Society. Lew Wallace Collection. M0292. Box 4. Folder 7. (**Wants martial law against confederacy of outlaws**)

Hayes, Rutherford B. "We are greatly obliged by your kindness." Letter to Lew Wallace. **January 9, 1881.** Indiana Historical Society. Lew Wallace Collection. M0292. Box 4. Folder 16. (**Thanking for gift of *Ben- Hur***)

HOYT, HENRY F.

AUTOBIOGRAPHICAL SOURCE FOR

Hoyt, Henry. *A Frontier Doctor.* Boston and New York: Houghton Mifflin Company. 1929. (**Describes Billy's superior abilities, pp. 93-94.**)

CONTEMPORARY SOURCES (CHRONOLOGICAL)

Bonney, William H. Bill of Sale to Henry Hoyt. **October 24, 1878.** Collection of Panhandle-Plains Historical Museum. Canyon, Texas. (Item No. X1974-98/1)

Hoyt, Henry F. "This time it is me who is apologizing for the long delay in answering ..." Letter to Lew Wallace Jr. (Lew Wallace's grandson) **April 27, 1927.** Indiana Historical Society. Lew Wallace Collection. M0292. Box 14, Folder 11.

_____. "Copy of a bill of sale written by Wm H. Bonney ..." Letter to Lew Wallace Jr. **April 27, 1927.** Indiana Historical Society. Lew Wallace Collection. M0292. Box 14, Folder 11. (**Handwritten note on back of Bill of Sale copy calls Billy Bonney a "remarkable character" and "a natural leader of men"**)

JONES, BARBARA ("MA'AM") AND FAMILY

Ball, Eve. *Ma'am Jones of the Pecos.* Tucson: University of Arizona Press. 1969.

KELLY, EDWARD M. "CHOCTAW"

Rasch, Philip J. "The Curious Case of Edward M. Kelly." *Quarterly of the National Association and Center for Outlaw and Lawman History* (NOLA) Volume 22, Issue 2, Fall 1987, Pages 8, 16-17. Boise, Tennessee, State University. Special Collections. Second Floor. Box 291.1. (**About Billy Bonney's Santa Fe jail cell-mate, and impossibility of Blandina Segale's claimed jail visit including him**)

KIMBRELL, GEORGE

Kimbrell, George. "I have the honor to request that you will furnish me a posse ..." Letter to Lieutenant Millard Filmore Goodwin. **February 20, 1879.** Indiana Historical Society. Lew Wallace Collection. Box 4, Folder 3.

KINNEY, JOHN

BIOGRAPHICAL SOURCE

Mullin, Robert N. "Here Lies John Kinney." *Journal of Arizona History.* 14 (Autumn 1973). Pages 223 - 242.

CONTEMPORARY SOURCES (CHRONOLOGICAL)

No Author. "Charges against Jessie Evans and John Kinney." Doña Ana County Criminal Docket Book. **August 18, 1875 to November 7, 1878.** Herman Weisner Collection. New Mexico State University Library at Las Cruces. Rio Grande Historical Collections. Accession No. Ms 0249. Box 13. Folder V-3. Folder Name: "Venue, Change of."

No Author. "Obituary of John Kinney." *Prescott Courier.* **August 30, 1919.** Obituary Section.

No Author. Obituary. "Over the Range Goes Another Pioneer." *Journal Miner.* Tuesday Morning, **August 26, 1919.**

LEONARD, IRA E.

CONTEMPORARY SOURCES (CHRONOLOGICAL)

LETTERS FROM HUSTON CHAPMAN'S FATHER

Chapman, W.W. "Yours of the 1st inst. came ..." Letter to Ira E. Leonard. **March 20, 1879.** Indiana Historical Society. Lew Wallace Collection. M0292. Box 4. Folder 6.

_____. "Since receiving yours of the 1st March ..." Letter to Ira Leonard. **May 8, 1879.** Indiana Historical Society. Lew Wallace Collection. M0292. Box 4. Folder 10.

COURT OF INQUIRY OF LIEUTENANT COLONEL N.A.M. DUDLEY

Leonard, Ira E. "You are perhaps fully aware of the outrages that have been perpetrated in Lincoln County ..." Letter to Secretary of War George McCrary. **March 4, 1879.** From *Proceedings of a Court of Inquiry in the Case of Lt. Col. N.A.M. Dudley (May 2,1879 – July 5, 1879).* File No. QQ1284. (Boxes 3304, 3305, 3305A); Court Martial Files 1809-1894. Records of the Office of the Judge Advocate General – Army. Record Group 153. Old Military and Civil Branch. National Archives and Records Administration. Washington, D.C. (**Accusing N.A.M. Dudley of murders of A.A. McSween and H.I. Chapman and arson of McSween house**)

_____. "Charges and specifications against Lieutenant Colonel N.A.M. Dudley, Commander at Fort Stanton, New Mexico." **March 4, 1879.** *Proceedings of a Court of Inquiry in the Case of Lt. Col. N.A.M. Dudley (May 2,1879 – July 5, 1879).* File No. QQ1284. (Boxes 3304, 3305, 3305A); Court Martial Files 1809-1894. Records of the Office of the Judge Advocate General – Army. Record Group 153. Old Military and Civil Branch. National Archives and Records Administration. Washington, D.C. (**As Susan McSween's lawyer, Leonard assisted the military prosecutor, Henry H. Humphreys, and was present in court.**)

LETTERS TO AND FROM LEW WALLACE

Leonard, Ira E. "Dear Gov. You have undoubtedly learned ere this of the assassination ..." Letter to Lew Wallace. **February 24, 1879.** Indiana Historical Society. Lew Wallace Collection. M0292. Box 4. Folder 3. (**On Chapman murder.**)

Wallace, Lew. "It is important to take steps to protect the coming court ..." Letter to Ira Leonard. **April 6, 1879.** Indiana Historical Society. Lew Wallace Collection. M0292. Box 4. Folder 8.

Leonard, Ira E. "You may have learned the result of the cattle examination ..." Letter to Lew Wallace. **April 8, 1879**. Indiana Historical Society. Lew Wallace Collection. M0292. Box 4. Folder 8. (**Mentions the ongoing "cruel war"**)

_____. "One Wm Wilson, a saloon keeper ..." Letter to Lew Wallace. **April 9, 1879**. Indiana Historical Society. Lew Wallace Collection. M0292. Box 4. Folder 9.

Wallace, Lew. "Your favors both received." Letter to Ira Leonard. **April 9, 1879**. Indiana Historical Society. Lew Wallace Collection. M0292. Box 4. Folder 9. (**Wallace's "martyr" letter: "all the world against you"**)

_____. "Mr. Howell goes to the Plaza to give bond ..." Letter to Ira Leonard. **April 9, 1879**. Indiana Historical Society. Lew Wallace Collection. M0292. Box 4. Folder 9.

_____. "Referring to the testimony in Mr. Howell's cattle case ..." Letter to Ira Leonard. **April 9, 1879**. Indiana Historical Society. Lew Wallace Collection. M0292. Box 4. Folder 9.

Leonard, Ira. "Yours received it might perhaps be a good idea to surrender the cattle to Mr Howell." Letter to Lew Wallace. **April 9, 1879**. Indiana Historical Society. Lew Wallace Collection. M0292. Box 4. Folder 9.

_____. "... *if the wind does not blow so I can't.*" Letter to Lew Wallace. **April 9, 1879**. Unpublished. Personal communication from Frederick Nolan. July 29, 2005.

_____. "I was disappointed in not seeing you ..." Letter to Lew Wallace. **April 12, 1879**. Indiana Historical Society. Lew Wallace Collection. M0292. Box 4. Folder 9. (**Anxious about hard looking characters coming into Lincoln**)

Wallace, Lew. "Your favor, with the prisoner received." Letter to Ira Leonard. **April 13, 1879**. Indiana Historical Society. Lew Wallace Collection. M0292. Box 4. Folder 9. (**About writs of habeas corpus to free his Fort Stanton prisoners**)

Leonard, Ira. "Yours was received last night ..." **April 13, 1879**. Indiana Historical Society. Lew Wallace Collection. M0292. Box 4. Folder 9. (**Enforcing vagrancy and gun laws in Lincoln**)

_____. "The air is filled tonight with 'rumors of wars ... Letter to Lew Wallace. **April 20, 1879**. Indiana Historical Society. Lew Wallace Collection. M0292. Box 4. Folder 9. (**About District Attorney Rynerson: "He is bent on going for the Kid"**)

_____. "When you left here I promised to write you concerning events transpiring here ..." Letter to Lew Wallace. **May 20, 1878 [sic - 79]**. Indiana Historical Society. Lew Wallace Collection. M0292. Box 4. Folder 10. (**Has quote on the Murphy-Dolan party as: "part and parcel of the Santa Fe ring that has been so long an incubus on the government of this territory."**)

_____. "I write to you with pencil because I am laboring for breath ..." Letter to Lew Wallace. **May 23, 1879**. Indiana Historical Society. Lew Wallace Collection. M0292. Box 4. Folder 11. (**With quote "we are pouring the 'hot shot' into Dudley." With enclosed letter of May 20, 1879**)

_____. "Dudley commenced on the defense Thursday afternoon ..." Letter to Wallace. **June 6, 1879**, Indiana Historical Society. Lew Wallace Collection. M0292. Box 4. Folder 11. (**Quote: "I am thoroughly and completely disgusted with their proceedings ..."**)

_____. "Yours of the 7th inst reached me ..." Letter to Lew Wallace. **June 13, 1879**. Indiana Historical Society. Lew Wallace Collection. M0292. Box 4. Folder 11.

ARTICLES

No Author. "[He] attracted special commendation by his fearless action in the suppression of disorder..." *St. Louis Globe* of September 7, 1872. Unpublished. Personal communication from Frederick Nolan. July 29, 2005.

No Author. Obituary. **July 6, 1889**. Las Cruces *Rio Grande Republican*. Unpublished. Personal communication from Frederick Nolan. July 29, 2005.

LeROY, BILLY (ARTHUR POND)
BIOGRAPHICAL SOURCES (CHRONOLOGICAL)

No Author. No title. **March 2, 1881.** Pueblo, Colorado *Colorado Daily Chieftain.* www.coloradohistoricnewspapers.org. **(Jailing of Billy LeRoy in Pueblo, Colorado; no mention of a "Billy the Kid" moniker)**

No Author. "Billy Le Roy, The Story of His Escape From Cantril, Detailed Minutely to a Reporter of the News, by the "Solid Pard" of the Bold Stage Robber, Who Put Up the Job and Successfully Executed It, Billy's Girl, Who Loves Him Most Devotedly, Lends a Helping Hand to the Scheme, The Deputy's Fatal Drink of Water at the Tank, Which Had Been Dosed With Croton Oil, While Cantril Was in the Toilet Room, Billy Le Roy in a Twinkling Don's Women's Attire, And Settles into The Arms of His Pard, The Cleverest Piece of Work in the Annals of Crime." **April 9, 1881.** *The Daily News: Denver.* (Private collection)

No Author. "Le Roy's Luck, Colorado's Stage Robber and Road Agent, Goes Through a Kansas City Pawn Shop, Securing Several Thousand Dollars Worth of Jewelry, And Returns to Denver With His Booty, How He Spent Last Sabbath Day in Our Midst." **Tuesday, April 12, 1881.** *The Daily News: Denver.* (Private collection) **(No mention of a "Billy the Kid" moniker)**

No Author. "Le Roy is Dead, He Falls Victim to Del Norte's Hemp ... Lynched at Del Norte." **May 23, 1881.** *The Daily News: Denver* of Monday. (Private Collection) **(No mention of "Billy the Kid" moniker)**

No Author. "Lynched, The Story of Le Roy's Capture Saturday, After a Tedious Trail Through the Mountains ... Details of the Scenes at Del Norte When the Prisoners Were Hung to a Tree." **Wednesday, May 25, 1881.** *The Daily News: Denver.* (Private Collection) **(No mention of "Billy the Kid" moniker, and showing he could not have been in the Santa Fe jail when Blandina claimed)**

No Author. Editorial: "Billy Le Roy, The Last Act in the Drama of His Life, Captured by the Sheriff of Rio Grande County, He is Conveyed With His Brother to the County Jail in the Town of Del Norte, From Thence They are Taken By the Lynchers, Who Hang Them on the Banks of the River, A Terrible End to a Career of Outrageous Crime." **May 24, 1881.** *The Daily News: Denver.* (Private Collection) **(No mention of "Billy the Kid" moniker)**

Cline, Donald. *Alias Billy the Kid: The Man Behind the Legend.* Santa Fe, New Mexico: Sunstone Press. **1986. (Unsupported claims of "two Billy the Kids," with Billy LeRoy as a "Billy the Kid" preceding Billy Bonney)**

Daggett, Thomas F. "Billy LeRoy, the Colorado Bandit; or, The King of American Highwaymen. A Complete and Authentic History of This Famous Young Desperado, His Crimes and Adventures." *Police Gazette Series of Famous Criminals.* Published by Richard K. Fox. New York: Police Gazette. **1881.** From Newberry Library's American West online collection, http://www.americanwest.amdigital.co.uk/Documents/Details/Graff_968.

Dugan, Mark. *Bandit Years, A Gathering of Wolves.* Santa Fe: Sunstone Press. **1987. (Biography of Billy LeRoy)**

Louden, Richard. "Local legend about Sister Blandina and Billy the Kid is a case of mistaken ID: Creative exaggerations of his violent life created such myths as the one that by the time he was killed at age 21, he had killed that many men." **August 30, 1991.** Trinidad, Colorado, *Chronicle.* Sisters of Charity of Cincinnati Archives, Mount Saint Joseph, Ohio. Blandina Segale Collection. Box 5, Folder 73. **(Explaining the Billy the Kid fabrications as being a second Billy the Kid, Billy LeRoy)**

McClarey, Donald R. "Sister Blandina and the Original Billy the Kid." **October 12, 2012.** *The American Catholic.* **(States that Blandina's "Billy the Kid" was William LeRoy as the "original" Billy the Kid)**

Rezac, Mary. "Nuns, guns and the Wild West – the extraordinary tale of Sr. Blandina." **August 31, 2015**. Catholic News Agency. Sisters of Charity of Cincinnati Archives, Mount Saint Joseph, Ohio. Blandina Segale Collection. Box 16, Folder 2. **(Publicizing by using Billy Bonney, but ambiguously calling him William LeRoy as Billy the Kid)**

MAXWELL FAMILY

Cleaveland, Agnes Morley. *No Life for a Lady*. Boston: Houghton Mifflin. 1941.

_____. *Satan's Paradise: From Lucien Maxwell to Fred Lambert*. Boston: Houghton Mifflin Company. 1952.

Cleaveland, Norman. *The Morleys - Young Upstarts on the Southwest Frontier*. Albuquerque, New Mexico: Calvin Horn Publisher, Inc. 1971.

Dunham, Harold H. "New Mexican Land Grants with Special Reference to the Title Papers of the Maxwell Grant." *New Mexico Historical Review*. (January 1955) Vol. 30, No. 1. pp. 1 - 23.

Freiberger, Harriet. *Lucien Maxwell: Villain or Visionary*. Santa Fe, New Mexico: Sunstone Press. 1999.

Keleher, William A. *The Maxwell Land Grant. A New Mexico Item*. Albuquerque, New Mexico: University of New Mexico Press. 1964.

Lamar, Howard Roberts. *The Far Southwest 1846 - 1912. A Territorial History*. New Haven and London: Yale University Press. 1966.

Miller, Kenny. Descendant of Lucien Bonaparte Maxwell. Personal communication. 2011 to 2012.

Montoya, María E. *Translating Property. The Maxwell Land Grant and the Conflict Over Land in the American West, 1840-1900*. Berkeley and Los Angeles, California: University of California Press. 2002.

Murphy, Lawrence R. *Lucien Bonaparte Maxwell. Napoleon of the Southwest*. Norman: University of Oklahoma Press. 1983.

Pearson, Jim Berry. *The Maxwell Land Grant*. Norman: University of Oklahoma Press. 1961.

Poe, Sophie. *Buckboard Days*. Albuquerque, New Mexico: University of New Mexico Press. 1964.

Taylor, Morris F. *O. P. McMains and the Maxwell Land Grant Conflict*. Tucson, Arizona: The University of Arizona Press. 1979. **(Origins of Santa Fe Ring)**

No Author. "Mrs. Paula M. Jaramillo, 65 Died Here Tuesday." *The Fort Sumner Leader*. Official Newspaper County of De Baca. December 20, 1929. No. 1158, Page 1, Column 1. **(Death of Paulita Maxwell Jaramillo, Billy Bonney's sweetheart)**

McSWEEN, ALEXANDER

Bristol Warren. "Writ of Embezzlement." **December 21, 1877**. Writ of Embezzlement. New Mexico State University Library at Las Cruces. Rio Grande Historical Collections. Lincoln County Papers. New Mexico State University Library at Las Cruces. Rio Grande Historical Collections. Accession No. Ms 0249. Box No. 10. Folder M-13. "Will and Testament A. McSween." **(Emilie Fritz Scholand's sworn complaint against Alexander McSween)**

Fritz, Charles. Affidavit sworn before John Crouch, Clerk of Doña Ana District Court, for Writ of Attachment issued against property of Alexander A. McSween. Probate Court Record. **February 6, 1878**. (private collection).

_____. Fritz, Charles and Emilie Scholand. Attachment Bond sworn before John Crouch, Clerk of Doña Ana District Court, against Alexander A. McSween for indebtedness to them. **February 6, 1878**. (private collection).

Bristol, Warren. Action of Assumpsit to command Sheriff of Lincoln County to attach goods of Alexander A. McSween. **February 7, 1878**. District Court Record. (private collection).

_____. Preprinted form in his name for "Writ of Attachment" (Printed and sold at the office of the Mesilla News) filled out to command the Sheriff of Lincoln County to attach goods of Alexander McSween for a suit of damages for ten thousand dollars. **February 7, 1878.** (private collection).

McSween, Alexander. "It looks as though the agent were the property of J.J. Dolan & J.H. Riley, known here as Dolan & Co." Letter to Secretary of Interior Carl Schurz. **February 11, 1878.** From Frederick Nolan. *The Life and Death of John Henry Tunstall.* Albuquerque, New Mexico: The University of New Mexico Press. 1965. Page 266.

_____. "Will and Testament A. McSween." **February 25, 1878.** Herman B. Weisner Papers, ca. 1957-1992. New Mexico State University Library at Las Cruces. Rio Grande Historical Collections. Accession No. Ms 0249. Box 10. Folder M15. Folder Name. "Will and Testament A. McSween."

McSween, A.A. and B.H. Ellis. Secretaries. "The undersigned have the Honor of transmitting you, as requested, a copy of the proceedings of a meeting held by the citizens of Lincoln County ..." Letter to President Rutherford B. Hayes; with attached proceedings of the April 1878 Lincoln Grand Jury. **April 26, 1878.** Microfilm File Case Number 44-4-8-3. Record Group 48. Microfilm No. M750. Roll 1. National Archives and Records Administration. U.S. Department of Justice. Washington, D.C.

McSween, Alexander. Deposition to Frank Warner Angel. **June 6, 1878.** Pages 5-183 of Frank Warner Angel report *In the Matter of the Examination of the Causes and Circumstances of the Death of John H. Tunstall a British Subject.* Report filed **October 4, 1878.** Angel Report. Microfilm File Case Number 44-4-8-3. Record Group 48. Microfilm No. M750. Roll 1. National Archives and Records Administration. U.S. Department of Justice. Washington, D.C.

Angel, Frank Warner. *In the Matter of the Lincoln County Troubles.* To the Honorable Charles Devens, Attorney General. **October 4, 1878.** Angel Report. Microfilm File Case Number 44-4-8-3. Record Group 48. Microfilm No. M750. Roll 1. National Archives and Records Administration. U.S. Department of Justice. Washington, D.C.

McSWEEN, SUSAN

BIOGRAPHICAL SOURCE

Chamberlain, Kathleen P. *In the Shadow of Billy the Kid: Susan McSween and the Lincoln County War.* Albuquerque: University of New Mexico Press. 2013.

CONTEMPORARY SOURCES (CHRONOLOGICAL)

Dudley, Nathan Augustus Monroe. "I am in receipt of a copy of letter written by one H.I. Chapman, calling himself the Attorney ..." **November 9, 1878.** Letter to Lew Wallace. From *Proceedings of a Court of Inquiry in the Case of Lt. Col. N.A.M. Dudley (May 2,1879 - July 5, 1879).* File No. QQ1284. (Boxes 3304, 3305, 3305A); Court Martial Files 1809-1894. Records of the Office of the Judge Advocate General - Army. Record Group 153. Old Military and Civil Branch. National Archives and Records Administration. Washington, D.C. (**Forwarding the Susan McSween defamatory affidavits in answer to the charges made by Chapman**)

Wallace, Lew. "In a communication ... I requested for reasons stated, a safe-guard for Mrs. McSween ..." Letter to Edward Hatch. **November 9, 1878.** Indiana Historical Society. Lew Wallace Collection. M0292. Box 3. Folder 17.

McSween, Susan. Testimony in Court of Inquiry for Lieutenant Colonel N.A.M. Dudley. **May 23-24, 26, 1879.** *Proceedings of a Court of Inquiry in the Case of Lt. Col. N.A.M. Dudley (May 2,1879 - July 5, 1879).* File No. QQ1284. (Boxes 3304, 3305, 3305A); Court Martial Files 1809-1894. Records of the Office of the Judge

Advocate General – Army. Record Group 153. Old Military and Civil Branch. National Archives and Records Administration. Washington, D.C.

Waldo, Henry. "Nothing has been accomplished in the least that connects Col. Dudley with anything which transpired in the town of Lincoln on the occasion of his presence there on the 19th..." Closing argument for Dudley Court of Inquiry. **July 5, 1879**. *Proceedings of a Court of Inquiry in the Case of Lt. Col. N.A.M. Dudley (May 2,1879 – July 5, 1879)*. File No. QQ1284. (Boxes 3304, 3305, 3305A); Court Martial Files 1809-1894. Records of the Office of the Judge Advocate General – Army. Record Group 153. Old Military and Civil Branch. National Archives and Records Administration. Washington, D. C.

No Author. Verdict on Civil Cause 298 for arson of Susan McSween's house. *Mesilla News*. **December 6, 1879**. Unpublished. personal communication from Frederick Nolan. July 29, 2005. (**Dudley exonerated**)

SEE ALSO: Alexander McSween; Huston Chapman; Ira Leonard

MEADOWS, JOHN P.

Meadows, John P. "Billy the Kid to John P. Meadows on the Peñasco, May 1-2, 1881." *Roswell Daily Record*. February 16, 1931. Page 6.

Meadows, John P. Ed. John P. Wilson. *Pat Garrett and Billy the Kid as I Knew Them: Reminiscences of John P. Meadows*. Albuquerque: University of New Mexico Press. 2004.

MURPHY, LAWRENCE G.

Murphy, Lawrence G. "Will of Lawrence G. Murphy." Herman B. Weisner Papers, ca. 1957-1992. New Mexico State University Library at Las Cruces. Rio Grande Historical Collections. Accession No. Ms 0249. Box 11. Folder P15. Folder Name: "Murphy, Lawrence G."

PATRÓN, JUAN

Wallace, Lew. "Be good enough to send word to all your men to turn out soon as possible ..." Letter to Juan Patrón. **March 19, 1879**. Indiana Historical Society. Lew Wallace Collection. M0292. Box 4. Folder 6. (**Reports escape of Jessie Evans and Billy Campbell from Fort Stanton**)

Patrón, Juan. First letter to Lew Wallace on **March 29, 1879**. Indiana Historical Society. Lew Wallace Collection. M0292. Box 4, Folder 7.

_____. Second letter to Lew Wallace on **March 29, 1879**. Indiana Historical Society. Lew Wallace Collection. M0292. Box 4, Folder 7.

_____. Letter to Rosa. **April 12, 1879**. Indiana Historical Society. Lew Wallace Collection. M0292. Box 4, Folder 9.

POE, JOHN WILLIAM

Poe, John W. "The Killing of Billy the Kid." (a personal letter written at Roswell, New Mexico to Mr. Charles Goodnight, Goodnight P.C., Texas) July 10, 1917.

_____. *The Death of Billy the Kid*. (Introduction by Maurice Garland Fulton). Boston and New York: Houghton Mifflin Company. 1933.

Poe, Sophie. *Buckboard Days*. Albuquerque, New Mexico: University of New Mexico Press. 1964.

RILEY, JOHN

Dolan, James J. "Answer to A Taxpayer's Complaint." Mesilla *Independent*. **January 29, 1878**. (**Response to J.H. Tunstall's exposé of him, William Brady, and John Riley for tax fraud with T.B. Catron**)

McSween, Alexander. "It looks as though the agent were the property of   J.J. Dolan & J.H. Riley, known here as Dolan & Co." Letter to Secretary of Interior Carl Schurz. **February 11, 1878**. From Frederick Nolan. *The Life and Death of John Henry Tunstall*. Albuquerque, New Mexico: The University of New Mexico Press. 1965. Page 266.

Rynerson, William. "Friends Riley & Dolan, Lincoln N.M. I have just received letters from you mailed 10th inst." **February 14, 1878**. Letter to James Dolan and John Riley. Copy as Exhibit B in June 6, 1878 deposition of Alexander McSween. Frank Warner Angel report. *In the Matter of the Examination of the Causes and Circumstances of the Death of John H. Tunstall a British Subject*. Report filed October 4, 1878. Interior Department Papers 1850-1907; Appointments Division and Subsequent Actions. Microfilm File Case Number 44-4-8-3. Record Group 48. Microfilm No. M750. Roll 1. National Archives and Records Administration. U.S. Department of Justice. Washington, D.C. (James J. Dolan Deposition. June 20, 1878. pp. 235-247.) **(Planned killing of J.H. Tunstall)**

Riley, John. Letter to N.A.M. Dudley. **May 19, 1878. (Fabricated Regulator theft from Catron-Dolan Pecos Cow Camp)** Cited by Victor Westphall, *Thomas Benton Catron and His Era*, Page 87.

RYNERSON, WILLIAM L.

Rynerson, William. "Indictments of the April, Lincoln County Grand Jury." **April 28, 1879**. Herman B. Weisner Papers, ca. 1957-1992. New Mexico State University Library at Las Cruces. Rio Grande Historical Society Collection. Accession No. Ms 0249. Box 4/39. Folder E-Z. Folder Name: "Jessie Evans Accessory to Murder." **(Billy's testimony indicts J.J. Dolan, Billy Campbell, and Jessie Evans fulfilling his pardon bargain)**

_____. "Friends Riley & Dolan, Lincoln N.M. I have just received letters from you mailed 10th inst." Letter to James Dolan and John Riley. **February 14, 1878**. Copy as Exhibit B in June 6, 1878 deposition of Alexander McSween. Frank Warner Angel report. *In the Matter of the Examination of the Causes and Circumstances of the Death of John H. Tunstall a British Subject*. Report filed October 4, 1878. Interior Department Papers 1850-1907; Appointments Division and Subsequent Actions. Microfilm File Case Number 44-4-8-3. Microfilm No. M750. Roll 1. National Archives and Records Administration. U.S. Department of Justice. Washington, D.C. (James J. Dolan Deposition. June 20, 1878. Pages 235-247.) **(Planned killing of J.H. Tunstall)**

Angel, Frank Warner. "I have just been favored by a call from W.L. Rynerson ..." Letter to Secretary of Interior Carl Schurz. **September 6, 1878**. Microfilm File Case Number 44-4-8-3. Record Group 48. Microfilm No. M750.   Roll 1. National Archives and Records Administration. U. S. Department of Justice. Washington, D.C.

Rynerson, William. Venue Change. **April 21, 1879**. Herman B. Weisner Papers, ca. 1957-1992. New Mexico State University Library at Las Cruces. Rio Grande Historical Collection. Accession No. Ms 0249. Box 1. Folder 14-D. Folder Name: "Billy the Kid Legal Documents."

SALAZAR, YGINIO

Salazar, Yginio. "Salazar's Affidavit." No Date. (July, 1878 likely) Herman B. Weisner Papers, ca. 1957-1992. New Mexico State University Library at Las Cruces. Rio Grande Historical Collections. Accession No. Ms 0249. Box. 12. Folder 56. Folder Name. " Salazar, Higinio."

Kimbrell, George. "I have the honor to request that you will furnish me a posse ..." Letter to Lieutenant Millard Filmore Goodwin. **February 20, 1879**. Indiana Historical Society. Lew Wallace Collection. Box 4, Folder 3. **(For pursuit of William Bonney and Yginio Salazar)**

Goodwin, Millard Filmore. ""I have the honor to submit the following report regarding my duties performed ..." Letter to Fort Stanton Post Adjutant John Loud. **February 23, 1879**. Indiana Historical Society. Lew Wallace Collection. Box 4, Folder 3. **(Assisting pursuit of William Bonney and Yginio Salazar)**

Wallace, Lew. "I beg to submit to you a list of persons ... to arrest ..." Letter to Henry Carroll. **March 11, 1879**. Indiana Historical Society. Lew Wallace Collection. M0292. Box 4. Folder 5. **(Lists Ygenio Salazar and "the Kid)**

Salazar, Joe. (Grandson of Yginio Salazar). Personal Interviews 1999-2001.

TOLBY, FRANKLIN J.

BIOGRAPHICAL SOURCES

Cleaveland, Norman. *The Morleys - Young Upstarts on the Southwest Frontier.* Albuquerque, New Mexico: Calvin Horn Publisher, Inc. 1971.

Taylor, Morris F. *O.P. McMains and the Maxwell Land Grant Conflict.* Tucson, Arizona: The University of Arizona Press. 1979. **(Traces origins of the Santa Fe Ring)**

CONTEMPORARY SOURCES (CHRONOLOGICAL)

Morley, William Raymond and Frank Springer. On Oscar McMains's citizen's Meeting. *Cimarron News and Press.* **November 10, 1875**. In Mary McPherson, Letters and Petitions to President Rutherford B. Hayes re: Removal Governor Axtell and the Santa Fe Ring. 1977. Interior Department Papers 1850-1907; Appointments Division and Subsequent Actions. Microfilm File Case Number 44-4-8-3. **Record Group 48**. Microfilm Roll M750. National Archives and Records Administration. **(Colfax County citizens meeting on F.J. Tolby murder by Santa Fe Ring**.)

_____. " 'The Territory of Elkins.' Assassination of Supposed Sun Correspondent. The Murder of the Rev. F.J. Tolby in New Mexico. A Probate Judge Accused of Complicity in the Crime. Indignation Meeting." New York *Weekly Sun*. **December 22, 1875**. Interior Department Papers 1850-1907; Appointments Division and Subsequent Actions. Microfilm Roll M750. National Archives and Records Administration. Record Group 48. Microfilm Case File Number 44-4-8-3. U.S. Department of Interior. Washington, D. C. **(From May 1, 1877 letter to President Hayes as "Mary E. McPherson and W.B. Matchett 'Make certain charges against the U.S. Officials in the Territory of New Mexico.' "**)

No Author. Report on murder trial for Franklin Tolby. Pueblo, Colorado *Chieftain*, May 25, 1876 quoting from *Daily New Mexican*, **May 1, 1876**. From Morris F. Taylor. *O.P. McMains and the Maxwell Land Grant Conflict.* Tucson, Arizona: The University of Arizona Press. 1979. Page 49. **(Ring-biased jury instructions by Judge Henry Waldo)**

Lambert, J.J. "At It Again." Pueblo, Colorado, *Enterprise and Chronicle*. **April 21, 1877**. Interior Department Papers 1850-1907; Appointments Division and Subsequent Actions. Microfilm File Case Number 44-4-8-3. Record Group 48. Microfilm No. M750. Roll 1. National Archives and Records Administration. U.S. Department of Justice. Washington, D.C. **(Description of Santa Fe Ring control of courts and malicious prosecution of opponents like Oscar McMains in the Franklin Tolby murder; used in: "W.B. Matchett and Mary E. McPherson 'Make Certain Charges Against the U.S. Officials in the Territory of New Mexico.' " Letter to President Rutherford B. Hayes. Received and filed May 1, 1877. Interior Department Papers 1850-1907; Appointments Division and Subsequent Actions. Microfilm File Case Number 44-4-8-3. Record Group 48. Microfilm No. M750. Roll 1. National Archives and Records Administration. U. S. Department of Justice. Washington, D.C.)**

McPherson, Mary and W.B. Matchett. "To The President. Please make the enclosed part of the evidence in the case of "Charges Against New Mexican Officials" Letter to President Rutherford B. Hayes. **May 3, 1877**. McPherson, Mary E. Letters and Petitions to President Rutherford B. Hayes re: Removal Governor Axtell and the Santa Fe Ring. Interior Department Papers 1850-1907; Appointments Division and Subsequent Actions. Microfilm File Case Number 44-4-8-3. Record Group 48. Microfilm Roll M750. National Archives and Records Administration. U.S. Department of Justice. Washington, D.C. (**Addendum to their May, 1877 charges**)

McPherson, Mary and W.B. Matchett. "The Secretary of the Interior, Sir – Accompanying please find copy of charges, &c., against S.B. Axtell, Governor, and other New Mexican Officials ..." "Charges Against New Mexican Officials." Letter to Secretary of the Interior Carl Schurz. **May 5, 1877**. McPherson, Mary E. Letters and Petitions to President Rutherford B. Hayes re: Removal Governor Axtell and the Santa Fe Ring. Interior Department Papers 1850-1907; Appointments Division and Subsequent Actions. Microfilm File Case Number 44-4-8-3. Record Group 48. Microfilm Roll M750. National Archives and Records Administration. U.S. Department of Justice. Washington, D.C.

TUNSTALL, JOHN HENRY

BIOGRAPHICAL SOURCES

Nolan, Frederick W. *The Life and Death of John Henry Tunstall*. Albuquerque, New Mexico: The University of New Mexico Press. 1965.

CONTEMPORARY SOURCES (CHRONOLOGICAL)

Tunstall, John Henry. "A Taxpayer's Complaint ... January 18, 1878." Mesilla *Independent*. **January 26, 1878**. (**Exposé of William Brady, James Dolan, and John Riley for tax fraud; T.B. Catron then paid that bill**)

Dolan, James J. "Answer to A Taxpayer's Complaint." Mesilla *Independent*. **January 29, 1878**. (**Response to J.H. Tunstall's tax exposé**)

Rynerson, William. "Friends Riley & Dolan, Lincoln N.M. I have just received letters from you mailed 10th inst." Letter to James Dolan and John Riley. **February 14, 1878**. Copy as Exhibit B in June 6, 1878 deposition of Alexander McSween. Frank Warner Angel report. *In the Matter of the Examination of the Causes and Circumstances of the Death of John H. Tunstall a British Subject*. Report filed October 4, 1878. Interior Department Papers 1850-1907; Appointments Division and Subsequent Actions. Microfilm File Case Number 44-4-8-3. Record Group 48. Microfilm No. M750. Roll 1. National Archives and Records Administration. U. S. Department of Justice. Washington, D.C. (James J. Dolan Deposition. June 20, 1878. pp. 235-247.) (**Planned killing of J.H. Tunstall**)

Wilson, John, George B. Barker, Robert M. Gilbert, John Newcomb, Samuel Smith, Benjamin Ellis. "We the undersigned Justice of the Peace and Coroners Jury who sat upon the inquest held this 19th day of February 1878 on the body of John H. Tunstall ..." Coroner's Jury Report for John Tunstall. **February 19, 1878**. (**Naming Tunstall's murderers**)

Springer, Frank. "I hope you have received a full account of the Troubles in Lincoln County from your nephew ..." Letter to Senator Rush Clark. **April 9, 1878**. Herman B. Weisner Papers, ca. 1957-1992. New Mexico State University Library at Las Cruces. Rio Grande Historical Collections. Accession No. Ms 0249. Box 4/39. Folder D-6. Folder Name "Frank Springer Letter to Rush Clark." (**Links Santa Fe Ring to murder of J.H. Tunstall**)

Angel, Frank Warner. *In the Matter of the Examination of the Causes and Circumstances of the Death of John H. Tunstall a British Subject*. Report filed **October 4, 1878**. Angel Report. Records of the Justice Department. Record

Group 60. Class 44 Litigation Files. Container 21. National Archives and Records Administration. U.S. Department of Justice. Washington, D.C. or Microfilm File Case Number 44-4-8-3. Record Group 48. Microfilm Roll No. M750. Roll 1. National Archives and Records Administration. U.S. Department of Justice. Washington, D.C.

_____. *In the Matter of the Lincoln County Troubles. To the. Honorable Charles Devens, Attorney General.* **October 4, 1878**. Angel Report. Microfilm Case File No. 44-4-8-3. Record Group 48. Microfilm Roll No. M750. National Archives and Records Administration. U.S. Department of Justice. Washington, D.C.

VICTORIO

Ball, Eve and James Kaywaykla. *In the Days of Victorio. Recollections of a Warm Springs Apache.* Tucson, Arizona: The University of Arizona Press. 1997.

Thrapp, Dan L. *Victorio and the Mimbres Apaches.* Norman: University of Oklahoma Press. 1974.

No Author. "Glory! Hallelujah!! Victorio Killed." Wednesday, October 20, 1880. *Thirty-Four Newspaper.* Las Cruces, New Mexico. Page 1, Column 4.

WALDO, HENRY

Morley William Raymond. "I was astonished beyond measure at your proceedings, and have fears as to the result ..." Letter to Mary McPherson. **March 6, 1877**. McPherson, Mary E. Letters and Petitions to President Rutherford B. Hayes re: Removal Governor Axtell and the Santa Fe Ring. Interior Department Papers 1850-1907; Appointments Division and Subsequent Actions. Microfilm File Case Number 44-4-8-3. Record Group 48. Microfilm Roll M750. National Archives and Records Administration. U.S. Department of Justice. Washington, D. C. (**Hopes she can help fight against Santa Fe Ring, in Mary McPherson's "Charges Against U.S. Officials in the Territory of New Mexico."**)

Morley, William Raymond. "Your letter of the 7th came last night and it was a good long newsy letter ..." Letter to wife, Ada McPherson Morley. **August 15, 1878**. Collection of Norman Cleaveland. Quoted in Norman Cleaveland, *The Morleys: Young Upstarts in the Southwest.* Albuquerque, New Mexico: Calvin Horn Publisher, Inc. 1971. Pages 152-155. (**Waldo's link to Catron and Elkins**)

Waldo, Henry. *Proceedings of a Court of Inquiry in the Case of Lt. Col. N.A.M. Dudley (May 2,1879 – July 5, 1879).* File No. QQ1284. (Boxes 3304, 3305, 3305A); Court Martial Files 1809-1894. Records of the Office of the Judge Advocate General - Army. Record Group 153. Old Military and Civil Branch. National Archives and Records Administration. Washington, D.C. (**Defense attorney for Dudley**)

WALLACE, LEW

BIOGRAPHICAL SOURCES

Cooper, Gale. *The Lost Pardon of Billy the Kid: An Analysis Factoring in the Santa Fe Ring, Governor Lew Wallace's Dilemma, and a Territory in Rebellion.* Albuquerque, New Mexico: Gelcour Books. 2017.

Grant, Ulysses S. "General Lew Wallace and General McCook at Shiloh: Memoranda on the Civil War." *Battles and Leaders of the Civil War. Century* magazine. 30 [n.s. 8], 776. August, 1885. Vol. I, Page 468. (**Quote damning Wallace for Shiloh**)

_____. *Personal Memoirs.* New York: Charles L. Webster. 1885. (**Same quote from *Century* magazine damning Lew Wallace for Shiloh**)

Jones, Oakah L. "Lew Wallace: Hoosier Governor of Territorial New Mexico. 1878-81." *New Mexico Historical Review. 59(1)* (January, 1984).

Morsberger, Robert E. and Katherine M. Morsberger. *Lew Wallace: Militant Romantic.* New York: McGraw-Hill Book Company. 1980.

Paarlberg, Larry. Height of Lew Wallace. (Personal communication. Head of Lew Wallace Museum, Crawfordsville, Indiana. 2014) (**Height from Civil War Records is 5'10" - 5'11"**)

Perret, Geoffrey. *Ulysses S. Grant: Soldier and President.* New York: Random House. 1997. (**Pages 170-171, 185, 188, 191**)

Stephens, Gail. "Shadow of Shiloh: Major General Lew Wallace in the Civil War." Indianapolis: Indiana Historical Society Press. 2010.

Wallace, Lew. *An Autobiography. Vol. I.* New York and London: Harper and Brothers Publishers. 1997.

_____. *An Autobiography. Vol. II.* New York and London: Harper and Brothers Publishers. 1997.

AUTHORSHIP OF BOOKS

Wallace, Lew. *An Autobiography. Vol. I.* New York and London: Harper and Brothers Publishers. 1997.

_____. *An Autobiography. Vol. II.* New York and London: Harper and Brothers Publishers. 1997.

_____. *Ben-Hur: A Tale of the Christ.* New York: Harper & Brothers, Franklin Square. 1880.

_____. *Commodus: An Historical Play.* 1872. Unpublished manuscript. Wallace MSS., Lilly Library, Indiana University, Bloomington, Indiana.

_____. *Prince of India: Or Why Constantinople Fell.* 1893. Manuscript. Wallace MSS., Lilly Library, Indiana University, Bloomington, Indiana.

_____. *The Fair God: A Tale of the Conquest of Mexico.* 1873. Manuscript. Wallace MSS., Lilly Library, Indiana University, Bloomington, Indiana.

COLLECTED PAPERS OF

Wallace, Lew. Collected Papers. Microfilm Project Sponsored by the National Historical Publications Commission. Microfilm Roll No. 99. Santa Fe, New Mexico: State of New Mexico Records Center and Archives. 1974.

_____. Lew and Susan Wallace Collection. Indiana Historical Society. M0292.

_____. Collected Papers. Lilly Library. Bloomington, Indiana.

SECRETLY RECEIVED ANGEL NOTEBOOK ON SANTA FE RING

Angel, Frank Warner. "To Gov. Lew Wallace, Santa Fe, N. M., 1878." Notebook. **1878**. Indiana Historical Society. Lew Wallace Collection. M0292. Microfilm No. F372. (**Notebook made for Lew Wallace listing names for the Santa Fe Ring**)

Theisen, Lee Scott. "Frank Warner Angel's Notes on New Mexico Territory, 1878." *Arizona and the West: A Quarterly Journal of History.* Winter 1976. Volume 18. Number 4. Pages 333-370. (**About the Angel notebook**)

SECRETLY RECEIVED BOOKLET ON SANTA FE RING

McPherson, Mary and W.B. Matchett. "*In the Matter of Charges vs. Gov. S.B. Axtell and Other New Mexico Officials. Submitted to the Departments of the Interior and Justice.* **August, 1877.** Printed as a 31 page booklet. No publisher listed. Indiana Historical Society. Lew Wallace Collection. M0292. Box 3. Folder 20. (**Exposé about Santa Fe Ring, Catron, and Elkins; in Lew Wallace's possession**)

OATH OF OFFICE OF (NEW MEXICO TERRITORY GOVERNORSHIP)

Wallace, Lew. "Oath of Office, Governor, New Mexico Territory. **October 1, 1878**. Indiana Historical Society. Lew Wallace Collection. DNA; RG 48, M364. [Copy in

New Mexico Archives: Records of Secretary of Territory of New Mexico (Acc# 1971-001), Series B-02: Executive Record Book 2, 1867-1882.]

AMNESTY PROCLAMATION OF

Wallace, Lew. "Proclamation by the Governor." **November 13, 1878**. Indiana Historical Society. Lew Wallace Collection. M0292. Box 3. Folder 17. (**Amnesty Proclamation for Lincoln County War fighters**)

PARDONS ISSUED AS GOVERNOR

Wallace, Lew. "Whereas it has been made known to the undersigned that Ursula Montoya ..." **October 24, 1878**. Indiana Historical Society. Lew Wallace Collection. M0292. Box 3. Folder 16. (**Pardon granted with affidavit**)

_____. Pardon of Jacob B. Matthews, William B. Powell, John Long, and John Hurlie et al. April, 1879 District Court. Filed **May 1, 1879**. (Under Attorneys S.B. Newcomb, Sidney Wilson, and Catron & Thornton). Herman B. Weisner Papers, ca. 1957-1992. New Mexico State University Library at Las Cruces. Rio Grande Historical Society Collection. Accession No. Ms 0249. Box 1. Folder 4. Folder Name: "Amnesty." (**Condoned pardon for Ringites**)

_____. Pardon of Marian Turner. April, 1879 District Court. Filed **May 1, 1879**. (Under Attorneys Catron & Thornton and S.B. Newcomb). Herman B. Weisner Papers, ca. 1957-1992. New Mexico State University Library at Las Cruces. Rio Grande Historical Society Collection. Accession No. Ms 0249. Box 1. Folder 4. Folder Name: "Amnesty." (**Condoned pardon for a Ringman**)

DUDLEY COURT OF INQUIRY TESTIMONY

Wallace, Lew. Testimony in Court of Inquiry for Lieutenant Colonel N.A.M. Dudley. **May 12-15, 1879**. *Proceedings of a Court of Inquiry in the Case of Lt. Col. N.A.M. Dudley (May 2,1879 – July 5, 1879)*. File No. QQ1284. (Boxes 3304, 3305, 3305A); Court Martial Files 1809-1894. Records of the Office of the Judge Advocate General – Army. Record Group 153. Old Military and Civil Branch. National Archives and Records Administration. Washington, D.C.

INTERVIEW NOTES ON BILLY BONNEY'S STATEMENTS

Wallace, Lew. "Statements by Kid, made Sunday night **March 23, 1879**." (Cover sheet reads: "Fort Stanton, March 20, 1879. William Bonney ("Kid") relative to arrangement with him." Indiana Historical Society. Lew Wallace Collection. M0292. Box 4. Folder 6.

REWARD NOTICES FOR WILLIAM BONNEY

Wallace, Lew. "Billy the Kid: $500 Reward." Las Vegas *Gazette*. **December 22, 1880**.
_____. "Billy the Kid. $500 Reward." May 3, 1881. *Daily New Mexican*. Vol. X, No. 33. Pages 1, c. 3.

REWARD POSTERS FOR WILLIAM BONNEY

Greene, Chas. W. "To the New Mexican Printing and Publishing Company." **May 20, 1881**. (Bill to Lew Wallace for Reward posters for "Kid"). Indiana Historical Society. Lew Wallace Collection. M0292. Box 4. Folder 18.
_____. "I enclose a bill ..." Letter to Lew Wallace for "Kid" wanted posters. **June 2, 1881**. Indiana Historical Society. Lew Wallace Collection. M0292. Box 4, Folder 18.

DEATH WARRANT FOR WILLIAM BONNEY

Wallace, Lew. "To the Sheriff of Lincoln County, Greeting ..." **April 30, 1881**. Indiana Historical Society. Lew Wallace Collection. M0292. Box 9, Folder 11.

LETTERS (ALPHABETICAL, THEN CHRONOLOGICAL)

TO AND FROM WILLIAM BONNEY (See William H. Bonney)

FROM, TO, AND ABOUT ATTORNEY HUSTON CHAPMAN

Chapman, Huston I. "You will please pardon me for presuming so much upon your kindness ..." **October 24, 1878.** Indiana Historical Society. Lew Wallace Collection. M0292. Box 3. Folder 16.

Wallace, Lew. "I enclose you a copy of a letter from Las Vegas ..." Letter to Edward Hatch. **October 28, 1878.** Indiana Historical Society. Lew Wallace Collection. M0292. Box 3. Folder 16.

Chapman, Huston I. "You must pardon me for so often presuming upon your kindness ..." **November 29, 1878.** Indiana Historical Society. Lew Wallace Collection. M0292. Box 3. Folder 18.

TO AND FROM COMMANDER N.A.M. DUDLEY

Dudley, Nathan Augustus Monroe. "I am in receipt of a copy of letter written by one H.I. Chapman, calling himself the Attorney ..." **November 9, 1878.** Letter to Lew Wallace. From *Proceedings of a Court of Inquiry in the Case of Lt. Col. N.A.M. Dudley (May 2,1879 – July 5, 1879).* File No. QQ1284. (Boxes 3304, 3305, 3305A); Court Martial Files 1809-1894. Records of the Office of the Judge Advocate General – Army. Record Group 153. Old Military and Civil Branch. National Archives and Records Administration. Washington, D.C. (**Forwarding the Susan McSween affidavits in answer to the charges made by Chapman**)

Wallace, Lew. "Your favor containing the duplicate accounts of the messenger who posted the President's Proclamation ..." Letter to N.A.M. Dudley. **November 30, 1878.** Indiana Historical Society. Lew Wallace Collection. M0292. Box 3. Folder 18.

Dudley, Nathan Augustus Monroe. "An Open Letter, By Lieut. Col. N.A.M. Dudley, 9th Cavalry, to His Excellency Governor Lew Wallace." Letter to Lew Wallace. Santa Fe *Weekly New Mexican*. **December 14, 1878.** Reprinted in *Mesilla News.* December 21, 1878. As Exhibit 13 from *Proceedings of a Court of Inquiry in the Case of Lt. Col. N.A.M. Dudley (May 2,1879 - July 5, 1879).* File No. QQ1284. (Boxes 3304, 3305, 3305A); Court Martial Files 1809-1894. Records of the Office of the Judge Advocate General - Army. Record Group 153. Old Military and Civil Branch. National Archives and Records Administration. Washington, D.C. (**Attacks Wallace's Amnesty Proclamation as applying to the military**)

Wallace, Lew. "The public interests with which I am charged make it, in my judgment, exceedingly improper for me to answer publicly your letters in the New Mexican ..." Letter to N.A.M. Dudley and other Fort Stanton officers. **December 16, 1878.** Indiana Historical Society. Lew Wallace Collection. M0292. Box 3. Folder 19.

Dudley, Nathan Augustus Monroe Dudley. "This being regular report day, I respectfully state ..." **March 1, 1879.** Indiana Historical Society. Lew Wallace Collection. M0292. Box 4. Folder 4. (**Blaming Lincoln County "troubles" on rustlers**)

TO SHERIFF PATRICK F. GARRETT

Wallace, Lew. "To the Sheriff of Lincoln County, New Mexico, Greeting ..." **April 30, 1881.** Indiana Historical Society. Lew Wallace Collection. M0292. Box 9. Folder 11. (**Death Warrant for William Bonney**)

TO LINCOLN COUNTY SHERIFF GEORGE KIMBRELL

Wallace, Lew. "The duty of keeping the peace in the county and arresting offenders is devolved by the law upon you ..." **April 2, 1879.** Indiana Historical Society. Lew Wallace Collection. Box 4, Folder 8.

FROM ARCHBISHOP OF SANTA FE J.B. LAMY

Lamy, J.B. "Permit me to thank you for your fine book, Ben Hur ..." **March 17, 1881.** Indiana Historical Society. Lew Wallace Collection. Box 4, Folder 16.

TO AND FROM IRA E. LEONARD

Wallace, Lew. "I enclose a paper, signed by all the leading attorneys ..." Letter to Carl Schurz. **November 13, 1878.** Indiana Historical Society. Lew Wallace Collection. M0292. Box 3. Folder 17. (**Urging judgeship for Ira Leonard**)

Leonard, Ira E. "You have undoubtedly learned ere this of the assassination of H.I. Chapman ..." **February 24, 1879.** Indiana Historical Society. Lew Wallace Collection. M0292. Box 4. Folder 3. (**Announcing Chapman murder**)

Wallace, Lew. "It is important to take steps to protect the coming court." Letter to Ira Leonard. **April 6, 1879.** Indiana Historical Society. Lew Wallace Collection. Box 4, Folder 8.

_____. "Your favors both received. The arrest of Wilson was a blow at the right time ..." **April 9, 1879.** Indiana Historical Society. Lew Wallace Collection. M0292. Box 4. Folder 9. (**With quote: "To work trying to do a little good, but with the world against you, requires the will of a martyr"**)

Leonard, Ira E. "I was disappointed at not seeing you when I went to the Fort." Letter to Lew Wallace. **April 12, 1879.** Lew Wallace Collection. M0292. Box 4. Folder 9. (**Reports seeing hard looking characters in Lincoln before court**)

Wallace, Lew. "Your favor, with the prisoner received." Letter to Ira Leonard. **April 13, 1879.** Indiana Historical Society. Lew Wallace Collection. M0292. Box 4. Folder 9. (**About the writs of habeas corpus being made to free his Fort Stanton prisoners**)

Leonard, Ira. "Yours was received last night ..." Letter to Lew Wallace. **April 13, 1879.** Indiana Historical Society. Lew Wallace Collection. M0292. Box 4. Folder 9. (**Enforcing vagrancy and gun laws in Lincoln**)

Leonard, Ira. "The air is filled to night with "rumors of wars ..." Letter to Lew Wallace. **April 20, 1879.** Indiana Historical Society. Lew Wallace Collection. M0292. Box 4, Folder 9. (**Quote on D.A. Rynerson: "He is bent on going for the Kid"**)

_____. "When you left here I promised to write you concerning events transpiring here ..." Letter to Lew Wallace. **May 20, 1878 [sic - 79].** Indiana Historical Society. Lew Wallace Collection. M0292. Box 4. Folder 10. (**Quote: Murphy-Dolan party as: "part and parcel of the Santa Fe ring that has been so long an incubus on the government of this territory."**)

_____. "I write to you with pencil because I am laboring for breath ..." Letter to Lew Wallace. **May 23, 1879.** Indiana Historical Society. Lew Wallace Collection. M0292. Box 4. Folder 11. (**Quote: "we are pouring the 'hot shot' into Dudley." With enclosed letter of May 20, 1879**)

_____. "Dudley commenced on the defense Tuesday afternoon ..." Letter to Wallace. **June 6, 1879.** Indiana Historical Society. Lew Wallace Collection. M0292. Box 4. Folder 11. (**With quote: "I am thoroughly and completely disgusted with their proceedings."**)

_____. "Yours of the 7th inst reached me ..." Letter to Lew Wallace. **June 13, 1879.** Indiana Historical Society. Lew Wallace Collection. M0292. Box 4. Folder 11. (**Important quotes: "... they would not enter our objections ..." "... would not allow us to show the conspiracy formed with Dolan beforehand ..." "I tell you Governor as long as the present incumbent occupies the bench all that Grand Juries may do to bring to justice these men every effort will be thwarted by him and the sympathizers ...")

TO AND FROM SECRETARY OF INTERIOR CARL SCHURZ

Schurz, Carl. "I transmit herewith an order from the President ..." Letter to Lew Wallace. **September 4, 1878.** Indiana Historical Society. Lew Wallace Collection. M0292. Box 3. Folder 14. (**Suspension of New Mexico Governor S.B. Axtell and his appointment as replacement Governor**)

Wallace, Lew. "I have the honor to inform you ..." Letter to Carl Schurz. **October 1, 1878.** Indiana Historical Society. Lew Wallace Collection. M0292. Box 3. Folder 15. (**Informing Schurz that he informed Axtell of suspension and that he now qualified as Governor**)

_____. "I have the honor to enclose herewith a requisition ..." **October 4, 1878.** Letter to Carl Schurz. Indiana Historical Society. Lew Wallace Collection. M0292. Box 3. Folder 15. (**Requesting arms from Secretary of War**)

_____. "As the basis of the request which I have to prefer relative to the affairs in the county of Lincoln ..." Letter to Carl Schurz. **October 5, 1878.** Indiana Historical Society. Lew Wallace Collection. M0292. Box 3. Folder 15. (**Requesting President to declare martial law**)

_____. "In further exemplification of affairs in Lincoln county accept extract received ..." Letter to Carl Schurz. **October 5, 1878.** Indiana Historical Society. Lew Wallace Collection. M0292. Box 3. Folder 15. (**N.A.M. Dudley's report of "Wrestlers" raping in Lincoln County**)

_____. "I received by mail last night a petition signed by the Probate Judge ..." Telegram to Carl Schurz. **October 14, 1878.** Indiana Historical Society. Lew Wallace Collection. M0292. Box 3. Folder 15. (**Giving situation and asking martial law for Lincoln and Doña Ana Counties**)

_____. "I have the honor to inform you that since the posting of the President's Proclamation ...." Letter to Carl Schurz. **October 22, 1878.** Indiana Historical Society. Lew Wallace Collection. M0292. Box 3. Folder 16.

_____. "I have appointed Mr. Epifanio Vigil, of this city, Interpreter and Translator ...." **October 22, 1878.** Indiana Historical Society. Lew Wallace Collection. M0292. Box 3. Folder 16.

_____. "Herewith please find bond ...." **October 22, 1878.** Indiana Historical Society. Lew Wallace Collection. M0292. Box 3. Folder 16.

No signatures. (But in Lew Wallace's handwriting). "Yesterday, at the request of Governor Wallace the undersigned, physicians ...." **October 23, 1878.** Indiana Historical Society. Lew Wallace Collection. M0292. Box 3. Folder 16. (**Focus on refurbishing Palace of the Governors**)

Wallace, Lew. "Be good enough, at your earliest convenience, to call attention of the President ...." **October 24, 1878.** Indiana Historical Society. Lew Wallace Collection. M0292. Box 3. Folder 16.

_____. "I enclose a paper, signed by all the leading attorneys ..." Letter to Carl Schurz. **November 13, 1878.** Indiana Historical Society. Lew Wallace Collection. M0292. Box 3. Folder 17. (**Urging judgeship for Ira Leonard**)

_____. "I have the honor to forward to you the following report." **November 13, 1878.** Indiana Historical Society. Lew Wallace Collection. M0292. Box 3. Folder 17. (**About Presidential Proclamation and issuing his own Amnesty Proclamation**)

Schurz, Carl. "In reply to your letter ..." **November 14, 1878.** Indiana Historical Society. Lew Wallace Collection. M0292. Box 3. Folder 17. (**Given bond for arms**)

_____. "Replying to your two telegrams ..." Letter from Carl Schurz. **November 15, 1878.** Indiana Historical Society. Lew Wallace Collection. M0292. Box 3. Folder 17. (**Ira Leonard's requested judgeship appointment**)

_____. "I acknowledge the receipt of your letter of the 13th instant ..." Letter from Carl Schurz. **November 23, 1878.** Indiana Historical Society. Lew Wallace Collection. M0292. Box 3. Folder 18. (**Amnesty Proclamation, has approval of President**)

Wallace, Lew. "It has not unexpectedly happened that delay, involving expense ..." Letter to Carl Schurz. **November 26, 1878.** Indiana Historical Society. Lew Wallace Collection. M0292. Box 3. Folder 18. (**Wants extradition of fugitive criminals**)

Schurz, Carl. "In compliance with the suggestion of the Secretary of State ..." **November 30, 1878.** Indiana Historical Society. Lew Wallace Collection. M0292. Box 3. Folder 18. (**About extradition of fugitive criminals**)

_____. "I have received your letter ..." Letter to Lew Wallace. **December 9, 1878.** Indiana Historical Society. Lew Wallace Collection. M0292. Box 3. Folder 19. (**Answer about anyone in Senate trying to defeat his confirmation as Governor**)

Wallace, Lew. "I have the honor to report that affairs of the Territory are moving on quietly ..." Letter to Carl Schurz. **December 21, 1878.** Indiana Historical Society. Lew Wallace Collection. M0292. Box 3. Folder 19. (**N.A.M. Dudley's indignation about the Amnesty Proclamation**)

Schurz, Carl. "I have received your report ..." **December 28, 1878.** Indiana Historical Society. Lew Wallace Collection. M0292. Box 3. Folder 19.

Wallace, Lew. "I have the honor to enclose you a copy of a communication ..." Letter to Carl Schurz. January 17, 1879. Indiana Historical Society. Lew Wallace Collection. M0292. Box 4. Folder 1. (**Bad condition of Palace of the Governors**)

_____. "... I have just returned from Trinidad, Col ..." Letter to Carl Schurz. **February 5, 1879.** Indiana Historical Society. Lew Wallace Collection. M0292. Box 4. Folder 2. (**Bringing his family to Santa Fe**)

_____. "I beg to call your attention to the condition of the house called the 'Palace' ...." Letter to Carl Schurz. **February 12, 1879.** Indiana Historical Society. Lew Wallace Collection. M0292. Box 4. Folder 2.

_____. "One H.I. Chapman, lawyer, was assassinated ...." Letter to Carl Schurz. **February 27, 1879.** Indiana Historical Society. Lew Wallace Collection. M0292. Box 4. Folder 3. (**Reacting to Chapman murder by using troops to track "outlaws" – meaning the Regulators. Start of the pardon saga**)

Schurz, Carl. "I have the honor to acknowledge the receipt of your letter of the 1st inst." Letter to Lew Wallace. **March 11, 1879.** Indiana Historical Society. Lew Wallace Collection. M0292. Box 4. Folder 5. (**Presidential permission for "arresting the disturbances" in Lincoln County**)

Wallace, Lew. "My time has been so constantly occupied in getting my work into operation ..." Letter to Carl Schurz. **March 21, 1879.** Indiana Historical Society. Lew Wallace Collection. M0292. Box 4. Folder 7. (**Progress report with multiple enclosures; one listing "The Kid -William Bonney in anti-outlaw campaign of "taking the head off the evil."**)

_____. "To day I forwarded a telegram to you, with another to the President ..." Letter to Carl Schurz. **March 31, 1879.** Indiana Historical Society. Lew Wallace Collection. M0292. Box 4. Folder 7. (**Mention of "precious specimen nicknamed 'The Kid'"**)

_____. "I have official information that a court of inquiry for Col. Dudley has been ordered ..." Letter to Carl Schurz. **April 4, 1879.** Indiana Historical Society. Lew Wallace Collection. M0292. Box 4, Folder 8.

_____. "I have the honor to inform you that affairs in Lincoln County are progressing favorably ..." Letter to Carl Schurz. **April 18, 1879.** Indiana Historical Society. Lew Wallace Collection. M0292. Box 4, Folder 9.

_____. "In a recent letter descriptive of the situation in Lincoln County, I alluded to the necessity of breaking up illicit transactions in cattle." **April 25, 1879**. Indiana Historical Society. Lew Wallace Collection. M0292. Box 4, Folder 9.

_____. "I enclose account in duplicate for services in overhauling and removing Territorial archives ..." **May 1, 1879**. Indiana Historical Society. Lew Wallace Collection. M0292. Box 4, Folder 10.

_____. "I have the honor to inform you that all the recent reports, military and otherwise, justify me in saying Lincoln County is enjoying a term of peace." Letter to Carl Schurz. **May 5, 1879**. Indiana Historical Society. Lew Wallace Collection. M0292. Box 4. Folder 10.

_____. "I had the honor a few weeks ago of writing you respecting a balance of contingent fund due this Executive Office ..." **May 5, 1879**. Indiana Historical Society. Lew Wallace Collection. M0292. Box 4. Folder 10.

_____. "Enclosed please find a copy of the report of the commandant at Fort Stanton." Letter to Carl Schurz. **June 11, 1879**. Indiana Historical Society. Lew Wallace Collection. M0292. Box 4. Folder 11. (**Self-serving progress report of quelling disturbances**)

Schurz, Carl. "I have received your letter of the 3ᵈ inst., and am glad to know ..." Letter to Lew Wallace. **July 10, 1879**. Indiana Historical Society. Lew Wallace Collection. M0292. Box 4. Folder 12.

Wallace, Lew. "The accompanying document received from Fort Stanton which will explain itself." Letter to Carl Schurz. **July 30, 1879**. Indiana Historical Society. Lew Wallace Collection. M0292. Box 4. Folder 12. (**Describes progress, but calls Dudley Court of Inquiry corrupt**)

Bell, A. "Referring to your letter of the 30ᵗʰ ultimo ..." **August 29, 1879**. Indiana Historical Society. Lew Wallace Collection. M0292. Box 4. Folder 12. (**Acting Secretary of the Interior and Secretary of War George McCrary placate Wallace about the corrupt Court of Inquiry outcome**)

Wallace, Lew. "In reply to the communication of Acting Secretary Bell ..." **September 15, 1879**. Letter to Carl Schurz. Indiana Historical Society. Lew Wallace Collection. M0292. Box 4. Folder 13. (**On John Jones killing John Beckwith, and Bob Olinger killing John Jones**)

_____. "The enclosed communication received yesterday from Mr. Louis Scott, U.S. Consul ..." **December 29, 1879**. Indiana Historical Society. Lew Wallace Collection. M0292. Box 4. Folder 13.

_____. "I have the honor to inform you that the Legislature of this Territory adjourned ..." **February 16, 1880**. Letter to Carl Schurz. Indiana Historical Society. Lew Wallace Collection. M0292. Box 4, Folder 14. (**Important proof of T.B. Catron as head of the Santa Fe Ring, and Wallace's Ring opposition**)

Schurz, Carl. "I have received your letter ..." **May 24, 1880**. Indiana Historical Society. Lew Wallace Collection. M0292. Box 4. Folder 15.

Wallace, Lew. "I have returned from a tour through the counties ..." Letter to Carl Schurz. **July 23, 1880**. Indiana Historical Society. Lew Wallace Collection. M0292. Box 4. Folder 14. (**Reporting on south counties, Victorio, and recommends Ira Leonard for judgeship replacing Warren Bristol.**)

_____. "I have the honor to report that I returned to this city ..." **November 30, 1880**. Letter to Carl Schurz. Indiana Historical Society. Lew Wallace Collection. M0292. Box 4, Folder 14. (**Reports Victorio is dead, and Navajo problems**)

_____. "From private advices received from Lincoln county ..." **December 7, 1880**. Indiana Historical Society. Lew Wallace Collection. M0292. Box 4. Folder 15. (**Reports pursuit of outlaws by people in Lincoln County**)

_____. "I have private business urgently requiring my presence in New York City ..." Letter to Carl Schurz. **December 14, 1880**. Indiana Historical Society. Lew Wallace Collection. M0292. Box No. 4. Folder 15. (**Mention's - without giving names - the deputy sheriff [Garrett] tracking the "leader of the outlaws" [Billy] for whom Wallace has set a "$500 reward."**)

_____. "I have the honor to submit the following matter for consideration ..." **December 15, 1880.** Indiana Historical Society. Lew Wallace Collection. M0292. Box 4. Folder 15.

TO AND FROM JUSTICE OF THE PEACE JOHN B. WILSON

Wallace, Lew. "I hasten to acknowledge receipt of your favor of the 11th Jan. ult. ..." **January 18, 1879.** Indiana Historical Society. Lew Wallace Collection. M0292. Box 4. Folder 1. (**Says that Lincoln County was carrying on a revolution**)

_____. "Your favors are both in hand and place me under renewed obligation. ..." February 6, 1879. Indiana Historical Society. Lew Wallace Collection. M0292. Box 4. Folder 2.

_____. "I understand that affidavits will be filed with you against the prisoners. ..." Letter to John B. Wilson. **March 8, 1879.** Indiana Historical Society. Lew Wallace Collection. M0292. Box 4. Folder 4.

_____. "I enclose a note for Bonney." Letter to John "Squire" Wilson. March 20, 1879. Indiana Historical Society. Lew Wallace Collection. M0292. Box 4. Folder 6.

ARTICLES BY AND ABOUT (CHRONOLOGICAL)

No Author. "Gen. Lew Wallace Reached Home ..." Crawfordsville *Saturday Evening Journal.* **December 16, 1876.** Indiana Historical Society. The Papers of Lew and Susan Wallace. Microfilm Edition. Indianapolis, Indiana: Indiana Historical Society Press. 2008. (**Denying election fraud in Rutherford B. Hayes's Florida election results**)

No Author. "Fighting the Indians. Sketches of General Lew Wallace's Plan for Conducting the Frontier Warfare." *Indianapolis Journal.* **August 28, 1877.** Indiana Historical Society. The Papers of Lew and Susan Wallace. Microfilm Edition. Indianapolis, Indiana: Indiana Historical Society Press. 2008.

No Author. "For Delegate Benito Baca. County Ticket Juan C. Armijo." *Albuquerque Review.* **October 5, 1878.** Indiana Historical Society. The Papers of Lew and Susan Wallace. Microfilm Edition. Indianapolis, Indiana: Indiana Historical Society Press. 2008. (**Wallace's arrival and swearing in by Warren Bristol**)

Wallace, Lew. "Statement by the Governor." **November, 1878.** Indiana Historical Society. Lew Wallace Collection. M0292. Box 18. Folder 1. (**In a Lew Wallace scrapbook. About the Amnesty Proclamation**)

No Author. "Wallace and Lincoln County." Grant County *Herald.* **March 1, 1879.** Indiana Historical Society. The Papers of Lew and Susan Wallace. Microfilm Edition. Indianapolis, Indiana: Indiana Historical Society Press. 2008. (**Ridicule about Huston Chapman's murder**)

No Author. Editorial on Governor Wallace's letter to Carl Schurz. *Denver Daily Tribune.* **May 7, 1879.** Indiana Historical Society. The Papers of Lew and Susan Wallace. Microfilm Edition. Indianapolis, Indiana: Indiana Historical Society Press. 2008. (**Blames Lincoln County for outlawry**)

No Author. "Governor Lew Wallace's Rose Colored Account of Them. Inexhaustible Deposits of Gold, Silver, Copper and Lead – An Open Invitation." New York *Daily Graphic.* **March 24, 1880.** Indiana Historical Society. The Papers of Lew and Susan Wallace. Microfilm Edition. Indianapolis, Indiana: Indiana Historical Society Press. 2008.

No Author. "General Wallace's Proclamation." Santa Fe *Daily New Mexican.* **June 12, 1880.** Reprinted in Santa Fe *Weekly New Mexican* of June 14, 1880. Indiana Historical Society. The Papers of Lew and Susan Wallace. Microfilm Edition. Indianapolis, Indiana: Indiana Historical Society Press. 2008. (**Contemplated proclamation for citizens to "take the field" against Indians**)

No Author. "General Lew Wallace Interviewed." Chicago *Daily Inter Ocean*. **January 3, 1881.** Indiana Historical Society. The Papers of Lew and Susan Wallace. Microfilm Edition. Indianapolis, Indiana: Indiana Historical Society Press. 2008. **(About his attempted repeal of the Posse Comitatus Act)**

No Author. "Wallace's Words ..." January 3, 1881), Chicago *The Daily Inter Ocean*. **January 4, 1881.** p. 2, c. 4. Indiana Historical Society. The Papers of Lew and Susan Wallace. Microfilm Edition. Series I. Reel 15. Indianapolis, Indiana: Indiana Historical Society Press. 2008. **(Interview with Wallace conducted in Washington, D.C.)**

No Author. "Governor Wallace. Chat About the Use of Troops in New Mexico and His New Book." *Crawfordsville Journal*. **February 26, 1881.** Indiana Historical Society. The Papers of Lew and Susan Wallace. Microfilm Edition. Indianapolis, Indiana: Indiana Historical Society Press. 2008. **(Trying to stop Posse Comitatus Act and the success of *Ben-Hur*)**

No Author. "Richard Dunham's May 2, 1881 encounter with Billy the Kid.", Santa Fe Daily New Mexican, May 5, 1881, p.4, c. 3.

No Author. "The Thug's Territory. Stage Robbers and Cut-Throats Have Things Their Own Way in New Mexico. Gen. Lew Wallace Anxious to Punish the Crime That is So Prevalent – A Chapter About "Billy the Kid' – The Governor has a Narrow Escape From Being Spanked." *St. Louis Daily Globe-Democrat*. Monday Morning, **May 16, 1881.** Page 2, Columns 5 and 6. (private collection)

No Author. O.L. Houghton's Conversation with Lew Wallace. *The Las Vegas Daily Optic*, **May 26, 1881**, p.4, c.4.

No Author. "Interview With General Lew Wallace Relative to Affairs in New Mexico." Chicago *Daily Inter Ocean*. **June 4, 1881.** Indiana Historical Society. The Papers of Lew and Susan Wallace. Microfilm Edition. Indianapolis, Indiana: Indiana Historical Society Press. 2008.

No Author. "General Wallace's Serenade: A Welcome Home by his Neighbors and Friends - What the General Said." **June 4, 1881.** Indiana Historical Society. The Papers of Lew and Susan Wallace. Microfilm Edition. Indianapolis, Indiana: Indiana Historical Society Press. 2008.

No Author. "Billy the Kid, General Wallace Tells Why the Young Desperado of New Mexico Wanted to Kill Him." (Lew Wallace interviewed on June 13, 1881), Crawfordsville *Saturday Evening Journal*, **June 18, 1881.** Indiana Historical Society. The Papers of Lew and Susan Wallace. Microfilm Edition. Indianapolis, Indiana: Indiana Historical Society Press. 2008.

No Author. "Gen. Lew Wallace. Visit to His Pleasant Home in the Athens of Indiana. Crawfordsville *Saturday Evening Journal*. **January 16, 1886.** Indiana Historical Society. The Papers of Lew and Susan Wallace. Microfilm Edition. Indianapolis, Indiana: Indiana Historical Society Press. 2008. **(Rationalizing Shiloh)**

No Author. "General Wallace Said ..." Crawfordsville *Saturday Evening Journal*. **January 16, 1886.** Indiana Historical Society. The Papers of Lew and Susan Wallace. Microfilm Edition. Indianapolis, Indiana: Indiana Historical Society Press. 2008.

No Author. "General Wallace in Cincinnati." Weekly *Crawfordsville Journal*. **April 4, 1893.** Indiana Historical Society. The Papers of Lew and Susan Wallace. Microfilm Edition. Indianapolis, Indiana: Indiana Historical Society Press. 2008.

No Author. "Lew Wallace at Shiloh. What the General Has to Say Further on This Question – Buell's Army." *Indianapolis News*. **September 13, 1893.** Indiana Historical Society. The Papers of Lew and Susan Wallace. Microfilm Edition. Indianapolis, Indiana: Indiana Historical Society Press. 2008. **(Wallace still blaming Grant for Shiloh in attempt to vindicate himself)**

No Author. "Lew Wallace's Foe. Threatened by 'Billy the Kid.' The Writing of 'Ben Hur' Interrupted. An Incident of the Soldier-Author's Career in New Mexico. *San Francisco Chronicle*. **December 10, 1893.** Indiana Historical Society. Lew Wallace Collection. M0292. Box 14. Folder 11.

No Author. "Street Pickings," Weekly *Crawfordsville Review - Saturday Edition*, **January 6, 1894**. Indiana Historical Society. The Papers of Lew and Susan Wallace. Microfilm Edition. Series I. Reel 27. Indianapolis, Indiana: Indiana Historical Society Press. 2008.

No Author. "General Lew Wallace." (Interview.) *Cincinnati Post*. **February 10, 1894**. Reprinted in Crawfordsville *New Review*. July 8, 1899. Indiana Historical Society. The Papers of Lew and Susan Wallace. Microfilm Edition. Indianapolis, Indiana: Indiana Historical Society Press. 2008. (**Calling *Ben-Hur* better than Dickens**)

No Author. "Author of Ben-Hur, Gen. Lew Wallace, of Indiana, spends the Day in the City. Talks Politics and Books." St. Paul *Dispatch*. **October 5, 1894**. Indiana Historical Society. The Papers of Lew and Susan Wallace. Microfilm Edition. Indianapolis, Indiana: Indiana Historical Society Press. 2008.

No Author. "Lew Wallace at Shiloh. Through an Orderly's Error He Took the Wrong Road." Spokane *Weekly Spokesman-Review*. **October 11, 1894**. Indiana Historical Society. The Papers of Lew and Susan Wallace. Microfilm Edition. Indianapolis, Indiana: Indiana Historical Society Press. 2008. (**New excuse of blaming the orderly for Shiloh as well as Grant**)

No Author. "Lew Wallace Honored, The People of Seattle Extend Him a Hearty Greeting." Tacoma, Washington *Daily Ledger*. **October 14, 1894**. Indiana Historical Society. The Papers of Lew and Susan Wallace. Microfilm Edition. Indianapolis, Indiana: Indiana Historical Society Press. 2008. (**Mentions writing a secret book**)

No Author. "About His Works. A Chat With General Lew Wallace." *San Francisco Chronicle*. **October 29, 1894**. Indiana Historical Society. The Papers of Lew and Susan Wallace. Microfilm Edition. Indianapolis, Indiana: Indiana Historical Society Press. 2008.

Lewis, E.I. "Gen. Wallace's Feud with Billy the Kid, When the General Was Governor of New Mexico and Billy Bonne Was the Most Dangerous Western Outlaw. He Was a Waif and Was Reared in Indiana. *The Indianapolis Press*. Saturday, **June 23, 1900**. Page ?. Indiana Historical Society. Lew Wallace Collection. M0292. Box 14. Folder 11.

No Author. "An Incident. Gen. Lew Wallace Tells of His First Meeting With His Stepmother in Crawfordsville." *Crawfordsville Journal*. **March 20, 1901**. Indiana Historical Society. The Papers of Lew and Susan Wallace. Microfilm Edition. Indianapolis, Indiana: Indiana Historical Society Press. 2008. (**About father's cruel introduction of step-mother**)

No Author. "Home From Shiloh. Gen. Lew Wallace and Capt. Geo. R. Brown Pleased With the Work of the Commission." Weekly *Crawfordsville Journal*. **December 6, 1901**. Indiana Historical Society. The Papers of Lew and Susan Wallace. Microfilm Edition. Indianapolis, Indiana: Indiana Historical Society Press. 2008.

No Author. "An Old Incident Recalled," *The* (Crawfordsville) *Weekly News-Review*, **December 20, 1901**.

Wallace, Lew. "Indiana is Now Literary Center, General Lew Wallace Gives His Views on Present Day Writers, Is Working on New Book." Cincinnati *Commercial Tribune* reprinted in Crawfordsville *Weekly News-Review*. **April 15, 1902**. Indiana Historical Society. The Papers of Lew and Susan Wallace. Microfilm Edition. Series I. Reel 27. Indianapolis, Indiana: Indiana Historical Society Press. 2008.

_____. "General Lew Wallace Writes a Romance of 'Billy the Kid,' Most Famous Bandit of the Plains." *New York World Magazine*. Sunday, **June 8, 1902**. Page 4. Indiana Historical Society. Lew Wallace Collection. M0292. Box 14. Folder 11.

No Author. "The Statehood Bill, General Wallace and Delegate Rodey Take Opposite Views. Wallace for New Mexico As a Single State But Rodey Says His People Are Reconciled to the Union With Arizona." Weekly *Crawfordsville Journal*. **January 6, 1905**. Indiana Historical Society. The Papers of Lew and Susan Wallace. Microfilm Edition. Indianapolis, Indiana: Indiana Historical Society Press. 2008.

WILD, AZARIAH

Brooks, James J. *1877 Report on Secret Service Operatives.* "On Azariah Wild." **September 26, 1877.** Page 392. Department of the Treasury. United States Secret Service. Washington, D.C.

Nolan, Frederick. "Biography of Azariah Wild." Unpublished and personal communications, June 11, 2005 and October 9, 2005.

Wild, Azariah F. "Daily Reports of U. S. Secret Service Agents, Azariah F. Wild. Microfilm T-915. Record Group 87. Rolls 306 **(June 15, 1877 - December 31, 1877),** 307 **(January 1, 1878 - June 30, 1879),** 308 **(July 1, 1879 - June 30, 1881),** 309 **(July 1, 1881 - September 30, 1883),** and 310 **(October 1, 1883 - July 31, 1886).** National Archives and Records Department. Department of Treasury. United States Secret Service. Washington, D. C.

WILSON, BILLY (POSSIBLE AKA DAVID L. ANDERSON)

SOURCES ABOUT

Lavash, Donald. *Wilson and the Kid.* College Station, Texas: Creative Publishing Company. 1990.

Keleher, William A. *Violence in Lincoln County 1869-1881.* Albuquerque, New Mexico: University of New Mexico Press. 1957.

No Author. "Outlaws of New Mexico. The Exploits of a Band Headed by a New York Youth. The Mountain Fastness of the Kid and His Followers - War Against a Gang of Cattle Thieves and Murderers - The Frontier Confederates of Brockway, the Counterfeiter." *The Sun.* New York. **December 22, 1880.** Vol. XLVIII, No. 118, Page 3, Columns 1-2.

Wild, Azariah F. "Daily Reports of U. S. Secret Service Agents, Azariah F. Wild. Microfilm T-915. Record Group 87. Rolls 306 **(Reports of October 6 and 10, 1880).** National Archives and Records Department. Department of Treasury. United States Secret Service. Washington, D. C.

WILSON, JOHN B. "SQUIRE"

Wilson, John, George B. Barker, Robert M. Gilbert, John Newcomb, Samuel Smith, Benjamin Ellis. "We the undersigned Justice of the Peace and Coroners Jury ..." Coroner's Jury Report for John Tunstall. **February 19, 1878.**

LETTERS TO JOHN "SQUIRE" WILSON

Bonney, William Henry. "Friend Wilson ..." **March 18, 1879.** Indiana Historical Society. Lew Wallace Collection. M0292.

Wallace, Lew. "I enclose a note for Bonney." **March 20, 1879.** Indiana Historical Society. Lew Wallace Collection. M0922. Box 4. Folder 6.

INDEX

Abbott, E.C. "Teddy Blue" – 108, 318
Abbott's saloon – 291
Alamosa, Colorado – 352
Albuquerque Journal – 14, 51, 56
Albuquerque, New Mexico – 15, 33, 47, 53, 56, 67, 117, 119, 135, 178, 413
A Frontier Doctor – 107
Allison, Clay – 362-365, 420
Allison, John – 363
Alias Billy the Kid – 7
Alias Billy the Kid: The Man Behind the Legend – 68, 343-350
Amnesty Proclamation – 88, 257
Anderson, David L. (See Billy Wilson)
Anderson, Gilbert M. "Broncho Billy" – 268
Angel, Frank Warner – 84, 86-87, **deposition of William Bonney to:** 84
Antrim, Catherine – 64, 78
Antrim, Henry (see William Henry Bonney)
Antrim is My Stepfather's Name – 9, 78, 186, 419
Antrim, Joseph "Josie" – 78, 419-420
Antrim, William Henry Harrison – 78
Arapahoe County jail – 351
Arizona Territory – 77, 79
Armstrong, Lew M. – 341, 353, 358-359
Associated Press – 51, 55-58, 67
Atkins Cantina – 79
At the End of the Santa Fe Trail books (see Blandina Segale)
"At the End of the Santa Fe Trail" magazine articles (see Blandina Segale)
"At the End of the Santa Fe Trail" Saint Hood TV series (see Blandina Segale)
Axtell, Samuel Beach – 83-84, 86-87
"Ballad of Billy the Kid" – 112
Baker, Frank – 82, 92, 97, 261
Bandit Years – 68, 344, 351
Barlow and Sanderson stage coach – 352
bay mare – 96, 214, 313, 334
Billy LeRoy: The Colorado Bandit or The King of American Highwaymen – 264-266, 320-342
Bell, James W. – 78, 97-98, 104-105, 247-248
"Bill's gang" (see Blandina Segale)
Billy the Kid (see William H. Bonney)
"Billy the Kid" (see Blandina Segale)
"Billy the Kid gang" (see Blandina Segale)
Billy the Kid moniker (see William Bonney)
Billy the Kid reward notices (see William H. Bonney)
"Billy the Kid" reward notices" error (see Blandina Segale)
Billy the Kid's Pretenders: Brushy Bill and John Miller – 5, 7
Billy the Kid's Writings, Words, and Wit – 412
Billy the Kid: The Outlaw – 111
Blazer's Mill – 83, 96, 100, 262
Bonita, Arizona – 37, 39-41, 75, 79, 205, 275, 278, 283, 410, 418-419, 422
Bonney, William Henry "Billy" (William Henry McCarty, Henry Antrim, Billy Bonney, the Kid, Billy the Kid) – 3-5, 7-8, 14, 17-18, 21-22, 26, 29-31, 37, 39-47, 52, 54-55, 57, 59, 64, 68-69, 71, 75-111, 113, 117-120, 127, 130-132, 134, 137-138,

146, 150, 153, 157, 161, 173-174, 181-183, 185-186, 189-190, 194, 196-197, 202, 204-206, 208-209, 214, 219, 224, 237-239, 243, 252, 257-260, 262-263, 275, 277-280, 283, 288-289, 291, 293-295, 297-301, 309-315, 317-320, 323, 326, 333, 337, 339, 341, 343-344, 347-348, 350-351, 355-356, 360, 400, 402, 404-407, 409-413, 415-426; **biography of:** 75-110; **tintype of:** 13, 18, 21, 47, 52, 55, 67, 83, 92, 118, 120, 137-138, 169; **contemporary friends of:** 100-107; **"Little Casino" nickname of:** 91; **Billy the Kid moniker of:** 3-4, 30, 310-318, 320; **bi-culturalism of:** 78, 99-100, 107, 111; **"Regulator Manifesto" by:** 85, 87, 106, 109-110; **Lincoln County War freedom fighter:** 8, 52, 75, 77, 95, 109, 111, 173, 186, 192, 257, 293, 415, 424; **federal indictment No. 411 against:** 83-84, 96; **Hoyt Bill of Sale of:** 87, 106; **eye-witness to Huston Chapman murder by:** 88, 106, 196, 257, 310; **pardon bargain with Lew Wallace of:** 7, 19, 21, 31, 43-44, 76, 78, 88-90, 94-95, 103, 106, 132, 174, 181, 196, 222, 224, 226, 228, 244, 252-253, 255, 257, 260, 262-263, 310; pardon bargain letter of March 13, 1879 by: 88, 257-258; pardon bargain letter of March 20, 1879 by: 259; pardon bargain meeting of March 17, 1879 with Wallace by: 89, 252, 257-263; Wallace "pardon in your pocket" quote about: 233, 256, 263; **sham arrest and jailing of:** 89, 94, 221, 258, 310; Lew Wallace **interview of March 24, 1879 of:** 260-263;

letter of December 12, 1880: 4, 194, 208, 312; **Santa Fe jail letter of March 4, 1881:** 263, 288, 293; **guerilla rustling by:** 76, 109, 257; **gambling by:** 87, 90, 181; **men killed by:** 82, 84, 92, 97-98; **outlaw press of:** 205-238, 242-256; **Secret Service reports about:** 239-241; **Lew Wallace reward notices for:** 88, 94, 180-182, 209, 217, 246, 250, 266, 312, 314; **Coyote Springs ambush of:** 94, 213, 331; **Greathouse ranch ambush of:** 94; **Stinking Springs capture of:** 78, 95-96, 197, 228, 294, 313; **transport to Santa Fe jail of:** 39; **Santa Fe jailing of:** 44, 76, 95, 110, 181, 263, 287-289, 291, 293-295, 298-299, 309, 340, 343, 347-348, 351-352, 359, 373, 399, 404; **transport from Santa Fe jail of:** 313; **transport to Mesilla jail of:** 44, 313; **Mesilla hanging trial of:** 44, 76, 78, 90, 103, 110, 182, 288; **letter of April 15, 1881 to Edgar Caypless by:** 96; **Lincoln County courthouse-jail jailbreak by:** 45, 78, 94, 104, 182, 223, 299-300, 314-315; **killing of by Pat Garrett:** 4, 7, 30, 46, 59, 76-77, 92, 98, 271; **Coroner's Jury Report of:** 315

Bosque Grande ranch – 87, 211-212, 329, 331, 405

Bowdre, Charles "Charlie" – 59, 78, 83, 87, 91, 93, 95-97, 106, 209, 311

Brady, William – 80-84, 87-88, 92, 96-97, 100-101, 106, 195

Brewer, Richard "Dick" – 82-83, 97, 102, 192

Briscoe, Joe – 90

Bristol, Warren H. – 81, 89-90, 95-96

Brockway, William – 210, 214, 264, 323, 333, 355, 406
Brooks, James J. – 93
"Broncho Billy and the Baby" – 268
Brown, Henry – 96
Bruce Publishing Company – 15-16, 18, 20, 138, 140
Buchanan, Veronica – 370, 377-378, 413, 422
Buell, George – 183-184
Burns, Walter Noble – 5, 9, 22, 176, 185-186, 188-202, 242, 268, 371
Cahill, Frank "Windy" – 79, 82, 84, 92, 97
Campbell, Billy – 88-89, 259
Cañon City county jail – 409
Carbonateville, New Mexico Territory – 288-292
Carlyle, Jim – 94, 98, 213, 332
Casey, Robert – 80
Cassano, Carmela – 140, 377-379, 381-383
Catholic Family Weekly – 66
Cathectical Guild Educational Society –62
Catholic Digest – 70
Catholic Health Initiatives (CHI) – 16, 117
Catholic Heritage Curricula – 69
Catron, Thomas Benton – 32-33, 35-36, 75, 77, 80-81, 83, 85-91, 93, 96, 100, 106, 108-110, 134-136, 178, 199, 202, 239, 257, 401
Caypless, Edgar – 96, 289, 301, 407
Cerrillos, New Mexico – 296, 347-348
Cerrillos Mining District –290, 296
Chambers, William T. "Persimmon Bill" – 360-361
Chapman, Huston I. – 76, 88-90, 105-106, 196, 220, 222, 226, 233, 252, 256-258, 263
Chavez, Peso – 54, 57, 117, 404, 410, 413

"Chism" – 24,38, 124, 144, 161, 194, 206, 277, 280, 340
Chisum, John Simpson – 81, 83-84, 193-194, 220, 222, 226, 238, 279, 339-340
Cicagna, Italy – 14
Cimarron, New Mexico Territory – 23, 36-37, 87, 123, 157, 166, 272, 275-276, 305, 346, 354, 362-363, 408, 410, 420, 424
Cimarron News and Press – 275
Cincinnati, Ohio –14-16, 18, 20, 58, 117, 138-139, 156, 179, 379-380, 384, 388, 390-391
Cincinnati Enquirer – 65, 69
Cincinnati Post – 16
Clancy, Frank – 33, 135
Clark, Frank – 351, 359
Cline, Donald – 68, 343-350
Coe, Frank – 83, 101
Coe, George – 18, 83, 96, 100-104, 318
Coghlan, Pat – 87
Colfax County, New Mexico – 36, 77, 87, 362-363, 402
Colfax County War – 77, 109, 402
Colorado Chieftain – 279-280, 355, 363, 369
Colorado Daily Chieftain – 400
Colorado Weekly Chieftain – 280
Columbian Press – 18
Comello, Lucy – 140
Comello-Cassano paper – 377, 379, 383, 414
Cooper, Thomas "Tom" – 93
Contreras, Russell – 56, 58
Copeland, John – 84
Coroner's Jury Report –
 for Billy LeRoy: 341, 353, 359;
 for Frank "Windy" Cahill: 79
 for John Tunstall: 82
 for William Bonney: 7-8, 99, 185, 315
counterfeiter, counterfeiting – 76, 87, 93-94, 189, 208-210, 214, 239-241, 264, 311, 323, 333, 355, 405-406, 408

"Cowboy Business" – 267
Cracking the Billy the Kid Case Hoax – 5, 7
Crawfordsville, Indiana – 219-220, 224, 254
Crawfordsville Review – 316
Crawfordsville *Saturday Evening Journal* – 219, 243, 254, 315, 339
Daeger, Albert O. – 142
Daggett, Thomas – 264-266, 320, 322-328, 332-333, 335-341, 343-344, 350
DailyMail.com – 51-52, 55
Daily New Mexican – 94, 181-182, 291-294, 313-314
"dark and moonless night" error – 8, 306
Daughters of Charity Provincial Archives – 425
Davis, Rosemary – 65
Dayton, Ohio – 14, 56
Dedrick, Dan – 87, 93-94, 405, 408
Del Norte, Colorado – 177, 340-341, 349, 353, 358-359
Demasters, George – 362
Denver Catholic Register – 65-66
Dillon, Richard Charles – 142, 162
Dirks, Tim – 268
DNA hoax – 5-6, 51
Dolan, James – 85-86, 88-90, 93, 96, 106, 193, 239, 258
Doctor Cushing – 370, 372
Doctor Michael Beshoar – 366, 370, 372 (see Blandina Segale)
Doctor Menger brothers – 366, 372 (see Blandina Segale)
Doctor Palmer – 366, 372 (see Blandina Segale)
Doctor Rogers – 370, 372
Doña Ana County, New Mexico Territory – 89
Donnlson, R.I. "Happy Jack" – 370, 372, 417
Dudley, Nathan Augustus Monroe – 85-90, 105-106, 222, 310-311; **Court of Inquiry for:** 89-90, 106, 222, 310-311

Dugan, Mark – 68, 344, 350, 353-355
Elkins, Stephen Benton – 77, 91, 93, 108, 199
Engle, Sam – 63, 65
Evans, Jessie – 79, 82, 88-89, 226
Exchange Hotel – 404
Faber, Charles – 363
federal indictment Number 411 – 96
Feliz River – 80, 261
Feliz River Ranch – 82
Findsen, Owen – 69
Ford, John – 268
Fort Stanton – 80, 85, 196, 198, 260-261, 310
Fort Sumner – 4, 34, 59, 76-78, 87, 90-95, 98, 157, 175, 199-201, 210-211, 214, 237, 239-241, 249, 305, 311, 313, 315, 326, 328-329, 333, 389, 405, 410
Foster, Jack – 63
Fountain, Albert Jennings – 96
Fox Film Corporation – 267
Franciscans – 176
"friend Murphy" error (see Blandina Segale)
Fritz, Charles –106, 259
Fritz, Emil – 80-81
Garrett, Patrick Floyd "Pat" – 4-5, 7, 9, 13, 18, 22, 30, 44, 46, 76, 78, 90-92, 94-100, 107, 111-113, 130, 176, 181, 185-197, 199, 202, 212-213, 222, 228-230, 235-237, 241-242, 246-247, 249, 251, 268, 271, 313, 315, 319-320, 331, 371, 389, 403, 406, 413, 415
Gauss, Gottfried – 97, 104, 111, 315
Geronimo – 138, 154, 184
Gibson, Hoot – 267
Girolamo, Michael – 139
Gomez, Adrian – 51
Gordon, Hol. – 369, 371
"Grant County Declaration of Independence" – 109
Grant County *Herald* – 349

Grant County, New Mexico Territory – 77
Grant County Rebellion – 109
Grant, Joe – 92, 97
Greathouse's ranch – 211, 213, 328, 332-333
"Great Train Robbery" – 267
Grimmesman, Henry J. – 121
Gutierrez, Apolinaria – 91-92
Gutierrez, Celsa – 91-92, 98
Gutierrez, Juanita – 91-92
Gutierrez, Saval – 92, 98
Hall, Warren – 63-64
Hammerstein, Oscar – 426
"Happy Jack" (see R.I. Donnlson; see Blandina Segale)
Hargrove's Saloon – 90, 92
Hatch, Edward – 184
Hayes, Rutherford B. – 31, 84, 87, 133, 246, 283
Hindman, George – 83, 88, 92, 96-97, 100
Homestead Act – 80, 100, 109
Hotel de Luna – 410
Hoyt, Henry – 18, 87, 106-107, 111
Hunt, James Winford – 175
Indiana Historical Society – 182
Indianapolis, Indiana – 217, 220, 225, 237, 322
Indianapolis Press – 224, 244, 255, 316
"insult to mother" error (see Blandina Segale)
James, Jesse – 220, 226, 233
Johnson, E. Dana – 142
Jones, Buck – 267
Joe Dyer's saloon – 188
Jones family – 262
Jones, Jim – 262
Jones, John – 262
Kansas City, Missouri – 295, 326, 352, 357-358
Kaplan, Sarah – 56
Keleher, William – 8, 185, 406, 408-409
"Kelly" – 151-152, 284-286, 288-293, 296, 298-301, 340, 348, 405-406, 409, 415, 421

Kelly, Edward "Choctaw" – 288-292, 296, 298-299, 301, 347-349, 405-407
Kid-Wilson gang - 405
Kimbrell, George – 88, 94, 259
Kinney, John – 85, 92, 98-99, 110
Kitt Carson Museum – 417
Kitt, Georgia – 55, 425
Koogler, J.H. – 208, 294, 311, 412
La Glorieta, New Mexico Territory – 24, 39, 125, 144, 166
Lake City, Colorado – 349, 352, 357, 370
La Fonda Hotel – 404
Lamy, Jean-Baptist – 25, 40, 126, 167, 207, 349, 411
"land-grabbers" – 4, 32, 35, 75, 91, 108, 134, 136
Las Cruces ("Cruces"), New Mexico – 237, 261-262, 313
Las Cruces *Thirty-Four Newspaper* – 183
Las Portales, New Mexico Territory – 5, 195, 208-212, 312, 328-331, 412
Las Vegas Daily Gazette – 94, 209, 312-313
Las Vegas Daily Optic – 292
Las Vegas Gazette – 5, 180-181, 195, 208-209, 240, 294, 300, 311-312, 412
Las Vegas jail – 95, 216, 294, 406, 412
Las Vegas, New Mexico – 81, 88-89, 95, 207, 209-210, 214, 216, 239, 289, 291-292, 301, 311, 326, 333, 401, 407
Legislature Revolt of 1872 – 109
Leonard, Ira E. – 89-90, 93, 96, 105-106, 293, 313
LeRoy, Billy – 53-54, 57, 68-69, 71, 117, 119-120, 263-266, 295, 297-299, 301, 309, 318, 320, 422, 424-425; **biography of:** 351-353; **dime novel about:** 263-266, 320-341; **Donald Cline book about:** 343-350; **contemporary press of:** 354-358

Lincoln County courthouse-jail –
44, 69, 78, 96, 104, 182, 220,
234-235, 244, 247-248, 256,
297, 315
Lincoln County Leader – 104, 315
Lincoln County, New Mexico
Territory – 4, 27, 30-31, 43, 46,
75-76, 78, 80, 83-84, 87-90, 92-
94, 96, 100, 106, 108-109, 113,
128, 130, 133, 147, 149-150,
153, 162, 180, 193, 196, 198,
203-204, 212, 214, 220, 222,
229, 233, 241, 244, 246, 250,
252, 259-260, 283, 304, 310,
318, 331, 334, 336-340
Lincoln County troubles – 108,
220, 318, 339
Lincoln County War – 4, 7-8, 31,
42, 44, 47, 52, 76-77, 80, 82, 85-
86, 88-89, 91-92, 94-95, 97-98,
100, 102-104, 106-107, 109,
134, 148-150, 161-162, 167,
173, 183, 191-192, 194-196,
202-205, 228, 238, 243, 257-
258, 288-289, 295, 304, 309-
310, 340, 345, 347, 402
Lincoln County War Battle – 76,
85, 88, 109, 229, 283
*Lincoln County War: A
Documentary History* –
Lincoln County War Battle – 76,
88, 109, 229, 283
Lincoln, New Mexico – 43-45, 69,
76, 78, 80-83, 85-89, 93, 96-97,
102-108, 110, 112, 148, 150,
161, 182, 193, 195-196, 215,
217-218, 227, 257-258, 260,
299-300, 314, 337-338
Little Casino" – 91
Longwill, Robert H. – 36
"Los Corrilos" error (see Blandina
Segale)
Louden, Richard – 68
Lovato, María Paula – 199
Mackie, John – 79
MacNab, Frank – 83-84, 98
Martinez, Atanacio – 82
Martinez, Romulo – 291
Martin, Therese – 18, 20-22, 24,
30-31, 33-34, 39, 46, 48, 120,
176, 186, 202
Martinez, Mariano – 177
Mason, Barney – 92, 98
Matthews, Jacob Basil "Billy" –
83, 90
Maxwell family mansion – 4, 8
Maxwell Land Grant – 77, 91,
199, 362
Maxwell, Lucien Bonaparte – 77,
91, 199
Maxwell, Luz Trotier de Beaubien
– 34, 91, 156-157, 199-200, 315
Maxwell, Paulita – 77-78, 91, 98,
157, 163, 199-202, 305-306
Maxwell, Peter "Pete" – 77, 92, 98,
249
"Maxwell's ranch" – 30, 34, 46,
156, 163
Mayeux, Lucie E. – 67-68
McCarty, Catherine (see
Catherine Antrim)
McClarey, Donald R. – 53
McKinney, Thomas "Kip" – 92, 98-
99
McNicholas, John T. – 121
"McSwain" error (see Blandina
Segale)
McSween, Alexander – 75-76, 80-
82, 84-86, 88-89, 97, 146-147,
162, 195, 203-205, 304
McSween house – 86, 261
McSweens – 84, 86, 94
McSween, Susan – 86, 88-90, 105,
310
Meadows, John P. – 18, 107, 111,
317-318
Mescalaro Indian Reservation –
80, 83-84, 96
Mesilla jail – 96
Mesilla, New Mexico Territory –
44, 69, 81, 90, 95-96, 243, 289,
291, 298, 407
Mesilla News – 288
Metz, Judith – 55, 425
Mexican-American War – 108
Middleton, John – 83, 96
Milner, Bill "California Bill" – 351

Minogue, Anna – 121-122, 141, 158-159, 163
Mix, Tom – 268
Mooar, J. Wright – 175, 184
Morgan, William A. (see Bill Milner)
Morris, Harvey – 85-86, 89
Morrison, William V. – 7
Morton, William "Buck" – 82, 92, 97
Moulton, Ed – 187-189
Mount St. Vincent Academy – 14-15
Murphy-Dolans – 85-86
Murphy, Eugene P. – 59
Murphy-Kenney party – 110
Murphy, Lawrence G. – 26, 30, 42, 80, 85, 104, 127, 132, 146-149, 153, 156-157, 161-163, 167-168
New York Sun – 93, 175, 209, 240, 264-265, 312, 323, 326, 355, 405, 409, 419
New York World Magazine – 231, 255, 262, 317
Nolan, Frederick – 8, 185-186
Nordhaus, Hannah – 54
Nun's Tale Hoax (see Blandina Segale)
O'Brien, Katie – 69
O'Carroll, L.G. – 62, 387
O'Folliard, Tom – 59, 78, 85, 87-88, 91, 93-95, 106, 240, 323, 341
Ohio City, Colorado – 351
Olinger, Robert "Bob" – 97-98, 104-105, 247
"O'Phallier, Tom" – 215, 240, 313, 323-325, 341 (see Tom O'Folliard)
Our Sunday Visitor – 67
Palace of the Governors – 33, 198, 245-247, 257, 287, 300
Panhandle – 209-210, 264, 326-328, 331, 339, 364
Panhandle Transportation Company" – 212-213, 330
"Paoline Maxwell" error (see Blandina Segale)
"Parish Bulletin for Youth of St. Mary's" – 66

Parrell, Louise – 64
Parsons, Louella O. – 65
Patrón, Juan – 80, 87, 89, 260
Pecos River – 91, 212, 261, 331
Pecos valley – 193, 203, 210, 326, 402
Peñasco River – 80
Peñasco River ranch – 90
Peppin, George – 84-86, 88, 260
People of God – 57
Pickett, Tom – 94-95, 406
Poe, John William – 8, 90, 98-99
Police Gazette Series of Famous Criminals – 264, 319
"Pomeroy" – 279
Pond, Arthur (see Billy LeRoy)
Pond, Silas aka Sam Potter – 326, 328, 341, 344, 351-353
Portales, New Mexico Territory – 5, 195, 208-212, 312, 328-331, 412
Porter, Edwin S. – 267
Posse Comitatus Act – 85-86, 90
Potter, Sam (see Silas Pond)
Pueblo, Colorado – 15, 279-280, 295, 352, 355-356, 359, 363, 369, 400
"Ranch Life in the Great Southwest" – 268
Rasch, Philip – 289, 291-292, 348
Rawley, Ellen Rita – 66
Reardon, John – 288-292, 296
Regulators of 1878 – 75, 77, 83-87, 91, 96-97, 100-102, 106, 110, 134, 148, 161-162, 257, 283
"Regulator Manifesto" (see William H. Bonney)
Rezac, Mary – 16, 56-57, 119
rewards for Billy the Kid (see William Henry Bonney)
Richardson, Bill – 51
"Riders of the Purple Sage" – 268
Riley, John – 80
Roberts, Andrew "Buckshot" – 83, 92, 96-97, 100
Roberts, Oliver "Brushy Bill" – 6-8, 14, 19, 67, 271, 306; **true-believers of:** 67, 413
Rocky Mountain News – 63

Romero, Vincente – 85-86, 89
Roscoe, Burton – 351
Ross, Edmund G. – 178
Roswell, New Mexico Territory –
    4, 92, 107, 261, 317, 389
Rudabaugh, Dave "Dirty Dave" –
    93-95, 209-210, 213, 216, 288-
    289, 291-294, 299, 311, 313,
    323, 328, 331, 406-407, 421
Rudolph, Milnor – 98-99, 315
Rynerson, William L. – 81, 89, 106
Saint Blandina – 14
Saint Hood Productions – 52-53,
    58, 422, 425-426
Sánchez, Allen – 16, 18, 52-54, 56-
    58, 117-120, 137, 245, 266, 343,
    381, 390, 403-404, 410, 413,
    422, 425-426
Sanchez, Thomas – 53, 58, 71, 426
Salazar, Yginio – 84-86, 98
San Francisco Chronicle – 244,
    316
San Miguel County, New Mexico
    Territory – 94, 209
San Patricio, New Mexico
    Territory – 82, 84-85, 259
Santa Fe County – 288-290
Santa Fe Daily New Mexican – 94,
    181-182, 291-292, 294, 313-314,
    419
Santa Fe jail – 15, 21, 28, 39, 44-
    45, 54, 69, 76, 95, 110, 129, 138,
    151, 161-162, 168, 181, 206,
    263, 266, 284-285, 287-289,
    291, 293-295, 297-299, 301-302,
    309, 313, 340, 343, 347-348,
    351-352, 359, 373, 399, 404-
    407, 409, 412, 415-416, 421-
    422,424
Santa Fe, New Mexico Territory –
    14, 33, 52, 54, 58, 70, 109, 134,
    142, 145-146, 148, 156, 162,
    217-218, 226, 230, 244, 246,
    248, 251, 253, 281, 292, 294,
    305, 316, 336, 345, 347
Santa Fe New Mexican – 58, 142
Santa Fe Ring (the Ring) – 4-5, 8,
    32-35, 37, 42, 52, 75, 77, 79, 87,
    91-92, 99-100, 106, 108-109,
    113, 134-135, 161, 173-175,
    181, 186, 192, 194, 196-197,
    199, 202, 204-205, 208, 220,
    229, 239, 257, 260, 264, 310-
    312, 362, 415
Santa Fe Trail – 59, 207, 273, 404
Santa Maria Institute – 15-16, 18,
    20, 58, 117, 131, 138-140, 158,
    160, 202, 303, 377, 383-384,
    388, 390-391
scalping – 6, 23, 39, 52, 63, 124,
    144, 152, 166, 168, 179, 183-
    184, 206, 272, 276, 279-280,
    346, 355, 365, 371-372, 410,
    415, 418-419, 422-424
Scanland, John M. – 111-112
Schatznov, Thomas – 267
"Schneider" – 23-24, 38, 62, 124,
    143-144, 155, 161, 166, 168,
    265, 268, 271-277, 283, 335,
    346, 365-367, 371-373, 386,
    397-398, 400, 403
Schurz, Carl – 310
Scurlock, Josiah "Doc" – 88, 96,
    102
Secret Service – 27, 93, 98, 181,
    194, 208, 239, 283, 311,405
Segale, Blandina (Rosa Maria) –
    3, 6, 8-9, 13-19, 47-48, 51-71,
    75, 99, 108-1111, 113, 117-122,
    137-140, 163-165, 169, 173-181,
    184-185, 187, 189, 191-206,
    238-239, 242, 251-252, 263,
    266, 271, 277, 281, 284, 289,
    293-294, 301-303, 309-310, 318,
    320, 324, 328, 334-336, 340-
    341, 343-355, 359-360, 362,
    364-367, 369, 371-373, 377-398,
    400-401, 404-423, 425-426;
    biography of: 9, 14-17, 21;
    true-believers of: 413, 422;
    19th century journal by: 3, 9,
    13, 15-20, 22, 25, 30-32,36, 40,
    47-48, 51, 58, 66, 69, 75, 113,
    118-123, 131-132, 137-146, 148,
    150-155, 159-161, 163-166, 169,
    173-174, 177-179, 183-186, 199,
    202, 205-207, 219-220, 224,
    238, 242-244, 251, 263-264,

266-268, 271, 274, 278, 280-281, 283, 285, 291, 295, 197, 301-303, 306, 309-310, 318, 328, 335, 340, 343, 347-348, 360, 369, 371, 377-383, 386, 388, 390-392, 404, 414, 417, 423; "At the End of the Santa Fe Trail" magazine articles by: 16, 18, 20, 48, 58, 121-122, 131-132, 138-165, 169, 173, 176, 180, 186, 192, 199, 202, 204-205, 271, 275-276, 278, 283, 286, 302-305, 371, 377-381, 383-384, 388, 413, 423; *At the End of the Santa Fe Trail* books by: 8-9, 13, 17-19, 22-48, 58-59, 68, 70, 111, 118-138, 166-169, 173, 184, 186, 202, 303, 343, 377, 383, 391, 401, 422-423, 425-426; 1932 edition: 121-137, 166-169, 303-305, 309, 334, 365-367, 377, 381, 383, 385-386, 389, 414; 1948 edition: 22-48, 120, 166-169, 176, 186, 202, 251, 291, 348, 401, editor of (see Therese Martin); 1996 edition: 137, 2014 edition: 16, 137-138; At the End of the Santa Fe Trail" TV series about: 53; *Topix* comic book about: 13, 59-62; "The Fastest Nun in the West" CBS Special about: 13; "At the End of the Santa Fe Trail" 2017 Saint Hood TV series about: 13-14, 52-53, 58, 416; **press about:** 51-70; **summary of journal entry dates' alterations of:** 166-169; **research ability of:** 175-179; **second-hand sources of Pat Garrett, Walter Noble Burns, and Ralph Emerson Twitchell used by:** 173-174, 185-205, 268, 401-402, 414-415, 423; **second-hand sources of contemporary press used by:** 205-238, 242-256, 360-373, 414-415, 423; **indirect use of Secret Service reports by:** 239-241; **second-hand source of Billy LeRoy dime novel used by:** 263-266, 268, 320-342; **Hollywood Westerns as possible secondary sources for:** 266-268; **first-hand encounters with "Schneider/Snyder" by:** 23, 37-38, 40, 123-124, 143, 166, 272-276, 373, 416-419, 423-424; **first encounter with on-the-loose "Billy the Kid" by:** 23-24, 38, 124, 144, 151, 166, 277-280, 373; **second encounter with on-the-loose "Billy the Kid" by:** 26, 41, 126-127, 146, 167, 281-283, 373; **Santa Fe jail meeting with "Billy the Kid" and "Kelly" by:** 28-29, 45, 129-130, 151-152, 162, 168, 284-301, 373; **first-hand magazine-only encounter in her hospital with "Billy the Kid" by:** 146-147, 303-305, 373; **first-hand encounter with Victorio by:** 302, 373, 404, 424; **first-hand magazine-only encounter in her hospital with "friend Murphy" by:** 146-147, 303-305, 373, 420-422, 424; **first-hand magazine-only encounter with "Paoline" Maxwell by:** 305-306, 373, 421, 424; **"The Trinidad Enterprise" referenced by:** 22, 37 69, 123, 272, 275, 346, 354-355, 408; **"Billy the Kid" referenced by:** 9, 13, 15, 17, 19, 21-30, 36-48, 53, 56, 58, 62, 66, 69, 71, 75, 111, 113, 119-121, 123-132, 137-139, 141, 143-155, 157, 159-163, 165, 169, 174-175, 179, 186, 190-191, 198-199, 204-208, 242, 252, 263-264, 266-268, 271, 276-289, 294-296, 298, 302-305,

309, 340, 365, 371-372, 385-386, 389, 404-406, 408-426; "Billy the Kid gang" referenced by: 15, 17, 21-27, 30-31, 37-42, 46-47, 51, 55-57, 59, 62, 64, 66, 68-70, 123-227, 131, 133, 143-147, 152, 154-155, 161, 165-169, 174-175, 179, 189, 194, 205-208, 238, 267-268, 271-283, 294, 302, 341, 354, 367, 372, 379, 405, 408-410, 412, 416-420, 422-423, 425; "Bill's gang" references by: 22-23, 123, 272, 275, 345, 354, 362, 408, 420; "Schneider" referenced by: 23-24, 38, 62, 124, 143-144, 155, 161, 166, 168, 265, 268, 271-277, 283, 335, 346, 365-367, 371-373; "Snyder" referenced by: 155, 169, 274-276, 367; actual "Snyder" in the press: 370-373 (see John M. Snyder); "Happy Jack" referenced by: 23, 38, 155, 273-276, 345-346, 365, 367, 371-373; actual "Happy Jack" press: 367-373 (see R.I. Donnlson); Trinidad doctors facing scalping referenced by: 17, 20-21, 23-24, 38, 51-52, 55-58, 62-70, 121, 124, 144, 152, 166, 168, 206, 265, 273-274, 276, 278-279, 345-346, 366, 419, 423-424; names given by: 366 (see Doctors Beshoar, Menger, Palmer); press on actual doctors: 370 (see Doctors Cushing, Beshoar, Rogers); Santa Fe Ring referenced by: 32-36, 135; Thomas Benton Catron referenced by: 32-33, 35, 134-135, 178; Dr. Robert Longwill referenced by: 36; Land-grabbers referenced by: 35, 136; Victorio referenced by: 36, 47-48, 136, 154, 163, 180, 182, 271, 302, 306, 373, 404, 424;

"tenderfoot miner patient" reference by: 28-29, 44-45, 129, 151, 168, 243, 284-286, 290, 295-296; "Kelly" referenced by: 151-152, 168, 284-286, 289-290, 292, 298, 300-301, 340, 348, 405; "Billy the Kid" errors by summarized: 36-46; "*The Trinidad Enterprise*" error by: 37, 275, 353, 361; "Lew Wallace Billy the Kid rewards" error by: 27, 31, 43, 127-128, 133, 180-182, 196; "Lew Wallace Billy the Kid interviews" error by: 27, 31-32, 43, 133, 196, 252-263; "Lew Wallace threatened by Billy the Kid" error: 28, 32, 44, 128-129, 133-134, 197-198, 242-251, 286-287, 296; "Lew Wallace's attempted attack by Billy the Kid" error by: 28, 32, 44, 129, 134; Lincoln County War" magazine only error by: 149-150, 203; "McSwain" magazine only error by – 146-148, 203; "friend Murphy" magazine only error by: 146-150, 153, 161-162, 168, 203-205, 303-305, 420-422, 424; "Santa Fe jail Billy the Kid and Kelly" errors by: 295-301; "Los Corrilos" error by: 284, 286, 290, 296, 347; "Patrick Garret" error by: 130, 153, 340; "twelve year old murderer" error by: 28, 46, 130, 153, 187; "insult to mother" error by: 28, 46, 130, 153; Victorio error by: 182-184; 302, ,404, 424

"Paoline Maxwell" error by: 156-157, 169, 199-202, 305-306, 421, 424; "Snyder" "error" by: 364-369; "Happy Jack" "error" by: 364-369; Billy LeRoy explanation for

(two Billy the Kid's theory for): – 54, 68-69, 119, 309, 320, 341, 343-345, 347, 350, 373, 422, 425; **Billy Wilson explanation for:** 404-409; **addled nun explanation for:** 48, 404-409, 421; **lack of disclaimer by:** 131, 141, 162, 199, 383, 390, 413-414, 416; **"damage done to Billy the Kid history by:** 9, 52, 75, 110-111, 113, 263, 415, 424
Segale, Justina (Maria Maddelena) – 14-16, 18-19, 22, 29, 37, 45, 47, 55, 122, 130, 138, 140-141, 152, 159, 164-165, 174, 176, 180-181, 285, 299, 347-348, 378-380, 386, 388, 391-393, 425
Selig Polyscope – 268
Seton, Elizabeth – 16
Seven Rivers, New Mexico Territory – 97, 259, 261
Seven Rivers rustlers – 84-85, 98
Shedd's Ranch – 261-262
Sheehan, Michael J. – 16
Sheldon, Lionel – 287, 300-301
Silver City, New Mexico Territory – 64, 75, 78-79, 187-188, 220, 261-262, 418-419
Sister Augustine – 25, 281-283
Sister Catherine – 47, 136, 156, 182, 302
Sisters of Charity of Cincinnati – 14-16, 18, 20, 22, 25, 34, 55, 66-67, 118, 120, 137-138, 140, 143, 155-156, 158, 164, 174, 176, 179, 184, 271, 343, 370, 377, 384, 388, 390, 392-393, 413, 416, 421-422, 425-426
"Sleuthing Hoaxbusting Clues" – 3, 13, 30, 36, 51, 75, 117, 120, 132, 137, 138, 164, 166, 173, 179, 185, 205, 239, 242, 252, 263, 266, 271, 272, 277, 281, 284, 303, 309, 310, 319, 320, 343, 351, 354, 360, 377, 382, 384, 390, 400, 404, 410, 411, 413

Smithsonian Magazine – 54
"Smoking Guns For a Hoax" – 9, 48, 71, 113, 119, 132, 137, 138, 163, 165, 168, 169, 184, 199, 202, 205, 238, 251, 263, 266, 268, 276, 280, 283, 301, 302, 305, 306, 319, 341, 350, 353, 359, 373, 381, 383, 387, 390, 400, 403, 404, 409, 410, 411, 422
"Snyder" – 155, 169, 274-276, 365, 367, 370-373, 403 (see John M. Snyder; see Blandina Segale)
Snyder, John M. – 370-373, 404, 417-418, 424; **obituary of:** 370, 417
"Sound of Music" – 426
South, W.L. – 362
Spencerian handwriting – 78, 89, 106, 257
Staab, Adolph (carriage ride of family) – 25, 40-41, 62, 126, 145-146, 161, 207, 281, 324, 347, 398-399, 410, 415-416, 420-421, 424
Staked Plain – 210, 237
Steubenvillle, Ohio – 14
Stewart, Frank – 96, 212, 313
Stinking Springs, New Mexico Territory – 78, 95-96, 197, 228, 294, 313, 406, 412
St. Francis of Assisi Basilica Cathedral – 16
St. James Hotel – 410
St. Joseph Academy – 57, 200
St. Joseph's Children Community Health – 16, 53, 117
St. Mary's convent school – 201
Sunnyside, New Mexico Territory – 98
Tansey, Anne – 66
Tascosa, Texas – 42, 87, 106, 195
Tekakwitha, Kateri – 16
"tenderfoot" patient (see Blandina Segale)
Terrazas, Joaquín – 183
The American Catholic – 53
The American Weekly – 63

The Authentic Life of Billy the Kid – 4, 9, 22, 100-101, 176, 186, 190, 315, 319-320, 403
The Cincinnati Enquirer – "At the End of the Santa Fe Trail" TV series (see Blandina Segale) 65, 69
The Cincinnati Post – 16, 67
The Colorado Chieftain – 279-280, 355, 363, 369
The Colorado Springs Gazette and El Paso County News – 279
"The Curious Case of Edward Kelly" – 289, 348-349
The Daily News: Denver – 355-358
The Denver Catholic Register – 65-66
The Denver Tribune – 351
The Eagle Valley Enterprise – 364
The Enterprise and Chronicle – 37, 275, 354, 370, 417
"The Fastest Nun in the West" CBS Special (see Blandina Segale)
"The Great K & A Train Robbery" – 268
"the House" – 80, 90, 104, 161
The Indianapolis Press – 224, 255, 316
The Irish Digest – 62, 64, 387
"The Iron Horse" – 268
The Leading Facts of New Mexico History – 202
The Lincoln County War: A Documentary History – 8, 186
The Lost Pardon of Billy the Kid – 8, 174
The Magazine of the South – 175, 184
The Salida Mail – 363
The Saga of Billy the Kid – 5, 9, 22, 176, 186, 200
The Santa Maria magazine – 15, 121-122, 161, 186, 276, 302, 390
"The Son of a Gun" – 268
The Trinidad Enterprise – 22, 37, 69, 123, 174, 272, 275, 346, 354-355, 362, 408
The West of Billy the Kid – 8

Thornton, William T. – 33, 110, 135
tintype (see William H. Bonney)
Tolby, Franklin J. – 36
Topix comic book (see Blandina Segale)
Treasury Department – 93, 239
Treaty of Guadalupe Hidalgo – 108
Tres Castillos, Mexico – 183
Trinidad, Colorado – 14-15, 17, 20-26, 30, 37-41, 46, 52, 56-58, 62-63, 65-71, 119-121, 123-126, 131, 143-145, 152, 154-157, 161, 163, 166, 168, 174-175, 200-202, 206-208, 265, 272-273, 281-282, 298, 302, 305, 318, 334, 344-348, 351, 355, 362, 365-367, 371-373, 385-386, 388, 392-393, 397-399, 408-410, 415-424
Trinidad, Colorado *Chronicle* – 353-354
Trinidad doctors facing scalping (see Blandina Segale)
Trinidad doctors (newspaper listing of) – 370
Trinidad jail – 347
Tunstall, John Henry – 26-27, 30, 42, 75-76, 79-84, 87-90, 97-98, 100, 102, 104, 109-110, 127, 132, 146-148, 167, 186, 192-193, 195, 202-205, 261, 283, 303-304, 310
Twain, Mark – 14, 52
"twelve year old murderer" error (see Blandina Segale)
Twitchell, Ralph Emerson – 202-205, 268, 401
"Two Billy the Kids Theory" – 54, 68-69, 119, 309, 320, 341, 343-345, 347, 350, 373 (see Billy LeRoy; see Blandina Segale)
Upson, Marshall Ashmun "Ash" – 41, 92, 99, 187, 319
Veritas magazine – 15, 18, 58, 131, 138-146, 148-151, 153, 156, 158-159, 161, 164, 166-168, 202-203, 205, 272, 297,

300, 303-304, 365-366, 378-380, 384, 388-390
Victorian magazine – 64
Victorio – 36, 47-48, 52, 136, 154, 163, 180, 182-184, 271, 302, 306, 373, 404, 424
Wagon Wheel Gap, Colorado – 358
Waite, Fred Tecumseh – 80, 82-83, 96
Waldo, Henry – 89
Wallace, Lew – 4, 7, 18, 21, 26-28, 30-33, 42-44, 76-78, 87-90, 94-95, 103, 106, 127-129, 132-134, 147, 149-150, 167, 180-182, 184, 194-198, 207-208, 215-238, 242-266, 285-286, 288, 283, 296-297, 301, 303, 310, 312, 314-317, 320, 334-339, 401, 412, 415, 422; **betrayed pardon bargain with Billy Bonney:** 7, 18, 21, 43-44, 76-77, 89, 94, 132, 174, 181, 228; **"precious specimen" letter to Carl Schurz by:** 310; **interviews of Billy Bonney by:** 32, 89, 133, 150, 196, 256-263, 266; **death warrant for Billy Bonney by:** 96; **betrayed pardon bargain guilty obsession of:** 76, 95, 174, 219, 244, 252; **outlaw myth articles by:** 197-198, 216-238, 242-256, 264-265, 286-287, 297, 314-317, 335; **reward notices for Billy the Kid by:** 88, 94, 180-182, 209, 215, 265, 312, 314, 336; **books by:** *Autobiography*: 197-198, 231, 237, 242, 317; *The Fair God*: 87; *Ben-Hur: A Tale of the Christ*: 28, 32, 44, 87, 128, 133, 151, 198, 231, 242, 244-245, 248, 257, 317; *Prince of India*: 245
Walz, Edgar – 88, 93, 106, 110, 239
Weddle, Jerry – 9, 186, 419, 422

Weekly *Crawfordsville Review* – 249, 316
West, W.H. – 405
White Oaks livery – 87, 93-94, 405
White Oaks, New Mexico Territory – 87, 93-94, 97-98, 181, 209, 212-213, 215, 331, 406
Wilcox, Lucius "Lute" – 209, 294, 300, 313
Wild, Azariah – 93-95, 98, 194, 208, 239-241, 283, 311, 405, 408
Wilson, Billy (possible aka David L. Anderson) – 93-95, 210, 213, 215, 239-241, 288-289, 291, 293-294, 299-300, 313, 328, 331, 341, 404-409; **"Kid-Wilson gang of:** 405; **Billy Wilson explanation for** (see Blandina Segale)
Wilson, John "Squire" – 82-84, 86-87, 89, 258
Wooten, Dick – 155, 274, 367

www.ingramcontent.com/pod-product-compliance
Lightning Source LLC
Chambersburg PA
CBHW060447090426
42735CB00011B/1938